Great Gourmet Weekends in Australia

Contents

Above (left to right):
table set for service
at The Stag, South-
West Coast, Victoria;
foamed egg white
crowned with edible
gold at Absynthe, Gold
Coast and hinterland,
Queensland; an idyllic
vineyard setting at
Warrenmang Vineyard,
Ballarat and Pyrenees,
Victoria; blue cheese
from Grandvewe
Cheeses, Southern
Valleys, Tasmania;
produce for sale at
A Slice of Orange,
Central Tablelands,
New South Wales

Introduction

Australia is home to some of the world's best food and wine destinations and to experience them *Great Gourmet Weekends in Australia* takes you on a gastronomic journey of discovery. This book covers everything from fine-dining restaurants, breezy cafes and up-market produce stores, to farm-gate stalls, cheesemaking factories, olive groves, boutique breweries and cellar doors. With so many fabulous options, you could eat out – and drink out – every day for the next few years!

But even if you're more of a home chef, this book will tell you where to purchase produce from the source: everything from dukkah to ducks, chocolates to cheese, olives to oils, pastries to pies, lobster to marron, venison to wagyu, and berries to bugs. And for wine lovers, you will find Australia's veritable A–Z of wines and where to taste them, varietals such as arneis, cinsaut, refosco and zinfandel, not to mention the more familiar cabernet, shiraz, semillon, chardonnay and sauvignon blanc.

Together with our knowledgeable writers, who are keen to showcase all that their state has to offer, we have selected what we believe are the country's most rewarding areas for gourmet tourism. The book is divided by state and then regional areas, with information on where to stay, festivals and a wealth of suggestions on where to stop for your next treat. Region maps will also assist you in creating your own itinerary.

The text is peppered with interesting details about all things local – chefs, gourmet producers, winemakers and food and wine festivals. And wherever you go, you will discover much about the pioneering people who have created the incredible range of fresh produce that this country has to offer. So whether you want to travel the back roads of New South Wales' coastal hinterland to find a distillery making Australia's only potato vodka (*see* Coffs Harbour and hinterland, p. 60), learn the art of Thai cooking in Queensland (*see* Sunshine Coast, p. 364) or go truffle hunting in Tasmania (*see* Central North, p. 410), this book will take you on an extraordinary journey of culinary delights.

Left (clockwise from top left): nougat squares at The Larder, Cape to Cape, Western Australia; gourmet produce display at Bottega Rotolo, Adelaide, South Australia; a delightful dish at Clairault, Cape to Cape, Western Australia; wine barrels at Pipers Brook/Kreglinger, Central North, Tasmania

About the writers

SALLY HAMMOND
New South Wales and Victoria's South-West Coast

Sally Hammond is a Sydney-based author and freelance food and travel writer. She has written many books and guides and her food and travel articles have been published in numerous newspapers and magazines in Australia and overseas. She is never happier than when exploring country areas and discovering what the country does best. With her husband, Gordon, she publishes the *Australian Regional Food Guide*; www.australianregionalfoodguide.com.au

TRICIA WELSH
Victoria

Tricia Welsh is a Melbourne-based freelance journalist who specialises in writing about food and travel. She has visited more than 70 countries and all seven continents, yet is just as happy discovering the rich joys and culinary delights of her home state, writing regular regional food and wine articles and restaurant reviews for Melbourne publications.

QUENTIN CHESTER
South Australia

Quentin Chester is a freelance travel and nature writer, who has also had extensive experience in the wine and hospitality industries, including stints as an outback cook. He is the author of six books, among them *The Kimberley: Horizons of Stone* and *Australia's Wild Islands*, as well as two story collections, *The Wild Calling* and *Tales from the Bush*. A regular contributor to *Australian Geographic* and *Wild* magazines, Quentin now calls Kangaroo Island home.

CARMEN JENNER
Western Australia

Carmen Jenner is a Perth-based freelance travel and food writer and a regular contributor to *Cravings* food magazine. Her work has appeared in numerous books, magazines and national newspaper *The Australian*. She is also an ongoing contributor and restaurant reviewer for the *Top 50 Restaurant Guide Western Australia 2010*.

LIZ JOHNSTON
Queensland

Liz Johnston is a Queensland-based travel, food and wine writer and in this capacity has been reporting on her home state for leading national newspapers and magazines since the 1970s. She has also travelled extensively overseas for many years, publishing articles in Australia on the wine and food of Scandinavia, Europe, United Kingdom and North America. She is the author of the 2009 publication *Wolf Blass, Behind the Bow Tie*.

SUE MEDLOCK
Tasmania

Sue Medlock is a writer with a passion for gourmet food. She has degrees in ecology and journalism and has travelled across Australia, working at universities in Adelaide, Perth and Melbourne, before returning to live in Hobart. She pursues her zest for travel with explorations of Tasmania's countryside, researching its bountiful larder at wineries, farm gates and restaurants along the way. Sue has contributed to Explore Australia publications since 2003.

New South Wales

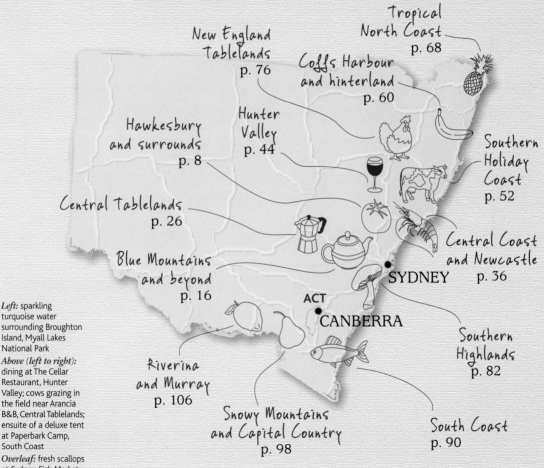

Tropical
North Coast
p. 68

New England
Tablelands
p. 76

Coffs Harbour
and hinterland
p. 60

Hawkesbury
and surrounds
p. 8

Hunter
Valley
p. 44

Southern
Holiday
Coast
p. 52

Central Tablelands
p. 26

Blue Mountains
and beyond
p. 16

Central Coast
and Newcastle
p. 36

SYDNEY

ACT

CANBERRA

Southern
Highlands
p. 82

Riverina
and Murray
p. 106

Snowy Mountains
and Capital Country
p. 98

South Coast
p. 90

Left: sparkling
turquoise water
surrounding Broughton
Island, Myall Lakes
National Park

Above (left to right):
dining at The Cellar
Restaurant, Hunter
Valley; cows grazing in
the field near Arancia
B&B, Central Tablelands;
ensuite of a deluxe tent
at Paperbark Camp,
South Coast

Overleaf: fresh scallops
at Sydney Fish Market

Sydney

Sydney Harbour and the beaches specialise in views of course, and a sunny slice of Sydney panorama is the natural side-serve with many meals; understandably seafood is high on the list of cuisines, but so are all types of Asian food.

Sydney ~ an overview

Sydney, capital of New South Wales and Australia's largest city, is a diverse and multicultural place. In the CBD, high-rise five-star hotels loom over streets packed with bars and cafes – many of which serve world-class coffees – as well as restaurants and takeaway food outlets. Sydney Harbour and beachfront venues specialise in views of course, and a sunny slice of Sydney panorama is the natural side-serve with many meals. Understandably seafood is high on the list of cuisines, but so are all types of Asian food.

It is a trendy city. Farmers' markets in several locations are extremely popular, tapas and shareable dishes have become the way to dine, especially in the inner city, and cafe breakfasts are de rigueur. The good news is that 'modern Australian', the ubiquitous term for a fusion-type cuisine, has at last morphed into 'contemporary'.

While the inner east and west of the city have perhaps the largest number of eating places, the suburbs are notable for their ethnic mix. Sydneysiders head to Campsie for Korean food, Cabramatta and Bankstown for Vietnamese, Chinatown or Chatswood for Chinese, Kingsford for Indonesian, Leichhardt, Haberfield and Five Dock for Italian, Marrickville for Greek, or Lakemba and several southern suburbs for Middle Eastern food.

The best thing about these precincts is that not only can you have an authentic dining experience but it is possible to shop there too, and pick up the ingredients to create your own ethnic feast at home. That said, these suburbs are always changing and it pays to keep up with the trends via the local newspapers, internet or dining guides.

Outer-city gourmet experiences

In alphabetical order, here are some suggestions for ten suburban 'finds', half an hour or more from the CBD but well worth the trip.

Above (left to right): stylish dining at Barrenjoey House, Palm Beach; pier on the Hawkesbury River leading to Cottage Point Kiosk; preparing loaves for the oven at Brasserie Bread Bakery Cafe, Banksmeadow; the contemporary interior of Ormeggio at The Spit, Mosman

Barrenjoey House: this grand old eating house with a new lease on life is still one of the best places to get the feel of 'Palmie'; 1108 Barrenjoey Rd, Palm Beach; (02) 9974 4001; www.barrenjoeyhouse.com.au

Brasserie Bread Bakery Cafe: just-baked bread and pastries, freshly roasted coffee and light meals in an unlikely but unforgettable location; 1737 Botany Rd, Banksmeadow; 1300 966 845; www.brasseriebread.com.au/bakery-cafe

Cavallino: owner-chef Giovanni Pilu's Middle Harbour restaurants feature standout Sardinian food and now he does wood-fired pizzas at this out-of-town venue on the edge of a national park; Cnr McCarrs Creek Rd and Yulong Ave, Terrey Hills; (02) 9450 1777; www.cavallino.com.au

Cottage Point Inn: a former boatshed with absolute-waterfront views, water taxi and seaplane access, fine contemporary cuisine and relaxed elegant surroundings; 2 Anderson Pl, Cottage Point; (02) 9456 1011; www.cottagepointinn.com.au

Cottage Point Kiosk: the lovely Hawkesbury River to Sydney's north has many bays and inlets and this laid-back waterside eatery has it all – views, easy dining, and a great feel; Cottage Point Rd, Cottage Point, Ku-ring-gai Chase National Park; (02) 9456 3024; www.cottagepointkiosk.com.au

Jonah's: this restaurant with a breathtaking aerial view of the beach far below serves topnotch cuisine to match; boutique accommodation is available on-site; 69 Bynya Rd, Whale Beach; (02) 9974 5599; www.jonahs.com.au

Oliveto: come here for Sunday lunch and you will have to pinch yourself to realise that you have not slipped away to Tuscany; it's busy, it's vibrant, and the wood-fired oven goes non-stop, and there are even water views; Bray's Bay Reserve, 443 Concord Rd, Rhodes; (02) 8765 0006; www.oliveto.com.au

Ormeggio at The Spit: Chef Pavoni has come from a top Sydney hotel, but it is here, with its uninterrupted views of lovely Middle Harbour, that he can convey his home region of Lombardy; D'Albora Marinas, The Spit, Mosman; (02) 9969 4088; www.ormeggio.com.au

Pilu at Freshwater: Sardinian food in a heritage former beach cottage is award-winning, and so is the wine list; Moore Rd (at the end), Freshwater; (02) 9938 3331; www.piluatfreshwater.com.au

Sahra by the River: Lebanese food hardly gets better than in this modern place beside the Parramatta River; 2/76 Philip St, Parramatta; (02) 9635 6615; www.sahrabytheriver.com.au

Hawkesbury and surrounds

Residents around the Hawkesbury River and its environs are well placed. Close enough to commute to the city in one direction on weekdays, they can go the other way at weekends to trawl through farmers' markets or visit orchards, olive groves and gardens.

Some call this area the Sydney Basin, the lush lowlands between the city sprawl and the mountains. Others call one part of it the Hawkesbury Harvest region. If you download the map for the self-guide Hawkesbury Harvest Trail (www.hawkesburyharvest.com.au), producers, attractions and restaurants are colour-coded, making it easy to see what sort of delight might be just down the road. A small chart lists all the produce available in the area, alongside a calendar clearly marked to show when each item is in season, as well as the places where it can be found. Although the trail is a great help, there are far too many options for one day. Ideally you should plan a couple of days, remembering that many producers keep the weekends free for 'open days' at their properties and get down to business during the week. The good thing is you can always come back again, next weekend. Whatever you do, whether you are planning just a daytrip or

Above: the old-world entrance to Sassafras Creek Cafe, Kurrajong Village
Opposite: fresh fruit for sale in the Hawkesbury region

Festivals

**Autumn Harvest Food &
Wine Festival:** a celebration
of nature's bounty; Mount
Tomah Botanic Garden; May;
(02) 4567 2154;
www.mounttomahbotanic
garden.com.au

Where to stay

**The Sebel Resort & Spa
Hawkesbury Valley:** spa resort
and luxury country hotel;
61 Hawkesbury Valley Way, Windsor;
(02) 4577 4222;
www.mirvachotels.com/sebel-
resort-hawkesbury

Tizzana Winery B&B: heritage
treasure (*see* feature, p. 14);
518 Tizzana Rd, Ebenezer;
(02) 4579 1150;
www.winery.tizzana.com.au

Above (left to right): fresh fruit and a working tractor at Enniskillen Orchard, Grose Vale; rustic charm at Apple Bar, Bilpin; farm fresh eggs on sale at The Local Harvest, Bilpin

several days, there is one important rule: don't forget to bring your shopping bag!

The historic towns of Richmond and Windsor are the stepping-off points, and to get yourself organised a visit to the busy and bustling markets in Windsor's mall area on George Street is a good idea. Here, you'll find herbs and seasonal fruits and vegetables as well as other market things. With time to spare, you might want to take a gentle three-horsepower clip-clop through the streets of old Windsor in a horse-drawn former omnibus called, appropriately, **Clydesdales**. A tour and dining experience combined, dishes are picked up en route from local restaurants and served in style on board.

Enniskillen Orchard on Grose Vale Road beyond Richmond is a must. Owner John Maguire has added a covered verandah and tables with the ideal view of his orchard, herb garden and the long rolling slopes of the Hawkesbury Valley. Inside, the shop is full of a magnificent array of local and Australian products. Varieties of honey, jams, sauces, and pickles line the shelves in the centre of the store. Mounds of potatoes,

pumpkins and onions, and boxes of apples and peaches, and – most important for people with a busy day of touring – good coffee are all to be found here.

You could wander around these back roads and valleys without any plan really. Depending on the season you will see hand-lettered signs beginning to pop up on the roadsides even around Dural and Castle Hill – promising farm-fresh eggs, strawberries, peaches, even 'poo' for sale (chicken, cow or horse, of course) and buckets of flowers.

Take the Bells Line of Road from Richmond. It is the alternative (and some say much more scenic) route to the Blue Mountains, with long views towards the coast and Sydney, now just a smudge on the horizon, and plenty of orchards just begging you to drop in for crunchy fresh apples or stone fruit. Kurrajong is a lovely place to break your journey with a couple of places serving fine mountain fare. Natalie Smith, the owner of **Sassafras Creek Cafe**, has established a concept that is deceptively simple. More than just a cafe, here a gallery and lifestyle store melds with a space where local produce

features as much as possible in dishes on the menu. Think local goat's curd tart with roasted pumpkin salad, or flaky beef pies. It all comes together in a light and airy weatherboard cottage with indoor dining as well as a brick paved courtyard at the front and umbrella-shaded tables at the back.

There must be something in the mountain air in these parts, as just up the road is the esteemed **Lochiel House**, where owner-chefs Monique Maul and Anthony Milroy deliver dishes such as goat's cheese soufflés, freshly baked bread and perfectly cooked duck breast. In many shops in the area you'll also come across **Kurrajong Australian Native Foods**' wide range of products using native Australian fruits and herbs.

Even higher at the acclaimed apple capital of the mountains, Bilpin, the aptly named **Apple Bar** is the spot where city escapee and former Neil Perry apprentice, Michael Jaggard, shows how completely he has adapted to country life and style. Generous portions, hearty flavours, chunky soups and wood-fired pizzas suit this cooler climate. If you only have

time for some ice-cream or a snack, there's **Tutti Fruitti** (you'll recognise it by the eye-catching purple and green cottage), which also sells local produce. So, too, does **Shields Orchard** at Bilpin, which grows several varieties of apples and has a sideline in the folk-art crates decorated by Bill Shields' wife, Julie. A wooden box with apples painted on the side and some apples to go in it is a really classy gift for a friend back home. If you can part with it!

You can roll up your sleeves and get in the country spirit at **Bilpin Springs Orchard** when you pick your own apples. Check their website for what is in season when you plan to visit. Outlets with plenty of choice include the **Bilpin Fruit Bowl** selling a good range of the local produce and **The Local Harvest** just across the road. Its specialty is apple pies, freshly baked daily, but there are also figs in season, an eclectic mix of eggs (including pullet eggs), beans, red bird's-eye chillies, pears, apples, and pumpkins.

Just a little further along Bells Line of Road you will catch the heavenly scent of more freshly baked apple pies, enough to lure you into **Cottage Orchard** where they are laid out in their crusty sugary glory. There are many orchards worth visiting along this road, so take your time and stock up. It's just like a strung-out farmers' market. You could spend days just in Bilpin. And there are some surprising finds. **Wirraninna Ridge** makes apple cider vinegar. The business began in 1986, using apples from the Kindler's own orchard, and the product is still made only from Bilpin apples.

At Mount Tomah Botanic Garden, about as high as you can get in this part of the mountains, **Restaurant Tomah** is a popular spot for functions, but also a place to rest with coffee and a light meal after an exploration of Sydney's cool-climate gardens. There are dozens of other places so do yourself a favour and check Hawkesbury Harvest's map before you head off. It would be a shame to miss anything in this lovely area. If time is limited or you just want to sit back and be taken there, contact Hawkesbury Sight-seeing Tours on (02) 4575 1421. And if you arrive home with a basketful of things you don't know how to use, next time check in first for an **Urban Graze** hands-on cooking class at Kellyville, on the brink of the region.

Many restaurants in the area make good use of the local produce. Expect to be able to sample **Pepe's Ducks** from South Windsor, **Willowbrae**'s delectable goat cheeses made at Wilberforce to the north, and quail, guinea fowl, rabbit, venison or almost any less-familiar meat from Galston's **Game Farm**.

This region also includes other places. The Penrith and Camden area, while easily combined with a Hawkesbury visit, is also a simple day trip from Sydney. From here, it's the ideal opportunity to have time to enjoy some of the places lower in the Blue Mountains, often in danger of being overlooked in the rush to gain altitude. It turns out to be much easier to include them in a loop from Penrith instead.

While in Penrith, a major town on the Nepean River, drop in at **Go-Shu Sake**. The visitor centre is open weekdays and brewery tours are available by appointment. This is serious business, producing sake (using Australian rice), which is so good it is exported to Japan. Sake brewing commenced in Australia in 1988 when Sun Masamune, along with the Australian Rice Growers Co-operative, began testing a small brewing plant at Leeton, located not far south-east of Griffith in the Riverina region of New South Wales. The Japanese characters for Go-Shu mean Australian Sake, and phonetically it sounds like 'Australia' in Japanese, which is a particularly apt double meaning!

At Blaxland, just a few minutes towards the mountains from Penrith, **Restaurant Como** is one of the leading dining lights in the area. Far too good to bypass, it is a destination in itself, and just ten minutes from the end of the freeway. Chef Grant Farrant's slow-cooked duck leg and duck sausage, served with spiced poached pear, toasted sour cherry risotto, and a splash of calvados, is artistry on the plate – and the palate. A mention of roast fillet of monk fish that arrives with a crisp chicken wing, golden beetroot, kipfler fondant, sweetcorn purée, and (wait for it) citrus air, hints at some serious innovation and expertise in the kitchen.

Don't abandon this part of the mountains and return home before you visit one of the region's best little secrets. **Zokoko** 'bean-to-bar' artisan chocolate has to be tasted to be experienced. The elegant sleek tasting place at Emu Heights is the perfect backdrop for the delights of this fine chocolate, and best of all you can stay on with a coffee, some cake or order something else chocolaty to go with it.

If you have stayed the night– and the mountains do B&B and guesthouse accommodation so well, so you should – **Mash Cafe** at Glenbrook, serving fine Fair Trade coffee, is a good place for breakfast or a lunch to fortify you for your return to the stress of city traffic.

Opposite (above, left to right): sake bottle and a traditional Japanese wooden sake cup at Go-Shu Sake, Penrith; Tutti Fruitti's eye-catching purple and green cottage, Bilpin
Below: view over the Hawkesbury River and valley

Winemaking heritage

Time out at Tizzana Winery

Not many think of the Hawkesbury area as a wine region, yet vines were originally planted in the centre of Sydney (on the site of the present Hotel InterContinental, for instance) soon after European settlers arrived. Quite naturally, as emigrants moved into nearby areas, they decided to see if wine grapes could be grown there too.

Tuscany to the upper Hawkesbury is a long voyage, yet it was made in the 1880s by a young surgeon from Florence, Dr Thomas Fiaschi, who settled in the remote area of Ebenezer, well north of Windsor. It was here that he planted one of the state's oldest vineyards, no doubt reflecting on his homeland, and keen to recreate Italy in this new land. He succeeded, but sadly the stone-built winery burned down in 1955. From the ashes the present cellars have been faithfully restored to National Trust specification, and a range of wines are still made here, keeping alive Fiaschi's dream. The much newer five-star B&B accommodation (see Where to stay) above the cellars fulfils guests' wish-list items too. Dining with a view of the surrounding area is a delight, especially when matched with a taste of the past in a glass.

Tizzana Winery
(02) 4579 1150
Open: Saturday, Sunday & Public Holiday.
Noon - 6.00pm other times by Appointment
Functions, Tastings & Cellar Door Sales
Bed & Breakfast

Contacts for Hawkesbury and surrounds

EATERIES

Apple Bar: 2488 Bells Line of Road, Bilpin; (02) 4567 0335; www.applebar.com.au

Clydesdales: 1 Thompson Sq (rear), Windsor; (02) 4577 4544; www.clydesdalesrestaurant.com.au

Lochiel House: 1259 Bells Line of Road, Kurrajong; (02) 4567 7754; www.lochielhouse.com

Mash Cafe: 19 Ross St, Glenbrook; (02) 4739 5908; www.mashcafe.com.au

Restaurant Como: 134 Great Western Hwy, Blaxland; (02) 4739 8555; www.restaurantcomo.com.au

Restaurant Tomah: Mount Tomah Botanic Garden, Bells Line of Road, Bilpin; (02) 4567 2060; www.restauranttomah.com.au

Sassafras Creek Cafe: 83 Old Bells Line of Road, Kurrajong Village; (02) 4573 0988; www.sassafrascreek.com.au

Tutti Fruitti: 1917 Bells Line of Road, Bilpin; (02) 4567 8436; www.tuttifruitti.com.au

Zokoko: Unit 3, 84–90 Old Bathurst Rd, Emu Heights; (02) 4735 0666; www.zokoko.com

STORES

Bilpin Fruit Bowl: 2093 Bells Line of Road, Bilpin; (02) 4567 1152

The Local Harvest: Cnr Johnsons Rd and Bells Line of Road, Bilpin; 0414 671 154.

MARKETS

Camden Produce Markets: Lower John St; 2nd and 4th Sat each month, morning; 0403 617 333

Hawkesbury Harvest Farmers' & Fine Food Market: Castle Hill Showground, 2nd Sat each month, morning, 0406 237 877; Joan Sutherland Performing Art Centre, High St, Penrith, 1st Sat each month, morning, 0406 237 877; School of Arts Hall, March St, Richmond, 2nd Sat each month, morning, 0406 237 877

Penrith Original Farmers' Market: Penrith Showground, Station St; 1st and 3rd Fri each month; (02) 9744 5252

Windsor Mall Craft Market: George St Mall, Windsor; Sun each month except Jan; 0418 869 685; www.windsormallcraftmarket.com

GOURMET PRODUCE

Bilpin Springs Orchard: 2550 Bells Line of Road, Bilpin; (02) 4567 1294; www.bilpinspringsorchard.com.au

Cottage Orchard: 3158 Bells Line of Rd, Bilpin; (02) 4567 2193

Enniskillen Orchard: 753 Grose Vale Rd, Grose Vale; (02) 4572 1124; www.enniskillenorchard.com.au

Game Farm: 51 Crosslands Rd, Galston; (02) 9653 2113; www.gamefarm.com.au

Kurrajong Australian Native Foods: Kurrajong; (02) 4577 8711; www.bushtuckershop.com

Pepe's Ducks: 17 Walker St, South Windsor; (02) 4577 4233

Shields Orchard: 2270 Bells Line of Road, Bilpin; (02) 4567 1206; www.shieldsorchard.com

Willowbrae Chevre Cheese: 143 Singleton Rd, Wilberforce; (02) 4575 1077

Wirraninna Ridge: 134 Kurts Rd, Bilpin; (02) 4567 1240; www.wirraninnaridge.com.au

WINERIES

Tizzana Winery: 518 Tizzana Rd, Ebenezer; (02) 4579 1150; www.winery.tizzana.com.au

BREWERIES

Go-Shu Sake: 29 Cassola Pl, Penrith; (02) 4732 2833; www.sun-masamune.com.au

COOKING SCHOOLS

Urban Graze: 6 Patterson Ave, Kellyville; (02) 9862 3042; www.urbangraze.com.au

Blue Mountains and beyond

Try to imagine those early explorers attempting to cross the Blue Mountains. These ranges, tinged a deceptively benign pale blue by the mists from multitudes of eucalypts, were in reality treacherous. The men hoped to break through to a panorama of plains and undulating countryside. But there were many disappointments as they were continually confronted by yet more steep bluffs and wild gorges coated with seemingly impenetrable bushland. This is wild, untouched country. It was here that a prehistoric tree, the Wollemi pine, was much later discovered – still growing and propagating – and it is here that there are still purported sightings of wild black panthers.

Early last century many Sydneysiders came to the higher altitude for health cures. Medlow Bath was a popular spa and the once-glamorous Hydro Majestic is now in the throes of being revitalised. Thousands of visitors still make the two-hour trip from the city for the mountains' clean air and outdoor activities, the breathtaking views creating endless photo opportunities and the delights of the chain of villages along the highway on the ascent. These small towns are places where you can linger over

Festivals

Yulefest: cold-climate food and activities; throughout the Blue Mountains; June–Aug; www.yulefest.com or www.katoomba-nsw.com/Yulefest.html

Mudgee Wine and Food Fair at Balmoral: Mudgee's prime produce on show at the beach; Aug; www.mudgeewine.com.au

Mudgee Fine Food Awards: highly respected nationally; presentation dinner Sept; www.mudgeefinefoods.com.au/awards.htm

Mudgee Wine Festival: spectacular month-long fiesta; Sept; www.mudgeewine.com.au

Where to stay

Echoes Boutique Hotel & Restaurant: magnificent views and luxury; 3 Lilianfels Ave, Katoomba; (02) 4782 1966; www.echoeshotel.com.au

Mountain Heritage Hotel & Spa Retreat: gracious and comfortable (*see* feature, p. 22); Cnr Apex and Lovel sts, Katoomba; (02) 4782 2155; www.mountainheritage.com.au

Old Leura Dairy: eco-friendly rustic charm; 61 Kings Rd, Leura; (02) 4782 0700; www.oldleuradairy.com.au

Pericoe Retreat: homestead retreat; 12R Cassandra Dr, Dubbo; (02) 6887 2705; www.pericoeretreat.com.au

Wombadah and Tierney House: grand accommodation amid the vines; 46 Tierney La, Mudgee; (02) 6373 3176; www.wombadah.com.au *and* www.tierneyhouse.com.au

Above (left to right): coffee to go, and coffee to stay, at Fresh Espresso, Katoomba; horseriding in the Blue Mountains; local produce on display

coffee and cake, browse crammed shops for souvenirs and antiques, or simply soak up the atmosphere. The more hardy can lace on hiking boots and hit the bushwalking trails, but others see the area as the place to come in summer when Sydney, a thousand metres below at sea level, is sweltering.

Katoomba, one of the highest towns, and the largest, was the prescription in the late 19th century when Sir Frederick Darley, then Sydney Chief Justice, learned that his 22-year-old-daughter Lilian had contracted tuberculosis. Hoping that the pure mountain air would save her, he set about building a house there that, sadly, she did not live to see. Many owners later, this elegant home at last realised its potential in 1992 when, after an entire refurbishment and restoration, it opened as the site of **Darley's** restaurant, along with Lilianfels Blue Mountains, a top-class, 86-room country house located on the same grounds.

A meal at Darley's has ever since been a coveted special occasion. The hushed and polished dining room transports diners back more than a century

and the menus of the succession of fine chefs have followed the tradition of making the best of local mountain produce. Chef Carl Middleton's menu showcases it well with an entrée of baby beet salad and heirloom tomatoes teamed with Bent Back goat's cheese from nearby Jannei Dairy. A main course of tender Mandagery Creek venison loin comes with baby carrots, Warrigal greens, and kipfler fondant potatoes, with a red wine reduction.

The ideal option is to stay in the area for several days so that you can pace yourself, dining at several of the other options nearby. At **Echoes**, clinging to the cliff top across the road from Lilianfels, the restaurant's menu explores a spectrum of flavours from truffle béarnaise over duck breast to a finger lime dessert. Then there's **Arjuna** for good Indian curries and naan, or a trip back in time at **The Rooster**, for French cuisine and spectacular views of the Jamieson Valley.

Make it your business too, to search out **Blue M**, the definitive place to buy Blue Mountains products,

or better still sit back and have them served to you, slowly, at a table in the garden. Slow is the right word because Katoomba was recognised as Australia's second Cittaslow in 2007. There are obvious sympathies with Slow Food, but the concept extends further, to nurturing and protecting artisans, traditions, environment and culture. Locally grown fruit and vegetables are available at the **Blue Mountains Food Co-op** too.

In Katoomba's steeply rising main street, Katoomba Street, do stop at **Hominy Bakery** for some of the best organic sourdough you'll find, and the old-style milk bar **Paragon Restaurant** with its handmade chocolates, or any number of other cafes. Keep alert for good aromas of coffee and baking and you can't go wrong. **Fresh Espresso** is always worth a visit and the carbon-neutral cafe is eco-friendly. Take a detour to **Blue Mountains Chocolate Company** for some handmade chocolates or the house specialty, chocolate-coated toffees, or better still, watch a demonstration or book in for a course with the European chocolatier!

If you spend a few days in the rarefied atmosphere of the mountains, you too may feel your pace slowing. Loiter in lovely Leura, with its quintessential village atmosphere. Here you will discover busy cafes such as **Leura Gourmet**, **Red Door Cafe** or **Stockmarket Cafe**. Go for breakfast. You could easily still be there for lunch. Nearby, **Silk's Brasserie**, a Leura classic, can provide for your finer dining needs. A stayer, it has been here 15 years, but remains contemporary. A fine wine list, many by the glass, accompanies an up-to-the-minute menu, with dishes such as pan-fried snapper fillet on baked polenta cake, with tomato relish, chorizo and Kalamata olive butter.

If you want a side order of spectacular views, the aptly named **Solitary** restaurant at Leura Falls is a must. Chefs John Cross and David Povelsen have recently created a more family- and budget-friendly menu. Seated outside with a meze or charcuterie plate and no other buildings in sight, you could be excused for feeling that you own the mountains.

Travel on a little further west to nearby Blackheath, the highest point in the mountains, to

Above *(left to right):* mountain views from the deck at Echoes Restaurant, Katoomba; heritage splendour at Glenella, Blackheath; owner Glenys Lilley rolling pastry at Foxwood Farm Fine Food Cafe, Running Stream; Huntington Estate cellar door, Mudgee

Ashcrofts (save room for Corinne Evatt's burnt almond ice-cream), long-time favourite Philip Searle's wood-fired dishes at **Vulcans**, and the recently revitalised **Glenella** with guesthouse attached. Here you will drool over the wagyu, blue-eye and venison dishes, but don't skip dessert. If you are lucky, the rose geranium panna cotta, orange compote, strawberry salsa and dark chocolate might be on the menu.

But wait, there's more. A slew of gourmet daytime delights awaits, including handmade chocolates at **Cafe Josophan's** (also at Leura), and sourdough bread at **Bakehouse on Wentworth** (also at Springwood and Leura). Take a trip towards Govetts Leap (yes, there is a history to the name) and you'll find **Bush Rock Cafe**, just what it sounds, homely and welcoming with an eclectic organic menu. If you like that sort of thing you'll also want to stop off at the **Conservation Hut** in Wentworth Falls on the way back down the mountains, for either the panoramic views or as the well-earned reward after a bushwalk in the adjoining national park.

At Medlow Bath, one must-see is the **Whisk & Pin Store and Cafe** in the recycled Post Office. W&P's trademark muesli is served here, making this an essential breakfast stop, but don't miss the excellent cafe fare. It's a shop, too, so stock up on gourmet goodies if you are self-catering or picnicking.

It is about here that you must make a choice. If this is a daytrip from Sydney, or an overnight break, you will most probably need to turn back. You could swing off from Blackheath towards the often overlooked but stunning Megalong Valley. You'll discover a heritage farm, an olive grove, and **Megalong Valley Tearooms**, which has been family owned and operated for over 50 years. Understandably it has become famous for its Devonshire teas.

For others, the lure of the west is pulling and you keep going. Finally you crest the ranges that those explorers sweated over and swoop down towards Hartley, a golden sandstone heritage township. **Hartley Valley Teahouse**, at Little Hartley, provides just what you would want and expect in this

location – a Devonshire tea, some jam or a pot plant to take home. Not far away, along with farming necessities, **Adam's Shed** has a wide variety of produce available from all around the Central Tablelands and Blue Mountains regions and tasting of local wines is available at the weekends.

Take the road to Mudgee and shortly on the right you will see the multi-awarded **Jannei Goat Dairy**. While not officially a tourist stop, you will see the flock of goats that provides some of the state's finest goat curd and cheeses. An important stop for coffee lovers is **Foxwood Farm Fine Food Cafe**. The home-baked pies are a signature, so have a slice of apple pie to begin with then take another home.

Mention Mudgee, and most people's thoughts turn to either wine or honey (Mudgee Honey has become almost a byword with honey lovers). There are a couple of dozen wineries in the area and the signposts on key corners in the valley make deciding where to visit almost impossible. **Abercorn Wine** is important for its fine shiraz, and **Botolobar** (try the preservative-free dry red to see for yourself) and

Thistle Hill specialise in organic reds. **Huntington Estate**'s big red Block 3 cabernet is worth experiencing too. **Robert Stein Vineyard & Winery** has great rieslings and **Logan Wines**' sauvignon blanc is getting good reviews. The best way is to pick up a wine map in town and wander the back roads and laneways, stopping to taste anywhere that takes your fancy.

But don't think of this as a new wine region. Craigmoor Winery was established in 1858 by German immigrant Adam Roth, and is one of Australia's oldest wineries. It became Poet's Corner and is now **Robert Oatley Vineyards**. Many German immigrants followed Roth, and for a time the area was like a mini Barossa. Roth's wife would make cheeses and take them to market in Mudgee. At that time the bush was so dense that they had to mark blazes on the trees so she could find her way back home again!

Mudgee's assets are disproportionately large. Wineries, restaurants and cafes abound, and food producers of honeys and mustards, trout, yabbies, lamb, nuts, jams, jellies, fruit and vegetables make the area almost self-sufficient. See much of it at **Mudgee Gourmet** in the beautifully restored railway station. You are spoiled for choice when planning your dining. **Blue Wren Wines**, **Burrundulla** and **High Valley Wine** (& Cheese Co) have dining at their cellar doors.

Bechora and Sybil **Deeb's Kitchen, Restaurant and B&B** in an old schoolhouse on the Cassilis Road is a must to visit at the weekends. Bechora's soft creamy yoghurt and sheep's cheese are signature items, born of his Lebanese heritage, and they feature in many of his dishes. A meal here is like dining with friends. Good friends, who cook magnificently.

In town there is the **Wineglass Bar & Grill** at the Cobb & Co Hotel for hearty country food, **Eltons Brasserie** for delicious wood-fired pizzas and an Italian-inspired menu, and **Rajarani** for good Indian fare. Breakfasts and coffees are good at the always-busy **Butcher Shop Cafe**. It has a sibling in nearby Gulgong as well. But you can also score a great way to start the day at **High Valley Wine & Cheese and Fromagerie Cafe** (and snap up some of their fabulous cheeses to take home as well) near **Deeb's**, or the **Quaff Shop Gallery Cafe** in town. Later in the day, you can factor in a stop at **Roth's Wine Bar**, for some bar food (think, meze) and local tipples, including beers from the **Mudgee Brewing Company**.

A detour to Wellington is a good idea as you can schedule a stop for lunch or a coffee at **Cactus Gallery**. In the cool and lofty surrounds of this former Catholic Infant's School, there is cafe fare, indoor or outdoor dining and an artistic and eclectic gift shop. If time permits, make sure you visit Dubbo, home to an amazing inland zoo, but also with much else to offer. Dubbo's dining history has been a little chequered, but currently **Rose Garden Thai** is the salvation of those wanting good food. It is spicy (of course) and largely vegetarian, but there are prawn and chicken dishes as well. Over wine at **Two Doors Tapas & Wine Bar** you may feel you're back in the city somewhere, while **Newtown Providores**, generously stocked with gourmet goodies, is inner-city bountiful. On a visit (open Friday–Sunday) to the much-awarded **Lazy River Estate**, just 3 kilometres out of town, you can dine simply at the cafe by the river and vines, or pick up a hamper and take it where you please.

If you want one more treat, **Lime Grove** at Narromine grows 10 000 chemical-free lime trees, and has recently opened a cafe. If you travel the extra 40 kilometres from Dubbo you can experience Moroccan lamb or lime tart enhanced by limes grown just metres away, and take home a bag of fresh ones too.

Below (left to right): crisp white table linen sets the scene in the dining room at Glenella, Blackheath; forest-fringed walkway in the Blue Mountains

Yuletide

Christmas in July

They say it all began with the Irish, when a band of nostalgic visitors one chilly night in 1980 encountered the sort of crisp, clear winter weather that reminded them of Ireland, right there, in the mountains. In mid-July! They were relaxing at the **Mountain Heritage Hotel & Spa Retreat** (*see* Where to stay) at Katoomba, at an altitude of 1000 metres, in front of a roaring log fire. Host and owner Garry Crockett listened enthralled as his guests remembered snowy Christmases thousands of kilometres away. It's not the same in Australia, they all agreed. Crockett, of Irish ancestry himself, decided there was no reason why an Aussie Christmas could not be celebrated in our winter. He decided to re-create a Yuletide atmosphere on his premises. Assuring his other guests this was no Irish joke, he sourced a Christmas tree and decorations (no easy feat mid-year) and prepared a feast of traditional foods – turkey, mulled wine and Christmas pudding – then capped it off with carol singing and a visit from Santa. Of course it was such a success that it soon became a mountain tradition. Now known as Yulefest, this three-month event warms the hearts of visitors to the Blue Mountains in the winter months (*see* Festivals).

Contacts for Blue Mountains and beyond

EATERIES

Arjuna: 16 Valley Rd, Katoomba;
(02) 4782 4662

Ashcrofts: 18 Govetts Leap Rd, Blackheath;
(02) 4787 8297; www.ashcrofts.com

Blue M: 1 Kanimbla St, Katoomba;
(02) 4782 2650; www.bluemfood.com

Blue Wren Wines Restaurant:
433 Ulan Rd, Mudgee; (02) 6372 6205;
www.bluewrenwines.com.au

Burrundulla: 234 Castlereagh Hwy,
Mudgee; (02) 6372 9532;
www.burrundulla.com.au

Bush Rock Cafe: 198 Evans Lookout Rd,
Blackheath; (02) 4787 7111

Butcher Shop Cafe: 49 Church St,
Mudgee, (02) 6372 7373;
113 Main St, Gulgong, (02) 6374 2622

Cactus Gallery: 33–35 Warne St,
Wellington; (02) 6845 4647;
www.cactuscafe.com.au

Conservation Hut: Fletcher St,
Wentworth Falls; (02) 4757 3827;
www.conservationhut.com.au

Darley's: Lilianfels, Lilianfels Ave,
Katoomba; (02) 4780 1200;
www.lilianfels.com.au

Deeb's Kitchen, Restaurant and B&B:
Cnr Cassilis Rd and Buckaroo La, Mudgee;
(02) 6373 3133

Echoes Restaurant: Echoes Boutique
Hotel & Restaurant, 3 Lilianfels Ave,
Katoomba; (02) 4782 1966;
www.echoeshotel.com.au

Eltons Brasserie: 81 Market St, Mudgee;
(02) 6372 0772

Foxwood Farm Fine Food Cafe:
Castlereagh Hwy, Running Stream;
(02) 6358 8251;
www.foxwoodfarm.com.au/Welcome.html

Fresh Espresso: Shop 5, 181 Katoomba St,
Katoomba; (02) 4782 3602;
www.freshcafe.com.au

Glenella: 56 Govetts Leap Rd, Blackheath;
(02) 4787 8352;
www.glenellabluemountainshotel.com.au

Hartley Valley Teahouse: Cnr Great
Western Hwy and Baaners La, Little Hartley;
(02) 6355 2048;
www.hartleyvalley.com.au

**High Valley Wine & Cheese and
Fromagerie Cafe:** see Gourmet Produce

Lazy River Estate: see Wineries

Leura Gourmet: 159 Leura Mall, Leura;
(02) 4784 1438

Megalong Valley Tearooms and Kiosk:
Megalong Rd, Megalong Valley;
(02) 4787 9181;
www.megalongtearooms.com

Paragon Restaurant & Chocolatierie:
65 Katoomba St, Katoomba;
(02) 4782 2928

Quaff Shop Gallery Cafe: 13 Lewis St,
Mudgee; (02) 6372 4940;
www.thequaffshop.com

Rajarani: 75 Church St, Mudgee;
(02) 6372 3968

Red Door Cafe: 134 The Mall, Leura;
(02) 4784 1328

Rose Garden Thai: 208 Brisbane St,
Dubbo; (02) 6882 8322

Roth's Wine Bar: 30 Market St, Mudgee;
(02) 6372 1222;
www.rothswinebar.com.au

Silk's Brasserie: 128 The Mall, Leura;
(02) 4784 2534; www.silksleura.com

Solitary: 90 Cliff Dr, Leura;
(02) 4782 1164; www.solitary.com.au

Stockmarket Cafe: 179 The Mall, Leura;
(02) 4784 3121

The Rooster: 48 Merriwa St, Katoomba;
(02) 4782 1206; www.jamisonhouse.com

Two Doors Tapas & Wine Bar:
215B Macquarie St, Dubbo; (02) 6885 2333;
www.twodoors.com.au

Vulcans: 33 Govetts Leap Rd, Blackheath;
(02) 4787 6899

Whisk & Pin Store and Cafe: 1 Railway
Pde, Medlow Bath; (02) 4788 1555;
www.whiskandpin.com.au

Wineglass Bar & Grill: Cobb & Co Court
Boutique Hotel, cnr Market and Perry sts,
Mudgee; (02) 6372 3417;
www.cobbandcocourt.com.au

STORES

Adam's Shed: Great Western Hwy,
Hartley; (02) 6355 2096

Bakehouse on Wentworth:
10 Wentworth St, Blackheath,
(02) 4787 7255; 209 Macquarie Rd,
Springwood, (02) 4751 5788;
208 The Mall, Leura, (02) 4784 3588

Blue Mountains Food Co-op: Shops 1–2,
Hapenny La, Katoomba; (02) 4782 5890;
www.bluemtnsfood.asn.au

Hominy Bakery: 185 Katoomba St,
Katoomba St; (02) 4782 9816

**Mudgee Gourmet @ The Railway
Station:** Railway Station, Inglis St, Mudgee;
(02) 6372 0030;
www.mudgeehampers.com.au

Newtown Providores: 62 Wingewarra St,
Dubbo; (02) 6882 0055

Opposite (left to right): warm atmosphere at
Roth's Wine Bar, Mudgee; intimate dining room
at Ashcrofts, Blackheath; dining room at Silk's
Brasserie, Leura

MARKETS

Blackheath Growers' Market: Blackheath Community Hall, cnr Great Western Hwy and Gardiner Cres; 2nd Sun each month, morning; (02) 4572 6260

Dubbo Farmers' Market: Visitor Centre; 1st and 3rd Sat each month, morning; (02) 6885 4300

Mudgee Farmers' Market: grounds of St Mary's Catholic Church, cnr Church and Market sts; 3rd Sat each month, morning; (02) 6362 2677; www.mudgeefinefoods.com.au

GOURMET PRODUCE

Blue M: see Eateries

Blue Mountains Chocolate Company: 176 Lurline St, Katoomba; (02) 4782 7071; www.bluemountainschocolate.com.au

Cafe Josophan's: 12 Govetts Leap Rd, Blackheath, (02) 4787 6333; 187a The Mall, Leura, (02) 4784 3833; www.josophans.com.au

High Valley Wine & Cheese and Fromagerie Cafe: 137 Cassilis Rd, Mudgee; (02) 6372 1011; www.highvalley.com.au

Jannei Goat Dairy: Castlereagh Hwy, Lidsdale; (02) 6355 1107

Lime Grove: 4606 Mitchell Hwy, Narromine; (02) 6889 1962; www.limegrove.net.au

Whisk & Pin Store and Cafe: see Eateries

WINERIES

Abercorn Wine: 679 Ulan Rd, Mudgee; (02) 6373 3106; www.abercornwine.com.au

Blue Wren Wines: see Eateries/Blue Wren Wines Restaurant

Botolobar: 89 Botolobar Rd, Mudgee; (02) 6373 3840; www.botolobar.com

Burrundulla: see Eateries

Lazy River Estate: 29R Old Dubbo Rd, Dubbo; (02) 6882 2111; www.lazyriverestate.com.au

Logan Wines: Castlereagh Hwy, Mudgee; (02) 6373 1333; www.loganwines.com.au

High Valley Wine & Cheese Co: see Gourmet Produce

Huntington Estate: Cassilis Rd, Mudgee; (02) 6373 3825; www.huntingtonestate.com.au

Robert Oatley Vineyards: Craigmoor Rd, Mudgee; (02) 6372 2208; www.robertoatley.com.au

Robert Stein Vineyard & Winery: Pipeclay La, Mudgee; (02) 6373 3991; www.robertstein.com.au

Thistle Hill: McDonalds Rd, Mudgee; (02) 6373 3400; www.thistlehill.com.au

BREWERIES

Mudgee Brewing Company: 4 Church St, Mudgee; (02) 6372 6726; www.mudgeebrewing.com.au

COOKING SCHOOLS

Blue Mountains Chocolate Company: see Gourmet Produce

Central Tablelands

What do you make of a district that bears the name of one fruit, but grows another? This is just one of the surprises you will discover around Orange in the Central Tablelands region. At one time eager gold-diggers worked the fields in the central west of the state. Now the picks and shovels have been replaced by knives and forks as people come seeking gold of another kind. In fact the 1800s gold rush was relatively short-lived. Farming soon took over but for generations pastoralists battled drought. In desperation, many changed course, diversifying from wheat and sheep into other industries such as wine grapes, fruit, lavender or olive-growing, or raising trout, deer, alpaca, chickens or rabbits. Aussie farmers are nothing if not inventive, and some built B&Bs, cafes and outlets for the produce on their properties. In fact if you take a leisurely trip around this region you will certainly meet many of these people, all with a story to tell.

The Central Tablelands is a region bounded by the two 'anchor cities' of Bathurst and Orange, and the smaller centres of Cowra and Young. It's rich land, some of it high altitude and ideal for growing many fruits as well as grapes for cool-climate wines. Many people mistakenly only associate

Above: Cows grazing in the field near Arancia B&B, Orange

Opposite (top to bottom): a fresh truffle just dug from the ground at A Slice of Orange; guest room at Bishop's Court hotel, Bathurst

Festivals

Bathurst Harvest Festival: Apr;
(02) 6332 2333 or 1800 681 000;
www.bathurstharvestfestival.com

Orange FOOD Week: local wine,
food, arts and culture; Orange,
Cabonne and Blayney area; Apr;
(02) 6362 5151 or 1800 069 466;
www.orangefoodweek.com.au

Central Ranges Truffle Festival:
celebratory tours and dinners;
Orange; July; (02) 6360 1990;
www.trufflefestival.com.au

Orange Wine Week: Oct;
(02) 6360 1990;
www.tasteorange.com.au

Young Cherry Festival: harvest
festival; Dec; (02) 6382 3394;
www.visityoung.com.au/pages/
national-cherry-festival

Where to stay

Arancia B&B: tranquil retreat;
69 Wrights La, Orange; (02) 6365 3305;
www.arancia.com.au

**Bishop's Court Estate Boutique
Hotel:** grand historic house;
226 Seymour St, Bathurst;
(02) 6332 4447;
www.bishopscourtbathurst.com.au

Black Sheep Inn: shearing shed meets
luxury (*see feature, p. 33*); 91 Heifer
Station La (off Forbes Rd), Borenore;
(02) 6369 0662; blacksheepinn.com.au

Everview Retreat: romantic luxury
stone cottages; 72 Cultowa La, 'The
Vines', Canowindra; (02) 6344 3116;
www.everview.com.au

Five Frogs Guest House: luxury
lodgings in a historic village; 3 Belubula
St, Carcoar; (02) 6367 3155;
www.fivefrogs.com.au

Above (left to right): minimalist decor at Cobblestone Lane, Bathurst; peaceful water flows at Cowra Japanese Garden; a graceful gum casts shade at Grove Estate cellar door, Young; regional food and wine are on offer at Absolutely Delicious, Bathurst

Bathurst with motor racing, particularly the Bathurst 1000, a high-octane event that draws rev-heads from all over the country each October. The easiest (and tastiest) way to find out what else the town does best is to drop in to **Absolutely Delicious**, a cafe and regional food and wine centre next door to the Bathurst Visitor Centre. It's the ideal way to calibrate your tastebuds for the exciting journey you are about to have through this diverse region.

A quick visit to **Legall Patisserie** is always a must. Here French owner-chef Philippe Legall dispenses meltingly delicate cakes and pastries and chocolate confisserie. Two doors away **The Hub Espresso Bar** serves these delicacies along with excellent locally roasted **Fish River Roasters** coffee, and good cafe fare. On some evenings, there's a side order of cool jazz in the courtyard. A block away, on the main street, **Country Fruit** has an amazing range of fruit and vegetables and almost any good food you can imagine.

Another place to include in your travels is the oft-awarded **Cobblestone Lane** in the main street,

where owner-chef Heath Smith does good things with the local produce. For example, a Bombaldry rabbit and thyme terrine comes with pickled rhubarb and toasted brioche. If that doesn't get your mouth watering then maybe his roasted Blayney suckling pork, pear, prune and Pedro Ximenez compote will.

Just under a scenic 40 kilometres west is Orange, which many wrongly assume to be a citrus centre because of its name (inexplicably the town was named in the 1820s for Prince William of Orange, the Crown Prince of Holland). Instead, because of the altitude and climate, the area is much better known for crisp flavoursome apples and other cool-climate fruits. The conditions here are well suited to winegrowing too. The entire Orange–Cowra–Young (Hilltops wine region) area has over 50 wineries. Many have also planted olives and as well as cellar doors for wine-tasting have branched into olive-oil-tasting, cafes and sales of local produce. Worth seeing are **The Quarry Restaurant & Cellar Door** at Cowra Estate and the **Mill Cellar Door & Function Centre** at **Windowrie Wines**, where you should taste The Mill verdelho.

The Orange area has the most wineries in this region and **Canobolas-Smith**'s premium handmade chardonnays are exceptional, while **Philip Shaw Wines**' shiraz viognier is particularly well respected. **Chalkers Crossing** in Young has excellent shiraz and, also in the Hilltops wine region, **Grove Estate**'s rare sommita nebbiolo is worth trying. For tasting and sales, **Union Bank Wine Store** is centrally located in Orange and stocks most local wines.

With a population of nearly 40 000, Orange is large enough to provide something for everyone. The restaurant scene is diverse and of a high standard. For a start, Union Bank Wine Store's name belies its role. This is not just another wine store. Its competence in providing food at the adjoining bar and restaurant to match its stellar wine list is much valued in the town. Lunch or dinner inside by the fire or outdoors under the trees and umbrellas is one of the better things to do in Orange.

Originally the owner of renowned Selkirks restaurant, these days Michael Manners works with Michael Borg at **Manners & Borg**, providing traiteur-style meals from a small shopfront opposite the supermarket. The place is always busy, with diners seated on stools at the side counter enjoying food that would sit well in any Paris bistro. Others take away containers of lasagne, Thai chicken curry, roast pork or lamb hot pot, secure in the knowledge they will dine on food from a five-star chef at home that night.

The old Selkirks site is now occupied by **Bistro Ceello**. Former Selkirks sous-chef Scott Want (more recently at Union Bank Wine Store) is in charge, offering dishes that track the seasons such as house-made terrine, local venison from **Mandagery Creek**, or a glistening dish of lamb rump with ratatouille and rosemary polenta at bistro-affordable prices. All are sensibly matched with local wines. Stay on for desserts of Orange mountain ice or fig and almond tart.

Lolli Redini, named for a family friend of the owner, is another popular restaurant in town, noted for its approachable food that features Chef Simonn Hawke's wonderfully sensual take on contemporary cuisine.

Above (left to right):
wine on display at
Totally Local, Orange;
gifts and goodies at
A Slice of Orange;
cooking class at Urban
Graze, Millthorpe;
convivial atmosphere
at Union Bank Wine
Store, Orange

One bite of her meltingly wonderful Jannei goat's
cheese, hazelnut, sorrel and asparagus tartlet with the
counterpoint of truffle honey dressing and crisped
pancetta will explain her food's enduring popularity.

Out of town on the Lake Canoblas Road is **Racine
Restaurant** at **La Colline Wines**, where chefs Shaun
Arantz and Tom Grasso are passionate about local
produce. One week they may feature local pork,
another it will be goat. **Sister's Rock Restaurant** at
Borrodell on the Mount also promotes the local
products. Why wouldn't they? This rich area is a
chef's wonderland and the Borrodell property has its
own amazing range of produce including truffles.

Two places in town, the aptly named **A Slice of
Orange** and **Totally Local**, are both crammed with
the bounty of the area. Here you're likely to find
Anna's Cuisina's award-winning condiments and
relishes, Fish River Roasters coffee, **Huntley Berry
Farm** jams and condiments, **Greentrees Gourmet
Preserves**, **Trunkey Bacon & Pork** and enough of
other things to fill your shopping bag (or car boot!)
for your return journey.

Similarly, in an elegant historic building in the
main street of Cudal, to the west of Orange, the
Cabonne Food, Wine & Cultural Centre showcases
the rich history, food, wine and attractions of the
region. There's an extensive range of local produce
and crafts, making this the ideal place to stop for a
country cuppa.

If you have the time and would like to learn what
to do with this largesse, Lesley Black's **Orange
Regional Cooking School** will answer your questions.
The Essential Ingredient in the centre of Orange
stocks gourmet ingredients and the equipment to
create your dishes. **Hawkes General Store** (formerly
Fem's) multi-tasks, living up to its name and
providing accoutrements for all phases of your life,
especially the kitchen, even allowing a place to stop
for a coffee and consider your shopping list.

Cafes abound in Orange. **Bills Beans**' comfy
corner cafe has a faithful following, no doubt lured
by the aroma of Bill Parianos' freshly roasted beans.
Very popular with vegetarians is **Bodhi Garden**, ideal
for a meatless yum cha and a teahouse experience.

And if it's a good old-style meat pie you're after, go for **Whitey's Pies on Sale**, the iconic pies originally sold at the old Smoko Shed, which some will remember fondly. Best of all, the pies are handmade daily and are uncompromisingly good. If you're making your own pies and looking for local meat, all **M & J's Butchery**'s meats are hung for at least 14 days for maximum tenderness.

As you travel around the area – and ideally you'll need plenty of time – make sure you visit the cluster of villages in a triangle close to both Bathurst and Orange. Millthorpe is notable for its fine-dining restaurant, **Tonic**. Here owner-chef Tony Worland's produce-driven menu lures diners from near and far. Little wonder when in the right season you could be tucking into Blayney pork loin with braised red cabbage, walnuts and Jerusalem artichokes in the beautifully restored 19th-century building. Nearby, newly opened **la boucherie** deals with local appetites too, with Single Origin Coffee, and lighter, yet absolutely luscious offerings. Also in the town is the flower-flanked **Old Mill Cafe & Restaurant** and

newly located **Urban Graze** cookery school. The fledgling **Millthorpe Truffles** is also here, and Urban Graze has tours planned to explore these in season.

At nearby Blayney, **Sallydale Orchard** is the oldest organic farm in New South Wales, still producing heritage apples, and drying some of them to crisp perfection. Lovely old Carcoar, the third town to be established west of the Blue Mountains, has revived its **Royal Hotel** and new life has been breathed into the dining room. Others flock to the **O'Connell Cafe & Deli** beyond Bathurst for meals matched with vegetables home-grown just outside the door, or to the **Beekeepers Inn** at Vittoria to settle back to enjoy the views and the range of local products as well as the coffee and food.

To the east of Orange, the community of Borenore has a sprinkling of places worth visiting. **Hillside Orchard**, for a wide range of apples and stone fruits, and **Norland Fig Orchard**, are worth a visit in season. **The Old Convent** is a cafe-lover's magnet on Sundays, while the small and unassuming old **Borenore Store** turns out to be the quintessential country find – great coffee, good wine selection and a smiling welcome.

Heading south, Canowindra with its dog-legged main street is well preserved and a delightful step back in time, even more so when you take time to visit **Deli Lama** in the main street and pick up some 'food for the soul' – gourmet local products, homemade meals and maybe a just-baked cake and some coffee. Also in town is **taste Canowindra**, a skilful blend of wine, art and food in a unique award-winning restaurant and art gallery. Come here for wines from ten local vineyards, lunch any day, or for the scheduled theatre restaurant evenings and art exhibition openings. The Canowindra region is often called Australia's hot air ballooning capital, and you can see how floating over the patchwork of paddocks, vines and olive groves would be, literally, an 'uplifting experience'.

Neila restaurant in Cowra is a long-time favourite, with its door now almost covered by awards, as it brings the local flavours together better than anywhere else. Owners Jerry and Anna Wong have set about making this cosy restaurant into a home-like haven with food that would sit well in a large city fine-diner. Anna's touch with citrus caramel pork hock or slow-cooked duck leg served with saltwater breast and prunes explains those many awards. Better still, much of the produce originates just a few kilometres away on the Wongs' farm.

It's hard to imagine that Young, a small town set in lovely farming country 376 kilometres west of Sydney, was once the site of vicious race riots and bloodshed during its short-lived gold rush in 1860. On the cusp of both the Riverina and Capital Country it is now the self-styled cherry capital of Australia. Come here in cherry season (especially for the annual festival late in the year) and you'll pass through many kilometres of orchards, some with the freshly picked produce for sale at the orchard gate. Or check with the visitor centre about which places will allow you to pick your own fruit. And cherries are not the only stone fruit grown in this area. **Verity Prunes** are processed from local plums, and you should be able to find these along with local duck, rabbit, organic chicken, squab, locally milled flour, honey, Yandilla mustard seed oil, and Hilltop wines in the local **IGA Supermarket**.

Best of all, the town of Young now has access to great coffee. **Art of Espresso** recently moved its roasting operations here from Greenthorpe, about 40 kilometres away. The owners say they had outgrown their tin shed on the farm and needed more space and a shopfront. The new premises include an espresso bar, a retail section for home coffee connoisseurs, accredited barista-training facilities and, of course, the roaster. Also in town, the long-established **Zouch Restaurant** is still a warm and cosy dinner restaurant with an outdoor courtyard. Head chef Nathan Beasley's confit pork belly appropriately comes with Madeira-soaked prunes, and you can bet that in season there will be cherries on the menu too.

Below (left to right): fresh baguettes at A Slice of Orange; Liz Frencham performs in the restaurant at taste Canowindra, and the venue's art gallery space

Shearing-shed chic

A night at the Black Sheep Inn

If you grew up in the country, you may have found shearing sheds interesting but smelly and dirty. Never in a million years would you have considered spending the night in one! Prepare to have your ideas about these places upended. A couple of years ago the Napier family, owners of a sheep-raising property, set about turning their hundred-year-old corrugated-iron shearing shed into a place of unpredictable beauty and comfort. The makeover uncovered the best features and retained them, while gently smoothing out the damage caused by years of use. So you have pieces of shearing equipment still in place and lanolin-soaked original floorboards in the central space forming a sort of great hall and dining area, alongside the latest in creature comforts.

The five guest suites are country-comfortable with enough rustic charm to make them authentic and the 'inn' ideal for families or groups. There are fluffy towels and thick doonas, and plenty of cushions, open fires and glossy magazines to make a sublime getaway. With all this, and stunning views across rolling pastures, possibly what guests remember most is Helen Napier's stunning homestead breakfasts. You'll wish you could find dishes like hers in your favourite cafe back home.

Contacts for Central Tablelands

EATERIES

Beekeepers Inn: 2319 Mitchell Hwy, Vittoria; (02) 6368 7382

Bills Beans: 148 McLachlan St, East Orange; (02) 6361 1611; www.billsbeans.com.au

Bistro Ceello: 179 Anson St, Orange; (02) 6361 1179; www.bistroceello.com.au

Bodhi Garden: 341 Summer St, Orange; (02) 6360 4478

Cobblestone Lane: Webb Chambers, 2/173–179 George St, Bathurst; (02) 6331 2202; www.thecobblestonelane.com

Deli Lama: 87 Gaskill St, Canowindra; (02) 6344 1006

la boucherie: 25 Victoria St, Millthorpe; (02) 6366 3656

Legall Patisserie: 56 Keppel St, Bathurst; (02) 6331 5800

Lolli Redini: 48 Sale St, Orange; (02) 6361 7748; www.lolliredini.com.au

Manners & Borg: Rear 166 Summer St, Orange; (02) 6362 2037; www.mannersandborg.com

Neila: 5 Kendal St, Cowra; (02) 6341 2188; www.neila.com.au

O'Connell Cafe & Deli: 2431 O'Connell Rd, O'Connell; (02) 6329 4880

Old Mill Cafe & Restaurant: 12 Pym St, Millthorpe; (02) 6366 3188; www.orange-nsw.com/TheOldMill.htm

Racine Restaurant: La Colline Wines, 42 Lake Canobolas Rd, Nashdale; (02) 6365 3275; www.racinerestaurant.com.au

Royal Hotel: 6 Belubula St, Carcoar; (02) 6367 3009

Sister's Rock Restaurant: Borrodell on the Mount, 298 Lake Canobolas Rd, Orange; (02) 6365 3128; www.borrodell.com.au

taste Canowindra: 42 Ferguson St, Canowindra; (02) 6344 2332; www.tastecanowindra.com.au

The Hub Espresso Bar: 52 Keppel St, Bathurst; (02) 6332 1565

The Old Convent: Convent La, Borenore; (02) 6365 2420; www.oldconvent.com.au

The Quarry Restaurant & Cellar Door: Cowra Estate, 7191 Boorowa Rd, Cowra; (02) 6342 3650

Tonic: Cnr Pym and Victoria sts, Millthorpe; (02) 6366 3811; www.tonicmillthorpe.com.au

Union Bank Wine Store: Cnr Byng and Sale sts, Orange; (02) 6361 4441; www.unionbank.com.au

Zouch: 26 Zouch St, Young; (02) 6382 2775; www.zouch.com.au

STORES

A Slice of Orange: 200 Anson St, Orange; (02) 6369 0396; www.asliceoforange.com.au

Absolutely Delicious: 1 Kendal Ave, Bathurst; (02) 6334 2588; www.bathurst-nsw.com/AbsolutelyDelicious.html

Borenore Store: 595 Borenore Rd, Borenore; (02) 6365 2261

Cabonne Food, Wine & Cultural Centre: Main St, Cudal; (02) 6364 2038

Country Fruit: 165 George St, Bathurst; (02) 6331 1742

Hawkes General Store: 46 Sale St, Orange; (02) 6362 5851; www.hawkesgeneralstore.com.au

IGA Supermarket: 159 Boorowa St, Young; (02) 6382 2443

M & J's Butchery: 30 Moulder St, Orange; (02) 6362 2037; www.orange-nsw.com/MJButchery.html

Mill Cellar Door: 6 Vaux St, Cowra; (02) 6341 4141; www.windowrie.com.au

The Essential Ingredient: 145 Summer St, Orange; (02) 6361 8999; www.theessentialingredient.com.au

Totally Local: 426 Mitchell Hwy, Orange; (02) 6360 4604; www.totallylocal.com.au

Union Bank Wine Store: see Eateries

Whitey's Pies on Sale: 26B Sale St, Orange; (02) 6362 6263; www.whiteyspies.com.au

MARKETS

Bathurst Region Farmers' Markets: Bathurst Showground, Sydney Rd, Kelso; 4th Sat each month, morning; (02) 6368 1104

Cowra Region Farmers' Market: Cowra Showground; 3rd Sat each month, morning; (02) 6342 9225

Orange Region Farmers' Market: Orange Showground; 2nd Sat each month, morning; (02) 6362 0039

GOURMET PRODUCE

Anna's Cuisina: 1/207 McLachlan St, Orange; (02) 6362 9613; www.annascuisina.com.au

Art of Espresso: 35 Main St, Young; (02) 6382 1151; www.artofespresso.com.au

Borrodell on the Mount: 298 Lake Canobolas Rd, Orange; (02) 6365 3425; www.borrodell.com.au

Fish River Roasters: Bathurst;
(02) 6329 4860;
www.fishriverroasters.com.au

Greentrees Gourmet Preserves:
33 Pinnacle Rd, Orange; (02) 6361 4546

Hillside Orchard: 1209 Escort Way,
Borenore; (02) 6365 2247

Huntley Berry Farm: Huntley Rd,
via Orange; (02) 6365 5282

Mandagery Creek Venison:
PO Box 37, Orange; (02) 6365 6171;
www.mandagerycreek.com.au

Millthorpe Truffles: Millthorpe;
(02) 6366 3348

Norland Fig Orchard: 'Norland',
Bradley Rd, Borenore; (02) 6365 2225

Sallydale Orchard: 225 Marshalls La,
Blayney; (02) 6368 2550

Trunkey Bacon & Pork: Shop 9, Kurim
Shopping Centre, Kurim Ave, Orange;
(02) 6369 1381

Verity Prunes: 43 Nasmyth St, Young;
(02) 6382 2656; www.verityfruits.com.au

WINERIES

Borrodell on the Mount: see Gourmet
Produce

Canobolas-Smith: Boree La (off Cargo Rd),
Orange; (02) 6365 6113;
www.canobolassmithwines.com.au

Chalkers Crossing: 285 Henry Lawson
Way, Young; (02) 6382 6900;
www.chalkerscrossing.com.au

Cowra Estate: see Eateries/The Quarry
Restaurant & Cellar Door

Grove Estate: 4100 Murringo Rd, Young;
(02) 6382 6999; www.groveestate.com.au

La Colline Wines: 42 Lake Canobolas Rd,
Nashdale; (02) 6365 3275;
www.orange-nsw.com/LaCollineWines.html

Philip Shaw Wines: Koomooloo Vineyard,
Caldwell La, Orange; (02) 6365 2334;
www.philipshaw.com.au

Windowrie Wines: 6 Vaux St, Cowra;
(02) 6341 4141; www.windowrie.com.au

COOKING SCHOOLS

Orange Regional Cooking School:
169 Hill St, Orange; (02) 6361 3336;
www.learntocook.com.au

Urban Graze: 6 Patterson Ave, Millthorpe;
(02) 9862 3042; www.urbangraze.com.au

Below (left to right): produce for sale at A Slice of
Orange; a pyramid of venison and red date salad at
Neila, Cowra

Central Coast and Newcastle

The Central Coast is a stunningly beautiful yet complicated place to drive around. Notched by bays, inlets and lagoon-like lakes, as well as the mouth of the mighty Hawkesbury River, there are many delightful small communities tucked in wherever there's a view. So, rather than try to follow a logical route, it is best just to wander and enjoy the serendipity of discovery.

This part of the coast has always been a fruitful area. In 1830 John Moore, an Irish army officer, was granted a tract of land here, which he named Avoca. There he grew date palms, wine grapes, pears and maize. Now this part of the Central Coast is known as Avoca Beach. Just an hour or so from Sydney by road, the area is richer than ever, making it an ideal daytrip from Sydney. Be prepared to change your mind, though. Chances are you will find so much to explore, one day will not be long enough. However, there is an abundance of comfortable B&Bs, guesthouses and luxury lodges with room for you to rest after your hectic days of sightseeing, beachcombing, surfing and dining.

Above: seagulls survey the foreshore at Terrigal

Opposite (top to bottom): cool blues and pale timber floors at Bells at Killcare, Killcare Beach; salmon and salmon roe at Berowra Waters Inn

Festivals

Wine & Waves Festival: fine wine and food from Newcastle and the Hunter Valley; Merewether (Newcastle); Mar; (02) 4961 3200; www.wine-and-waves.com.

Terrigal Food & Wine Fair: Terrigal Haven; Terrigal; Oct; 0434 427 667; www. terrigalfoodandwinefair.com.au

Bitter & Twisted International Boutique Beer Festival: Maitland Gaol, East Maitland; Nov; (02) 4931 2888; www.bitterandtwisted.com.au

Where to stay

Bells at Killcare Boutique Hotel Restaurant and Bar: beach and country accommodation, fine food; 107 The Scenic Rd, Killcare Beach; (02) 4360 2411; www.bellsatkillcare.com.au

Crowne Plaza Newcastle: premier foreshore hotel; Cnr Merewether St and Wharf Rd; (02) 4907 5000; www.crowneplaza.com

Kims Beach Hideaway: idyllic beachside bungalows; 16 Charlton St, Toowoon Beach; (02) 4332 1566; www.kims.com.au

Magenta Shores – Quay West Resort: family friendly resort; 1 Magenta Dr, Magenta; 1800 095 764; www.mirvachotels.com.au

Pretty Beach House: exclusive guesthouse; Bouddi Peninsula; (02) 4360 1933 or 1300 773 889; www.prettybeachhouse.com

Above (left to right): louvred windows welcome the river-cooled breezes in summer at Berowra Waters Inn; chefs at work, and a lobster and prawn creation, at rocksalt on Newcastle Marina; Berowra Waters Inn jetty

The region's bounty also includes honey and free-range eggs, sourdough bread, fruit, vegetables, herbs and chillies. The monthly **Avoca Beach Growers' Market** brings together a good mix of food to buy to take home, and food to eat there, as well as knick-knacks and trinkets, jewellery and pot plants. There is a carnival atmosphere and it is evident the locals enjoy the excuse for a community get-together while shopping. But wait, there's more. Not everything happens on land. The Hawkesbury River is a great source of prime rock oysters, and there are many oyster farmers in the region. Brooklyn is a great place to get some, as well as fish and seafood caught locally. **J J's at the mouth of the Hawkesbury River** sells some of the best and the Crab and Oyster Cruise, also based at Brooklyn, will allow you to learn more about how the oysters are farmed. Call (02) 9985 8237 for details.

Up and down the coast there are places where you can try your own skill at fishing, and the good news is that bream, blackfish, flathead, whiting and prawns are in abundance. If your luck is out, there

are other ways to enjoy some fish. Most restaurants serve local seafood, and **Seasalt** at the Crowne Plaza in Terrigal goes a step further with a magnificent seafood platter.

Looking for somewhere to enjoy a leisurely, sunny breakfast? Go to **Coast Bistro and Lounge** in Terrigal. Lunch by the beach? Try the all-day breakfast at **Zanziba**, or specials at **Bellyfish Cafe**, both in Terrigal. While here at the seaside, fish and chips is a must. Locals say that **The Snapper Spot** is the best. Not completely satisfied? Then how about some entertainment while you dine? **Lizotte's** at Kincumber has jazz, blues and rock acts booked year-round.

One of the region's biggest surprises is **Flair** at Erina Heights, located in a shopping centre yet serving standout food that reflects the expertise of owner-chef Jason Martin (ex-Lamiche). His wife's Latin influence is apparent in the signature dish of ceviche of scallops with prawn mayonnaise, and twice-cooked pork belly with squid and chorizo.

It must be something in the air here. The well-respected **Lamiche** at Wamberal near Forresters

Beach certainly does not need to curry favour, yet a complimentary amuse-bouche and petit fours appear as a standard part of the hospitality. You get the feeling you have just been invited to dine with your new best friends. Chef Catherine Amos is now in charge of the stoves and, of course, there is yet another stunning view from this restaurant. Night-time dining is mandatory too at **The Cowrie**, with its panoramic views of the starry lights of Terrigal below and the sea beyond.

Gourmet experiences are seemingly endless in this region. For instance at Blue Bay near The Entrance you may go for lunch at **Ocean Restaurant**, known for its ultra-local produce (Empire Bay oysters, samphire from the rocks below), then discover that Italian-leaning **Onda** (the name means 'wave') just down the coast at Terrigal is an ideal plan for the following day. Or evening. After all, house-made gnocchi or pasta is quite an inducement, and the view of the lagoon and beach will seal the deal. At the southern end, **Reef Restaurant** almost paddles in the sea.

Then, of course, there's **Pearls on the Beach** at Pearl Beach, a secluded enclave that the locals may not wish to have publicised too much. However, this is too good to ignore because news of fine beachside dining must be shared. Eat light, on sushi-grade yellowfin tuna tataki with tamarind, chilli and ginger pickled vegetables, or forget the plan and go for grain-fed beef or Berkshire loin of pork. It's a win-win choice.

All long-time food lovers in Sydney have a **Berowra Waters Inn** memory. For 20 years this riverside restaurant, just north of Sydney but accessible only by boat or seaplane, was the love-child of some of the most gifted chefs in the country, attaining almost mythical status. Then it closed and stayed that way until a couple of years ago, when chef Dietmar Sawyere (former owner of Forty One in Sydney) took it over. Now, a new generation of gourmands will experience the magic of this location partnered once again by the finest food and wines. The interior has been lovingly brought up to date with elegant chairs and new polished timber floorboards, outdoors there is a new balcony for alfresco dining, and Sawyere's food is as confidently brilliant waterside as it was at 42 storeys up, overlooking Sydney Harbour. The degustation menu matched with wines makes a leisurely experience of this location stretch over several hours. The tastes are Mediterranean more than French, even veering towards North Africa. Spanish jambon, brik pastry, and gnocchi meet Australian yabbies and Murray cod on the menu.

Completely different but also remote is **Peats Bite Restaurant** on a tiny island upriver in the Hawkesbury. Again you need a boat, water taxi or floatplane to arrive here in style, but expect a location like no other and leisurely dining on a succession of small dishes banquet-style. Holiday unit accommodation is also available just in case you can't bear to tear yourself away.

Not as inaccessible, yet equally desirable, is **Bells at Killcare**, where former Belmondo chef Stefano Manfredi has established a gourmet locavore base. Better still the attached hotel offers accommodation so that you need not hit the highway for the return trip. To dine on the sunny verandah overlooking the lawns and bushland is a true delight, eclipsed only by a dish of Manfredi's modern Italian fare, rustic beef cheeks on pea purée, and home-style touches of fresh bread and pasta.

Killcare is an emerging food-loving haven it seems. The **Deli Goose** is a popular holiday spot for breakfast (muesli, eggs cocotte) or for its pizzas, a saviour for those who can't bear to cook on their time off. Not far away **Yum Yum Eatery** at Hardy's Bay is a sunny place for Sunday breakfast or later-in-the-week lunches and dinners.

If you are into 'assembling' rather than cooking while travelling, a visit to award-winning **Taste Gourmet Grocer & Cafe** at East Gosford is in order. You'll find almost anything that's delicious here, and if you come over all lazy, stay on and let them feed you with their delicious sandwiches, pies and light meals. For those on a serious health-kick, nearby

Ooomph has all the organic fresh produce anyone could need and **Bodyfuel** at Gosford (also at Terrigal and Tuggerah) does much the same but with coffee. **Caffe Jam** in East Gosford is great for deli dallying, and **Sweet Solutions** in Terrigal is ideal for old-style confectionery. Why not indulge? The whole area has a back to childhood holiday feel!

And while we're talking about beautiful black 'break fluid' you owe yourself a visit to **Caesar's Coffee** in Erina, where they blend and roast to perfection. Many also pick up gourmet treats to take back to their self-catering premises. There is even a Central Coast winery, albeit a fruit one. **Firescreek Fruit Wines** at Holgate produces fascinating fruit, flower and herb wines. Fancy a tipple of delicately dry apricot wine? Or maybe a complex dry Herb Royale might suit your palate more.

A whizbang discovery is **St Fiacre Distillery**, on the former Fragrant Garden site in Erina, where distiller-extraordinaire Phillip Moore produces what he calls 'heavenly spirits for earthly bodies'. This translates to Australian native spirits made using lemon and aniseed myrtle, mountain pepperberry, wild lime or mandarin.

Yarramalong Macadamias, well inland near Kulnura and established almost 40 years ago, is another interesting place to visit, if only to see how these rock-hard nuts are cultivated and to stock up on some to take home. There are tours, and a cafe serves light meals.

Of course the real drawcard to any coastal area is the seafood, and the Central Coast does this superbly. Most eateries serve at least one or two seafood dishes. You can pick up freshly caught fish and farmed seafood easily, and naturally many of the oysters you might be served have been raised in beds that are clearly visible in the Hawkesbury as you travel along the freeway. From the Central Coast it is an easy drive to Newcastle (*see* feature, opposite) and the Hunter Valley (*see* p. 44). So the biggest decision is whether to press on and be tempted by even more delights or to turn for home.

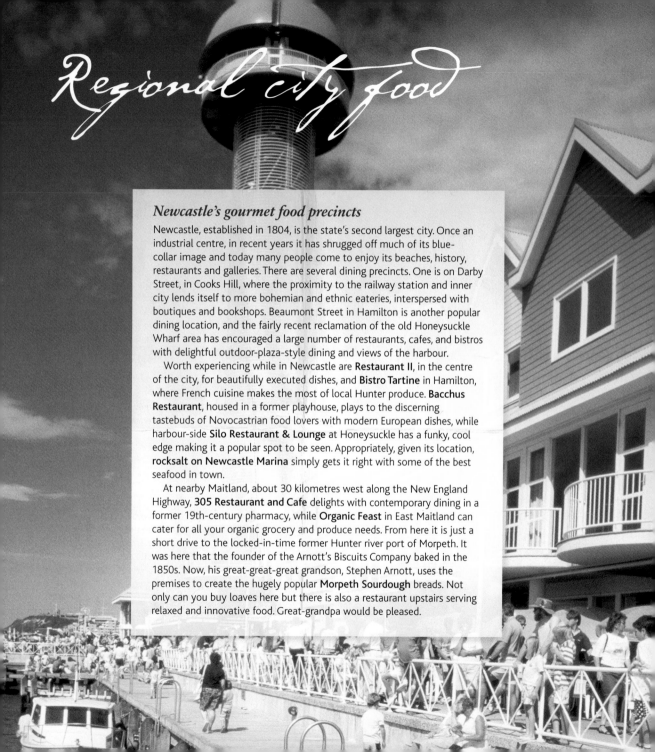

Regional city food

Newcastle's gourmet food precincts

Newcastle, established in 1804, is the state's second largest city. Once an industrial centre, in recent years it has shrugged off much of its blue-collar image and today many people come to enjoy its beaches, history, restaurants and galleries. There are several dining precincts. One is on Darby Street, in Cooks Hill, where the proximity to the railway station and inner city lends itself to more bohemian and ethnic eateries, interspersed with boutiques and bookshops. Beaumont Street in Hamilton is another popular dining location, and the fairly recent reclamation of the old Honeysuckle Wharf area has encouraged a large number of restaurants, cafes, and bistros with delightful outdoor-plaza-style dining and views of the harbour.

Worth experiencing while in Newcastle are **Restaurant II**, in the centre of the city, for beautifully executed dishes, and **Bistro Tartine** in Hamilton, where French cuisine makes the most of local Hunter produce. **Bacchus Restaurant**, housed in a former playhouse, plays to the discerning tastebuds of Novocastrian food lovers with modern European dishes, while harbour-side **Silo Restaurant & Lounge** at Honeysuckle has a funky, cool edge making it a popular spot to be seen. Appropriately, given its location, **rocksalt on Newcastle Marina** simply gets it right with some of the best seafood in town.

At nearby Maitland, about 30 kilometres west along the New England Highway, **305 Restaurant and Cafe** delights with contemporary dining in a former 19th-century pharmacy, while **Organic Feast** in East Maitland can cater for all your organic grocery and produce needs. From here it is just a short drive to the locked-in-time former Hunter river port of Morpeth. It was here that the founder of the Arnott's Biscuits Company baked in the 1850s. Now, his great-great-great grandson, Stephen Arnott, uses the premises to create the hugely popular **Morpeth Sourdough** breads. Not only can you buy loaves here but there is also a restaurant upstairs serving relaxed and innovative food. Great-grandpa would be pleased.

EATERIES

305 Restaurant and Cafe: 305 High St, Maitland; (02) 4933 9989

Bacchus Restaurant: 141 King St, Newcastle; (02) 4927 1332; www.bacchusnewcastle.com.au

Bells at Killcare: 107 The Scenic Road, Killcare Beach; (02) 4360 2411; www.bellsatkillcare.com.au

Bellyfish Cafe: Shop 4, 112 The Esplanade, Terrigal; (02) 4385 6838

Berowra Waters Inn: Public Wharves, Kirkpatrick Way, Berowra Waters; (02) 9456 1027; www.berowrawatersinn.com

Bistro Tartine: 52 Cleary St, Hamilton; (02) 4965 3648

Bodyfuel Cafe: Shop 1, William Crt, Gosford, (02) 4385 3627; 2/12 Kurrawyba Ave, Terrigal, (02) 4385 3627; Shop 7, Tuggerah Business Park, 1 Pioneer Ave, Tuggerah, (02) 4351 0834; www.bodyfuel.com.au

Caffe Jam: Shop 4, 103 Victoria St, East Gosford; (02) 4324 8708

Coast Bistro and Lounge: 5 Kurrawyba Ave, Terrigal; (02) 4385 3100

Deli Goose: Shop 3, Killcare Rd, Killcare; (02) 4360 1888

Flair: 1/488 The Entrance Rd, Erina Heights; (02) 4365 2777

J J's at the mouth of the Hawkesbury River: 8 Dangar Rd, Brooklyn; (02) 9985 7106

Lamiche: 80 Oceanview Rd, Wamberal; (02) 4969 2060

Lizotte's: Lot 3, Avoca Dr, Kincumber; (02) 4368 2017; lizottes.com.au

Morpeth Sourdough: 148 Swan St, Morpeth; (02) 4934 4148; www.morpethsourdough.com.au

Ocean Restaurant: Oceanfront Motel, 102 Ocean Pde, Blue Bay; (02) 4334 4600; oceanrestaurant.com.au

Onda: 150 Terrigal Rd, Terrigal; (02) 4384 5554; www.onda.com.au

Pearls on the Beach: 1 Tourmaline Ave, Pearl Beach; (02) 4342 4400

Peats Bite Restaurant: Sunny Corner, Hawkesbury River; (02) 9985 9040; www.peatsbite.com.au

Reef Restaurant: On the beach, The Haven, Terrigal; (02) 4385 3222; www.reefrestaurant.com.au

Restaurant II: 8 Bolton St, Newcastle; (02) 4929 1233

rocksalt on Newcastle Marina: 91 Hannel St, Newcastle; (02) 4961 1676; www.rocksaltnewcastle.com.au

Seasalt: Level 1, Crowne Plaza, Pinetree La, Terrigal; (02) 4384 9133; www.seasaltrestaurant.com.au

Silo Restaurant & Lounge: 18/1 Honeysuckle Dr, The Boardwalk, Newcastle; (02) 4926 2828; www.silolounge.com.au

The Cowrie: 109 Scenic Hwy, Terrigal; (02) 4384 3016; www.thecowrie.com.au

The Snapper Spot: 104b The Esplanade, Terrigal; (02) 4384 3780

Yum Yum Eatery: 60 Araluen Dr, Hardys Bay; (02) 4360 2999; www.yumyumeatery.com.au

Zanziba: 1/18 Church St, Terrigal; (02) 4385 9144

STORES

Caesar's Coffee: 222 The Entrance Rd, Erina; (02) 4365 1988; www.caesarscoffee.com.au

Ooomph: 26a Adelaide St, East Gosford; (02) 4321 1133; www.ooomph.com

Organic Feast: 10–12 William St, East Maitland; (02) 4934 7351; www.organicfeast.com.au

Sweet Solutions: Shop 5, 42 The Esplanade, Terrigal; (02) 4385 6722

Taste Gourmet Grocer & Cafe: 73 Victoria St, East Gosford; (02) 4324 2130; www.tastegourmet.com.au

Left: coffee and gourmet items on sale at Caesar's Coffee store, Erina

Opposite (top to bottom): succulent mussels and fresh seafood at rocksalt on Newcastle Marina; fruit enticements at Firescreek Fruit Wines, Holgate

MARKETS

Avoca Beach Growers' Market: Hunters Park, cnr Avoca Dr and Vale St; 1st Sun each month, morning; (02) 4572 6260

Kurri Kurri Farmers' Market: Rotary Park, Lang St; 2nd Sat each month, morning; (02) 4937 2640 or 0409 153 628; www.kurrikurri.com/kurri-farmers-market.php

Maitland Fresh Produce Markets: Heritage Mall, High St; Thurs (Jan–Sept, all day; Oct–Dec, morning); (02) 4934 1981

Maitland Markets: Maitland Showground, Blomfield St; 1st Sun each month (Feb–Sept) and 1st and 3rd Sun each month (Oct–Dec); (02) 4962 5522

Newcastle City Farmers' Markets: Newcastle Showground, Griffiths Rd, Broadmeadow; Sun morning; (02) 4930 5156; www.newcastlefarmersmarket.com.au

GOURMET PRODUCE

Morpeth Sourdough: *see* Eateries

Yarramalong Macadamias: RMB 1253, Yarramalong Rd, Yarramalong; (02) 4356 1170; www.yarramalongvalley.com.au/ yarramalong_attractions/macadamia_nut_ farm.html

WINERIES

Firescreek Fruit Wines: 192 Wattle Tree Rd, Holgate; (02) 4365 0768; www.firescreek.com.au

DISTILLERIES

St Fiacre Distillery: 25 Portsmouth Rd, Erina; (02) 4365 3968; www.st-fiacredistillery.com

Hunter Valley

Murrurundi

Scone

BARRINGTON
TOPS
NATIONAL
PARK

Muswellbrook

Denman

Singleton

North Rothbury

Branxton

Broke

Rothbury

Pokolbin

Lovedale

Cessnock

Around two hours drive from Sydney the Lower Hunter Valley, established in the 1820s, was Australia's first wine region. Producing all styles of wine, including some from relatively rare grape varieties, the region has enough wineries (latest count 130 wineries and 100 cellar doors) to keep visitors happily tasting for days. The tasting venues are backed up with a range of bars, cafes and restaurants, everything from casual to elegant, and accommodation that also spans all pockets and preferences. Added to all this are special attractions, world-class musical events and bacchanalian festivals. It is now the most visited wine region in the country. And just as the rich alluvial soil on the flood-prone Hunter riverbanks grows almost anything, so too the vineyards keep popping up.

As you travel around the area passing signs for **Tyrrell's**, **Wyndham Estate** (established in 1828), **Tamburlaine**, **Tempus Two**, **McGuigan Cellars**, **Lindemans**, **Drayton's** and **Hungerford Hill**, you could be forgiven for fantasising that you are taking a drive through someone's prime cellar. If time is a problem, the **Small Winemakers Centre** in Pokolbin is ideal for those who prefer tasting prestige wines from the smaller hidden wineries without extensive travelling. Better still it's next door to the **Australian Regional Food Store & Cafe**, a great place to pick up supplies or a coffee. Lunch is served all day to allow you to tour the vineyards knowing that whenever you tire, a light meal, whether it's dishes such as prosciutto with baby figs in season or specialty cheeses, pâtés, meats, and bread, will fit in to your plans.

One of the great things about the Hunter, apart from the views that go on forever across folding hills striped with vines, and those wines, is that the rich area produces so much else as well. Beef, cheeses, duck, game, olives (and of course sumptuous olive oils), stone fruits and honey are made good use of by local restaurants as they realise that diners are craving a real taste of the region.

Geographically, the Hunter region stretches from the coast where the mighty river enters into the ocean at Newcastle, to the Upper Hunter high in the hills past Muswellbrook, extending to Scone and Murrurundi, then Barrington Tops at its source. The area is large – Cessnock (the key town for the Lower Hunter) is 22 kilometres from Branxton on the New

Festivals

Hunter Uncorked at Pyrmont: Hunter wines come to the city; Apr; (02) 4991 4533; www.hunteruncorked.com.au

Lovedale Long Lunch: progressive lunch; Lovedale Rd and nearby wineries, Lovedale; 3rd weekend in May; www.lovedalelonglunch.com.au

Hunter Valley Wine and Food Month: June; (02) 4991 4533; www.hunterwineandfood.com.au

Hunter Valley Semillon & Seafood: Oct; www.huntersemillonandseafood.com.au

Hunter Uncorked Balmoral: Hunter wines come to the city; Nov; (02) 4991 4533; www.hunteruncorked.com.au

Where to stay

Crowne Plaza Hotel Hunter Valley: city-style hotel amid vines; 430 Wine Country Dr, Lovedale; 1800 899 960; www.crowneplaza.com

Hunter Valley Cooperage B&B: contemporary vineyard accommodation; Lot 41, Kelman Vineyards, 2 Oakey Creek Rd, Pokolbin; (02) 4990 1232; www.huntervalleycooperage.com

Peppers Guesthouse: country-house charm; Ekerts Rd, Pokolbin; (02) 4993 8999; www.peppers.com.au/guest-house

Tower Lodge: luxury gourmet; Halls Rd, Pokolbin; (02) 4998 7022; www.towerestate.com

Above (left to right): chocolate parfait and crème brûlée dome with raspberry mille-feuille at Henri's Brasserie, Singleton; a pasta dish of seasonal produce laced with barbera wine at Margan Restaurant, Broke; Crystal Bay prawns with crab, zucchini and pine-nut tortellini in a saffron and tomato broth at The Cellar Restaurant, Pokolbin; outdoor dining at Bistro Molines, Mount View

England Highway and 35 kilometres from Broke. To allow more time for what you've come for (to be honest, wine tasting and sampling the local food), it's better to break the area up. There is just far too much to explore in a day, or even a weekend. Which is great news as it means you have an excellent excuse to return.

The epicentre is Pokolbin, a sprawling area encompassing some of the country's best vineyards and all that goes with them. To list everything here is impossible. The best idea on arrival is to drop in at the visitor centre on Wine Country Drive, next to the airport, pick up an armful of brochures then retire to the adjoining cafe to work through them and make your choices. The wineries cater for all palates from sparkling wines and dry whites to fruity reds and everything in between. With around 60 restaurants in the Hunter Valley, there are far too many to list them all. It's easiest to say that there is something for everyone.

Look for cafe food at **Cafe Enzo** at Peppers Creek for up-market lunches, and **Cracked Pepper**

Restaurant, next to Iiulis Winery, for lighter fare. **Firestick Cafe** (at **Poole's Rock Winery**), the recipient of many awards, is noted for its model-thin pizza bases and, at the opposite end of the spectrum, hearty lamb shank pies. Elsewhere, many cellar doors do tasting platters of local cheeses and other produce to enjoy along with their own wines, often served outdoors with those stunning Hunter Valley panoramas as an added appetite (not to mention thirst!) stimulant.

For relaxed evening fine dining, **Margan Restaurant** at Broke is ideal (*see* feature, p. 49). Poole's Rock Winery has fine dining at **Rock Restaurant**, a must-do, and winner of even more awards than its cafe. Chef Andrew Clarke's sublime dinner menu may (it changes seasonally) begin with squab breast with black grapes, squab crepinette, truffle vodka and grape seed dressing then progress to wagyu hanger steak with mushroom, pea and bacon, pan-fried sweetbread and remoulade. Considerately he offers infinite options, with each dish available in three sizes.

Many breathed a sigh of relief a while ago to see that venerated chef Robert Molines has not yet hung up his apron. Now his unashamedly French menu at **Bistro Molines** at Tallavera Grove is again drawing former fans and newcomers to the Hunter. His deft hand with offal is in evidence, and so are his duck dishes and pâté, appearing, as they should, seasonally and using locally sourced produce. If the wealth of vineyards reminds you more of Piedmont, though, then a bowl of gnocchi or other northern Italian fare at **Il Cacciatore** should sit just right with you.

Food shopping is a joy in this part of the Hunter. The **Hunter Valley Smelly Cheese Shop** at Pokolbin (now also with an outlet at **Tempus Two Winery**) may not sound attractive, but it is a cheese-lover's heaven, with all the things you need to go with the carefully matured cheeses from its cheese room.

The Hunter has some simple divisions according to its various roads. Don't feel confused by it all. Boards at each intersection clearly announce the winery names. At Hungerford Hill, **Muse Restaurant** is many people's introduction to the area. Lunch at

Muse is one of life's delights and dishes such as a gamy loin braise and roast of Hunter Valley white rabbit with spinach tagliatelle show that owner-chef Troy Rhoades-Brown is clearly enjoying working with and enhancing the local produce.

At the junction of McDonalds and Broke roads, the mighty McGuigan Cellars (the outlet for **McGuigan Wines**) with the **Hunter Valley Cheese Company**, is a must to visit. Take a cheese platter and some wine onto the lawn outside and count your blessings. Look for **Amanda's on the Edge** on McDonalds Road, a country-friendly favourite. Fortunately the name refers to the owner's choice of location (at Windsor's Edge Vineyard) and not her emotional health. At Pokolbin Village resort you'll find **Winehouse Bar & Restaurant**, where a contemporary feel has been injected into Mediterranean food (think ricotta-stuffed butternut pumpkin cannelloni with almonds and muscatels), and at the award-winning Bimbadgen Estate, **Esca Bimbadgen**'s chef Bradley Teale continues to wow diners with his faultless mix of cuisines.

Next door, along Broke Road, Hunter Valley Gardens provides retail therapy at its mini village of shops, which include **Bliss Coffee Roasters** and a branch of the **Hunter Valley Chocolate Company**. When you tire of shopping, there is always **The Cellar Restaurant** as a handy place for lunch or dinner.

Hermitage Road holds other treats such as **La Trattoria at Beltree,** formerly Cafe Beltree, the ideal place to immerse yourself in a bowl of mussels or some other Mediterranean bliss-food, or to stock up on **Binnorie Dairy**'s range of soft cheeses made only with locally sourced milk. Across the road is **Bluetongue Brewery Cafe**, where you can taste handcrafted beers and stay for lunch as well if you like.

For small town charm, continue on from here to Broke. Margan Restaurant is here as well as **Pickled and Pitted**, selling premium olive products. At Lovedale, Lovedale Road, to the east of Wine Country Drive, is the venue for the annual Lovedale Long Lunch, a weekend of outdoor dining and entertainment at the many wineries there. Certainly worth checking out are **Leaves and Fishes, Mojo's on Wilderness** and **Majors Lane Restaurant** (with its **Lovedale Smokehouse** and cookery classes as well). Here you will also find the Hunter Valley Chocolate Company factory and showroom with enough temptations to turn anyone into a serious chocoholic!

Long-time local favourite, **Shakey Tables** is not far away at North Rothbury, and **Redsalt Restaurant** at the Crowne Plaza Hotel is the ideal place for a healthy sunny buffet breakfast. Close by **Potters Hunter Valley Hotel Brewery Resort** at Nulkaba provides an alternative to wine, with Hunter Beers brewed in Potters Brewery. If this cornucopia of wining and dining has made you itch to dust off your apron and get back into the kitchen then you can. **Majors Lane Cooking School**, in Lovedale, has Saturday classes in Asian cookery, and **Sandalyn Wilderness Estate** offers pasta-making classes every weekend, at Rothbury.

Heading north along the New England Highway, Singleton is a quiet Hunter Valley town, removed from the bustle of the wine-lands. In its modern main street location, **Henri's Brasserie** has set the dining tone for this end of the Hunter. Chef Tony Klasen proudly affirms that fresh produce is integral to his restaurant's success. 'Everything on the menu is made on the premises, from the bread to the tomato paste,' he says. Many of the popular products used in the dishes may be bought from **Henri's Pantry** on the ground floor. Upstairs, menu items may include seared scallops with crispy prosciutto and pumpkin sauce, or cauliflower soup with bug tail and white truffle oil.

Muswellbrook, 48 kilometres north, is home to **Hunter Belle Cheese,** which produces award-winning boutique handmade dairy products from a herd of Swiss Brown cows that graze nearby. There is a tasting room in the round dairy building, so make sure you try the cleverly named cheeses (camembelle, a camembert-style cheese, and bluebelle, fromagebelle, and others). Buy here or from other local outlets. Towards Denman you will find **Pukara Estate**'s olive grove and press, which also welcomes visitors and here you may taste the various oils produced by this oft-awarded producer.

Once you reach Scone the farmland has changed and you are in pastoral country and the equestrian capital of the state. The appropriately named **Canter** restaurant in a renovated cottage is a little piece of diner heaven, busy but controlled, with marvellous offerings. Owners Tom and Nicole Jordan set up here a couple of years ago and have made a name for their country fare, which depending on the season includes treats such as a salad of fresh figs, endive, candied macadamias and gorgonzola. All the customer drawcards are here: a monthly farmers' market, accommodation and even a toy store. Elsewhere in town is **Kerv Espresso** (coffee, antiques and deli items), **The Larda** (great breakfasts and coffee), and **Paddock to Pantry**, the ideal place to stock up on supplies or order a hearty sandwich to go.

Don't bypass Murrurundi at the northernmost edge of the Hunter. Better still, time your visit for lunchtime and drop in to **Cafe Telegraph** for a simple lunch of lovingly cooked food under the trees by the riverside. **Bacco's Bakeries**, home of Bacco's Leaves, those so-special gourmet crispbreads and biscotti, is just up the street. Bet you can't resist nibbling on them as you depart the Hunter and travel on! Or regretfully return home.

Margan Restaurant at Margan Estate

Lisa Margan from Margan Restaurant proudly proclaims they 'recycle everything'. Chickens eat the green scraps from the kitchen; manure from the chicken house is raked up to enrich the garden soil. In return, the chickens supply eggs for the menu. 'Our one-acre fruit and vegetable garden is a labour of love as well as a sustainable way we can reduce our food miles,' says Lisa.

Even the restaurant building looks organic. Neutral tones, rammed earth walls, timber chairs and a terracotta and red painting on one wall all add to the feeling that this place has arisen naturally from the Hunter soil. Cushions softening the banquettes and white linen on the tables add balance. And then there's the food: duck tortellini in broth, osso buco on mushroom risotto, roasted root vegetables, saddle of rabbit. Salt of the earth, taste of the seasons, that's the core of the menu. Only seasonal produce is used, either home-grown or sourced locally. 'We create our menus around the seasons and, in particular, what we are harvesting from the garden right now. The water falls from the sky so we offer you fresh rainwater, filtered and free. The wine comes from the grapes grown on our vineyards right here in Broke.' What could possibly be a better offer? Margan Restaurant at **Margan Family Winegrowers Estate** is open for breakfast on Sunday, lunch Friday to Sunday, and dinner Friday to Saturday.

Contacts for Hunter Valley

EATERIES

Amanda's on the Edge: Windsor's Edge Vineyard, McDonalds Rd, Pokolbin; (02) 4998 7900; www.amandas.com.au

Australian Regional Food Store & Cafe: McDonalds Rd, Pokolbin; (02) 4998 6800; www.australianregionalfoods.com.au

Bistro Molines: 749 Mount View Rd, Mount View; (02) 4990 9553; www.bistromolines.com.au

Bluetongue Brewery Cafe: Hunter Resort, Hermitage Rd, Pokolbin; (02) 4998 7777; www.hunterresort.com.au

Cafe Enzo: Peppers Creek Winery, cnr Broke and Ekerts rds, Pokolbin; (02) 4998 7233; www.pepperscreek.com.au

Cafe Telegraph: 155 Mayne St, Murrurundi; (02) 6546 6733

Canter: 111 Susan St, Scone; (02) 6545 2286; www.canterrestaurant.com.au

Cracked Pepper Restaurant: 1616 Broke Rd, Pokolbin; (02): 4998 7076; cracked-pepper.com.au

Esca Bimbadgen: 790 McDonalds Rd, Pokolbin; (02) 4998 4666; www.bimbadgen.com.au

Firestick Cafe: Poole's Rock Winery, 576 DeBeyers Rd, Pokolbin; (02) 4998 6968; www.rockrestaurant.com.au

Henri's Brasserie: Level 1, 85 John St, Singleton; (02) 6571 3566; www.henris.com.au

Il Cacciatore: 609 McDonalds Rd, Pokolbin; (02) 4998 7639; www.hermitagelodge.com.au

Kerv Espresso Bar: 108 Liverpool St, Scone; (02) 6545 3111

La Trattoria at Beltree: 266 Hermitage Rd, Pokolbin; (02) 6574 7216; www.aroundhermitage.com.au

Leaves and Fishes: 737 Lovedale Rd, Lovedale; (02) 4930 7400; www.leavesandfishes.com

Majors Lane Restaurant: 64 Majors La, Lovedale; (02) 4930 7832; www.majorslane.com

Margan Restaurant: 1238 Milbrodale Rd, Broke; (02) 6579 1372; www.margan.com.au

Mojo's on Wilderness: 84 Wilderness Rd, Lovedale; (02) 4930 7244; www.mojos.com.au

Muse Restaurant & Cafe: 1 Broke Rd, Pokolbin; (02) 4998 6777; www.musedining.com.au

Redsalt Restaurant: Crown Plaza Hotel, 430 Wine Country Dr, Lovedale; (02) 4991 0900; www.ichotelsgroup.com

Rock Restaurant: Poole's Rock Winery, 576 DeBeyers Rd, Pokolbin; (02) 4998 6968; www.rockrestaurant.com.au

Shakey Tables: Hunter Country Lodge, 1476 Wine Country Dr, North Rothbury; (02) 4938 1744; www.shakeytables.com.au

The Cellar Restaurant: Hunter Valley Gardens Village, Broke Rd, Pokolbin; (02) 4998 7584; www.the-cellar-restaurant.com.au

The Larda: 122 Kelly St, Scone; (02) 6545 9533

Winehouse Bar & Restaurant: Pokolbin Village, 2188 Broke Rd, Pokolbin; (02) 4998 7945; www.pokolbinvillage.com.au

STORES

Australian Regional Food Store & Cafe: see Eateries

Henri's Pantry: see Eateries/Henri's Brasserie

Hunter Valley Smelly Cheese Shop: Shop 3, Pokolbin Village, 2188 Broke Rd, Pokolbin, (02) 4998 6960; Tempus Two Winery, Hall 1, 2144 Broke Rd, Pokolbin, (02) 4998 6713; www.huntervalleysmellycheeseshop.com.au

Paddock to Pantry: 135 Kelly St, Scone; (02) 6545 9851; www.paddocktopantry.com

Small Winemakers Centre: McDonalds Rd, Pokolbin; (02) 4998 7668; www.smallwinemakerscentre.com.au

MARKETS

Broke Community Markets: McNamara Park; Sat morning; (02) 6579 1334

Dungog Community Markets: Presbyterian Church grounds; 1st Sat each month; (02) 4992 1806

Gresford Markets: Clevedon, Gresford Rd, East Gresford; 3rd Sun each month

Laguna Markets: Old Northern Trading Post; 3rd Sun each month, morning

Singleton Farmers and Craft Market: Singleton Showground, Bathurst St; 4th Sat each month, morning; (02) 4930 5156

Opposite (left to right): vineyard views at Lindemans Wines, Pokolbin; cellar door lounge area at Margan Family Winegrowers Estate, Broke, with a glimpse of the restaurant framed in the rear doorway

GOURMET PRODUCE

Bacco's Bakeries: 13 Mayne St,
Murrurrundi; (02) 6546 6822;
www.baccos.com.au

Binnorie Dairy: Cnr Hermitage Rd and
Mistletoe La, Pokolbin; (02) 4998 6660;
www.binnorie.com.au

Bliss Coffee Roasters: Shop 2, Hunter
Valley Gardens Village, Broke Rd, Pokolbin;
(02) 4998 6700; www.blisscoffee.com.au

Hunter Belle Cheese: 75 Aberdeen St,
Muswellbrook; (02) 6541 5066;
www.hunterbellecheese.com.au

Hunter Valley Cheese Company:
McGuigan's Complex, McDonalds Rd,
Pokolbin; (02) 4998 7744;
www.huntervalleycheese.com.au

Hunter Valley Chocolate Company:
Shop 5, Hunter Valley Gardens Village, Broke
Rd, Pokolbin, (02) 4998 7221; Factory and
Showroom, 820 Lovedale Rd, Lovedale,
(02) 4930 7388; www.hvchocolate.com.au

Lovedale Smokehouse: see Eateries/
Majors Lane Restaurant

Pickled and Pitted: 67 Wollombi St,
Broke, (02) 6579 1063;
www.riverflatsestate.com.au

Pukara Estate: 1440 Denman Rd,
Muswellbrook; (02) 6547 1055;
www.pukaraestate.com.au

WINERIES

Bimbadgen Estate: 790 McDonalds Rd,
Pokolbin; (02) 4998 7585;
www.bimbadgen.com.au

Drayton's Family Wines: 555 Oakey
Creek Rd, Pokolbin; (02) 998 7513;
www.draytonswines.com.au

Hungerford Hill: 1 Broke Rd, Pokolbin;
(02) 4998 7776; www.hungerfordhill.com.au

Lindemans Wines: McDonalds Rd,
Pokolbin; (02) 4998 7684;
www.lindemans.com

Margan Family Winegrowers Estate:
see Eateries/Margan Restaurant

McGuigan Wines: Cnr Broke and
McDonalds rds, Pokolbin; (02) 4998 7402;
www.mcguiganwines.com.au

Poole's Rock Winery: DeBeyers Rd,
Pokolbin; (02) 4998 7356;
www.poolesrock.com.au

Tamburlaine: 358 McDonalds Rd,
Pokolbin; (02) 4998 7570;
www.tamburlaine.com.au

Tempus Two Winery: Cnr Broke and
McDonalds Rd, Pokolbin; (02) 4993 3999;
www.tempustwo.com.au

Tyrrell's Wines: 1838 Broke Rd, Pokolbin;
(02) 4993 7000; www.tyrrells.com.au

Wyndham Estate: 700 Dalwood Rd,
Dalwood; (02) 4938 3444;
www.wyndhamestate.com

BREWERIES

Bluetongue Brewery Cafe: see Eateries

**Potters Hunter Valley Hotel Brewery
Resort:** Old Brickworks, Wine Country Dr,
Nulkaba; (02) 4991 7922;
www.pottersbrewery.com.au

COOKING SCHOOLS

Majors Lane Cooking School: see
Eateries/Majors Lane Restaurant

Sandalyn Wilderness Estate: Wilderness
Rd, Rothbury; (02) 4930 7611;
www.huntervalleyboutiques.com.au/
pasta_class.html

Southern Holiday Coast

Frederickton
Kempsey
Port
Wauchope Macquarie
Byaburra
Comboyne   Kew
Lorne
Laurieton
Wingham
Cundletown
Taree
Forster-
Tuncurry
Wootton   Boomerang
Bulahdelah   Beach
Blueys
Beach   TASMAN
SEA
Raymond
Terrace Nelson Bay
Shoal Bay

Imagine the surprise – no, make that, amazement – of explorer John Oxley and his men when, in 1818, they broke out of harsh bushland and encountered a magical view of the sparkling Pacific Ocean and sweeping white beaches. Trekking through the mountainous inland they had come upon the area that we now know as Port Macquarie. This major town is roughly halfway between Sydney and Brisbane on the Pacific Highway (Highway 1), or the Pacific Coast Touring Route as it is now termed. Getting there is certainly easier these days, but the rewards and surprises are just as great. It makes a delightful stopping point.

The Southern Holiday Coast is part of the extensive Northern Rivers region of New South Wales. Wide rivers dawdle through lush landscapes before emptying into the ocean at regular intervals along the coast between Newcastle, on the Central Coast, and Tweed Heads, on the Tropical North Coast. These rich floodplains will grow almost anything, including macadamias, avocadoes, kiwi fruit, coffee and bananas, and the sweet pastures plump out the udders of the many herds of black and white dairy cattle that dot the paddocks.

While you can easily drive from Sydney to Port Macquarie in five or so hours, it is well worth looping off occasionally for some unexpected treats. Just beyond Raymond Terrace, north of Newcastle, a turn to the right will soon have you in the town of Nelson Bay on lovely Port Stephens. This natural harbour is larger than Sydney Harbour and its entrance is flanked by the twin exclamation marks of striking former volcanic hills.

Nelson Bay, for such a small town, has a welcome number of good eating spots. Glenn Thompson, the chef at **Zest** restaurant, has for two years running won the Signature Dish Competition held annually in Port Macquarie. The competition attracts chefs from the region who favour fresh, regional, seasonal produce. This year Chef Thompson's dish was a ballotine of farmed Macleay rabbit wrapped in prosciutto with pickled eschalots, black olive paint and sauce aigre doux matched with Cassegrain edition 2008 pinot noir. **Ritual Restaurant**, also in Nelson Bay, is very different, and perhaps destined to become the elBulli of this region. Chef Carl Kenzler prepares avant-garde cuisine that upends any preconceived

Festivals

Oysters in the Vines: oysters and wines; Cassegrain Wines, Port Macquarie; Jan; www.cassegrainwines.com.au

Annual Grape Stomp: vintage celebration; Bago Vineyards, Wauchope; 2nd Sun in Feb; www.bagovineyards.com.au

Slice of Haven Food & Wine Festival: Laurieton; May; www.camdenhaveninfo.org.au

Tastings of the Hastings: food and wine; Port Macquarie; Oct; www.tastingsofthehastings.com.au

Tastes of the Bay Food & Wine Festival: food, wine and jazz; Nelson Bay foreshore; Nov; www.bluewatercountrymusic.com.au/Tastes_At_The_Bay.html

Where to stay

Bank Guest House and Tellers Restaurant: elegant and stylish; 48 Bent St, Wingham; (02) 6553 5068; www.thebankandtellers.com.au

Gypsy Falls Retreat: peaceful waterfall and forest retreat; Lorne; (02) 6556 9702; www.gypsyfalls.com.au

Lotus Retreat: accommodation in rural surrounds; 812 Wattley Hill Rd, Wootton; (02) 4997 7320; www.lotusretreat.com.au

Peppers Anchorage Port Stephens: luxury hotel right at the marina; Corlette Point Rd, Corlette; (02) 4984 2555; www.peppers.com.au/anchorage

Above (left to right): night reflections at Peppers Anchorage near Port Stephens; 'avant-garde' dessert at Ritual Restaurant, Nelson Bay; unpretentious sign points the way to Brush Turkey Cafe, Wootton; flower-framed cellar-door tasting area at Bago Vineyards, Wauchope

notions diners have of how flavours should (and indeed could) be presented (*see* feature, p. 58).

At **Catch at Shoal Bay Resort & Spa** you may be in luck if your visit coincides with one of the bi-monthly Tastes of the Hunter dinners. You won't want to miss one of these, but if you do, don't despair. The chef, Patrick Power, does reliably fine things with local seafood and meats every day (think, a seafood platter for *one*, if you happen to be dining alone, or your partner is seafood-sensitive, and wagyu with a marble score of 8) and the view of the bay is sensational. Good news too is that **Murray's Craft Brewing Co** (the same one that put the beer back in the Pub with No Beer at Taylors Arm near Coffs Harbour) has relocated its brewing operation to just outside the town.

Back on the highway and further north, take a right. **Kingfisher Restaurant** at Blueys Retreat on secluded Blueys Beach is yet another surprise. Owner-chefs Nick and Jane Samaras's touch with country-raised beef, especially a roasted beef fillet crusted with hot English mustard and served with

baked autumn vegetables and beetroot jam, makes a detour worthwhile. A little further on, at Boomerang Beach, local Wallis Lake oysters and prawns are on the menu in season and there's a daily seafood special at **M Bistro** (formerly Restaurant Two Forty) at Breakfree Mobys Resort.

If you choose to stay on the highway, then there's the rustic community-run **Brush Turkey Cafe**, at Wootton, north of Bulahdelah, open only at weekends, but serving homespun food (think apple pie and hearty lasagne and the freshest salads made from herbs and vegetables in the cafe's own garden) from local volunteer cooks. It is a portal to rural Australia circa 1955.

Wingham is the sometimes forgotten backwater of Taree, the much larger town on the Manning River, but it's definitely worth the extra couple of kilometres. Donna Carrier's multi-award-winning cafe, **Bent on Food**, is the sort of place every country town should have. Serving great coffee, light meals and stocked full of local products, it has a wonderful vibe attracting everyone from mums with

toddlers to passing travellers in the know. Recently Donna added the only thing hitherto missing and opened a gourmet kitchenware shop a couple of doors away.

For a sensory experience of another kind you must drop into **Mentges Master Meats** in Chatham, just outside Taree, where a family of artisan butchers continues owner Rudi Mentges 700-year German family tradition making sausages and smallgoods. It's wurst at its best with all the favourites such as weisswurst, pepperwurst and bratwurst, but the biggest hit with customers – cheese kranski – is a beautiful blend of pork and beef with low-fat cheeses. Only open on Thursdays and Fridays, it is understandably packed on those days. There's also good local meat at **Cundletown Butchery** nearby.

On the highway, just north of Taree, at **Ghinni Ghinni Wines**, ex-dairy farmer Tony Hammond turned to making home-grown raspberry, blueberry, chilli, ginger and pumpkin wines after the deregulation of the milk industry, and now sells them from the cellar door on his property. His

ten-year-old honey mead is worth savouring too. As you drive north from Taree, it's not hard to see that the Hastings area is a dairying region. The scene of black and white cows dotting the rich green river flats creates a one-thousand-and-one-dalmatians effect. The milk churns at the farm gates are always a dead giveaway, indicating that you have entered serious milking country, although most are now recycled and serving as letterboxes. The Dairy Fresh signs are the real cue that this is where your daily milk begins its journey.

By now your appetite has been well and truly sharpened, so what is there to eat in Port Macquarie? The good news is there is so much. **The Restaurant at Cassegrain** (formerly Ca Marche), part of the winery outside Port Macquarie, has long been highly regarded and its lovely rose garden-vineyard setting is perfect for a leisurely lunch. But wait, there's more. When chef Lindsey Schwab opened **Fusion 7** in a Port Macquarie cafe-shopping strip a couple of years ago, he was pleasantly surprised to find he'd hit on a formula – laid-back ambience coupled with sensational food. Schwab had worked with the 'godfather' of fusion cuisine, Peter Gordon, in London, hence the restaurant's name. Twice he has won the People's Choice Award at the Signature Dish competition. This year they loved his line-caught local kingfish on fried Ricardoes green tomatoes with spring pea and black bean vinaigrette, coriander and Comboyne potato wafer.

Rydges is a major hotel in Port Macquarie and its **Compass Restaurant**, headed by Michael Schubert, makes good use of the abundant and fresh local seafood. **The Stunned Mullet** is also well respected and serves contemporary food in a relaxed alfresco setting. Make sure you try the crispy skinned local mulloway if it is on the menu when you go there.

For those now tempted to learn what to do with all the bounty of this region, The Company Farm, spectacularly located on a property inland from Wauchope, offers classes (**Cooking with Company**) for around a dozen people at a time in a commercial kitchen and plenty of time to relax and enjoy the meal afterwards. And then there's coffee, expertly roasted and blended by the well-named **Peak Coffee**. Owners Sean and Kris Edwards have long been involved with coffee. Sean is a coffee consultant who travels the state training baristas so understandably the couple is meticulous about their product, prepared in their premises. Coffee machines and equipment are also available.

Cross the mighty Hastings River, just north of Port Macquarie, and watch out for a large sign providing a clue that one of the state's hidden gems is nearby. In 2005, brothers Anthony and Richard Sarks opened **Ricardoes Tomatoes**. They wanted to raise the best and brightest and most flavourful hydroponic tomatoes. With that accomplished, they then added equally bright red strawberries and recently, changing the colour coding, introduced lettuces. Now there is an eatery, **Cafe Red**, and market selling tomatoes and strawberries as well as other local produce and products and farm tours available at 11am on weekdays. Visitors may pick their own strawberries and several varieties of hydroponic lettuce year-round. It is definitely worth a visit.

The heritage of this area is vital. It is best discovered at Kempsey's Wigay Aboriginal Culture Park, where local Aboriginal people guide visitors on bush medicine and Indigenous food tours, then treat them to a feast of damper and barbecued locally caught bream wrapped in paperbark. Call (02) 6567 1013 for more details. The aptly named **Bliss in the Bush Cafe**, just north of Kempsey, is a real find, too. First glance says it's a farm shed, but inside you'll discover a bustling cafe and an eclectic mix of interesting crafty goods for sale. If you only want a quick snack, nothing beats one of the fifty or so varieties of pies baked daily at the legendary **Fredo Pies** in Frederickton just north of Kempsey. There is now a cafe next door and local Peak Coffee is made to perfection here.

Below (left to right): alfresco dining area at The Restaurant at Cassegrain, Port Macquarie; light and bright M Bistro, Boomerang Beach; rural landscapes at Wingham

It would be a mistake to think this area is only about food, though. The North Coast Wine Trail includes Port Macquarie's **Cassegrain Wines**, noted for its delectable chambourcin and shiraz, and several other grape growers and wine producers. The trail meanders along both sides of the Pacific Highway, from just south of Coffs Harbour to just north of Kew. All offer cellar-door facilities. **Long Point Winery** is best known for its chambourcin rosé, and this grape has also made a name for **Bago Vineyards**. To balance the cellar, **Inneslake Vineyards** makes a fine Little Fish summer white, and **Sherwood Estate Wines** has a range of soft, full-bodied reds and whites. Catering for all tastes, Port Macquarie has its own brewery, **The Little Brewing Company**, which turns out a boutique range of unpasteurised natural beers three of which are whimsically tagged Wicked Elf, as well as Mad Abbot, a Belgian-style strong ale.

Stray inland from Wauchope on the Ellenborough Falls road and you will be pleasantly surprised by tiny Byabarra. Only a handful of cars pass each day, yet most can't resist stopping at **Blue Poles** cafe-gallery, which also offers studio accommodation. On this back road south to Wingham, a stop at Comboyne is a must for several reasons. One is that this is where you will discover soft ripened boutique cheeses par excellence. Ron Lindsay attended cheesemaking workshops at Wingham in 2004 at **Duck Under the Table** and was inspired to develop **Comboyne**

Culture cheese, a range of European-style cheeses including camembert and washed rind bluembert. Lindsay blue cheeses are available locally and at markets such as the Great Lakes Great Produce Market on the third Saturday each month. Farmers' markets are the ideal way to see as many producers as possible (*see* Markets, p. 59).

The other reason for stopping at tiny Comboyne is to visit **Baba Lila**, where handmade chocolates are created using the chocolatier's Russian heritage. There are the fillings you'd expect such as trad rum and raisin and prune and brandy of course, but an interesting twist is Baba Lila's Aussie range, where she uses native flavours such as wattle seed and Kakadu plum (as well as locally grown aniseed or lemon myrtle) inside her decadent, hand-rolled, dipped and wrapped chocolates. Look for them also at local farmers' markets.

Be very glad if you need to self-cater along the way north. Forster–Tuncurry, a seafood-lovers' paradise, has the vibrant **Wallis Lakes Fishermen's Co-operative** selling only fish and seafood directly from the boats. Fat local oysters are opened daily at nearby **Barclay Oysters**, and **The Big Oyster** at Port Macquarie does the same, also offering handy cooked-prawn packs. With so much to taste and experience on a trip north along the Pacific Highway, it is easy to see how there's a whole new meaning to 'Highway Number One'.

Tasting journey

Breaking the culinary boundaries at Ritual Restaurant

'I am the scientist and Carl is the chef,' says Kelie Kenzler. The couple are owners of possibly the state's most groundbreaking restaurant. These brave and talented people, who describe their cuisine as 'avant-garde', are extending culinary boundaries in the style of molecular gastronomy experts such as Spain's Ferran Adrià and the United Kingdom's Heston Blumenthal.

Be aware that this is no ordinary food (think, a palate cleanser of pickled ginger cloud, a cube of intensely flavoured foam) so come with an open mind, prepared for textures, flavours and delivery you could never have anticipated. The ten-course or more 'tasting journey' will take your tastebuds where they have never before ventured. Along the way you might encounter deconstructed bruschetta comprising a crumbed onion ring flanking tomato ravioli and a basil leaf suspended in balsamic gel; or a finale of tri apple pie, three creative bites of the traditional apple pie served with custard squares and ice-cream shards. Or maybe not. The Kenzlers are dreaming up new combinations and juxtapositions constantly. Relying on matching mainly organic and biodynamic (and often local) produce according to its chemical composition, often employing unusual combinations, the result is without exception mind-blowing but delightful.

Chef Kenzler's experience on the Sunshine Coast and his wife's science degree makes this a unique partnership. Despite the menu, perhaps the most surprising thing of all is that this place is tucked away in an ordinary suburban shopping strip, a little away from Nelson Bay's main drag. You should plan to dine here soon, as the space is limited and dinner, daily, is by reservation only. As Winner of Best New Restaurant, 2008 (Newcastle & Surrounds) and Best Specialty Restaurant (NSW) 2009, Ritual Restaurant is beginning to get a lot of attention. Who knows, elBulli-like waiting lists could be ahead.

Contacts for Southern Holiday Coast

EATERIES

Bent on Food: 95 Isabella St, Wingham; (02) 6557 0727; www.bentonfood.com

Bliss in the Bush Cafe: 42 Turners Flat Rd, Turners Flat; (02) 6561 7559; www.bliss-in-the-bush.com

Blue Poles: 1086 Comboyne Rd, Byabarra; (02) 6587 1167; www.bluepoles.com.au

Brush Turkey Cafe: 1633 Wootton Way, Wootton; (02) 4997 7296; www.wootton.org.au/cafe.htm

Cafe Red: Ricardoes Tomatoes and Strawberries, 221 Blackman's Point Rd, Port Macquarie; (02) 6585 0663; www.ricardoes.com

Catch at Shoal Bay Resort & Spa: Beachfront, Shoal Bay; 1800 181 810; www.shoalbayresort.com/restaurants-and-bars.aspx

Compass Restaurant: Rydges Port Macquarie, I Hay St, Port Macquarie; (02) 6589 2888; www.rydges.com/hotel/1/RNPMAC/Rydges-Port-Macquarie/restaurants.htm

Fredo Pies: 75 Macleay St, Frederickton; (02) 6566 8226; www.fredopies.com.au

Fusion 7: Shop 6, 124 Horton St, Port Macquarie; (02) 6584 1171; www.fusion7.com.au

Kingfisher Restaurant: Blueys Retreat, 285 Boomerang Dr, Blueys Beach; (02) 6552 9222; www.blueysretreat.com.au

M Bistro: Breakfree Mobys Resort, 4 Redgum Rd, Boomerang Beach; (02) 6554 0766; www.masticate.com.au

Ritual Restaurant: Shops 1–2, Austral Street Shopping Village, Nelson Bay; (02) 4981 5514 or 0422 445 263; www.ritualcuisine.com.au

The Restaurant at Cassegrain: 764 Fernbank Creek Rd, Port Macquarie; (02) 6582 8320; www.cassegrainwines.com.au

The Stunned Mullet: Shop 1,12 William St, The Sandcastle, Port Macquarie; (02) 6584 7757; www.thestunnedmullet.com.au

Zest: 16 Stockton St, Nelson Bay; (02) 4984 2211; www.zestrestaurant.net.au

STORES

Barclay Oysters: Cnr Mark and Little sts, Forster; (02) 6554 7455

Cundletown Butchery: 55 Main St, Cundletown; (02) 6553 9302

Mentges Master Meats: 4 Milligan St, Chatham; (02) 6552 6878

Ricardoes Tomatoes and Strawberries: see Eateries/Cafe Red

The Big Oyster: Hastings River Dr, Port Macquarie; (02) 6584 3803

Wallis Lakes Fishermen's Co-operative: 1 Wharf St, Tuncurry; (02) 6554 6149

MARKETS

Great Lakes Great Produce Market: Tuncurry, 3rd Sat each month; (02) 6554 4184

Hastings Farmers' Market: Port Macquarie, 2nd Sat each month; Wauchope, 4th Sat each month; (02) 6585 9324

Wingham Farmers' Market: 1st Sat each month; (02) 6550 5761

GOURMET PRODUCE

Baba Lila: 12 River St, Comboyne; 0400 384 311; www.babalila.com.au

Comboyne Culture: 12 River St, Comboyne; (02) 6550 4054; www.comboyneculture.com

Peak Coffee: 1/30 Jambali Rd, Port Macquarie; (02) 6581 2677; www.peakcoffee.com.au

WINERIES

Bago Vineyards: Milligans Rd, off Bago Rd, Wauchope; (02) 6585 7099; www.bagovineyards.com.au

Cassegrain Wines: Cnr Fernbank Creek Rd and Pacific Hwy, Port Macquarie; (02) 6582 8377; www.cassegrainwines.com.au

Ghinni Ghinni Wines: Pacific Hwy, Cundletown; (02) 6553 8191

Inneslake Vineyards: The Ruins Way, off Oxley Hwy, Port Macquarie; (02) 6581 1332; www.inneslake.com.au

Long Point Winery: Cnr Long Point Dr and Cooinda Pl, Lake Cathie; (02) 6585 4598; www.longpointvineyard.com.au

Sherwood Estate Wines: 1187 Gowings Hill Rd, Sherwood via Kempsey; (02) 6566 9414; www.sherwoodestatewines.com.au

BREWERIES

Murray's Craft Brewing Co: 3443 Nelson Bay Rd, Bobs Farm; (02) 4982 6411; www.murraysbrewingco.com.au

The Little Brewing Company: Unit 1, 58 Uralla Rd, Port Macquarie; (02) 6581 3949; www.thelittlebrewingcompany.com.au

COOKING SCHOOLS

Cooking with Company: The Company Farm, 3470 Oxley Hwy, Gannons Creek; (02) 6585 6495; www.cookingwithcompany.com.au

Duck Under the Table: 22 Bent St, Wingham; (02) 6553 4057; www.duckunder.com

Coffs Harbour and hinterland

TASMAN SEA

Iluka
Yamba
Maclean
Angourie
Grafton
Halfway Creek
Woolgoolga
Emerald Beach
Dorrigo
Coffs Harbour
Bonville
Sawtell
Bellingen
Urunga
Bowraville
Valla
Nambucca Heads
Macksville
Taylors Arm

If you had visited this part of the coast in the mid-1800s, you would have found Korff's, not Coffs Harbour, and Boat Harbour instead of Bellingen. To further confuse things, if you had visited Bellingen, about 30 kilometres from Coffs, a few years ago, you may have been surprised to see the name 'Clarence' displayed on some public buildings. You would have also seen movie cameras, lights, action and about a fifth of the locals happily employed as extras in the film, *Danny*, starring Miranda Otto, which was being shot on location. Bellingen had been selected as a place with enough old-world charm and solid main-street buildings to suit the backdrop for the film. Locals queued for bit parts, the former timber and farming town spruced itself up and the whole place was abuzz with movement and excitement, for a while.

But change is perhaps the only constant in this area that is forever evolving. Not only names change but so does the focus. If you conjure up the Big Banana, that huge yellow tourist-focused mega market, when you think of Coffs, it's time to take another look. Many farmers are pulling out their bananas and some are replanting with coffee. In the beginning, timber-getting was the original industry in the region, along with gold, then later dairying and fishing – and of course bananas. But inevitably, tourism quickly followed.

Indeed, how could you keep people away from those lush forests, clean glistening beaches, and surf that has had nowhere to break since South America? Today's Coffs, with its subtropical climate, is one of the state's major tourism destinations outside Sydney. The CSIRO rates the climate of this region as one of the most liveable in Australia. Summer is warm, winter is cool and mild, and autumn and spring are delightfully balmy. Travelling north, just 162 kilometres of Highway 1 separates what the locals call 'Port' and 'Coffs', yet somewhere along the way changes occur, morphing the climate from temperate to subtropical.

Every Australian of a certain age has heard of **The Pub With No Beer**. Not everyone realises it actually exists at Taylors Arm in breathtaking hinterland just 25 kilometres from the coast. If you wish, you could continue on that very scenic 'back road' from Macksville to Kempsey, but

Festivals

Chilli Festival: regional restaurateurs serve up Australia's leading chilli products; First Ave, Sawtell; July; www.sawtellchillifestival.com.au

Gate to Plate: celebration of Clarence Valley produce; Grafton Showground; Sept; www.gatetoplate.com.au

Toast Urunga Food and Wine Festival: family fun and food stalls on the waterfront; Urunga; Sept; 0409 817 864; www.coffscoast.com.au/WhatsOn/

Cool Creek Rhythms: music, food and wine; Park Beach Reserve, Coffs Harbour; Oct; 1300 369 070; www.coffscoast.com.au

Where to stay

Bonville Golf Resort: comfortable accommodation; North Bonville Rd, Bonville; (02) 6653 4002 or 1300 722 444; www.bonvillegolf.com.au

Breakfree Aanuka Beach Resort: beachside resort; 11 Firman Dr, Coffs Harbour; (02) 6652 7555; www.breakfreeaanukabeachresort.com.au

Casa Belle Country Guest House: luxury Mediterranean-style villa accommodation; 90 Gleniffer Rd, Bellingen; (02) 6655 9311; www.casabelle.com

Observatory Holiday Apartments: luxury self-contained apartments; 30–36 Camperdown St, Coffs Harbour; (02) 6650 0462 or 1300 302 776; www.theobservatory.com.au

Saltwater: luxury rooms with ocean views; 104 Fiddaman Rd, Emerald Beach; (02) 6656 1888; www.saltwateronthebeach.com

most can't resist sinking a few cold ones on the expansive verandah overlooking that enormous view. Murray's Craft Brewing Co was established here but a couple of years ago the brewing operations moved south to Port Stephens. However, the large range of handcrafted beers is still on tap at the pub (because of its legendary status, contact details for the pub are listed, under Breweries.) Meat lovers are equally well served in nearby Macksville. Dan has left **Dangerous Dan's Butchery** but new owners Peter and Karen Wharton are carrying on the high traditions and still making those trademark bushman and swagman pork and beef sausages that won Dan so many awards.

There are plenty of reasons to stop on this stretch of coastline. Just north at Nambucca Heads, time your arrival for dinner from Wednesday to Saturday and you could be tucking into fragrant olive-studded house-baked sourdough at **Ocean Chill** overlooking the Nambucca River. Chef Matthew Knight has been praised for his slow-cooked blade steak and fearless use of less exotic ingredients such as cabbage, chicken wings and sweetcorn.

In a secluded location at Valla, just up the road, is **Quigley's Smokehouse**. Don't worry if you miss it,

the delicate smoked yellowfin tuna and Quigley's Tuna Dust are available locally. If oysters are more your thing, then family-owned **Lindsay's Oyster Barn** at Urunga will proudly open-to-order their oysters raised 'just up the river'.

At Coffs Harbour everything begins to feel more languid, somehow more bountiful and laid-back. This is resort territory. Lovely beachside Aanuka Beach Resort with its day spa and seafood-focused **Finz on the Beach** restaurant will soon have you in holiday mode. Some visitors choose to stay in these places, cocooned in luxury, playing in the pool, coming out long enough for a pedicure or massage. But you'd short-change yourself if this was all you did in Coffs Harbour. The place has a raft of topnotch eating places, as well as good shopping, and activities that range from whale- and dolphin-watching cruises, to canoeing, golf, deep-sea fishing, and diving.

At the end of town is what the locals call the 'jetty strip' with a range of casual dining places. From here you can walk to **Wild Harvest Seafood Restaurant** in the Coffs Harbour Fishermen's Co-op at the marina for dinner, or pick up simply the best

Below (left to right): casual atmosphere at Split Cafe, Sawtell; tastings on the iron-roofed verandah at Red Dirt Distillery, Dorrigo; Toni and Ray Urquhart at No 2 Oak Street, their cottage restaurant at Bellingen; wining and dining at Flooded Gums, Bonville

fish and chips in town or some prawns to take to the beach. **Fiasco Ristorante and Wine Bar** is not far from this area, at ground level of an apartment building. The lucky residents can pop down any night except Monday for some of chef Stefano Mazzina's northern Italian spaghetti vongole or one of his trademark baked polenta dishes.

In the green and lush hinterland, this tiny wedge of the state has become a bolthole for the rich and famous, the city-weary, and those simply looking for a clean green tree-change. Russell Crowe owns Nana Glen, a property north of Coffs, and locals drop other big names when asked: George Negus, Wendy Matthews, or David Helfgott, for instance.

When Susanne and Fritz Dimmlich decided to retire from Melbourne, they wanted sun and peace and they found plenty of it just outside Bellingen. Here, in a commanding position on the other side of the river from the town, on 13 acres of former dairy land, they built Casa Belle Country Guest House (*see* Where to stay), a cool hacienda draped in bougainvillea, and lit the courtyard by night with chunky Spanish candles. Charming, private, luxurious and welcoming, you may never even make it on to

Coffs. While in Bellingen be sure to dine at **No 2 Oak Street**, a restaurant located in a former bungalow. It's a serial award-winner and after a meal here, you'll know why. Front of house Toni Urquhart lets nothing slip, while husband, Ray, is equally in control in the kitchen. If the night is warm, head to the verandah that encircles the former cottage. Soak up the balmy night air as you tuck into flowerpot house-made breads and Mediterranean-inspired mains. Whatever you do save room for the chocolate and espresso assiette dessert.

A main-street place in Bellingen, **Lodge 241**, makes excellent coffee, as does **Hearth Fire Organic Wood-Fired Bakery**, which is a must for some of the best yeast-free baked goods (and that goes for croissants as well) that you'll find anywhere.

Take time to drive into the mountains to explore the national park and the small but vibrant former logging town of Dorrigo. Even if the 70-kilometre trip leaves you time-poor, at least stop for a coffee and something delicious at **Lick the Spoon**, which is packed with local products and shares the premises with a cellar door. This company, originally known as Waterfall Winery, and sourcing premium local and

Above (left to right): view from Breakfree Aanuka Beach Resort, home of Finz on the Beach, Coffs Harbour; cutting up yellowfin tuna at Quigly Smokehouse, Valla; Wild Harvest Seafood Restaurant in the Coffs Harbour Fishermen's Co-op is famous for the best fish and chips in town; fishing trawlers at Coffs Harbour

regional fruits to produce its fruit wines, moved from Bellingen to Dorrigo in 2005 because of the excellent quality of the water in the mountain town. Now called **Red Dirt Distillery**, it also produces Australia's only potato vodka using Dorrigo red soil Sebago potatoes. A tasting is definitely in order here!

Back near the coast, at Bonville Golf Resort, chef Lee O'Carroll at **Flooded Gums** restaurant has won a steady fan base. Sydney chef George Francisco from Jonah's at Palm Beach acts as his consultant, inspiration and mentor. A dish of Woolgoolga lobster and angel hair pasta, dried chilli and lemon zest reflects the area, while a butter-tender eye fillet of locally grown Black Angus served with wilted spinach, summer beans, jus aioli and pink peppercorns could be the perfect excuse to come back again.

Also in this vicinity is a shop with an absolutely fabulous name. **Absolutely Fabulously Local** is just what it says. Everything stocked in this neat and spotless store comes from somewhere in the region. Because this is an abundant growing area, you can pick up the makings of an entire meal, including local free-range eggs, meat, bacon, Quigley's smoked

yellowfin tuna, pasta, sauce, cheese, bread, fruit, vegetables and much more.

Sawtell, 6 kilometres south of Coffs, seems cut and pasted from another era. First Avenue, the main street, is almost entirely filled by eating spots. **Taste Restaurant** serving good honest contemporary food, just down the street from a revived Art Deco movie theatre, is worthy of a visit, and across the road **Split Cafe** is a must for superb 'as good as Melbourne' coffee.

A little further north along the coast from Coffs, the waterfront **Saltwater Cafe and Restaurant** at Emerald Beach has made a name for its Asian-accented dishes such as kaffir and kingfish wontons and chilli spiced prawns, coconut rice and lemongrass dressing. Desserts are just as appealing and irresistible – chocolate hazelnut meringue torte, maybe? Diners can get so engrossed in the standout meals they forget to be awed by the beautiful ocean view, but the good news is if they have been savvy enough to book a room, they can enjoy it at their leisure.

Drive half an hour north of Coffs to Woolgoolga, or 'Woopi' as it is known in these parts, to find a massive Hindu temple unexpectedly dominating the

skyline. This area is home to the largest Sikh population in the Southern Hemisphere and hosts an annual Curry Festival each April. But despite the temple's breathtaking looks, the various indoor-outdoor cafes serving just the sort of laid-back meals you need at the beach seem to get more attention from many visitors.

Travellers passing north along the highway mark their progress by the huge northern rivers they cross. First it's the Manning at Taree, the Hastings at Port Macquarie, then the Clarence, which meanders past Grafton and Maclean before emptying lazily into the sea at Yamba and Iluka. Don't zoom past these towns. Grafton's Jacaranda Festival each October is a drawcard, but any time of year it's worth visiting **Georgie's at the Gallery**. This well-established restaurant at the rear of the Grafton Regional Gallery is the ideal place to take a break after some 'culture' or to visit out of gallery hours. Expect fine local produce with some surprises such as tasty Brahman hump sausages or duck confit with bacon.

Maclean calls itself the Scottish Town in Australia and many street signs are also written in Gaelic. Even the telegraph poles have painted tartan bands,

with clan names helpfully added. Look for suitably Scottish-inspired products such as haggis sausage in the local butchers, and shortbread and sweeties, slice sausage, haggis-burgers and rumbletythump at various restaurants and cafes in the town.

At the coast, Angourie on the southern side of the estuary has **Frangipan** open for dinner and weekends, its tropical name a clue to how far north you've come. The contemporary menu surfs the world, though, from local seafood to feather-light gnocchi, delicate desserts and good coffee. Yamba, on the northern arm, is a busy surfing spot and **Pippi's Cafe & Bar**, at the Yamba Beach Motel, is a favourite cafe by day, but pulls out the tablecloths for dinner service. For a quick snack or breakfast, there's the ever-popular **Beachwood**, but you may need to wait for a table. On menus in the area, watch out for Carrs Peninsula olives and olive oil, Challacombe strawberries and products, local seafood and coffee. Surprises are everywhere along this part of the coast. Make sure you allow yourself enough time to discover them.

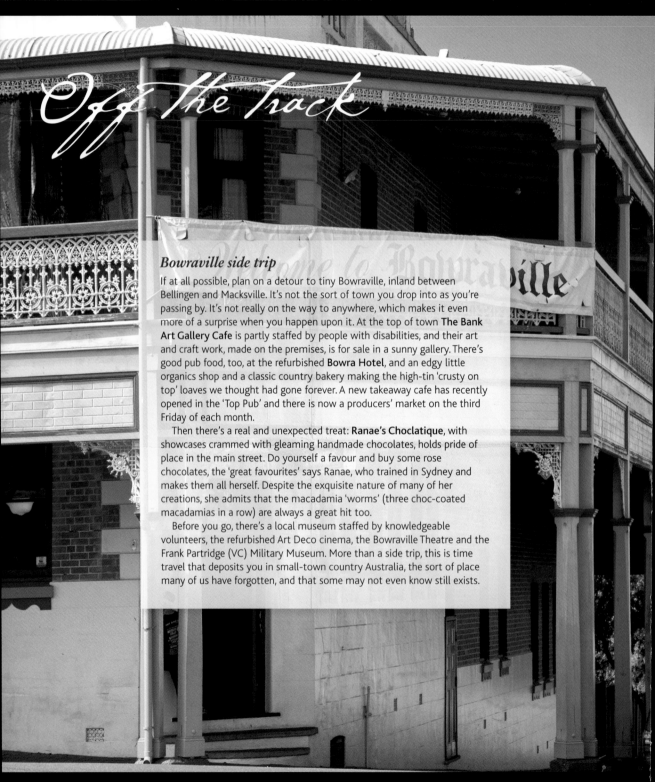

Off the track

Bowraville side trip

If at all possible, plan on a detour to tiny Bowraville, inland between Bellingen and Macksville. It's not the sort of town you drop into as you're passing by. It's not really on the way to anywhere, which makes it even more of a surprise when you happen upon it. At the top of town **The Bank Art Gallery Cafe** is partly staffed by people with disabilities, and their art and craft work, made on the premises, is for sale in a sunny gallery. There's good pub food, too, at the refurbished **Bowra Hotel**, and an edgy little organics shop and a classic country bakery making the high-tin 'crusty on top' loaves we thought had gone forever. A new takeaway cafe has recently opened in the 'Top Pub' and there is now a producers' market on the third Friday of each month.

Then there's a real and unexpected treat: **Ranae's Choclatique**, with showcases crammed with gleaming handmade chocolates, holds pride of place in the main street. Do yourself a favour and buy some rose chocolates, the 'great favourites' says Ranae, who trained in Sydney and makes them all herself. Despite the exquisite nature of many of her creations, she admits that the macadamia 'worms' (three choc-coated macadamias in a row) are always a great hit too.

Before you go, there's a local museum staffed by knowledgeable volunteers, the refurbished Art Deco cinema, the Bowraville Theatre and the Frank Partridge (VC) Military Museum. More than a side trip, this is time travel that deposits you in small-town country Australia, the sort of place many of us have forgotten, and that some may not even know still exists.

Contacts for Coffs Harbour and hinterland

EATERIES

Beachwood: 22 High St, Yamba;
(02) 6646 9781

Bowra Hotel: 33 High St, Bowraville;
(02) 6564 7041;
www.bowraville.org.au/bowrahotel/index.
htm

Fiasco Ristorante and Wine Bar:
22 Orlando St, Coffs Harbour;
(02) 6651 2006; www.caffefiasco.com.au

Finz on the Beach: Breakfree Aanuka
Beach Resort, 11 Firman Dr, Coffs Harbour;
(02) 6652 7555;
www.breakfreeaanukabeachresort.com.au

Flooded Gums: Bonville Golf Resort,
North Bonville Rd, Bonville; (02) 6653 4002;
www.bonvillegolf.com.au/dining

Frangipan: 11–13 The Crescent, Angourie;
(02) 6646 2553

Georgie's at the Gallery: Grafton
Regional Gallery, 158 Fitzroy St, Grafton;
(02) 6642 6996; www.georgiescafe.com.au

Lick the Spoon: 51–53 Hickory St,
Dorrigo; (02) 6657 1373

Lodge 241: 117–212 Hyde St, Bellingen;
(02) 6655 2470;
www.bellingen.com/the lodge

No. 2 Oak Street: 2 Oak St, Bellingen;
(02) 6655 9000; www.no2oakst.com.au

Ocean Chill: 58 Ridge St, Nambucca
Heads; (02) 6568 8877;
www.oceanchill.com

Pippi's Cafe & Bar: Yamba Beach Motel,
cnr Clarence and Queen sts, Yamba;
(02) 6646 1425

Saltwater Cafe and Restaurant:
104 Fiddaman Rd, Emerald Beach;
(02) 6656 1888;
www.saltwateronthebeach.com/restaurant-
mainmenu-73

Split Cafe: Shop 3, 4 First Ave, Sawtell;
(02) 6658 3026

Taste Restaurant: 11 First Ave, Sawtell;
(02) 6658 3583

The Bank Art Gallery Cafe: 88 High St,
Bowraville; (02) 6564 7677

Wild Harvest Seafood Restaurant: Coffs
Harbour Fishermen's Co-operative Ltd,
69 Marina Dr, Coffs Harbour;
(02) 6652 2811; www.coffsfishcoop.com.au

STORES

Absolutely Fabulously Local:
340 Pinecreek Way (Old Pacific Hwy),
Bonville; (02) 6653 5225;
www.absolutelyfabulouslylocal.com.au

Dangerous Dan's Butchery: 13 Princess
St, Macksville; (02) 6568 1036;
www.here.com.au/dans/default.htm

Ranae's Choclatique: Shop 2, 43 High St,
Bowraville; (02) 6564 7133

MARKETS

Bellingen Growers' Market: Bellingen
Showground, Black St; 2nd and 4th Sat each
month, morning; (02) 6653 5288

Bowraville Producers' Market: Main St;
3rd Fri each month; 0404 887 473

Coffs Coast Growers' Market: City
Square, Harbour Dr; Thurs;
(02) 6648 4084

Grafton Farmers & Growers' Market:
Market Square; Thurs morning;
(02) 6642 9700

Maclean Farmers' Market: Maclean
Showground; 1st Sat each month, morning;
(02) 6645 1980

GOURMET PRODUCE

**Hearth Fire Organic Wood-Fired
Bakery:** 73–75 Hyde St, Bellingen;
(02) 6655 0088

Lindsay's Oyster Barn: Pacific Hwy,
Urunga; (02) 6655 3399

Quigley's Smokehouse: Pacific Hwy, Valla;
(02) 6655 3600;
www.quigleyssmokehouse.com.au

BREWERIES/DISTILLERIES

Red Dirt Distillery: 51–53 Hickory St,
Dorrigo; (02) 6657 1373;
www.reddirtdistillery.com.au

The Pub with No Beer: Taylors Arm;
(02) 6564 2100;
www.pubwithnobeer.com.au

Tropical North Coast

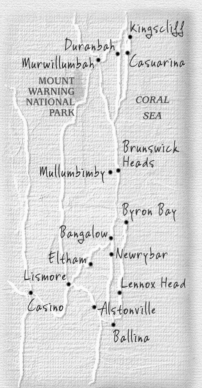

How's this for a potent mix of visitor drawcards? An extinct volcanic caldera now lushly carpeted with rainforest and pasture land; the nation's most easterly point, which welcomes Australia's sunrise each day; surfing beaches that stretch on forever; stunningly magnificent scenery; and hippie communities and alternative lifestyles. And that's even before you get to the food, dining and accommodation hideaways on offer in this region.

Lismore, on the Wilson River, is situated on yet another of the wide, sometimes flood-prone rivers that punctuate the state's coastal strips from Taree northwards. Here and around nearby Casino the lush pastures make for prime beef-raising country and Casino holds an annual Beef Week to celebrate. Vegetarians and the health-conscious need not move straight along to the beansprout- and tofu-munching areas further north. Lovers of sourdough will be impressed with Lismore's **Goanna Bakery & Cafe**, a well-established organic sourdough bakery serving a wide range of vegetarian, vegan and gluten-free dishes. Make sure you also enjoy a wood-fired pizza at **Fire in the Belly** and try its fruit of the sea version, crammed with local seafood from the ocean just some 30 kilometres away. At **Paupiettes,** chef David Forster's fusion of flavours in dishes such as the Bangalow pork belly with apple and fennel, make it an ideal choice for dinner.

Alstonville is the birthplace of **Father Mac's Heavenly Puddings**. He was a real priest and there is something rather supernatural about his rich fruit Christmas puddings, which were originally made to raise funds to rebuild the parish school. They are available all year at the Alstonville factory.

This subtropical area does not support wine production, but if you are more interested in drinks than dessert, then a tour of Alstonville's **Northern Rivers Brewing Company** is in order. The company is proud of their range of all-natural, preservative- and chemical-free handcrafted beers. Pick up other delicacies at **Eltham Valley Pantry**, between Lismore and Byron Bay. The property grows pecans and coffee, and you can take a tour and learn how it's done, buy the products, or settle down for morning tea or lunch overlooking the groves.

The roughly 100 kilometres between Ballina and the Queensland border is so packed with interest that you may need days to explore it all. The

Tweed Valley Banana Festival: art, craft, banana display and street parade; Murwillumbah; Aug; (02) 6672 3723; www.tweed.nsw.gov.au

Where to stay

Peppers Salt Resort & Spa: up-market beach resort; Bells Blvd, Salt Village, South Kingscliff; (02) 6674 7777 or 1300 987 600; www.peppers.com.au/salt

SanBah: funky seaside apartments; 16 Rayner La, Lennox Head; (02) 6685 3844; www.swellproperty.com.au

Tallaringa Views: cabins in rainforest retreat; 1344 Eltham Rd, Alstonville; (02) 6628 5005; www.tallaringa.com.au

The Byron at Byron Bay: resort-style rainforest retreat; 77–97 Broken Head Rd, Byron Bay; (02) 6639 2000 or 1300 554 362; www.thebyronatbyron.com.au

The Garden Burées of Byron Bay: unique tropical bungalows; 17 Gordon St, Byron Bay; (02) 6685 5390; wwwgardenburees.com.au

advice is to take it slowly and soak up the unique atmosphere. The hardest decision will be choosing where to stay, as the area is full of all levels of accommodation from quaint and quirky to outright luxurious. Then there's the dilemma of where to eat. It's a shame to limit yourself to just three meals. Try grazing – a coffee here, a burger there, some oysters, a gelato, another coffee …

On the coast, Ballina is a friendly relaxed seaside town and it's hard to resist stopping at the **Ballina Fishermen's Co-op** for some fresh-from-the-boat seafood, or **Richmond Oysters** where you can enjoy their farmed oysters with a view of the lagoon. If you are craving something more, something wonderful with chairs and tables and a view, **The Point Ballina** now has executive chef Perry Hill (previously in Sydney at Boathouse on Black Wattle Bay) at the stoves.

Travelling north by car, you're sure to be lured briefly off the highway to Lennox Head. For weekend breakfasts or lunches it will be hard to go past **O-pes**. It's casual sand-on-feet friendly, yet the Persian lamb shanks or duck curry (yes, the chef is Thai) make it an ideal place to return to in the evening for dinner. And if you are looking for a lazy breakfast of home-baked cannellini beans with chorizo, good coffee and views of Seven Mile Beach, award-winning **Blackboard at the Beach** ticks all the right boxes: laid-back, friendly and efficient.

As you drive north you'll pass groves of macadamias and coffee plantations. Drop in to see **Zentveld's Coffee** at Newrybar, 15 minutes south of Byron Bay and surely one of the largest and most professional operators in the industry. And do make time to cross the highway to **Harvest Cafe**. This airy cottage with wide verandahs shaded by poinciana trees would be coveted as a site for many a suburban restaurant, and the superb menu welcome in any city. Good coffee, magazines to browse, and a relaxed ambience, combined with Tristan Grier's unswerving allegiance to organic and natural foods, make it so popular. Come for chef Joseph Griffin's contemporary dishes, often using produce from Tristan's family garden. Chances are you'll never feel the same way about Caesar salad again. Here it comes topped with a poached organic egg.

Five minutes away, Bangalow is doing it right too. A peek into **Utopia**'s slender silvery space with its unique chain drapes, and the aroma of well-made coffee (blended to their own specifications) and shelves of provisions and a tempting menu, lure most people inside. In fact the main street is a full of tempting places. **Satiate** restaurant and its companion cafe **Ate** (subtitled 'the Art of Food') are located in a delightful old-style building. Former Tetsuya's chef Shannon Debreceny is responsible for the five-course degustation menu, which includes braised Bangalow sweet belly pork, as well as a

Below (left to right): leafy surrounds at Eltham Valley Pantry, Eltham; luscious dessert in a glass at Mavis's Kitchen, Mount Warning; Zentveld's Coffee plantation, Newrybar; chilli burrito at Ozy-Mex Cafe, Byron Bay

gratefully received matching degustation for vegetarians. **Fresca** at the Bangalow Hotel, its dining deck shaded by a gigantic frangipani tree, does good Mediterranean flavours.

Fishheads is now in Bangalow, as well as in Byron Bay where it is appropriately housed in the 1951 former Bathers' Pavilion. Both places are ideal for takeaways and a more leisurely meal. Do try scallops with finger lime, which are the locally grown indigenous sensation.

For some, it is a relief to know that Byron Bay has morphed into more than simply a drop-in centre for feral kids with dreadlocks. You'll see them of course, brightening the town especially on market day, and the main street is pretty colourful too with signs for crystals and sprouts, mantras and massages. But Byron suits all comers, including whale-watchers, bushwalkers and those seeking respite and a healthy alternative. To the east, massive waves and ruler-straight beaches keep the surfers returning.

Others come for the food. Here you could plant a stick and it would sprout leaves, and locals now grow the widest choice of tropical fruit in the state – everything from avocadoes and chillies to exotic finger limes that feature as a tart, green, caviar-like garnish on some dishes around the area. If you want an overview, Foodscape Tours has coach or walking tours of Byron Bay and the Northern Rivers; call (02) 6685 9995 for details. On these excursions you get to meet producers, eat their food and see the countryside as well.

In food terms Byron Bay has something for everyone: coffee freaks head for **Bay Leaf Cafe**; those needing a chilli fix go to **Ozy-Mex Cafe** founded by the local Byron Bay Chilli Company; lovers of French pastries and bread seek out **L'Ultime Patisserie**; and organic-meat eaters go to **Wholly Smoked Organic Foods**. **Fishmongers** (or Mongers, depending how you read the sign over this superb back-lane, hole-in-the-wall eatery) serves up A-grade fish, hand-cut chips, and healthy salads packed in a box, with oysters shucked to order. Choose to eat in or outside (if you can find a seat) or take your meal off to the beach.

At the other end of the dining spectrum is **The Restaurant at The Byron at Byron**, which is open and relaxed with a view of the pool and palms. It is here you can settle back to enjoy Gavin Hughes' take on the local produce – Bangalow pork, Alstonville chicken, Yamba prawns, Hervey Bay sea scallops – that he is so proud to use. To further show off the region's bounty he is available to escort guests each Thursday on a tour of the Byron Farmers' Market, one of the best of its kind in the state.

Other places worth making room for in your dining plans in Byron are **Dish Restaurant** (think, house-smoked quail or a trio of lemon desserts),

Olivo for the plumpest scallops, **Orient Express Eatery**'s modern take on all things Asian, and the reliable **Pacific Dining Room** where it's hard to know which is better, the food, the view or just the whole Byron package.

Self-caterers should locate **The Green Garage** in Byron Bay for it is here they will find the largest range of absolutely local produce under one roof. The provenance of some fruits and vegetables is listed according to distance away *in minutes!* There is a juice bar serving sandwiches too, so you don't need to waste precious surfing or sightseeing time making lunch. And if you want a biscuit to go with your afternoon tea, **Byron Bay Cookie Company** is the place to go, and if you're lucky there may be some seconds you can pop in and buy from the factory to munch on your way north.

The pace slows even further as you head into the hinterland around Mullumbimby and Murwillumbah on the Tweed River. Soon the increasingly steep slopes become clothed with banana plantations, while pale green sugarcane covers the rest. If France was tropical, you could expect it to feel just like Mullumbimby's **La Table**. Take a garden courtyard seat and sit back prepared to enjoy local produce with a Provençal accent in dishes such as double-baked blue cheese soufflé with pecan crust and yummy grilled figs, Bangalow ham, beetroot and mustard seed chutney.

There are several fruit shops in town heavily reliant on the lush growing conditions of the surrounding volcanic soils. **Eden's Landing** specialises in organic, farm-fresh produce and even home delivers. **Mullumbimby Fruit Market** and **Santos Trading** are worth checking too, and for a more decadent stop go to the **Mullumbimby Chocolate Shop**, which in addition to the world's best chocolate brands, also serves local Myocum coffee.

Mullumbimby is like a mini Byron. For the size of the town, the range of cafes is staggering. See for yourself: **Poinciana**'s charming courtyard, organic foods at **D'Lush**, and **Milk and Honey**'s wood-fired pizzas and salads are all worth making time for. If you've taken the coast road, then **fatbellykat**'s modern Greek menu at Brunswick Heads is as fresh and catchy as its name.

Almost hidden in the hills of this area is one of Australia's most fascinating spots. Over three decades ago, the plantation here began as one man's dream. It has grown and been nurtured until now **Tropical Fruit World** has over 500 varieties of tropical and rare fruit and you can join a tour that will explain their provenance and use, then return to the cafe to sample platters and fresh juices containing fruits you have possibly never heard of. Lemon meringue fruit, anyone? Miracle fruit?

Near Murwillumbah, take a weekday tour of **Madura Tea Estates**, which produced Australia's first, and still its most popular, green tea and has been recognised by consumer magazine *Choice* as one of the cleanest teas sold in Australia, with no detectable levels of pesticides or insecticides.

Bamboo Restaurant and Lounge Bar at the luxurious Santai Resort at Casuarina Beach is a must if you like relaxed tapas-style dining in an up-market environment. But don't expect too little. The kitchen can tackle the finest fine-dining dishes too. Close to the border, take the time for a fun excursion. Catch-A-Crab and Oyster Farm Cruises will have you hauling up crab pots, and pumping for yabbies. Best of all you get to enjoy the catch cooked on board for lunch. Call (07) 5599 9972 for details.

Kingscliff's up-to-the-minute dining precinct lets you go international, enjoying an affordable meal at the **Kathmandu Kitchen** with Nepalese and Tibetan cuisine. The nearby Salt Village has several places (**Saltbar**, **Sea Salt**) to dine on appropriately fishy fare. Sweeping ocean and park views are the ideal backdrop at **Roughies** at Peppers Salt Resort & Spa for a menu that should please anyone.

Many make the journey this far north simply to sample acclaimed chef Steven Snow's cooking at **Fins**. Understandably, given the location and surfer-Steve's love of the waves, the cuisine is seafood based and at its best in a menu that veers from a Portuguese version of bouillabaisse to tempura soft-shell crab via a Moroccan tagine.

The magical far north coast of New South Wales will always be a place that people choose for escape of course. It is a place to recharge and re-evaluate, to gain perspective, or make a new beginning. To be reinvigorated by the magic of that surf. To eat and drink and … eat and drink some more!

Mavis's Kitchen at Mount Warning

Owners Peter, Sandi and Charlie must have agreed that Mavis deserved a namesake of her own, as she now has in this delectable white-painted Queenslander perched in the foothills of Mount Warning, the totem of this corner of the state. Mavis is Charlie's mother, a passionate foodie in her time, and if the menu is anything to go by a memorable cook, herself. Charlie calls her 'legendary'. The kitchen at this unique and delightful place uses only biodynamic, home-grown, free-range and organic produce wherever possible and the blackboard menu changes according to what is available. Just steps from the kitchen there is a lovingly tended cook's garden packed with greens and herbs and other salad things and their freshness makes any dish here at least twice as good as elsewhere. It seems like that, anyway, if you're seated on the verandah with those views, surrounded by the similar approval of other diners.

Better still, Mavis's Kitchen is hospitable as well and diners don't need to eat and run. There is self-contained accommodation in a converted dairy and a log cabin on the property. These have kitchens, but why would you cook much here, apart from breakfast — the makings of which are provided. Mavis's Kitchen serves lunch from Wednesday to Sunday and dinner on Friday and Saturday nights. The restaurant is licensed and offers Australian and organic wines as well as beers.

Contacts for Tropical North Coast

EATERIES

Ate: 33 Byron St, Bangalow; (02) 6687 2555; www.ate.net.au

Ballina Fishermen's Co-op: Cnr Pacific Hwy and Keppel St, Ballina; (02) 6686 2533

Bamboo Restaurant and Lounge Bar: Santai Resort, 9 Dianella Dr, Casuarina Beach; (02) 6670 5555; www.santairesort.com.au/dining

Bay Leaf Cafe: Shop 8, 87 Jonson St, Byron Bay; (02) 6685 8900

Blackboard at the Beach: 50 Pacific Pde, Lennox Head; (02) 6687 4333; www.blackboard.net.au

D'Lush: 28 Burringbar St, Mullumbimby; (02) 6684 1660

Dish Restaurant: Shop 4, cnr Marvel and Jonson sts, Byron Bay; (02) 6685 7320; www.dishbyronbay.com.au

fatbellykat: 26 Tweed St, Brunswick Heads; (02) 6685 1100; www.fatbellykat.com

Fins: 5/6 Bells Blvd, Salt Village, South Kingscliff; (02) 6674 4833; www.fins.com.au

Fire in the Belly: 109 Dawson St, Lismore; (02) 6621 4899; www.fireinthebelly.com.au

Fishheads Restaurant & Takeaway: 1 Jonson St, Main Beach, Byron Bay, (02) 6680 7632; Shop 1, 2 Byron St, Bangalow, (02) 6687 2883; www.fishheadsbyron.com.au

Fishmongers: Bay La, rear of Beach Hotel, Byron Bay; (02) 6680 8080; www.mongers.com.au/byron.html

Fresca: Bangalow Hotel, 1 Byron St, Bangalow; (02) 6687 1711; www.fresca.net.au

Goanna Bakery & Cafe: 171 Keen St, Lismore; (02) 6622 2629; www.goannabakery.com.au

Harvest Cafe: 18 Old Pacific Hwy, Newrybar, (02) 6687 2644; www.harvestcafe.com.au

Kathmandu Kitchen: 2/106 Marine Pde, Kingscliff; (02) 6674 5746

La Table: 72 Burringbar St, Mullumbimby; (02) 6684 2227; www.latable.com.au

Mavis's Kitchen and Cabins @ Mt Warning: 64 Mt Warning Rd, Mt Warning; (02) 6679 5664; www.maviseskitchen.com.au

Milk and Honey: Shop 5, 59A Station St, Mullumbimby; (02) 6684 1422

O-pes: 90–92 Ballina St, Lennox Head; (02) 6687 7388

Olivo: 34 Jonson St, Byron Bay; (02) 6685 7950

Orient Express Eatery: 1/2 Fletcher St, Byron Bay; (02) 6680 8808

Ozy-Mex Cafe: 8 Jonson St, Byron Bay; (02) 6685 7157; www.byronbaychilli.com/ozymexmenu.html

Pacific Dining Room: Beach Hotel, Bay St, Byron Bay; (02) 6680 7055; www.pacificdiningroom.com.au

Paupiettes: 56 Ballina St, Lismore; (02) 6621 6135

Poinciana Cafe: 55 Station St, Mullumbimby; (02) 6684 4036; www.poincianacafe.com

Richmond Oysters: The Serpentine, Ballina; (02) 6686 3270

Roughies: Peppers Salt Resort & Spa, Bells Blvd, Salt Village, South Kingscliff; (02) 6674 7766; www.peppers.com.au/salt/dining/

Saltbar: Bells Blvd, Salt Village, South Kingscliff; 1300 725 822; www.saltbar.com.au

Satiate: 33 Byron St, Bangalow; (02) 6687 1010; www.ate.net.au/satiate/index.html

Sea Salt: Shop 1, Bells Blvd, South Kingscliff; (02) 6674 3613

The Point Ballina: 2 Martin St, Ballina; (02) 6618 1188; www.thepointballina.com.au

The Restaurant at The Byron at Byron: The Byron at Byron Resort, 77–97 Broken Head Rd, Byron Bay; (02) 6639 2111; www.thebyronatbyron.com.au

Utopia: 13 Byron St, Bangalow; (02) 6687 2088; www.utopiacafe.com.au

STORES

Eden's Landing: 4 Stuart St, Mullumbimby; (02) 6684 1007

Eltham Valley Pantry: 713 Boatharbour Rd, Eltham; (02) 6629 1418; www.elthamvalley.com.au/pages/home.asp

L'Ultime Patisserie: Feros Arcade, 3 Lawson St, Byron Bay; (02) 6685 5822

Mullumbimby Chocolate Shop: 1/104 Dalley St, Mullumbimby; (02) 6684 4825; www.mullumbimbychocolateshop.com.au

Mullumbimby Fruit Market: 65 Burringbar St, Mullumbimby; (02) 6684 2169

Santos Trading: Cnr Burringbar and Stuart sts, Mullumbimby; (02) 6684 3773; santostrading.com.au/local_shops/mullumbimby/index.html

The Green Garage: 63 Tennyson St, Byron Bay; (02) 6680 8577; www.greengarage.com.au

Wholly Smoked Organic Foods: Shop 7, 130 Jonson St, Byron Bay; (02) 6685 6261

MARKETS

Bangalow Farmers' Market: Bangalow Hotel carpark, Bangalow; Sat morning; (02) 6687 1137

Above: grilled fish at Fins, South Kingscliff

Byron Farmers' Market: Butler St Reserve, Byron Bay; Thurs morning; (02) 6687 1137; www.byronfarmersmarket.com.au

Kingscliff Farmers & Friends Markets: Beachfront, Marine Pde, Kingscliff; 2nd and 4th Sat each month; (02) 6674 0827

Lismore Farmers' Market: Lismore Showgrounds, North Lismore; Sat morning; (02) 6621 5916

New Brighton Produce Markets: Tues morning; (02) 6684 5390

GOURMET PRODUCE

Ballina Fishermen's Co-op: Cnr Pacific Hwy and Keppel St, Ballina; (02) 6686 2533

Byron Bay Cookie Company: Bakehouse Outlet Store, Shop 1, BP Ozigo Complex, cnr Ewingsdale Rd and Bayshore Dr, Byron Bay; (02) 6685 7633; www.cookie.com.au

Father Mac's Heavenly Puddings Ltd: 9 Perry St, Alstonville; (02) 6628 5474; www.fathermac.org.au

Madura Tea Estates: 753 Clothiers Creek Rd, Murwillumbah; (02) 6670 6000; www.maduratea.com.au

Tropical Fruit World: Duranbah Rd, Duranbah; (02) 6677 7222; www.tropicalfruitworld.com.au

Zentveld's Coffee: 193 Broken Head Rd, Newrybar; (02) 6687 2045; www.zentvelds.com.au/

BREWERIES

Northern Rivers Brewing Company: 57 Northcott Cres, Russellton Industrial Area, Alstonville; (02) 6628 8737

New England Tablelands

Gold, guns, gems and granite. Once this would have summed up the wild northern tablelands of this state perfectly. For this was bushranger country 150 years ago and the romantically named Captain Thunderbolt (aka Fred Ward) was king of these rocky ranges. Today the region has tamed. People still find smidgens of gold and gems, but now the air reverberates to guitars – in Tamworth, anyway, where the nation's best country music festival draws thousands each year. And replacing musket fire, further north, more recently there's the gentle popping of wine corks.

New England is one of the newer wine regions in New South Wales and the dozen or so wineries spread between Bendemeer and Tenterfield (almost on the Queensland border) are drawing critical acclaim. Varieties best suited to the often chilly uplands include chardonnay, riesling and sauvignon blanc, although wineries in this region are winning medals as well for their shiraz and cabernet sauvignon.

At the far south of the region, **Blickling Estate** at Bendemeer produces some great chardonnay and riesling, while **Why Worry Wines**, in Thunderbolt's former stamping grounds at Uralla, grows a number of grape

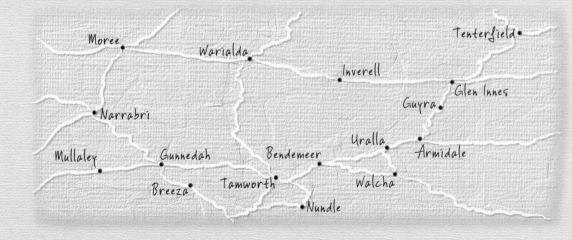

Moree
Warialda
Tenterfield
Inverell
Glen Innes
Guyra
Narrabri
Uralla
Armidale
Mullaley
Gunnedah
Bendemeer
Breeza
Tamworth
Walcha
Nundle

Festivals

Guyra Lamb & Potato Festival: market stalls, entertainment, wine tastings, sheep-shearing demonstrations; Rotary Park, New England Hwy; Jan; 0412 647 518 (Neil Donnelly); www.nnsw.com.au/guyra/tourism. html#GLAPF

Nosh on the Namoi: food, wine, art, music and performance; Narrabri Tourist Information Centre; Mar; (02) 6799 6760

Moree on a Plate: regional menu, music and entertainment; Moree Secondary College; May; 0433 447 178; www.moreeonaplate.com.au

Gourmet in the Glen: over 35 food stalls; Glen Innes Park; Sept; www.gourmetintheglen.com.au

Tenterfield Food & Wine Festival: 1st weekend in Nov; 0401 305 572; www.tenterfieldfoodandwine.org.au

Where to stay

Kings Plains Castle: castle folly with luxury accommodation; Kings Plains Rd, Inverell; (02) 6733 6808; www.kingsplainscastle.gleninnes.biz

Peterson's Armidale Winery & Guesthouse: beautifully restored heritage homestead; Dangarsleigh Rd, Armidale; (02) 6772 0422; www.petersonsguesthouse.com.au

The Retreat at Froog-Moore Park: eclectic decor and luxury touches; 78 Bligh St, Tamworth; (02) 6766 3353; www.froogmoorepark.com.au

varieties, with the whites proving quite exceptional. At **Deetswood Wines** in Tenterfield, the cellar door is only open from Friday to Monday but it's worth dropping in on those days to sample boutique wines made with handpicked grapes. The winery's semillon has done well, and the Staggering Cow shiraz was named Best Unfinished Wine at the New England Wine Show in 2009. A humorous poem on their website explains that unusual name.

Local plates are filled with good things too – fine lamb, pork, trout, beef and poultry. Honey, berries, tomatoes, potatoes, cherries and other stone fruit, apples, olives and olive oil, yabbies, Murray cod, goat's cheese, milk, eggs and many types of organic foods. In fact you can construct a whole menu (and some do) just from the bounty of this surprising area.

The wheat lands on the plains to the west of the ranges yield grains that Bellata uses in its fine durum wheat pasta so watch for this in local shops and restaurants. There's linseed grown in the region too, west of Gunnedah at Mullaley, and Demeter's Farm Mill at Breeza, west of Tamworth, has long been the hub of organic grain milling in the state.

If approaching from the south, by the time you reach Tamworth on the Peel River, the Hunter and its upper reaches have fallen behind. This is different country, rising swiftly into the New England ranges and ultimately the high tablelands. Country music makes January the biggest month of the year in Tamworth. For good food, **Monty's** at Quality Hotel Powerhouse is the place to go. Chef Ben Davies is passionate about local produce. Just pray that his sensational confit sea trout, on an Arc-en-Ceil trout rösti served with green bean salad and a champagne and trout caviar butter sauce is on the menu when you go. The hotel's sibling at Armidale also has a good restaurant, **Cattleman's Grill**, for various cuts of grass-fed beef, and also crispy Inglegreen pork belly, or a whole Nundle trout on warm panzanella salad.

Let's hope you have taken the time before Tamworth for a detour through Nundle, a flyspeck on the map but with a vibrancy that makes it one of the most rewarding places to visit. Make it an add-on trip from January's Tamworth music festival, go blackberry picking in February, or attend other regional food fairs during the year. Nundle's woollen mill has been revived, and knitting or spinning weekends draw eager visitors. Although the much-loved Jenkins Street Guesthouse has closed, **The Peel Inn**, a favourite with

travellers for 146 years, offers cosy accommodation, and on its menu you'll find local flavours such as whole Nundle trout, tender grass-fed local beef, and of course the local blackberries.

Also off the New England Highway before Armidale is Walcha with its amazing outdoor sculptures. This is the junction for Thunderbolt's Way, formerly the less evocatively named Bucketts Way, which connects with Raymond Terrace north of Newcastle. If Captain Thunderbolt were around today, he'd be proud of the wide new road, delighted with its name, of course, and much in favour of the tipple so readily available in this region. There is also a shortcut (and scenic route) from here across to Port Macquarie.

For the food-loving traveller **Cafe Graze**, in Walcha, serves good Allpress coffee and hearty breakfasts and lunches. Stock up in town with natural goodies at **High Country Organics** (also known as Balnagowan Organics). This co-op has been created to provide chemical-free, certified organically grown produce at competitive costs.

By Armidale you will have climbed to almost 1000 metres and this, the largest city in the region, attains academic and cultural heights too. Established in 1840, it has orchestras, choirs, ensembles, and a conservatorium of music. There are 17 schools, six secondary schools and the University of New England. Two gold booms in the 1800s got the town going, but these days it is made lovelier by another metal – iron lace on the older buildings, much of it made at nearby Uralla's foundry, which is also worth a visit.

But you can only take in so much culture, so with a well-earned thirst do check out the latest developments in the local wine scene. A good place to start your investigation is at **Petersons Wines'** cool-climate winery cellar door in the heritage-listed stables of the old Dangar family homestead, on Armidale's outskirts. The tasting list runs almost the entire gamut from chardonnay to merlot and, when you are finished, there is also elegant accommodation in beautifully restored rooms of the 1912 homestead.

Armidale's tables are well stocked with local produce. Top favourite with many is **Green Papaya**, where the authentic green papaya salad is made with organic papaya sourced from Bellingen just across the ranges. The menu is packed with fragrant-yet-fiery north-eastern Thai dishes and the locals love it. By day Armidale's **Caffiends on Marsh** will capably deal with your coffee or tea needs in its relaxed cafe, and if you want an Italian accent with that, then **Bottega Caffe and Delicatezza** is the place to visit. Here you can enjoy biscotti with an espresso, order a Black Mountain ham on Morpeth Sourdough panini, or just a see what cakes 'nonna' might have made. There isn't a real nonna here, of course. Phillip and Donella Tutt are in charge, but you feel like there's a benign Italian grandmotherly influence in the food. Other places that take their coffees seriously are **Bistro on Cinders** and **Goldfish Bowl Espresso**.

Travelling north of Armidale, en route to Glen Innes you will pass paddocks littered with huge granite boulders as the landscape flattens somewhat, becoming less hospitable but still breathtakingly lovely. Guyra, a tiny yet thriving town just beyond 'Thunderbolt's Cave', celebrates its local lamb and potatoes at a festival each January, but few know it also raises **Black Mountain Free-range Pork**, as well as the Blush tomatoes that you see in fruit markets, and rabbits, eels and rainbow trout.

Glen Innes has earned a name as the Celtic capital of the highlands and the annual Celtic Festival in April–May is well attended. So too is Gourmet in the Glen in September. Australia's doyenne of cookery, Margaret Fulton, grew up in Glen Innes. Good places to taste the local produce include **The Hereford Steakhouse** at the Rest Point Motor Inn, and **Highland Lodge Restaurant** where you can deal with the often-chilly evenings by a blazing open fire. You may even find locally reared goat from **AusGoat** on menus in the area. By day **The Tasting Room** is a popular cafe in the town. But for a super-local treat many people visit **The Super Strawberry** (*see* feature, p. 80).

Inverell, 67 kilometres west of Glen Innes, is olive-growing country and **New England Olive Processors** (formerly the pioneering Gwydir Olives) offers a tour of its processing facility. What better way to follow this than with a visit to an olive grove? **Olives of Beaulieu** is on the Copeton Dam Road, 10 kilometres towards Warialda from Inverell. There you can walk through the grove, see different varieties of trees and enjoy morning or afternoon tea.

Just before the Queensland border town of Wallangarra, lovely Tenterfield with its glowing autumn colours and brittle icy winters delivers one final course to food and wine lovers. The infant wine industry has several cellar doors and often blends into the Granite Belt's more established region just across the border in Queensland. It may surprise you to know that this small town was pivotal in Australia's history. It was here, in 1889, that Sir Henry Parkes delivered his famous 'Birth of a Nation' speech, which began a move towards Federation in 1901. More recently, singer Peter Allen immortalised the town with his song 'Tenterfield Saddler'.

Poor Captain Thunderbolt had to rob and hunt for every mouthful all those many years ago. How lucky are we now to travel this area and find it absolutely bursting with good things to eat and drink?

*Below (**left to right**):* vine rows at Deetswood Wines, Tenterfield; relaxed dining at Caffiends on Marsh, Armidale

local produce

The Super Strawberry

You can see the strawberry farm through the back window of this shop, just a kilometre south of the Glen Innes town centre on the busy New England Highway. It's no wonder your strawberry thick shake is so full of flavour. Cecily and David Tarrant have been doing this for 30 years now: growing the berries then making the strawberry jam and ice-cream, and serving up strawberries and cream with their irresistible sponges and pavlovas.

The tiny shop, hardly more than a roadside kiosk, is a temple to all things to do with strawberries – jams, sauces, souvenirs – and of course those thick shakes, which are more a dessert than a drink. The Tarrants grow their own berries during the summer then source strawberries from other growers in winter. The business was the idea of Cecily Tarrant's father, Ivan March, and today the strawberries are still harvested using a machine that he designed and manufactured.

To round out the offerings, there is also local honey, fresh Guyra tomatoes, homemade local jams, chutneys and sauces, and Byron Bay coffee to enjoy with fresh scones and strawberry jam at a table outside in the sunshine. The shop is open daily 9am–5.30pm.

Contacts for New England Tablelands

EATERIES

Bistro on Cinders: 14 Cinders La, Armidale; (02) 6772 4273

Bottega Caffe and Delicatezza: Shop 2, 14 Moore St, Armidale; (02) 6772 6262

Cafe Graze: 21n Derby St, Walcha; (02) 6777 2409

Caffiends on Marsh: Shop 1,110 Marsh St, Armidale; (02) 6771 3178

Cattleman's Grill: Quality Hotel Powerhouse, 31 Marsh St, Armidale; (02) 6772 7788; www.qualityhotelpowerhouse.com.au

Goldfish Bowl Espresso: Shop 10, 206 Beardy St, Armidale; (02) 6771 3271

Green Papaya: Shop 1, Girraween Shopping Centre, Queen Elizabeth Dr, Armidale; (02) 6771 3611

Highland Lodge Restaurant: New England Motor Lodge, 160 Church St, Glen Innes; (02) 6732 2922; www.neml.com.au/dining.html

Monty's: Quality Hotel Powerhouse, New England Hwy, Tamworth; (02) 6766 7000; www.qualityhotelpowerhouse.com.au

The Hereford Steakhouse: Rest Point Motor Inn, New England Hwy, Glen Innes; (02) 6732 2255; www.restpointmotel.com.au/glen-innes-restaurants.htm

The Peel Inn: Jenkins St, Nundle; (02) 6769 3377; www.peelinn.com.au

The Super Strawberry: 9922 New England Hwy, Glen Innes; (02) 6732 1210; www.superstrawberry.com.au

The Tasting Room: 296 Grey St, Glen Innes; (02) 6732 6500

STORES

High Country Organics (Balnagowan Organics): Balnagowan, Walcha; (02) 6769 2269

MARKETS

Tamworth Farmers' Market: Liquor Stax, Dowle St, Tamworth; 2nd Sat each month, morning; (02) 6755 4504

GOURMET PRODUCE

AusGoat: 311 Grey St, Glen Innes; (02) 6732 2144; www.ausgoat.com

Black Mountain Free-range Pork: PO Box 225, Guyra; (02) 6771 5130; www.blackmountain.com.au

New England Olive Processors: 35 Brissett St, Inverell; (02) 6721 2727; www.gwydirolives.com.au

Olives of Beaulieu: 439 Copeton Dam Rd, Beaulieu via Inverell; (02) 6722 1458; www.olivesofbeaulieu.com.au

WINERIES

Blickling Estate: Green Valley Rd, Bendemeer; (02) 6769 6786

Deetswood Wines: 209 Washpool Creek Rd, Tenterfield; (02) 6736 1322; www.deetswoodwines.com.au

Petersons Wines: Dangarsleigh Rd, Armidale; (02) 6772 0422; www.petersonswines.com.au/cellardoor.htm

Why Worry Wines: Kingston Rd, Uralla; (02) 6778 4147; www.whyworrywines.com.au

Below (left to right): wine and cheese at Petersons Wines, Armidale; vines surrounded by eucalypt bushland at Deetswood Wines, Tenterfield

Southern Highlands

Above: cheese from Small Cow Farm, Robertson

Opposite (top to bottom): cellar door at Bluemetal Vineyard, Berrima; colourful dining-room bar at Pizzas in the Mist, Robertson

The Southern Highlands is in Sydney's commuter zone – with good conditions it's an hour and a half to the CBD – but why do that? After a few days here, it's not hard to see why many residents choose to hunker down in acreage mansions instead of hitting the highway each day. The main towns of Mittagong, Bowral, Moss Vale, Sutton Forest and Berrima form a closely knit enclave – stay in one of these and the others are a stone's throw away. And not far to the east is the Illawarra, the highlands' beachside cousin. In less than a 90-kilometre scenic drive across the range from Moss Vale you can be surfing at Shellharbour. Further north, the city of Wollongong is just 20 kilometres along the coast.

In the highlands you couldn't really refer to the rolling green on green fields as 'paddocks' – they've been transplanted from the Britain, it seems. The sheep are woolly white, too, apples ripen crisp and juicy, and the list of local cool-climate wineries just keeps on growing. Up here (the altitude nudges around 700 metres) it's cold enough for open fires many months of the year; frost nips most mornings in winter; and a jovial pig (remember *Babe?*) briefly made one town in the area world-famous.

Festivals

Cool Flavours Festival: celebration of local attractions; various venues; June; (02) 4871 2524

Where to stay

Fitzroy Inn: comfort meets history; 1 Ferguson Cres, Mittagong; (02) 4872 3457; www.fitzroyinn.com.au

Peppers Manor House: grand country house; Kater Rd, Sutton Forest; (02) 4860 3111; www.peppers.com.au/Manor-House/

Pleasant Heights B&B: suites with a view; 77 New Mt Pleasant Rd, Wollongong; (02) 4283 3355; www.pleasantheights.com.au

Tumbling Waters Retreat: luxury with panoramic views; Stonehaven Rd (end of road), Stanwell Tops; (02) 4294 1888; www.tumblingwatersretreat.com

Above (left to right): assorted bites at Zweefers Divine Cakes, Fairy Meadow; timber-lined interior of Pizzas in the Mist, Robertson; pumpkin tortellini at Caveau, Wollongong; cascading wisteria at Joadja Winery cellar door, Berrima

Locals love the definite transition between the seasons, and their bookshops, galleries, second-hand shops, antique stores and good food. Visitors come to the highlands for all this, but also to take garden tours and, during one blazing autumn event, to worship tulips in Bowral. This is the area of small growers and boutique producers of truffles (watch for them in coming years), berries, apples, lavender, free-range eggs, and mushrooms. Plenty of other places stir up a storm in their kitchens, creating chutneys, relishes, sauces and mayonnaise.

Montrose Berry Farm at Sutton Forest welcomes pick-your-own visitors. Call ahead to see if your favourite berry is ready to pick, but even if it is not, there should be plenty of frozen berries on hand at any time of the year. Many small producers are too busy for visitors, and it's counterproductive to attempt to chase them up at their premises as the goodies are easily found proudly displayed in the local stores or mentioned on menus. Look for **Cuttaway Creek**'s fine raspberry sauces, vinegars and jams, **Li-Sun Exotic Mushrooms**, **Doodles Creek**

gourmet mayonnaises, **Spring Hill Beef**, **Highland Organics** and **Small Cow Farm** cheeses. The local **Highland Hamper Company** can put together a taste of your trip to order, if you'd rather.

While most people feel spoiled for choice in the Southern Highlands when choosing a place to dine out, be glad if one evening you need to self-cater, or if a picnic is in order. You could stock up for an absolute gourmet experience with cheeses at **The Cheese Store** and charcuterie and deli items at **Il Topolino** at Bowral. Then condiments from **The Little Hand-Stirred Jam Shop** at Berrima, shortbread and marmalade from **Little Piece of Scotland** at Sutton Forrest, and luscious pastries and breads from any of **Gumnut Patisserie**'s three outlets.

Many Southern Highlands' small villages such as Barrengarry, **Exeter** and **Burrawang** have general stores, and these are well worth visiting for local products and a country welcome. Many have regular farmers' markets too, so see what is on offer if you visit on a weekend. For local farm-raised meats,

Mauger's Meats in Burrawang is the place to head for. Of course you could conduct your wine and food tasting in style with a wine tour and limousine transfer from Highland Wine Tours (02) 4872 3038, or Southern Crush Wine Tours (02) 8516 0031, or go with a local foodie to meet the producers on a FoodPath tour (02) 4872 4884.

The Southern Highlands is a growing wine region. **Bluemetal Vineyard** has a small cafe and also accommodation and makes good cabernet sauvignon and pinot gris. **Centennial Vineyards** is known for its range of wines including reserve riesling and a good sparkling wine. It has a fine lofty restaurant, which is often booked for functions. **Joadja Vineyards & Winery**'s cabernet triple blend is well respected.

But let's not forget beer. The highlands have two breweries: **Fish Rock Beer** at Mittagong, using the slogan 'award winning beers brewed by winemakers who love beer!', and **Bowral Brewing** known for its Pigs Fly craft beers. In the Illawarra, **Five Islands Brewing Company**, established in 2001, has won many awards for its range of traditionally brewed beers made with natural ingredients, free from preservatives.

If you want to come to grips with some cooking techniques while in the area, why not book in for a cheesemaking course at **Small Cow Farm** in Robertson, or join a group in the friendly environment of **Blue Bowl Brown Sugar** at Mittagong. For an elegant chef-inspired class, you could go for the hands-on experience from the well-respected **Caveau** restaurant in Wollongong.

Dining in the area is diverse and options are maddeningly difficult to decide upon. Do you go for open fires and manor-house ambience such as at **Katers** at Peppers in Sutton Forest? Or perhaps age rules. Then it has to be **The Black Swan**, once the Crown Inn in the mid-1800s, now revitalised with a contemporary menu. **Eschalot** at Berrima is a consistent favourite and why not when owner-chef Richard Kemp turns out dishes such as his smoked eel parfait, or pan-fried mulloway with samphire, squid ink and red mullet?

If you feel like Italian, even that gets tricky. **Onesta Cucina** in Bowral is known for its golden-crusted polenta with mushrooms and gorgonzola or unforgettable pasta dishes, while **Esco Pazzo**'s Roman cuisine offerings such as crispiest crust pizzas, duck ravioli or veal boscaiola are almost irresistible.

History is everywhere in this area. **Red Olive** has opened in an 1860s stone cottage at Mittagong, doing very contemporary tapas and chilli squid, making it a good casual choice for lunch in the midst of sightseeing. At Moss Vale, **Post Cafe & Bar** has taken over the old post office, built in 1895, doing the cafe-by-day, restaurant-at-night trick very successfully with comfort foods such as braised lamb shanks and baked vegetables, and decadent chocolate desserts.

One of the region's finest, the **Journeyman Restaurant & Bar**, lived up to its name and has recently moved from Berrima to Bowral. Fortunately owner-chef Tim Pratt packed his recipes for the sublime ragoût of pork and mushrooms with handmade beetroot pasta and fresh herbs, and his pan-fried apple and date bread and butter pudding, and so much more. The new elegant dining room is proving the ideal backdrop for his fine contemporary cuisine, which has won him so many accolades.

As expected in a winegrowing region, there are wineries where you can taste, then eat, then maybe taste again and buy later. At Sutton Forest, **Stones** at Eling Forest Vineyard & Winery is a perfect example, and Mark Stone, formerly from the Sofitel Wentworth in Sydney, has brought his formidable patisserie (and other) skills to this lovely spot with outdoor dining overlooking the gardens. If your love of steaks is greater than your need for fine surroundings then the **Royal Brasserie and Steakhouse** at Bowral should rate a visit, as should **The Magpie Cafe** in Berrima for the steak sandwich that has set this eatery apart in the minds of many (the place is often overwhelmed by tourists).

Of course a holiday spot that draws plenty of visitors who love the area as much as the lucky locals needs cafes and there are plenty of these too. Any of the three **Gumnut Patisserie** outlets aside, **Gilbert's** at Bowral is good value, **Gastronome** is hyper popular, and you should save at least one visit for **The Milk Factory Gallery Cafe** at Bowral. The latter's lofty gallery gives you a reason to begin with the excellent coffee and cakes and return for a light lunch after your gallery gazing.

If you head to the coast, Robertson is around halfway, a blip on the map, home of the Big Potato, an enigmatic roadside concrete sculpture, and Babe's former stamping ground. At least this is where the film was made. Just a small place, it is at the transition between the Southern Highlands and the coastal Illawarra area. The main claim to fame has always been the rich red volcanic basalt soil, known as Robertson soil. This, plus a dependable rainfall and chilly winters, are the ideal formula for potato growing, and so the village is regarded as the centre of the largest potato-growing area in the state.

Yet there are high spots nearby that allow expansive views of the gently rolling almost-British landscape dotted with cattle, and amazing panoramas across the coastal plains to the ocean. See this, and you realise that dairying is also basic to the area. Little wonder the **Robertson Cheese Factory** was established here. Today you can still break the trip and pick up some hearty sandwiches, homemade cake and scones at the on-site cafe. The huge wood-fired oven at **Pizzas in the Mist** is the place to come to warm up from the chill mountain air and also for some of the best pizzas as well as dishes made from natural produce, often from the restaurant garden. Further on, at Kangaroo Valley, **Cafe Bella** is as much about the convivial vibe as the food.

There are stupendous views of Wollongong (*see* feature opposite) as you near the coast. It is a big city, third largest in the state, tenth in the country, but it's no longer purely an industrial centre. Today it is both a dormitory city for Sydney, and a lush getaway for city folks. A slew of recent luxury B&Bs and other accommodation caters to these newer needs. Once you reach the coast, if you make a stop it should be at **Zweefers Divine Cakes** at Fairy Meadow. The range of delights here lives up to the name.

One thing is certain as you travel the truly scenic road along the coast north of Wollongong, you won't go hungry. The real difficulty will be in deciding whether to stop for fresh juices at **AustiBeach Cafe** in Austinmer, or breakfast at **Ruby's Kitchen** at Stanwell Tops. Maybe soup or one of their excellent coffees might lure you to **The Palms Cafe** at Stanwell Park. Or perhaps a hearty, relaxed, family-friendly dinner at **Samuels** at Thirroul may be just the best way to finish a circuit of these appealing food areas within such a short distance from Sydney.

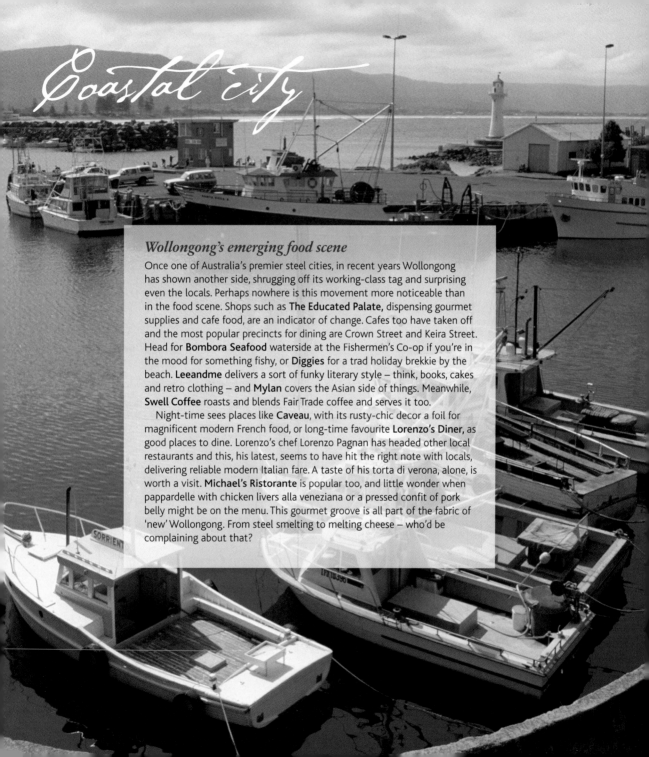

Coastal city

Wollongong's emerging food scene

Once one of Australia's premier steel cities, in recent years Wollongong has shown another side, shrugging off its working-class tag and surprising even the locals. Perhaps nowhere is this movement more noticeable than in the food scene. Shops such as **The Educated Palate**, dispensing gourmet supplies and cafe food, are an indicator of change. Cafes too have taken off and the most popular precincts for dining are Crown Street and Keira Street. Head for **Bombora Seafood** waterside at the Fishermen's Co-op if you're in the mood for something fishy, or **Diggies** for a trad holiday brekkie by the beach. **Leeandme** delivers a sort of funky literary style – think, books, cakes and retro clothing – and **Mylan** covers the Asian side of things. Meanwhile, **Swell Coffee** roasts and blends Fair Trade coffee and serves it too.

Night-time sees places like **Caveau**, with its rusty-chic decor a foil for magnificent modern French food, or long-time favourite **Lorenzo's Diner**, as good places to dine. Lorenzo's chef Lorenzo Pagnan has headed other local restaurants and this, his latest, seems to have hit the right note with locals, delivering reliable modern Italian fare. A taste of his torta di verona, alone, is worth a visit. **Michael's Ristorante** is popular too, and little wonder when pappardelle with chicken livers alla veneziana or a pressed confit of pork belly might be on the menu. This gourmet groove is all part of the fabric of 'new' Wollongong. From steel smelting to melting cheese – who'd be complaining about that?

Contacts for Southern Highlands

EATERIES

AustiBeach Cafe: 104 Lawrence Hargrave Dr, Austinmer; (02) 4268 5680

Bombora Seafood: Fishermen's Co-op, Endeavour Dr, Wollongong; (02) 4229 7011; www.bomboraseafood.com

Burrawang General Store Cafe: 11 Hoddle St, Burrawang; (02) 4886 4496; www.bgsc.com.au

Cafe Bella: 151 Moss Vale Rd, Kangaroo Valley; (02) 4465 1660

Caveau: 122–124 Kiera St, Wollongong; (02) 4226 4855; www.caveau.com.au

Diggies: 1 Cliff Rd, Wollongong; (02) 4226 2688

Eschalot: 24 Old Hume Hwy, Berrima; (02) 4877 1977; www.eschalot.com.au

Esco Pazzo: 84 Main St, Mittagong; (02) 4872 2400

Exeter General Store: Cnr Exeter and Middle rds, Exeter; (02) 4883 4289

Gastronome: 23A Boolwey St, Bowral; (02) 4861 3614

Gilbert's: Shops 4–5, 88 Main St, Mittagong; (02) 4872 2399

Journeyman Restaurant & Bar: 5 Boolwey St (cnr Argyle La); Bowral; (02) 4861 2442; www.journeymanrestaurant.com.au

Katers: Peppers Manor House, 52 Kater Rd, Sutton Forrest; (02) 4860 2355; www.peppers.com.au/manor-house/katers-restaurant

Leeandme: 87 Crown St, Wollongong; (02) 4244 0695; www.leeandme.com.au

Lorenzo's Diner: 119 Keira St, Wollongong; (02) 4229 5633; www.lorenzosdiner.com.au

Michael's Ristorante: Shop 1, 50 Crown St, Wollongong; (02) 4225 9542; www.michaelsristorante.com.au

Mylan: 193 Keira St, Wollongong; (02) 4228 1588

Onesta Cucina: Shop 2, The Penders, Wingecarribee St, Bowral; (02) 4861 6620

Pizzas in the Mist: 42 Hoddle St, Robertson; (02) 4885 1799; www.pizzasinthemist.com

Post Cafe & Bar: 494 Argyle St, Moss Vale; (02) 4868 3878

Red Olive: 3/185 Old Hume Hwy, Mittagong; (02) 4871 2298

Robertson Cheese Factory Cafe: 1 Illawarra Hwy, Robertson; (02) 4885 1133; www.robertsoncheesefactory.com

Royal Brasserie and Steakhouse: The Royal Hotel, 255 Bong Bong St, Bowral; (02) 4862 5588

Ruby's Kitchen Cafe: 91A Lawrence Hargraves Dr, Stanwell Tops; (02) 4294 1822

Samuels: 382 Lawrence Hargrave Dr, Thirroul; (02) 4268 2244

Stones: Eling Forest Vineyard & Winery, Hume Hwy, Sutton Forest; (02) 4878 9499; www.elingforest.com.au

The Black Swan: 11 Old Hume Hwy, Berrima; (02) 4877 2222

The Magpie Cafe: Old Hume Hwy, Berrima; (02) 4877 2008

The Milk Factory Gallery Cafe: 31 Station St (rear), Bowral; (02) 4862 1077; www.milkfactorygallery.com.au

The Palms Cafe: 111 Lawrence Hargraves Dr, Stanwell Park; (02) 4294 3371; www.thepalmscafe.com.au

STORES

Gumnut Patisserie: Grand Arcade, Bong Bong St, Bowral (also Berrima and Mittagong); (02) 4862 2819

Il Topolino Alimentari Delicatessen: Grand Arcade, Bong Bong St, Bowral; (02) 4861 4957

Little Piece of Scotland: Cnr Illawarra Hwy and Exeter Rd, Sutton Forest; (02) 4868 3492; www.shortbread.com.au

Mauger's Meats: Hoddle St, Burrawang; (02) 4886 4327

The Cheese Store at Bowral: Shop 6B, Corbett Plaza, 14 Wingecarribee St, Bowral; (02) 4862 3749; www.thecheesestore.com.au

The Educated Palate: 87 Crown St (rear), Wollongong; (02) 4225 0100

The Highland Hamper Company: PO Box 1430, Bowral; (02) 4868 2909; www.thhc.com.au

The Little Hand-Stirred Jam Shop: Shop 1, 9 Old Hume Hwy, Berrima; (02) 4877 1404

MARKETS

Berrima Food Market: Courthouse, cnr Wilshire and Argyle sts; 4th Sat each month, morning; (02) 4877 1164

Bowral Farmers' Market: Bowral Public School, Bendooley St; 2nd Sat each month, morning; 0437 136 693

Bundanoon Village Markets: Soldiers Memorial Hall, Railway Pde; 1st and 3rd Sun each month (except Jan); (02) 4869 3016

Opposite (left to right): expansive pool at Tumbling Waters Retreat, Stanwell Tops; children's cooking school at Blue Bowl Brown Sugar, Mittagong; an enticing slice of mango and coconut cake at Zweefers Divine Cakes, Fairy Meadow

Colo Vale Markets: Colo Vale Hall, Railway Ave; 4th Sat each month; (02) 4862 4910

Mittagong Markets: Cnr Albert and Alice sts; 3rd Sat each month and 5th Sat; (02) 4684 1261

Wollongong Produce & Creative Traders Market: Crown St Mall; Fri; 0422 781 920

GOURMET PRODUCE

Cuttaway Creek: Old Hume Hwy, Mittagong; (02) 4871 1201

Doodles Creek: PO Box 2349, Kangaloon; (02) 4888 2085; doodlescreek.com/default.aspx

Highland Organics: 113 Lackey St, Moss Vale; 0424 088 937

Li-Sun Exotic Mushrooms: 16 Davey St, Mittagong; (02) 4871 2879; li-sunexoticmushrooms.com.au

Montrose Berry Farm: Ormond St, Sutton Forest; (02) 4868 1544; www.montroseberryfarm.com.au

Small Cow Farm: 70 Pearsons La, Robertson; (02) 4885 1241; www.smallcowfarm.com

Spring Hill Beef: Spring Hill Southern Highlands Retreat, Lot 2, Hoddle St, Burrawang; (02) 4886 4479; springhillbeefhamper.com.au

Swell Coffee: Shop 3, 135 Crown St (rear), Wollongong; (02) 4229 5579; www.swellcoffee.com.au

Zweefers Divine Cakes: 43–45 Princes Hwy, Fairy Meadow; (02) 4285 4155; www.zweefers.com.au

WINERIES

Bluemetal Vineyard: 112 Compton Park Rd, Berrima; (02) 4877 1877; www.bluemetalvineyard.com

Centennial Vineyards: Centennial Rd, Bowral; (02) 4861 8722; www.centennial.net.au

Joadja Vineyards & Winery: Joadja Rd, Berrima; (02) 4878 5236; www.joadja.com

BREWERIES

Bowral Brewing: 13 Loftus St, Bowral; (02) 4862 1313; www.pigsfly.net.au

Fish Rock Beer: Mundrakoona Estate, Old Hume Hwy, Mittagong; (02) 4872 1311; www.fishrockbrewery.com.au

Five Islands Brewing Company: Eastern Tce, WIN Entertainment Centre, Crown St, Wollongong; (02) 4220 2854; www.fiveislandsbrewery.com

COOKING SCHOOLS

Blue Bowl Brown Sugar: Mittagong; 0414 855 087; www.bluebowl.com.au

Caveau: 122–124 Kiera St, Wollongong; (02) 4226 4855; www.caveau.com.au

Small Cow Farm: 70 Pearsons La, Robertson; (02) 4885 1241; www.smallcowfarm.com

South Coast

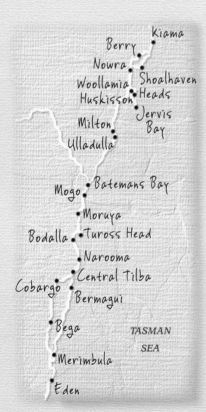

Dr Alexander Berry made a definite impression on the New South Wales South Coast. You see his name honoured in the cosy little town of Berry and you savour his handiwork in the vineyards at Coolangatta Estate (*see* feature, p. 95), where the first vines to be grown in this area were planted well over 180 years ago. This Scottish-born surgeon would smile if he knew what has happened since then. The area has turned into a holiday-makers' paradise, and food and wine lovers come out best. The coastline is rich with seafood, which is hauled in on boats each day. Oysters are farmed, bread baked, fish smoked, jams and relishes stirred and bottled, honey collected and olives gathered. Several local wineries (*see* feature, p. 95) provide the right drop to match.

Scenic Kiama is the centre for the northern part of the region, with a local bistro, **55 on Collins**, that just about sums up the area — bright, busy and airy, it buzzes by day and sparkles at night. The menu swerves from Spain (think, tapas plates) to South-East Asia where lemongrass blesses a fragrant blue swimmer crab and coconut soup. Nearby Gerringong has a boutique resort, **Bellachara**, to be proud of. Its restaurant, a consistent dining award-winner, now has London-born chef Dudley Wood at the stoves, his mandate stated as 'both imaginative and accessible'.

Lazy weekends call for provisioning — and good coffee. The **Seahaven Cafe & General Store** at Gerroa is perfect for this. Pocket-sized, with lagoon and park views, you may not want to eat anywhere else. Regardless, many visitors head straight for Berry, and who can blame them when the **Berry Wood-fired Bakery**, one of the state's finest sourdough bakeries, turns out loaf after crusty loaf of traditional handcrafted wood-fired breads. Brothers Jelle and Joost Hilkemeijer won even more fans when they added a cafe and plenty of seating and began serving brioche, croissants and delicious tarts, breakfasts and lunches, with mandatory great coffee, too.

Think of Berry (and indeed much of this stretch of coastline) as a sort of coastal Mudgee, if you like. City refugees have flocked here in the past ten or twenty years, lured by the ocean just five minutes away, an emerging winery scene, the magnificent hinterland of rolling farmland, some of it with distant views of the sea — and the town itself, small enough to be personal, yet with

Where to stay

Bannisters Point Lodge: cliff-top boutique hotel; 191 Mitchell Pde, Mollymook; (02) 4455 3044; www.bannisterspointlodge.com.au

Bellachara: luxury boutique hotel; 1 Fern St, Gerringong; (02) 4234 1359; www.bellachara.com.au

Driftwood: lakeside house; 14 Prior St, Lake Conjola (near Milton); 0412 292 822 or 0407 950 768; www.driftwoodlakeconjola.com.au

Paperbark Camp: glamour camping; 571 Woollamia Rd, Woollamia; (02) 4441 6066; www.paperbarkcamp.com.au

Tathra Beach House Apartments: beach resort; 57 Andy Poole Dr, Tathra Beach; (02) 6499 9900; www.tathrabeachhouse.com.au

Above (left to right): seafood smorgasboard at On the Pier, Batemans Bay; wine barrels at Silos Estate, Jaspers Brush; dining in the treetops at The Gunyah Restaurant, Paperbark Camp, Woollamia; exterior and cosy interior, of Valley Edge Cafe, Cobargo

a variety of shops and boutique businesses only dreamed of in suburbia. Just on two hours south of the centre of Sydney, it's no wonder people have 'emigrated' here. Those who don't move in permanently, take up residence at weekends and in holiday periods, sunning themselves at the footpath tables of the thirty or so eateries in the town.

Several other places in town also get the thumbs up from locals and visitors. **Hungry Duck** does modern Asian with real flair and prime local produce, much of it organic. Fish comes from the boat out of Ulladulla, oysters from Greenwell Point, crayfish from Jervis Bay, herbs and vegetables from the restaurant's own garden.

Visit **The Posthouse** for good rustic food, **Silos Restaurant** for spectacular vineyard views just out of town, and pick up sandwiches and supplies at **The Emporium Food Company** in the main street or the newly opened **South Coast Providores**, which is doing fascinating things combining gallery exhibitions with special events such as a 'citrus day' or 'tomato day'. One smart idea is their South Coast Food Bowl –

literally that, a quality china bowl packed with goodies grown and made on the south coast.

The Shoalhaven, stretching from Berry to Batemans Bay, is second only to Sydney for state visitor numbers, with an annual tally of almost three million people who find plenty do in the area: shopping, sightseeing, dolphin-watching, and now dining and wine-tasting. Jervis Bay, the large bay that takes a massive bite out of the coastline just south of Nowra, is pronounced as it is spelled. None of this JARvis Bay stuff, say the locals. Here you'll find a slew of beachside eating places so you'll need to factor in a few extra days to get around them all.

A quick trip to nearby shopping town Nowra is in order for dining at **River Deli Cafe,** with its Paddock to Plate concept of slow food. After your lunch collect some local deli items and sausages for your beach house barbecue that night. Watch out all along the south coast, especially around Greenwell Point, Batemans Bay, Ulladulla and Merimbula, for roadside signs and small stalls selling locally raised oysters and other seafood.

If you are self-catering around Huskisson, you will want to make the acquaintance of the friendly folk at **Hyams Beach Cafe** and **Supply** – each has a gourmet provedore side (although you should front up for takeaways and coffee too) – and **Husky Bakery** for pies and slices. **Locavore**, as its name suggests, also prefers to use local, organic, and generally 'slow food' ingredients. Also in the vicinity, a transformed butter factory is winning awards for dining excellence. **The Butter Factory Restaurant** has featured in Restaurant and Caterings NSW's awards over the past four years. Evening diners also flock to Huskisson's multi-award-winning **Seagrass Brasserie**, secure in the knowledge that owner-chef Kierrin McKnight will serve up something seafood-y and sumptuous such as local Shoalhaven oysters or a whole fish of the day with a red curry dressing.

A little away from Husky's main drag is Paperbark Camp, where permanent en suite safari tents make this the ideal location for a spot of bird- or wildlife-watching. In the spacious main hall, **The Gunyah**, guests enjoy restaurant dining often in front of a roaring log fire as evenings can get a little nippy here.

By the time you reach Milton, this lush and lovely area will have you firmly in its grip. It's snack-time territory too, luckily with choices of **Brill on the Green** (fine Allpress coffee and cakes or super-healthy organic treats and juices at **Pilgrims Wholefood**. On the highway to the south of town are some of the best pies in the state at **The Rainbow Pie Shop**, although other aficionados hold out until **Hayden's Pies** at Ulladulla.

Once you've come this far, take some time to check out these twin towns that make the ideal full stop on the exclamation point of any trip south, with Mollymook playing surfin' sister to the more staid fishing port of Ulladulla. Latest wow-factor in these parts is the newish ownership of Bannisters Point Lodge's restaurant in Mollymook, now retagged **Rick Stein at Bannisters**. Yes, *that* Rick Stein, the United Kingdom's celebrity TV chef, who attributes his unexpected choice of an antipodean address to fond memories of eating the local seafood here years ago. 'I knew that one day I would open up a restaurant celebrating local fish and shellfish but keeping it really simple,' he says. Uncompromising quality is another given.

Otherwise there is also good dining in Ulladulla at **Elizan's Restaurant** at Ulladulla Guesthouse, **The Vineyard Kitchen**, where a weekday lunch overlooking the vines might trick you into thinking you have followed the menu to France or Italy, and local firm-favourite **Millards Cottage Restaurant** in an 1868 stone cottage opposite the harbour.

Batemans Bay marks the border of the Eurobodalla region. **North Street Cafe & Bar** is well worth visiting for a leisurely breakfast or a light lunch. For dinner many choose **On the Pier**, in a former punt house on the Clyde River, which has won awards for its fresh-as seafood. Oyster lovers are in bivalve heaven with offerings harvested from leases adjacent to the restaurant. Other places for farm-fresh Clyde oysters are **The Pearly Oyster Bar & Farm**, and **Bay Marlin Seafood**, which also has lovely fresh fish and lobsters.

The Princes Highway snakes along the coastline, often too narrow for speedy travel, which is a good thing as otherwise you could miss tiny Mogo. Take a detour to the zoo here for some exercise and excitement or hunker down under a willow tree at **Sydney Street Cafe** for a driver-reviver of good coffee and some luscious cakes. The good thing about driving this highway is that there is always something to call you off the road – a roadside stall selling strawberries, the sign to a quaintly named bay, a cafe, or a picnic spot just asking for a blanket to be thrown down.

Pray that you'll be passing through Moruya later in the week (Wednesday onwards) for that is when the delightful restaurant, **The River Moruya**, opens for lunch and dinner. The menu is termed 'European', so think full flavours and grand techniques, as displayed in the assiette of pork, making use of loin, belly, trotters and ham with exceptional skill. The outlook, though, of a wide sleepy river almost at the doorstep, with distant hills beyond, is pure Australia.

But all is not lost if your timing fails. **Red Box Pizza** at nearby Tuross Head will restore your faith in pizzas, country service and life in general. Just leave enough room to be in good shape to enjoy an old-fashioned creamy milkshake at the aptly named **Bodalla Dairy Shed**. Down this way there are towns with supermarket cheese names such as Bodalla and

Bega and, yes, you will find **Bega Cheese Heritage Centre** easily. The countryside has morphed quite obviously into dairying land as the pastures turn a deeper shade of green. Driving on side roads in the late afternoon you may be temporarily held up by lumbering herds of 'ladies' off to have the burdens of their massive udders relieved in the milking shed.

Narooma is one of the most scenic of this scenic coast's beauty spots. Many come to see the seasonal migrations of whales up and down the coast. Others come for **The Whale Restaurant,** at the motor inn of the same name. A revelation for those a little unsure of motel restaurants, here the signature dish of kelp-crusted salmon is superb and the menu is reassuringly local slow-food leaning. At the beach, actually in the surf club, **Michael's by the Sea** does it all sensationally. It's easy, uncomplicated fare – think fish and chips, local mussels, salads and burgers – in a laid-back environment. Most importantly, owner-chef Michael Stokes knows the provenance of all his ingredients, which are as local as it gets. He even makes his own salami and other smallgoods.

Still picking your way through some of the state's most delightful countryside, pause at Tilba Tilba for a garden-surrounded experience at **Love at First Bite**, and the film-set-ready Central Tilba where the award-winning **ABC Cheese Factory** beckons, and the **Rose & Sparrow** will make you feel right at home. The country-chic **Valley Edge Cafe**, just south in Cobargo, feels like an inner-city place. Maybe it's the panini. But more likely it's the aroma of the roasted-on-the-premises coffee. Try to make nearby **Saltwater** at Bermagui in time for dinner or lunch (eat in or takeaway, it's all good) for great seafood dishes, or simple fish and chips to enjoy with the never-ending interest of the harbour views.

About as far south as you can go, the menu at **Zanzibar Cafe** at Merimbula is unashamedly parochial with Hobbitt Farm goat's cheese, local mussels and anything else that's seasonal. If you just want to indulge in seafood, **Wheelers Oyster Farm & Seafood Restaurant** should be able to help you. They have been producing oysters on this spot for a century. With luck you will also find places in the region selling or serving the amazingly flavoursome fish smoked at **Sapphire Coast Smoked Fish** with its premises on the wharf at Eden. Sadly it seems that just as you have at last found Eden, the trip is over, and finally it is time to turn towards home.

Colonial beginnings

Dr Berry's Coolangatta Estate legacy

Surely the good Scottish doctor who had such a vision for the South Coast would be delighted if he could return and see what has happened here since his time. **Coolangatta Estate** was the vineyard that he established in 1822, in the foothills of Mount Coolangatta near the village of Shoalhaven Heads. The original convict-built hamlet is now surrounded by sprawling vineyards and landscaped grounds and accommodation is available in the houses. Although Dr Berry grew grapes in the mid-1800s on this site, the plantings lapsed and it wasn't until the 1980s that the current owners, Greg and his father Colin Bishop, re-established them. Today the vineyard produces many grape varieties including semillon, verdelho, chardonnay, sauvignon, chambourcin, tannat, cabernet sauvignon and tempranillo.

The maritime climate and coastal breezes of the area seem to suit vine growing, and nearby **Cambewarra Estate**'s range includes fine cabernet sauvignon, verdelho and chardonnay. The cellar door at **Crooked River Wines** at Gerringong is beautifully sited overlooking the valleys and vines. The winery makes 40 wines and five ports, and has a restaurant that also offers alfresco dining. With views like that it's little surprise many choose to eat outside. **Silos Estate**, established in 1870, just outside of Berry, has boutique B&B accommodation as well as an elegant restaurant. Available at the cellar door are wines made from seven varieties of grapes, which are grown unirrigated on the estate and are hand-pruned and hand-picked. The winery furthest south, **Kladis Estate** at Wandandian, is close to St Georges Basin, and has won many wine awards in Australia and overseas. There are now 15 wineries in the Shoalhaven region. Och, aye, Dr Berry would be proud of them all.

Contacts for South Coast

EATERIES

55 on Collins: 55 Collins St, Kiama; (02) 4232 2811

Bellachara Restaurant & Wine Lounge: 1 Fern St, Gerringong; (02) 4234 1359; www.bellachara.com.au

Berry Wood-fired Bakery: 23 Prince Alfred St, Berry; (02) 4464 1617

Bodalla Dairy Shed: 52 Princes Hwy, Bodalla; (02) 4473 5555; www.bodalladairyshed.com.au

Brill on the Green: 107 Princes Hwy, Milton; (02) 4454 0640

Elizan's Restaurant: Ulladulla Guesthouse, 39 Burrill St, Ulladulla; (02) 4455 1796; www.guesthouse.com.au

Hayden's Pies: 166 Princes Hwy, Ulladulla; (02) 4455 7798

Hungry Duck: 85 Queen St, Berry; (02) 4464 2323; www.hungryduck.com.au

Husky Bakery: 11 Currambene St, Huskisson; (02) 4441 5015; www.tourismjervisbay.com.au/huskybakery/

Hyams Beach Cafe: 76–78 Cyrus St, Hyams Beach; (02) 4443 3874; www.tourismjervisbay.com.au/hyams_beach_cafe

Locavore: Shop 2, 66 Owen St, Huskisson; (02) 4441 5464

Love at First Bite: Shop 1, Lot 401 Corkhill Dr, Tilba Tilba; (02) 4473 7055

Michael's by the Sea: Ballingalla St, Narooma; (02) 4476 5500

Millards Cottage Restaurant: 81 Princes Hwy, Ulladulla; (02) 4455 3287

North Street Cafe & Bar: 5 North St, Batemans Bay; (02) 4472 5710

On the Pier: Old Punt Rd, Batemans Bay; (02) 4472 6405; www.onthepier.com.au

Pilgrims Wholefood: Shop 8, The Settlement, Princes Hwy, Milton; (02) 4455 3421

Red Box Pizza: 93B Trafalgar Rd, Tuross Head; (02) 4473 8537; www.turosshead.org/Businesses/RedBox.htm

Rick Stein at Bannisters: Bannisters Point Lodge, 191 Mitchell Pde, Mollymook; (02) 4455 3044; www.bannisterspointlodge.com.au

River Deli Cafe: 84 Kinghorne St, Nowra; (02) 4423 1344; www.riverdeli.com.au

Rose & Sparrow: 4 Bate St, Central Tilba; (02) 4473 7229

Saltwater: 59 Lamont St, Bermagui; (02) 6493 4328

Seagrass Brasserie: 3 Currambene St, Huskisson; (02) 4441 6124; www.seagrass.net.au

Seahaven Cafe & General Store: 19 Riverleigh Ave, Gerroa, (02) 4234 3796

Silos Restaurant: Silos Estate, B640 Princes Hwy, Jaspers Brush; (02) 4448 6082; www.thesilos.com

Supply: 1/54 Owen St, Huskisson; (02) 4441 5815

Sydney Street Cafe: 34 Sydney St, Mogo; (02) 4474 5572; www.mogovillage.com.au/sydney-street-cafe.html

The Butter Factory Restaurant: 739 Greenwell Point Rd, Pyree; (02) 4447 1400; www.butterfactory.com.au

The Emporium Food Company: 127B Queen St, Berry; (02) 4464 1570

The Gunyah Restaurant: Paperbark Camp, 571 Woollamia Rd, Woollamia; (02) 4441 6066; www.paperbarkcamp.com.au

The Posthouse: 137 Queen St, Berry; (02) 4464 2444; www.berryposthouse.com.au

The Rainbow Pie Shop: 197–201, Princes Hwy, Milton; (02) 4455 1013

The River Moruya: 16b Church St, Moruya; (02) 4474 5505; www.therivermoruya.com.au

The Vineyard Kitchen: Cupitt's Winery, 58 Washburton Rd, Ulladulla; (02) 4455 7888; www.cupittwines.com.au

The Whale Restaurant: 104 Wagonga St (Princes Hwy), Narooma; (02) 4476 2411; www.whalemotorinn.com.au

Valley Edge Cafe: 59 Princes Hwy, Cobargo; (02) 6493 6007; www.valleyedge.net

Zanzibar Cafe: Shop 8, Main St, Merimbula; (02) 6495 3636

STORES

Bay Marlin Seafood: Shops 8–9, Bridge Plaza, Clyde St, Batemans Bay; (02) 4472 3244

South Coast Providores: 78 Queen St, Berry; (02) 4447 0571

The Pearly Oyster Bar & Farm: 6 North St, Batemans Bay; (02) 4472 4233

MARKETS

Bega Farmers' Market: Littleton Gardens, Zingel Pl; 1st and 3rd Fri each month, morning; (02) 6492 0161

Berry Country Fair Markets: Berry Showground, Alexandra St; 1st Sun each month; (02) 4464 1476

Opposite (left to right): dining with a view at The Whale Restaurant, Narooma; tempting array of cheeses on display at ABC Cheese Factory, Central Tilba

Gerringong Markets: Gerringong Town Hall; 3rd Sat each month; (02) 4234 1494

Kiama Produce Market: Black Beach; 4th Sat each month, morning; (02) 4232 3322

Moruya Markets: Riverside Park, 1 Ford St; Sat morning; (02) 4474 2796; www.eurobodalla.com.au/operator. asp?code=37703

Shoalhaven Heads Seafood & Produce Fair: Shoalhaven Heads Hotel, 51–55 River Rd; Sat morning; (02) 4422 7844

Tilba Growers' Markets: Big Hall, Bate St, Central Tilba; Sat morning; (02) 4473 7284

GOURMET PRODUCE

ABC Cheese Factory: Bate St, Central Tilba; (02) 4473 7387; www.tilba.com.au/abc_cheese.htm

Bega Cheese Heritage Centre: Bega Cooperative Society Ltd, 18–36 Ridge St; (02) 6491 7777; www.begacheese.com.au

Sapphire Coast Smoked Fish: PO Box 436, Eden; (02) 6496 2331; www.smo-kingovens.com.au/Sapphire_ Coast_Seafood.htm

Wheelers Oyster Farm & Seafood Restaurant: 162 Arthur Kaine Dr, Merimbula; (02) 6495 6089; www.wheelersoysters.com.au

WINERIES

Cambewarra Estate: 520 Illaroo Rd, Cambewarra; (02) 4446 0170; www.cambewarraestate.com.au

Coolangatta Estate: 1335 Bolong Rd, Shoalhaven Heads; (02) 4448 7131; www.coolangattaestate.com.au

Crooked River Wines: Cnr Princes Hwy and Willowvale Rd, Gerringong; (02) 4234 0975; www.crookedriverwines.com.au

Kladis Estate: Princes Hwy, Wandandian; (02) 4443 5606; www.kladisestatewines.com.au

Silos Estate: see Eateries/Silos Restaurant

Snowy Mountains and Capital Country

98

Have you ever wondered what this area would have been called if the national capital had not been located here? This random collection of small towns, mainly involved with agriculture of one sort or another, now goes under the collective name of Capital Country. Should it perhaps have been called Classic New South Wales instead? Surely those long views, the stands of gum trees, smoky-blue horizons and meandering rivers speak of the scenes chosen by early Australian landscape artists.

This was land taken up early in the 1800s when explorers then pastoralists pushed out from Sydney. Goulburn was established in 1833 and farmers were quick to see this was ideal land for sheep rearing and it soon became the centre of the wool industry in colonial times. The Snowy's economic prominence came later, with the huge 25-years-in-the-making, hydro-electric scheme, completed in 1974. Before this, the river was part of our mythology, embedded in our psyche by Banjo Paterson's iconic poem *The Man from Snowy River,* written in 1890. Perhaps now this high country is best known as a premier winter sports destination.

But what of the food and wine? There are now around 35 wineries in this region, most in New South Wales and a couple in Canberra's surrounds. Winegrowing attracts fine dining and a general love of good food. With that comes comfortable accommodation, galleries, and other complementary attractions. In this region, the proximity of Canberra, the nation's capital, and therefore the base for consulates and staff from many countries, has added yet another dimension.

The multicultural city has attracted and relocated people with international tastes and expectations. It is the ideal place for those who would appreciate a smokehouse like **Poacher's Pantry** (*see* feature, p. 104), for example, or the fine goat's cheeses made by **Hobbitt Farm**, or sourdough breads and the cool-country offerings of apples, pears, cherries, plums – even black truffles – from nearby producers. Farmers' markets and regular festivals emphasise the local bounty. Pack an insulated shopping bag if you visit this region as you will surely want to bring some of it home with you!

With time to spare, the ideal way to travel from Sydney is to take a lazy loop that follows the Hume Highway beyond Gundagai before turning east

Festivals

Festival of the Falling Leaf: events and entertainment; Tumut; Apr; www.fallingleaffestival.org

Harvest Festival: vineyards celebrate latest vintage; Apr; www.canberrawines.com.au

Capital Country Truffle Festival: restaurants and wineries; June; www.trufflefestival.com.au

Fireside Festival: winter food and wine; Canberra region; Aug; www.canberrawines.com.au

Murrumbateman Moving Feast: local food and wine; Murrumbateman area; Oct; www.murrumbateman.org.au

Snowy Mountains Regional Food Fair: Snowy River, Dalgety; Oct; www.snowymountains.org.au/snowyfoodfair.html

Wine, Roses and all that Jazz: spring festival of food, wine and music; Capital Country wineries; Nov; www.canberrawines.com.au

Where to stay

Alpine Habitats: luxury self-contained 'eco habitats'; Cnr Alpine Way and Wollondibby Rd, Crackenback; (02) 6457 2228; www.alpinehabitats.com.au

Country Guesthouse Schonegg: relaxed retreat with great dining; 381 Hillview Dr, Murrumbateman; (02) 6227 0344; www.schonegg.com.au

Kerrowgair B&B: classic country luxury-chic; 24 Grampian St, Yass; (02) 6226 4932; www.kerrowgair.com.au

The Carrington at Bungendore: old-style hospitality; 21 Malbon St, Bungendore; (02) 6238 1044; www.thecarringtoninn.com.au

Above (left to right): warming bowl of sweetcorn veloute at Crackenback Cottage, Thredbo Valley; in the barrel room at Clonakilla, Murrumbateman; a vintage car, and scenic views, at Thredbo Valley Distillery & Cafe, Jindabyne

and cutting through the massive Kosciuszko National Park. Detour if you wish to the snow regions (remember they are just as interesting out of the ski season) then take a lap around the Capital Country highlights before returning. At the northern entrance is Goulburn, with its lovely Art Deco buildings and interiors, such as the **Paragon Cafe**, seemingly cut and pasted from the 1930s, untouched and utterly charming. Another step back in history is the **Old Goulburn Brewery**, which has been brewing up amber liquids for 180 years.

Goulburn's importance in the wool industry is commemorated by the Big Merino, a 15-metre-high ram created in 1985, which recently made a precarious but effective transit to the other side of the highway. Now it stands opposite something more recently established and more interesting to food lovers, **The Bakery of Goulburn**, offering a range of breads including a San Francisco sourdough made to a traditional recipe that demands a rising time of two days. There are other breads too, and pies, good coffee and cakes – all the things a

road-weary traveller needs. Above the tables, one wall has a mural with the intriguing long-ago Aussie-bush story of how the owner, Keith (known as The Trapper), became a baker.

Tucked away in the valleys above Goulburn is the delightful **Willow Vale Mill** at Laggan. The restored flour mill has a touch of Tuscany about it. Owner-chef Graham Liney's bounteous food is home-style, help-yourself Mediterranean-style fare at its finest. There are also charming country-style bungalows on the property. Some 70 kilometres west of Goulburn, Yass is a quintessential historic country town, but travellers are also lucky enough to find an award-winning coffee shop, **Cafe Dolcetto,** where they can expect reliably good coffee, hearty sandwiches and generous country breakfasts.

If you are not hungry enough for lunch at Yass, you should be by Jugiong, home of the evocatively named **Long Track Cafe & Pantry**. While the swinging wire doors, wooden floorboards and counters set the scene for old-fashioned country service, the menu would sit well in the inner city.

Pantry products such as pear and vanilla jam and autumn chutney have shelves to themselves, and the blackboard menu announces the seasonal dishes on offer that day. There may be potato, leek and bacon soup, or lamb, olive and spinach pie made from local lamb, and of course always a selection of home-baked cakes – think, orange champagne cake, or coconut and rhubarb, to get the idea. This is more than enough to make any driver take the tiny detour off the highway into the town.

Further on, Coolac, a speck on the map just north of Gundagai, is home to the annual Bald Archy Art Prize, a light-hearted take on the prestigious Archibald Prize. It is judged by Maud, the curator Peter Batey's white cockatoo, and has a cult following, although the entries are hung in a gallery in Canberra for viewing. Watch out for local fruit and vegetables at the store.

Turning onto the Snowy Mountains Highway takes you through Adelong, and Tumut with its willow-flanked river, which celebrates autumn each year with a strangely named event, the Festival of the Falling

Leaf. Actually there are many leaves in autumn at this colourful cool-climate spot, and it is a photographer's delight. There is also trout fishing in the rivers, as well **Snowy Mountains Trout Farm,** the state's largest, where if you don't trust your skill in waders with a rod, you can buy fresh trout to take home.

The Batlow–Adelong area is well known for apples. **Batlow Apples**, the large apple-processing co-operative, is not open to the public, but there are three Batlow Apples road stalls close to town on the Tumut Road, which sell apples in season. Many growers have roadside stalls that are open to the public from late February to June each year, selling fresh apples and freshly squeezed apple juice.

From Batlow you can choose to head further south through Tumbarumba to Thredbo and Jindabyne, or take the Snowy Mountains Highway to Cooma. It's a win-win choice. With time to spare, take a couple of days, pausing at Thredbo as much as anything to dine at one of the fine eateries there. Newly opened in time for the 2010 ski season, **The Knickerbocker**, owned and run by Thredbo distillery

Above (left to right): eclectic dining room at Crackenback Cottage, Thredbo Valley; brewery tower at Old Goulburn Brewery, Goulburn; relaxing at Country Guesthouse Schonegg, Murrumbateman

owner Brad Spalding, offers fast efficient European mountain food, with Spalding's Wild Brumby schnapps naturally the après-ski tipple of choice. **Terrace** offers fine dining with a tasting degustation and matched wines. Those looking for something good and quick and easy find themselves at **Gourmet Forty Two**. The coffee, made with G42's own blend, is alone worth the visit.

Jindabyne is the other major centre here, but you must make two stops before reaching that town 35 kilometres to the east. Kerry Henderson has only owned **Crackenback Cottage** since 2007, but the original stone cottage, about ten minutes from Jindabyne, is much older. Already there is a new feel to this rustic restaurant with its eclectic decor. New chef, local produce such as rabbit, venison, veal, cheese and berries, and a happy buzz from the diners has brought it alive. A must-try is the rich duck pâté, or anything made using the schnapps from the **Thredbo Valley Distillery** across the road (there is a cafe here as well). A visit to the distillery allows you to huddle around the huge copper still

tasting peach nectar or sour apple schnapps or one of the other amazing flavours, then stay on for lunch in its cafe overlooking the garden from which the menu derives much of its herbs and vegetables.

Jindabyne, as a skiing base, has something for everyone's appetite. Plenty of quick and filling fare, of course, for carbo-needy skiers, but it is also the base for **Snowy Mountains Cookies**, Hobbit Farm with its amazing chèvres, and **Snowy Mountains Brewery**. Look for the latter's ales in all the best local watering holes. If you are driving through and self-catering and want to use local produce and products, stop off at **Iona Gardens Cafe & Nursery** in Dalgety, or **Snowy Mountains Gourmet** at Bredbo, on the way towards Canberra, for freshly baked pies and smoked trout.

Cooma is the centre for the Snowy region, and the best place to gain your bearings is over a cup of coffee at the **Lott Food Store Bakery & Cafe**. Always busy, with a dozen aromas of coffee, frying eggs, cakes, cheese, and deli items, it's a good place to

stock up, take stock, or just slow down and enjoy the sunny location. From here it's easy to take in historic Braidwood, once a bustling gold-rush town but quieter now. In Wallace Street, **The Albion** is a friendly country pub that emphasises regional and seasonal flavours. Just along the street, the old-style **Braidwood Bakery** is worth a stop for French-style sourdough breads, but a few doors further along you may drop in and watch the baker at work on the revered Dojo bread, which is also available at **Braidwood Natural Foods**. In the other direction, **Braidwood Traditional Ales** has a range of artisan beers that you can taste at the source, the microbrewery behind the Braidwood Deli.

This area is so rich in food-loving points of interest that it has been documented in the Poachers Way Food Trail (www.thepoachersway.com.au). **Country Guesthouse Schonegg** (*see* Where to stay) at Murrumbateman provides a comfortable base. People repeatedly remark on the tranquillity, the comfort of the rooms, the hospitality and, of course, the food!

At Gundaroo, the old Royal Hotel has been taken over by **Grazing**, which is not to be missed, nor are the gourmet pizzas at **Cork Street Cafe**. In Hall, Poacher's Pantry's **Smokehouse Cafe** is an important stop (*see* feature, p. 104) and, as you head unwillingly away from the area, make one final stop at **Cafe Lerida** at Lake George's **Lerida Estate** to try some of Anne's delicious homemade scones, seasonal local produce and superb espresso coffee. This winery is just one of several that should be included in any visit to the area. **Clonakilla**, at Murrumbateman, is a standout winery, revered for its shiraz viognier. Nearby, **Shaw Vineyard Estate** also makes some good reds, although the rieslings are very popular. For a great pinot gris, you should go to **Lambert Vineyards** and perhaps stay for a meal at the cafe. **Lark Hill**, at Bungendore, produces excellent riesling as well as pinot noir, and **Mount Majura**'s shiraz and riesling get good results. For a sparkling wine, **Gallagher Wines**' blanc de blanc méthode champenoise will raise your spirits, even if you are on the point of leaving this lovely region.

Success in Diversification

Poacher's Pantry smokehouse

When the family farm was looking at a downturn in the rural economy, rather than packing their bags and leaving their home of 30 years, the Bruce family simply got creative. Diversification seemed the key to economic survival so in 1991 Poacher's Pantry was born, cashing in on the culinary and management skills of the team, but still situated firmly on the property, just off the Barton Highway, 25 minutes from Canberra.

After identifying a need in the market for hot and cold smoked meats, poultry and game, they set about meeting that demand by establishing a gourmet smokehouse, one of the first of its kind. The standout products they developed earned them handfuls of awards and a place in most quality delis and gourmet shops throughout Australia. Now the company turns out a range of high-quality wood-smoked or brandy-cured meat, poultry, game and vegetables that are unique to the business. And while the Italian-style bresaola is always popular, so is the kangaroo or emu prosciutto. Susan Bruce, the spokesperson for the company, is also proud of the Smokehouse Cafe on the property, which is also the cellar door of **Wily Trout Vineyard**. 'The cafe is located in an old farm cottage that has been restored with a smart but casual feel,' she says. 'The terrace overlooks the 1870s slab woolshed and has views of the rolling hills with only the sheep and cockatoos to disturb the peace.' Open daily 10am–5pm, it's worth making a booking to get an outdoor table for lunch, particularly on weekends.

Contacts for Snowy Mountains and Capital Country

EATERIES

Cafe Dolcetto: 129 Comur St, Yass; (02) 6226 1277

Cafe Lerida: Federal Hwy, Lake George; (02) 6295 6640; www.leridaestate.com.au

Cork Street Cafe: Cork St, Gundaroo; (02) 6236 8217

Crackenback Cottage: Alpine Way, Thredbo Valley; (02) 6456 2601; www.crackenback.com

Gourmet Forty Two: Shop 4, 100 Mowamba Pl, Thredbo; (02) 6457 7500

Grazing: Old Royal Hotel, cnr Cork and Harp sts, Gundaroo; (02) 6236 8777; www.grazing.com.au

Iona Gardens Cafe & Nursery: Cnr Barnes and Campbell sts, Dalgety; (02) 6456 5130

Long Track Cafe & Pantry: Riverside Dr, Jugiong; (02) 6945 4144; www.longtrackpantry.com.au

Lott Food Store Bakery & Cafe: 178–180 Sharp St, Cooma; (02) 6452 1414

Paragon Cafe: 174 Auburn St, Goulburn; (02) 4821 3566

Smokehouse Cafe: Poacher's Pantry, 431 Nanima Rd, Hall; (02) 6230 2487; www.poacherspantry.com.au

Terrace Restaurant at The Denman Hotel: Diggings Tce, Thredbo; (02) 6457 6222; www.thedenman.com.au/restaurant

The Albion: 119 Wallace St, Braidwood; (02) 4842 1422

The Bakery of Goulburn: 1 Sowerby St, Goulburn; (02) 4821 4477; www.bakeryofgoulburn.com.au

The Knickerbocker: Riverside Cabins, Thredbo; (02) 6457 6844

Willow Vale Mill: Mill Rd, Laggan; (02) 4837 3319

STORES

Braidwood Bakery: 99 Wallace St, Braidwood; (02) 4842 2541

Braidwood Natural Foods: 56a Wallace St, Braidwood; (02) 4842 1311

Snowy Mountains Gourmet: Monaro Hwy, Bredbo; 02 6454 4200

MARKETS

Bredbo Village Markets: Bredbo Community Hall, Monaro Hwy; last Sun each month; 0402 620 335

Capital Region Farmers' Market: Exhibition Park, Canberra; Sat morning; 0400 852 227

Hall Craft and Home Produce Markets: Cnr Dalby and Mildura sts, Hall; Thurs–Sun; (02) 6295 0606

Old Bus Depot Markets: Wentworth Ave, Kingston, ACT; Sun; (02) 6239 5306; www.obdm.com.au

Rotary Markets: Tumut: 2nd Sun each month; (02) 6947 1239

GOURMET PRODUCE

Batlow Apples: 74 Forest Rd, Batlow; (02) 6941 4200; www.batlowapples.com.au

Dojo Bread: Rear Lane, 91 Wallace St, Braidwood; 0438 648 468; www.dojobread.com.au

Hobbitt Farm Goat Cheese: Barry Way, Jindabyne; (02) 6457 8171

Poacher's Pantry: see Eateries/ Smokehouse Cafe

Snowy Mountains Cookies: 7 Lee Ave, Jindabyne; (02) 6457 1333; www.snowycookies.com.au

Snowy Mountains Trout Farm: Blowering Dam Rd, Tumut; (02) 6947 3612; www.snowymountainstrout.com.au

WINERIES

Clonakilla: 3 Crisps La, Murrumbateman; (02) 6277 5877; www.clonakilla.com.au

Gallagher Wines: 2770 Dog Trap Rd, Murrumbateman; (02) 6227 0555; www.gallagherwines.com.au

Lambert Vineyards and Cafe: 810 Norton Rd, Wamboin; (02) 6238 3866; www.lambertvineyards.com.au

Lark Hill Biodynamic Winery: 521 Bungendore Rd, Bungendore; (02) 6238 1393; www.larkhillwine.com.au

Lerida Estate: see Eateries/Cafe Lerida

Mount Majura Vineyard: RMB 314, Majura Rd, Majura; (02) 6262 3070; www.mountmajura.com.au

Shaw Vineyard Estate: 34 Isabel Dr, Murrumbateman; (02) 6227 5827; www.shawvineyards.com.au

Wily Trout Vineyard: Smokehouse Cafe, 431 Nanima Rd, Hall; (02) 6230 2487; www.wilytrout.com.au

BREWERIES/DISTILLERIES

Braidwood Traditional Ales: 91 Wallace St, Braidwood; (02) 4842 1317

Old Goulburn Brewery: 23 Bungonia Rd, Goulburn; (02) 4821 6071; users.tpg.com. au/adslcy22/Brewery/Products.html

Snowy Mountains Brewery: PO Box 666, Jindabyne; 0418 226 027; www.snowymountainsbrewery.com.au

Thredbo Valley Distillery & Cafe: Cnr Wollondibby Rd and The Alpine Way, Jindabyne; (02) 6457 1447; www.wildbrumby.com

Riverina and Murray

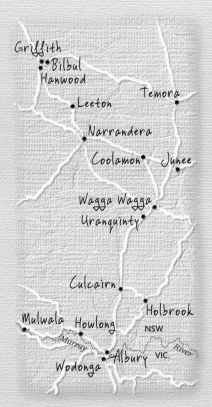

It's easy to talk about the Riverina, yet forget why it bears this name. It derives from the mighty Murrumbidgee River, which flows for 900 kilometres from high in the Great Dividing Range until it joins the Murray beyond Balranald at the Victorian border. As rivers go, it has it all. You can take a boat down it, swim in it, fish there, or just gaze at the waters and learn to recognise its various moods. But its greatest economic use is in irrigating the agricultural land along its banks, the riverine areas, especially since 1916 when the population centre of Griffith was established as part of the Murrumbidgee Irrigation Area project.

So fertile and productive is this land, that even if it was cut off from the rest of the state, you feel it could almost remain self-sufficient. In the Riverina you can find eggs, poultry, rice, lamb, wine grapes, citrus and stone fruits, vegetables, canola, wheat, cattle, pistachio nuts, olives and tomatoes, all being grown or raised on land that mainly owes its productivity to the waters of that river. The list of produce just goes on and on. Soon there may even be licorice growing at Junee's innovative Green Grove Organics (*see* feature, p.112).

Yet while the river brought essential water to irrigate and nourish the otherwise dry plains, something else was almost as crucial to the success of this land. The first wave of Italian migrants came during the Depression in the 1930s. In the postwar period of the late 1950s and early 1960s, more followed, bringing with them their core values of industrious labour and innovation. Their hard-won knowledge of food cultivation and winegrowing, which had been passed down over centuries as their families had worked and mastered the equally difficult countryside in their homeland, was vital too.

Roughly 60 per cent of Griffith's population of around 24 000 claim an Italian background and it shows in the type of foods grown and made here, and also in the cafes and eateries in the town. The long-term favourite, **La Scala Restaurant**, could have been cut and pasted from some home-town trattoria in Italy, with its exceptional pizzas, pasta and so much more. Just a few doors away, the showcases of **Dolce Dolce Pasticceria** are guaranteed to make your mouth water and your feet refuse to move until you have ordered and sat down with your coffee and something wonderfully

Festivals

La Festa: international music, wine and food; Griffith; Easter Sat; (02) 6964 7555; www.lafesta.org.au

UnWINEd in the Riverina: wine tastings, long lunches and music; various locations; June; www.unwined-riverina.com

Where to stay

Centrepoint Apartments: convenient and comfortable; Cnr Yambil and Ulong sts, Griffith; (02) 6960 2000; www.centrepointapartmentsgriffith. com.au

Chifley Albury: centrally located suite and studio accommodation; Cnr Dean and Elizabeth sts, Albury; (02) 6021 5366; www.chifleyhotels.com.au

Wilga Park Cottage B&B: self-contained B&B; 6 Condon Rd, Bilbul; (02) 6968 1661; www.wilgaparkcottage.com.au

Above (left to right): ripening olives at Wollundry Grove Olives, Wagga Wagga; elegant dining area at Zest BYO, Temora; rows of well-tended vines at De Bortoli Wines, Bilbul

decadent such as a silky lemon tart or crisp biscotti. Return later for lunch of pasta or a focaccia. And more coffee.

Also worth experiencing is **The Monastery Brasserie**, the name a tribute to the building's heritage, and not at all an indicator of an abstemious menu or wine list. Even though the menu has some Italian-inspired dishes (antipasti, rotolo of spinach, ricotta and mushrooms) you are just as likely to be won over by a duo of rabbit, the loin wrapped with bacon and the slow-braised leg served on a celeriac purée.

The award-winning restaurant **The Clock**, in a former main street bank building, is another local favourite not to be missed. Come here if you like fresh produce that has not been fussed with, such as orange blossom glazed duck breast, or baked salmon with a basil crust, served with a leek and caper risotto.

Throughout town on shelves or menus you will see products from **Riverina Grove**, a local food-processing business that has been established for over 20 years. You can shop at the warehouse and maybe meet managing director Louis Marangon as you browse the many items then, with true Italian-style, stay on for a local Art of Espresso coffee. Take a big bag as the products range from sun-dried tomatoes to pickled onions (descriptively named Bum Hummers), tapenades, antipasto vegetables, pasta sauces and salsas, and much more. Just don't leave Griffith without visiting **Bertoldo's Bakery**, established for almost 60 years. The bread, pastries and gelato are excellent, but the nougat is world-renowned. It makes an ideal take-home gift for your family and friends, too.

Grape growing was the first form of horticulture in the Griffith area and was started at Hanwood in 1913 by John James McWilliam. Soon wines were made and fruit and orchards were planted. At Hanwood, the **Catania Fruit Salad Farm** is one of the oldest farms in the area, a working example of how the early migrants became self-sufficient. You can take a tour and see plums drying, pick nuts, taste fresh fruit and purchase homemade, preservative-free wine, olives, jams, prunes in port, and mustard.

Griffith is the state's largest premium wine-producing area, accounting for about a quarter of the country's wine. Wine-tasting is an ideal way to become acquainted with the important producers. A specialty of the region is the internationally renowned 'sticky' botrytis semillon. **De Bortoli Wines**, one of the region's most successful wineries, has been awarded many trophies for its Noble One Botrytis Semillon. A third-generation family company established by Italian migrants in 1928, its vineyards now extend to the Hunter Valley and south of the border to Victoria's Yarra and King valleys.

McWilliam's Hanwood Estate is a family-owned winery as well, and a key part of a winemaking empire that stretches across three states. Another family concern, **Nugan Estate**, is a premium producer of estate-grown wine and one of Australia's top 20 wine exporters, while **Casella Wines**, founded by Sicilian immigrants, is responsible for the popular and highly drinkable Yellow Tail, Yendah and Mallee Point wine labels. **Westend Estate Wines** has a range that includes fine pinot grigio and sauvignon

blanc, interesting because the winemaker, Bill Calabria, is teetotal.

But not all wineries have big brands. **Lillypilly Estate Wines** at Leeton is establishing a reputation for its unique tramillon wine as well as Noble Blend. **Charles Sturt University Winery** at its Wagga campus is producing some premium varietals and teaching the art of winemaking too (it also produces good cheeses and you can book in for a cheesemaking course). Also in Wagga, **Borambola Wines** has award-winning vintages from chardonnays to shiraz utilising 'organic and environmental best practice'. At the boutique **Harefield Ridge Wines** near Wagga, the good news is that you don't have to leave after tasting their wines, because their restaurant, **Cottontails on the Ridge**, is the Riverina's newest and most exclusive eatery.

Leeton is the home of the Murrumbidgee Irrigation Area's rice industry. **Leeton SunRice Centre** is based there and those interested can book a tour or watch cooking demonstrations and learn more about this fascinating industry, which began in 1950.

This Australian-owned food business is one of the largest rice-producing companies in the world and its harvest is said to feed typically up to 40 million people per day in over 60 countries.

At **Pagès on Pine**, in Leeton, rice appears in risotto but the accompaniments may be steak and ratatouille because this Provençal-style restaurant is inspired by the Riverina's warm dry climate, and echoes it in the dishes. In the region's north-east, at Temora, known for its Aviation Museum, a pause for a light lunch at the relaxed and popular **Zest BYO** makes a welcome break too.

Around Wagga Wagga, the largest centre of the Riverina, the countryside begins to undulate, leaving behind the flatter western plains which, incidentally, the explorer Oxley said were so uninteresting (pre-irrigation) that no one would ever venture there again. How wrong he turned out to be! Restaurants in town that feature fresh local produce are the rustic **Magpie's Nest** with a lovely view over town, and **Three Chefs Restaurant**, a city-style eatery serving business lunches by day, and contemporary seasonally changing menu with a regional twist at night. Before leaving town, do drop in to **Premium Coffee Roasters** for award-winning, small-batch, house-roasted coffee and healthy snacks. There's more good-for-you organic food at **The Red Pomegranate** but if all you want is a top-rating pie, then **Mick's Bakehouse** in Wagga (or Leeton) is the place to go. Each year many of the pies, breads, cakes and pastries from this bakery win a slew of awards at the Sydney Fine Foods Show and other industry competitions.

The dry Mediterranean climate makes the Riverina an excellent place to grow olives, another high-quality product of the region. On the grounds of Charles Sturt University is one of the oldest olive groves in Australia, which still produces award-winning olive oil. Not far away is **Wollundry Grove Olives**, home of premium table olives and olive oils.

Just a little south of Wagga a dot on the map, Uranquinty, gives you a great excuse to stop. The **Quinty Cake & Bakehouse** (the owners call it a 'home-grown slice of Australia') has been so successful that **Quinty on the Run** has now opened in Wagga, where the sourdough breads and gelato are just as popular.

At the far edge of the Riverina, and geographically in the Murray region, Albury on the New South Wales–Victorian border makes a fitting endpoint to a food and wine journey through this area. As you would expect in a large provincial city, there are numerous places serving many cuisines. At **sourcedining**, chef Jodie Jones' adventurous cuisine combines high-tech control with playfulness, presenting a new dimension without sacrificing taste and enjoyment – as, for example, a jellied gazpacho terrine.

If you're craving Thai hawker food, you'll find it at **Baan Sabai Jai**, while the stripy precinct of **Green Zebra** should provide an adequate pasta fix (plus mandatory espresso) just when you need it. There is a little cross-border action going on here too, with a Victorian business, **Beechworth Bakery,** now in residence. Nobody minds, however, because their breads and other baked goods are so delectable.

A trip to **Butts' Gourmet Smokehouse** is a good idea, especially if a picnic is planned, and while shopping in town watch out for some local **Riverina Cheese** (the feta won an award recently) to go with your cold cuts. In local butcher shops, you may find **Bultarra Saltbush Lamb**, an up-and-coming gourmet meat from farmland on the banks of the Murray, and **Mirrool Creek Lamb** near Griffith.

Come night-time, the **Border Wine Room Restaurant** is the place to go for fine wines, tapas and other diminutive treats to match with the huge range of wines selected and collected by owner and wine expert David Sutherland. In fact, an evening here could form a fitting finale to a trip through such a rich and varied region.

Opposite (above, left to right): wine packing at Casella Wines, Yenda; a drop of red wine to taste at De Bortoli Wines, Bilbul
Below (left to right): scrumptious dessert at Zest BYO, Temora; ornamental vine shows off its autumn colours at Westend Estate Wines, Griffith

Riverina Roots

Green Grove Organics: from flour-milling to licorice

Neil Druce, one of the family members who run **Green Grove Organics**, a unique project in the small Riverina town of Junee, half an hour from Wagga Wagga, is justly proud of what has been achieved here. The family business had been milling grain since 1962 on its property, but needed a larger, more central location. The town mill closed in the 1970s and, after a fire gutted the end section, it was bought in 1998 by Green Grove Organics and carefully restored. Adding the **Junee Licorice & Chocolate Factory** to the family business was an ideal mix as flour is a major ingredient of licorice confectionery, that black, chewy sweet we all love. While the powdered organic licorice root is still imported, Druce hopes one day to have his own plants growing to provide for the needs of the factory.

For the chocolate side of things, he uses organic Belgian-style couverture to make 40-kilogram batches of chocolate-coated fruit and nuts, polished to a rich gloss using a true-blue Aussie substance – knobs of acacia gum. This takes place in huge gleaming copper barrels, and the public can watch the process through viewing windows. Heritage is vital to Green Grove and all flour milling is still gravity-fed and, along with the many types of yummy sweets and chocolates, the product is available in the shop next to the cafe (open daily 10am–4pm, with tours available).

Contacts for Riverina and Murray

EATERIES

Baan Sabai Jai: 459 Smollett St, Albury; (02) 6021 2250

Border Wine Room Restaurant: Upstairs, 492 Dean St, Albury; (02) 6021 0900; www.borderwineroom.com.au

Cottontails on the Ridge: Harefield Ridge Wines, 562 Pattersons Rd, Wagga Wagga; (02) 6928 4554; www.cottontailwines.com.au

Dolce Dolce Pasticceria: 449 Banna Ave, Griffith; (02) 6962 1888

Green Zebra: 484 Dean St, Albury; (02) 6023 1100; www.greenzebra.com.au

La Scala Restaurant: 455 Banna Ave, Griffith; (02) 6962 4322

Magpie's Nest: 20 Pine Gully Rd, Wagga Wagga; (02) 6933 1523

Pagès on Pine: 119 Pine Ave, Leeton; (02) 6953 7300

sourcedining: 664 Dean St, Albury; (02) 6041 1288; www.sourcedining.com

The Clock Restaurant & Wine Lounge: 239–243 Banna Ave, Griffith; (02) 6962 7111; www.theclockgriffith.com.au

The Monastery Brasserie: 18 Church St, Griffith; (02) 6931 8288; www.themonastery.com.au

Three Chefs Restaurant: 70 Morgan St, Wagga; (02) 6921 5897; www.threechefs.com.au

Zest BYO: 168 Hoskins St, Temora; (02) 6978 0332

STORES

Beechworth Bakery: Shop 11, Myers City Centre, Albury; (02) 6021 1010; www.beechworthbakery.com.au

Mick's Bakehouse: 67 Baylis St, Wagga Wagga, (02) 6925 9599; 56 Pine Ave, Leeton, (02) 6953 2212; www.micksbakehouse.com.au

Quinty Cake & Bakehouse: 42 Morgan St, Uranquinty; (02) 6922 9119; www.qbakehouse.com

Quinty on the Run: Cnr Best and Forsyth sts, Wagga Wagga; (02) 6931 9931; www.qbakehouse.com

The Red Pomegranate: Shop 15, 117 Baylis St, Wagga Wagga; (02) 6931 0223

MARKETS

Wagga Wagga Farmers' Markets: Wollundry Lagoon, Civic Centre Gardens, Tarcutta St; 2nd Sat each month, morning; (02) 6922 9221

GOURMET PRODUCE

Bertoldo's Bakery: 342 Banna Ave, Griffith; (02) 6964 2514

Bultarra Saltbush Lamb: Perricoota Rd, Womboota; (02) 5729 8029; www.bultarra.com.au

Butts' Gourmet Smokehouse: 417 Tribune St, Albury; (02) 6021 3987

Catania Fruit Salad Farm: Farm 43, Cox Rd, Hanwood; (02) 6963 0219; www.cataniafruitsaladfarm.com.au

Junee Licorice & Chocolate Factory: Green Grove Organics, 45–61 Lord St, Junee; (02) 6924 3574; www.greengroveorganics.com

Leeton SunRice Centre: Calrose St, Leeton; (02) 6953 0596; www.rga.org.au

Mirrool Creek Lamb: see website for NSW/Vic. outlets; (02) 6974 3258 or 0407 262 395; www.mirroolcreek.com.au

Premium Coffee Roasters: 34 Trail St, Wagga Wagga; (02) 6921 4155; www.premiumcoffeeroasters.com.au

Riverina Cheese: 470-482 Hovell St, Albury; (02) 6023 5325

Riverina Grove: 4 Whybrow St, Griffith; (02) 6962 7988; www.riverinagrove.com.au

Wollundry Grove Olives: Mary Gilmore Rd, Wagga Wagga; (02) 6924 6494; www.wollundrygroveolives.com.au

WINERIES

Borambola Wines: 1734 Sturt Hwy, Wagga Wagga; (02) 6928 4210; www.borambola.com

Casella Wines: Wakley Rd, Yenda; (02) 6961 3000; www.casellawines.com

Charles Sturt University Winery: McKeown Dr, Wagga Wagga; (02) 6933 2435; www.csu.edu.au/winery

De Bortoli Wines: De Bortoli Rd, Bilbul; (02) 6966 0100; www.debortoli.com.au

Harefield Ridge Wines: see Eateries/ Cottontails on the Ridge

Lillypilly Estate Wines: 47 Lillypilly Rd, Leeton; (02) 6953 4069; www.lillypillywines.com.au

McWilliam's Hanwood Estate: Jack McWilliam Rd, Hanwood; (02) 6963 3400; www.mcwilliamswine.com/OurWines/hanwood_wines.asp?v=CHD

Nugan Estate: 72 Banna Ave, Griffith; (02) 9362 9993; www.nuganestate.com.au

Westend Estate Wines: 1283 Brayne Rd, Griffith; (02) 6969 0800; www.westendestate.com.au

COOKING SCHOOLS

Charles Sturt University: Borooma St, Wagga Wagga; (02) 6933 2170; www.csu.edu.au

Victoria

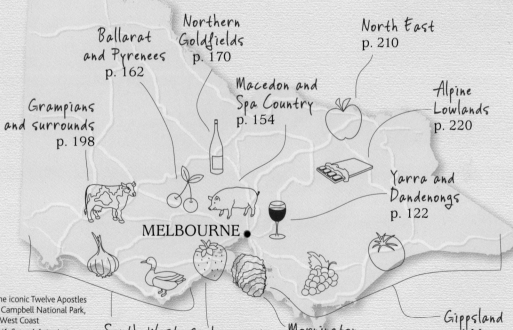

Mildura
and environs
p. 206

Ballarat
and Pyrenees
p. 162

Northern
Goldfields
p. 170

North East
p. 210

Macedon and
Spa Country
p. 154

Alpine
Lowlands
p. 220

Grampians
and surrounds
p. 198

Yarra and
Dandenongs
p. 122

MELBOURNE

South-West
Coast
p. 188

Geelong and
Bellarine
p. 178

Mornington
Peninsula
p. 134

Gippsland
p. 144

Left: the iconic Twelve Apostles in Port Campbell National Park, South-West Coast

Above (left to right): plating up ravioli parcels at Pickled Sisters Cafe in Wahgunyah, North East; TarraWarra Estate in the Yarra Valley; The Dispensary Enoteca in Bendigo, Northern Goldfields

Overleaf: wonderful European-style coffee shops abound in Melbourne

Melbourne

Embracing its rich multicultural society, the restaurant scene covers the full spectrum of traditional and ethnic cuisines, from fine à la carte dining and romantic restaurants to buzzy bistros, casual cafes and wonderful European-style coffee shops.

Right (left to right):
bicycle in the city's
Flinders Lane; Time
Out Cafe in the city's
Federation Square; Cafe
Vue @ Heide, Bulleen
Below: Melbourne's
laneway ambience,
Degraves Street

Melbourne ~ an overview

Melbourne has an international reputation for its fine food
and celebrates the fact with the annual Melbourne Food and
Wine Festival held over several weeks in March. Embracing
its rich multicultural society, the restaurant scene covers the
full spectrum of traditional and ethnic cuisines, from fine à la
carte dining and romantic restaurants to buzzy bistros, casual
cafes and wonderful European-style coffee shops. Explore
the rejuvenated city laneways crammed with tiny cafes and
eateries, with their tables spilling out onto the pavements. Take
a walk down cosmopolitan Acland Street in St Kilda and marvel
at the mouth-watering towers of cakes on display in many of
the windows. The city boasts many 'eat streets': Fitzroy Street
and the aforementioned Acland Street in St Kilda; Lygon Street
('little Italy') in Carlton; Victoria Street ('little Saigon' or 'little
Vietnam') in Richmond; Little Bourke Street, the city's lively
Chinatown; Bridport Street in Albert Park; Chapel Street in
Prahran; and, of course, Brunswick Street in Fitzroy, the grunge
capital of things quirky and funky. While these places exemplify
the variety of gourmet Melbourne, the good-food ripple extends
into the near and outer suburbs as well.

OUTER-CITY GOURMET
EXPERIENCES
* Attica
* Cafe Vue @ Heide
* Kimchi Grandma
* Le Petit Bourgeois
* Noodle Kingdom
* Oasis Bakery
* Rob's British and Irish
  Butchery
* Shira Nui
* The Baths Restaurant
* Va Tutto

See following pages...

Outer-city gourmet experiences

Here are some very good restaurants and food shops and stores just out of the city proper, but well worth the slight detour.

Above (left to right): dark chocolate tart with caramelised popcorn and popcorn ice-cream at The Baths Restaurant, Brighton; Lebanese coffee and biscuits are a treat in the cafe at Oasis Bakery, Murrumbeena; potato cooked in the earth it was grown in, and chef Ben Shewry adding the finishing touches to a dish, at Attica, Ripponlea

Attica: chic restaurant with all the 'wow' factors – including molecular gastronomy – of some of the inner city's best eateries; 74 Glen Eira Rd, Ripponlea; (03) 9530 0111; www.attica.com.au

Cafe Vue @ Heide: a little taste of what the hallowed kitchens of chef surpremo Shannon Bennett produce at his celebrated city establishment, Vue de Monde; 7 Templestowe Rd, Bulleen; (03) 9852 2346; www.heide.com.au

Kimchi Grandma: as its name suggests, this bustling eatery specialises in authentic stews and claypots that make Korean visitors homesick; 125 Koornang Rd, Carnegie; (03) 9569 2399

Le Petit Bourgeois: longstanding eatery that has been pleasing regulars for more than 20 years with its well-cooked and well-balanced French-style dishes; 330 Waverley Rd, Malvern East; (03) 9571 0909

Noodle Kingdom: this might just be noodle heaven – made fresh in the window and available in all sizes, with dumplings; 469 High St, Preston; (03) 9478 8885

Oasis Bakery: more than just a bakery, you will find a great range of spices and Middle Eastern products on sale here as well as top felafels, kebabs and shawarmas; 9/993 North Rd, Murrumbeena; (03) 9570 1122; www.oasisbakery.com.au

Rob's British and Irish Butchery: excellent range of meats based on English, Scottish, Welsh and Irish recipes, including gammon ham, haggis and Cumberland sausages; 177 Lonsdale St, Dandenong; (03) 9792 5188

Shira Nui: this place has an enviable reputation for its top Japanese food so trust the chef and opt for the theatrical omakase, or chef's choice; 47 Springvale Rd, Glen Waverley; (03) 9886 7755

The Baths Restaurant: enjoy gorgeous bay views while dining on contemporary, mainly seafood dishes; 251 The Esplanade, Brighton; (03) 9539 7000; www.middlebrightonbaths.com.au

Va Tutto: serves great modern Italian cuisine with a seafood bent and an occasional Asian and Middle Eastern touch; 226 Upper Heidelberg Rd, Ivanhoe; (03) 9499 7769; www.vatutto.com.au

Yarra and Dandenongs

The beautiful Yarra Valley, surrounded by rolling hills, lies north-east of Melbourne and not more than an hours drive away. As far back as the mid-1800s wine put the valley on the map but the huge proliferation of vineyards has only occurred in the last two or three decades and it is only in recent years that the area has become known for its quality regional food. And as this wine district has extended its boundaries, the range of fine eateries and gourmet produce stores has spread into the nearby Dandenong Ranges. Today there is almost a surfeit of good food outlets throughout the region, in part due to most wineries operating quality restaurants and cafes where menus complement the estate-grown wines.

The unofficial gateway to the wine-rich valley is the small suburban enclave of Coldstream, after which the Maroondah Highway forks off towards Healesville in one direction and Yarra Glen in the other. On the southern outskirts of Coldstream you can enjoy spectacular valley views from **Vines Restaurant at Helen's Hill**, while dining on very good modern Australian food to match estate-grown wines – perhaps Thai calamari and chargrilled wagyu beef rump. If you are looking to buy meat to take home,

Above: vineyard views from the restaurant at Rochford Wines, Coldstream
Opposite (top to bottom): showcasing local gourmet produce at Yarra Valley Dairy, Yering; landscaped surrounds at TarraWarra Estate

Festivals

Kellybrook Cider Festival:
1st weekend in May;
(03) 9722 1304;
www.kellybrookwinery.com.au

Smaller Wineries Shortest Lunch: progressive lunch at 14 boutique wineries; 3rd weekend in June; (03) 5964 3015; www.shortestlunch.com.au

Melba Festival: wine, food and music; multiple venues; Sept; 1300 765 584; www.melbafestival.com.au

Shed Fest Wine Festival: various Warburton Hwy winery sheds; 2nd weekend in Oct; (03) 9730 2800; www.shedfest.com.au

Where to stay

3Kings B&B: luxury apartments; 2480 Warburton Hwy, Yarra Junction; 0409 678 046; www.3kingsbnb.com

Chateau Yering Historic House Hotel: luxury accommodation; 42 Melba Hwy, Yering; (03) 9237 3333; www.chateauyering.com.au

Gracedale Yarra Valley: architect-designed home; 619 Healesville–Kooweerup Rd, Healesville; (03) 5962 1248; www.gracedaleyarravalley.com.au

Lochiel: four cottages, one family home; 1590–1596 Mt Dandenong Tourist Rd, Olinda; (03) 9751 2300; www.lochielaccommodation.com

The Sebel Heritage Yarra Valley: luxury country retreat; 2 Heritage Ave, Chirnside Park; (03) 9760 3333 or 1800 002 105; www.mirvachotels.com/sebel-heritage-yarra-valley

Above (left to right): scenic countryside surrounds Vines Restaurant at Helen's Hill, Coldstream; lunchtime buzz at Shantell Vineyard Restaurant, Dixons Creek; tending the vines at Kellybrook, Wonga Park

Little Creek Cattle Company (not far away at Seville) has great local grass-fed beef.

In Coldstream, the North Gateway shopping centre houses factory outlets for several local producers. You can pick up panforte, organic jams, chutneys, sauces and Bio-grape fruit pastes at **Australian Harvest**, and old-fashioned chutneys, preserves, sauces, real-fruit breakfast jams and the pungent Count Vaciliev's Russian mustard at **Cunliffe & Waters**. On the suburb's northern fringe, **Coldstream Brewery** offers palate-cleansing ales including a pilsner and an English-style ale, as well as a refreshing cider made from crisp local apples to complement tasty light meals such as sticky spiced pork spare-ribs and chargrilled prawns in vine leaves.

Appealing to a younger market, cider is also being made at two other local wineries. **Kellybrook**, at Wonga Park (west of Coldstream), makes three ciders using Yarra Valley apples – Kelly Brothers sparkling cider, champagne cider and old gold cider – and an apple brandy. They even have their own cider festival each May. Along the short St Huberts Road, which

links the Melba and Maroondah highways not far from Coldstream, the winemaking Napoleone family of **Punt Road Wines** are fourth-generation orchardists. Their estate-grown fruit goes into their sparkling apple and pear ciders, marketed under the Napoleone and Co brand. Also on St Huberts Road, **Stones of the Yarra Valley** offers some of the region's best views from their excellent restaurant set in a renovated barn house. Dishes are mostly European-inspired, such as a vodka-cured salmon carpaccio with fennel panna cotta, green olives and preserved lemon. There's also a more casual meze bar.

If you head towards Healesville after St Huberts Road, **Domaine Chandon**, established by the prestigious French champagne house Moët et Chandon in 1986, is the region's landmark wine-producing operation. Take a tour of the state-of-the-art winery and atmospheric riddling room before sampling the latest releases, including their sparkling shiraz. If time permits, dine in the **Green Point Room** where soaring architectural windows look out over vineyards to the Black Spur Ranges. Flexible menus

offer seafood tastes or cheese and antipasto dishes while an à la carte list has more substantial dishes such as rack of saltbush lamb for two – and even a children's menu.

A little further on, just after a sharp bend in the road, is the cellar door for **Badger's Brook** vineyard. Perched on a hill surrounded by vines, the eucalypt-green cottage shares premises with the wonderful **Bella Vedere**, where high-profile chef Gary Cooper holds the reins. The warm timber interiors provide the setting for daytime cafe breakfasts, exceptional lunches, weekend degustation dinners and an artisan bake-house producing terrific sourdough and olive breads and stunning almond croissants. When you enter, you have to run the gamut of the daily desserts that are displayed on the kitchen bench – they do irresistible tarts using seasonal fruit such as quinces, and enticing chocolate creations made with locally produced Kennedy & Wilson chocolate. You can book into one of Cooper's hands-on cooking classes; if you are the only one, it's likely you'll be cooking in the restaurant kitchen.

Not far away, **Rochford Wines Restaurant** enjoys an idyllic location with windows overlooking a lake, vineyard and amphitheatre for summer concerts on the green. Sample Yarra Valley chardonnay, Macedon Ranges pinot noir and Macedon Ranges pinot gris, then enjoy them in the restaurant with dishes such as smoked salmon risotto or slow-cooked pork shoulder followed by cumquat delicious pudding.

Along this stretch of the highway, heading towards Healesville, you look right across rich undulating hills, home to some of the region's original and best wineries. At **Dominique Portet**, you might meet winemakers Dominique or son Ben at the French-style cellar door as you try their barrel-fermented sauvignon blanc, rosé or sparkling rosé. The outdoor tables overlooking the vineyard make for a picturesque setting for lunch or maybe a glass of sparkling and a croissant from Melbourne's Laurent Bakery. Established in the late 1980s by noted wine author and judge James Halliday, **Coldstream Hills** produces award-winning chardonnay, pinot noir and cabernet. Nearby **Yarra Yering**, founded by the late

Above (left to right): tempting soufflé at Chateau Yering's Eleonore's, Yering; a variety of cheeses at Yarra Valley Dairy, Yering; mist-shrouded vines at Bulong Estate, Yarra Junction

Bailey Carrados, has taken over the dining room of his house as its cellar door. In what is a personal tribute to the local pioneering legend, visitors can now enjoy his powerful wines complete with fabulous views. While the majority of the wines here cost over $60 a bottle, the complexity of flavours – found in the likes of the Portuguese-style No. 3 dry red – make them worthwhile purchases. And, on the same road, prepare to be charmed by the cellar-door folk at another of the valley's originals, **Warramate Wines**, which also makes individual big wines from their dry-grown vines such as cabernet merlot, older-style shiraz and riesling (one of the few made in the region).

Also tucked-away in these hills, at Medhurst Wines' cellar door, the **Red Shed Cafe** is a modern eatery that serves imaginative breakfasts all day and light tasty lunches, such as Healesville pasta, local smoked Yarra Valley trout sandwiches, and cheese and antipasto platters – to eat in or as a picnic on the grass – all to complement estate wines.

Healesville is an attractive country town with a busy tree-lined main street and a few typical-looking country pubs. But the award-winning **Healesville Hotel** is no ordinary pub, although you certainly can sit in the front bar and enjoy a very good bar menu. However, it is the hotel's French-themed dining room, with its wicker chairs, dark timber floors and alluring paintings, that excels, turning out meals sourced from as much local produce as possible – local Harvest Farm tomatoes, Yellingbo yabbies, local Yeringberg lamb and free-range pork. And every dish is beautifully executed, such as the handmade potato gnocchi with spiced pumpkin purée, hazelnuts, buffalo mozzarella and shaved fennel.

If you fancy something a little more casual, go next door to the hotel's smart offshoot, **Harvest Cafe**. Choose from the interesting fresh salads (perhaps a niçoise using local Buxton salmon, brown rice with Yarra Valley Dairy Persian feta and sweet potatoes or chargrilled Mediterranean vegetables), flavoursome ready-to-go sandwiches, great muffins and more. Next door to the cafe is their more general store, **Kitchen & Butcher**. Pick up homemade Toulouse sausages, Angus steaks, ham, cold chicken,

Buxton trout, salmon fillets, crisp Turkish pita breads and Fruition sourdough bread. And nearby is **Barrique Wine Store** with an amazing range of international wines.

Healesville boasts a plethora of gourmet produce outlets. Family-based **Ricci's Bikkies** is not only about hand-making great bickies – sticky date and ginger, chilli and parmesan, white chocolate and macadamia nut, bittersweet chocolate and orange praline –but they also make flavoured Turkish breads, muesli, nuts and dipping sauces. **The Beef Joint** makes a good range of sausages including pork with apple, sage and rosemary; rabbit and apple; Italian pork and fennel; beef, mustard and sweet herbs; lamb, honey, rosemary and mint; and hot Mexican chorizo. And you must stock up on sublime handmade chocolates from chocolatiers **Kennedy & Wilson** – perhaps their nouvelle framboise (raspberry and chilli), trois frères (toffee-coated hazelnuts dipped in dark chocolate), dark, milk and white mint frogs, mint and orange chocolate bars and their own scrumptious chocolate ice-cream.

Nearby, greengrocer **Toscano's** sources local seasonal fruit and vegetables such as stone fruit, berries, persimmons, apples, pears, tomatoes and capsicum. And if it's the makings of a pre-prepared meal that you want, the Colaneri family hand-make silken pasta at **Yarra Valley Pasta**, including traditional beef lasagne, hand-cut gnocchi, and pumpkin or smoked Buxton trout and Yarra Valley Dairy goat's cheese ravioli. They also prepare packs of fresh pasta such as cracked pepper fettuccine and lemon and parsley linguine, along with homemade sauces.

On the northern outskirts of town, funky **Giant Steps/Innocent Bystander** is a must-visit complex with winery, cellar door, bakery (their sourdough is a winner), cheese shop, wood-fired pizzeria, and amazing coffee roasted on site. A favourite watering hole for winemakers of the valley, it pumps on weekends. Sample wines (the pink moscato is gorgeous if you enjoy something fresh and bubbly), nibble on cheese or settle in for a little grazing – pumpkin and Meredith goat's cheese arancini, salt cod brandade or kingfish sashimi with white miso

Above (left to right): autumn, the 'season of mists and mellow fruitfulness' at Mandala Wines, Dixons Creek; fine-dining room, and picture-perfect semifreddo, at Eleonore's, Yering; stylish steel and glass house Zonzo restaurant at Train Trak Vineyard, Yarra Glen

sauce – or something more substantial such as duck and mushroom pie or tagine of blue-eye cod. Sharing the same carpark as Giant Steps is **White Rabbit Brewery**, where you can watch beer being made in open fermentation vats. This open-plan boutique brewery makes tasty dark ale – with food to match at its cafe. There's often a barbecue on weekends, where you can pick up a quick sausage with onions to accompany your brew.

If you head out of town on the picturesque Healesville–Yarra Glen Road, you must visit **TarraWarra Estate**, an impressive complex with winery, cellar door, **Wine Bar Cafe** and the stunning TarraWarra Museum of Art, established by the arts-loving Besen family. Enjoy valley and lake views as you sip wines and dine on goat's cheese in crispy vine leaves with pickled figs, Serrano ham with manchego fritters, bollito misto or perhaps duck pithivier. But if you don't have time for a meal, even a quick tour of the beautifully landscaped grounds and gallery (before or after tasting their Tin Cow and reserve wines) is worthwhile. Also on this road you

can call in at **Zonzo** at Train Trak Vineyard for great pizzas with traditional toppings. They also do succulent (pre-ordered) fall-off-the-bone roasts cooked in the pizza oven and simple pasta dishes to accompany Train Trak wines.

Before exploring Yarra Glen, turn right onto the Melba Highway where you will find **Rae's Restaurant** at **Balgownie Estate Vineyard Resort & Spa**. It boasts a beautiful contemporary rammed-earth cellar door, winery and cafe with casual dining in a beautiful setting. Typical dishes include bouillabaisse, duck and venison sausage on du Puy lentils, almond- and prune-crusted saddle of lamb, and lime-cured kingfish on calamari and pineapple risotto. And if you want to stay the night, check out their luxury spa accommodation. Further along the road, at Dixons Creek, cheese affineur Richard Thomas oversees the downstairs cheese room at **De Bortoli Winery** and ensures the wide selection of Australian and imported cheese is perfectly matured for optimum flavour. Enjoy wine and cheese tastings and look for Richard's homemade butter, clotted cream and yoghurts.

Upstairs, dine on rustic Italian fare in the winery restaurant, **Locale**, where head chef Tim Keenan cooks exceptional Italian dishes such as hand-rolled linguine with ragù of rabbit and pancetta, slow-cooked salt bush lamb shoulder and heavenly panna cotta and tiramisu. Learn his secrets of feather-light gnocchi, pasta and sauces at one of his monthly cooking classes at **On the Vine Cooking School**.

Also in this vicinity pretty hillside **Shantell Winery Restaurant** serves dishes such as seafood gnocchi, grilled rainbow trout, pork fillet and vegetarian Wellington to complement their estate-grown wines. Guests at nearby **Cafe Immerse** can start the day with a smoked salmon omelette, zucchini and corn fritter or ricotta hotcakes, while at lunch they might consider sharing a tasting plate followed by confit of duck or fillet of Tasmanian salmon. Also in this area, one of the newest wineries is the architecturally designed **Mandala Wines**, providing an appropriate modern setting for their great wines and contemporary fare – all with matching wine suggestions. Typical entrées are braised oxtail and

tempura zucchini flowers filled with Yarra Valley goat's cheese followed by perhaps slow-cooked lamb shanks and hand-rolled ricotta gnocchi.

Backtrack to Yarra Glen, where the renovated gracious **Yarra Valley Grand Hotel** in the main street puts on good live music on Thursday nights and Sunday afternoons and surprisingly good pub food and wine list. Perhaps share a ploughman's platter and then a banquet of curries, fish and chips or a wagyu beef burger. Nearby and housed in an elegant old 1886 bank, the **Hargreaves Hill Brewery Co** offers its range of hand-crafted brews on tap in the front bar and good restaurant food featuring local produce. You can sample six brews on a 'tasting paddle' that might include Hefeweizen wheat and barley beer, the ESB and pale ale. Their beer-battered fat chips with garlic aioli are knockout.

If you turn back towards Melbourne on the Melba Highway you will experience more delights before leaving the valley. Beautifully located behind a screen of tall cypress pines and overlooking vineyards at Yering, the magnificent 1850s **Chateau Yering**

Historic House Hotel is a luxury establishment set amid heritage gardens and boasting two very good restaurants. **Sweetwater Cafe** offers more casual meals in a bright and airy 'conservatory' room while **Eleonore's** is fine dining in the true sense of the word. Think special-occasion dining with both à la carte and eight-course degustation menu, with dishes such as pearl meat in XO sauce, slow-cooked rabbit and Serrano terrine, coffee-roasted venison and roasted Grimuld duck breast. Next door, the stylish **Wine Bar Restaurant** at **Yering Station** sources top local produce to match estate wines – and some of the best views in the region. French-trained head chef Laura Webb-James adds Asian flavours to dishes such as crispy pork belly and scallop dumpling in consommé, and blue-eye in lemongrass marinade with crispy coconut prawn and Thai salad, perhaps followed by Kennedy & Wilson chocolate chilli mousse with churros. In the old winery building (c. 1859), there's the more casual **Matt's Bar** (upstairs; open at weekends), with a great selection of tasting plates to share. Downstairs is a gourmet food store next to the cellar door wine-tasting area, which also doubles as a small art gallery.

After you leave the impressive Yering Station complex, do not miss the turn-off for the hundred-year-old **Yarra Valley Dairy**, where you can buy handmade farmhouse cheese – fresh chèvre, goat's curd, matured white-mould cheese and award-winning Persian feta. If you are exploring the upper reaches of the Yarra River, near Warburton, you can avoid the valley crowds and linger over excellent cafe fare at beautiful **Bulong Estate** in Yarra Junction.

The mountain villages nestled in the Dandenong Ranges east of Melbourne are approachable from Healesville and Yarra Glen. You could return to the city from the Yarra Valley via the Dandenongs but you may be better to visit the ranges on a separate trip. Food enclaves are mainly found in and around the towns of Sassafras and Olinda. Look for the **Wild Oak Restaurant and Wine Bar**, a contemporary eatery serving modern Australian food with a French influence, and **Ripe – Australian Produce**, a shop-front crammed with gourmet produce and local wines that makes terrific home-style dishes to eat in or take away. In summer aim for a table on the rear terrace. In the Sassafras main street, the somewhat touristy **Miss Marple's Tea Room** offers gigantic servings of country-style cottage pie or the ploughman's lunch, followed by a skyscraper-high sundae or brick-size 'scones'. The small eatery doesn't take bookings so arrive early or expect to wait. A stroll around the local shops, such as the lovely **Tea Leaves** store selling teapots of every shape and size, will quickly pass the time.

At Olinda, check out **Credo** for modern Italian food and **Ranges** for modern cuisine with an eclectic mix of flavours. **The Ivy Cafe and Restaurant** also specialises in Italian fare, even flying in their authentic buffalo mozzarella, and offers a popular seafood barbecue on Sundays. At **Coonara Springs** garden lovers can dine on King Island steak, Glenloth chicken and Flinders Island lamb with a variety of sauces as they absorb views over the hundred-year-old botanic garden and the Yarra Valley away in the distance. Have a cocktail on the terraced lawns before eating in one of the sprawling array of dining rooms that once comprised an early 20th-century mountain home. At Mount Dandenong, the pinnacle of the ranges, enjoy one of the best panoramic views over Melbourne and surrounds from **SkyHigh Restaurant**. The contemporary cafe and family bistro has something for everyone from oysters, lamb rump and confit duck to pasta, burgers and a special children's menu.

local market

Yarra Valley Regional Food Group Farmers' Market

Handmade chocolates, fabulous biscuits, just-pressed olive oils, real fruit jams, local farmhouse cheeses and even buffalo sausages. You would not normally expect to find such gourmet products at a country location. However, the monthly farmers' market held in the historic wooden barn of Yering Station is anything but average and is the first and longest running market of its kind in Australia. Located within the manicured grounds of the winery, the barn is possibly the only traditional indoor farmers' market in the country. It literally lifts its galvanised tin sides to accommodate up to 40 stallholders and small producers who come from all corners of the fertile valley to show and sell their wares. The market is a tangible by-product of the innovative Yarra Valley Regional Food Group, which was established in 1998 to promote the region's bountiful and diverse produce. Spearheaded by passionate local food- and wine-lover Suzanne Halliday, the group publishes an innovative food trail map showing how, when and where to sample and buy everything from pasta and peaches to exotic mushrooms and mysterious witlof. From an initial few dozen farm gates and fresh-produce outlets in the region, the easy-to-follow street-by-street map now celebrates a hundred individual endeavours. The market is a great way to sample them in one location.

Contacts for Yarra and Dandenongs

EATERIES

Bella Vedere: Badger's Brook, 874 Maroondah Hwy, Coldstream; (03) 5962 6161; www.badgersbrook.com.au

Bulong Estate: 70 Summerhill Rd, Yarra Junction; (03) 5967 1358; www.bulongestate.com.au

Cafe Immerse: 1548 Melba Hwy, Dixons Creek; (03) 5965 2300; www.immerse.com.au

Coldstream Brewery: see Breweries/Cider-makers

Coonara Springs: 129 Olinda–Monbulk Rd, Olinda; (03) 9751 1043; www.coonarasprings.com.au

Credo: 543 Mt Dandenong Tourist Rd, Olinda; (03) 9751 1844; www.credorestaurant.com.au

Eleonore's: Chateau Yering Historic House Hotel, 42 Melba Hwy, Yering; (03) 9237 3333; www.chateauyering.com.au

Giant Steps/Innocent Bystander: 336 Maroondah Hwy, Healesville; (03) 5962 6111; www.innocentbystander.com.au

Green Point Room: see Wineries/Domaine Chandon

Hargreaves Hill Brewery Co: see Breweries

Harvest Cafe: see Healesville Hotel below

Healesville Hotel: 256 Maroondah Hwy, Healesville; (03) 5962 4002; www.healesvillehotel.com.au

Locale: see Wineries/De Bortoli Winery

Mandala Wines: 1568 Melba Hwy, Dixons Creek; (03) 5965 2016; www.mandalawines.com.au

Matt's Bar: see Wineries/Yering Station

Miss Marple's Tea Room: 382 Mt Dandenong Tourist Rd, Sassafras; (03) 9755 1610; www.missmarples.com.au

Rae's Restaurant: Balgownie Estate Vineyard Resort and Spa, 1309 Melba Hwy, Yarra Glen; (03) 9730 0700; www.balgownieestate.com.au

Ranges at Olinda: 5 Main St, Olinda; (03) 9751 2133; www.ranges.com.au

Red Shed Cafe: Medhurst Wines, 24 Medhurst Rd, Gruyere; (03) 5964 9022; www.redshedcafe.com.au

Ripe – Australian Produce: see Stores

Rochford Wines Restaurant: Cnr Maroondah Hwy and Hill Rd, Coldstream; (03) 5962 2119; www.rochfordwines.com.au

Shantell Vineyard Restaurant: 1974 Melba Hwy, Dixons Creek; (03) 5965 2155; www.shantellvineyard.com.au

SkyHigh Restaurant: 26 Observatory Rd, Mount Dandenong; (03) 9751 0443; www.skyhighmtdandenong.com.au

Stones of the Yarra Valley: 14 St Huberts Rd, Coldstream; (03) 9739 0900; www.stonesoftheyarravalley.com

Sweetwater Cafe: Chateau Yering Historic House Hotel; see Eleonore's above

The Ivy Cafe & Restaurant: 540 Mt Dandenong Tourist Rd, Olinda; (03) 9751 2388; www.theivycafe.com.au

Vines Restaurant at Helen's Hill: 16 Ingram Rd, Coldstream; (03) 9739 0222; www.helenshill.com.au

Wild Oak Restaurant and Wine Bar: Cnr Ridge and Mt Dandenong Tourist rds, Mt Dandenong; (03) 9751 2033; www.wildoak.com.au

Wine Bar Cafe: TarraWarra Estate, 311 Healesville–Yarra Glen Rd, Tarrawarra; (03) 5957 3510; www.tarrawarra.com.au

Wine Bar Restaurant: see Wineries/Yering Station

Yarra Valley Grand Hotel: 19 Bell St, Yarra Glen; (03) 9730 1230; www.yarravalleygrand.com.au

Zonzo: Train Trak Vineyard, 957 Healesville–Yarra Glen Rd, Yarra Glen; (03) 9730 2500; www.zonzo.com.au

STORES

Australian Harvest: Shops 7–10, North Gateway Plaza, Coldstream; (03) 9739 0203; www.australianharvest.com.au

Barrique Wine Store: 260 Maroondah Hwy, Healesville; (03) 5962 6699; barriquewinestore.com.au

Kitchen & Butcher: 258 Maroondah Hwy, Healesville; (03) 5962 2866; www.kitchenandbutcher.com.au

Ripe – Australian Produce: 376–378 Mt Dandenong Tourist Rd, Sassafras; (03) 9755 2100

Tea Leaves: 380 Mt Dandenong Tourist Rd, Sassafras; (03) 9755 2222; www.tealeaves.com.au

The Beef Joint: 179 Maroondah Hwy, Healesville; (03) 5962 4905; thebeefjoint.healesville.biz

Toscano's: 211 Maroondah Hwy, Healesville; (03) 5962 4808

MARKETS

Healesville Community Market: River St carpark; 1st Sun each month; (03) 5962 5875

Healesville Organic Market: Tourist Railway Station; Sat; (03) 5962 5070

Healesville Racecourse Harvest and Craft Market: Healesville–Kinglake Rd; 1st Sun each month, morning; (03) 5974 4710

Healesville Racecourse Market: Healesville–Kinglake Rd; 3rd Sun each month; (03) 5962 5875

Marysville Community Market: 11 Murchison St; 2nd Sun each month, morning; (03) 5963 3353

Mont De Lancey Farmers' Market: Mont De Lancey Historical Home, Wellington Rd, Wandin; 2nd Sat each month, morning; (03) 5964 2088

St Andrews Community Market: Cnr Kangaroo Ground–St Andrews Rd and Heidelberg–Kinglake Rd (opposite St Andrews pub); Sat; 0408 416 392; www.standrewsmarket.com.au

Tatong Village Market: Tatong Tavern Hotel, Fernhill Rd; 1st Sat each month, morning; (03) 57672192; www.tatongvillagemarket.com

Yarra Glen Station Market (Railway Place Market): Yarra Glen Station, Melba Hwy; 4th Sun each month, morning; 0425 742 323

Yarra Valley Regional Farmers' Market: Yering Station, Melba Hwy; 3rd Sun each month; (03) 9739 0122

Yarrawood Estate Market: 1275 Melba Hwy, Yarra Glen; 2nd Sun each month; (03) 9730 2003

GOURMET PRODUCE

Cunliffe & Waters: 2 North Gateway Plaza, Coldstream; (03) 9739 0966; www.cunliffeandwaters.com.au

Kennedy & Wilson: 203 Maroondah Hwy, Healesville; (03) 5962 6448; www.kennedyandwilson.com.au

Little Creek Cattle Company: 90 Douthie Rd, Seville; 0419 887 712; www.littlecreekbeef.com

Ricci's Bikkies: 2/281 Maroondah Hwy, Healesville; (03) 5962 1294; www.riccisbikkies.com

Yarra Valley Dairy: McMeikans Rd, Yering; (03) 9739 0023; www.yvd.com.au

Yarra Valley Pasta: 321–325 Maroondah Hwy, Healesville; (03) 5962 1888; www.yarravalleypasta.com.au

WINERIES

Badger's Brook: see Eateries/Bella Vedere

Balgownie Estate Vineyard Resort and Spa: 1309 Melba Hwy, Yarra Glen; (03) 9730 0700; www.balgownieestate.com.au

Coldstream Hills: 31 Maddens La, Coldstream; (03) 5960 7099; www.coldstreamhills.com.au

De Bortoli Winery: Pinnacle La, Dixons Creek; (03) 5965 2271; www.debortoli.com.au

Domaine Chandon: Green Point, Coldstream; (03) 9738 9200; www.chandon.com.au

Dominique Portet: 870 Maroondah Hwy, Coldstream; (03) 5962 5760; www.dominiqueportet.com

Giant Steps/Innocent Bystander: see Eateries

Helen's Hill: see Eateries/Vines Restaurant at Helen's Hill

Kellybrook: see Breweries/Cider-makers

Mandala Wines: see Eateries

Rochford Wines: see Eateries/Rochford Wines Restaurant

TarraWarra Estate: see Eateries/Wine Bar Cafe

Train Trak Vineyard: see Eateries/Zonzo

Warramate Wines: 27 Maddens La, Gruyere; (03) 5964 9219; www.warramatewines.com.au

Yarra Yering: Briarty Rd, Coldstream; (03) 5964 9267; www.yarrayering.com

Yering Station: 38 Melba Hwy, Yarra Glen; (03) 9730 0100; www.yering.com.au

BREWERIES/CIDER-MAKERS

Coldstream Brewery: 694 Maroondah Hwy, Coldstream; (03) 9739 1794; www.coldstreambrewery.com.au

Hargreaves Hill Brewery Co: 25 Bell St, Yarra Glen; (03) 9730 1905; www.hargreaveshill.com.au

Kellybrook: Winery & Distillery, Fulford Rd, Wonga Park; (03) 9722 1304; www.kellybrookwinery.com.au

Punt Road Wines: 10 St Huberts Rd, Coldstream; (03) 9739 0666; www.puntroadwines.com.au

White Rabbit Brewery: 316 Maroondah Hwy, Healesville; 1300 722 850; www.whiterabbitbeer.com.au

COOKING SCHOOLS

Bella Vedere: see Eateries

On The Vine Cooking School: see Wineries/De Bortoli Winery

Mornington Peninsula

Right on Melbourne's doorstep, the Mornington Peninsula is ringed by beautiful surf and bay beaches fringed with old-fashioned bathing boxes, and is characterised by undulating hills covered with orchards and vineyards, quaint villages and a comfortable country-meets-the-sea lifestyle. The region's burgeoning wine industry began in the 1970s when Baillieu (Bails) Myer and his wife Sarah planted the first vines on their Elgee Park property in Merricks North. Today, vines in the area cover some 920 hectares with more than 200 vineyards, 55 cellar doors and impressive wineries open to the public. Vineyard restaurants champion the excellent local produce such as seafood, cheese, apples, avocados, berries and stone fruit, while many small producers sell direct through pick-your-own or farm-gate sales.

Before setting off to tour the region, pick up a Mornington Peninsula gourmet produce guide and map, and a 'Get Fresh at the Farm Gate' brochure from the peninsula's visitor centre in Dromana; call (03) 5987 3078 or 1800 804 009 for further details or a copy of the brochure.

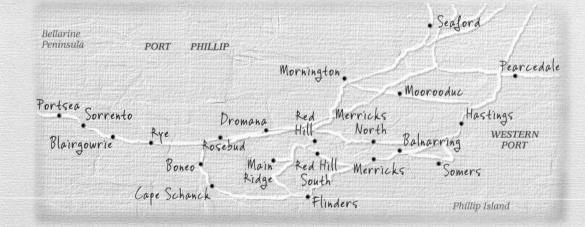

Festivals

Mornington Peninsula International Pinot Noir Celebration: ticketed biennial event, odd-numbered years, last weekend in Jan; (03) 5989 2377; www.mpva.com.au

Peninsula Piers and Pinots: wine, food and music; various wineries; Mar (Sun, Labour Day weekend); (03) 5989 2377; www.mpva.com.au

Winter Wine Weekend: new wine release tastings; various venues; June (Queen's Birthday weekend); (03) 5989 2377; www.mpva.com.au

October Pinot Week: dinners, tastings and cellar-door events; 1st week in Oct; (03) 5989 2377; www.mpva.com.au

Where to stay

Aquabelle Apartments: architect-designed bayside apartments; Level 1, 2331–2335 Point Nepean Rd, Rye; 1300 880 319; www.aquabelle.com.au

Lakeside Villas at Crittenden Estate: contemporary villas; Crittenden Estate, Harrisons Rd, Dromana; (03) 5987 3275; www.lakesidevillas.com.au

Lindenderry at Red Hill: luxury country house; 142 Arthurs Seat Rd, Red Hill; (03) 5989 2933; www.lancemore.com.au/lindenderry

Max's Retreat: vineyard retreat and self-contained cottage; 9 Station Rd, Red Hill South; (03) 5989 3007; www.maxsretreat.com.au

Woodman Estate: boutique hotel and spa retreat; 136 Graydens Rd, Moorooduc; (03) 5978 8455; www.woodmanestate.com

Above (left to right): tasting platter and wine at Stillwater at Crittenden, Dromana; chocolate treats at Mornington Peninsula Chocolates, Flinders; food preparation at Foxey's Hangout, Red Hill; raspberry mille-feuille and lavender ice-cream at La Petanque, Main Ridge

There are a few worthy dining options in Mornington's main street. **Afghan Marco Polo** serves family-style Afghan food with tasty dishes to share – kebabs, kormas and other curry-like dishes – while **Brass Razu Wine Bar**, with its quirky baroque mix of leather banquettes and chandeliers, offers dozens of wines by the glass with tasty snacks such as a slice of pâté or terrine, as well as gourmet pies and pizzas. Attached to the Mornington Yacht Club, **The Rocks** specialises in seafood, with crayfish, mud crabs and Moreton Bay bugs (live from tanks) and has great views over the local fishing fleet, charter boats and yachts in the picture-postcard marina.

There's good coffee and traditional Italian fare at **Via Boffe**, while **Coffee Traders** is a small but quaint space just off the town's main road with delicious cakes, biscuits and a range of flavoured coffee beans. For an enjoyable dinner, **Harba Oyster Bar and Grill** on The Esplanade delights with its bay views, good grills and freshly shucked oysters served natural and cooked, perhaps kilpatrick or Thai-style.

Also just off the main street, **Houghton's Fine Food** is chock-full of mostly homemade gourmet goodies, along with take-home meals, desserts and salads, plus a good range of local wines, cheese, olive oils, antipasto items, smallgoods and specialty breads including fabulous French, Italian and sourdough breads from **Peninsula Baker Boys**.

If you love seafood, on weekends in summer you can buy plump Mount Martha-grown **Bay Sea Farms** blue mussels from the Mornington Pier–based ship/shop *Sabrina II*, as well as seasonal oysters, prawns, scallops and abalone. For fresh bay scalefish such as snapper, flathead, whiting, pike and mullet, check out **Hutchins Brothers**, fifth-generation fishermen who sell their day's catch from an old beach box on Fishermans Beach. On the other side of the peninsula, the **Hastings Jetty Fish Shed** is the place to go for similar ocean bounty.

At Dromana, the people at **Heronswood**, the home of The Digger's Club, have been propagating millions of seeds annually to sell through their mail

order business for more than 25 years. With 62 000 members, it is Australia's largest garden club. The on-site cafe, **Fork to Fork**, uses just-picked fruit, vegetables and herbs from their production garden and gives a whole new meaning to 'fresh, local and seasonal'. Also at Dromana is **Stillwater at Crittenden**, a lovely lakeside winery restaurant, where Zac Poulier creates modern Australian cuisine featuring free-range and regional produce to match the Crittenden range of wines and more. Not far from here, at Arthurs Seat, keen cooks can learn cooking techniques and flavours of Mediterranean, south-east Asian or classic French cuisine at a two- or three-day residential cooking class at **Georges Boutique B&B & Culinary Retreat**.

Away from the sea are the small centres of Merricks and Merricks North. The quaint 1920s **Merricks General Wine Store** retains its rustic charm despite refurbishment as a bistro and cellar door for three local wineries – Elgee Park, Baillieu and Quealy. Nearby is one of the peninsula's first

vineyards, **Stonier Winery**, established in 1978 and specialising in the region's two classics, chardonnay and pinot noir. Winery restaurant **Salix** at **Willow Creek Vineyard** enjoys one of the prettiest vineyard locations at Merricks North, with a casual cellar door cafe and a more upmarket restaurant, where chef Bernard McCarthy uses local produce such as bay snapper and Red Hill cherries in dishes to match the estate-grown wines.

At Red Hill, **Foxey's Hangout** is an appealing winery that produces a good sparkling range, particularly the sparkling shiraz. The cellar door doubles as an intimate but casual cafe offering a series of small dishes that can be enjoyed individually or ordered en masse to share as a more substantial meal – perhaps spiced meatballs, barbecued quail or mushrooms wrapped in vine leaves. In warmer months, look for a space on the wooden deck and enjoy magnificent views of the vines in the valley below. Red Hill is also the place where chef Bernie Furness bakes a great range of

Above (left to right):
Tuscan porchetta, and
room with a view, at
Max's Restaurant, Red
Hill Estate; Scotch ale
at Red Hill Brewery,
Red Hill South; warm
vegetable salad at La
Petanque, Main Ridge

home-style goodies in his **Red Hill Kitchen**, many of
the ingredients fresh-picked from his kitchen garden.
He cooks pies such as duck, chicken, rabbit or
perhaps fish, savoury and sweet tarts, sausage rolls,
pâtés, dips, biscuits, jams, chutneys and preserves.

At Red Hill South, the **Red Hill Baker** uses
traditional baking methods to produce breads
including its signature wine-bread, perfect with
cheese, and also bakes a good range of pies, cakes
and pastries. For restaurant dining, you'll forgive and
soon forget **The Long Table**'s shopping-strip location
as you savour co-owner and chef Andrew
Doughton's outstanding combination of flavours –
perhaps pan-fried scallops, jamon and apples with
black rice – as well as his tasty tapas offerings.
Sunday night is BYO when local winemakers often
bring along unlabelled wines to try.

Wineries in this vicinity are numerous. Sample
wines at **Paringa Estate**, one of the most awarded in
the country, before deciding which you might like to
accompany your meal at the excellent winery

restaurant. They make an admirable pinot noir.
Nearby, **Red Hill Estate** is another winery with a
good reputation, mostly for chardonnay and dessert
wine. It's also worth picking up a bottle of their
Briars Cabernet with its rich berry flavours and subtle
tannins (only available from the cellar door). At
Max's Restaurant at **Red Hill Estate** the view is one
of the best on the peninsula; the food's good too,
and do try Max's balsamic-style vinegar.

At **Red Hill Cheese**, Trevor, Jan and Burke Brandon
produce excellent cheeses such as the delicate
award-winning Misty Valley goat's cheese, Mountain
Goat Blue and semi-matured Paradigm Log. Nearby,
Red Hill Brewery handcrafts a range of top ales
including Golden Ale, Wheat Beer and Scotch Ale,
plus seasonal ales, while their cafe serves traditional
European dishes to match. **Vines of Red Hill** is a
restaurant and cellar door set in a delightful Tuscan
garden overlooking vines to a lake beyond.
Acclaimed chef James Redfern really adheres to
seasonal and regional produce and, being located

between two bays, fresh local seafood. Book in to one of his monthly cooking classes.

Well sited overlooking vineyards and an olive grove, **Montalto Vineyard and Olive Grove**, with its sculpture garden and wetlands, has won many tourism awards as well as many for its wine and food. In the renowned restaurant, the French-influenced menu features organic herbs and vegetables from the kitchen garden as well as other local produce. Another impressive winery complex in this vicinity is **Port Phillip Estate** (*see* feature, p. 140).

Adjoining Red Hill, Main Ridge is dotted with terrific restaurants and wineries such as **Main Ridge Estate,** one of the earliest wineries on the peninsula and noted for its pinot noir. Another noteworthy vineyard is the curiously named **Ten Minutes by Tractor** (its three vineyards are all ten minutes apart by tractor). The slick restaurant with vineyard views has a European-style menu that is guaranteed to please, with the likes of spice roasted duck breast, cabbage compote, quince, beetroot terrine and a

port and pepper sauce. Each dish is matched with a wine, not only the winery's own, but also a number of international drops. Nearby neighbour is **T'Gallant**, where winemaker Kevin McCarthy's Juliet pinot grigio and pinot noir are considered benchmarks, and those with an appetite can tuck into pizzas or rustic Italian fare at the winery's **La Baracca Trattoria**, in a converted tractor shed. Almost opposite is **La Petanque**, where indeed diners can bowl a few boules on the gravel piste, between elegant courses orchestrated by charming Frenchman Philippe Marquet. And if you need more exercise after all this dining, pick-your-own strawberries, raspberries and cherries in season at **Sunny Ridge Strawberry Farm** (open daily) and, of course, savour fruit wines, liqueurs, ice-cream, jams and preserves.

En route to Sorrento and Portsea, the **Blue Mini Cafe** at Rosebud is a good pit-stop serving good coffee, homemade goodies, filled wraps and all-day breakfasts – try their tapas offering with Spanish-style eggs with chorizo or the New Zealand farmhouse mixed grill. At Blairgowrie, you can buy fresh fish from **Cornell's Fresh Seafood.**

Sorrento is an enormously popular resort town, packed with sun lovers during the Christmas holiday period and summer weekends. The holiday-makers come for the casual atmosphere, easy shopping and relaxed lifestyle. **Stringers Stores of Sorrento** stock much of the local produce and wine (look for acclaimed Dexter Wines), while opposite, **Just Fine Food** does a good trade in homemade soups, quiches and salads, and have cornered the vanilla slice market, selling some 1400 a day in high season. Dining options are good and varied from **Acquolina**, where northern Italian flavours sing at dinner time only, **Loquat Restaurant & Bar** with its Mediterranean menu that pleases locals, **Smokehouse Sorrento** where pizza is king, and **The Baths**, where any closer to the beach and you'd have sand in your shoes. This eatery is noted for its seafood and does great fish and chips.

On the ocean side of the peninsula, you'll have to book ahead to score a seat at the charmingly rustic **La Campagna**, near Cape Schanck, where Helen and Ted Ori serve casalinga-style Italian dishes using home-grown olives, bake their own breads and

pizzas and make traditional lasagne like nonna used to make. Further east along the coast, you use an old-fashioned honesty box to pay for your hydroponic tomatoes at **Flinders Farm**, where Andrew Stephens grows flavoursome round varieties and Roma tomatoes year-round. Flinders village might be small, but it's here you can buy fresh lobster in season from the **Flinders Village Cafe**, while at the **Red Hill Baker at Flinders**, breadmaker Ray Johns, as well as baking great breads, entertains with live jazz on Sunday afternoons.

Nearby, you can sample **Mornington Peninsula Chocolates**, handmade daily on the premises from Belgian, French and Swiss couverture – perhaps chilli and tequila, mascarpone cheese or strawberries and cream. At Balnarring, you can enjoy home-grown figs with prosciutto and traditional Italian dishes such as seared sliced rare beef with rocket, parmesan, balsamic and roasted home-grown heirloom tomatoes at **Ciao Bella Pizzeria and Wine Bar.** Not far away, the 1927 **Somers General Store**, with beautiful views over Western Port to Phillip Island, has a full kitchen that produces grazing platters, homemade pies and antipasto plates to eat in, and fresh daily salads, homemade cakes and filled focaccia to go.

Below: outdoor area at Port Phillip Estate, Red Hill South

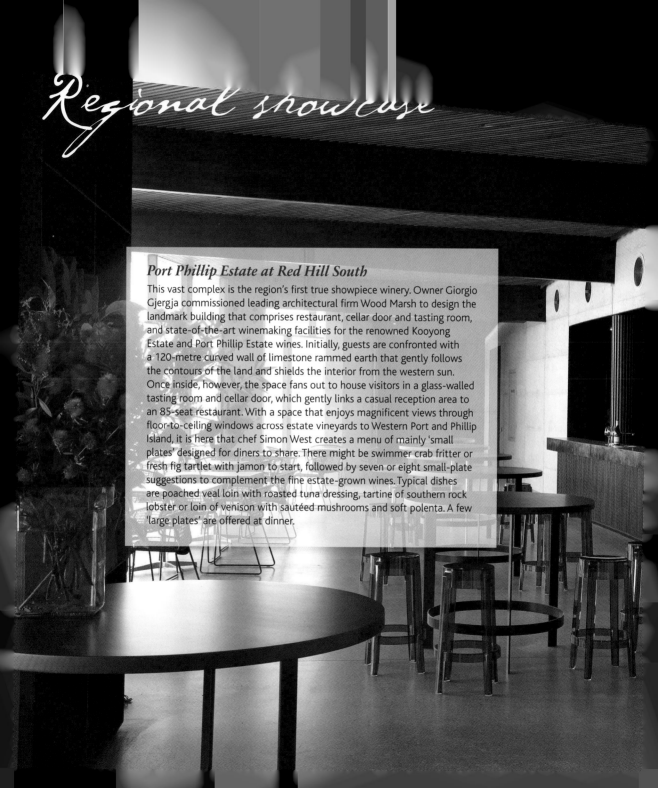

Port Phillip Estate at Red Hill South

This vast complex is the region's first true showpiece winery. Owner Giorgio Gjergja commissioned leading architectural firm Wood Marsh to design the landmark building that comprises restaurant, cellar door and tasting room, and state-of-the-art winemaking facilities for the renowned Kooyong Estate and Port Phillip Estate wines. Initially, guests are confronted with a 120-metre curved wall of limestone rammed earth that gently follows the contours of the land and shields the interior from the western sun. Once inside, however, the space fans out to house visitors in a glass-walled tasting room and cellar door, which gently links a casual reception area to an 85-seat restaurant. With a space that enjoys magnificent views through floor-to-ceiling windows across estate vineyards to Western Port and Phillip Island, it is here that chef Simon West creates a menu of mainly 'small plates' designed for diners to share. There might be swimmer crab fritter or fresh fig tartlet with jamon to start, followed by seven or eight small-plate suggestions to complement the fine estate-grown wines. Typical dishes are poached veal loin with roasted tuna dressing, tartine of southern rock lobster or loin of venison with sautéed mushrooms and soft polenta. A few 'large plates' are offered at dinner.

Contacts for Mornington Peninsula

EATERIES

Acquolina: 26 Ocean Beach Rd, Sorrento; (03) 5984 0811

Afghan Marco Polo: 9–11 Main St, Mornington; (03) 5975 5154; www.afghanmarcopolo.com.au

Blue Mini Cafe: 1455 Point Nepean Rd, Rosebud; (03) 5982 1455; www.bluemini.com.au

Brass Razu Wine Bar: 13 Main St, Mornington; (03) 5975 0108

Ciao Bella Pizzeria and Wine Bar: 2998 Frankston–Flinders Rd, Balnarring: (03) 5931 3098; www.ciaobellapizza.com.au

Coffee Traders: 3 Blake St, Mornington; (03) 5977 1177

Fork to Fork: Heronswood, 105 LaTrobe Pde, Dromana; (03) 5984 7900

Foxey's Hangout: 795 White Hill Rd, Red Hill; (03) 5989 2022; www.foxeys-hangout.com.au

Harba Oyster Bar and Grill: 786 The Esplanade, Mornington; (03) 5975 1100; www.harba.com.au

La Baracca Trattoria: T'Gallant, 1385 Mornington–Flinders Rd, Main Ridge; (03) 5989 6565; www.tgallant.com.au

La Campagna: 176 Rogers Rd, Cape Schanck; (03) 5988 5350

La Petanque: 1208 Mornington–Flinders Rd, Main Ridge; (03) 5931 0155; www.lapetanque.com.au

Loquat Restaurant & Bar: 3183 Point Nepean Rd, Sorrento; (03) 5984 4444

Max's Restaurant: Red Hill Estate, 53 Shoreham Rd, Red Hill South; (03) 5989 0177; www.maxsrestaurant.com.au

Merricks General Wine Store: 3460 Frankston–Flinders Rd, Merricks; (03) 5989 8088; www.mgwinestore.com.au

Montalto Vineyard and Olive Grove: 33 Shoreham Rd, Red Hill South; (03) 5989 8412; www.montalto.com.au

Paringa Estate Restaurant: 44 Paringa Rd, Red Hill; (03) 5989 2669; www.paringaestate.com.au

Port Phillip Estate: 263 Red Hill Rd, Red Hill South; (03) 5989 4444; www.portphillipestate.com.au

Salix Restaurant: Willow Creek Vineyard, 166 Balnarring Rd, Merricks North; (03) 5989 7640; www.willow-creek.com.au

Smokehouse Sorrento: 182 Ocean Beach Rd, Sorrento; (03) 5984 1246

Stillwater at Crittenden: 25 Harrisons Rd, Dromana; (03) 5981 9555; stillwateratcrittenden.com.au

Ten Minutes by Tractor: 1333 Mornington–Flinders Rd, Main Ridge; (03) 5989 6080; www.tenminutesbytractor.com.au

The Baths: 3278 Point Nepean Rd, Sorrento; (03) 5984 1500; www.thebaths.com.au

The Long Table: Red Hill Village, 159 Shoreham Rd, Red Hill South; (03) 5989 2326; www.thelongtable.com.au

The Rocks: Mornington Yacht Club, 1 Schnapper Point Dr, Mornington; (03) 5973 5599; www.therocksmornington.com.au

Via Boffe: 74 Main St, Mornington; (03) 5975 7499

Vines of Red Hill Restaurant: 150 Red Hill Rd, Red Hill; (03) 5989 2977; www.vinesofredhill.com.au

STORES

Houghton's Fine Food: 59 Barkley St, Mornington; (03) 5975 2144

Just Fine Food: 23 Ocean Beach Rd, Sorrento; (03) 5984 4666

Merricks General Wine Store: see Eateries

Red Hill Baker: 5 Point Leo Rd, Red Hill South; (03) 5989 2733

Red Hill Baker at Flinders: 37 Cook St, Flinders; (03) 5989 0067

Red Hill Kitchen: 67 Prossors La, Red Hill; (03) 5931 0186

Somers General Store: 2 The Boulevard, Somers; (03) 5983 2070; www.somersgeneralstore.com

Stringers Stores of Sorrento: 2–8 Ocean Beach Rd, Sorrento; (03) 5984 2010

MARKETS

Balnarring Racecourse Community Market: Emu Plains Reserve; 3rd Sat each month (Nov–Apr), morning; 0401 016 626

Boneo Community Market: Boneo Recreation Reserve, Boneo Rd, Rosebud; 3rd Sat each month; 0418 418 302

Mornington Farmers' Market: Peninsula Lifestyle Centre, Bungower Rd; 4th Sun each month, morning; (03) 5664 0096

Mornington Racecourse Market: Racecourse Rd; 4th Sat each month; (03) 5974 4710

Pearcedale Farmers' Market: Pearcedale Community Centre, 710 Baxter–Tooradin Rd; 3rd Sat each month, morning; (03) 59786620

Opposite: floor-to-ceiling glass at Max's Restaurant, Red Hill South

Red Hill Community Market: Arthur's Seat Rd; 1st Sat each month (Sept–May), morning; (03) 5974 4710

Seaford Farmers' Market: Broughton St Reserve; 3rd Sat each month, morning; 0419 870 698

GOURMET PRODUCE

Bay Sea Farms: Sabrina II, Mornington Pier; 0412 522 544

Cornell's Fresh Seafood: 2961 Point Nepean Rd, Blairgowrie; (03) 5988 8311

Flinders Farm: Boneo Rd, Flinders; (03) 5989 0047

Flinders Village Cafe: 49 Cook St, Flinders; (03) 5989 0700

Hastings Jetty Fish Shed: 2 Marine Pde, Hastings; (03) 5979 3556

Heronswood: see Eateries/Fork to Fork

Hutchins Brothers: 94 Fishermans Beach, Mornington; (03) 5975 3090

Mornington Peninsula Chocolates: 45 Cook St, Flinders; (03) 5989 0040; www.mpchocolates.com.au

Peninsula Baker Boys: 1140 Nepean Hwy, Mornington; (03) 5976 1911

Red Hill Cheese: 81 William Rd, Red Hill; (03) 5989 2035; www.redhillcheese.com.au

Sunny Ridge Strawberry Farm: Cnr Mornington–Flinders and Shands rds, Main Ridge; (03) 5989 4500; www.sunnyridge.com.au

WINERIES

Crittenden Estate: 25 Harrisons Rd, Dromana; (03) 5981 8322; crittendenwines.com.au

Main Ridge Estate: 80 William Rd, Red Hill; (03) 5989 2686; www.mre.com.au

Montalto Vineyard and Olive Grove: see Eateries

Paringa Estate: see Eateries/Paringa Estate Restaurant

Port Phillip Estate: 261 Red Hill Rd, Red Hill South; (03) 5989 4444; www.portphillipestate.com.au

Red Hill Estate: 53 Shoreham Rd, Red Hill South; (03) 5989 2838; www.redhillestate.com.au

Stonier Winery: 2 Thompsons La, Merricks; (03) 5989 8300; www.stonier.com.au

Ten Minutes by Tractor: see Eateries

T'Gallant: 1385 Mornington–Flinders Rd, Main Ridge; (03) 5989 6565; www.tgallant.com.au

Willow Creek Vineyard: see Eateries/ Salix Restaurant

BREWERIES

Red Hill Brewery: 88 Shoreham Rd, Red Hill South; (03) 5989 2959; www.redhillbrewery.com.au

COOKING SCHOOLS

Georges Boutique B&B & Culinary Retreat: 776 Arthurs Seat Rd, Arthurs Seat; (03) 5981 8700; www.georgesonarthurs.com.au

Vines of Red Hill: see Eateries

Gippsland

Gippsland is possibly the country's largest and most fertile agricultural region. It stretches from the New South Wales border in the east and follows the Victorian coastline to Phillip Island and the outskirts of Melbourne, extending northwards in grassy finger-like valleys into the lush high plains. Its diverse geography encompasses snow-clad mountainsides, trout-filled rivers and lakes, stretches of pristine white-sand beaches and rocky headlands. In the midst of all this are pastoral flatlands that are a mosaic of market gardens and small-crop farming, and undulating pastures that produce succulent beef, lamb and dairy cattle – the origin of the region's superb farmhouse cheese, which makes the ideal accompaniment to the region's signature wine varieties of chardonnay and pinot noir. Regular farmers' markets and food and wine festivals celebrate the local bounty.

Exploring this vast region requires more than a daytrip. The suggested route leaves Melbourne on the Princes Highway, passing through the major centres of Morwell, Sale and Bairnsdale. Many of the recommended food producers, eateries and wineries are off the highway; some locations such as Noojee (north of Warragul) and Tongio near Swifts Creek (north of

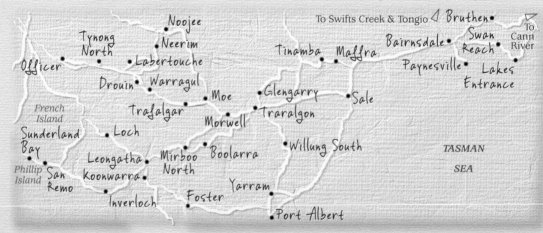

Boolarra Folk Festival: last Sat in Feb; (03) 5169 6275; www.boolarrafolkfestival.com

A Palate of Passions: food, wine and culture; West Gippsland; Feb–Mar; 0407 230 043; www.westgippsland.com.au

Jindi Harvest of Gippsland: produce, jazz and blues; 1st Sun in Mar; (03) 5626 1373; www.lardnerpark.com.au

Inverloch Food and Wine Festival: 2nd Sat in Mar; 1300 366 433; www.visitinverloch.com

Loch Village Food & Wine Festival: June (Queen's Birthday weekend); (03) 5659 4215; www.loch.org.au

Where to stay

5 Knots: luxury waterside apartments; 42 Metung Rd, Metung; (03) 5156 2462; www.5knots.com.au

Captain's Cove: two-storey architect-designed apartments; 13 Mitchell St, Paynesville; (03) 5156 7223; www.captainscove.com.au

Eugenie's Luxury Accommodation: luxury B&B; 16 Ramsay Blvd, Inverloch; (03) 5674 6121; www.eugenies.com.au

Minnies B&B: contemporary arty home; 202 Gibsons Rd, Sale; (03) 5144 3344; www.minnies.com.au

RACV Resort Inverloch: resort with beach views; 70 Cape Paterson–Inverloch Rd, Inverloch; (03) 5674 0000; www.racv.com.au

Above (left to right): exterior of Wildfish, Port Albert; preparing the signature dish at Jindi Harvest of Gippsland Festival; a disused railway viaduct provides a venue for the annual long lunch, Gippsland

Bairnsdale) are a fair way off the main road. The most easterly town to visit is Cann River in the far south-east of the state. To return to Melbourne the trail takes the South Gippsland Highway from Sale then the Bass Highway from Leongatha.

On the outskirts of the city, at Officer, you can choose up to eight apple-juice varieties and eating apples from **Summer Snow Apple Juice**, then visit one of the closest cellar doors to Melbourne, the small intimate winery **Cannibal Creek Vineyard** at Tynong North. Patrick and Kirsten Hardiker produce beautifully balanced chardonnay, crisp sauvignon blanc and top pinot noir. (You can also learn how to build your own pizza oven at one of their workshops.) Other wineries around here with welcoming cellar doors include **Gypsy Creek Winery** at Labertouche and **Kouark Vineyard & Winery** at Drouin South.

At **View Cafe at Brandy Creek Winery** in Drouin East you can share tapas-style dishes in one of the prettiest vineyard settings you will find anywhere. Start with dips then progress to grilled whole

prawns, grilled calamari, honey-roasted pumpkin and warm lamb salad complemented by their tempranillo or rosé. Do save room for desserts – perhaps light-as-air Spanish drunken sponge cake. More spectacular views abound from nearby **Parnassus Vineyard** where the French-inspired menu of **Helena at Parnassus** features local produce such as rabbit in white wine or steamed asparagus on potato and bacon ragoût. Try their sparkling pinot chardonnay and unwooded chardonnay. On Sundays, perhaps stop by for high tea.

It is worth taking a detour to Noojee, some 38 kilometres north of Warragul. Historic **Swaffields** at Neerim South dates from 1900 when it was the district's general store and haberdashery. Today it has morphed into a gourmet deli-cum-cafe with local cheese and smoked meats, antipasti, home-baked goodies and gourmet pies. They have a second store in Trafalgar. If you make it to Noojee, you will find **The Outpost Retreat** in an old farmhouse, where acclaimed chef John Snelling prides himself on sourcing the best local produce in the region.

There might be Noojee Smoked Trout Pâté, pot roast of lamb or roasted pork belly followed by Jindi Brie and Strawberry gum panna cotta. Also in this area is **Piedmont Wines**, where the cellar door welcomes visitors at weekends and public holidays.

Some 5 kilometres north of Warragul, at Lillico, **Clearly Delicious** uses traditional recipes to make gourmet jams, jellies, chutneys, pickles, sauces and cordials, sourcing fresh fruit and vegetables from their own gardens and elsewhere in the Gippsland region. Try their cumquat and passionfruit preserve, rhubarb relish and elderflower cordial. In Warragul **The Courthouse Restaurant**, housed in an historic 1887 courthouse, has a good reputation for its Italian fare and pizzas, or you can eat-in or order takeaway at **The Grange Cafe and Deli,** a food and wine store specialising in local produce. Also in town, you can buy hydroponic tomatoes that burst with flavour by the kilogram or case from **Flavourite Tomatoes**. And if you simply can't get to your favourite winery's cellar door, you can stock up on local wines at **The Press Cellars**. Just out of

Warragul, **Wild Dog Winery** restaurant offers a modern Australian menu with wine suggestions for each dish – perhaps carpaccio of Gippsland eye fillet with the estate pinot noir or braised lamb shank with estate cabernet franc. If the sun's shining, dine alfresco on the deck and enjoy vineyard and olive-grove views to the Strzelecki Ranges.

Yarragon village is an ideal spot to stretch the legs with some good window-shopping in its myriad shops. You can choose from a wide selection of local produce at **Gippsland Food & Wine**, such as regional cheeses from Jindi, Tarago River, Berry's Creek and Capra Cheese, smoked trout from Alpine Trout Farm in Noojee, and exceptional Hope Farm sourdough bread. This bountiful store also has weekend hampers to go, and will make to order.

South of the highway you can pick your own raspberries, blackberries and strawberries in season (November–May) at **Sunny Creek Berry Farm**, a certified organic family-owned farm at Trafalgar South. You can also pick your own seasonal fruit such as raspberries, boysenberries, blackberries and kiwi fruit at **Waterwheel Orchards** at Boolarrra South, then pay per kilogram at the farm gate. **Brushtail Bush Foods** is also located near here (you can order their produce on the internet). They grow, process and package an unusual range of spices including warrigal greens, apple berry, strawberry gum, mountain pepper leaf and berries. And while the area might abound with wineries, **Grand Ridge Brewery** at nearby Mirboo North crafts a range of delicious beers including Moonshine, a limited edition extra strong pure malt beer, and their enormously popular Gippsland Gold.

Gaztronomy and Gazbah are two eateries housed in a former bank in Morwell. Gaztronomy offers casual dining by day and is a more formal affair at night. The eclectic menu has strong Middle Eastern flavours with dishes such as quail bisteeya, Spanish seafood stew, slow-poached salmon and braised leg of rabbit. The intimate **Gazbah** next door offers a good Middle Eastern and Mediterranean tapas-style menu. In Traralgon, up-market **Neilsons** is one of the best places to eat in the region. Expect the unexpected, but also expect terrific flavours such as their signature slow-braised wagyu ox cheek in velvety black vinegar and tamarind glaze topped with yoghurt, cucumber salad and dukkah. Look for Jilly Cross's superb handmade Chocodence (*see* p. 149) truffles and fudges at local retail outlets and farmers' markets.

At Glengarry, **Narkoojee** is an award-winning boutique winery producing premium wines that reflect both varietal and regional character. Try the Lily Grace chardonnay, the Isaac shiraz and their

sparkling chardonnay, Harriet – all named after owner Harry and Val Friend's grandchildren. Halfway between Traralgon and Yarram, at Willung South in the Strzelecki Ranges, **Toms Cap Vineyard**'s stylish complex is a little oasis with its own terrific accommodation. Ann and Graham Morris didn't set out to open a restaurant here, but **The Vines** is ideal to showcase their wines as well as a few other local labels. Try their sauvignon blanc, cabernet sauvignon, unwooded chardonnay or crisp riesling with some of their dishes – Thai fish cakes, macadamia-crusted Atlantic salmon, twice-cooked duck on du Puy lentils, pan-seared tuna fillet or perhaps spicy warm lamb salad.

Bis Cucina is a city-chic cafe that is part of Sale's main entertainment centre. Ricotta hotcakes are a breakfast hit, while wraps and rosemary lamb burgers are popular lunchtime snacks. More substantial dishes include salt and pepper calamari, fresh local fish and Gippsland eye fillet. Near Maffra, look for the **Tinamba Hotel**, a gastropub that rears its own chooks, ducks and turkeys and has a thriving kitchen garden of assorted herbs and vegetables. Start with flash-fried crisp squid with wasabi aioli followed perhaps by homemade gnocchi with slow-cooked Moroccan spiced lamb shoulder, veal saltimbocca or Gippsland beef cheeks slow-braised in dark ale.

The lakes area has much to offer. Housed in beautiful historic former stables, **The River Grill** in Bairnsdale offers fine dining in a peaceful riverside setting. Contemporary dishes might be homemade gnocchi with slow-braised lamb shoulder, veal

Below (left to right): entrance to the farmhouse eatery at The Outpost Retreat, Noojee; Grand Ridge Brewery, Mirboo North; mortar and pestle at Culinaire Cooking School, Swan Reach; plated and ready to go at Tinamba Hotel, Tinamba

scaloppine and honey crème brûlée. Around Bairnsdale, pick up a 'Twin Rivers Food and Wine Trail' brochure, outlining farms, orchards and wineries in the area where you can meet the producers and buy from their farm gates. **Capra Cheese** (*see* feature, p. 150) is situated near Mount Taylor, north of Bairnsdale. At **Nicholson River Winery** you can sample Ken Eckersley's award-winning and very individual wines: syrah (shiraz), chardonnay, pinot noir and semillon sauvignon blanc. Rare back vintages are available only at the cellar door.

At Johnsonville, buy peaches, nectarines and plums from four-generation orchardists at the **Fruitfarm Johnsonville**, vine-ripened gourmet truss tomatoes from **Tambo Hydroponics** and seasonal blueberries, homemade jams and free-range eggs from **Blueberry Fields**. In Swan Reach, you can ramble through Chris Philip's lush parterre herb and vegetable garden, select from her range of homemade preserves and gifts in her garden shop and book a cooking class at her **Culinaire Cooking School Herb and Kitchen Garden**.

For fresh seafood, buy direct from the **Lakes Entrance Fisherman's Co-operative** and **Paynesville Seafoods**. If you fancy a fresh seafood meal, **The Boathouse Restaurant** at Lakes Entrance has been voted one of the top ten seafood restaurants in the state. Also located in town is independent greengrocer **The Fresh Food Group**, sourcing as much local produce as possible including a good range of organic produce and hard-to-find items such as tropical fruits, zucchini blossoms, enoki and

shiitake mushrooms, galangal, lemongrass, lime and curry leaves. They also have a dry-pantry section with unusual rice, dried porcini mushrooms and lots of local cheese. There are wineries in this area as well and you can sample chardonnay, riesling, merlot and pinot noir at **Wyanga Park Winery**, the oldest winery in Gippsland, and dine at on-site **Henry's Winery Cafe** on simple but tasty food such as tomato and basil soup and beef and port pie. Nearby Metung is the home base of those superb **Chocodence** truffles and fudges.

At Bruthen, follow the signs to **McConnells Berry Farm** for export-quality raspberries, blackberries, boysenberries and redcurrants in season (December–January), and homemade jams and sauces. If you have time on your side, take the trip north along the Great Alpine Road to Tongio, just past Swifts Creek. When olives are in (May–June), you can view them being pressed here at **Nullamunjie Olive Oil**, and enjoy coffee and cake. A light lunch at weekends is available over summer in **The Pressing Shed Cafe** (mid-October – mid-March), the olive grove's on-site eatery with views over the Tambo Valley. The cafe also doubles as the cellar door for olive oil sales.

At Cann River, seek out the mudbrick cellar door, restaurant and gallery of **Noorinbee Selection Vineyards,** perhaps the most easterly winery in Victoria. Modelling their wines on those of the famed Medoc region in Bordeaux, they produce mainly merlot, cabernet sauvignon, malbec, cabernet franc and petit verdot.

If you are returning to Melbourne, take the South Gippsland Highway from Sale. On the coast at Port

Albert, former professional fisherman Michael Hobson has set up a terrific waterfront restaurant **Wildfish**, with an adjacent fish and chippery that offers fresh fish for sale as well. Further west at Foster, **Windy Ridge Vineyard and Winery** is the oldest vineyard in South Gippsland, with arguably the best views over Wilsons Promontory. Let Graeme Wilson show you his range of terrific pinot noirs and interesting traminer.

Koonwarra is a real foodies' destination. The **Koonwarra Food, Wine and Produce Store** is a cafe, provedore and wine store specialising in handmade, regional, seasonal and organic produce. At **The Organic Fix** check out the quality organic fruit and vegetables from local growers. Opposite, at the **Peaceful Gardens Organic Cooking School**, hands-on classes cover a wide range of techniques including breadmaking, cooking with chocolate, preparing gluten-free dishes and preserving, as well as sessions for children. There is also a cafe.

With a name derived from an Aboriginal term for 'willie wagtail', **djinta djinta Winery and de Vine Restaurant** at Kardella serves a seasonal menu of modern Australian food at weekends. Typical entrées are pan-fried garlic prawns on rice, Mediterranean vegetable and feta tart and salt and pepper squid, with main courses of prime Angus porterhouse with garlic and rosemary potatoes and succulent lamb cutlets, with feta, rocket and tomato salad. Try their Classique Bubbles, their Classique table wine blend, their medal-winning sauvignon blanc and semillon.

Inverloch, known for its safe coastal surfing and inlet beaches is home to **Vela 9,** a stylish restaurant and wine bar that serves excellent contemporary fare. Tony Richardson and partner Felicity O'Dea are industry professionals. With more than 16 years experience in kitchens in Sydney and Spain, and parts in between, they make all their own breads, pastries, pasta, ice-creams and sorbets, and serve tender organic local lamb, their signature two-toned squid-ink tagliatelle with squid and prawns and possibly the best sirloin in Gippsland.

The friendly **Tomo Modern Japanese** restaurant in the centre of Inverloch is a contemporary space with walls displaying modern Japanese artworks, and there is a Japanese-style bamboo garden at the back. Owner-chef Tomo Ezaki cooked at one of Melbourne's favourite Japanese restaurants, Ocha,

for several years and already has a loyal following of locals here. If you are fond of chilli, let Tomo know and he'll spice things up for you. His dishes are designed to share – even the steak with wasabi mash is cut for that purpose. Recommended are the gyoza (Japanese-style dumplings) and spicy calamari legs with chilli and garlic. The standout main course is touban duck, a fillet of duck breast cooked in a rich broth with mushrooms, leeks, soy, mirin, miso and chilli. Tucked away along a residential street, **Green Heart Organics** stocks a vast array of organic wholefoods from beans and peas to rice, pasta, nuts, dried fruits and takeaway meals. They also sell fresh local fruit and vegetables and gluten-free flours, cereal and grains.

The tiny Archies Creek, population about 40, is not where you'd expect to find a sophisticated lakeside restaurant such as **Archie's on the Creek.** Local businessman Vern Rickman converted his former shire-council-office premises into an inside/outside restaurant, wine bar, 20 000-bottle wine cellar, wedding venue and conference centre, with future plans for accommodation, spa, boutique brewery, old-fashioned butchery, winery and more. Beef (tartar and chargrilled) is the go here, and is dry-aged for more than 60 days for optimum flavour and tenderness.

Let chef Paul Stafford teach you the techniques of French provincial, Japanese, Thai, contemporary Chinese, Indian and Moroccan cuisines and more with hands-on classes at his **Spice Island Pantry and Cooking School** at Sunderland Bay on Phillip Island. The school has also opened the Churchill Island Cafe, showcasing their food prowess at breakfast and lunch. **Clay Pot Curry House and Cooking School** at Woolamai teaches authentic Sri Lankan dishes from Shirani Perera, including curries, sambals, perfect rice, spicy seafood and vegetarian dishes.

One final recommendation is a stop at the quaint village of Loch and the **Gilded Lily Bar and Restaurant.** Housed in a renovated Victorian cottage, it features fresh Gippsland produce on its seasonally changing menu, with enticing dishes such as mushrooms filled with Gippsland goat's cheese and date, Brandy Creek quail chargrilled, Gippsland lamb or a succulent eye fillet, all accompanied by Gippsland wines.

Cheese

Capra Cheese at Mount Lookout near Bairnsdale

Maverick cheesemakers Emma and Matthew Gurnsey started their Capra Cheese business in 2004 with just one goat in their carport, which they milked by hand. Self-taught, they learned the techniques of cheesemaking by trial and error and won two gold medals at the Australian Specialist Cheesemakers' Show with their first attempts. Today, on their 39-hectare farm at Mount Lookout near the town of Mount Taylor (north of Bairnsdale), their 80-strong herd produces six distinct boutique varieties of farmhouse cheese from certified organic goat's milk: Fresco, a soft fresh goat's milk curd; Allegro, a creamy yet tangy firm fresh cheese; Mountain Ash, an elegant pyramid-shaped ash-coated traditional French-style cheese; Cameo, an ashed creamy textured mature cheese with natural white mould rind; Velvet, Capra's signature cheese, which is a matured French-style barrel with white mould rind; and Serenade, a unique heart-shaped velvety cheese with a white mould rind and a layer of ash through its centre. A qualified naturopath, Emma is mindful of making healthy cheese that is produced using a slow-lactic acid fermentation. Capra cheeses are ideal for a cheese board, lightly grilled, tossed through a salad or crumbled through pasta.

Contacts for Gippsland

EATERIES

Archie's on the Creek: 81 Archies Creek Rd, Archies Creek; (03) 5678 7787; www.archiesonthecreek.com.au

Bis Cucina: 100 Foster St, Sale; (03) 5144 3388

djinta djinta Winery and de Vine Restaurant: see Wineries

Gaztronomy and Gazbah: 15 Church St, Morwell; (03) 5134 2913

Gilded Lily Bar and Restaurant: 35 Victoria Rd, Loch; (03) 5659 4488; www.gildedlily.com.au

Helena at Parnassus: 180 Lardners Track, Drouin East; (03) 5626 8522; www.parnassus.com.au

Henry's Winery Cafe: see Wineries/ Wyanga Park Winery

Neilsons: 13 Seymour St, Traralgon; (03) 5175 0100; www.neilsons.com.au

Peaceful Gardens Organic Cooking School and Farmhouse Kitchen cafe: 1 Koala Dr, Koonwarra; (03) 5664 2211

Swaffields: see Gourmet Produce

The Boathouse Restaurant: 201 The Esplanade, Lakes Entrance; (03) 5155 3055; www.bellevuelakes.com

The Courthouse Restaurant: 72 Smith St, Warragul; (03) 5622 2442

The Grange Cafe and Deli: 15 Palmerston St, Warragul; (03) 5623 6698

The Outpost Retreat: 38 Loch Valley Rd, Noojee; (03) 5628 9669; www.theoutpostretreat.com

The Pressing Shed Cafe: see Gourmet Produce/Nullamunjie Olive Oil

The River Grill: 2 Wood St, Bairnsdale; (03) 5153 1421

The Vines: Toms Cap Vineyard, 322 Lays Rd, Willung South; (03) 5194 2215; www.tomscap.com.au

Tinamba Hotel: 4–6 Tinamba–Seaton Rd, Tinamba; (03) 5145 1484; www.tinambahotel.com.au

Tomo Modern Japanese: Shop 1, 23 A'Beckett St, Inverloch; (03) 5674 3444

Vela 9: 9 A'Beckett St, Inverloch; (03) 5674 1188; www.velanine.com.au

View Cafe at Brandy Creek Winery: 570 Buln Buln Rd, Drouin East; (03) 5625 4498; www.brandycreekwines.com.au

Wild Dog Winery: Warragul–Korumburra Rd, Warragul; (03) 5623 1117; www.wilddogwinery.com

Wildfish: 40 Wharf St, Port Albert; (03) 5183 2007; www.wildfishrestaurant.com.au

STORES

Gippsland Food & Wine: 123 Princes Hwy, Yarragon; (03) 5634 2451

Green Heart Organics: 60 Dixon St, Inverloch; (03) 5674 2759; www.greenheartorganics.com.au

Koonwarra Food, Wine and Produce Store: South Gippsland Hwy, Koonwarra; (03) 5664 2285

The Fresh Food Group: 14 Myer St, Lakes Entrance; (03) 5155 4112

The Grange Cafe and Deli: see Eateries

The Organic Fix: 4–6 Koala Dr, Koonwarra; (03) 5664 2481

The Press Cellars: 1/80 Smith St, Warragul; (03) 5622 0494; www.thepresscellars.com.au

MARKETS

Bairnsdale East Gippsland Farmers' Market: Secondary College oval, McKean St; 1st Sat each month, morning; (03) 5156 9342

Bruthen Village Market: Bruthen Mechanics Hall, Main St; 4th Sat each month; (03) 5157 5110

Drouin Produce and Craft Market: Civic Park; 3rd Sat each month, morning; 0428 252 440

Inverloch Farmers' Market: The Glade; 3rd Sun each month, morning; (03) 5664 0096

Jumbunna Bush Market: Public Hall; Sun (phone for dates); (03) 5657 3241

Kongwak Market: Kongwak General Store and sheds; Sun; (03) 5672 2951

Latrobe Country Market: Latrobe Rd, Morwell; Sun morning; 0407 532 957

Loch Village Market: Loch Village Railway Siding; 2nd Sun each month (Nov–Apr), morning; (03) 5659 0212

Loch Winter Market: Loch Public Hall, Smith St; 2nd Sun each month (May–Sept), morning; (03) 5659 4305

Metung Farmers' Market: Village Green, Metung Rd; 2nd Sat each month, morning; (03) 9717 3404

Moe Art and Craft Market: Gippsland Heritage Park, Lloyd St; 4th Sat each month (Sept–May); (03) 5127 3082

Paynesville Market: Gilsenan Reserve, The Esplanade; 2nd Sun each month; (03) 5156 0225

Rokeby Community Market: Rokeby Hall and Reserve; 2nd Sat each month, morning; (03) 5626 8255

Sale Sunday Charity Variety Market:
Thompson River Canal Reserve; 3rd Sun
each month, morning; (03) 5144 1258

Traralgon Farmers' Market: Bert
Christensen Reserve, Kay St; 4th Sat each
month, morning; (03) 5174 2279

Traralgon Market: Kay St; 2nd Sat each
month, morning; (03) 5174 3494

**Yarragon Community Craft and
Produce Market:** Yarragon Public Hall,
Campbell St; 4th Sat each month;
(03) 5634 2138

Yarram Market: Guide & Scout Hall,
Commercial Rd; 1st Sun each month
(except Apr), morning; (03) 5182 5679

Wonthaggi Rotary Market: Apex Park,
Murray St; 2nd Sun each month (Nov–June);
(03) 5672 5204

GOURMET PRODUCE

Blueberry Fields: Lot 11, The Eyrie,
Johnsonville; (03) 5156 4495

Brushtail Bush Foods: 2045 Grand Ridge
Rd, Boolarra South; (03) 5664 8315

Capra Cheese: Mia Mia Farm, 125 Tices Rd,
Mt Lookout (via Mount Taylor);
(03) 5156 9312

Chocodence: 4 Leonie St, Metung;
(03) 5156 2111

Clearly Delicious: 243 Lillico Rd, Lillico;
(03) 5623 1592;
www.clearlydelicious.com.au

Flavourite Tomatoes: 318 Copelands Rd,
Warragul; (03) 5623 1693;
www.flavourite.com.au

Fruitfarm Johnsonville: 54 Bumberra Rd,
Johnsonville; (03) 5156 4549

**Lakes Entrance Fishermen's
Co-operative:** Bullock Island, Lakes
Entrance; (03) 5155 1688

McConnells Berry Farm: Engineers Rd,
Bruthen; (03) 5157 5527

Nullamunjie Olive Oil: 290 Bindi Rd,
Tongio; (03) 5159 4455;
www.nullamunjie.com.au

Paynesville Seafoods: 67a The Esplanade,
Paynesville; (03) 5156 6080

Summer Snow Apple Juice: 544 Brown
Rd, Officer; (03) 5943 2390;
www.summersnowjuice.com.au

Sunny Creek Berry Farm: 69 Tudor Rd,
Trafalgar South; (03) 5634 7526

Swaffields: 203 Main Rd, Neerim South,
(03) 5628 1667; 90 Princes Hwy, Trafalgar,
(03) 5633 1100; swaffields.com

Tambo Hydroponics: 430 Swan Reach Rd,
Tambo; (03) 5156 4434

Waterwheel Orchards: 250 Fishers Rd,
Boolarra South; (03) 5169 6622

WINERIES

Brandy Creek Winery: see Eateries/View
Cafe

Cannibal Creek Vineyard: 260 Tynong
North Rd, Tynong North; (03) 5942 8380;
www.cannibalcreek.com.au

**djinta djinta Winery and de Vine
Restaurant:** 10 Stevens Rd, Kardella;
(03) 5658 1163; www.djintadjinta.com.au

Gypsy Creek Winery: 43 School
Rd, Labertouche; (03) 5628 7679;
gypsycreekwines.com.au

Kouark Vineyard & Winery:
300 Thompson Rd, Drouin South;
(03) 5627 6337

Narkoojee: 170 Francis Rd, Glengarry;
(03) 5192 4257; www.narkoojee.com

Nicholson River Winery: 57 Liddells Rd,
Nicholson; (03) 5156 8241;
www.nicholsonriverwinery.com.au

Noorinbee Selection Vineyards:
53 Monaro Hwy, Cann River;
(03) 5158 6500

Piedmont Wines: 3470 Yarra Junction–
Noojee Rd, Noojee; (03) 5628 9675
(weekends); www.piedmontwines.com.au

Toms Cap Vineyard: see Eateries/The
Vines

Windy Ridge Vineyard & Winery:
527 Fish Creek–Foster Rd, Foster;
(03) 5682 2035;
www.windyridgewinery.com.au

Wyanga Park Winery: 246 Baades Rd,
Lakes Entrance; (03) 5155 1508;
www.wyangapark.com.au

BREWERIES

Grand Ridge Brewery: Main St,
Mirboo North; (03) 9778 6996;
www.grand-ridge.com.au

COOKING SCHOOLS

**Clay Pot Curry House and Cooking
School:** 733 Turnbull–Woolamai Rd,
Woolamai; (03) 9705 2370

**Culinaire Cooking School Herb and
Kitchen Garden:** 51 Cunningham Crt,
Swan Reach; (03) 5156 4091;
www.culinaire-cookingschool.com.au

**Peaceful Gardens Organic Cooking
School:** 1 Koala Dr, Koonwarra;
(03) 5664 2480

**Spice Island Pantry and Cooking
School:** 1A Hill St, Sunderland Bay,
Phillip Island; (03) 5956 7557;
www.spiceisland.com.au

Macedon and Spa Country

The distinctive form of Mount Macedon rises from the surrounding volcanic plains just north-west of Melbourne. In the 19th and early 20th centuries, it provided a cool mountain retreat in summer for many of Melbourne's wealthy families. They built large rambling mansions and established spectacular gardens that flourished in the rich volcanic soil. These days it is a popular destination for plant lovers, with many of its landscaped gardens open to the public on certain days, particularly in autumn when the deciduous oaks, elm and maples showcase their brilliant reds and golds. And just north of Macedon is the famous Hanging Rock, shrouded in mystery but also the setting for popular picnic races and the namesake for a local cool-climate winery.

To the west of Macedon, the picturesque Daylesford–Hepburn Springs area has long been known as the country's leading spa region, boasting more than 70 of the state's 110 documented springs. Swiss-Italians settled here in the mid-1800s and, as well as appreciating the natural springs, they also brought with them their knowledge of farming, thus providing the foundations for a rich agricultural community. In recent years, the lush

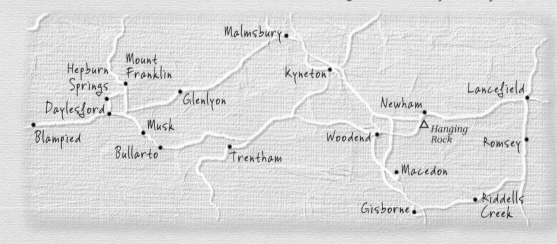

Malmsbury

Hepburn Springs

Mount Franklin

Kyneton

Lancefield

Daylesford

Glenlyon

Newham

Musk

Hanging Rock

Woodend

Romsey

Blampied

Bullarto

Trentham

Macedon

Gisborne

Riddells Creek

Festivals

New Year's Day Races: Hanging Rock; Jan; (03) 5422 1866; www.hangingrockracingclub.com.au

Regional Producers Day: Daylesford; 1st Sun in Feb; (03) 5348 3329; www.lakehouse.com.au

Harvest Picnic: music, cooking demonstrations and free children's activities; Hanging Rock; last Sun in Feb; (03) 9521 8844; www.harvestpicnic.com.au

Kyneton Olive Oil Harvest: oils, olives and tapanades; June (Queen's Birthday weekend); (03) 9384 6338; www.kynetonoliveoil.com.au

Swiss Italian Festa: food, wine and music; Hepburn Springs; 3rd week in Oct; 1800 353 354; www.swissitalianfesta.com

Budburst: food and wine festival; Macedon Ranges vineyards; 2nd weekend in Nov; (03) 5429 5565; www.macedonrangeswine.com.au

Where to stay

Apartment 61A: stylish B&B; 61 Piper St, Kyneton; (03) 5422 1211; www.macedonrangesinteriors.com.au/apartments

Lake House: picturesque lakeside country house; King St, Daylesford; (03) 5348 3329; www.lakehouse.com.au

Mollisons: luxury self-contained apartment; 116–118 Mollison St, Kyneton; 0419 001 518; www.mollisons.net.au

Peppers Springs Retreat & Spa: refurbished Art Deco guesthouse; 124 Main Rd, Hepburn Springs; (03) 5348 2202; www.peppers.com.au/springs

The White House: charming 1850s miner's cottage; 58 Albert St, Daylesford; 0416 032 111; www.thewhitehousedaylesford.com.au

undulating farmland between Daylesford and the Macedon area boasts an enviable reputation for its diverse, quality regional produce, excellent wines and thriving farmers' markets. Local growers, vignerons, chefs, restaurateurs, provedores, publicans and suppliers have even banded together to produce *A Tasty Little Pocket Guide* to the region, a small booklet celebrating the wealth and depth of its gastronomic produce (call 13 2842 for a copy).

Today, much of the regional produce is on sale at farm-gate shops, at some small wineries and village gourmet stores such as **Cliffy's Emporium**, housed in a quirky old produce store in Daylesford. It sells a range of items including Holy Goat fromage frais, Mount Zero olives, Fernleigh Farm free-range pork products and Verde Providore handmade organic dips.

The regional food renaissance in this area has its roots in Daylesford. For many years, energetic hotelier and restaurateur Alla Wolf-Tasker fought a lone battle championing regional food and wine at her iconic family-run country-style **Lake House** (*see* feature, p. 159). Today, her efforts have had a ripple-on effect, with many local restaurants tailoring their menus to reflect what is fresh, local and seasonal. Just out of neighbouring Hepburn Springs, for example, at the charmingly rustic **La Trattoria** at Lavandula Lavender Farm, you can sit under the trees overlooking the extensive lavender gardens to savour home-grown vegetables, antipasto platters of Istra smoked meats, homemade jams on lavender-flavoured scones and homemade lavender cordial.

In Daylesford's main street, **Frangos & Frangos** offers intimate candlelit dining with dishes such as local Istra prosciutto-wrapped buffalo mozzarella and well-aged steaks, while its almost-adjacent **Koukla** has more casual fare, creating terrific pizzas topped with Tuki smoked trout, Istra's chorizo, smoked hams or prosciutto and locally grown organic vegetables in season such as zucchini, heirloom tomatoes, capsicum, eggplant and local herbs. Similarly, local produce such as Spa Venison's venison, goat and wild rabbit, Tuki lamb, organic berries, zucchini flowers, and heritage beets from Mount Franklin feature on the creative menu at **Perfect Drop**, with dishes such as rabbit, black-eyed bean and chorizo fricassee and crumbed lamb cutlets with smoked eggplant and feta salad. **Mercato @ Daylesford** is another dining spot where you can savour the region's bounty. Housed in an

1864 timber cottage, it has a loyal following who come for the consistently good degustation and à la carte modern Australian fare.

The **Farmers Arms Hotel** manages to cater for all-comers: farmers who come in for a pint in the front bar, the weekly chook raffle and a really good bar menu; and those looking for a little more in a meal in the welcoming bistro at the rear. Expect dishes such as zucchini flowers stuffed with fresh Meredith goat's curd, pan-fried quail with local Istra spicy chorizo served with locally grown heirloom tomatoes dressed with Spanish sherry vinegar, and Western Plains cured pork and vegetable terrine with homemade pickles.

After an enjoyable lunch don't leave town before browsing the shops in the main street. Pick up gourmet items as you go: authentic Swiss-Italian bull boar sausages from **Albert Street Butchery**, where Danny Wanke produces more than 300 kilograms a month using a century-old recipe; and farm-raised venison and goat from **Spa Venison** as well as perhaps kangaroo, squab, rabbit, specialty pies, pâté and game sausages. At **Sweet Decadence at Locantro**, try some of the 35 different handmade chocolates including dark and light layered milkshake, tropical-flavoured Daylesford delight, rum and raisin or lavender chocolate. There are more chocolate delights at nearby Mount Franklin, north of town, where the **Chocolate Mill** produces 12 000 chocolates each week in 90 different varieties including irresistible hazelnut Frangelico truffles and caramel supremes.

Just south-east of Daylesford at Musk, the family-run **Istra Smallgoods** salt, cure and smoke European-style smallgoods such as hams, prosciutto, sausages, salamis and bacon, all available at their farm shop. At nearby Bullarto, Fiona Chambers has been championing organic animals and produce for more than 20 years at **Fernleigh Farms**. She rears organic rare breeds such as Wessex Saddleback pigs and Shropshire lamb and sells cuts through the farm shop along with organic farm-grown vegetables.

There's something extra special about fresh breads and pies from country bakehouses. In Trentham, **Red Beard Historic Bakery** is known for its great wood-fired organic sourdough breads baked in a 120-year-old Scotch oven: blonde Vienna loaf, Carmen Miranda spicy fruit loaf, stubble multigrain and brunette wholemeal loaf. At Malmsbury, north of Kyneton, the **Malmsbury Bakery** does a roaring trade with its range of hearty pies: steak and mushroom, gourmet, mushroom stroganoff, curry steak or vegetarian.

Kyneton is an attractive country centre, its streetscapes showcasing many heritage buildings that hark back to the gold-rush era when the town provided a welcome stopover point for those on the way to the goldfields. Today, the Piper Street precinct has emerged as a country destination in itself, with innovative specialty food outlets, appealing lifestyle boutiques and all manner of exciting dining facilities from cosy cafes to gastropubs such as the **Royal George Hotel**. Originally given the kiss of life by entrepreneurial Frank Moylan and Melissa Macfarlane, who had earlier revitalised the Farmers Arms in Daylesford, this gracious corner diner is now in the tender care of city slickers Neil Henson and Jim Lekakis. Enjoy a glass of premium local wine –they have a formidable list – in the public bar before taking your seat at linen-clad tables in the dining room. Nearby, the old mill has also found new life in the hands of Jessi and Jennifer Singh, who have converted the former bakery into an intimate

20-seater Indian restaurant, **Dhaba at the Mill**. Curries are cooked fresh daily, and the couple also give cooking classes in simple Indian meals using authentic ingredients 'not out of a jar' (contact the restaurant for details).

For an intimate dining experience, **Star Anise** really is a star turn. Housed in a charming 1900s timber cottage, there are just half a dozen tables, where Chris Chapple tends ably to front of house while wife Emma is in the kitchen. There are small plates to share for starters, followed by dishes such as their signature star anise-spiced duck, rack of lamb and kingfish with a cashew and almond crust. The tip here is to keep room for dessert.

Across the street you can pick up specialty cheese, local smallgoods and more from **Ladle Foodstore**; and stunning biscuits and pastries from **Inner Biscuit**, whose owner Mara Szoke gleaned her expertise from some of the best including Greg Brown – try her buttery ginger slice. Cross the street again to **Slow Living** for some of Rachel McLindin's wide range of organic and regional produce or take a seat on the verandah and enjoy a light snack with a cup of organic coffee.

Below (left to right): interior of the Farmers Arms Hotel, Daylesford; grilled semolina with ratatouille purée, roasted baby root vegetables, smoked eggplant and walnut butter at Star Anise, Kyneton

Although Steven and Sarah Rogers honed their culinary skills in the hallowed kitchens of innovative French chef Jacques Reymond, they insist their **Little Swallow Cafe** fare is more the type of food they like to eat themselves. They serve breakfast all day – classic eggs Benedict, homemade baked beans with feta or roasted field mushrooms then hearty soup and perhaps simple braised dishes for lunch, such as chicken with smoked paprika, preserved lemon, green olives, tomato and couscous. Almost next door, Damien Sandercock and his wife Bryanna run the welcoming family-friendly **Pizza Verde**, producing great thin-based pizzas with daily-changing toppings as well as slow-roasted oven-baked dishes on Sundays. Ask about their special seasonal dinners, their cooking classes (for children and adults) as well as classes on how to use a wood-fired oven at home.

At the western end of the street is **Annie Smithers' Bistrot**, the sublime casual French-style dining base of the pioneer who was the first to open a chic restaurant in Piper Street and start the culinary trend to Kyneton. She offers a daily-changing plat du jour and an à la carte menu of French classics such as soup du jour, chicken livers and steak tartare, followed by main courses of trout amandine, chive-crusted snapper fillet, free-range duck confit and eye fillet steak. Many dishes feature her home-grown produce. Around the corner in Mollison Street, husband and wife Simon and Bec Fenwick have set up a European-style deli, **Monsieur Pierre**, in a restored butcher shop. They cook ready-to-go meals, beautifully presented, to take home, gourmet lunch items and stock a great range of local produce.

At picturesque Woodend (in gold-rush times, literally the end of the woods north of Melbourne, a haunt of bushrangers and robbers, through which gold seekers and other travellers had to pass), **Maloa House** is a stylish produce and home-wares store that stocks fresh bread, cheese, dips and soups, while **Cafe Colenso** serves terrific coffee and homemade treats. Set in tranquil grounds, **Campaspe Country House** has long championed quality regional food on its menu. Book in for high tea or Sunday lunch in the Edna Walling landscaped garden beneath established trees.

Woodend is also home to the award-winning **Holgate Brewhouse**, which produces a range of

Holgate beers including Pilsner, Mt Macedon Ale, ESB and Temptress. Housed in a historic 19th-century hotel, the premises include a restaurant and accommodation, as well as a bar of course. Another historic building, this time an 1860 Victorian country house, is home to the renowned **Diana Marsland Cooking** school. Cordon Bleu-trained in London, Diana has been running her classes for almost 20 years and is a passionate promoter of the region's produce and the slow food movement. Courses here are non-residential but there are plenty of accommodation options nearby. Down the road, in the shadow of the mountain at tiny Macedon, **Sitka Foodstore & Cafe** is a deli, foodstore and eatery, serving up breakfast, lunch and takeaway meals (closed Tuesday).

This whole region is dotted throughout with vineyards that thrive in the cool mountain climate. Outstanding among these are **Hanging Rock Winery**, where John and Ann Ellis produce the exceptional Macedon sparkling as well as their top Jim Jim sauvignon blanc and Heathcote shiraz; **Curly Flat Vineyard** at Lancefield, where Phillip and Jeni Moraghan produce multi-award-winning chardonnay and pinot noir; **Cobaw Ridge** at Kyneton, a small hands-on winery where Alan and Nelly Cooper create award-winning estate-grown wines, including the spicy savoury Italian varietal, lagrein, the first to be commercialised in Australia; **Granite Hills Winery** at Baynton (north-east of Kyneton), where second-generation vigneron/winemaker Llew Knight is still kicking goals with his outstanding peppery shiraz and iconic cool-climate rieslings; and **Captains Creek Organic Wines** at Blampied (west of Daylesford), where the May brothers make the only organic wines in the region.

Some wineries offer tasting platters and casual lunches at weekends to complement their wines, such as **Ellender Estate** at Glenlyon, where kangaroos hop about while you munch on wood-fired pizza or savour a regional platter in the winery cafe with its outdoor terrace; and, not far from Melbourne, **Gisborne Peak Winery** that serves antipasto, bruschetta and wood-fired pizzas. Also in the Gisborne area is **Mount Gisborne Wines**, its cellar door open Wednesday–Sunday for tastings.

Humble beginnings

Alla Wolf-Tasker, founder of Lake House

Without doubt, Alla Wolf-Tasker has single-handedly changed the face of country dining in the Daylesford–Macedon Ranges region. As co-owner and restaurateur, she is the driving force behind the multi-award-winning Lake House country restaurant, one of Australia's most celebrated gourmet retreats. From a food-focused Russian émigré background, she has been championing regional, seasonal and organic produce for more than 25 years, encouraging small local producers along the way. Today, the huge variety of regional produce features strongly on the restaurant's constantly changing menu. A browse through her recent book reveals delights such as beef carpaccio with crisp twice-cooked potatoes and sauce Gribiche, cabbage roll of boned quail with pork farce and roasting juices, and sublime desserts such as honey panna cotta with quince soup. From humble beginnings as a 45-seater country dining room in a 'food and wine wilderness', Lake House has evolved into a chic boutique hotel and restaurant with waterfront accommodation and an excellent Salus Spa. Alla is a director of Tourism Victoria, a member of the Victorian Food & Wine Council, founding convener of the Daylesford and Macedon Produce Group and is patron of the region's innovative kitchen garden that flourishes in the grounds of Daylesford Primary School. In 2007 she received an Order of Australia for her services to the tourism and hospitality industries.

Contacts for Macedon and Spa Country

EATERIES

Annie Smithers' Bistrot: 72 Piper St, Kyneton; (03) 5422 2039; www.anniesmithers.com.au

Cafe Colenso: 42 Anslow St, Woodend; (03) 5427 2007

Campaspe Country House: Goldies La, Woodend; (03) 5427 2273; www.campaspehouse.com.au

Dhaba at the Mill: 18 Piper St, Kyneton; (03) 5422 6225; www.dhabaatthhemill.com

Farmers Arms Hotel: 1 East St, Daylesford; (03) 5348 2091; www.farmersarms.com.au

Frangos & Frangos: 82 Vincent St, Daylesford; (03) 5348 2363; www.frangosandfrangos.com

Koukla: 82 Vincent St, Daylesford; (03) 5348 2363; www.frangosandfrangos.com

La Trattoria: Lavendula Lavender Farm, 350 Hepburn–Newstead Rd, Shepherds Flat, Hepburn Springs; (03) 5476 4393; www.lavendula.com.au

Lake House: King St, Daylesford; (03) 5348 3329; www.lakehouse.com.au

Little Swallow Cafe: 58A Piper St, Kyneton; (03) 5422 6241; www.littleswallowcafe.com

Mercato @ Daylesford: 32 Raglan St, Daylesford; (03) 5348 4488; www.mercatorestaurant.com.au

Perfect Drop: 5 Howe St, Daylesford; (03) 5348 3373; www.aperfectdrop.com

Pizza Verde: 62 Piper St, Kyneton; (03) 5422 7400; www.pizzaverde.com

Royal George Hotel: 24 Piper St, Kyneton; (03) 5422 3409; www.royalgeorge.com.au

Slow Living: 37C Piper St, Kyneton; (03) 5422 3818; www.slowliving.com.au

Star Anise: 29A Piper St, Kyneton; (03) 5422 2777; www.staranisebistro.com

STORES

Cliffy's Emporium: 30 Raglan St, Daylesford; (03) 5348 3279

Inner Biscuit: 34 Piper St, Kyneton; (03) 5422 1129; www.innerbiscuit.com

Ladle Foodstore: 30 Piper St, Kyneton; (03) 5422 2430; www.ladlefoodstore.com.au

Malmsbury Bakery: 73–77 Malison St, Malmsbury; (03) 5423 2369

Maloa House: 95 High St, Woodend; (03) 5427 1608

Monsieur Pierre: 143 Mollison St, Kyneton; (03) 5422 1136; www.whoispierre.com.au

Sitka Foodstore & Cafe: Shop 4, 23 Victoria St, Macedon; (03) 5426 3304; www.sitka.com.au

Slow Living: see Eateries

MARKETS

Daylesford Farmer's Market: Daylesford Primary School, Vincent St; 1st Sat each month (except May and Aug), morning; (03) 5664 0096

Gisborne Olde Time Market: Cnr Hamilton and Aitken sts; 1st Sun each month (Oct–May), morning; 0431 563 566; www.gisborneoldetimemarket.org.au

Gisborne Village All Seasons Market: Gisborne Village Shopping Centre, Brantome St; 1st Sun each month; 0447 526 145

Kyneton Country Market: 52–56 Mollison St; Sat and Sun; 0458 400 168; kynetonmarket.com

Kyneton Farmers' Market: St Paul's Park, Piper St; 2nd Sat each month, morning; (03) 5422 1863

Lancefield and District Farmers' Market: Centre Plantation, High St; 4th Sat each month (3rd Sat in Dec), morning; (03) 5429 1214

Lancefield–Romsey Lions Club Market: Main St; 4th Sat each month (except Jan and June–July); 0438 414 245

Riddells Creek Farmers' Market: Riddells Creek Primary School; 3rd Sat each month (except Dec); (03) 5428 7683

Trentham Farmers' Market: Trentham Town Sq; 3rd Sat each month, morning; (03) 5424 1185

Woodend Market: High St; 3rd Sun each month (Sept–May); (03) 5427 2321

GOURMET PRODUCE

Albert Street Butchery: 3/22 Albert St, Daylesford; (03) 5348 2679

Chocolate Mill: 5451 Midland Hwy, Mount Franklin; (03) 5476 4208; www.chocmill.com.au

Fernleigh Farms: 1070 Trentham Rd, Bullarto; (03) 5348 5566; www.fernleighfarms.com

Istra Smallgoods: 36 Wheelers Hill Rd, Musk; (03) 5348 3382

Red Beard Historic Bakery: 38A High St, Trentham; (03) 5424 1002; www.redbeardbakery.com.au

Spa Venison: Shop 3, 9 Howe St, Daylesford; (03) 5348 3551; www.spavenison.com.au

Sweet Decadence at Locantro: 87 Vincent St, Daylesford; (03) 5348 3202; www.sweetdecadence.com.au

WINERIES

Captains Creek Organic Wines: Kangaroo Hills Rd, Blampied; (03) 5345 7408; www.captainscreek.com

Cobaw Ridge: 31 Perc Boyers La, East Pastoria, Kyneton; (03) 5423 5227; www.cobawridge.com.au

Curly Flat Vineyard: 263 Collivers Rd, Lancefield; (03) 5429 1956; www.curlyflat.com

Ellender Estate: 260 Green Gully Rd, Glenlyon; (03) 5348 7785; www.ellenderwines.com.au

Gisborne Peak Winery: 69 Short Rd, Gisborne South; (03) 5428 2228; www.gisbornepeakwines.com.au

Granite Hills Winery: 1481 Burke and Wills Track, Baynton; (03) 5423 7273; www.granitehills.com.au

Hanging Rock Winery: 88 Jim Rd, Newham; (03) 5427 0542; www.hangingrock.com.au

Mount Gisborne Wines: 83 Waterson Rd, Gisborne; (03) 5428 2834; www.mountgisbornewines.com.au

BREWERIES

Holgate Brewhouse: 79 High St, Woodend; (03) 5427 2510; www.holgatebrewhouse.com

COOKING SCHOOLS

Dhaba at the Mill: see Eateries

Diana Marsland Cooking: The Gables, 19 Brooke St, Woodend; (03) 5427 1155; www.dianamarslandcooking.com.au

Pizza Verde: see Eateries

Below (left to right): Lavandula Lavender Farm, home of La Trattoria, Hepburn Springs; Royal George Hotel, Kyneton; Red Beard Historic Bakery, Trentham; Ellender Estate, Glenlyon; Holgate Brewhouse, Woodend

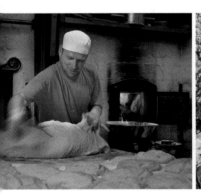

Ballarat and Pyrenees

This central Victorian region comprising the Pyrenees and the goldfields area of Ballarat and surrounds is dotted with small hamlets and quaint country towns linked by verdant pastoral lands. Ballarat is Victoria's largest inland city, built on the wealth of the region's goldfields, and it was here that the famous miners' rebellion in 1854 resulted in the raising of the Eureka flag and a bloody confrontation between miners and police – seen by many as the origins of the Australian belief in equity and a 'fair go' for workers. Today the city's preserved streetscapes boast magnificent gold-rush architecture amid growing contemporary style. Included in this region are other gold-rush centres north-east of Ballarat, including the historic town of Castlemaine and the smaller but beautifully preserved village of Maldon. The Pyrenees wine-producing area lies north-west of Ballarat, spreading out from the town of Avoca. Shiraz is the premium drop here and the big names are Blue Pyrenees, Taltarni and Dalwhinnie.

At Scotsburn just south of Ballarat, Sandra Armstrong and partner Robert Taylor have taken over running her family's **Mount Buninyong Winery**, turning the cellar door into a quirky cafe furnished with retro kitchen pieces and a wonderful collection of electric mixers. Known for their fortified wines, the couple are justifiably proud of their white port, chardonnay liqueur and chilli port.

The gracious thoroughfare of Sturt Street in Ballarat is edged with pavement cafes. Standouts are the long-established **L'espresso**, where broody Italian good looks and the wine bar appeal as much as the coffee itself; nearby **Europa Cafe**, where an outside table is the place to be; and **Cafe Bibo**, with its bowling-alley space filled with 1950s retro pieces. At the **Lydiard Wine Bar** in Lydiard Street you can sink into lovely club leather chairs, while listening to moody music and sipping on a glass of local wine. This quietly sophisticated wine bar and dining room, housed in a former Bank of New South Wales, offers a mix of Asian and Mediterranean dishes on its menu. If its fresh farm produce you want, stock up at **Wilson's Fruit and Vegetables**, much of it locally grown. This huge family-owned grocer also has specialty breads, cheese, olive oils, verjuice, preserves and a range of meals to go.

Festivals

Ballarat Begonia Weekend:
Botanic Gardens; Mar (Labour Day
weekend); 1800 446 633;
www.ballaratbegoniafestival.com

Maldon Easter Fair: Easter:
(03) 5475 2262;
www.maldoneasterfair.com.au

Mount Avoca Races: legalised
two-up, winery stalls, children's
activities; Anzac Day;
1800 206 622;
www.avocaraceclub.com

Ballarat Heritage Weekend:
cultural celebration; 2nd weekend
in May; (03) 5320 5620;
www.ballaratheritageweekend.com

Pyrenees Escapade: European-
style food and wine festival; last
Sun in Oct; 1800 206 622;
www.pyrenees.org.au

THE EMPYRE

LUXURY ACCOMMODATION ~ CAFE & BAR

Where to stay

Eco-Luxe at Mount Avoca: three
eco-luxury lodges; Moates La, Avoca;
(03) 5465 3282; www.mountavoca.com

Moonbeam Cottages: mudbrick
cottages; 92 Mountain Creek Rd,
Moonambel; (03) 5467 2350;
www.moonbeam.com.au

The Ansonia: B&B-style hotel;
32 Lydiard St South, Ballarat;
(03) 5332 4678;
www.theansoniaonlydiard.com.au

The Empyre Boutique Hotel:
six beautiful suites; 68 Mostyn St,
Castlemaine; (03) 5472 5166;
www.empyre.com.au

Warrenmang Vineyard & Resort:
chalets and luxury suites (*see* feature,
p. 167); 188 Mountain Creek Rd,
Moonambel; (03) 5467 2233;
www.warrenmang.com.au

Ballarat and Pyrenees

163

GREAT GOURMET WEEKENDS *in Australia*

Tucked away in historic Camp Street, the **Phoenix Brewery Restaurant** doesn't actually make its own brews but does offer a good selection of beers and wines to complement its terrific tapas and à la carte menus. Share lamb koftas, saganaki or grilled prawns before main courses of seafood laksa or rack of lamb stuffed with goat's cheese. If you want to try a regional beer, look out for **Three Troupers** local brews – a pale ale, pilsner, amber ale and a wheat ale – made from locally grown wheat and barley and local natural spring water. The brewery is located at Beaufort, some 50 kilometres north-west of Ballarat. Housed in an old two-storey pub, **Mason's Cafe** is where Viv Mason makes much of the gourmet produce on sale and she has coaxed an Italian nonna to make authentic gnocchi, ravioli and pasta sauces.

Just out of the main CBD near Lake Wendouree, **Eclectic Tastes** makes great coffee and is the ideal spot for breakfast. Try the three-cheese omelette folded in a piadina. Everything is made on the premises including lemon curd, hummingbird and rhubarb and walnut muffins and seasonally flavoured lamingtons – perhaps strawberry and rosewater, mandarin or passionfruit and pineapple.

If you travel north-east of Ballarat to the small town of Smeaton, it's a 2-kilometre private drive through a historic Stoney Rises sheep-grazing property to reach **Tuki** farmhouse belonging to Robert and Jan Jones, who have been sharing their farm experiences with guests for more than 25 years.

There are some 2000–3000 Tukidale sheep on the property as well as beef cattle, and rainbow trout stocked in seven ponds. Guests can buy or dine on home-grown produce such as smoked trout pâté, fresh trout or pasture-fed Tuki lamb or beef – or indeed catch their own fish. North of here, on the Pyrenees Highway, the tiny village of Newstead has a population of perhaps 200, but boasts an excellent butcher, **Newstead Meat Supply**, where Ross Barker sources quality local beef, lamb and pork and makes his own bull boar sausage, patties, hamburgers, kebabs and pies.

There is also a trendy corner cafe and wine bar in town called **Dig**, which offers breakfast and lunch daily and dinner and pizzas at the weekends. There is always a risotto, perhaps with house-smoked salmon; pasta, possibly linguini with home-smoked chicken sausages; and homemade bread and dips and toasted Turkish breads with fillings.

Continuing in a north-easterly direction leads you to the historic township of Maldon, classified by the National Trust as Australia's first notable town. One of the most photogenic and most photographed towns in the state, its beautiful old buildings within the preserved streetscape house everything from boutique clothes, collectibles and local produce. Look for handmade chocolates at **Chocolade**, which also acts as cellar door for **Chaperon Wines** on the outskirts of town (try their rosé or shiraz); organic and biodynamic produce and vegetarian dishes at

Below (left to right): autumn-coloured vines, and a plate of pan-fried scallops on French lentils de puy with Pyrenees smoked bacon and salsa verde, at Warrenmang Vineyard, Moonambel; formerly an old pub, The Good Table at Castlemaine; machine harvesting at Blue Pyrenees, Avoca

Zen Eden Produce; and good coffee with homemade treats at **Penny School Gallery/Cafe**, housed in a former schoolhouse that is one of only six Victorian heritage-listed buildings in town. **Goldfields Provender** showcases many locally produced goodies including table olives and extra virgin olive oil from **Maldon Olive Grove**. Over summer, **Maldon Cherry Farm** on the outskirts of town has a self-serve honesty box system to sell its just-picked organic cherries and apricots.

Some 18 kilometres south-east of Maldon is the leafy town of Castlemaine. It came into being some 150 years ago when the news spread that gold had been found at nearby Specimen Gully. More than 30 000 would-be miners flocked to this part of the Victorian goldfields to seek their fortune. The town grew overnight and some 30 hotels sprang up, one on nearly every corner and several in between. **The Empyre Boutique Hotel,** formerly the Albion Hotel, was one of them and today, after extensive renovations, offers elegant accommodation and fine and casual dining with the best coffee in town. With several years experience at the famed Daylesford Lake House, chef Michael Nam creates beautifully presented dishes with layers of flavours and textures using vegetables and herbs from the kitchen garden. Start with Caprese-style salad with home-grown heirloom-tomatoes and Shaw River buffalo mozzarella or house-made squid ink cannelloni filled with scallop mousseline and Yarra Valley salmon

pearls. Recommended main courses include Kyneton Black Angus eye fillet of beef with braised ox cheek and crepinette of lamb loin on a cassoulet of borlotti beans. The wine list includes many good local drops.

Former MoVida chef Alexander Perry has come back to his hometown Castlemaine to set up **The Good Table** in a former 1860s gold-rush-era pub, the Council Club Hotel. Meals are designed to be shared, with lots of small tapas-style dishes including zucchini flowers stuffed with ricotta, lemon and olive then deep-fried in the lightest batter, smooth rich duck liver pâté with shiraz jelly, pickled octopus and kingfish cerviche. Larger dishes include pan-fried Tuki trout with chestnuts and lemon beurre blanc or the stunning homemade ravioli filled with gorgonzola and accompanied by confit pear with burnt sage butter – a triumph.

Almost opposite Perry's establishment, former French Lettuce patisserie chefs John and Annie Stekerhols operate **Apple Annie's Bakery Cafe**, a cheery space for light meals. It houses a commercial kitchen for baking their delicious pastries, cakes, energy slice, and range of gluten-free cakes such as orange, almond and poppy seed cake, baked citrus cheese cake, Belgian chocolate tort and passionfruit and raspberry friands. Try their signature 'mouna', a delicious French–Algerian orange-flavoured doughnut–brioche hybrid.

Housed in an old miner's cottage, **Togs Place** has become a local institution, with pavement tables,

seating inside around a warming fire in winter, and even on the roof in summer with views over the rooftops of town. Popular for breakfast, they offer all the usual suspects, but done well, and sell muffins by the tonne. The same people own **Mulberry's Fine Foods** next door, a deli and provedore with a gourmet range of antipasto, pâtés, local and European cheeses and delicious take-home meals such as lamb rogan josh, lasagne and more.

A coffee shop and roaster a few minutes out of town, **Coffee Basics** has freshly roasted coffee beans and blends, as well as some ten different coffee blends available to drink on-site. While in this area you should also look for **Michel's Fine Biscuits**, which are baked in town and available at local outlets. Made from mostly organic ingredients, free-range eggs and using no preservatives, flavours include ginger and almond, triple Belgian chocolate and almond, macadamia, almond and white Belgian chocolate and sticky date pecan and almond.

Some 23 kilometres north of Maryborough, the small village of Dunolly, with a population of about 700, is not known as a gourmet centre but it does have a collection of superb old buildings and it does have **Wright on Broadway**. Fiona Lindsay is a passionate local who rescued this old licensed grocer shop that had been serving the local community since 1857. Today she sources quality local produce from within the Ballarat–Bendigo area and wines within the Loddon catchment area. She serves coffee and cakes all day and easy-to-prepare dishes made with chicken fillet and lamb. Shelves are stocked with local pistachio from Rheola and dukkah made from the same nuts, Dunolly garlic, yellow box honey from 'a bloke up the road', olive oil from Newbridge and Moonambel olives.

Avoca is at the centre of the Pyrenees wine region. In town, gourmet pies are all the go. At **Shear Delights Bakery** you can watch baker Sam Beavis as he rolls, cuts, fills and bakes various traditional pies including chicken, mushroom, curry, beef, and drovers (with an egg); while opposite, **Pyrenees Pies, Pizza & Take Away** bakes more than 70 varieties from crocodile, camel, buffalo, emu, venison and ostrich. Duane Gibson at **Pyrenees Gourmet Butchers** sources meat locally, makes his own

smallgoods and smokes whole local trout and sides of salmon. For light lunches, homemade cakes, more pies and deli and pantry items, go to **Janie's Kitchen**, where owner Jane Howe will also do hampers to order or take-home meals. Alternatively you can enjoy a light lunch or Devonshire tea at **Olive & Lavender Store**, where owner Trish Godfrey also makes her own jams and preserves under the Doctors Creek label, as well as stocking lots of other local produce, gifts and home wares.

For more than 20 years, **Warrenmang Vineyard & Resort** has offered warm hospitality, outstanding wine and excellent regional food from its secluded ridge-top location at Moonambel (*see* feature, opposite). The restaurant features local produce with dishes such as Pyrenees white rabbit terrine, Greenhams natural grass-fed sirloin and Bazzani shiraz-braised lamb.

The Pyrenees is noted for its premium shiraz and cabernets. Vineyards in the undulating hills around here are household names: **Dalwhinnie**, **Mount Avoca**, **Blue Pyrenees** and **Taltarni**. Most offer antipasto platters to accompany wine tastings at the cellar door. **St Ignatius Vineyard** at Lamplough (just south-east of Avoca) offers an occasional Argentinean-style grill with chimichurri sauce to complement its Hangman Gully wines. Other wineries worth a visit include the boutique **Pyrenees Ridge Winery**, also at Lamplough, with views to the eponymous Pyrenees. Graeme and Sally-anne Jukes run this bush vineyard, specialising in shiraz – try their flagship Pyrenees Shiraz 2008. At the self-sustainable microwinery **Gwynnyth Vineyard**, Adrian van den Bergen trellises vines shoulder-high, out of reach of grazing wallabies, to produce a refreshing fumé chenin blanc. He also makes a sparkling cider and a tawny plum port, as well as packing and selling local salted capers, caper and olive paste, tapenade and olive oil.

Closer to Ballarat, **Quoin Hill Vineyard** is the southernmost vineyard in the Pyrenees wine region. Its cafe is open at weekends for light lunches and tasting platters to complement the estate-grown wines (and Holgate Brewery beers from Woodend; *see* Macedon and Spa Country).

Family Traditions

The Bazzani family of Warrenmang Vineyard & Resort

Luigi and Athalie Bazzani of Warrenmang are legendary figures in country Victoria, particularly in the Pyrenees. Having grown up on a vineyard in Italy's Emilia-Romagna, where good food and fine wine went hand in hand, it was probably only natural that Luigi would follow this path. The Bazzanis' first venture was the impressive La Scala restaurant in Ballarat, offering arguably some of the best country dining rooms in Victoria. In 1978, they bought a 60-hectare vineyard near Moonambel, 'so Luigi could have his own wine to sell in his restaurant', says Athalie. Over the years, they have built vineyard accommodation and opened an on-site restaurant championing regional and seasonal produce so they can share their love for the region with guests. In the restaurant, the saddle of Pyrenees hare became their signature dish. More than 30 years since he started the vineyard, Luigi continues to produce exceptional wines; his flagship multi-award-winning Black Puma Shiraz sells around the world and his Torchio and Bazzani Tribute blends are not far behind. Luigi has twice been honoured by the Wine and Food Society of Australia for elevating the standards of wine and food.

Contacts for Ballarat and Pyrenees

EATERIES

Apple Annie's Bakery Cafe: 31 Templeton St, Castlemaine; (03) 5472 5311

Cafe Bibo: 205 Sturt St, Ballarat; (03) 5331 1255

Dig: Lyons St, Newstead; (03) 5476 2744

Eclectic Tastes: 2 Burbank St, Ballarat; (03) 5339 9252

Europa Cafe: 411 Sturt St, Ballarat; (03) 5331 2486; www.europacafe.com.au

Janie's Kitchen: 160 High St, Avoca; (03) 5465 3022

L'espresso: 417 Sturt St, Ballarat; (03) 5333 1789; www.ballarat.com/lespresso.htm

Lydiard Wine Bar: 15 Lydiard St North, Ballarat, (03) 5327 2777; www.heritageonlydiard.com.au/bar

Mason's Cafe: 32 Drummond St North, Ballarat; (03) 5333 3895

Olive & Lavender Store: 106 High St, Avoca; (03) 5465 3777; www.pyreneestourism.com.au/oliveandlavenderstore/

Penny School Gallery/Cafe: 11 Church St, Maldon; (03) 5475 1911; www.pennyschoolgallery.com.au

Phoenix Brewery Restaurant: 10 Camp St, Ballarat; (03) 5333 2686; www.ballarat.com/phoenix

The Empyre Boutique Hotel: 68 Mostyn St, Castlemaine; (03) 5472 5166; www.empyre.com.au

The Good Table: 233 Barker St, Castlemaine; (03) 5472 4400; www.thegoodtable.com.au

Togs: 58 Lyttleton St, Castlemaine; (03) 5470 5090

Warrenmang Vineyard & Resort: see Wineries

Wright on Broadway: see Stores

STORES

Goldfields Provender: 12 Main St, Maldon; (03) 5475 2444; www.goldfieldsprovender.com.au

Janie's Kitchen: see Eateries

Mason's Cafe: see Eateries

Mulberry's Fine Foods: 60 Lyttleton St, Castlemaine; (03) 5472 1651

Pyrenees Pies, Pizza & Take Away: 120 High St, Avoca; (03) 5465 3280

Shear Delights Bakery: 105 High St, Avoca; (03) 5465 3517

Wilson's Fruit and Vegetables: 85–91 Mair St, Ballarat; (03) 5329 1900

Wright on Broadway: 127 Broadway, Dunolly; (03) 5468 1245

Zen Eden Produce: 6 Main St, Maldon; 0408 319 188

MARKETS

Avoca Riverside Market: Dundas St; 4th Sun each month, morning; 0488 177 647

Ballarat Lakeside Market: Ballarat Fine Arts Gallery; 2nd and 4th Sat each month; (03) 5320 5858

Ballarat Trash and Trivia Market: Wendouree Pde, Lake Wendouree; Sun; (03) 9569 4767

Beaufort Market: Memorial Park, Havelock St; 1st Sat each month (Sept–Apr), morning; (03) 5349 1184

Buninyong Farmer's Market: Buninyong Town Hall, Learmonth St; 1st Sun each month; (03) 5334 3380

Castlemaine Farmers' Market: Mostyn St; 1st Sun each month (except Jan), morning; 0429 518 885

Talbot Farmers' Market: Scandinavian Cres; 3rd Sun each month; (03) 5463 2001

GOURMET PRODUCE

Chocolade: 30 Main St, Maldon; (03) 5475 1150

Coffee Basics: 1 Halford St, Castlemaine; (03) 5470 6270; www.coffeebasics.com

Maldon Cherry Farm: Cnr Bridgewater and Watersons rds, Maldon; (03) 5475 2178

Maldon Olive Grove: Allens Rd, Maldon; (03) 9391 8261

Michel's Fine Biscuits: 36 McGrath St, Castlemaine; (03) 5472 4274; www.michelsfinebiscuits.com.au

Newstead Meat Supply: 23 Lyon St, Newstead; (03) 5476 2217

Pyrenees Gourmet Butchers: 110 High St, Avoca; (03) 5465 3110

Tuki: 60 Stoney Rises Rd, Smeaton; (03) 5345 6233; www.tuki.com.au

WINERIES

Blue Pyrenees: Vinoca Rd, Avoca; (03) 5465 1111; www.bluepyrenees.com.au

Chaperon Wines: see Gourmet Produce/Chocolade

Dalwhinnie: 448 Taltarni Rd, Moonambel; (03) 5467 2388; www.dalwhinnie.com.au

Gwynnyth Vineyard: 87 McAdams La, Moonambel; 0409 944 757; www.gwynnythvineyards.com

Mount Avoca: Moates La, Avoca; (03) 5465 3282; www.mountavoca.com

Mount Buninyong Winery:
205–210 Platts Rd, Scotsburn;
(03) 5341 8360;
www.mountbuninyongwinery.com.au

Pyrenees Ridge Winery: 532 Caralulup
Rd, Lamplough; (03) 5465 3320;
www.pyreneesridge.com.au

Quoin Hill Vineyard: Quoin Hill Rd,
Waubra; (03) 5343 5365;
www.quoinhill.com.au

St Ignatius Vineyard: 5434 Sunraysia
Hwy, Lamplough; (03) 5465 3542;
www.stignatiusvineyard.com.au

Taltarni: 339 Taltarni Rd, Moonambel:
(03) 5459 7900;
www.taltarni.com.au

Warrenmang Vineyard & Resort:
188 Mountain Creek Rd, Moonambel:
(03) 5333 2121; www.warrenmang.com.au

BREWERIES

Three Troupers: RMB 762, Beaufort;
(03) 5349 7377

Right (top to bottom): graceful aspect of Blue
Pyrenees, Avoca; friendly ambience at Phoenix
Brewery Restaurant, Ballarat

Northern Goldfields

The Northern Goldfields region is a small area within and around a rural triangle comprising Bendigo at the apex, and Harcourt to the south-west and Heathcote to the south-east. Bendigo, an opulent boom town spawned by the gold decade of the 1850s, is notable for its flamboyant neo-classical public buildings, its vintage trams and the shady expanses of its public gardens that form a picturesque backdrop to the architectural extravagance. This extraordinary provincial city, surrounded by the dry hills and eucalypt woodlands of central Victoria, is but one of the region's many surprises.

Perhaps the greatest surprise of all is the region's outstanding Heathcote shiraz being produced by the many local wineries. Wine writer Max Allen has described Heathcote's soil as 'some of the most exciting grape-growing dirt in Australia'. It's as if any shiraz produced from Heathcote grapes has a golden touch – the rich, velvety and full-bodied flavours are guaranteed to please any red-wine drinker. More and more wineries are producing a 'Heathcote shiraz' to cash in on the area's powerful soil.

Above: seafood-topped risotto at Heathcote Winery, Heathcote

Opposite (top to bottom): tree-lined entrance to Sandhurst Ridge, Marong; Balgownie Estate, Maiden Gully

Bridgewater On Loddon

Leichardt

Maiden Gully

Marong

Bendigo

Mandurang

Heathcote

Harcourt

Redesdale

Tooborac

Festivals

Harcourt Applefest: food, wine, cider and local talent; Mar (Labour Day weekend); 0409 229 331; www.harcourtapplefest.org.au

Bendigo Winemakers' Festival: Easter Sun; (03) 5474 8250; www.bendigowine.org.au

Heathcote Wine and Food Festival: 1st weekend in Oct; 1800 813 153; www.heathcotewineandfoodfestival.com.au

Bendigo Heritage Uncorked: food and wine; 2nd weekend in Oct; (03) 5434 6100; www.bendigowine.org.au

Where to stay

Bendigo Balgownie House: vineyard accommodation; Hermitage Rd, Maiden Gully; (03) 5449 6222; www.balgownieestate.com.au/bendigo

Hut on the Hill: luxury B&B; 720 Dairy Flat Rd, Heathcote; (03) 5433 2329; www.hutonthehill.com.au

Spa Eleven: stylish accommodation; 11 Forest St, Bendigo; (03) 5444 5123; www.spaeleven.com.au

The Hotel Shamrock: modernised historic hotel; Cnr Pall Mall and Williamson St, Bendigo; (03) 5443 0333; www.hotelshamrock.com.au

The Redesdale: luxury cottage and auberge; 2640 Kyneton–Heathcote Rd, Redesdale; (03) 5425 3111; www.theredesdale.com.au/accommodation

Balgownie Estate

Added to the exceptional quality of the wine is the high standard of restaurants, wine bars and cafes in Bendigo and the quality ciders and old-fashioned perry being fashioned from crisp Harcourt apples. **Henry of Harcourt** is one of the two cider-makers in the region. Drew Henry and his wife, Irene, bought their property about 15 years ago and today grow 4500 apple trees, the largest commercial orchard of English and French cider apples in Australia. Currently they make 14 different ciders including the Kingston Black and Yarlington Mill, perry, plus a golden delicious fortified cider – the only one made in Australia. And do try their tangy cider vinegars.

A gaggle of geese, domestic chooks and flighty guinea fowl are likely to be your welcoming committee at **Bress** winery, just north of Harcourt. Owner-winemaker Adam Marks spent a vintage near Beaujolais in France at Bourg-en-Bresse, famous for their fat-breasted table chickens. He loved the concept, came home, raised and showed chooks for a while then bought the vineyard, gradually turning it into a biodynamic property. Today, all his wines salute chooks with labels such as Silver Chook, Gold Chook and the latest addition, Le Grand Coq Noir. At weekends, the people here stoke up a wood-fired oven and prepare rustic Sicilian-style dishes such as lamb shanks with couscous, rolled roast loin of pork

and perhaps chicken cacciatore and whole orange Sicilian cake or figs soaked in their own sweet bonbon **Bress Cider**. A nearby production garden supplies rocket, silver beet, chard, broad beans, salad greens and herbs for the restaurant kitchen.

A few years ago, Laurie Whelan couldn't find any good sourdough bread that he was happy with in Bendigo, so he learned how to make his own. He took over the heritage-listed former Beaurepaire's Tyre Centre, a circular building on the edge of the CBD, installed commercial ovens and transformed the space into an all-day bakery, **The Good Loaf**, and adjacent aroma-filled cafe for breakfast and casual lunch. He also sells his terrific breads – try his pumpkin semi-sourdough loaf or his corn and semolina rolls.

The centre of Bendigo is made for walking and several streets are pedestrian-only. Call in to **Indulge Fine Belgian Chocolates** where Hayley Tibbett creates and makes her own range of chocolate treats using Callebaut couverture. Local creations are a special chocolate bar incorporating the region's iconic Castlemaine Rock and chocolates filled with Bendigo honey. Nearby in quaint Bath Lane, **The Green Olive Cafe** is a good spot for a restorative coffee, to pick up some gourmet produce or to relax with friends under the ornamental pear trees at

Below (left to right): coffee to stay at The Green Olive Cafe, Bendigo; verandahed exterior of The Redesdale; inside, and outside, at The Dispensary Enoteca, Bendigo

pavement tables. Their signature breakfast is called 'The Tassie Devil' and comprises English muffins topped with Tasmanian smoked salmon, two poached eggs, avocado, and Hollandaise sauce. At other times, you can snack on Thai beef salad, chicken risotto, spaghetti carbonara, chicken club sandwiches, Caesar salad, gourmet steak sandwiches and a good range of vegetarian dishes.

Around the corner in Mitchell Street, Norm Quin has been selling fresh fruit and vegetables at **Quins Bluebird** greengrocers for more than 50 years. He knows all his customers by name and is a wealth of knowledge concerning his quality local produce. Further up the street is **Favourite Flavours**, a family-oriented shop that sells lots of home wares and ice-cream paraphernalia as well as the best selection of ice-cream in town. Steve Virtue creates flavours such as pumpkin pie, sticky date pudding, shortbread, golden syrup dumplings with hot fudge sauce, chocolate chilli, zabaglione and his signature lemon meringue. Everything is made on the premises and available in cone, cup or take-home packs.

At **The Epicurean Delicatessen**, Tony, Cathy and Maria Ciancio dispense warm hospitality with good coffee, homemade food to eat in or take away – think quiches, pasta, salads, and arguably the best selection of cheese in town, both local and imported.

Bendigo Wholefoods takes the term 'local produce' seriously, sourcing much from within a hundred-kilometre radius. Expect to find seasonal fruit and vegetables, free-range eggs, breads, meat, pasta, dips, spices, preserves, dressings, marmalades, relish and their own kitchen garden plants. If you are looking for a good pie, **Gillies Pies** has been synonymous with Bendigo since 1950. They sell so many pies – about 50 dozen a day – that they have a special 'hole-in-the-wall' window for pie sales only. Choose between traditional beef pies, steak and mushroom, steak and pepper, steak and onion, chicken and mushroom, curry chicken, chicken and vegetable, tuna with potato, pizza pies and more. The pies are made each morning on the premises using local beef and poultry and handmade pastry.

With a population of around 100 000, Bendigo has always been a well-heeled regional centre and it is served by some excellent restaurants. Enjoy pre-dinner drinks and tapas at either **La Piazza Wine Bar & Restaurant**, or at the atmospheric **Wine Bank on View**, in its bottle-lined vault-like interior room or under market umbrellas on the pavement. Nearby, **Whirrakee Restaurant** offers fine dining in an elegant high-ceilinged Art Nouveau room overlooking the city's landmark Alexandra Fountain. It is housed in the former 1908 Royal Bank, one of a

string of banks handling the gold during the gold-rush era. There is a degustation menu with matching wines as well as an à la carte list with all the little trimmings – amuse-bouche, palate-cleansing sorbets and petits fours. Entrées might be roasted butternut pumpkin ravioli on du Puy lentils or prawn tortellini with scallops, followed by Glenloth free-range chicken breast on a gnocchi galette or roasted Leverton Park lamb rump on quinoa risotto. **The Dispensary Enoteca** with its wall of wine is a slice of Melbourne transported to the country. Tucked away down a historic lane off the main Pall Mall, it serves good coffee, great breakfasts (try the field mushrooms with taleggio and thyme on cornbread), snacks at the bar and traditional Italian-style dishes.

In Maiden Gully, just north-west of town, historic **Balgownie Estate** has been producing outstanding wines for more than 40 years. Try their non-vintage cuvee brut sparkling, their flagship shiraz or estate chardonnay. At weekends they offer Italian-style plates to share, such as thin-based pizzas perhaps topped with zucchini, caramelised onion and blue cheese, Tuki trout salad and Istra smallgoods platters.

Wineries are prolific throughout the region but look for **Sandhurst Ridge** in its picturesque bush setting at Marong; **Connor Park** with a small but still noteworthy production at Leichardt; **Mandurang Valley**, which makes a very good chardonnay and riesling; and **Water Wheel Vineyards** at Bridgewater

on Loddon, which produces consistently high-quality wines alongside the property's historic 1841 Memsie homestead.

Near Heathcote, Greg and Natala Flynn have set up **Flynn's Wines & Heathcotean Bistro**, in the former winery. Now there is a cosy cellar door surrounded by barrels to which they have added an appealing bistro area with views through a draping cabernet grapevine to vineyards beyond, giving it an air of Tuscany or Provence. Open only at weekends, they serve a Mediterranean-inspired menu with dishes such as homemade pizza, slow-cooked pork belly on Asian-style salad, and chocolate tart with morello cherry ice-cream with cherry and shiraz glaze. Fresh-picked vegetables and fruit come from the home garden and orchards. Naturally try their shiraz, but also their verdelho and sangiovese, one of the first in the region.

Heathcote Winery is in the main street where Cravens Cafe serves casual meals in the central garden space, with a gallery of local art and cellar door. Share a tasting plate and sample their flagship Curagee shiraz or perhaps the MCV White – an elegant blend of marsanne, chardonnay and viognier. **Cellar & Store**, also located on Heathcote's main street, is an independent wine outlet in a charming corner store that was once the local saddlery and family home. Local sheep farmers Eleanor and Adrian Dempster bought the building in 2005 and converted it into a chic light-filled space to

Below (left to right): enjoying a glass of red at Sandhurst Ridge, Marong; a showcase of wines at Cellar & Store, Heathcote; gourmet produce at The Green Olive Cafe, Bendigo; tree-lined drive at Water Wheel Vineyards, Bridgewater on Loddon; simplicity of style marks the interior of The Redesdale

showcase local produce, stylish home wares, outdoor seating in the garden and a wine room filled with some 80 different labels from the Heathcote region. It also acts as cellar door for wineries such as Stefani Estate, Heathcote Estate, Wanted Man Greenstone and Tatiara. If you'd like to sample any wine, just tell them and they'll open the bottle – making the rest available by the glass on their cafe wine list.

Jasper Hill's elegant shiraz labels, Georgia's Paddock and Emily's Paddock, are so difficult to come by that anyone who finds a bottle should snap it up immediately (and cellar it for at least eight years to enjoy the wine's full complexities). The winery will accept visitors by appointment only, but you may be able to find a bottle at Cellar & Store (see above).

Wild Duck Creek Estate is another winery deserving mention. Their Duck Muck shiraz has a cult following with its big, bold flavours and high alcohol content. The heady wine came about by accident in 1994 when winemaker David Anderson discovered several rows of grapes that hadn't been picked during the harvest. All the fermentation vats were full but he and a friend quickly picked the grapes and discovered the must had an extremely high acidity level. The yeast used to ferment the wine worked perfectly and a bottle can now sell for over $500 in Australia (overseas a bottle costs over $1000).

Other Heathcote cellar doors worth a visit include Louis De Castella Wine, where biodynamic principles are used to produce shiraz only (organic fare is available for lunch); and Shelmerdine, Stephen Shelmerdine's vineyard, where good use is made of local ingredients in the Whistler Cafe. Or perhaps you feel like a beer? The historic bluestone Tooborac Hotel has a state-of-the-art brewery that produces three brews all celebrating the region's heritage: a Stonemason's Pale Ale, a Woodcutter's Amber Ale and a Blacksmith's Porter.

Until recently, there was very little at Redesdale except a rather exotic bridge over the Campaspe River and the pub. The latter, built in the 1860s of local bluestone, was in bad need of some TLC when entrepreneurial couple Peter and Suzanne Williams, who already owned Redesdale Estate nearby, bought it and converted it into a chic gastropub, The Redesdale. They maintained the prerequisite front bar and gave it a good bar menu, converted a former dairy into a private dining room and have plans for a regional wine centre in the old stone stables. Restaurant and bar manager James Bone, a former sommelier at Daylesford's renowned Lake House, sees that the 60-seater runs smoothly, dispensing local ciders and wines to complement the contemporary menu. Share a charcuterie plate of homemade smoked veal and duck sausages, slow-braised kid and Istra smallgoods followed by potato gnocchi, prosciutto-wrapped wild rabbit or rack of lamb. The wine list includes Redesdale's own excellent shiraz and cabernets as well as imports.

Apples

Harcourt Valley – apple centre of Victoria

The Harcourt Valley, located at the foot of Mount Alexander, has long been known as the apple centre of Victoria. At the end of the 19th century it was possibly the biggest apple-growing area in Australia. The intense flavour and crispness of the apples are due to the cool climate and sandy soils derived from the granite rocks around the base of the mountain. The first apple orchard in the district was planted in 1859 by brothers Henry and William Ely and fellow Englishman William Eagle, who had grown up among apple orchards in Suffolk. From just three trees, further plantings followed, and the industry expanded rapidly with the development of the Coliban Irrigation System in the 1860s, which brought water to the surrounding goldfields. The first shipment of Harcourt apples to England was for the Colonial and Indian Exhibition of 1886 in London. Today, with some 402 hectares under apples, there is more land cultivated for apple-growing than there is for vines. Some 16 years ago there were 30 growers and although today that figure has halved, apples still make up the largest rural industry in the Mount Alexander Shire, with a combined annual income in a good year of more than $20 million.

Contacts for Northern Goldfields

EATERIES

Cellar & Store: see Stores

Flynn's Wines & Heathcotean Bistro: 29 Lewis Rd, Heathcote: (03) 5433 6297; www.flynnswines.com

La Piazza Wine Bar & Restaurant: 4 Bank St, Bendigo; (03) 5444 4499

The Dispensary Enoteca: 9 Chancery La, Bendigo; (03) 5444 5885; www.thedispensaryenoteca.com

The Good Loaf: see Gourmet Produce

The Green Olive Cafe: 11 Bath La, Bendigo; (03) 5442 2676; www.thegreenolive.com.au

The Redesdale: 2640 Kyneton–Heathcote Rd, Redesdale; (03) 5425 3111; www.theredesdale.com.au

Whirrakee Restaurant: 17 View St, Bendigo; (03) 5441 5557; www.whirrakeerestaurant.com.au

Whistler Cafe: see Wineries/Shelmerdine

Wine Bank on View: 45 View St, Bendigo; (03) 5444 4655; www.winebankonview.com

STORES

Bendigo Wholefoods: 314 Lyttleton Tce, Bendigo; (03) 5443 9492; www.bendigowholefoods.com.au

Cellar & Store: 105 High St, Heathcote; (03) 5433 2204; www.cellarandstore.com.au

The Epicurean Delicatessen: 79 Mitchell St, Bendigo: (03) 5443 2699; www.epicureandeli.com.au

MARKETS

Bendigo Community Farmers' Market: Williamson St; 2nd Sat each month, morning; 0422 031 859; www.bcfm.org.au

Bendigo Prince of Wales Showgrounds Market: Bendigo Showgrounds, 42–72 Holmes Rd; Sun; 0407 094 805; www.bendigoshow.org.au/themarket.html

Bridge Street Market: Bridge St, Bendigo; 3rd Sat each month; www.bridgestreetmarket.com.au

Heathcote Bush Market: Cnr Barrack Reserve and High St; 1st Sat each month, morning; (03) 5433 3555

GOURMET PRODUCE

Favourite Flavours: 37 Mitchell St, Bendigo; (03) 5444 2147

Gillies Pies: 266 Hargreaves St, Bendigo; (03) 5443 4965; www.gilliespies.com.au

Indulge Fine Belgium Chocolates: Shop 26, Fountain Crt, Bendigo; (03) 5441 1770

Quins Bluebird: 22 Mitchell St, Bendigo; (03) 5443 6781

The Good Loaf: 404 Hargreaves St, Bendigo; (03) 5444 2171

The Green Olive Cafe: see Eateries

WINERIES

Balgownie Estate: 46 Hermitage Rd, Maiden Gully; (03) 5449 6222; www.balgownieestate.com.au/bendigo-cellar-door

Bress: 3894 Calder Hwy, Harcourt; (03) 5474 2262; www.bress.com.au

Connor Park: 59 Connor Rd, Leichardt; (03) 5437 5234

Flynn's Wines & Heathcotean Bistro: see Eateries

Heathcote Winery: 185 High St, Heathcote; (03) 5433 2595; www.heathcotewinery.com.au

Jasper Hill: Drummonds La, Heathcote; (03) 5433 2528; www.jasperhill.com

Louis De Castella Wine: 68 Pink Cliffs Rd, Heathcote; (03) 5433 3958; www.louisdecastellawines.com.au

Mandurang Valley Wines: 77 Fadersons La, Mandurang; (03) 5439 5367; www.mandurangvalleywines.com.au

Redesdale Estate: Redesdale Rd North, Redesdale; (03) 5425 3236; www.redesdale.com

Sandhurst Ridge: 156 Forest Dr, Marong; (03) 5435 2534; www.sandhurstridge.com.au

Shelmerdine: Lancefield Rd, Tooborac; (03) 5433 5188; www.shelmerdine.com.au

Water Wheel Vineyards: Raywood Rd, Bridgewater on Loddon; (03) 5437 3060; www.waterwheelwine.com

Wild Duck Creek Estate: 762 Spring Flat Rd, Heathcote; (03) 5433 3133

BREWERIES/CIDER-MAKERS

Bress Cider: 3894 Calder Hwy, Harcourt; (03) 5474 2262; www.bress.com.au

Henry of Harcourt: 219 Reservoir Rd, Harcourt; (03) 5474 2177; www.henrycider.com

Tooborac Hotel & Brewery: 5155 Northern Hwy, Tooborac; (03) 5433 5201; www.tooborachotel.com.au

Geelong and Bellarine

The regional centre of Geelong, Victoria's second largest city, is the gateway to this area just an hour or so from Melbourne. The bustling port city grew with the state's wool industry and was once the wool export centre of the world (this heritage is proudly showcased in the excellent wool museum in Moorabool Street). Car manufacturer Ford established a plant here in the 1920s and the city became known as the 'home of Ford'. Today the redeveloped Eastern Beach Waterfront district features cafes, restaurants and colourful sculptured bollards that evoke characters past and present, from colonial seafarers to AFL football identities.

The Bellarine Peninsula juts out into Port Phillip, its south-easterly point overlooking the entrance to the bay at the tiny historic town of Point Lonsdale. Vines were first planted in the region in the 1840s but were uprooted during the 1870s phylloxera outbreak. Today's industry was established in the 1960s and there are now around 20 wineries. More recently the Bellarine Peninsula – even its name sounds slightly Italian – is becoming well known for its Mediterranean tastes and flavours. Depending on the season, you might come across plump table olives and quality extra

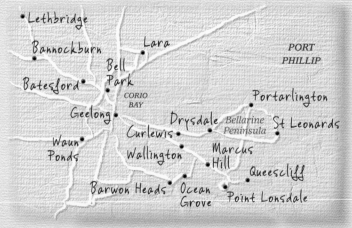

Above: fresh produce at McKenzie Ebbels Food Store, Queenscliff
Opposite (top to bottom): Clyde Park Vineyard and Bistro, Bannockburn; fine seafood at Fishermen's Pier, Geelong

Festivals

Portarlington Mussel Festival:
2nd Sat in Jan; 0409 254 265;
www.portarlingtonmusselfestival.
net.au

Wallington Strawberry Fair: 1st
Sun in Mar; (03) 5258 2219;
www.wallington-ps.vic.edu.au

Ocean Grove Apple Fair:
Mar (Labour Day weekend);
(03) 5255 1340; www.ogps.vic.edu.au

Lara Food and Wine Festival:
Pirra Homestead, 108 Windermere
Rd, Lara; 4th Sun in Mar;
www.larafoodandwinefestival.com.au

Queenscliff Seafood Festival:
Easter Fri; (03) 5258 3682;
www.seafoodfeast.org

Toast to the Coast: food and
wine festival; Geelong; Nov;
www.winegeelong.com.au/toast_
to_the_coast

Queenscliff Music Festival: last
weekend in Nov; (03) 5258 4816;
www.qmf.net.au

Where to stay

**Benambra B&B and Historic
Cottage:** charming boutique B&B;
15 Hesse St, Queenscliff;
(03) 5258 2606;
www.benambraqueenscliff.com.au

Hawthorn Suites at 13th Beach:
modern and self-contained; Barwon
Heads Rd, Barwon Heads;
(03) 5254 1777;
www.hawthornsuites.com.au

Mercure Hotel Geelong: luxury suites
and apartments; Cnr Gheringhap and
Myers sts; (03) 5223 6200;
www.mercuregeelong.com.au

Springhill House on Pardalote:
premium B&B; 13 Pardalote Cl, Point
Lonsdale; (03) 5258 4330;
www.springhillhouse.com.au

Waterfront Apartments Geelong:
self-contained luxury; Cnr Eastern Beach
Rd and Yarra St; (03) 5222 1370;
www.stayingeelong.com.au

Above (left to right): wine-tasting straight from the barrel at Park Vineyard and Bistro, Bannockburn; vine-side dining at Bellarine Estate, Portarlington; just-baked baguettes at McKenzie Ebbels Food Store, Queenscliff; wine racks at Leura Park Estate, Curlewis

virgin olive oil, excellent local goat's cheese, succulent strawberries and blueberries, exceptional sourdough breads, terrific farmed mussels, fresh bay scalefish and exceptional premium wines that constantly win awards nationally. While many immediately associate the peninsula with Queenscliff (that elegant seaside resort established in the 1920s, where grand hotels and mansions still grace the wide streets) or Barwon Heads (the location of Pearl Bay in the successful ABC series *Sea Change*), gourmet destinations are far more wide-ranging and visitors are spoilt for choice as more and more entrepreneurs move in to the area to make their own sea change, becoming involved in exciting new enterprises in the process.

Geelong also has a solid core of food-related businesses especially along central Pakington Street. Family-run **V & R Fruit and Vegetable Market** has cornered the market with a huge range of local breads, an extraordinary selection of cheese, smallgoods and quality fruit and vegetables. At the other end of Pakington Street, **Warren and Hutch**

Provedores stocks free-range chickens and rare breed pork, fresh farmed rabbits, dried fruits, olive oils and a vast array of jams, chutneys and preserves. Opposite is **Geelong Fresh Foods**, which among other things sells Kossie's grain-fed free-range eggs from Stonehaven, which local chefs insist are the best they've ever tasted.

Welcome newcomer to the Geelong dining scene is the Cantonese **Man Bo**, where locals have embraced its 'no expense spared' attitude; while **Fishermen's Pier** with its fantastic bay views continues to draw seafood lovers for its signature fish and chips using fresh local whiting with homemade tartare sauce. At weekends, choose from flake, barramundi or salmon, either grilled or battered, in the cafe.

On the north-western outskirts of Geelong is **Moorabool Valley Chocolates by Design**, where Lynne Meek makes a huge variety of European-style truffles, moulded and dipped chocolates with flavours such as chilli, summer peach and chardonnay from nearby Clyde Park Vineyard

(see p. 184) and a range of Australian native flavours such as lemon myrtle and lillypilly berry. On the south-western side of the city, at Waurn Ponds, **Pettavel Winery & Restaurant** (see feature, p. 185) consistently receives accolades for its food and wine. Using home-grown produce from its kitchen garden and elsewhere, the set menu of five or eight courses offers beautifully crafted dishes with matching wines (don't plan on doing much more after lunch!). More casual fare is available at the open-plan cellar door – their pinot noir is very good.

Breads are in abundance too. Select from the full range of authentic sourdough breads at the **Irrewarra Sourdough Shop & Cafe** – ciabatta, spicy fruit and nut loaves, even chocolate panforte – and, on weekdays only, lunch on gourmet sandwiches, Irrewarra club sandwiches, filled panini, fruit tarts, chocolate brownies and more. In Bell Park (in Geelong's north), call in to **La Madre Bakery**, an artisan bakery that produces organic sourdough, legendary ciabatta sourdough, other traditional breads using old-fashioned techniques, and fruit

tarts and seasonal desserts. Nearby, **Siketa Meats** has attracted a loyal clientele over nearly 50 years with their quality meats and smallgoods. Locals queue on Saturday mornings for the spicy skinless Croatian-style *cvuappe*, presswurst, chorizo, smoked ham hocks, tyroler and homemade black pudding.

On the peninsula, Drysdale is the home of celebrated **Drysdale Goat Cheese**. Corinne and Peter Blacket, both chemists, have won many medals for their cheeses, which include three types of shev (a play on the French chèvre), four different fettina and the strong and smooth Corio Bay mature. They are not open to the public, but you will find their product in local stores. Also at Drysdale you will discover thriving olive groves – the peninsula is proving a perfect site for growing these oil-producing fruits. At **Lighthouse Olive Mill** you can buy oils, marinated olives and many olive-oil-based products from the on-site shop, while **Manzanillo Grove** is open only by appointment. **Mason's Creek Olive Grove** at nearby Portarlington is also open to visitors only by appointment.

Above the Lighthouse Olive Mill Shop is **Loam Restaurant**, one of the most exciting dining ventures to open in the region in many years. Run by husband and wife team Aaron and Astrid Turner, this stylish place overlooks the 11 000 trees in the olive grove and has two sections: inside where you trust the chef to create either a two-, four- or seven-course meal based on what you *don't* like; or outside on the deck where a more regular, rustic menu is the go. Surprise courses might be Western Plains suckling pig with melon and yoghurt or brined and braised beef tongue with quinoa.

Fruit picking always makes for a great family day out as you can enjoy the 'fruits' of your labour and at **Tuckerberry Hill Blueberries** you can pick your own blueberries in summer and take home frozen ones year-round. They also grow lemons and organic garlic. Started by industry pioneers John and Margaret Tucker, this second-generation business also has a smart cafe, serving great coffee with all things blueberry from cup cakes to ice-cream and blueberry spiders! At Wallington, **Oakdene Vineyard & Restaurant** is the total package with vineyard, restaurant, cellar door, accommodation and lavender and orchid farm. The restaurant in a converted farmhouse serves contemporary dishes to complement the estate-grown wines.

Portarlington is synonymous with mussels. A sleepy seaside village, it comes alive at weekends when families descend to enjoy its safe beaches, try their luck with a rod off the pier and indeed buy plump mussels from **Mr Mussel** on Portarlington Pier. Alternatively you can order from **Seabounty**, whose processing factory is nearby. Locals know to look for Peter and Ben Jenkins' fishing boat and watch for these fifth-generation fishermen to emerge from the water at Portarlington with their daily catch, which is sold direct from their shop **Jenkins & Son** at the rear of their house. Fresh local fish is also available from wholesalers **White Fisheries** in St Leonards (mornings only).

While graceful Queenscliff still evokes images of a bygone era, in recent years the number of gourmet shops, cafes and restaurants has grown at an incredible rate. Tucked away on a quiet side street is the star turn on the peninsula, **Athelstane House**. By day, aim for a table outside on the deck under market umbrellas, but you'll have to book for dinner as word is spreading about the exceptional,

innovative food created by young chef Tyler Vakidis. Expect dishes such as molten egg, marinated cherry tomatoes, string beans with pea purée and pickled fennel or yellowtail kingfish with scallop omelette, peas, rice noodles and dashi broth. A few doors away, the same people have opened **McKenzie Ebbels Food Store**, a welcome retail food outlet offering restaurant-prepared take-home dishes and local gourmet produce, including cheese, honey, olive oils and breads.

Around the corner is **Raw Ingredients**, where Vicki Beale sells mostly bulk items but also stocks terrific Zeally Bay organic sourdough bread from Torquay. **Farm Foods** is a one-stop shop specialising in quality meats (much of it sourced from the Western District), cheese and lots of local wines. There is a huge range of other gourmet produce – local and from further afield. Sublime handmade Belgian chocolates and hot Italian chocolate in 23 different flavours are on offer at **Chocolatté on Hesse** – try the orange and cinnamon or fiery chilli that tingles your tongue.

Queenscliff Harbour has been given a boost with the impressive two-storey Rathbone Wine Group's wood, copper and limestone building, **360Q**, which houses a smart waterside cafe with observation tower overlooking the town and bay. Ex-Yering Station head chef Colin Swalwell creates innovative dishes such as curry-dusted prawns on chargilled tuna and share plates of crab and scallop-filled zucchini flowers with chilli and lime sauce. Near the Point Lonsdale turn-off look for **Lonsdale Hydroponics**, where Andrew Pearson grows plump round, Roma and cherry truss tomatoes, fresh lettuce and basil.

At Barwon Heads, Heather McCarthy opened **Peppercorn Foods** more than 12 years ago, cooking home-style food to go. She's famous for her savoury quiches and tarts and signature flourless orange cake. Almost opposite is **Annie's Provedore**, a produce store where the displays of fresh herbs and organic tomatoes are so beautiful you won't want to disturb them. There is also a cafe here, with local produce and take-away options as well as great pizzas, pies and more. On the breadmaking front, **Starfish Bakery**, originally from Melbourne, produces a seriously good casalinga sourdough as well as croissants and daily muffins.

Dotted throughout the region are a number of wineries consistently producing quality premium

Opposite (clockwise from top left): loaves fresh from the oven at La Madre Bakery, Bell Park; food and wine at Leura Park Estate, Curlewis; rows of vines at Clyde Park Vineyard, Bannockburn

wines. For years, the two iconic regional wineries were Bannockburn Vineyards in the Moorabool Valley and Scotchmans Hill at Bellarine. While these two still more than hold their own, others are also emerging to produce outstanding wines, giving credence to the whole area as a serious winegrowing region. In the case of **Bannockburn Vineyards**, although not open to the public, if you phone ahead winemaker Michael Glover will happily show you their shiraz, chardonnay and pinot noir (one of the country's best).

Nearby, at **Lethbridge Wines**, Ray Nadeson produces outstanding wines. Last year he won all five trophies at the Geelong Wine Show including the award for the best pinot noir, shiraz and chardonnay. Plan to visit and sample some of the dozen wines at **Clyde Park Bistro and Vineyard** on a weekend, when owners Terry and Sue Jongebloed match them with a menu of mostly local produce and thin-crust pizzas. You can settle back and enjoy the views overlooking the Moorabool Valley.

On the Bellarine, **Barrgowan Vineyard** is a small boutique winery at Curlewis, where winemaker Dick Simonsens makes exceptional shiraz. Open only by appointment, you might have to beg for a bottle as he produces only 150 cases a year. **Leura Park Estate** draws wine lovers on Sundays with live music and rustic dishes, often cooked on hot rocks to

accompany your choice from their 13 wines. **Scotchmans Hill** has relocated its cellar door to historic Spray Farm at Portarlington, where you can enjoy spectacular views over Corio and Port Phillip bays as you sample their chardonnay, pinot noir or Cornelius Syrah. At **Bellarine Estate** the cellar door is open for wine and beer tastings daily. As well as a good range of wines, some with quirky names such as the award-winning Two Wives shiraz and Phil's Fetish pinot noir, the estate's **Bellarine Brewing Company** produces quality lagers, ales, pilsners and stouts. This is the only microbrewed beer on the peninsula. An on-site restaurant is open Wednesday–Sunday for lunch, with an extensive menu showcasing the regional produce.

If you are into cars, then head for **McGlashans Wallington Estate** at Wallington. Owner Russell McGlashan puts on a changing car show at weekends, while you sip pinot, chardonnay or shiraz. An abalone diver, he often has this seafood delicacy on his tasting platters. From the quirky to the up-to-date, one of the newest wineries on the peninsula is **Banks Road Vineyard**. Here Will Derham offers a good range of wines including pinot grigio, sauvignon blanc and low-alcohol dolce grigio. The property is sprinkled with a changing sculpture exhibition and light lunches are offered at weekends.

Below (left to right): rows of exceptional shiraz at Barrgowan Vineyard, Curlewis; an artful dish of venison topside with pea mousse, pumpkin and a venison brik at Pettavel Restaurant, Waurn Ponds

Wine

Pettavel Winery & Restaurant

Swiss émigré David Louis Pettavel first planted vines at Waurn Ponds in 1848 and the wines he produced received recognition at international exhibitions. Celebrated artist Eugène von Guérard sketched Pettavel's vineyard in 1854 – at the time Geelong boasted the largest acreage of vineyards in Victoria, some 225 hectares being under cultivation by 1861. Sadly the vines disappeared after the devastation caused by phylloxera in the 1870s. In 2001 the Fitzpatrick family opened the Pettavel Winery cellar door with a range of cool-climate estate-grown wines, and the Pettavel Restaurant focusing on sourcing the freshest local products. Many of the fresh vegetables and herbs such as juicy raspberries, vine-ripened tomatoes, baby leeks, mignonette lettuce and garlic used in the dishes are picked from the restaurant's kitchen garden, and often served accented by Pettavel's estate-grown cold-pressed extra virgin olive oil. While the restaurant's hilltop location is magical, the food is exceptional. Since his arrival in 2007 executive chef Lyndon Betts has created quite a following. On the menu you may find such offerings as tortellini of goat's cheese sage and muscatels to start, 'Sher' wagyu rump with mustard and tomatoes to follow, and pithivier with apple, quince and caramel for dessert. You can choose from the degustation or à la carte menu at lunch, with or without matching wines, or a five-course dinner on Friday nights. These once-a-week dinners at the multi-award-winning restaurant are always something special (Saturday nights are reserved for weddings and private functions). The extensive wine list features over 150 wines from both national and international wine regions, in addition to 15 varietals available in complimentary wine tastings at the cellar door. Betts is also continuing the popular hands-on cookery classes, each of which concludes with students dining on their creations matched with a glass of Pettavel estate-grown wine. In 2009, over 300 food enthusiasts, ranging from beginners to practised cooks, participated in these classes.

Contacts for Geelong and Bellarine

EATERIES

360Q Cafe: 2 Wharf St, Queenscliff; (03) 5257 4200

Apostle: 79 Hess St, Queenscliff; (03) 5258 3097; www.apostlequeenscliff.com.au

Athelstane House: 4 Hobson St, Queenscliff; (03) 5258 1024; www.athelstane.com.au

Bellarine Estate: 2270 Portarlington Rd, Portarlington; (03) 5259 3310; www.bellarineestate.com.au

Clyde Park Vineyard & Bistro: 2490 Midland Hwy, Bannockburn; (03) 5281 7274; www.clydepark.com.au

Fishermen's Pier: Yarra St, Geelong; (03) 5222 4100; www.fishermenspier.com.au

Loam Restaurant: 650 Andersons Rd, Drysdale; (03) 5251 1101

Man Bo: 361 Moorabool St, Geelong; (03) 5221 7888; www.manbo.com.au

Oakdene Vineyard & Restaurant: 255 Grubb Rd, Wallington; (03) 5255 1255; www.oakdene.com.au

Pettavel Winery & Restaurant: 65 Pettavel Rd, Waurn Ponds; (03) 5266 1120; www.pettavel.com

Tuckerberry Hill Blueberries cafe: see Gourmet Produce

STORES

Annie's Provedore: Shop 2, 50 Hitchcock Ave, Barwon Heads; (03) 5254 3233

Farm Foods: 1 Symonds St, Queenscliff; (03) 5258 4744

Geelong Fresh Foods: 171 Pakington St, Geelong; (03) 5221 6004

Irrewarra Sourdough Shop & Cafe: 10 James St, Geelong; (03) 5221 3909; www.irrewarra.com.au

McKenzie Ebbels Food Store: 42–44 Hesse St, Queenscliff; (03) 5258 4829

Peppercorn Foods: 47 Hitchcock Ave, Barwon Heads; (03) 5254 2602

Raw Ingredients: 36B Hesse St, Queenscliff; (03) 5258 5275

Siketa Meats: 37 Hughes St, Bell Park; (03) 5278 2612

Starfish Bakery: 78 Hitchcock Ave, Barwon Heads; (03) 5254 2772

V & R Fruit and Vegetable Market: 5 Pakington St, Geelong; (03) 5222 2522; www.vandrfruit.com.au

Warren and Hutch Provedores: 156 Pakington St, Geelong; (03) 5229 7720; www.warrenandhutch.com.au

White Fisheries: Shop 3, Murradoc Rd, St Leonards; (03) 5257 1611

MARKETS

Central Geelong Farmers' Market: Little Malop St; 2nd Sat each month, morning; (03) 272 4938

Drysdale Community Market: Drysdale Reserve; 3rd Sun each month, morning; 0432 183 115

Point Lonsdale Primary School Market: Bowen Road; 2nd Sun each month; 0417 037 970

Portarlington Community Market: Ian Parks Hall, Newcombe St; last Sun each month; 0408 108 869

Queenscliff Community Market: Lower Princess Park; last Sun each month (Sept–May); 0408 340 932

Steampacket Garden Arts and Crafts Market: Steampacket Gardens, Eastern Beach, Geelong; 1st Sun each month: (03) 5229 0764

The Golden Plains Farmers' Market: Bannockburn; 1st Sat each month, morning; (03) 5220 7105; www.goldenplainsfarmersmarket.com.au

GOURMET PRODUCE

Chocolatté on Hesse: 13 Hesse St, Queenscliff; (03) 5258 2835

Drysdale Goats Cheese: 10 Newcombe St, Drysdale; (03) 5251 1449

Jenkins & Son: 10 Hood Rd, Portarlington; (03) 5259 3179

La Madre Bakery: 29 Milton St, Bell Park; (03) 5272 1727; www.lamadre.com.au

Lighthouse Olive Mill Shop: 650 Andersons Rd, Drysdale; (03) 5251 1100; www.lighthouseoliveoil.com.au

Lonsdale Hydroponics: 49 Yarram Creek La, Point Lonsdale; (03) 5258 2665

Manzanillo Grove: 150 Whitcombes Rd, Drysdale; (03) 5251 3621; www.manzanillogrove.com.au

Mason's Creek Olive Grove: 531–601 Queenscliff Rd, Portarlington; (03) 5257 3616

Moorabool Valley Chocolates by Design: 320 Ballarat Rd, Batesford; (03) 5276 1422; www.mooraboolvalleychocolate.com.au

Mr Mussel: Portarlington Pier, Portarlington; 0415 333 432

Seabounty: 160 Old St Leonards Rd, St Leonards; (03) 5257 1343; seabounty.com.au

Above: blackboard signage at Annie's Provedore, Barwon Heads

Tuckerberry Hill Blueberries: 35 Becks Rd, Drysdale; (03) 5251 3468

WINERIES

Banks Road Vineyard: 600 Banks Rd, Marcus Hill; (03) 5258 3777; www.banksroad.com.au

Bannockburn Vineyards: 100 Kelly La, off Midland Hwy, Bannockburn; (03) 5281 1363; www.bannockburnvineyards.com

Barrgowan Vineyard: 30 Pax Pde, Curlewis; (03) 5250 3861; www.barrgowanvineyard.com.au

Bellarine Estate: see Eateries

Clyde Park Vineyard & Bistro: see Eateries

Lethbridge Wines: 74 Burrows Rd, Lethbridge; (03) 5281 7279; www.lethbridgewines.com.au

Leura Park Estate: 1400 Portarlington Rd, Curlewis; (03) 5253 3180; www.leuraparkestate.com.au

McGlashans Wallington Estate: 225 Swan Bay Rd, Wallington; (03) 5250 5760

Oakdene Vineyard & Restaurant: see Eateries

Pettavel Winery & Restaurant: see Eateries

Scotchmans Hill: Spray Farm, 2275 Geelong–Portarlington Rd, Portarlington; (03) 5251 3176; www.scotchmanshill.com.au

BREWERIES

Bellarine Brewing Company: 2270 Portarlington Rd, Portarlington; (03) 5259 3310; www.bellarineestate.com.au

COOKING CLASSES

Pettavel Winery & Restaurant: see Eateries

Left: grilled lobster
at Chris's Restaurant,
Apollo Bay
Opposite (top to
bottom): the stylish
dining room, and a
dessert of flowers,
nectar and petals, at
Merrijig Inn, Port Fairy

South-West Coast

The South-West Coast draws more visitors to Victoria than any other region in the state. Its most famous asset, the Great Ocean Road, built between 1918 and 1932 as a memorial to Australian soldiers who died in World War I, is the scenic drive that hugs the coast between Torquay and Warrnambool. As it twists and turns it reveals hide-and-seek views of the ocean before plunging into the forests of the Otway Ranges, where you can walk through tall eucalypt woodlands, fern glades and ancient rainforests. Along the stretch known as the Shipwreck Coast, signs lure you off the main road with mysterious names – Moonlight Head, Wreck Beach and Devils Kitchen – before you arrive at the dramatic wave-torn cliffs and stacks near Port Campbell. Tantalising as this is, take time to make brief forays into the hinterland as well as taking in the historic villages and remote coastal beaches and bays beyond Warrnambool. Port Fairy, the city of Portland, and the pincer-like shapes of Cape Nelson and Cape Bridgewater that hold Bridgewater Bay within their grasp, are further along the coast and have much to offer.

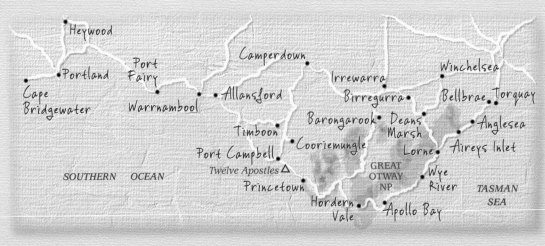

Heywood

Camperdown

Portland

Port
Fairy

Winchelsea

Cape
Bridgewater

Warrnambool

Allansford

Irrewarra

Birregurra

Bellbrae

Torquay

Barongarook

Deans
Marsh

Anglesea

Timboon

Port Campbell

Cooriemungle

Lorne

Aireys Inlet

SOUTHERN   OCEAN

Twelve Apostles △

GREAT
OTWAY
NP

Wye
River

TASMAN
SEA

Princetown

Hordern
Vale

Apollo Bay

Wood, Wine & Roses Festival: food festival; Village Green, Edgar St, Heywood; last Sat in Feb; www.woodwineroses.com/about-the-festival

Port Fairy Folk Festival: cultural dance and music festival; various locations; Mar (Labour Day Weekend); (03) 5568 2227; www.portfairyfolkfestival.com

Birregurra Weekend Festival: local produce on show; 2nd weekend in Oct; www.birregurra.com/festival

Where to stay

Aire Valley Guesthouse: sublime country accommodation and food; 2590 Great Ocean Rd, Hordern Vale; (03) 5237 9223; www.airevalleyguesthouse.com.au

Aqua Ocean Villas: self-contained luxury; 72 Merri St, Warrnambool; (03) 5562 5600; www.aquaoceanvillas.com.au

Bellbrae Harvest: romantic cottages; 45 Portreath Rd, Bellbrae; (03) 5266 2090; www.bellbraeharvest.com.au

Chris's Restaurant & Villas: contemporary villas and studios with stunning ocean views; 280 Skenes Creek Rd, Apollo Bay; (03) 5237 6411; www.chriss.com.au

Cumberland Lorne Resort: beachside apartments; 150 Mountjoy Pde, Lorne; (03) 5289 4444; www.cumberland.com.au

Elliminook: heritage homestead retreat; 585 Warncoort Rd, Birregurra; (03) 5236 2080; www.elliminook.com.au

Merrijig Inn: comfortable B&B accommodation in heritage inn; 1 Campbell St, Port Fairy; (03) 5568 2324; www.merrijiginn.com

Oscars Waterfront Boutique Hotel: riverside B&B; 41B Gipps St, Port Fairy; (03) 5568 3022; www.oscarswaterfront.com

Qdos: Japanese ryokan-style cottages in bushland; 35 Allenvale Rd, Lorne; (03) 5289 1989; www.qdosarts.com

Above (left to right): heritage-listed home of Ba Ba Lu Bar, Lorne; ocean views through the gums from Chris's Restaurant, Apollo Bay; Timboon Railway Shed Distillery, Timboon; braised rabbit with mushrooms, chestnuts and shallots at a la grecque, Aireys Inlet

The Twelve Apostles, those iconic, much-photographed 'standing stones' in the ocean just off the coast near Port Campbell, may be crumbling, but the area's food and wine scene is alive and well — from fine single malts to new artisan cheesemakers, luscious strawberries, blueberries, herbs and indulgent chocolate creations. It is only a few decades ago that this coast was almost bereft of gourmet-food options. This situation has been dramatically reversed as a result of the explosion in popularity of the major resort towns such as Lorne, the family-holiday appeal of the more laid-back centres such as Apollo Bay and Aireys Inlet, and of course the growing numbers of tourists who flock to catch the scenic wonders while they are still standing. Best of all there are now ample places delivering good coffee, a good reason to slow down and break your journey.

This is a road best travelled at a leisurely pace, whether you are touring from east to west or vice versa. Take your time and spend a few days in one or two places along the way. From Melbourne it takes little more than hour to reach Torquay, the 'surf

capital' of Australia, or some 75 minutes direct to Anglesea and the first of those spectacular ocean views. An alternative option is to drive the Princes Highway to Port Fairy, stay the night and start your explorations next day from there.

For those pushing off from the outskirts of Geelong, **Bellbrae Harvest Restaurant** at Bellbrae is the logical first stop. With a seasonally driven menu and bucolic surroundings (think, waterlilies on ponds, geese and ducks) this is the ideal stopover, as romantic cottage accommodation is also on offer (*see* Where to stay). At nearby Anglesea, the deck at **Pete's Place** suits anything from a lazy weekend breakfast enjoying the view, to dinner featuring local seafood or sausages from nearby Birregurra. Nestling behind the dunes, Aireys Inlet has long been linked to the iconic, whitewashed building housing **a la grecque**, serving Greek-Med food in surroundings that might make you feel a glimpse of the Aegean must be nearby. But the views here are all on the plate — beautiful dishes of locally caught whiting, mussels, octopus or fried calamari, and there is

plenty of lamb, prepared the Mediterranean way, of course. You can start your meal with a range of meze options then move on to the likes of lamb keftethes or chargrilled pork souvlaki. While many dishes will sound familiar, the food is a world apart from your local takeaway. The restaurant, owned by Pam and Kosta Talimanidis, members of the region's most famous food family, is open daily for breakfast, lunch and dinner.

Lovely Lorne, a little further on, is where you'll pull out the camera and begin snapping the coastal views in earnest. You'll also want to check out the local restaurant scene because it is very good. **Ba Ba Lu Bar** occupies a heritage-listed building near the entrance to town. The food here is strictly Spanish and tapas is king. Dishes are designed to share – Spanish meatballs, sherry-marinated mushrooms or perhaps authentic Spanish ham. The menu changes daily, the food is as fresh as can be and is all made in-house. Sunday is paella night, when this iconic seafood and rice dish is prepared with great ceremony in a huge communal paella pan, accompanied by live music.

Many Spanish wines, beers and sherries are available by the bottle or glass.

Lorne Ovenhouse, as the name suggests, specialises in crispy pizzas cooked in the imposing wood-fired oven, as well as roast meats and local seafood. Just along the street, **Marks'** owner Mark Purdie rejoices in the wealth of local produce, growing some himself, which makes dinner here (daily in summer) a true delight. And if you just crave some fish and chips by the water, join the locals at **The Pier Seafood Restaurant**, where you can eat inside or alfresco right beside the ocean after making your choice from the extensive seafood menu.

A slight detour into the bushland behind Lorne's main street will take you to **Qdos**, housing an art gallery, accommodation and cafe/restaurant. Breakfast or lunch is recommended so that you can walk among the outdoor sculptures (and possibly spot a koala in the trees) and peruse the current exhibition before or after your meal. The two-course breakfast 'packages' are indulgent but still suitable for those on a health kick, while lunch is a more exotic affair, with the likes of duck, labneh, cherries and rocket. All dishes are served on quirky pottery made on-site, which is also available for sale.

If you have time, at this point, you may want to take a drive inland to **Sunnybrae Restaurant & Cooking School** (*see* feature, p. 195) at Birregurra or at least mark it on the map as a place to pop into on the way back along the Princes Highway. Deans Marsh is nearby and it is here you will find **Gentle Annie Berry Gardens**, a good place to pick your own strawberries in summer, or simply take the easy way out and buy berries from the farm shop and settle down for a Devonshire tea or coffee (or a light lunch). **Old Lorne Road Olives** is relatively newly established, as olive groves go, but is already producing good oils that go nicely on the chef's platter or with its cafe fare of light meals.

Back on the coast road, pick up some provisions, grab lunch or have a coffee at **Wye River General Store**. Like many small local general stores, with its country-chic decor this old place now has new life as a busy stopping point for travellers and a welcome option for locals. Count your blessings if your itinerary allows a night at **Aire Valley Restaurant and Guest House** set in postcard-beautiful surroundings at Hordern Vale. Vegetables and herbs are picked from the garden in the early evening for the restaurant, meat is locally sourced from Colac and the fish is from local Victorian waters.

From it lofty perch high on the hillside near Apollo Bay, **Chris's Restaurant** is another of the region's much-loved eateries. First opened in 1979, the original restaurant burned down but has risen from the ashes – bigger, better and more contemporary but still with that spectacular view through overhanging gums. The hospitality of owner-host and chef Chris Talimanidis is legendary and the food is equally impressive. He keeps the Greek theme going with grilled and roasted meats, local crays in season, octopus and other seafood. Many dishes are given an Australian spin, such as the kakavia, a mix of seafood in a vegetable and garlic cream sauce. Open all day, it's a relaxed hospitable space, equally popular for breakfast as it is for other meals. Many guests stay a night or more in one of Chris's on-site contemporary villas or luxury studios (*see* Where to stay), all with that spectacular view.

Closer to town **La Bimba** has views aplenty too. There is something about this coastline that reminds people of the Mediterranean it seems, so here the cuisine reflects Moorish influences with plenty of tagines and couscous and brik pastry.

Twelve kilometres inland, **Otway Herbs** is the place to come to hone your herbal knowledge. In this fragrant environment, plants are grown using biodynamic principles, with compost-based potting mixes and no artificial fertilisers or chemicals. Nearby, Princetown has earned its place on the

Below (left to right): antipasti treats at Bellbrae Harvest Restaurant, Bellbrae; service with a smile at Bridgewater Bay Beach Cafe, Cape Bridgewater; sweet poached fruit dessert at Pippies by the Bay, Warrnambool; Gentle Annie Berry Gardens, Deans Marsh

foodie map with the arrival of decadently delicious **GORGE Chocolates**. Gorge? 'Great Ocean Road Gourmet Experience' is the apt explanation of the brand name for this range of dainties made using Belgian chocolate. Buy some and gorge on them as you travel on, stopping at the lookouts to view the Twelve Apostles near Port Campbell.

A side trip inland from the coast to Timboon will yield a little gem of a community. The former Mousetrap and Timboon Cheese have gone, but in their place there's **L'Artisan Cheese** in the care of a French couple, fourth-generation French cheesemakers and well worth a visit. You can also pick your own strawberries from November to March at **Berry World** or pick up berry products at other times. **Timboon Fine Ice Cream**, which began in 1999 using local milk from this rich dairying area, has relocated here and its products and a wide range of other local produce, much of it from the unofficial local 'food trail', are available at the **Timboon Railway Shed Distillery**. When the former railway building became available, Tim Marwood and Caroline Simmons decided to establish their operations in the town whose name they had made so well loved. A great new milestone is the distillery's first single malt. Nearby, at Cooriemungle, you'll find **Apostle Whey Cheese** prepared on the owner's family farm using milk produced by their 'contented herd of Jerseys and Friesians'. The farm shop is a good place to stock up on gourmet cheeses, gifts, and good-quality coffee.

Warrnambool is the key town for this area, and with a population of around 28 000 and a front row seat on the treacherous Southern Ocean you certainly won't go short of food and dining places here. For pizza, there's **Bojangles Pizza Restaurant** and good reliable meals at **Breakers Restaurant** or **Donnelly's**. For beer, **Flying Horse Bar and Brewery** is a very good microbrewery delivering well-named medal-winning tipples – such as Dirty Angel, Whale Ale and Mahogany Porter. Best for dining in town is the contemporary Italian-leaning cuisine at **Nonna Casalinga**, and **Pippies by the Bay** for honest cafe food, which is dished out with commendable care and attention. Locals also recommend a visit to the **Warrnambool Farmers' Market** on the first Saturday morning of the month or **Pronto Fine Food** at other times to pick up local produce and gourmet items.

At this point you need to make a decision. Depending on your time, you can wander on westwards or turn for home down the highway. However, if nothing else, at least make the short journey to the charming little town of Port Fairy, soaked in Irish heritage, its streets lined with quaint cottages, antique dealers and fantastic old pubs. Originally called Belfast, it was once a centre for the whaling industry; these days visitors are enticed by the old-world atmosphere, the historic bluestone

buildings, the small fleet of fishing boats that line the old wharf – and the exceptional food. You will find some of the best anywhere at the heritage **Merrijig Inn**, a modest colonial building dating from 1845. For the past few years, chef Ryan Sessions has been winning awards for his cutting-edge dishes. You might start with local crayfish with roe and coastal herbs, move on to Western Plains suckling pig with apple, fennel and morcilla, then finish with peaches 'three ways', sheep's milk gel and basil granita. There is a degustation menu, à la carte and plenty of choices for vegetarians. The great thing is that after such a memorable dining experience (dinner only) you can spend the night at this inn in cosy B&B accommodation (*see* Where to stay).

Elsewhere in town is the elegant and popular **Portofino on Bank**, serving fragrant and zesty dishes displaying strong Mediterranean influences, or **Saltra Brasserie**'s comfort food. Housed in one of the oldest corner buildings, **The Stag** restaurant has new owners bringing innovative ideas to the menu, with the emphasis on share-plates to start and hearty mains in the cooler months. **Wisharts at the Wharf** seafood cafe and wine bar is a busy spot day and night, while the **Port Fairy Farmers' Market** bustles on the third Saturday morning of each month. A little out of town is the ocean-side gem, **Time & Tide**, a gallery cafe with stunning views and fun and filling dishes.

The historic coastal city of Portland, the site of Victoria's first permanent settlement in 1834, marks the start of the Discovery Coast, a wilderness of stunning bays, pristine coastal lakes and long expanses of white sand that extend to the South Australian border. In Portland you'll discover some treasures such as **Clock by the Bay** in the former post office; **Lido Larder**, a cafe with excellent coffee; and **Tea Tree Gallery & Tearooms**, ideal for brunch or Devonshire teas. Time permitting, make the trip to Cape Bridgewater's **Bridgewater Bay Cafe** for some of the best fish and chips you'll find, seated almost

on the sand, and Cape Nelson's **Isabella's Cafe** at the Cape Nelson Lightstation, which serves up memorable views along with your lunch choices.

If you are now thinking of your return journey to Melbourne, take the Princes Highway rather than retrace your steps, but plan to punctuate the trip with stops at a number of fascinating places. Allansford, not far from Warrnambool, has been home to **Allansford Cheese World** for many years (this is the outlet for the Warrnambool Cheese and Butter Factory, located opposite). Here you can learn much about cheeses in general, and local cheese in particular, have lunch and stock up on all sorts of goodies. Further down the road in the main street of Camperdown, **Red Duck Provedore** at the **Red Duck Brewery** cellar door wraps up beer sales, gourmet produce and cafe fare. And then there is the delightful **Otway Estate Winery & Brewery** at Barongarook, near Colac. This is the major winery in this region and it also produces medal-winning beers. You can settle down for a relaxed meal in the cafe-restaurant and sample some of the local produce that features on its menu.

Pennyroyal Raspberry Farm at Murroon (fruit picking December–January only, with a teahouse open every day during those months) is also nearby as is Irrewarra, where the widely loved breads from **Irrewarra Sourdough**, sold throughout the region (*see* Geelong and Bellarine/Irrewarra Sourdough Shop & Cafe, p. 181), are made. You can see through the bakery by appointment but there are no on-site bread sales. Finally, at Winchelsea, there is one last highlight of the trip. **Winchelsea Larder** is a provedore (and online store **A Taste of the Region**) selling much of the produce that you have seen and tasted along this bounteous food trail. It is perfectly positioned for you to stock up on all the things – edible memories, if you like – that you have come to love along the way.

Birregurra

George Biron of Sunnybrae

Sunnybrae is one of regional Victoria's hidden gems. Renowned chef George Biron and partner Dianne Garrett run this welcoming farmhouse restaurant like an extension of their own historic 1868 tuck-point brick home. Located on the outskirts of the small village of Birregurra, they open only at weekends for lunch and offer hands-on cooking classes on Mondays where students can suggest techniques and ingredients used. A staunch advocate of slow food, Hungarian-born Biron grows much of his own fruit, vegetables, salad greens and herbs in his thriving kitchen garden and harvests olives from his adjacent grove for extra virgin olive oil to use in the restaurant. He bakes his own bread, makes his own preserves and cheese and cooks as much as possible in the outside wood-fired oven. Lunch at Sunnybrae is a much anticipated and leisurely affair, its fixed-price, multi-coursed offerings stretching over several hours. There might be a fish broth with whole farmed prawns and aioli to start, followed by half a dozen small plates to share. Main course might be Western Plains pork or Moroccan-style lamb. A mid-prandial wander through the garden is almost obligatory, before deciding on dessert. Championing all things local, Sunnybrae's wine list features outstanding labels, mostly from the Otway–Geelong region.

Contacts for South-West Coast

EATERIES

a la grecque: 60 Great Ocean Rd, Aireys Inlet; (03) 5289 6922; www.alagrecque.com.au

Aire Valley Restaurant and Guest House: 2590 Great Ocean Rd, Hordern Vale; (03) 5237 9223; www.airevalleyguesthouse.com.au

Ba Ba Lu Bar: 6A Mountjoy Pde, Lorne; (03) 5289 1808; www.babalubar.com.au

Bellbrae Harvest Restaurant: 45 Portreath Rd, Bellbrae; (03) 5266 2100; www.bellbraeharvest.com.au

Bojangles Pizza Restaurant: 61 Liebig St, Warrnambool; (03) 5562 8751; www.bojanglespizza.com

Breakers Restaurant: 79 Banyan St, Warrnambool; (03) 5561 3088

Bridgewater Bay Beach Cafe: 1661 Bridgewater Rd, Cape Bridgewater; (03) 5526 7155; www.bridgewaterbay.com.au

Chris's Restaurant & Villas: 280 Skenes Creek Rd, Apollo Bay; (03) 5237 6411; www.chriss.com.au

Clock by the Bay: Cnr Cliff and Bentinck sts, Portland; (03) 5523 4777; www.clockbythebay.com.au

Donnelly's: 78 Liebig St, Warrnambool; (03) 5561 3188

Gentle Annie Berry Gardens & Tea-Rooms: see Gourmet Produce

Isabella's Cafe: Cape Nelson Lightstation, Cape Nelson, via Portland; (03) 5523 5119

La Bimba: 125–127 Great Ocean Rd, Apollo Bay; (03) 5237 7411

Lido Larder: 5a Julia St, Portland; (03) 5521 1741

Lorne Ovenhouse: 46A Mountjoy Pde, Lorne; (03) 5289 2544; www.ovenhouse.com.au

Marks: 124 Mountjoy Pde, Lorne; (03) 5289 2787; www.marksrestaurant.com.au

Merrijig Inn: 1 Campbell St, Port Fairy; (03) 5568 2324; www.merrijiginn.com

Nonna Casalinga: 69 Liebig St, Warrnambool; (03) 5562 2051

Old Lorne Road Olives: 45 Old Lorne Rd, Deans Marsh; (03) 5236 3479; oldlorneroadolives.com.au

Pete's Place: 113 Great Ocean Rd, Anglesea; (03) 5263 2500

Pippies by the Bay: 91 Merri St, Warrnambool; (03) 5561 2188; www.flagstaffhill.com

Portofino on Bank: 26 Bank St, Port Fairy; (03) 5568 2251

Qdos: 35 Allenvale Rd, Lorne; (03) 5289 1989; www.qdosarts.com

Saltra Brasserie: 20 Bank St, Port Fairy; (03) 5568 3058; www.saltrabrasserie.com

Sunnybrae Restaurant & Cooking School: Cnr Cape Otway and Lorne rds, Birregurra; (03) 5236 2276; www.sunnybraerestaurantandcooking school.blogspot.com/

Tea Tree Gallery & Tearooms: 59 Percy St, Portland; (03) 5523 7376 or 0488 067 296; www.theteatreegallery.com.au

The Pier Seafood Restaurant: Lorne Pier, Lorne; (03) 5289 1119

The Stag: 22 Sackville St, Port Fairy; (03) 5568 3226; www.thestagportfairy.com.au

Time & Tide: 21 Thistle Pl, Port Fairy; (03) 5568 2134

Wisharts at the Wharf: 29 Gipps St, Port Fairy; (03) 5568 1884; www.wisharts.com.au

STORES

Allansford Cheese World: Great Ocean Rd, Allansford; (03) 5565 3130; www.cheeseworld.com.au

Pronto Fine Food: Shop 12, Norfolk Plaza, 743 Raglan Pde, Warrnambool; (03) 5561 5424; www.prontofinefood.com.au

Red Duck Provedore: see Breweries/Distilleries/Red Duck Brewery

Torquay Central Farmers' Market: Bristol Rd; Sat morning; 0418 315 026

Winchelsea Larder/A Taste of the Region: 40 Dicksons Rd, Winchelsea; (03) 5267 2832; www.atasteoftheregion.com.au

Wye River General Store: 35 Great Ocean Rd, Wye River; (03) 5289 0247

MARKETS

Birregurra Sunday Market in the Park: Main St; 2nd Sun each month; (03) 5236 2486

Port Fairy Community Market: Village Green, cnr Sackville and Bank sts; 2nd and 4th Sat each month; 0488 654 298

Port Fairy Farmers' Market: Village Green, cnr Sackville and Bank sts; 3rd Sat each month; (03) 5568 2421

Torquay Central Farmers' Market: Bristol Rd; Sat morning; 0418 315 026

Warrnambool Farmers' Market: Civic Green, Liebig St; 1st Sat each month; (03) 5562 7030

GOURMET PRODUCE

Apostle Whey Cheese: 9 Gallum Rd, Cooriemungle; (03) 5598 7367; www.apostlewheycheese.com.au

Berry World: Egan St, Timboon; (03) 5598 3240; www.berryworld.com.au

Gentle Annie Berry Gardens & Tea-Rooms: 520 Pennyroyal Valley Rd, Deans Marsh; (03) 5236 3391; www.gentleannie.com.au

GORGE Chocolates: 1231 Melrose Rd, Princetown; (03) 5598 8125; www.gorgechocolates.com.au

Irrewarra Sourdough: 85 Irrewarra School Rd, Irrewarra; (03) 5233 6219 or 0407 388 219; www.irrewarra.com.au

L'Artisan Cheese: 23 Ford & Fells Rd, Timboon; (03) 5598 3244; www.lartisancheese.com.au

Old Lorne Road Olives: 45 Old Lorne Rd, Deans Marsh; (03) 5236 3479; oldlorneroadolives.com.au

Otway Herbs: 155 Biddles Rd, via Wild Dog Creek Rd, Apollo Bay; (03) 5337 6318; www.otwayherbs.com.au

Pennyroyal Raspberry Farm: 115 Division Rd, Murroon; (03) 5236 3238

Timboon Fine Ice Cream: 630 Glenfyne–Brucknell Rd, Timboon; (03) 5595 0390; www.timboonicecream.com.au/contact.htm

Timboon Railway Shed Distillery: see Breweries/Distilleries

WINERIES

Otway Estate Winery & Brewery: 10–30 Hoveys Rd, Barongarook; (03) 5233 8400; www.otwayestate.com.au

BREWERIES/DISTILLERIES

Flying Horse Bar and Brewery: Cnr Mahoneys Rd and Raglan Pde, Warrnambool; (03) 5562 2254; www.theflyinghorse.com.au

Otway Estate Winery & Brewery: see Wineries

Red Duck Brewery: Red Duck Provedore, 243 Manifold St, Camperdown; (03) 5593 3303; www.redduckbeer.com.au

Timboon Railway Shed Distillery: The Railway Yard, 1 Bailey St, Timboon; (03) 5598 3555 or 0407 684 086; www.timboondistillery.com

COOKING SCHOOLS

Sunnybrae Cooking School: see Eateries

Below (left to right): showcasing local gourmet products at Pronto Fine Food, Warrnambool; old-world cottage atmosphere at Pennyroyal Raspberry Farm, Murroon

Left: artistry on a plate
at the Royal Mail Hotel,
Dunkeld

Opposite: outdoor
area and olive grove
at Mount Zero Olives,
Laharum

Grampians and surrounds

Grampians National Park is known for its natural rugged beauty, abundant
wildlife, challenging walking trails and scenic lookouts. Surrounding the
mountain peaks and lowlands of the national park, the Western District
farmlands support horticultural and pastoral properties, comprising olive
groves, small-crop farms and sheep and beef cattle. Some local beef, such
as that from **Greenvale Meats** and **Hopkins River Beef**, finds its way into
the kitchens of the country's leading restaurants. Also throughout this cool-
climate region are wineries that have long been winning awards for their
premium wines, notably shiraz and riesling. Vines were first grown here in
the 1860s and 1870s, with many of the original establishments such as
Best's and Seppelt still producing fine wines.

Ararat doctor Graeme Bertuch and his artist wife, Carolyn, have set up
the cellar door for Warrak-based **Mount Cole Wineworks** in a convenient
road-side lay-by at Buangor on the Western Highway. Called **'Off the
Beaten Track' Wine & Art Gallery**, it is housed in a smart corrugated iron
building where you can sip their excellent shiraz while admiring the artwork
of Carolyn and others. Nearby, **Mount Langi Ghiran** is one of those cellar

Festivals

Grampians Jazz Festival: various locations, Halls Gap; 2nd week in Feb; (03) 5572 2116; www.grampiansjazzfestival.com.au

Lake Bolac Eel Festival: celebrating Aboriginal culture and heritage; last Sat in Mar; (03) 5350 2204; www.eelfestival.org.au

Stawell Easter Gift: art and horseracing meets historic foot race; Easter weekend; (03) 5358 1326; www.stawellgift.com

Southern Grampians Promenade of Sacred Music: Hamilton; Apr; (03) 5573 0429; www.promenadeofsacredmusic. com.au

Grampians Grape Escape: Village Oval, Grampians Tourist Rd, Halls Gap; 1st weekend in May; 0408 811 459; www.grampiansgrapeescape.com.au

Discover Dunkeld: 1st weekend in Sept; 1800 807 056

Classics in Wartook Valley: cultural festival; Wartook; 2nd weekend in Sept; (03) 5382 9779; wartook.vic.au

Where to stay

Boroka Downs: spacious luxury villas; 51 Birdswing Rd, Halls Gap; (03) 5356 6243; www.borokadowns.com.au

DULC: secluded eco-cabins; Thryptomene Crt, Halls Gap; (03) 5356 4711; www.dulc.com.au

Kangaroos in the Top Paddock: self-contained retreat; 3062 Mt Victory Rd, Wartook; (03) 9497 2020; www.kangaroosinthetoppaddock.com.au

Meringa Springs: sophisticated five-star lodges; 2974 Northern Grampians Rd, Wartook; (03) 5383 6363; www.meringasprings.com.au

Mt Sturgeon Cottages: historic bluestone cottages; 98 Parker Street (Glenelg Hwy), Dunkeld; (03) 5577 2241; www.royalmail.com.au

doors that only those 'in the know' visit. It is set off the main highway so visitors here rarely just stumble upon the cellar door. It produces some of the best examples of cool-climate shiraz in the country. The winery produces its flagship Langi Shiraz from a 6-hectare single vineyard on the estate. Try the outstanding 2006 Langi Shiraz and the 2008 riesling. Also note that their Billi Billi shiraz is excellent quality for its reasonable price.

In Ararat, Mike Dilisio runs **Nectar Ambrosia**, a casual eatery and local produce store in a former 1859 pub, where you can enjoy a glass of wine or cup of coffee in comfy sofas by the fire. There are daily specials – perhaps a soup, pasta or chef's share plate – and more substantial offerings on the regular menu. The wine shop also acts as cellar door for smaller wineries such as Nowhere Creek, Jillian Wines and Moyston Hills. **The Vines Cafe** nearby has floor-to-ceiling doors that open out for pavement dining, and serves dishes such as twice-baked hazelnut-encrusted goat's cheese soufflé and great lemon tart.

Silvery green olive groves can be seen dotted throughout the region, which is known for its quality olives – many available through local stores. Look for

Mount Ararat Olives, Red Rock Olives, Toscana Olives, Grampians Olive Estate, the legendary Mount Zero Olives, and Laharum Grove, which has recently opened a cafe that has proved very successful. Mount Zero also sells salmon-pink salt from the large natural Dimboola Pink Lake, harvested in conjunction with the Barengi Gadjin Land Council.

The tiny township of Great Western is considered the birthplace of Australian sparkling wine. You can enjoy local cheese platters with shiraz jelly and Mount Zero olives at **Grampians Estate**'s cellar door, Great Western Wine Centre, as you sample their wines. If you're keen to learn more, book an informative Sunday afternoon wine tutorial with owner Tom Guthrie who will guide you through ten different wines and their processes. At iconic **Seppelt Great Western,** sample their latest releases in the historic Shaft House cellar door (their Salinger sparkling wine is excellent) and take a tour of the 3-kilometre National Trust–classified underground 'drives', where countless bottles are stored in atmospheric caves. Ask about their night-time ghost tours and ghost and gourmet dinners underground.

Family-owned **Best's Wines** now boasts its fifth generation of winemakers and still operates from its

Below (left to right): grazing in lush pastures at Greenvale Meats, Willaura; vaulted cellar at Best's Wines, Great Western; Mount Zero Olives, Laharum; handling rounds of cheese at Grampians Pure Sheep Dairy, Glenthompson

charming historic red-gum-slab cellar door on Concongella Creek, where an open fire lends a warming glow in winter. The hand-dug underground cellar, stables dating from 1869 and original 1860s nursery block are all an intrinsic part of local history. You can take a self-guide cellar walk, buy local produce and a bottle of wine and picnic in the lovely grounds. Their 'old vine' pinot meuniere deserves particular mention for its delicate raisin taste. Great Western is also the home of **Green Eggs**, not the Dr Seuss–coloured variety served with ham, but from the flock of free-roaming chooks owned by Shelley and Allan Green. Using sustainable and ethical farming methods, their birds graze on 480 hectares, enjoy state-of-the-art conditions, have won many awards and the eggs are available widely throughout Melbourne. Look for them in local Grampians' food outlets.

In need of a pick-me-up? **Salingers Cafe** offers coffee, cake and light lunches in a charming shopfront in the main street of Great Western. Check out the resident beehive where you can watch the busy bees at work in a special glassed-in observation space. Nearby Stawell, home of the legendary Stawell Gift footrace each Easter, is a great place to pick up fresh produce. Innovative producers **Bellellen Grampians Organics** grow organic fresh fruit, herbs, vegetables and olive products and have an honesty system for payment at the front gate.

Halls Gap is the main township for Grampians National Park. There is a string of shops in the Stony Creek Stores including the excellent **Halls Gap Bakery**, which has won numerous awards for its country-style meat pies and vanilla slices, and **Smugglers Hearth**, which makes a huge variety of fudge such as rum and raisin, Bailey's, peppermint and chocolate. A local institution, **The Kookaburra Bar & Bistro** serves modern Australian food along with a few old classics such as a pie of the day — perhaps lamb and rosemary. They breed their own venison, often used in their pies and sausages.

At Dadswells Bridge on the north-eastern edge of the national park, you will find that it's not just at Christmas that **Deutscher's Turkey Farm** is fattening their free-range birds. These antibiotic-free turkeys find a ready market year-round. Buy tray-packed and vacuum-sealed whole birds, or portions, as well as turkey and gluten- and preservative-free sausages from their farm shop (opposite the Giant Koala).

In Horsham, **Cafe Chickpea** is a modest little cafe that bakes most of the daily fare on the premises – spinach and feta pies, zucchini bakes, quiches and frittatas. Regulars come to breakfast on fresh fruit salad, cereal and local free-range eggs any way you like. Those with special dietary needs are particularly well catered for. Just south-west of town at Haven, apiarists Marion and Steve Sostheim of **Grampians Honey** move their 300 hives around the region to collect yellow box, yellow gum and grey box honeys. Call ahead and they will leave your order (500 grams, 1 kilogram, 3 kilograms, or more) out or deliver it if you are staying nearby.

A little further to the south-west, in Lower Norton, **Norton Estate** is one of Western Victoria's finest producers of boutique wines. Grapes are hand-picked, hand-pressed, fermented in open vats, and hand-plunged to produce truly handcrafted wines that consistently win national and international medals. Try their highly acclaimed Arapiles Run Shiraz.

In Hamilton, south-west of the national park, **Darriwill Farm Hamilton** is a chic produce/home-wares shop and wine store specialising in top regional produce and wine, much of which appears on the seasonal menu of **Darriwill Farm Cafe.** You can sit at the wine bar and enjoy oysters, prawns and antipasto straight from the deli cabinet or dine in the cafe on dishes such as crumbed calamari with Greek-style salad using Mount Zero olives, Meredith goat's feta and Doodles Creek lemon and caper mayonnaise or main courses of warm Greenvale beef salad or oven-baked rack of local lamb.

Nearby, **Roxburgh House** is a converted 1860s two-storey Victorian home furnished and decorated with gorgeous pieces from the family's antique shop next door. Dubbed 'The Rox', this is a fun wine bar and restaurant that serves great pizzas and terrific tapas dishes ideal for sharing. They have a good selection of local wines, serve the best coffee in town and make great hot Lindt chocolate. **Farm Foods Hamilton** is a family-owned-and-run retail butchery, liquor and mixed deli business known for its gourmet sausages and quality Western District beef and lamb. They grow their own certified Angus beef and make more than a dozen flavoured sausages, such as Birregurra beef, Guinness and beef with herbs, red wine and cracked pepper, chorizo and tandoori.

At Bochara, west of Hamilton is **Bochara Wines**, known for its sauvignon blanc, pinot noir, Picnic Train rosé and sparkling Arcadia. Its historic cellar door – once the 19th-century home of a returned World War I light horseman – was built originally at Tahara but transported to Bochara and restored to offer visitors a charming wine-tasting venue.

In Coleraine, Bavarian chocolatiers Erika and Manfred Kolberg create European-style truffles and fine continental-style chocolates at **Glenelg Fine Chocolates.** You can buy strawberry cream centres made from local strawberries, chocolates filled with cabernet sauvignon, rosé and Seppelt's dessert wine from their factory shop. Almost next door is **Fiona Wall Fine Foods Store**, where Fiona Wall has won international acclaim for her fabulous biscuits including chocolate florentines, melting moments, orange shortbread, organic anzacs, chocolate chip and gingerbread people.

Apart from a church, a school and a quaint antiques shop, there is not much else in Tarrington except the **Cafe Catalpa.** Formerly the old general store at this tiny place just south-east of Hamilton, it has been transformed into a lively cafe where hunting pictures and memorabilia hint that the menu leans heavily towards game. Entrées might be quail, smoked eel or local yabbies, while popular main courses include duck and shiitake mushroom pies, rabbit with Dijon mustard and slow-cooked hare with star anise. Go on Sunday when locals often arrive in gleaming vintage and veteran cars or on classic motorbikes.

The Grampians boasts one of the finest restaurants in the entire country. Over recent years, the **Royal Mail Hotel** (*see* feature opposite) has single-handedly put the tiny town of Dunkeld (population 440) on the map with its exceptional food and spectacular wine cellar. Also in town, the **Dunkeld Gourmet Pantry** is a cafe offering homemade vegetarian pasties and quiches, country-style pies and ready-to-go Turkish rolls, and a well-stocked larder featuring the region's fine local produce. Further east at Glenthompson, arrive early (or late) at **Grampians Pure Sheep Dairy** to see sheep being milked then sample farmhouse cheeses such as pecorino-style, a tasty cheddar, sheep's feta or seasonal styles such as Wesleydale, and yoghurts including lemon, vanilla, coconut and tangy natural.

Unsurpassed food

Royal Mail Hotel

Molecular gastronomy – the art of using scientific principles to create new flavours and textures in food – has taken many forms at restaurants around the world, with dishes often arriving smoking or bubbling at your table. While some may feel it's all just a case of 'smoke and bubbles', Dan Hunter of the Royal Mail Hotel in Dunkeld successfully marries molecular gastronomy with quality produce to create the ultimate dining experience. The renovated Art Deco–style hotel is one of the only establishments in the tiny town, but you'll need to book well in advance for the seasonal tasting menu. Every dish on the multi-course menu is a delicate and flavoursome work of art, using vegetables, herbs and edible flowers harvested from the restaurant's kitchen gardens. For winter, one dish may be moist venison placed beside roasted baby beets and caramelised apple, and accompanied by a chocolate sauce, while an autumn dessert could be rhubarb, licorice, almond and citrus that arrives like three decorated red cigars in a delicious pool of juice. The exceptional food is matched with equally exceptional wines. You may see sommelier Jeremy Scheill going across the road to the separate wine cellar that houses over 2000 labels, including one of the world's best collections of Bordeaux wines. A meal, together with matching wines, may be pricey, but it will certainly be one of the most memorable dining experiences of your life. The more reasonably priced bistro serves hearty country-style fare and there is also a most affordable bar menu.

Contacts for Grampians and surrounds

EATERIES

Cafe Catalpa: 7921 Hamilton Hwy, Tarrington; (03) 5572 1888

Cafe Chickpea: 30A Pynsent St, Horsham; (03) 5382 3998

Darriwill Farm Cafe: 99 Brown St, Hamilton; (03) 5571 2088

Nectar Ambrosia: 157–159 Barkly St, Ararat; (03) 5352 7344; www.nectarambrosia.com.au

Royal Mail Hotel: 98 Parker St, Dunkeld; (03) 5577 2241; www.royalmail.com.au

Roxburgh House: 64 Thompson St, Hamilton; (03) 5572 4857; www.roxburghhouse

Salingers Cafe: 98 Main St, Great Western; (03) 5356 2211

The Kookaburra Bar & Bistro: 125–127 Grampians Rd, Halls Gap; (03) 5356 4222; www.kookaburrabarbistro.com.au

The Vines Cafe: 74 Barkly St, Ararat; (03) 5352 1744

STORES

Darriwill Farm Hamilton: 169 Gray St, Hamilton; (03) 5571 2088; www.darriwillfarm.com.au/

Dunkeld Gourmet Pantry: 109 Parker St, Dunkeld; (03) 5577 2288

Fiona Wall Fine Foods Store: 89 Whyte St, Coleraine; (03) 5575 2732; www.fionawallfinefoods.com

Halls Gap Bakery: Shop 3, Stoney Creek Stores, Halls Gap; (03) 5356 4439

Nectar Ambrosia: see Eateries

'Off the Beaten Track' Wine & Art Gallery: 6669 Western Hwy, Buangor; (03) 5354 3216; www.mountcolewineworks.com.au

Smugglers Hearth: Shop 2, Stony Creek Stores, Halls Gap; (03) 5356 4383

MARKETS

Ararat Seasonal Farmers' Market: Alexandra Gardens, Vincent St; 2nd Sun each June, Sept and Dec; (03) 5355 0239

Halls Gap Primary School Craft Market: 10–14 School Rd; various Sundays (call to check); 0447 193 397

Natimuk Farmers' Market: Main St; 2nd Sun each month, morning; (03) 5387 1456

Pomonal Village Market: Ararat–Halls Gap Rd; last Sun each month; (03) 5356 6312

Stawell Fairdinkum Farm & Craft Market: Stawell Showgrounds, Patrick St; last Sat each month; (03) 5358 1947

Uncle Bobs Country Market: Napier St, St Arnaud; 2nd Sat each month; (03) 5495 1743

Wartook Community Bush Market: Wartook Pottery, Halls Gap–Horsham Rd; Easter and Sept; (03) 5383 6243

GOURMET PRODUCE

Bellellen Grampians Organics:
33 Bellellen Saleyards Rd, Stawell;
(03) 5358 1421

Deutscher's Turkey Farm: 5828 Western
Hwy, Dadswells Bridge; (03) 5359 5220

Farm Foods Hamilton: 119 Thompson
St, Hamilton; (03) 5752 4040

Glenelg Fine Chocolates: 99 Whyte St,
Coleraine; (03) 5575 2670

Grampians Honey: 21 Grahams Bridge
Rd, Haven; (03) 5382 0060

Grampians Olive Estate: 1800 065 483;
www.grampiansoliveestate.com.au

Grampians Pure Sheep Dairy: Glenelg
Hwy, Glenthompson; (03) 5577 4223

Green Eggs: 92 Green Hill La, Great
Western; (03) 5356 2458;
www.greeneggs.net.au

Greenvale Meats: 873 Willaura–Wickliffe
Rd, Willaura; (03) 5354 1343;
www.greenvale-homestead.com.au

Hopkins River Beef: Meadowbank,
PO Box 71, Dunkeld; (03) 5577 2336;
www.hopkinsriverbeef.com

Laharum Grove: 1603 Winfields Rd,
Laharum; 0429 136 319;
www.laharumgrove.com.au

Mount Ararat Olives: PO Box 384,
Ararat; (03) 5352 1751

Mount Zero Olives: 41 Mount Zero Rd,
Laharum; (03) 5383 8280 or 0412 324 683;
www.mountzeroolives.com

Red Rock Olives: Cnr Ararat–Halls
Gap Tourist Rd and Tunnel Rd, Pomonal;
(03) 5222 1005; www.redrockolives.com.au

Toscana Olives: 376 Olive Plantation Rd,
Laharum; www.toscanaolives.com.au

WINERIES

Best's Wines: 111 Best's Rd, Great Western;
(03) 5356 2250;
www.bestswines.com

Bochara Wines: 1099 Glenelg Hwy,
Bochara; (03) 5571 9309;
www.bocharawines.com.au

Grampians Estate: 1477 Western Hwy,
Great Western; (03) 5356 2400;
www.grampiansestate.com.au

Mount Cole Wineworks: 197 Mt Cole Rd,
Warrak; (03) 5354 3216;
www.mountcolewineworks.com.au

Mount Langi Ghiran: 80 Vine Rd,
Bayindeen; (03) 5354 3207;
www.langi.com.au

Norton Estate: 758 Plush Hannans Rd,
Lower Norton; (03) 5384 8235;
www.nortonestate.com.au

Seppelt Great Western: Moyston Rd,
Great Western; (03) 5361 2239;
www.seppelt.com.au

Below (left to right): casual outdoor dining at The
Vines Cafe, Ararat; Mount Cole Wineworks' cellar
door, 'Off the Beaten Track' Wine and Art Gallery
on the Western Highway, Buangor; National Trust–
classified underground 'drives' at Seppelt Great
Western; a dessert masterpiece of rhubarb, licorice,
almond and citrus at the Royal Mail Hotel, Dunkeld

Mildura and environs

The Murray River is the lifeblood of this region, resulting in the cultivation of fruit crops and the development of various riverside settlements. The city of Mildura, with its museums and galleries, excellent dining and surrounding wineries and orchards, is like a colourful Mediterranean oasis. This is an area once mainly known for its wine, table grapes, dried fruits and abundant orange crop, but today, because of one man, it is firmly on the radar of most gourmands. From humble beginnings in the cellar of his father-in-law's hotel, Quality Hotel Mildura Grand, Stefano de Pieri's name is now synonymous with this river town.

Over the years Stefano and his wife, Donata, have opened a cafe, bakery and produce store to showcase the regional bounty, an art gallery, a cellar door and bar, and are partners in a microbrewery. But dinner at **Stefano's** remains the main lure and is indeed a memorable experience. His five-course degustation menu reflects his passion for seasonal and regional produce and his northern Italian heritage. There is usually handmade silken pasta, perhaps Murray cod, and dishes created using the finest quality local lamb, beef or pork. Also in the hotel is the up-market **Spanish Bar & Grill**, considered one of the best steak restaurants in Australia. Chefs source cuts of prime beef aged on the bone from Loxton, Ouyen and Mildura farmers, cooking them over slow-burning red gum and mallee roots. As well as an eatery and a bakery, **Stefano's Cafe Bakery** is also a food store featuring quality regional produce. There are always just-baked breads, frittatas, marinated vegetables, filled focaccia, assorted cakes, slices and biscuits, a daily salad and many of Stefano's own labelled preserves and olive oils and more.

Adjacent to the Quality Hotel, **Seasons** serves uncommonly good fare – perhaps hand-rolled duck porcini ravioli with scallops, sage butter and romano pecorino or pumped mallee lamb with mashed potato and mustard fruits. At the **Mildura Brewery Pub** you can order a sample tray of five brews – Mallee Bull, Desert Premium, Honey Wheat (infused with local citrus blossom honey), Storm and Sun Light – and two seasonal brews. Housed in a former Art Deco theatre, all brews are made on site. If you are self-catering and wish to buy local saltbush lamb, grain- and grass-fed beef,

Festivals

Mildura Wentworth Arts Festival: Mar; (03) 5002 0005; www.artsmildura.com.au/wmaf

Mildura Cup Carnival: May; (03) 5032 2110; www.countryracing.com.au

Mildura Writers Festival: July; (03) 5002 0005; www.artsmildura.com.au/writers

Mildura Masters Games: biennial event, odd-numbered years, Aug; (03) 5018 8315; www.milduramasters.com.au

Mildura Country Music Festival: Sept–Oct; 1800 039 043; www.milduracountrymusic.com.au

Mildura Jazz, Food & Wine Festival: last weekend in Oct; (03) 5002 0005; www.artsmildura.com.au/jazz

Where to stay

Adventure Houseboats: luxury floating accommodation; 16 Sturt Hwy, Buronga; (03) 5023 4787 or 0427 211 469; www.adventurehouseboats.com.au

Emaroo Cottages: country-style cottages; 100 Magnolia Ave, Mildura; (08) 8595 7217; www.aperfectplace.com.au

Murray Haven on Thirteenth: country home; 118a Thirteenth St, Mildura; 0419 514 861; www.murrayhaven.com.au

Quality Hotel Mildura Grand: range of hotel rooms; Seventh St, Mildura; (03) 5023 0511; www.qualityhotelmilduragrand.com.au/

cooked yabbies and smallgoods, head for quality butchers **Wagner & Giddings**.

Using raw chocolate from the Yarra Valley's Kennedy & Wilson, the **Mildura Chocolate Company** produces excellent chocolate with flavours such as blood orange, roasted local almonds and dried local sultanas in a grape mould. The region produces 95 per cent of Australia's dried vine fruits, hence the **Australian Dried Fruits Association** offers a huge range of dried fruits and nuts including sultanas, muscatels, raisins, currants and pistachios, and dried tree-fruits such as apricots, peaches and pears, as well as locally made jams and chutneys. **The Angus Park Shop** at Irymple also specialises in dried fruits and nuts.

Over the bridge in Buronga, **Varapodio Estate** produces a wide range of items: extra virgin olive oil, pickled olives and even olive oil ice-cream (to order); homemade marinated mushrooms, eggplant and capsicum; caramelised balsamic vinegar; and local honey and almonds. Enjoy freshly squeezed orange juice from the 20-hectare orchard at **Orange World**, where Maria and Mario Mammone also grow other citrus fruits including mandarins, grapefruit, lemons, tangelos and limes, as well as avocadoes.

The historic riverside **Gol Gol Hotel** offers a good bistro menu with dishes such as salt and pepper squid and garlic prawns, grain-fed porterhouse or crumbed breast of Kulkyne chicken stuffed with mushrooms. Nearby, **Trentham Estate** winery restaurant matches food with their premium wines;

perhaps their gold-medal-winning Spanish-style Albarino to match a tangy goat's cheese tart and all with top river views. Executive chef Dag Demarkow bakes bread daily and makes a terrific dukkah using local pistachios.

The irrigated farmlands of the region are dotted with vineyards. Look for family-owned **Oak Valley Estate**, where Fred De Blasio makes muscatel and black muscatel and a very feminine Pink Contessa; and **Wooden Eye Estate**, a classy cellar door known for its semillon sauvignon blanc and chardonnay. Established more than 120 years ago by the town's founding Chaffey brothers, **Chateau Mildura** is the oldest winery on the Murray, much of the original complex now housing the Chaffey Wine & Horticultural Museum. The winery's three ranges – Smuggler, Heritage and Psyche – celebrate the rich local wine history. Out of town, **Lindemans Karadoc** has a 150-year history and is still producing first-class wines (new releases are only available at the cellar door). At Red Cliffs, **Nursery Ridge Estate** still uses traditional techniques, from hand-plunging to basket-pressing, to produce award-winning wines.

While in Mildura you may like to leave your car and take a Discover Mildura Tour to visit places not normally accessible to the public, such as award-winning pink **Murray River Salt** and the family home and table-grape vineyard **Tabletop Grapes**, owned by Gino and Elina Garreffa. Call (03) 5024 7448 for tour details.

Contacts for Mildura and environs

EATERIES

Gol Gol Hotel: Sturt Hwy, Gol Gol;
(03) 5024 8492; www.golgolpub.com.au

Seasons: Quality Hotel Mildura Grand,
Langtree Ave, Mildura; (03) 5023 0511;
www.seasonsmildura.com.au

Spanish Bar & Grill: Quality Hotel
Mildura Grand, Langtree Ave, Mildura;
(03) 5021 2377;
www.seasonsmildura.com.au

Stefano's: Quality Hotel Mildura Grand,
Langtree Ave, Mildura; (03) 5023 0511;
www.stefano.com.au

Trentham Estate: Sturt Hwy, Trentham
Cliffs; (03) 5024 8888;
www.trenthamestate.com.au

STORES

Stefano's Cafe Bakery: 27 Deakin Ave,
Mildura; (03) 5021 3627;
www.stefano.com.au

Wagner & Giddings Butchers: Cnr
Seventh St and San Mateo Ave, Mildura;
(03) 5023 1395

MARKETS

Sunraysia Farmers' Market: Australian
Inland Botanic Gardens, River Rd,
Mourquong; 1st and 3rd Sat each month;
(03) 5025 2342

GOURMET PRODUCE

Australian Dried Fruits Association:
31 Deakin Ave, Mildura; (03) 5023 5174

Mildura Chocolate Company:
141 Tenth St, Mildura; (03) 5023 6465;
www.mildurachocolateco.com.au

Murray River Salt:
(03) 5021 5355; www.sunsalt.com.au

Orange World: Silver City Hwy, Buronga;
(03) 5023 5197;
www.orangeworldmildura.com.au

Tabletop Grapes: PO Box 5101, Mildura;
(03) 5024 5355;
www.tabletopgrapes.com.au

The Angus Park Shop: 2132 Fifteenth St,
Irymple; (03) 5051 4444

Varapodio Estate: Block 60, Sturt Hwy
Buronga; (03) 5023 2292;
varapodioestate.com.au

WINERIES

Chateau Mildura: 191 Belar Ave, Irymple;
(03) 5024 5901;
www.chateaumildura.com.au

Lindemans Karadoc: Johns Ways,
Karadoc; (03) 5051 3285;
www.lindemans.com

Nursery Ridge Estate: 8514 Calder Hwy,
Red Cliffs; (03) 5024 3311

Oak Valley Estate: 3055 Deakin Ave,
Mildura South; (03) 5021 2379;
www.oakvalleyestate.com.au

Trentham Estate: see Eateries

Wooden Eye Estate: 48 Dewry Rd,
Irymple; (03) 5024 6126;
www.woodeneye.com.au

BREWERIES

Mildura Brewery Pub: 20 Langtree Ave,
Mildura; (03) 5021 5399;
www.mildurabrewery.com.au

Below (left to right): friendly service, and fresh
chillies and zucchini flowers, at Spanish Bar &
Grill, Mildura; Oak Valley Estate, Mildura South;
pavement tables at Stefano's Cafe Bakery, Mildura;
oranges are for sale throughout Mildura; Stefano de
Pieri in his restaurant kitchen

North East

Spreading south from the Murray River, the North East is a region of charming old gold towns, country hamlets that proudly showcase their bushranging heritage, and Rutherglen wineries that produce some of the world's great fortified wines. The region also boasts the thriving regional centres of Benalla and Wangaratta, the former housing one of the state's best regional art galleries and the latter offering all the services of a bustling rural city. Surrounding the population centres of the region lies a rich agricultural district that produces a diverse range of crops including kiwifruit, wine grapes, walnuts and wheat; and amid the farm country are areas of dense scrub, eucalypt woodland and tree-clad mountain ranges – once the hide-out of local bushrangers but now protected within national and state parks.

In the region's north-west is Rutherglen – its whole raison d'être revolving around wineries. They have been the heart and soul of this country community since the mid-1800s. From this early beginning, the vineyards were quick to establish an international reputation for fortified wines, particularly aged muscats, tokays and ports. Today many wineries

Above: a taste of red at Campbell's Winery, Rutherglen

Opposite (top to bottom): plating up ravioli parcels at Pickled Sisters Cafe, Wahgunyah; an eclectic mix of decor comes together at Beaumont's Cafe, Rutherglen

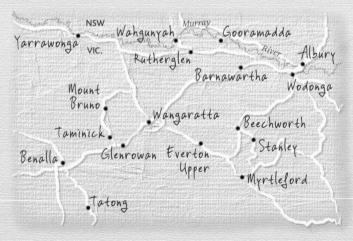

Festivals

Tastes of Rutherglen: wine festival; Mar; 1800 622 871; www.rutherglenvic.com

Trails, Tastings & Tales: Glenrowan; June (Queen's Birthday weekend); 1800 801 065; www.visitglenrowan.com

Rutherglen Winery Walkabout: June (Queen's Birthday weekend); 1800 622 871; www.rutherglenvic.com

Where to stay

1860 Luxury Accommodation: reconstructed slab hut; 4 Surrey La, Beechworth; 0408 273 783; www.1860luxuryaccommodation.com

Koendidda: historic B&B accommodation; RMB 2137, Barnawartha; (02) 6026 7340; www.koendidda.com.au

Provenance: luxury suites and fine food; 86 Ford St, Beechworth; (03) 5728 1786; www.theprovenance.com.au

The Hotel Nicholas: historic contemporary accommodation; 1A Camp St, Beechworth; (03) 5728 1051; www.hotelnicholas.com.au

The Vineyards at Tuileries: smart vineyard suites; 13–35 Drummond St, Rutherglen; (02) 6032 9033; www.tuileriesrutherglen.com.au

Above (left to right):
a rich muscat glaze
adorns a dish at
Pickled Sisters Cafe,
Wahgunyah; a seat in
the sun at Campbell's
Winery, Rutherglen;
Thai, Indian and
Moroccan influences
come to bear in
spectacular desserts
at Beaumont's Cafe,
Rutherglen; wine-
tasting at Campbell's
Winery, Rutherglen

are run by fifth- and sixth-generation winemakers
and their close familial relationship over 140 years
of continuous winemaking remains unique in
Australia's wine industry. Names like Bill Chambers,
Mick and David Morris, Norm Killeen, Bernard Gehrig
and Colin Campbell are legends in the industry.

At the end of a picturesque tree-lined driveway,
All Saints Estate, built in 1864 with a distinctive
castellated facade, is one of Australia's original
wineries and is run today by Eliza, Angela and
Nicholas Brown. The winery has a viewing area,
where you can watch winemakers handcraft the fine
wines using an old 1890 French basket press and
hand-plunging grapes in open fermentation vats. You
can sample limited-release wines at the cellar door
or move straight into **The Terrace Restaurant**, where
there are wine suggestions for each dish. Typical
offerings are suckling Rutherglen lamb, battered
Murray cod and Milawa organic chicken breast. Also
on site, you can enjoy a tasting platter of cheese
with All Saints wines at **The Indigo Cheese
Company** and buy Australian cheeses – many of

them Victorian, such as Tarago triple cream, Meredith
marinated feta and Gippsland Blue – along with
local olive oils and Jim Jam jams.

At **Campbells Winery**, sample wonderful white
wines, reds such as Bobbie Burns shiraz, and top
fortified wines; at **Jones Winery** in an enchanting
1860s stone cellar door, sample flagship shiraz from
110-year-old vines, just-released muscat and
cool-climate chardonnay; and at **Morris Wines** try
fifth-generation winemaker David Morris's multi-
award-winning durif and muscat. At **Chambers
Rosewood Winery** there is help-yourself wine-
tasting before buying some of the best-priced wines
in the region.

Attached to **Cofield's Winery**, **Pickled Sisters
Cafe** has long showcased local produce to match
with Cofield's wines. Share a vineyard platter with
their signature free-range chicken liver and muscat
pâté, free-range chicken terrine, honey- and
muscat-glazed confit duck or twice-baked Milawa
goat's cheese soufflé. **Vintara Winery & Cafe**
overlooks the Murray Valley and serves

contemporary Australian fare to match the estate-grown wines. Expect house-smoked rainbow trout with celeriac remoulade and house-baked bread, cassoulet of local rabbit with Formichi cotechino or local prime Hereford sirloin.

As elsewhere in Victoria, olives thrive among the vines. Sample naturally fermented table olives and buy award-winning extra virgin olive oils at **Gooramadda Olives**. At the mudbrick cellar door of **Calico Town Wines**, as well as wine-tasting you can buy **The Wicked Virgin Olives**, olive oil and tapenade.

Beaumont's Cafe serves some of the best food in town. You can sit in the lovely rear courtyard or dine inside on Thai, Indian, Moroccan and Italian dishes, such as their signature gnocchi, and red curry chicken. Locals catch up with friends at **Forks and Corks**, a food, wine and espresso bar serving casual meals with Mediterranean flavours, such as antipasto platters, gnocchi and gourmet steak sandwiches. And no visit to Rutherglen is complete without a visit to **Parker Pies**, where entrepreneurial owner Fred Parker has won more than a hundred awards for his pastry-filled

delights. Innovative fillings include green Thai chicken, tiger king prawns in creamy coconut and coriander sauce, lamb in mint and rosemary sauce and even crocodile and crabmeat with sweet chilli.

Wangaratta, locally known as 'Wang', is more a commercial hub than a gourmet centre. It does, however, boast the terrific **Rinaldo's Casa Cucina** restaurant, where King Valley chef Adam Pizzini mixes modern Mediterranean flavours with traditional Italian dishes. He grows his own vegetables and herbs and sources key ingredients from the region. His potato gnocchi is a knockout – perhaps with Myrrhee Welsh Black beef or King Valley free-range goat ragù.

Housed in a former tyre shop, **Tread** overlooks the Ovens River and serves very good modern Australian fare using fresh, local produce. There are traditional wood-fired pizzas but also dishes such as salmon gravlax with fennel remoulade and olive bread, pork belly with a plum purée and line-caught snapper with prawn colcannon. Just out of town, **Cherrybrook Cherry Farm** has some 4500 cherry trees and offers

Victoria

214

Above (left to right):
a sprinkle of parmesan
to finish a dish, and the
relaxed barn-like dining
space, at Rinaldo's Casa
Cucina, Wangaratta;
Cofield's Winery,
Wahgunyah; sweet
treat at Pickled Sisters
Cafe, Wahgunyah

all things cherry: fresh cherries, pipped cherries (fresh or frozen), cherry wine and more.

In the north-east of the region, steeped in history, Beechworth remains one of the best-preserved gold-rush-era towns in Victoria with more than 30 noteworthy buildings classified by the National Trust. Today its wide tree-lined streetscapes house local wine and produce stores, cafes and fine restaurants. One of the best is **Provenance Restaurant**, in an 1856 bank building, where Michael Ryan, long a champion of regional food and wine, offers à la carte as well as a six-course degustation menu and similar vegetarian list – with or without matching wines from his extensive wine cellar. Local ingredients often include Nug Nug goat, Sher wagyu beef, Stanley apples, pears, strawberries and raspberries and even white raspberries in summer. Luxury accommodation is also available here (*see* Where to stay).

The Green Shed Bistro is housed in a historic 1860s newspaper office that once covered stories such as Ned Kelly's exploits in and around the district. The menu at this casual bistro offers dishes packed with Asian and Middle Eastern flavours, particularly warming tagines and claypots to enhance the earthy flavours of the local Beechworth wines. Local Oxenbury Vineyard owners run **The Ox and Hound** and offer their Cow Hill wines to accompany the French-style fare. With an emphasis on fish and a 'from-farm-to-plate' concept, there might be Harrietville smoked trout, snapper pie or their own farmed milk-fed lamb. In season, look for their own pork and chestnut sausages and farmhouse terrine.

In a former old pub, **Wardens Food & Wine** boasts a wine bar with an interesting bar menu and offers modern Italian cuisine such as risotto with Portobello mushrooms, roasted quail with Sicilian flavours and fabulous warm spiced polenta cake. There are local and Italian wines to match (BYO on Tuesday and Wednesday nights). Visitors to town can stock up on local wines from wineries that don't have cellar doors (such as Giaconda, Castagna and Savaterre) as well as top local produce at **The Beechworth Provender**;

local fruits, nuts, saffron and more at the **Goldfields Greengrocer**; and deli products and homemade goodies from **Beechworth Pantry**.

On Sunday nights locals head for **Bridge Road Brewers**, a fun pizzeria and microbrewery with a beer-tasting menu, to sample their locally brewed ales such as Pale Ale and Australian Ale while grazing on good pizzas and pot pies (no table service). There are vineyards in the district as well; Beechworth wineries worth checking out are **Tinker's Hill Vineyard Cellar Door** in the Woolshed Valley, and **Indigo Vineyard** in the foothills of the Victorian Alps, which offers the Indigo Ultimate Taste Experience, a personal sensory journey for up to eight people.

Not far south-east of Beechworth, the tiny township of Stanley is well known for its apples – and **The Stanley Pub**. Built in 1857, this institution has a bar menu and seasonally changing bistro-style menu in the restaurant with dishes such as pan-seared scallops and black lentil salad, gnocchi with baby vegetables, Rutherglen milk-fed lamb, and their signature tarte tatin made with Stanley apples.

In the hills around Stanley, Michael and Annette Nuck have planted 300 000 crocus bulbs, which they hand harvest each autumn to produce **Stanley Saffron** – 300-millilitre vials are available at the Stanley Pub and other local outlets. Just out of Stanley you can buy quince paste, preserved lemons, Moroccan baked beans, piccalilli pickle, mango relish and fig paste, and all sorts of homemade jams including chestnut, from Maggie Mackenzie's farm-gate shop of **Jim Jam Foods**. You can pick your own blackberries, blueberries, raspberries, redcurrants, blackcurrants and American brambleberries at **High Grove Chestnut & Berry Farm** and, a little further south, buy seasonal apples, apricots, berries and nuts from a family-operated farm shop at **Snowline Fruits**.

Around the small tourist town of Glenrowan, the site of Ned Kelly's last stand, you will find more than just Kelly heritage and bushranging memorabilia. Two kilometres from town, nestled amid bushland on the slopes of Mount Glenrowan, you can join a wine school (on request; minimum of six) at

Morrisons of Glenrowan. Bob Morrison will talk you through perhaps semillon-sauvignon blanc, durif, shiraz, tempranillo or primitivo in his beautifully located mudbrick winery. A little further away, a cluster of heritage wineries is hidden in the foothills of the Warby Ranges at picturesque Taminick. Baileys Old Block Cafe at Baileys serves traditional wood-fired pizzas, terrines and salads to match their big reds, particularly their shiraz from old vines planted in 1904 and the 1920s. Also try their fruity frontignac and fortified wines (tokay and muscat) and check out the old Clydesdale stables and winemaking museum. On the same road, Nancy Reid has been serving her famous French provincial-style lunches for many years at Auldstone Cellars, built in 1891. Sip a sparkling shiraz by the fire with a Wine Taster's Platter including homemade pâté with sweet port then consider a rich vichyssoise, chicken and spinach-filled brioche or maybe pork, veal and pistachio terrine with a full-bodied red. Husband Michael makes dessert cakes such as deep-dish apple shortcake or chocolate and raisin cake – delicious with his liqueur muscat. Nearby at century-old Booths Taminick Cellars, you can meet fourth-generation winemaker James Booth and sample durif, shiraz, cabernet, trebbiano and muscat.

At the south-eastern tip of the region and just off the Hume Highway, Benalla has a surprising number of good dining options. Eat at the Benalla Gallery Cafe on a deck overlooking Lake Benalla in the town's botanical gardens. The blackboard menu changes daily depending on what's seasonal and fresh – perhaps Cajun-style chicken salad or grilled asparagus topped with smoked salmon and dill. Locals come often for the homemade cakes, slices and traditional melting moments and jam drops.

Housed in a lovely century-old building, Georgina's Restaurant offers modern Australian fare with an Asian influence with dishes such as chilli prawns, veal scaloppini and Indian-spiced squid, while the renovated 1905 Federation North Eastern Hotel serves modern regional fare including teriyaki chicken nori rolls, calamari salad and prosciutto-wrapped eye fillet. The hundred-year-old heritage building that is Raffety's Restaurant offers welcoming fires in winter and tables on a verandah in summer. Steaks are popular and there is always a pasta, risotto and fish of the day. And locals won't let them take the tangy lemon tart off the menu.

Sandy Leatham grows the beef and mutton that goes into her hearty pies, casseroles, osso buco and sausages that feature at Hook & Spoon in Benalla. She ages the beef for a minimum of three weeks, pickles onions for a month, uses cast-iron camp ovens and makes her own pasta. Gourmet pies include beef burgundy, beef with stout and mushroom, and luscious beef, fig and lemon – all in delicious homemade butter pastry.

Below (left to right): enjoying a glass of wine at Vintara Winery, Rutherglen; processing olives, and the ready-to-eat fruits, at Gooramadda Olives

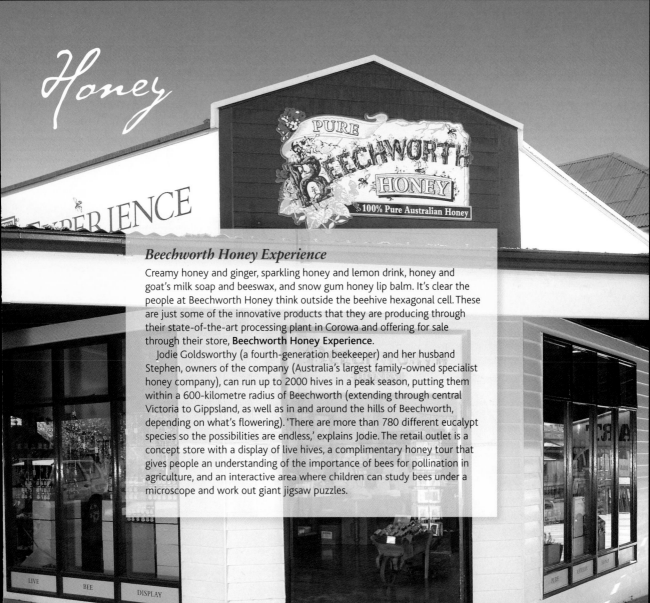

Honey

Beechworth Honey Experience

Creamy honey and ginger, sparkling honey and lemon drink, honey and goat's milk soap and beeswax, and snow gum honey lip balm. It's clear the people at Beechworth Honey think outside the beehive hexagonal cell. These are just some of the innovative products that they are producing through their state-of-the-art processing plant in Corowa and offering for sale through their store, **Beechworth Honey Experience**.

Jodie Goldsworthy (a fourth-generation beekeeper) and her husband Stephen, owners of the company (Australia's largest family-owned specialist honey company), can run up to 2000 hives in a peak season, putting them within a 600-kilometre radius of Beechworth (extending through central Victoria to Gippsland, as well as in and around the hills of Beechworth, depending on what's flowering). 'There are more than 780 different eucalypt species so the possibilities are endless,' explains Jodie. The retail outlet is a concept store with a display of live hives, a complimentary honey tour that gives people an understanding of the importance of bees for pollination in agriculture, and an interactive area where children can study bees under a microscope and work out giant jigsaw puzzles.

Contacts for North East

EATERIES

Auldstone Cellars: *see* Wineries

Baileys Old Block Cafe: 779 Taminick Gap Rd, Taminick, via Glenrowan; (03) 5766 2392; www.baileysofglenrowan.com.au

Beaumont's Cafe: 84 Main St, Rutherglen; (02) 6032 7428; www.beaumontscafe.com.au

Benalla Gallery Cafe: Bridge St East, Benalla; (03) 5762 3777; www.benallagallerycafe.com

Bridge Road Brewers: *see* Breweries

Forks and Corks: 82 Main St, Rutherglen; (02) 6032 7662

Georgina's: 100 Bridge St East, Benalla; (03) 5762 1334; www.georginas.net.au

North Eastern Hotel: 1 Nunn St, Benalla; (03) 5762 7333

Pickled Sisters Cafe: Cofield's Winery, Distillery Rd, Wahgunyah; (02) 6033 2377; www.pickledsisters.com.au

Provenance Restaurant: 86 Ford St, Beechworth; (03) 5728 1786; www.theprovenance.com.au

Raffety's Restaurant: 55 Nunn St, Benalla; (03) 5762 4066

Rinaldo's Casa Cucina: 8–10 Tone Rd, Wangaratta; (03) 5721 8800; www.rinaldos.com.au

The Green Shed Bistro: 37 Camp St, Beechworth; (03) 5728 2360

The Ox and Hound: 52 Ford St, Beechworth; (03) 5728 2123

The Stanley Pub: 1 Wallace St, Stanley; (03) 5728 6502; www.thestanley.com.au

The Terrace Restaurant: All Saints Estate, All Saints Rd, Wahgunyah; (02) 6035 2209

Tread: 56–58 Faithful St, Wangaratta; (03) 5721 4635; www.treadrestaurant.com.au

Vintara Winery & Cafe: 105 Fraser Rd, Rutherglen; 0447 327 517

Wardens Food & Wine: 32 Ford St, Beechworth; (03) 5728 1377; www.wardens.com.au

STORES

Beechworth Honey Experience: Cnr Ford and Church sts, Beechworth; (03) 5728 1432; www.beechworthhoney.com.au

Beechworth Pantry: 77 Ford St, Beechworth; (03) 5728 2456

Goldfields Greengrocer: 61 Ford St, Beechworth; (03) 5728 2303

Hook & Spoon: 16b Carrier St, Benalla; (03) 5762 2044

The Beechworth Provender: 18 Camp St, Beechworth; (03) 5728 2650

MARKETS

Hume Murray Food Bowl Farmers' Market: Gateway Village, Lincoln Causeway, Wodonga; 2nd Sat each month, morning; www.hmfb.org

Rutherglen Farmers' Market: Lions Park, Rutherglen St; 2nd Sun each month, morning; (02) 6033 6302

Tatong Farmers' Market: Tatong Tavern Hotel, 581 Benalla–Tatong Rd; 1st Sat each month, morning; (03) 5767 2210; www.tatongtavern.com

GOURMET PRODUCE

Cherrybrook Cherry Farm: 562 Jones Rd, Mt Bruno; (03) 5765 2331; www.cherryfarm.com.au

Gooramadda Olives: 1468 Gooramadda Rd, Gooramadda; (02) 6026 5658; www.olivesandoil.info

High Grove Chestnut & Berry Farm: 227 Mt Stanley Rd, Stanley; (03) 5728 6526; www.higrove.com.au

Jim Jam Foods: 89 Circular Creek Rd, Stanley; (03) 5728 6725; www.jimjam.com.au

Parker Pies: 86–88 Main St, Rutherglen; (02) 6032 9605; www.parkerpies.com.au

Snowline Fruits: 507 Stanley–Myrtleford Rd, Stanley; (03) 5728 6584

Stanley Saffron: (03) 5728 6520; www.stanleysaffron.com.au

The Indigo Cheese Company: All Saints Estate, All Saints Rd, Wahgunyah; (02) 6035 2250

The Wicked Virgin Olives: Calico Town Wines, Hopetoun Rd, Rutherglen; (02) 6032 7022; www.thewickedvirgin.com

WINERIES

All Saints Estate: All Saints Rd, Wahgunyah; (02) 6035 2222; www.prbwines.com.au

Auldstone Cellars: 296 Booth Rd, Taminick, via Glenrowan; (03) 5766 2237; www.auldstone.com.au

Baileys of Glenrowan: *see* Eateries/ Baileys Old Block Cafe

Booths Taminick Cellars: 339 Booth Rd, Taminick, via Glenrowan; (03) 5766 2282; www.taminickcellars.com.au

Calico Town Wines: *see* Gourmet Produce/The Wicked Virgin Olives

Campbells Winery: Murray Valley Hwy, Rutherglen; (02) 6032 9458; www.campbellswines.com.au

Chambers Rosewood Winery: Barkly St, Rutherglen; (02) 6032 8641; www.chambersrosewood.com.au

Cofield's Winery: Distillery Rd, Wahgunyah; (02) 6033 3798; www.cofieldwines.com.au

Indigo Vineyard: 1221 Beechworth–Wangaratta Rd, Everton Upper; (03) 5727 0233; www.indigovineyard.com.au

Jones Winery: 61 Jones Rd, Rutherglen; (02) 6032 8496; www.joneswinery.com

Morris Wines: Mia Mia Rd, Rutherglen; (02) 6026 7303; www.morriswines.com

Morrisons of Glenrowan: 30 Kays La, Glenrowan; (03) 5766 2734; www.morrisonsofglenrowan.com

Tinker's Hill Vineyard Cellar Door: 84 Sugarloaf La, Beechworth; (03) 5728 3327; www.tinkershillwines.com.au

Vintara Winery & Cafe: *see* Eateries

BREWERIES

Bridge Road Brewers: Old Coach House, Ford St, Rutherglen; (03) 5728 2703; www.bridgeroadbrewers.com.au

Left (top to bottom):
Pickled Sisters Cafe, Wahgunyah; barrel press and wine barrels at Chambers Rosewood Winery, Rutherglen

Left: ripe chestnuts at
Australian Gourmet
Chestnuts, Eurobin
Opposite: picturesque
setting at Boynton's
Feathertop Winery,
Porepunkah

Alpine Lowlands

Against a backdrop of the Victorian Alps, but away from the remoteness of the high plains and mountaintops, the Alpine Lowlands encompass the rich valleys of the Kiewa, Ovens and King rivers. With their headwaters in the Alpine National Park, high above Harrietville and Bright, these three mountain-fed streams wind through verdant green valleys and plains to the Murray River in the north of the state. This picturesque region, with its magnificent foliage in autumn and distant snow-capped peaks in winter, astounds with its diversity and quality of produce.

The flat plains of the valleys were once filled with fields of tobacco that kept this region, initially settled by Italian immigrants, economically viable in the 1950s. Rusting old drying kilns, remnants of a once-vibrant industry, still dot the landscape – some now converted into stylish accommodation. Over the years, tobacco has been replaced with quality vineyards, fruit and berry orchards, walnut, chestnut and lavender farms, olive groves and the odd hop plantation, all adding great charm to the peaceful agricultural scenes characteristic of the region. When the local railway was disbanded some years ago, 94 kilometres of rail track were converted to bicycle paths

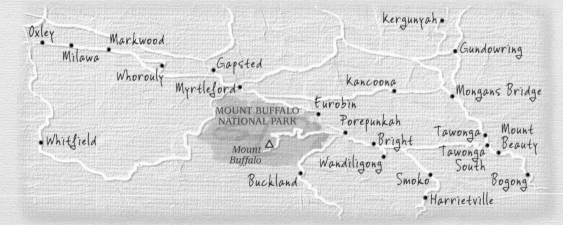

Where to stay

Lindenwarrah Country House Hotel: stylish boutique hotel; Milawa–Bobinawarrah Rd, Milawa; (03) 5720 5777; www.lancemore.com.au/lindenwarrah

Svarmisk: luxury self-contained apartments; 84 Bogong High Plains Rd, Mount Beauty; (03) 5754 4544; www.svarmisk.com.au

The Buckland Studio Retreat: eco-sensitive luxury suites; McCormack's La, Buckland; (03) 5756 2382 or 0419 133 318; www.thebuckland.com.au

The Kilns: architecturally reconstructed tobacco kilns; Cavedons La, Porepunkah: 0408 553 332; www.kilnhouse.com.au

The Odd Frog: contemporary bushland studios; 3 McFadyens La, Bright; 0418 362 791; www.theoddfrog.com

Villa Gusto: luxury Tuscan-style villa; 630 Buckland Valley Rd, Buckland; (03) 5756 2000; www.villagusto.com.au

Festivals

Mount Beauty Music Festival: Apr; (03) 5754 4008; www.musicmuster.org.au

Bright Autumn Festival: end Apr–early May; 1800 111 885; www.brightautumnfestival.org.au

Bright Spring Festival: last 2 weeks in Oct; 1800 111 885; www.brightspringfestival.com.au

Above (left to right):
olives and oils at The
Olive Shop, Milawa;
Lindenwarrah Country
House Hotel, Milawa;
relaxing in the groves
at EV Olive Groves,
Markwood; tastings
and sales at Milawa
Mustard, Milawa

to become the much-loved Rail Trail. As a natural enhancement to this, North East Valleys Food and Wine introduced a **Pedal to Produce** program, whereby you can hire bicycles fitted with wicker baskets then cycle around to cellar doors and farm-gate shops, picking up produce as you go.

If heading north on the Hume Highway from Melbourne, take the Oxley–Milawa turn-off shortly after Glenrowan. This road crosses the King River before following the Ovens River all the way to Bright. Hopefully you have brought a cooler bag so you can stop at **Blue Ox Berries** in Oxley to stock up on fresh raspberries in season (December–March), boysenberries and blackberries, and frozen berries year-round, as well as homemade berry jams, chutneys and sauces. There are wineries here too. At **Ciavarella Oxley Estate Winery**, try their excellent durif, gold-medal-winning chardonnay or zinfandel (one of the few made in the area); at **John Gehrig Wines** taste their signature riesling, chenin blanc or merlot; and at **Sam Miranda King Valley** sample their Italian-style sparkling prosecco or their flagship

Girls Block cabernet sauvignon blended with petit verdot.

There was a time when you could drive through Milawa and not realise you had done so. Now the streetscape is an enclave of gourmet food outlets and local produce is proclaimed on roadside signs, willing drivers to stop and sample the bounty of the area. With its concentration of gourmet produce, Milawa was one of the first regional produce trails in the state. At **Milawa Mustard**, housed in a charming colonial-style cottage, you can taste your way through a range of herb and flavoured mustards, chutneys, pickles, jams and vinegars, all made on the premises from mostly home-grown ingredients. **The Olive Shop** sells lots of local olives and local olive oil-related gifts, cosmetics, products and home wares. The Whitehead family of **Walkabout Apiaries** has been harvesting local blossoms for their range of honeys for more than 35 years and have a huge following for their flavoursome Mudgegonga stringybark and chestnut honey (the first in Australia) harvested from groves in the alpine region.

On Factory Road, in the historic former Murray–Goulburn butter factory, **Milawa Cheese** has been producing handmade cheeses since 1988. There are cheese tastings daily and you can sample award-winning cow's, goat's and sheep's milk cheeses – try the mild washed-rind King River Gold, mild creamy Milawa Blue and cow's milk Milawa camembert. Also on the premises is the **Milawa Bakery**, producing quality breads including French and fruit sourdoughs, while the seasonally changing menu at **The Ageing Frog Bistrot** on-site features local produce and always has a selection of gourmet pizzas topped with various local cheese and olives. At the adjacent **Milawa Chocolates** you can buy handmade delights such as fiery chilli blocks and more unusual lemon myrtle, lemon and cracked pepper and honey and mustard chocolates.

The district is supported by more than a dozen wineries including the long-established family-run **Brown Brothers**, among Australia's leading varietal winemakers. The region's first vines were planted here in 1885. You can sample wines at the cellar door or enjoy them with exceptional food at **The Epicurean Centre**, where rustic dishes are designed to complement the estate wines – perhaps roasted spatchcock with tempranillo or homemade gnocchi and cherry tomatoes with sauvignon blanc or a pinot meunier. Across the road, **Restaurant Merlot** is the stylish dining room of Lindenwarrah Country House Hotel (see Where to stay). The menu features regional wines as well as local produce – a typical entrée might be King Valley free-range pork sausage with Milawa Capricornia goat's cheese, red apple salad, Milawa honey mustard and pomegranate orange dressing.

If you can tear yourself away from Milawa, the next stop is the small hamlet of Markwood. Here you will find **EV Olive Groves**, where the olive trees thrive in the Mediterranean climate. Take a slight detour off the road to the tiny township of Whorouly and be surprised to find such a smart little store cafe as **The Whorouly Grocer**. Made of corrugated tin and fitted with retro collectibles, it stocks lovely imported pasta, cheese, gourmet fine

foods and local produce, and makes good coffee and light lunches. Farmers drop in with cases of farm-fresh produce such as Jerusalem artichokes, so you never know what you might find.

When you reach the Great Alpine Road, before heading to Myrtleford backtrack a short distance to Gapsted. In the vicinity, at **Valley Nut Groves**, let Gillian Gasser take you on a taste discovery tour of the walnut varieties her family has been growing since 1923. Back on the south side of town, you can sit on the terrace of **Gapsted Wines** overlooking the vines, while enjoying a tasting plate or à la carte lunch and sampling their innovative European-style wine varieties – perhaps the unusual Russian-style red saperavi or their luscious French-style riesling petite mansang (the only one made in Australia), both available at the cellar door only.

Although Myrtleford is the commercial centre for those travelling through to the snowfields, traders do realise locals, like skiers, need sustenance too. Housed in a 1906 converted butter factory, **The Butter Factory** is a cafe provedore that serves good

Above (left to right): luxury self-contained apartments at Svarmisk, Mount Beauty; jellies and jams for sampling at Milawa Mustard, Milawa; cafe space at The Butter Factory, Myrtleford; fresh raspberries at Blue Ox Berries, Oxley

Mediterranean-style meals, and sells loads of local produce as well as their own homemade butter and cheese. A strong supporter of slow foods, owner Naomi Ingleton also gives butter-making courses. While in this area, also check out the latest releases at the cellar door of **Michelini Wines**. Snowline Fruits (*see* North East) is also not far away.

As you head towards Bright, you pass through tiny Eurobin. Along Hughes Lane, you can dine on farmed venison and emu in the **Red Stag Restaurant** and take home packs of this and other game such as ostrich and goat. Also in town, you can sample homemade jams and fresh walnuts at **Bright Berry Farm**; buy raspberries, blueberries, blackberries, loganberries, youngberries, boysenberries, cherries, sylvanberries and blackcurrants in season; and frozen berries and ice-creams year-round. Nearby is **Australian Gourmet Chestnuts**, where Brian and Jane Casey sell chestnuts from end March to end July, harvested from their 2000 trees. Their crop is distributed locally and exported to Japan and France.

Last stop before Bright is Porepunkah. In autumn, an avenue of magnificent fiery liquid ambers announces the entrance to **Boynton's Feathertop Winery**. Try their sauvignon blanc, pinot gris and shiraz or for something different their prosecco-style sparkling, only available at the cellar door. At near neighbour **Ringer Reef** winery, on the site of an old gold mine, Bruce and Annie Holm are justly proud of their sparkling merlot and elegant rosé. And you don't have to be a cyclist to call into the cute little **Rail Trail Cafe** in town, although owner Jesse Rios does cater well for the lycra-clad legions who clamber for his sensational smoked ham, tomato and cheese toasted sandwiches, chicken and cheese quesadilla, yummy burritos, all-day breakfasts and great coffee. Just out of Porepunkah **Mount Buffalo Olives** is another good olive producer in the region.

From Porepunkah, the Buckland Valley, under the ramparts of Mount Buffalo, provides a scenic must-do detour. And it's here you'll find the wonderful Tuscan-style retreat, **Villa Gusto,** where its constantly changing five-course degustation menu reflects regional produce accompanied by High Country wines. Local ingredients on the enticing menu could be Roberts Creek duck, Milawa free-range quail, Mountain Fresh trout and salmon and Ovens Valley lamb, veal and beef. If you have time, why not stay a night or two in one of their on-site luxury suites (see Where to stay).

Bright is without doubt the autumn capital of Australia. Picturesque year-round, it literally shines from April until late May when golden and claret ashes are brilliant, elms, oaks and liquid ambers are aglow and Japanese and Canadian maples appear on fire. For many years, the sole gourmet light here was **Simone's Restaurant**, the multi-award-winning Italian restaurant of George and Patrizia Simone. Championing regional produce, Patrizia's fabulous rustic food was reason enough to visit the region. In recent years, son Anthony has joined her in the kitchen, his innovative style a happy blend with Patrizia's traditional dishes such as her signature gnocchetti (see feature, p. 227) or chestnut soup.

Poplars is a small restaurant serving French classics such as terrines, French onion soup, coq au vin, beef bourguignon and outstanding soufflés for dessert. Elsewhere you can relax over a cup of coffee at **Food Wine and Friends**. This convivial cafe stocks much local produce, and serves hearty winter soups and light lunches such as frittatas, picnic loaves and quiches all made on the premises. The region might be wine-rich, but **Bright Brewery** has a following for its many brews available on tap: fresh and natural Bright Lager, the aromatic Hellfire Amber Ale and the American-style Blowhard Pale Ale. The brewery uses fresh mountain water, home-grown grain and hops from the Alpine Valleys.

It's worth the pretty detour to Wandiligong to buy fresh apples – Fuji, Pink Lady, Golden Delicious, Red Delicious and Granny Smith – by the kilogram or box from **Nightingale Brothers Alpine Apples**; then continue on to Smoko to buy seasonal blueberries, raspberries, loganberries, tay berries, sylvan berries and blackberries from **Gunadoo Berries**. Further on at Harrietville buy or catch you own fish from **Mountain Fresh Trout and Salmon Farm**.

From Bright you can cut across to the Kiewa Valley. A right turn takes you into the foothills of Mount Bogong. The views across to this alpine peak and over the township of Mount Beauty make the ideal setting for the cutting-edge **A Skafferi**,

a Swedish-style deli (attached to luxury apartments, Svarmisk, *see* Where to stay) that serves simple platters of herring and cheese, light salads and soups. Back down the hillside at Tawonga South, **Treats Cafe** has an excellent reputation for pasta, soups, gourmet burgers, full meals and 'heat and eat' take-home foods. There are wineries in this area as well, most serving good food to complement their wines. At Tawonga try **Annapurna Estate Vineyard & Cafe**, with its contemporary fare and fabulous views, and pinot noir specialist **Bogong Estate**, which serves pizzas and Burgundian-style platters during major holidays. Near Mongans Bridge, **Ceccanti Kiewa Valley Wines** has a Tuscan-style cafe.

The Kiewa Valley runs northwards from Mount Beauty to Wodonga. Along the way you can stop at **Kancoona Valley Wines & Cafe**, then further north you pass through Upper Gundowring, where you will find **Alpine Olives**. Kiewa Valley is also home to the award-winning **Gundowring Ice Cream**, made on the family farm. Although not open for farm visits, you can sample their range of flavours a little further north in Kergunyah at **Waddington's**, a provedore and relaxed restaurant in a converted rustic timber barn. Choose perhaps from toasted honey and walnut, ginger, licorice, rhubarb, chocolate, raspberry, lime, fig or white chocolate and macadamia.

Below (left to right): beer-tasting at Bright Brewery; a relaxing late afternoon at Boynton's Feathertop Winery, Porepunkah

Gnocchetti

Simone's Umbrian gnocchetti con pomodoro
Serves 4

SAUCE

70 g butter
70 ml EV olive oil
1 onion, finely diced
salt to taste
400 g homemade tomato salsa *or*
   diced tomatoes
200 g fresh pecorino, ricotta salata
   tostata *or* parmigiano reggiano,
   to serve

GNOCCHETTI

500 g potatoes (such as Coliban),
   brushed
150 g plain flour
1 x 55 g egg
salt

Sauce method: Heat butter and oil together in a casserole pot then add onion and a little salt. Cook onions until soft. Add tomato and cook until oil separates from the sauce and sits on top. Check flavour, adding more salt if needed, ensuring the sauce remains sweet; this is the secret to this dish. Keep warm.

Gnocchetti method: Boil potatoes in their jackets until well cooked. When soft and while still warm, pass them through a mouli or push through a potato ricer (weigh to ensure you have 300 g cooked potato). Mix potato with flour and egg, add a little salt and work into a dough. Dust a work surface with a little flour, divide the dough into two equal parts and roll into long stick-like or snake shapes. Cut these into 1 cm cubes. Meanwhile, bring a large pot of salted water to the boil. Drop gnocchetti into the water, being careful not to let the water temperature drop too much. When gnocchetti rises to surface and floats, it is cooked. Carefully drain and add to sauce, mixing well with some grated pecorino. Spoon into bowl, grate extra pecorino on top, add fresh basil and serve.

Contacts for Alpine Lowlands

EATERIES

Annapurna Estate Vineyard & Cafe:
see Wineries

Food Wine & Friends: 2/6 Ireland Street,
Bright; (03) 5750 1312

Poplars: Shop 8, Star Rd, Bright;
(03) 5755 1655; www.poplars.com.au

Rail Trail Cafe: 2 Service St, Porepunkah;
0428 359 884; www.railtrailcafe.com.au

Red Stag Restaurant: 324 Hughes La,
Eurobin; (03) 5756 2365;
www.redstag.com.au

Restaurant Merlot: Lindenwarrah Country
House Hotel, 223 Milawa–Bobinawarrah Rd,
Milawa; (03) 5720 5777

Simone's Restaurant: 98 Gavan St, Bright;
(03) 5755 2266;
www.simonesrestaurant.com.au

The Ageing Frog Bistrot: Milawa Cheese,
Factory Rd, Milawa; (03) 5727 3589

The Butter Factory: 15 Myrtle St,
Myrtleford; (03) 5752 2300;
www.thebutterfactory.com.au

The Epicurean Centre: Brown Brothers,
239 Milawa–Bobinawarrah Rd, Milawa;
(03) 5720 5540;
www.brownbrothers.com.au

Treats Cafe: Bogong Ski Centre, Kiewa
Valley Hwy, Tawonga South; (03) 5754 1515

Villa Gusto: 630 Buckland Valley Rd,
Buckland; (03) 5756 2000;
www.villagusto.com.au

Waddington's: 2688 Kiewa Valley Hwy,
Kergunyah; (02) 6027 5393

STORES

A Skafferi: 84 Bogong High Plains Rd,
Mount Beauty; (03) 5754 4544;
www.svarmisk.com.au

Food Wine & Friends: see Eateries

The Butter Factory: see Eateries

The Olive Shop: 1605 Snow Rd, Milawa;
(03) 5727 3887; www.theoliveshop.com.au

The Whorouly Grocer: 577 Whorouly Rd,
Whorouly; (03) 5727 1220;
www.thewhoroulygrocer.com.au

MARKETS

Bright Market: Bright Shopping Centre;
3rd Sat each month, morning;
(03) 5755 2395

Mount Beauty Market: Main St; 1st Sat
each month, morning; (03) 5754 4097

**Myrtleford Community Produce
Market:** Anglican Church, cnr Clyde St and
Great Alpine Rd; Sat (Jan–Apr), morning;
(03) 5752 2505

GOURMET PRODUCE

Alpine Olives: 287 Mullagong Rd, Upper
Gundowring; (02) 6028 9265;
www.aplineolives.com.au

Australian Gourmet Chestnuts: 233
Hughes La, Eurobin; (03) 5756 2788;
www.cheznuts.com.au

Blue Ox Berries: 16 Smith Rd, Oxley:
(03) 5727 3397

Bright Berry Farm: 6300 Great Alpine Rd,
Eurobin; (03) 5756 2523

EV Olive Groves: Everton Rd, Markwood;
(03) 5727 0209

Gunadoo Berries: 1380 Great Alpine Rd,
Smoko; (03) 5759 2507

Gundowring Ice Cream: 1350
Gundowring Rd, Gundowring;
(02) 6027 5244;
www.gundowringfinefoods.com.au

Milawa Bakery: see Milawa Cheese below

Milawa Cheese: Factory Rd, Milawa;
(03) 5727 3589;
www.milawacheese.com.au

Milawa Chocolates: 2754 Factory Rd,
Milawa; (03) 5727 3500

Milawa Mustard: The Old Emu Inn,
Crossroads, Milawa; (03) 5727 3202;
www.milawamustard.com.au

**Mountain Fresh Trout and Salmon
Farm:** Stoney Creek Track, off Great Alpine
Rd, Harrietville; (03) 5729 2558

Mount Buffalo Olives: 307 Mt Buffalo
Rd, Porepunkah; (03) 5756 2143

Nightingale Brothers Alpine Apples:
Morses Creek Rd, Wandiligong;
(03) 5755 1318

Pedal to Produce:
www.pedaltoproduce.com.au

Valley Nut Groves: 235 Schlapps Rd,
Gapsted; (03) 5752 1251

Waddington's: see Eateries

Walkabout Apiaries: Snow Rd, Milawa;
(03) 5727 3468

WINERIES

**Annapurna Estate Vineyard &
Cafe:** 217 Simmonds Creek Rd, Tawonga;
(03) 5754 1356;
www.annapurnaestate.com.au

Bogong Estate: Cnr Mountain Creek and
Damms rds, Tawonga; (03) 5754 4347;
www.pinotnoir.com.au

Boynton's Feathertop Winery:
6619 Great Alpine Rd, Porepunkah;
(03) 5756 2356; www.boynton.com.au

Brown Brothers: 239 Milawa–
Bobinawarrah Rd, Milawa; (03) 5720 5500;
www.brownbrothers.com.au

Ceccanti Kiewa Valley Wines: 285 Bay
Creek La, Mongans Bridge; (03) 5754 5236;
www.ceccanti.com.au

Ciavarella Oxley Estate Wines: 17 Evans
La, Oxley; (03) 5727 3384;
www.oxleyestate.com.au

Gapsted Wines: 3897 Great Alpine Rd,
Gapsted; (03) 5751 1383;
www.victorianalpswinery.com.au

John Gehrig Wines: 80 Gehrigs Rd, Oxley;
(03) 5727 3395;
www.johngehrigwines.com.au

Kancoona Valley Wines & Cafe:
123 Morgans Creek Rd, Kancoona;
(02) 6028 9419

Michelini Wines: Great Alpine Rd,
Myrtleford; (03) 5751 1990;
www.micheliniwines.com.au

Ringer Reef: 6835 Great Alpine Rd,
Porepunkah; (03) 5756 2805;
www.ringerreef.com.au

Sam Miranda King Valley:
1019 Snow Rd, Oxley; (03) 5752 3888;
www.sammiranda.com.au

BREWERIES

Bright Brewery: 121 Great Alpine Rd,
Bright; (03) 5755 1301;
www.brightbrewery.com.au

COOKING SCHOOLS

The Butter Factory: *see* Eateries

Left (top to bottom): The Butter Factory,
Myrtleford; ultra-modern interior of Svarmisk,
Mount Beauty

Alpine Lowlands

GREAT GOURMET WEEKENDS *in Australia*

South Australia

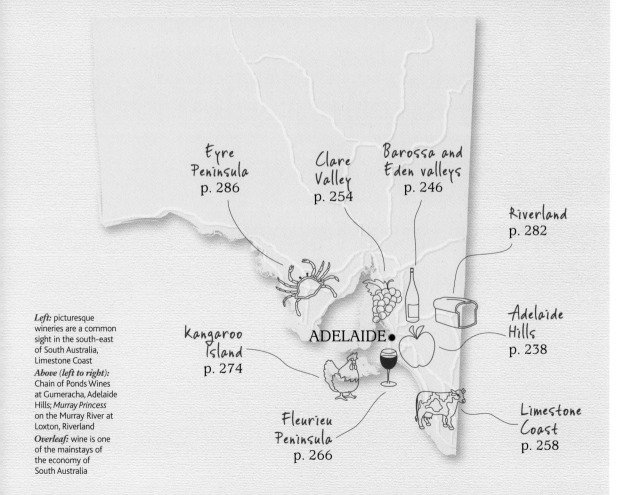

Eyre
Peninsula
p. 286

Clare
Valley
p. 254

Barossa and
Eden valleys
p. 246

Riverland
p. 282

Left: picturesque
wineries are a common
sight in the south-east
of South Australia,
Limestone Coast
Above (left to right):
Chain of Ponds Wines
at Gumeracha, Adelaide
Hills; *Murray Princess*
on the Murray River at
Loxton, Riverland
Overleaf: wine is one
of the mainstays of
the economy of
South Australia

Kangaroo
Island
p. 274

ADELAIDE

Adelaide
Hills
p. 238

Fleurieu
Peninsula
p. 266

Limestone
Coast
p. 258

Adelaide

Adelaide's climate and Mediterranean ethos encourage unhurried, open-air eating. And Adelaidians also know a thing or two about wine, with the Barossa, McLaren Vale and Adelaide Hills on their doorstep.

Adelaide ~ an overview

No other Australian capital has more food and wine blessings. The sheer proximity of so much fine produce gives Adelaide's chefs, and diners, a real edge. Whatever you choose from a restaurant menu, the chances are the ingredients have come fresh from a grower, farm gate or fishing boat within an hour or so from your table. There's no greater demonstration of these natural assets and the town's heady mix of cultural traditions than at Adelaide's Central Market. A few minutes here is enough to pique even the most jaded palate. And the constellation of eateries – be they Greek, Chinese, Argentinean, Italian, Thai, French, Indian or Spanish – on nearby Grote and Gouger streets is nothing short of phenomenal.

Being compact, there's a real sense of ease to the Adelaide dining experience. In half an hour you can be savouring seafood at a waterfront table overlooking Gulf St Vincent or enjoying pastoral bliss in the lush foothills. This ease extends to dining styles, with a climate and Mediterranean ethos that encourages unhurried, open-air eating. And Adelaidians also know a thing or two about wine. Having the Barossa, McLaren Vale and Adelaide Hills so close, adds terrific impetus to the local food scene – the shared passion for flavour and freshness. It's all part of a free flow of ideas between city and country, growers and consumers, and many different cultures.

OUTER-CITY GOURMET EXPERIENCES
* Bottega Rotolo
* Dhaba @ The Spice Kitchen
* El Choto
* Estia
* Penfolds Magill Estate
* Sammy's on the Marina
* Sarah's Cafe
* The Edinburgh Hotel & Cellars
* Utopia @ Waterfall Gully
* Windy Point Restaurant

See following pages...

Outer-city gourmet experiences

Here are some very good restaurants and provedores located outside the CBD but well worth the slight detour.

Above *(left to right)*: regional Indian dish at Dhaba @ The Spice Kitchen, Leabrook; cellar at Penfolds Magill Estate, Magill; Utopia @ Waterfall Gully; cheeseboard enticements at Bottega Rotolo, Norwood

Bottega Rotolo: Adelaide's finest gourmet food outlet with a fabulous collection of imported cheeses, artisan breads, oils and spices; 7 Osmond Tce, Norwood; (08) 8362 0455; www.bottegarotolo.com.au

Dhaba @ The Spice Kitchen: restaurant, cooking school and spice provedore, where chef Ragini Dey turns out inspired regional Indian dishes; 252 Kensington Rd, Leabrook; (08) 8431 4288; www.spicekitchen.com.au

El Choto: fun Spanish delicatessen with a range of brilliant cheeses, fine jamón, herb and spice mixes, chorizo, and coffee and churros too; 124 Port Rd, Hindmarsh; (08) 8346 1267; www.elchoto.com.au

Estia: casual seaside dining at its best – traditional Greek island mezedakia with flavour-rich dips and pita bread, grilled cheeses, meatballs and fried seafood; 255 Seaview Rd, Henley Beach Square; (08) 8353 2875; www.estia.com.au

Penfolds Magill Estate: striking venue honouring the birthplace of iconic Penfolds wines, where vine and city vistas accompany matchings of artful food and wine; 78 Penfold Rd, Magill; (08) 8301 5551; www.penfolds.com

Sammy's on the Marina: award-winning seafood restaurant featuring Greek-inspired dishes and platters in a busy, atmospheric waterfront locale; Marina Pier, Holdfast Shores, Glenelg; (08) 8376 8211; www.sammys.net.au

Sarah's Cafe: an enduring haven of fresh, unfussy vegetarian food, such as fragrant soups, rich moussaka and succulent pastry parcels (a house specialty); 117 Semaphore Rd, Semaphore; (08) 8449 5817

The Edinburgh Hotel & Cellars: hugely popular all-purpose bar, eatery and meeting place, where the bottle shop is a legendary treasure trove of Australian and imported wines; 1–7 High St, Mitcham; (08) 8373 2700; www.edinburgh.com.au

Utopia @ Waterfall Gully: historic gully hideaway provides an evocative setting for well-executed modern Australian cuisine with great local produce and wines; 170 Waterfall Gully Rd, Waterfall Gully; (08) 8379 2488; www.waterfallgully.com.au

Windy Point Restaurant: sublime views across Adelaide's twinkling city lights are the backdrop to this fine dining experience showcasing contemporary Australian cuisine; Windy Point Lookout, Belair Rd, Belair; (08) 8278 8255; www.windypoint.com.au

Adelaide Hills

When it comes to heavenly food and wine, the city of churches is truly blessed. No other Australian capital has such a bounty of produce right on its doorstep, and the Adelaide Hills is a mere 30-minute drive east across the ranges. Beyond Mount Lofty's summit ridge lies a wondrous patchwork of rolling hills, woodland and fertile river flats. Good rainfall and a cool climate have made these valleys a treasured source of vegetables and fruit, including cherries, apples, pears and raspberries. Recent years have also seen extensive vineyard plantings and a growing community of artisan bakers, brewers, cheesemakers, herb-growers and chocolatiers.

The fun begins in Piccadilly Valley, just below Mount Lofty's shaggy crown of stringybarks. With the best views in the hills, **Mount Lofty House** (*see also* Where to stay) is both a popular summer dining spot and an excellent breakfast venue for getting your bearings. Look out for local goodies such as venison, Lenswood apples and goat's cheese on the dinner menu plus an array of house-grown herbs and vegetables. Vineyards now crisscross the valleys below including those of pinot noir maestro Stephen George at **Ashton Hills Vineyard**, and nearby family-owned **Barratt Wines**. The latter also produces award-winning pinot noir, sourcing grapes from two small vineyards – Uley, where the cellar door is located, and Bonython.

As the South Eastern Freeway sweeps through the hills, every exit leads to a village with a compelling food story. The gateway town of Stirling has a fine range of suppliers and eateries. **The Organic Market and Cafe** is ever popular so drop in to try their super-fresh soups, salads, and bruschetta – there's also an Aladdin's cave of organic produce to explore. For crusty French-style breads and succulent pastries pay a visit to **Woodbake** down on the main street. As eateries go, **The Locovore** is proudly parochial: it only serves ingredients sourced within a hundred-mile radius. Offerings include tapas-style dishes highlighting local olives, almonds and smallgoods and heftier mains accented with hills-grown vegetables and herbs, including native pepper and lemon myrtle. The revamped **Stirling Hotel Bistro** has won a strong local following for its modern Australian fare – expect dishes such as lushly sauced lamb shanks or barbecued kangaroo fillet, plus there is often a tempting seafood special.

Festivals

Crush Adelaide Hills Wine & Food Festival: late Jan; 1300 305 577; www.crushfestival.com.au

Kuitpo Continuous Picnic: food and wine at 3 vineyards; Kuitpo; mid-June; (08) 8388 3700

Meadows Country Fair: Meadows Oval, Mawson Rd; 3rd Sun in Oct; 0438 114 994; www.meadowscountryfair.com.au

Where to stay

Cladich Pavilions: stylish contemporary B&B; 27–29 Wilpena Tce, Aldgate; (08) 8339 8248; www.cladichpavilions.com

Hannah's Cottage: self-contained cottages; Lot 14 Jones Rd, Balhannah; (08) 8388 4148; www.hannahscottage.com.au

Mount Lofty House: luxury boutique country house hotel; 74 Mt Lofty Summit Rd, Crafers; (08) 8339 6777; www.mtloftyhouse.com.au

The Manna of Hahndorf: suites, spa rooms and self-contained accommodation; 25 Main St, Hahndorf; (08) 8388 1000; www.themanna.com.au

Thorngrove Manor: private suites in a fantasy-style castle; 2 Glenside La, Stirling; (08) 8339 6748; www.slh.com/thorngrove

Above (left to right): scenic vineyard view at K1 by Geoff Hardy, Kuitpo; food preparation at Petaluma Restaurant, Bridgewater; Longview Vineyard, Macclesfield; Udder Delights, Hahndorf

Stirling is also home to the **Sticky Rice Cooking School**, with hands-on classes in Asian cuisine (no on-site accommodation). At nearby Heathfield you can visit **Nirvana Organic Farm**, a biodynamic orchard producing seasonal nuts and berries, where you can stock up on jams, marmalades, mustards and chutneys or choose from fresh raspberries, mulberries, gooseberries and blackcurrants in season.

A rolled-gold hills highlight is tucked away at the Bridgewater Mill, home to both Petaluma's cellar door and one of Australia's most acclaimed regional diners, **Petaluma Restaurant**. Wine industry visionary Brian Croser founded Petaluma and helped put the hills on the map as a versatile cool-climate wine region. The restaurant, housed in a heritage-listed restored stone flour mill, provides a rare opportunity to taste the full Petaluma oeuvre in the company of top-flight cuisine devised by executive chef Le Tu Thai. His seasonal lunch menus are graced with masterful flavour twists – everything from an ox-cheek pie with celeriac purée, figs and lager sauce,

to dapper desserts such as a coconut crème mille-feuille with roasted mango, green-tea ice-cream and passionfruit gel.

The hills form a vivid seasonal landscape and back-road drives to towns in the region's south, such as Echunga, Meadows and Macclesfield, are a delight in the colourful phases of spring and autumn. Apart from the historic pubs and bakeries there are hidden gems. At Macclesfield, **Longview Vineyard**, a former dairy farm, is now a postcard-perfect cellar door where a strong wine selection and vine views are teamed with an excellent tapas menu. There's even accommodation on site. A few minutes further south in the ranges, at Kuitpo, lurks **K1 by Geoff Hardy**, a lakeside chalet-style cellar door that somehow manages to be even more breathtaking. As well as crackerjack reds be sure to try Geoff's acclaimed arneis, a rare but zesty Italian white varietal.

If anything, the spread of vineyards is even more pronounced north of the freeway around Balhannah and Hahndorf. To savour examples of definitive Hills cool-climate chardonnay, shiraz, and sauvignon

blanc, visit the vineyards of **Shaw & Smith** (Balhannah) and nearby **Hahndorf Hill Winery** (also close to The Cedars, home of artist Hans Heysen). The latter also offers 'ChocoVino', an intriguing taste-matching experience of the label's red wines with premium chocolate. Yet more food and wine synergy is on offer at **The Lane Vineyard Bistro**, where breathtaking views north along the Onkaparinga Valley set the scene for a serious menu married to estate-crafted wines. Expect combos such as fresh and fleshy tuna carpaccio alongside the lemony zing of the sauvignon blanc semillon, or a rich viognier to go with braised pork belly partnered by squid and herb salad. **Nepenthe** has several vineyards in this area but the cellar door is at their Balhannah winery. In weekends you can enjoy a regional cheese platter with estate-grown sauvignon blanc, chardonnay and pinot noir (they won an award for the best chardonnay in the world in 2007). A willingness to toy with blends is evident at **Leabrook Estate** with Colin Best's 'Three-region' shiraz and cabernet sauvignon. The winery also turns

out excellent regional examples of pinot noir and chardonnay that are handcrafted and built to last.

German food heritage endures in Hahndorf with a string of main-street outlets serving all manner of wursts and kuchen. More recent traditions are on display at **Udder Delights** (*see* feature, p. 243), where the lushness of local pastures is reflected in a terrific range of goat and cow cheeses. At the eastern end of the street, take time to call in to **Beerenberg Strawberry Farm**, where you can pick your own delicious berries between mid-October and May. The on-site shop stocks the full range of Beerenberg jams, chutneys, sauces, jellies, mustards, pickles and more. If you are after something sweeter, visit **Chocolate @ No5**, a rustic 1850s cottage in Hahndorf's main street, for a selection of artfully decadent desserts, cakes and truffles. Offerings range from the simplicity of crisp Belgian sugar waffles to the ethereal layering in their mocha walnut gateaux.

The most recent addition (mid-2010) to the Hahndorf dining scene is **The Haus Hahndorf**, a cafe-bar open daily for breakfast, lunch and dinner.

This architect-designed eatery boasts an extensive menu using the freshest of local produce and a wide-ranging cellar showcasing local wines. Expect entrées such as rabbit and prune terrine with muscatel gel followed by traditional favourites such as steak and kidney pie or lamb shanks on creamy mash. There are German specialties, of course, and all come with sauerkraut, creamy potato bake and Beerenberg mustard. **Cocolat** in Balhannah is a specialist 'dessert cafe' where you can indulge in truffles, house-made gelato and cakes such as the notorious 'Wild Thing', a toffee-capped chocolate sponge pumped with chocolate mousse and plastered in dark ganache.

Located at Verdun, between Hahndorf and Balhannah, **Grumpy's Brewhouse** caters for those who long for a beer amid all this emphasis on wine. An all-grain boutique microbrewery, beers are made by hand using imported fine malts and hops and spring water from Mount Lofty. An on-site eatery serves up wood-fired pizzas. Returning to the wine theme, further east at Nairne you can savour **Howard Vineyard** wines at the cellar door or at the on-site **Pardalote Bistro**. Light lunches are the go on Saturday and during the week while Sunday has a popular tapas menu to match with the estate-grown cool-climate whites and reds.

Meanwhile, further up the valley to the north, Kris Lloyd continues to blaze the trail with a brilliant artisan selection at **Woodside Cheese Wrights**. Look out for her Capricorn, a luscious seasonal rendition of camembert using goat's milk, and the multi-award-winning Edith, an intense, ash-rolled chèvre. Woodside is also the home of **Melba's Chocolate Factory**, a full-on confectionary emporium. Here too is **Bird in Hand**, where the Nugent family not only produce an outstanding selection of estate wines, including sparkling pinot noir, but have their own range of olives and cold-pressed olive oils as well.

Further north, the old Onkaparinga Woollen Mill in the historic township of Lobethal has evolved into a real food and wine hub for the district. As well as the **Hills Market Kitchen** cooking school and the **Adelaide Hills Market** produce outlet, several boutique wine labels also have a presence here, including the talented team at **Tilbrook Estate**, whose small winery is on site. Their poised yet powerful sauvignon blanc and chardonnay are among the best in the hills. The relaxed **Golding Wines** cellar door is a unique opportunity to sample the local expression of sauvignon blanc alongside their own version of the same varietal from New Zealand's famous Marlborough region – plus a judicious blend of the two. The cellar door also offers cheese platters to enjoy indoors or out. Beer lovers will relish the handcrafted brews at the nearby **Lobethal Bierhaus**. Award-winning styles on tap include their intensely hopped India Pale Ale and Bohemian Philsner, a classic lighter, cold-fermented lager. As well as a cellar door, this microbrewery also has a restaurant and beer garden on site.

In the upper reaches of the Adelaide Hills carefully tended rows of apple and pear trees line steep-sided valleys. There's a lot to explore in the hidden landscapes around Lenswood and Gumeracha, including roadside fruit stalls and, increasingly, cellar doors. The high-country vineyards hereabouts are the unsung heroes of many big-name cool-climate wines. And being on site with the growers and makers is like having a backstage pass. At **Chain of Ponds** at Gumeracha, along with the estate-grown wines you can settle in for some substantial fare. Downstairs there's **Cafe Novello**, where you can tuck into a hearty pie or antipasto platter. Meanwhile, upstairs **The Balcony Restaurant** does full three-course dining. Expect Mediterranean dishes such as lemon and rosemary chicken breast involtini, or pork belly with eggplant ragoût – robust flavours that mesh well with this grower's strong suite of Italian varietals including nebbiolo and sangiovese.

Italian influences are dotted throughout the hills and, on the region's far northern outskirts, Tony Pipicella of **Uleybury Wines** has been scooping up awards for his handcrafted wines, especially his aged semillon. This variety seems to thrive on the warmer slopes around One Tree Hill, producing a ripe, richer style that nevertheless retains the necessary structure for long-term bottle maturation. On weekends the cellar door is also the venue for lunchtime wood-oven pizzas and tapas platters at **Bottega Restaurant**, while on Friday and Saturday nights the family turn out classic, big-flavoured pasta, and chicken and seafood dishes to complement their impressive wine selection.

Cheese

Udder Delights Cheese Cellar in Hahndorf

It all began with Nell and Nora, two goats that Trevor Dunford and wife, Estelle, bought back in 1995 to get their new farm rolling. Before long the herd was forty-strong and producing more milk than the Dunfords could sell. So necessity gave birth to the notion of cheesemaking. Four years later their daughter Sheree found herself in charge of the fledgling factory and learning on the job the subtle craft of creating artisan cheeses. Together with husband Saul, Sheree has steadily expanded the range to include versatile goat curd and chèvre styles along with distinctive goat's feta, brie and camembert. The latter is a standout for lovers of pungent, gooey Normandy-style camembert. Other highlights include Oscar, an ash-rolled goat's cheese with piquant aged characters, and their cow's milk Heysen Blue. The full complement of cheeses is up for tasting at the Udder Delights Cheese Cellar in Hahndorf, where Sheree also conducts specialist cheese- and wine-tasting sessions and her 'Easy Cheesey' cheesemaking classes.

Contacts for Adelaide Hills

EATERIES

Bottega Restaurant: *see* Wineries/
Uleybury Wines

Cafe Novello: *see* Wineries/Chain of Ponds
Wines

Mount Lofty House: 74 Mt Lofty Summit
Rd, Crafers; (08) 8339 6777;
www.mtloftyhouse.com.au

Pardalote Bistro: *see* Wineries/Howard
Vineyard

Petaluma Restaurant: Bridgewater Mill,
389 Mt Barker Rd, Bridgewater;
(08) 8339 9200; www.petaluma.com.au

Stirling Hotel Bistro: 52 Mount Barker
Rd, Stirling; (08) 8339 2345;
www.stirlinghotel.com.au

The Balcony Restaurant: *see* Wineries/
Chain of Ponds Wines

The Haus Hahndorf: 38 Main Rd,
Hahndorf; (08) 8388 7555;
www.haushahndorf.com.au

The Lane Vineyard Bistro: Ravenswood
La, Hahndorf South; (08) 8388 1250;
www.thelane.com.au

The Locavore: 1/49 Mt Barker Rd, Stirling;
(08) 8339 4416; www.thelocavore.com.au

The Organic Market & Cafe: 5 Druids
Ave, Stirling; (08) 8339 4835;
www.organicmarket.com.au

STORES

Beerenberg Strawberry Farm: *see*
Gourmet Produce

The Organic Market & Cafe: *see*
Eateries

MARKETS

Adelaide Hills Market: Old Woollen Mill,
1 Adelaide Rd, Lobethal; Fri–Sun;
(08) 8339 5615; www.marketsatheart.com

Echunga Market: Echunga Institute
carpark, Adelaide Rd; 1st Sat each month,
morning; (08) 8388 6457

Gumeracha Country Markets:
Gumeracha Town Hall, Albert St; 3rd Sun
each month; (08) 8389 1149;
www.gumeracha.com.au

Hahndorf Craft and Produce Market:
St Michaels Lutheran Church carpark; 4th
Sat each month, morning; (08) 8388 4578

Littlehampton Country Market:
Littlehampton War Memorial; 2nd Sat each
month, morning; 0435 017 991

Macclesfield Village Market: Davenport
Sq or Macclesfield Institute; Sun;
(08) 8388 9414

Meadows Country Market: Meadows
Memorial Hall; 2nd Sun each month;
(08) 8388 3224

Mylor Country Market: Mylor Oval;
1st Sun each month; (08) 8388 5334

Stirling Market: Druids Ave; 4th Sun each
month; 0418 877 124;
stirlingmarket.com.au

Uraidla Produce Market: Uraidla
Institute; 1st and 3rd Sun each month;
(08) 8339 3256

Wistow Country Market: Wistow Hall
and carpark; 3rd Sat each month, morning;
(08) 8391 5440

Woodside Market: Woodside Institute;
3rd Sat each month; (08) 8388 489

GOURMET PRODUCE

Beerenberg Strawberry Farm: Mount
Barker Rd, Hahndorf; (08) 8388 7272;
www.beerenberg.com.au

Chocolate @ No5: 5 Main St, Hahndorf;
(08) 8388 1835; www.chocolateno5.com.au

Cocolat: 83 Main Rd, Balhannah; (08) 83883 4666; www.cocolat.com.au

Melba's Chocolate Factory: Henry St, Woodside; (08) 8389 7868; www.melbaschocolates.com

Nirvana Organic Farm: 184 Longwood Rd, Heathfield; (08) 8339 2519; nirvanaorganicfarm.blogspot.com

Udder Delights: 91a Main St, Hahndorf; (08) 8388 1588; www.udderdelights.com.au

Woodbake: 73 Mt Barker Road, Stirling; (08) 8339 6757

Woodside Cheese Wrights: 22 Henry St, Woodside; (08) 8389 7877; www.woodsidecheese.com.au

WINERIES

Ashton Hills Vineyard: Tregarthen Rd, Ashton; (08) 8390 1243; a.h.v@bigpond.net.au

Barratt Wines: Uley Vineyard, Cornish Rd (off Collins Rd), Summertown; (08) 8390 1788; www.barrattwines.com.au

Bird in Hand: Cnr Bird in Hand and Pfeiffer rds, Woodside; (08) 8389 9488; www.birdinhand.com.au

Chain of Ponds Wines: Adelaide–Mannum Rd, Gumeracha; (08) 8389 1415; www.chainofponds.com.au

Golding Wines: Western Branch Rd, Lobethal; (08) 8389 5120; www.goldingwines.com.au

Hahndorf Hill Winery: Pains Rd, Hahndorf; (08) 8388 7512; www.hahndorfhillwinery.com.au

Howard Vineyard: Lot 1 Bald Hills Rd, Nairne; (08) 8188 0203; www.howardvineyard.com.au

K1 by Geoff Hardy: Tynan Rd, Kuitpo; (08) 8388 3700; www.k1.com.au

Leabrook Estate: Cnr Greenhill and Reserve rds, Balhannah; (08) 8398 0421; www.leabrookestate.com.au

Longview Vineyard: Pound Rd, Macclesfield; (08) 8388 9694; www.longviewvineyard.com.au

Nepenthe: Jones Rd, Balhannah; (08) 8398 8899; www.nepenthe.com.au

Petaluma: Bridgewater Mill cellar door, 389 Mt Barker Rd, Bridgewater; (08) 8339 9222; www.petaluma.com.au

Shaw & Smith: Lot 4 Jones Rd, Balhannah; (08) 8397 0500; www.shawandsmith.com

Tilbrook Estate: Building 17, Old Woollen Mill, 1 Adelaide–Lobethal Rd, Lobethal; (08) 8389 5318

The Lane Vineyard: see Eateries

Uleybury Wines: Uley Rd, One Tree Hill; (08) 8280 7335; www.uleybury.com

BREWERIES

Grumpy's Brewhaus: 115 Mount Barker Rd, Verdun; (08) 8188 1133; www.grumpys.com.au

Lobethal Bierhaus: Old Woollen Mills, 3A Main St, Lobethal; (08) 8389 5570; www.ahcb.com.au

COOKING SCHOOLS

Hills Market Kitchen: 1 Adelaide Lobethal Rd, Lobethal; (08) 8389 5615;

Sticky Rice Cooking School: 96 Old Mount Barker Rd, Stirling; (08) 8339 1314; www.stickyricecookingschool.com.au

Below (left to right): Longview Vineyard, Macclesfield; learning the art of spice-making at Sticky Rice Cooking School, Stirling; Howard Vineyard, Nairne; Hahndorf Hill Winery, Hahndorf; Stirling Hotel Bistro, Stirling; dining at Chain of Ponds Wines, Gumeracha

Barossa and Eden valleys

There's nowhere else quite like the Barossa. As one of the world's most revered wine regions, it's hardly surprising the view from Mengler Hill east of Tanunda reveals a grand patchwork of vineyards. But if you look more closely you will see the valley's tidy grid of roads is also dotted with hamlets, farms and needle-sharp church spires. The waves of German immigrants who settled here from the 1840s created a village life founded on artisan trades, religious faith, music and family-grown produce. These close-knit traditions endure and over six generations they have melded with a big-hearted Australian spirit to create a unique expression of place – rich, earthy and decidedly flavoursome.

This heritage is there for the tasting. This is the location of food doyen Maggie Beer's farm shop (near Nuriootpa). And every town boasts fine butchers, bakers and eateries, while the highways and byways are dotted with cellar doors. There are more than 70 venues for sampling the Barossa's wine styles, ranging from legends such as Yalumba and Penfolds, to a bevy of boutique producers. Behind the scenes some 700 grape-growing families secure the lifeblood of the region, tending to a priceless collection of vines.

Above: Jacob's Creek vineyard at Rowland Flat

Opposite (top to bottom): Maggie's Farm Shop at Nuriootpa; netted vines at Henschke Wines, Keyneton

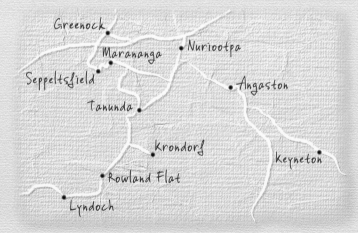

Festivals

Barossa Vintage Festival: various venues; biennial event, odd-numbered years, Apr; (08) 8563 0663; www.barossavintagefestival.com.au

Stew and Shiraz: Whistler Wines, Seppeltsfield Rd, Marananga; June (Queen's Birthday weekend); (08) 8562 4942

Barossa Gourmet Weekend: 66–68 Murray St, Tanunda; mid-Aug; (08) 8563 0600

Where to stay

Abbotsford Country House: traditional country retreat; Yaldara Dr, Lyndoch; (08) 8524 4662; www.abbotsfordhouse.com

Caithness Manor: antique-furnished B&B; 12 Hill St, Angaston; (08) 8564 2761; www.caithness.com.au

Goat Square Cottages: self-contained town houses; 33 John St, Tanunda; (08) 8524 5353; www.goatsquarecottages.com.au

The Louise: luxury vineyard retreat; cnr Seppeltsfield and Stonewell rds, Marananga; (08) 8562 2722; www.thelouise.com.au

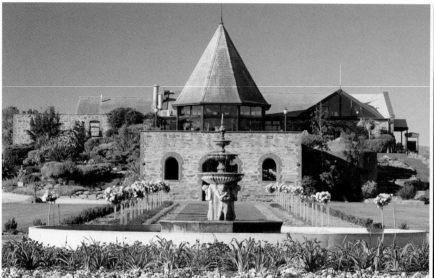

248

Above (left to right): impressive facilities at Grant Burge Wines, Tanunda; cappuccino at Blond Coffee, Angaston; irresistible offering of French toast with bananas at Maggie's Farm Shop, Nuriootpa; aged vine at Langmeil Winery, Tanunda

Best known for its plush, ripe shiraz, the Barossa comprises many subregions and soil types, each lending distinctive character to the fruit they grow. The most obvious division is between the valley floor – a stronghold for shiraz, grenache, mourvèdre and semillon – and the cooler reaches of the Barossa Ranges and Eden Valley where riesling, chardonnay and cabernet sauvignon flourish. The elevated wine-producing area of Eden Valley is regarded as a distinct region (only a small number of wineries here are open for tastings).

Approaching the Barossa from the south, the Barossa Valley Way extends through the valley gateway town of Lyndoch, which sets the scene. **Lyndoch Bakery & Restaurant** is both an outlet for traditional German fare such as sourdough loaves, pretzels and cakes as well as a restaurant for light meals. Tuck in to the authentic German offerings or opt for some of the Thai or Indian-influenced dishes.

Similarly, the family at nearby **Kies Wines** don't just tend a cellar door for their home-grown wines

but also provide a lunch cafe on site, serving light meals, plus an outlet for their specialist tea blends.

On the other end of the scale, the visitor centre at **Jacob's Creek**, up the road at Rowland Flat, is an imposing architectural statement, as befits a global brand. Yet **Jacob's Restaurant** also aims for authentic wine and food marriages, with this label's reserve range varietals teamed with local flavours such as local free-range pork cutlet wrapped in bacon with roesti and sauerkraut. And the views are spectacular. Between Rowland Flat and Tanunda, **Grant Burge Wines** nestles in picturesque landscaped gardens on the banks of Jacob Creek. As well as their shiraz and Semillon, try their late-harvest muscat.

There are many famous side roads but none more celebrated than Krondorf Road through the historic locality of Krondorf, just south of Tanunda. Here the virtues of old vines, traditional techniques and innovative thinking come together at **Rockford Wines**, where winemaker Robert O'Callaghan has mentored many of the industry's leading lights. While best known for their acclaimed and scarce

Basket Press Shiraz, Rockford's other wines, including their single vineyard series and Growers Semillon, are worth sampling. **Charles Melton Wines** is a little further along (*see* feature, p. 252*)* and further still is **Kabminye Wines**, with its cellar door and eatery housed in a barn-like building with stunning views overlooking the ranges. The vineyard showcases unusual varieties such as cinsaut, carignan and black frontignac as well as local shiraz and cabernet sauvignon. It is also home to the renowned **Krondorf Road Cafe**, where Ingrid Glastonbury honours the food traditions of her Silesian forebears with dishes such as smoky kassler with sweet and sour white cabbage, and unctuous blackobst (poached fruit) desserts.

On the southern side of Tanunda, long-established **Turkey Flat Vineyards** made its name with spicy crisp rosé. Its cellar door is housed in an old bluestone building, once the Schulz family butcher's shop. The town itself is the historic heart of the valley and a natural meeting place. Walk the backstreets and sites such as Goat Square to get the

feel of the village in earlier days. **Apex Bakery** offers unpretentious German cakes and honey biscuits baked in a wood oven that has been going since the 1920s. Among the town's many eateries, the **1918 Bistro & Grill** is a perennial local haunt with a homely atmosphere, with log fires in winter and a menu that straddles Mediterranean and Asian influences. That means everything from a rabbit and pistachio terrine with pickled cherries to a miso-crusted kangaroo fillet atop a soba noodle and mizuna salad. Tanunda is also the home base of **Carême Pastry**, which specialises in superb gourmet handcrafted pastry products, sold nationwide. Locally you can buy their products at Carême Patisserie at the Barossa Farmers' Market every Saturday morning in Angaston. The company also hosts a number of cooking classes and demonstrations throughout the year at various locations.

Some great vineyards encircle the north-western aspect of town. **Langmeil Winery** is custodian of shiraz vines dating back to 1843, growing on a small single vineyard that produces the mighty Freedom

Shiraz. And their other red blends, including the more reasonably priced Valley Floor Shiraz, and Eden Valley whites are also much sought after. A stone's throw away is **Peter Lehmann Wines**, with a tempting spread of wine styles unrivalled for consistency and value, not to mention some real hidden gems such as the Mentor Cabernet Sauvignon and Margaret Barossa Semillon. No experience could be more Barossan than swirling a Peter Lehmann wine under the shade of a river red gum while tucking into a cellar door platter of Linke's mettwurst and lachsschinken (smoked cured pork loin), Maggie Beer pâté, local cheese and crunchy Apex bakery bread. A historic and picturesque walking trail links the Langmeil and Peter Lehmann vineyards.

Head north-west and the palm-lined roads lead to **Seppeltsfield**. No visit to the region is complete without paying homage to this astonishing site — Australia's mecca for fortified wines. The sprawling estate is notable for its gardens, bluestone buildings and most of all a cellar that is home to 9 million litres of fortified wines — the oldest continuous collection in the world. A full range of tours and tastings are on offer here. The star of the show is the hundred-year-old Para Vintage Tawny but don't miss sampling their glorious tokay, sherry and muscat styles as well.

A very different cellar door experience — but still steeped in history — is at nearby **Hentley Farm**, a boutique operation on the gum-shaded banks of Greenock Creek. The western reaches of the Barossa have emerged as a key location for complex and concentrated red wine styles and this maker's The Beauty and The Beast are classic examples. It is also near Seppeltsfield that you will find **Appellation**, the regional standout for fine dining. Part of the feted vineyard accommodation retreat **The Louise** (see Where to stay), the elegant restaurant is under the deft guiding hand of executive chef Mark McNamara. With a sophisticated simplicity it presents chic creations that still capture the rustic essence of super-fresh local produce. This is on show with signature dishes such as the earthy and aromatic smoked duck breast partnered with ethereal liver parfait and rillettes, or local corn-fed chicken enriched with lachsschinken, garlic and sage.

Maggie Beer is the energetic grande dame of all things Barossan. On your way to Nuriootpa call into the lakeside **Maggie's Farm Shop** to see an ever-growing range of produce showcasing the

flavours of the region. Choose picnic fare such as pies, pâtés and cheeses from the all-day menu or simply gather food ideas and inspiration. A cooking demonstration kicks off at 2pm daily.

There's no more exalted name in Australian wine than **Penfolds** and their cellar door on the outskirts of Nuriootpa is the place to explore the full breadth of their output. The exceptional character of Barossa fruit has always underpinned the success of the brand's Bin range. As well as public tastings, you can also take advantage of more personalised encounters, including 'A Taste Of Grange' — an introduction to the philosophy and flavours of Australia's most celebrated wine, and the chance to get into the lab and 'make your own blend' using the components that make up Penfolds GSM Bin 138.

Downtown Nuriootpa can be bustling, but it's not all business. Food lovers have staked their claim with the takeover of an old bank to create **The Branch.** This cafe punches above its weight with an eclectic menu featuring everything from pizza and crunchy salads to a tangy saltbush goat curry infused with madras spices. **Linke's Central Meat Store** just up the street is also a valley institution — with mettwurst and double-smoked bacon that is among the best in a highly competitive local field. In the same street is **Linke's Nuriootpa Bakery & Tearoom**, which has been selling handmade pastries, breads and German cakes since 1938.

If you want a break from viticulture and wine, **Barossa Brewing Company** is located at Greenock, north-west of Nuriootpa on the other side of the Sturt Highway. This boutique brewery, housed in an 1860s wheat store, produces small quantities of traditionally brewed beers. Open at weekends, you can imbibe their Greenock Dark Ale, The Miller's Lager and Wheatstone Ale in the tasting room. Along the Sturt Highway in the other direction is the vineyard of the well-known maker, **Wolf Blass**, established here over 30 years ago.

As many-faceted as the valley floor can be, the gently folding hills to the east are no less alluring. Angaston has become a real food hub, with the Saturday Farmers' Market and a cluster of main street attractions. Victoria McClurg of the **Barossa Valley Cheese Company** is a veritable dairy dynamo with a passion for crafting both goat's and cow's milk cheeses, including her award-winning Washington Washrind, a hand-washed creation that

Opposite (top to bottom): Henschke Wines, Keyneton; handmade pastries at Carême Pastry, Tanunda

matures with incredibly rich and subtly sweet flavours. For many diehard locals their restaurant of choice is **Vintners Bar & Grill**. Chef Peter Clarke is a valley veteran with a sure touch in the kitchen and swag of great local produce to work with. Lots of gutsy Mediterranean flavours are at play here in dishes such as his potato gnocchi with gorgonzola piccante, prosciutto, and fried sage. Also popular for breakfast and lunch is the trendy **Blond Coffee**, where trained baristas deliver exceptional coffee to accompany light meals – maybe a tasty toasted panini or a frittata of roast pumpkin, caramelised onion, roast capsicum, spinach and feta. On site is Blond Store, where you can stock up on packaged and fresh gourmet produce. If it's cooked or cold meats you are craving, call in to **Schultz Butchers** for mettwurst, black and white pudding, smokehouse bacon, cooked beef silverside and fresh pork sausages. Now owned by Barossa Fine Foods, this business was first established in 1939.

Before you head out along the Eden Valley where cellar doors are thin on the ground, make a stop at **Taste Eden Valley** in Angaston. This shop gives you the inside running on many of the subregion's finest drops from a dozen or so high-country producers. Look out for crisp rieslings and a surprisingly strong showing of cool-climate reds. And on the southern outskirts of town, take a break at the captivating cellar door at **Yalumba**. There's a plethora of history here, and the Hill-Smith family story is a salutary reminder that not all the wine pioneering was German-driven. Yalumba's wine range is expansive but be sure to sample some of winemaker Louisa Rose's dazzling viognier.

Touring the ranges through Eden Valley reveals a wondrous landscape of flinty granite hills and secluded vineyards. Out east in the rolling farmland near Keyneton lies the home of **Henschke Wines**, one of the proudest names in Australia's wine firmament. The cellar door might be modest in scale but the scope of the winemaking on show – coupled with six generations of family history – makes this an unforgettable encounter. As well as single-vineyard icons such as Mount Edelstone and Hill of Grace, there's a swathe of fine varietal wines representing the best of Eden Valley and the Adelaide Hills – testament to the thoughtful teamwork of Stephen Henschke and his wife, Prue, among Australia's most respected viticulturists.

Grape crusader

Charlie Melton of Charles Melton Wines

Having been in the Barossa for a mere 30 years Charlie Melton might be a relative newcomer, yet his appreciation for the valley's vinous treasures runs deep. In the dire days of the 1980s when many growers were being urged to 'pull' vines, Charlie began crafting wines that drew on the strength of these venerable plantings. Inspired by visits to the Rhone Valley he created Nine Popes, a Barossan blend of grenache, shiraz and mourvèdre. At the same time his Rosé of Virginia set a new benchmark with its suite of vibrant, summer-berry flavours. 'Our wine styles are shaped by our community, our neighbours,' says Charlie. 'For me wine really comes together in a social sense.' That means working closely with a cadre of 20 loyal growers whose low-yielding, dry-grown vines bestow a distinctive richness and subtlety to the Melton range, which now includes single vineyard shiraz styles and the wonderfully floral and spice-laden Richelieu Grenache. This communal ethos extends to the barn-like cellar door with 'kitchen table' style tastings and verandah lunches with treats such as spinach and feta tarts or Hutton Vale lamb pies. Meanwhile, just across the vineyard stands the 'Kirche', a former neighbourhood church that Charlie and wife Virginia have converted into dapper guest accommodation. As with the wines it's a seamless merger of hospitality and heritage, another strand to an already inviting story. Or as Charlie puts it: 'Every time somebody opens one of our wines they're sharing the rewards of the life we're living here.'

Contacts for Barossa and Eden valleys

EATERIES

1918 Bistro & Grill: 94 Murray St, Tanunda; (08) 8563 0405; www. 1918.com.au

Appellation: The Louise, cnr Seppeltsfield and Stonewell rds, Marananga; (08) 8562 4144; www. appellation.com.au

Blond Coffee: 60 Murray St, Angaston; (08) 8564 3444; www.blondcoffee.com.au

Jacob's Restaurant: Barossa Valley Way, Rowland Flat; (08) 8521 3111; www.jacobscreek.com

Kies Wines cafe: see Wineries

Krondorf Road Cafe: Krondorf Rd, Tanunda; (08) 8563 0889; www.kabminye.com

Lyndoch Bakery & Restaurant: see Stores

The Branch: 15 Murray St, Nuriootpa; (08) 8562 4561; www.thebranch.com.au

Vintners Bar & Grill: Cnr Stockwell and Nuriootpa rds, Angaston; (08) 8564 2488; vintners.com.au

STORES

Apex Bakery: Elizabeth St, Tanunda; (08) 8563 2483

Linke's Central Meat Store: 27 Murray St, Nuriootpa; (08) 8562 1143

Linke's Nuriootpa Bakery & Tearoom: 40 Murray St, Nuriootpa; (08) 8562 1129

Lyndoch Bakery & Restaurant: 26 Barossa Valley Hwy, Lyndoch; (08) 8524 4422; www.lyndochbakery.com.au

Taste Eden Valley: 36A Murray St, Angaston; (08) 8564 2435; www.tasteedenvalley.com.au

MARKETS

Barossa Farmers Market: Cnr Nuriootpa and Stockwell rds, Angaston South; Sat morning; 0402 026 882; www.barossafarmersmarket.com

Williamstown Craft Market: Williamstown Institute, Main St; 1st Sun each month; (08) 8522 4234

GOURMET PRODUCE

Barossa Valley Cheese Company: 67b Murray St, Angaston; (08) 8564 3636; www.barossacheese.com.au

Carême Pastry: 7 Petras St, Tanunda; (08) 8563 1490; www.caremepastry.com

Maggie's Farm Shop: Pheasant Farm Rd (off Samuel Rd), Nuriootpa; (08) 8562 4477; www.maggiebeer.com.au

Schultz Butchers: 42 Murray Street, Angaston; (08) 8564 2145

WINERIES

Charles Melton Wines: Krondorf Rd, Tanunda; (08) 8563 3606; www.charlesmeltonwines.com.au

Grant Burge Wines: Barossa Valley Way, Tanunda; (08) 8563 7471; www.grantburgewines.com.au

Henschke Wines: Henschke Rd, Keyneton; (08) 8564 8223; www.henschke.com.au

Hentley Farm Wines: Jenke Rd, Seppeltsfield; (08) 8562 8427; www.hentleyfarm.com.au

Jacob's Creek: Barossa Valley Way, Rowland Flat; (08) 8521 3111; www.jacobscreek.com

Kabminye Wines: see Eateries/Krondorf Road Cafe

Kies Wines: Barossa Valley Way, Lyndoch; (08) 8524 4110; www.kieswines.com.au

Langmeil Winery: Cnr Langmeil and Para rds, Tanunda; (08) 8563 2595; www.langmeilwinery.com.au

Penfolds Wines: Tanunda Rd, Nuriootpa; (08) 8568 9408; www.penfolds.com

Peter Lehmann Wines: Para Rd, Tanunda; (08) 8563 2100; www.peterlehmannwines.com

Rockford Wines: Krondorf Rd, Tanunda; (08) 8563 2720

Seppeltsfield: Seppeltsfield Rd, Seppeltsfield; (08) 8568 6217; www.seppeltsfield.com.au

Turkey Flat Vineyards: Bethany Rd, Tanunda; (08) 8563 2851; www.turkeyflat.com.au

Wolf Blass Wines: 97 Sturt Hwy, Nuriootpa; (08) 8568 7311; www.wolfblass.com.au

Yalumba: Eden Valley Rd, Angaston; (08) 8561 3200; www.yalumba.com

BREWERIES

Barossa Brewing Company: Mill Street, Greenock; (08) 85634041; www.barossabrewingcompany.com

COOKING SCHOOLS

Carême Pastry: 7 Petras St, Tanunda; (08) 8563 1490; www.caremepastry.com

Clare Valley

Clare
Farrell Flat
Sevenhill
Mintaro
Penwortham
Watervale
Manoora
Auburn
Undalya
Riverton

Statuesque red gums and paddocks of golden wheat give this landscape a quintessentially Australian feel. A string of small, welcoming towns shows the way through the valley, from Auburn in the south to Clare in the north, while back roads swing past old homesteads and bush-clad ridges. This is classic sheep and cropping country – but with a twist. Amid the rustic, down-to-earth rural splendour, there are exceptional food and wine stories to track down, largely due to an array of fertile flats crisscrossed with vines.

Grapes have been grown here for 160 years, with the Jesuit priests and brothers of Sevenhill being among the pioneers. The valley is home to Australia's greatest rieslings, including intense, flinty dry styles from Polish Hill River and Watervale's elegant floral renditions. Other grape varieties to shine include cabernet sauvignon, semillon and shiraz. Alongside the vinous gems the district boasts a bounty of general farm produce: organic lamb, saltbush hogget, olives, organic fruit and vegetables, and free-range chicken. Such are the foundations for an authentic food culture on show in the region's many pubs, cafes and bakeries.

The southern village of Auburn epitomises the region's beguiling yet unruffled charms. Bluestone cottages and heritage buildings abound – **The Rising Sun Hotel** (1850) in the main-street is an ever-popular watering hole that also serves bistro fare and more substantial pub favourites such as schnitzels and beer-battered fish. On weekends you can visit the **Mount Horrocks** cellar door, housed in the Old Railway Station. Though Mount Horrocks' winemaker Stephanie Toole crafts just five styles, each wine is outstanding. The same goes for those of her husband, Jeffrey. His **Grosset Wines'** Polish Hill and Springvale rieslings are both consistently ranked among Australia's finest expressions of this variety. Grosset Wines cellar door at their Auburn vineyard is only open a few weeks a year, when you can purchase direct while stocks last (phone the winery for details). Just up the road, **Taylors** turns out a cavalcade of wines, but here too the quality is very even and their estate cabernet sauvignon is one of the region's signature drops. Their on-site cellar door is open daily.

Leisurely wine and food collaborations have always been a Clare Valley specialty and further up the road, near Penwortham, there is a cluster of

Festivals

Clare Gourmet Weekend: various wineries; mid-May; (08) 8843 0122; www.clarevalley.com.au

Fabulous Fortifieds: fortified wine celebration; Sevenhill Cellars, College Rd, Sevenhill; June (Queen's birthday weekend); (08) 8843 4222; www.sevenhill.com.au/events

Vintner's Picnic: Showgrounds, Main North Rd, Clare; early Oct; (08) 8843 0122; www.clarevalley.com.au

Where to stay

Brice Hill Country Lodge: luxury apartments; Warenda Rd, Clare; (08) 8842 2925

Molly's Chase: modern log cabin; Quarry Rd, Clare; 0412 265 031; www.mollyschase.com.au

Mundawora Mews: rural B&B cottage suites; Main North Rd, Clare; (08) 8842 3762; www.mundaworamews.com

Skillogalee: self-catering four-and five-star cottages; Trevarrick Rd, Sevenhill; (08) 8843 4311; www.skillogalee.com.au

excellent wineries. High in the Skilly Hills, west of Penwortham, lurks **Penna Lane**. Here you can sample their award-winning estate wines and at the same time enjoy a range of home-cooked fare, from tasty antipasto platters in summer to hearty soups in winter, all served with lashings of home-baked bread. And don't miss out on their famous poached figs served with creamy Greek yoghurt. Much of the food is sourced from the organic home vegetable patch and, served on the verandah overlooking the garden, this is an endearing way to taste the essence of Clare. You can also buy jams, sauces, relishes and chutneys to take away. On the same road, a little closer to Penwortham, you can visit **Kilikanoon** with its cellar door nestled in landscaped cottage gardens. For big-hearted cabernet sauvignon and shiraz styles it's hard to go past this producer's offerings.

In close proximity, up the road at Sevenhill, the old stone apple shed cellar door at **Mitchell Wines** is open seven days. Renowned for its long-lived rieslings and cabernet sauvignons, it also produces good semillon, grenache and shiraz. Nearby, **Skillogalee** was a trailblazer of vineyard dining. Their endearing 1850s cottage and perfumed garden is the venue for a seasonal menu of simple but stylish country-style food served with estate-grown wines. Local produce is to the fore – try the herb-crusted Burra lamb with goat's curd or the cured meats and vintage cheeses of their sturdy vine pruner's lunch. This is one of the standout restaurants in the valley, open seven days for lunch and luxury self-catering accommodation is also available (*see* Where to stay). For family-friendly atmosphere and reasonably priced meals, the **Sevenhill Hotel** in town offers an à la carte menu and an extensive list of premium Clare Valley wines.

Eminent, family-run wineries can be found throughout the region. East of Sevenhill, in the famed riesling subregion of Polish Hill River Valley, there are **Pikes Wines** and **Paulett Wines**. The cellar doors are open daily. Further east, over in the delightful heritage hamlet of Mintaro, a cute 1850s cottage serves as **Reilly's Wines & Restaurant**. For relaxed grazing there are excellent antipasto and cheese platters to share, perhaps with a bottle of Stolen Block Shiraz, or sturdier seasonal offerings such as roasted quail on mushroom risotto with their old bush vine grenache, or a seared lamb salad matched up with a dry-land cabernet sauvignon. Some of the produce is freshly picked from their home garden.

South of Clare, **Tim Adams Wines** is revered for its robust cabernet sauvignon and shiraz styles, while north of town **Jim Barry Wines** offer a stellar cast of varietals including their brooding, opulent shiraz, The Armagh, a true icon Australian wine. Both these vineyards house cellar doors that welcome visitors daily. In the heart of Clare township, **Wild Saffron** is the hub for all things gourmet from the region. They serve lunch Monday and Wednesday–Friday (licensed), and breakfast until noon at weekends. More than just a welcome venue for a coffee and a quick bite – though their muffins and cakes are topnotch – this is a great source of ideas and inspiration. And, if you're heading out on the Riesling Trail – Clare's famous walking and cycling pathway – this is the place to gather your picnic ingredients. There are also pre-packaged gift packs of local produce and gourmet dinners 'to go'.

Contacts for Clare Valley

EATERIES

Penna Lane Wines: *see* Wineries

Reilly's Wines & Restaurant: Cnr Hill and Burra sts, Mintaro; (08) 8843 9013; www.reillyswines.com.au

Sevenhill Hotel: Main North Rd, Sevenhill; (08) 8843 4217

Skillogalee Winery Restaurant: Trevarrick Rd, Sevenhill; (08) 8843 4311; www.skillogalee.com.au

The Rising Sun Hotel: Main North Rd, Auburn; (08) 8849 2015

Wild Saffron: 288 Main North Rd, Clare; (08) 8842 4255; www.wildsaffron.com.au

STORES

Penna Lane Wines: *see* Wineries

Wild Saffron: *see* Eateries

MARKETS

Burra Market Day: Best Pl; 1st weekend each month (Mar–Dec); (08) 8892 2772

Clare Showgrounds Country Market: Clare Showgrounds; 2nd Sat each month, morning; (08) 8842 3919

Clare Valley Food, Wine and Art Market: Ennis Park, Clare; 1st Sun each month, morning; (08) 8842 1880

Riverton Monthly Market: Riverton Community Hall; 3rd Sat each month, morning; (08) 8847 2705

Sevenhill Producers Market: Madonna Hall, Main North Rd; last Sat each month, morning; (08) 8843 4360

WINERIES

Grosset Wines: King St, Auburn; (08) 8849 2175 or 1800 088 223; www.grosset.com.au

Jim Barry Wines: Craigs Hill Rd, Clare; (08) 8842 2261; www.jimbarry.com

Kilikanoon: Penna La, Penwortham; (08) 8843 4206; www.kilikanoon.com.au

Mitchell Wines: Hughes Park Rd, Sevenhill; (08) 8843 4258; www.mitchellwines.com

Mount Horrocks: The Old Railway Station (cellar door), Curling St, Auburn; (08) 8849 2202; www.mounthorrocks.com

Paulett Wines: Polish Hill River Rd (Sevenhill–Mintara Road), Sevenhill; (08) 8843 4328; www.paulettwines.com.au

Penna Lane Wines: Lot 51 Penna La, Penwortham; (08) 8843 4364; www.pennalanewines.com.au

Pikes Wines: Polish Hill River Rd, Sevenhill; (08) 8843 4370; www.pikeswines.com.au

Reilly's Wines: *see* Eateries/Reilly's Wines & Restaurant

Skillogalee Wines: *see* Eateries

Taylors: Taylors Rd, Auburn; (08) 8849 1111; www.taylorswines.com.au

Tim Adams Wines: Warenda Rd, Clare; (08) 8842 2429; www.timadamswines.com.au

Below (left to right): winery building at Grosset Wines, Auburn; prawn and caper linguine at Wild Saffron, Clare; winery complex at Mitchell Wines, Sevenhill

Limestone Coast

Padthaway.

Kingston S.E.

Cape
Jaffa   Avenue Range

Naracoorte

Mount
Benson

Robe

Coonawarra

Penola

Beachport

Millicent

SOUTHERN   SA
OCEAN   VIC.

Mount Gambier.

Take ancient dunes and rich earth, add in a volcano or two, some cool breezes and mix with plenty of good rainfall – that's the recipe for the hearty flavours of South Australia's south-eastern corner. With a wild shoreline of surf beaches and fishing ports, the area is heaven for those who revel in the lush taste and texture of southern rock lobster. Inland you'll find a huge diversity of farm goods with fertile pastures supporting an array of boutique dairies, as well as beef and lamb producers. But the star of the show is the Coonawarra's famed terra rossa soil, which has been closely compared to the soils of Bordeaux. Sitting atop a bed of limestone, this hallowed ground has created an embarrassment of riches and ensured the Coonawarra a secure place in the pantheon of Australia's greatest wine regions. If you love good reds, particularly cabernet sauvignon, this is the place to come.

The Coonawarra's expanse of vines flanks the Riddoch Highway, extending north from the town of Penola. With all of the region's wineries closing in on the slender strip of terra rossa soil ('the cigar'), cellar doors are within a minute's drive from each other, making touring here very flexible. You could spend four or five days visiting every cellar door, but as a starting point it's hard to go past the iconic **Wynns Coonawarra Estate**, where canny Scot and vine pioneer John Riddoch got things rolling in 1891. For decades the reds released under the Wynns label have set varietal benchmarks for the region, and since 1982 their definitive cabernet sauvignon has been named in honour of their founder. However, lovers of elegant but full-bodied reds might find even more enjoyment with the Alex 88, a rich mixture of blackberry flavours and smooth oak tinges. The cellar door offers a smattering of back vintages, plus cheese platters and, for aficionados, hosted private tastings and 'make your own blend' tours (bookings essential).

Katnook Estate is another must-visit cellar door with a varietal to suit almost any palate. The estate riesling is a zesty mix of fruit with a hint of cinnamon, while the estate chardonnay has a sweet buttery finish. But the real excitement comes from the reds – especially if the Odyssey and Prodigy, the label's two limited release wines, are available for tasting. The

Cape Jaffa Seafood and Wine Festival: King Dr; Jan; 0409 571 438; www.capejaffafest.com.au

Taste the Limestone Coast Festival: Italian food and wine festival; Naracoorte Town Sq; Feb; 0437 916 683; www.thetastefestival.com.au

Seafari Beachport Festival: fresh produce, wine and entertainment; Beachport; last weekend in Feb; (08) 8735 8543; www.beachportfestival.com

Zema Estate's Great Cabernet Experience: cabernet tasting; Zema Estate, Riddoch Hwy, Coonawarra; 1st weekend in Aug; (08) 8736 3219; www.zema.com.au

Coonawarra Cabernet Celebrations: celebration of winemaking community; Riddoch Hwy, Coonawarra; Oct; (08) 8737 2392; www.coonawarra.org

Davidson Cottage: quaint 1860s cottage; Petticoat La, Penola; 0488 646 446; www.davidsoncottage.com.au

Merlot and Verdelho: two luxury townhouses; 14 Arthur St, Penola; (08) 8763 7132; www.merlotverdelho.com.au

Padthaway Estate Homestead: luxury Victorian guesthouse; Riddoch Hwy, Padthaway; (08) 8765 5555; www.padthawayestate.com

The Menzies Retreat: stunning contemporary accommodation amid vines; Yalumba Coonawarra Estate, Riddoch Hwy, Coonawarra; (08) 8737 3603; www.yalumba.com

The Shore: glittering beachfront residence; 11 Wrattonbully Rd, Robe; 1300 760 629; www.robelifestyle.com.au

Above (left to right): Hollick Wines, Coonawarra; a classic red from Rymill, Coonawarra; minimalist decor at fodder restaurant in Coonawarra; wine tasting at Wynns Coonawarra Estate

Odyssey, in particular, has won many awards with its velvety plum and mocha undertones. With this wine, senior winemaker Wayne Stehbens says his aim is to 'not only capture the essence of Coonawarra cabernet sauvignon, but to define it'.

Most of Australia's biggest wine brands feature Coonawarra styles in their portfolio. For Yalumba it started with their flagship cabernet sauvignon, The Menzies. In recent years this much-acclaimed wine has been joined by several regional siblings, all of which are up for tasting at **Yalumba Coonawarra Estate**. This modern, yet earthy venue also offers very smart on-site vineyard accommodation (*see* Where to stay/The Menzies Retreat). The region's other big producer is **Rymill**. Make sure to take in the views from the cellar door's balcony while sipping their crisp méthode champenoise sparkling white. The rosé is a very unusual mix of strawberry and other fruits that will interest even those who normally avoid the pink stuff.

A feature of the region is the number of established farmers and families who have

gravitated into making wine. Local stalwart Doug Balnaves is a case in point. After many years guiding vineyard development for others he and his family have built up **Balnaves of Coonawarra** to be one of the most respected producers in the district. That success is due in no small measure to the consummate winemaking skills of Peter Bissell. His flair with Coonawarra fruit is legendary and on show in top-flight wines such as The Tally (unfortunately, not often available for tasting), while this label's shiraz and chardonnay are also multi-award winning.

It's a similar tale with the Lynn brothers, Tony and Brian, one-time sheep farmers who, year by year, have become more involved with their premium range of reds at **Majella Wines**. The Malleea is a stunning cabernet and shiraz blend, layered with complex fruit characters, fine, dusty tannins and spicy oak, which is ranked as outstanding (the second tier) for Langton's well-respected Classification of Australian Wine. Their shiraz is another topnotch red and a bit of fun can be had with the sparkling shiraz.

Italian influences are to the fore in the traditional, handcrafted wines at **Zema Estate**. Their merlot is a real winner for its smooth texture and The Cluny is a well-balanced blend of cabernet sauvignon, merlot, cabernet franc and malbec. Italian neighbour **DiGiorgio Family Wines** offers an impressive spread of varietal styles, including sparkling whites and reds, from its Coonawarra and Lucindale vineyards. Another winery with a good range of reasonably priced wines is **Leconfield** – the Jette's viognier under the Richard Hamilton label is bursting with apricot blossom.

Of the local winemakers, Ian Hollick has always been ready to experiment and this is reflected in the mix at **Hollick Wines**. Mingling among traditional reds, such as the magnificent Wilgha Shiraz that is only released in years of excellence, you can find new varietals such as tempranillo, barbera, and the sweet, sparkling white frizzante that is simply a party in your mouth. The pinot noir is also an enjoyable wine with less of the smelly sock after taste characteristic of most pinot noirs. That same interest

in flavour marriages is a feature of the menu at **Upstairs at Hollick**, the estate's popular restaurant with the best vineyard views in the region. Regional produce is proudly deployed with dishes such as smoked Naracoorte venison highlighted by a tempranillo jelly, and a chunky fillet of Beachport snapper partnered with goat's cheese and soft herbs. Desserts also offer a spin on the classics, such as lemon verbena–scented panna cotta, and every dish is matched with a Hollick wine.

After lunch at Hollick, it's essential that you book for dinner at **Pipers of Penola** (*see* feature, p. 264), undoubtedly the region's best restaurant. However, you will also enjoy a good meal at **fodder**. Owned and run by husband and wife team Melissa and John Innes, the focus of this cafe/restaurant is actually on wines rather than food. John is Rymill's former winemaker and it's worth getting him to come over to your table for advice when perusing the extensive wine list, filled with both local and international drops. Despite the wine focus, the food here is still very good. John can be seen manning the wood-fired pizza oven that turns out thin-crust pizzas with simple but delicious toppings, while Melissa takes care of dishes such as steak and chips and gnocchi with a wild mushroom sauce, along with the best coffee in town.

Gourmet stores are not forgotten in this area. A range of food products, as well as cooking equipment and cookbooks, are available at **Koonara Wines**' cellar door in the middle of Penola's main street. At **The Poplars Winery**, their cellar door precinct has a cheese bar for cheese-tasting and **The Poplars Produce Store**, which sells a wide range of local goodies and gourmet products from South Australian and western Victorian producers. There is also **Kitchen @ The Poplars**, a casual cafe for breakfast or lunch (choose from such favourites as house-made lamb shank pie, blue swimmer crab pasta or pork tagliatelle). And for local labels that don't have a cellar door, the wine cellar at **Heyward's Royal Oak Hotel** in Penola is full of surprises (look out for back vintages of Reschke that sell out in weeks). It also offers some tastings. The heritage and National Trust-listed hotel has a history dating back to 1848 and a building to 1872. Pub meals are served in the dining room, bar or in the garden, and B&B accommodation is available.

Some 100 kilometres north of Coonawarra, along the Riddoch Highway, lies the small wine region of Padthaway, its climate slightly warmer but its soils enjoying some of the same characteristics as its southern counterpart. It is a more scenic landscape than Coonawarra, its gentle rolling hills contrasting to the latter's flat expanses. The fertile limestone plain, with its famous terra rossa soil, supports a small number of well-known wineries: Padthaway

Estate, Stonehaven (Hardy Wine Company), Henry's Drive, Browns of Padthaway, Fosters Estate, Orlando Wyndham and Morambro Creek. Only the first three wineries listed have cellar doors open for tastings and sales. The dominant wine style of the region is traditionally chardonnay while the cabernet sauvignon and shiraz is frequently blended with wines from elsewhere in the state.

The cellar door for the impressive **Padthaway Estate** is housed in a picturesque old stone stable block and is open daily. Renowned particularly for its sparkling wine, the estate has won recent awards for its 2002 Eliza Late Tirage Pinot Noir Chardonnay. As well as Padthaway Estate-grown wines visitors can also taste those produced under the Browns of Padthaway label. The winery's 1882 homestead provides luxury guesthouse accommodation (*see* Where to stay), situated near the red gums and stringybarks of Padthaway Conservation Park. Dinner is by arrangement and food focuses on local regional produce. You might find whole fresh Limestone Coast trout served with orange, maple syrup and macadamia nut sauce or a chargrilled terra rossa eye fillet served with a red wine jus, Swiss brown mushrooms and potato. The dessert list has a collection of old favourites such as traditional bread and butter pudding with homemade warm custard.

Stonehaven, one of the largest operations in the region, produces a range of well-priced wines including the regional stalwart chardonnay. It is also well regarded for its shiraz and, more recently, viognier. It welcomes visitors to its cellar door (open daily) for tastings and sales. **Henry's Drive Vineyards** offers regional food platters at their cellar door to complement the estate-grown wines available for

Below (left to right): Katnook Estate cellar door, Coonawarra; the burnt orange–red terra rossa soil is a feature of the region, including at Koonara Wines vineyard

tasting – try their shiraz. To purchase these labels and others produced in the region, call in to the **Padthaway General Store Bottle Shop**, open all day Monday–Saturday and Sunday morning.

Elsewhere in the Limestone Coast region, some successful vine plantings can be found at Mount Benson along the coastal strip from Kingston to Robe. Here the soothing effects of a maritime climate impart a different character to the wine styles, plus allowing other grape varieties to come to the fore. At **Wangolina Station** winemaker Anita Goode returned to the family farm to create a string of noteworthy drops, including her semillon and sauvignon blanc, both as straight varietals and blends. Even closer to the coast, the same duo is a feature of the range at **Cape Jaffa Wines**, where Derek Hooper has blazed a trail with the region's first fully certified biodynamic vineyard. Sporting eye-catching cotton cloth labels, his La Lune range includes powerful expressions of both cabernet sauvignon and shiraz.

Other coastal delights focus on gourmet food. However, before exploring the south-eastern fishing villages, head inland to Avenue Range where **Avenue Emus**, a working farm, offers a taste of emu meat products. Then return to Kingston SE where **Lacepede Seafood**, on the foreshore, is the place to go during the lobster season (October–May). You can pick up both live and cooked rock lobster straight off the boats, plus local prawns, King George whiting and flathead.

For more gastronomic pleasures it's a short drive south to the historic and picturesque fishing town of Robe. Being a busy holiday spot, there is a good choice of cafe-style venues. Commanding one of the best perches in town, **The Gallerie** caters for casual grazing on its spacious deck and more refined à la carte dining indoors. Seafood is the inevitable highlight here, with classics such as lobster thermidor and bouillabaisse often gracing the menu, while in the cooler months heartier venison, lamb and pork dishes come into their own. **The Caledonian Inn**, a historic, ivy-clad pub, has a beach cafe with familiar schnitzel, seafood and steak options, as well as a dining room that ventures into more exotic territory with European and Asian inspirations such as potted pork rillettes, tom yum prawn shooters, Korean tuna tartar and miso-marinated lamb rack. For devoted carnivores, the **Robe Butcher Shop** has multi-award-winning

smoked salami, mettwurst and bacon. Be sure to sample their stylish home-crafted sausages as well as local grain-fed beef and premium lamb cuts.

On the run down the coast call into Beachport where the grand old local pub has been reborn as **Bompas of Beachport**, a versatile accommodation and dining venue with a great foreshore location. In Millicent you can go right to the source at **Limestone Coast Trout** on a tour of its aquaculture facility and sample the home-farmed flavours in their fish and chip cones. With a herd of some 1100 wagyu cattle, nearby Mayura Station has become one of the nation's leading suppliers of full-blood wagyu beef (visits are by appointment only; (08) 8721 3000; www.mayurastation.com). Their multi-award-winning range features on top menus around the country. If you want to sample it locally, dine at **The Barn Steakhouse** on the southern side of Mount Gambier, where beef dishes take centre-stage. This landmark restaurant features a warm, elegant space and a menu with nearly a dozen different steak dishes, among them Mayura's wagyu. For devotees of prime aged cuts seared over mallee coals this is nirvana. And the wine list is suitably expansive with a host of back vintages from the region's top labels. Luxury accommodation in self-contained spa suites is also on offer here.

A very different atmosphere prevails at **Sorrento's Cafe**, an affable all-day eatery where you can dine outdoors or in an all-weather atrium courtyard. The emphasis is on quality local ingredients and easy dining with gourmet pizza and focaccia, plus heartier stir-fry and pasta dishes. Similarly, **Sage & Muntries** in the heart of town is a bright and breezy cafe catering to all tastes. Expect a diverse selection of pasta and risotto dishes, super-sophisticated burgers and seafood dishes accented with native bush spices and flavours. Of the mains, the house specialty is a boned half-duck, cooked with a crispy skin yet meltingly moist flesh and offset by a zingy plum and ginger sauce.

Among the products of local artisan producers, look out for the distinctive chocolate bars from **Sweet Business**, generally available from farmers' markets and gourmet food outlets across the region. The company has really embraced the melding of flavours with rich delights infused with everything from wattle seed and lemon myrtle to native pepperberries and locally ground coffee.

Fine dining

Pipers of Penola

Regional fine dining doesn't get more thoughtfully realised than this. Chef Simon Bowen hails from one of the region's best-known wine families (Bowen Estate), but he charted his own course, one that became a long journey home – via training in topnotch kitchens in the USA and Europe then Lake House at Daylesford in Victoria – before setting up shop in this revamped church. The premises might be modest in scale and simply dressed in timber, natural stone and white linen, but the food is exceptional. Earthy richness distinguishes Simon's confident, creative work. Thus, an eye fillet of Churchill beef is oak-smoked and teamed with duck liver parfait and duxelles (mushrooms), arriving at the table as a tower of ingredients topped off with a single potato crisp. Expect fine renditions of old classics such as a Waldorf side salad or, on the dessert list, an apple tarte tatin. But you'll find more exotic creations too, such as garlic-marinated quail served with roasted eggplant purée and labna, plus a lentil and pomegranate dressing. To complete the dining experience there's an excellent wine list, including aged Coonawarra gems with a proper quota of cellar years under their belt, and thoughtful table service coordinated by Simon's American-born wife Erika.

Contacts for Limestone Coast

EATERIES

Bompas of Beachport: 3 Railway Tce, Beachport; (08) 8735 8333; www.bompas.com.au

fodder: Memorial Dr, Coonawarra; (08) 8736 3170; www.fodder.net.au

Heyward's Royal Oak Hotel: 31 Church St, Penola; (08) 8737 2322; www.heywardshotel.com.au

Kitchen @ The Poplars: see Wineries/ The Poplars Winery

Limestone Coast Trout: 91 Lossie Rd, Millicent; (08) 8733 1407

Pipers of Penola: 58 Riddoch St, Penola; (08) 8737 3999; www.pipersofpenola.com.au

Sage & Muntries: 78 Commercial St West, Mount Gambier; (08) 8724 8400

Sorrento's Cafe: 6 Bay Rd, Mount Gambier; (08) 8723 0900

The Barn Steakhouse: Punt Rd (Nelson Rd), Mount Gambier; (08) 8726 8250; www.barn.com.au

The Caledonian Inn: 1 Victoria St, Robe; (08) 8768 2029; www.caledonian.net.au

The Gallerie: 2 Victoria St, Robe; (08) 8768 2256

Upstairs at Hollick: Cnr Ravenswood La and Riddoch Hwy, Coonawarra; (08) 8737 2752; www.hollick.com

STORES

Koonara Wines: 44 Church St; Penola; (08) 8737 3222; www.koonara.com

Padthaway General Store Bottle Shop: 15 Memorial Dr, Padthaway; (08) 8765 5020

The Poplars Produce Store: see Wineries/ The Poplars Winery

MARKETS

Limestone Coast Real Food Farmers Market: Riddoch Hwy, Penola; Sun morning; (08) 8737 3663; www.limestonecoastfood.com.au/farmers_market

Nangula Country Market: Nangula Hall, Princes Hwy; 2nd Sun each month; (08) 8734 4375

Naracoorte Country Market: Naracoorte Historic Vehicle Club, McDonnell St; 2nd Sat each month, morning; (08) 8762 1363

GOURMET PRODUCE

Avenue Emus: Thomas Rd, Avenue Range; (08) 8766 0085; www.avenueemus.com.au

Lacepede Seafood: Marine Pde, Kingston; (08) 8767 2549

Robe Butcher Shop: Union St, Robe; (08) 8768 2129

Sweet Business: PO Box 1018, Mount Gambier; (08) 8738 9291

WINERIES

Balnaves of Coonawarra: Riddoch Hwy, Coonawarra; (08) 8737 2946; www.balnaves.com.au

Cape Jaffa Wines: Limestone Coast Rd, Cape Jaffa; (08) 8768 5053; www.capejaffawines.com.au

DiGiorgio Family Wines: Riddoch Hwy, Coonawarra; (08) 8736 3222; www.digiorgio.com.au

Henry's Drive: Hodgson's Rd, Padthaway; (08) 8765 5251; www.henrysdrive.com

Hollick Wines: Cnr Ravenswood La and Riddoch Hwy, Coonawarra; (08) 8737 2318; www.hollick.com

Katnook Estate: Riddoch Hwy, Coonawarra; (08) 8737 0300; www.katnookestate.com.au

Koonara Wines: see Stores

Leconfield: Riddoch Hwy, Coonawarra; (08) 8737 2326; www.leconfieldwines.com

Majella Wines: Lynn Rd, Coonawarra; (08) 8736 3055; www.majellawines.com.au

Padthaway Estate: Riddoch Hwy, Padthaway; (08) 8765 5505; www.padthawayestate.com

Rymill: Riddoch Hwy, Coonawarra; (08) 8736 5001; www.rymill.com.au

Stonehaven: Riddoch Hwy, Padthaway; (08) 8765 6166; www.stonehavenvineyards.com.au

The Poplars Winery: Riddoch Hwy, Coonawarra; (08) 8736 3065 or (08) 8736 3309 (AH); www.thepoplarswinery.com

Wangolina Station: Limestone Coast Rd, Mount Benson; (08) 8768 6187; www.wangolina.com.au

Wynns Coonawarra Estate: Memorial Dr, Coonawarra; (08) 8736 2225; www.wynns.com.au

Yalumba Coonawarra Estate: Riddoch Hwy, Coonawarra; (08) 8737 3603; www.yalumba.com

Zema Estate: Riddoch Hwy, Coonawarra; (08) 8736 3219; www.zema.com.au

Fleurieu Peninsula

In their final flourish the Mount Lofty Ranges sweep south along the Fleurieu Peninsula. Bounded on both sides by the sea, these rolling highlands are among the most productive and best-watered landscapes in South Australia. For generations the region has been home to dairy farms and beef cattle, while the gentle flats cradled by the Willunga hills were closely planted with vineyards and almond orchards. It was a sleepy kind of place people drove through to get to the coast's holiday spots such as Victor Harbor.

This is no longer the case. Since the 1980s the region has blossomed as one of the state's most vibrant meeting points for boutique wines and fine fare. A big-hearted community of artisan producers has gathered here to grow fruits, olives and berries, make cheese and farm everything from rainbow trout and venison to quail, goat and pheasant. Together with the winemaking fraternity they have also cultivated a wonderfully welcoming and often downright quirky tradition for hospitality. Make no mistake, there are serious flavours on the table here, but with the allures of the bush and seaside so close the mood is surprisingly relaxed.

Above: gardens at Coriole winery at McLaren Vale

Opposite (top to bottom): fishing boats at Goolwa; Wirra Wirra winery at McLaren Vale

Festivals

Sea & Vines: various venues, McLaren Vale; June (Queen's Birthday weekend); (08) 8323 8999; www.mclarenvale.info/seaandvines

Willunga Almond Blossom Festival: Willunga Recreation Park, Main Rd; late July; (08) 8223 9889; www.willungafestivals.com

Fleurieu Folk Festival: Willunga Oval, Willunga; last weekend in Oct; (08) 8327 2797; www.fleurieufolkfestival.com.au

Where to stay

Bellevue Bed & Breakfast: immaculate contemporary suites; 12 Chalk Hill Rd, McLaren Vale; 0432 868 402; www.bellevuebnb.com.au

Coorong Beach House: artfully presented holiday home; 1 Goolwa Channel Dr, Hindmarsh Island; (08) 8383 0504; www.mclarenridge.com/coorong_beach_house

McLaren Ridge Log Cabins: boutique vineyard accommodation; Whitings Rd, McLaren Vale; (08) 8383 0504; www.mclarenridge.com

Silver Sands: stylish and secluded beach-side apartments; 277 Esplanade, Aldinga; (08) 8557 4002; www.silversandsbnb.com.au

The Summer House: ultra-smart spacious units; 7 Charlotte St, Port Elliot; (08) 8363 4510; www.pebe.com.au/summer_house

Above (left to right):
Flying Fish Café by
the beach Port Elliot;
d'Arenberg's father and
son winemaking team,
d'Arry and Chester
Osborn, overseeing a
vintage; cellar door at
Coriole, McLaren Vale

Located just 50 minutes drive from the heart of Adelaide also gives the region a real buzz. This is a lively hub where food and wine merge with art, music and all manner of festivals. Mediterranean influences abound. Italian families are prominent among the local grape growers and Spanish and Italian varieties are increasingly in favour. Nowhere else in South Australia has a more engaging choice of vineyard restaurants or seafront cafes – places where you can be outdoors on vine-shaded decks and terraces or inside with wood-ovens doing their thing, and sharing food nurtured in the landscape before you.

The McLaren Vale wine region is one of the peninsula's star attractions, and one of the flag bearers for the joyful union of food and wine is **d'Arry's Verandah Restaurant** (*see feature, p. 272*), nestled under the same cottage roof as **d'Arenberg Wines**. Other wineries to celebrate the marriage include **Woodstock** with **The Coterie** where, amid a relaxed atmosphere, house specialties run the gamut from handsomely laden regional platters of smoked

meats and antipasto treats to spicy Thai-flavoured squid salads and hefty Black Angus steaks. Just down the road **The Currant Shed** at **Hoffmann's** winery is equally informal (cellar door and restaurant closed Wednesday). Here the honest simplicity of chargrilled meats and earthy vegetable dishes are given a lift with local cheese and fruit accents – plus there is the occasional flourish such as prosciutto-wrapped brains adorned with an apple, celeriac and hazelnut remoulade.

McLaren Vale's vinous reputation is built on the spicy berry notes of grenache and the chocolate richness of shiraz. Yet many other varieties shine here and there's a terrific diversity of blends and winemaking skills on show. The portfolio at **Wirra Wirra** includes benchmark shiraz styles yet cabernet sauvignon is the star of their blockbuster The Angelus label and the crowd-pleasing Church Block blend. From here you can head onto the ridge overlooking the wilds of the Onkaparinga Valley to sample the glorious grenache and shiraz at **Samuel's Gorge**, where winemaker Justin McNamee also

crafts a delightfully soulful and savoury tempranillo (an increasingly popular Spanish varietal).

Nearby, **Coriole** turns out a strong selection of traditional varietals but they also have a longstanding Italian love affair with sangiovese and nebbiolo. While at the cellar door be sure to try the Lloyd family's excellent olives, oils and verjuice. Whereas Coriole inhabits historic bluestone cottages, the Grilli family have created a modern incarnation of Euro chic at **Primo Estate**. Yet more oils and aged vinegars are up for grabs here, plus a beguiling range of Italian-inspired wines. Be sure to sample the apple and pear hints in their crisp pinot grigio, and the coveted Joseph Moda, a many-layered cabernet sauvignon and merlot blend handcrafted in time-honoured amarone style.

In the town of McLaren Vale, there's a cluster of tempting eateries. Occupying a quaint 1851 cottage, **The Salopian Inn** is a seasoned veteran on the Fleurieu dining scene. As well as its own three-roomed wine cellar downstairs, the inn now also hosts the tasting rooms for Dowie Doole and

Gemtree Vineyards. Expect to see Peninsula produce, such as Encounter Bay garfish, Normanville lamb and wild rabbit, treated with ingenuity. Further along McMurtrie Road lurks **Red Poles**, an affable cafe with great verandahs for drifting through an afternoon of wine and food – often with live music too. The menu features dishes such as marron ravioli, and tofu, spinach and black bean fritters, plus heftier chicken and lamb courses with Mediterranean touches. And despite being ensconced in a corrugated iron shed at **Penny's Hill** cellar door, **The Kitchen Door** is a refined venue overlooking paddocks and vines. There's a very keen focus on all things seasonal and regional with rustic flavours such as the earthy mellowness of their braised lamb neck. A great value option is the five-course tasting selection, each course married with wines by Ben Riggs. Back in downtown McLaren Vale, **Blessed Cheese** is both a complete gourmet outlet and popular lunchtime cafe. There are local dairy delights from Paris Creek, Hindmarsh Valley and beyond, plus smallgoods, olive oils and Small World's irresistible sourdough loaves. For gathering picnic provisions this is the place to go.

Follow Main Road south and you arrive at Willunga, tucked at the foot of the Sellicks Hill Range escarpment. Every Saturday morning the town square is transformed by the Willunga Farmers' Market. **Fino** restaurant is right on the doorstep of all the market action so it's hardly surprising that the agenda here is driven by the freshest possible local produce. The authentic simplicity of its 1850s cottage also chimes beautifully with the dining ethos: rustic, Mediterranean-inspired dishes that honour the integrity of their ingredients. Signature creations include duck with beetroot, lentils and wilted greens, a salted-snapper brandade, and baked goat's cheese with olives and herbs.

Wherever you travel in the Vales, you're never far from the sea. Breathtaking water views bewitch patrons at the fabled **Star of Greece**, on the coast at Port Willunga. This revamped 1950s beachfront kiosk offers a well-balanced menu but it's hard to go past the artfully prepared whiting, garfish and squid dishes. For sweet tooths, the stylish desserts are real show stoppers. Just along the coast to the south, **Victory Hotel** is perched atop a hill and provides the full gulf and vines panorama. This is a favourite haunt for locals so the food is topnotch (think fresh local seafood and succulent steaks) and the wine cellar is a real Aladdin's cave. The establishment also has three serviced B&B cottages with sweeping views of vineyards and the coast.

Cheese is one the region's genuine highlights so as you head across to the other side of the peninsula stop in at the **Alexandrina Cheese Company** just south of Mount Compass. Try their multi-award-winning range, including aged jersey milk cheddars and buttery gouda and romano styles.

Being a lively holiday haunt, the coastal strip from Victor Harbor through to Goolwa is dotted with cafes and seafood is the natural highlight. Some, such as Goolwa's waterfront **Aquacaf Gourmet Cafe**, belie their low-key aura with exceptional food choices. Thus, savvy kitchen skills result in surprising dishes such as a humble seafood pasty featuring a luscious blend of mulloway pieces in a creamy herb sauce. Similar revelations are found in the cafe's reworking of classic dishes, such as their beef burger and flavoursome seafood chowder. Lighter fare includes a choice of alluring salads and baguettes. If you want to stay in Goolwa, **The Boathouse at Birks Harbour** in Liverpool Road is highly recommended, with B&B accommodation and self-catering facilities; call (08) 8555 0338 for further details.

Being smack bang on the seafront at Port Elliot, it's predictable that the **Flying Fish Cafe** is famous for its fish and chips on the deck. Yet this wonderful venue also proffers sophisticated lunch and dinner fare. Seafood is to the fore with superb oysters, rich fish stews and beer-battered King George whiting with tangy remoulade. Terra firma tastes are also catered for with dishes such as eye fillet steak on artichoke purée or peppered duck breast with sweet potato crepes. With fine ocean views and deft, innovative cooking, this is seaside dining at its best.

Of all Australia's wine regions it's hard to imagine a quieter achiever than Langhorne Creek, located in the region's west and fed by water and alluvial soils from the Bremer River. Vineyards have been a part of this floodplain landscape since the late 1850s and for generations its rich, ripe cabernet sauvignon and shiraz have been a major – but unsung – contributor to many high-profile wines. But the times are changing. The past 20 years has seen vineyard plantings increase more than tenfold. At the same time, several family producers have won plaudits on the national stage and thrown open their new cellar doors. The Willson sisters, Rebecca and Lucy, for example, have propelled **Bremerton Wines** into the top echelon of wine brands with the stunning success of their Old Adam Shiraz and other premium reds. A restored stone barn is an atmospheric cellar door and popular lunch venue with hearty platters and winter soups and pies.

Elsewhere at Langhorne Creek there are similar success stories. Ever since long-time grape growers the Follet family launched their **Lake Breeze** label it has become a byword for wines of outstanding consistency. Over the past 16 years they have won a staggering 23 trophies and 76 gold medals for their wines, including Greg Follett's archetypal shiraz and cabernet sauvignon blend, The Bernoota. And finally, for history, it's impossible to go past the legendary tales of **Bleasdale Wines** and the Potts family who first planted vines beside the Bremer River in 1858. Four years later Frank Potts built a basket press using a 10-metre, 3.5-tonne red gum tree as a lever! It survives today, along with an ever-reliable range of richly flavoured wines.

Opposite (clockwise from top left): cheese varieties at McLaren Vale's Blessed Cheese; McLaren Vale landscape; the entrance to Flying Fish Cafe, Port Elliot; sign at Bleasdale Wines, started by the Potts family in 1858 at Langhorne Creek

Vineyard Dining

d'Arry's Verandah Restaurant at McLaren Vale

Given Chester Osborn's knack for crafting all manner of harmonious blends for d'Arenberg wines, it's only fitting that deft kitchen teamwork is the hallmark of this classic cellar-door restaurant. Consistency is the greatest challenge for any top eatery, and co-chefs Peter Reschke and Nigel Rich deliver the goods year after year. Part of their secret is taking a winter break to gather fresh inspiration interstate and overseas. However, the real impetus for their ongoing success is working with the seasonal harvest emerging from farms right on their doorstep. This kitchen's passion for neighbourhood produce – olives, cheeses, nuts, fruits, game meats and shellfish – is legendary.

The dreamy vine views rolling all the way to the coast puts you in the mood from the moment you take your seat, especially if tastebuds are revved after a pre-lunch tasting of d'Arenberg's fine drops. While there's exquisite touch in entrées such as a lobster medallion with blue swimmer crab and prawn ravioli, Peter and Nigel are best known for their willingness to plate up punchy flavours – such as a tantalising slow-roasted pork belly with citrus jam or a brik of braised kangaroo tail with charry kangaroo fillet, beetroot confit and horseradish cream. The desserts are no slouches either, with house specialties such as an ethereal passionfruit soufflé. If any winery can produce a range of wines to serve as a foil for so many complex tastes and aromas, then it's d'Arenberg. Add to the adventure and try various wine flights and museum stock, plus an impressive array of imports.

Contacts for Fleurieu Peninsula

EATERIES

Aquacaf Gourmet Cafe: Barrage Rd, Goolwa; (08) 8555 1235

d'Arry's Verandah Restaurant: d'Arenberg, Osborn Rd, McLaren Vale; (08) 8329 4848; www.darrysverandah.com.au

Fino: 8 Hill St, Willunga; (08) 8556 4488; www.fino.net.au

Flying Fish Cafe: 1 Foreshore, Port Elliot; (08) 8554 3504; www.flyingfishcafe.com.au

Red Poles: McMurtrie Rd; McLaren Vale; (08) 8323 8994

Star of Greece: The Esplanade, Port Willunga; (08) 8557 7420

The Coterie: Woodstock Wines, Douglas Gully Rd, McLaren Flat; (08) 8383 0156; www.woodstockwine.com.au

The Currant Shed: Hoffmann's, Ingoldby Rd, McLaren Flat; (08) 8383 0232; www.hoffmannswine.com.au

The Kitchen Door: Penny's Hill, Main Rd, McLaren Vale; (08) 8556 4000; www.pennyshill.com.au

The Salopian Inn: McMurtrie Rd, McLaren Vale; (08) 8323 8769

Victory Hotel: Main South Rd, Sellicks Beach; (08) 8556 3083; www.victoryhotel.com.au

STORES

Blessed Cheese: 150 Main Rd, McLaren Vale; (08) 8323 7958

MARKETS

Inman Valley Craft and Produce Market: Memorial Hall, Main Rd; 1st Sat each month, morning; (08) 8558 8134

Moana Market: Moana Pioneers Memorial Hall, Nashwauk Cres; 2nd Sun each month; (08) 8327 0480

Victor Harbor Country Market: Esplanade, Victor Harbor; 2nd and 4th Sun each month; (08) 8556 8222

Victor Harbor Farmers' Market: Grosvenor Gardens, Torrens St; Sat morning; 0439 849 824; www.victorharborfarmersmarket.com.au

Willunga Artisans Market: Old Show Hall, Main St; 2nd Sat each month, morning; (08) 8386 0132

Willunga Farmers' Market: Willunga town square; Sat morning; (08) 8556 4297; www.willungafarmersmarket.com

Willunga Quarry Market: Aldinga Rd; 2nd Sat each month, morning; (08) 8556 2502; www.willungaquarrymarket.com

GOURMET PRODUCE

Alexandrina Cheese Company: Sneyd Rd, Mount Jagged, Mount Compass; (08) 8554 9666; www.alexandrinacheese.com.au

WINERIES

Bleasdale Wines: Wellington Rd, Langhorne Creek; (08) 8537 4022; www.bleasdale.com.au

Bremerton Wines: Strathalbyn Rd, Langhorne Creek; (08) 8537 3093; www.bremerton.com.au

Coriole: Chaffeys Rd, McLaren Vale; (08) 8323 8305; www.coriole.com

d'Arenberg: Osborn Rd, McLaren Vale; (08) 8329 4800; www.darenberg.com.au

Gemtree Vineyards: Cellar Door at Salopian Inn Restaurant, cnr Willunga and McMurtrie rds, McLaren Vale; (08) 8323 7428; www.gemtreevineyards.com.au

Hoffmann's: see Eateries/The Currant Shed

Lake Breeze Wines: Step Rd, Langhorne Creek; (08) 8537 3017; www.lakebreeze.com.au

Penny's Hill: Main Rd, McLaren Vale; (08) 8556 4460; www.pennyshill.com.au

Primo Estate: McMurtrie Rd; McLaren Vale; (08) 8323 6800; www.primoestate.com.au

Samuel's Gorge: Chapel Hill Rd, McLaren Vale; (08) 8323 8651; www.gorge.com.au

Wirra Wirra: McMurtrie Rd, McLaren Vale; (08) 8323 8414; www.wirra.com.au

Woodstock Wines: see Eateries/The Coterie

Below: sea views from
Bay of Shoals Wines,
Kingscote
**Opposite (top to
bottom):** hand-picked
malbec grapes at Islander
Estate, Parndana; dining
area at Sea Dragon
Lodge, Cape Willoughby
(see Where to stay)

Kangaroo Island

From day one of European landfall this has been a place of feasting. Back in March 1802 when navigator Matthew Flinders named the island he wasn't merely observing its abundance of kangaroos. The real reason was gratitude for the 31 animals he and the ship's company cooked up within hours of going ashore. Given it was their first fresh food in four months – who could blame them?

Kangaroo is still a feature on menus here, alongside an ever-growing array of local produce. As a result KI – as Australia's third largest island is known locally – has become a veritable frontier of food experiences. And this region has natural credentials like nowhere else. Its fresh air, quality soils and reliable rainfall make it the cleanest, greenest landscape in South Australia and, in addition, the absence of foxes, rabbits and many other environmental headaches gives growers terrific leeway to focus on quality, stress-free produce. Here, for example, chooks really can range free.

With a lively mix of cafes and venues, the emphasis here is on authentic, home-grown flavours. KI's output is eclectic to say the least, from wonderful honey and a range of sheep's cheeses to farmed marron,

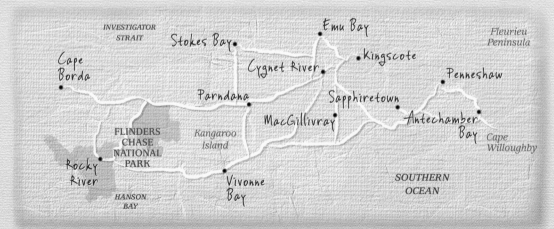

Festivals

Kangaroo Island Gourmet Gallop: food, wine and racing; Cygnet River bank; Jan; (08) 8553 1185; www.tourkangarooisland.com.au

Kangaroo Island Art Feast: wine, food and art festival; island-wide venues; 1st week in Oct; (08) 8553 1185; www.tourkangarooisland.com. au/ArtFeast

Where to stay

Hog Bay Hill: smart, contemporary-style B&B; Wrights Rd, Penneshaw; 0428 922 515; www.hogbayhill.com

Lifetime Private Retreats: stunning north-coast residences; Snelling Beach, North Coast Rd, via Kingscote; (08) 8559 2248; www.life-time.com.au

Sea Dragon Lodge: secluded coastal hideaway; Willoughby Rd, Cape Willoughby; (08) 8553 1449; www.seadragonlodge.com.au

Southern Ocean Lodge: ultra-luxury cliff-top retreat; Hanson Bay Rd, Hanson Bay; (02) 9918 4355; www.southernoceanlodge.com.au

free-range eggs and superb lamb. With 540 stunning kilometres of coastline, it's not hard to find seafood highlights, especially southern rock lobster, oysters and King George whiting. Meanwhile, vineyards dot the island's interior with 30 local growers pushing this wine region onto the national stage.

For travellers arriving by ferry the gateway town of Penneshaw is their first port of call. It's a handsome headland location with views across Backstairs Passage and a fine local beach. For casual meals try the **Dudley Wines Cellar Door and Cafe**. There is a bit of everything here – souvenirs, gallery, and a cellar door for one of KI's wine pioneers. Both breakfast and lunch menus incorporate regional flavours with tasting platters and heartier dishes such as their crispy panko-crumbed calamari with coddled egg tartare or local lamb rogan josh. Just across the road the historic **Hog Bay Hotel**'s expanded dining space features conventional pub fare, but you will find more adventurous options among the entrées and daily specials.

Part of the Kangaroo Island Seafront Resort, **Sorrento's Restaurant** offers the island's most complete dining experience. Here, island ingredients such as American River oysters, free-range chicken, Andermel marron, and South Rock lamb are confidently interpreted with Asian and Mediterranean flavours. Sorrento's is also the cellar door for the full range of **False Cape Wines**. Though more modest in appearance, **Fish** is not just an acclaimed seafood takeaway, but also the tip of a culinary iceberg. From October to April, English-born and trained chef Sue Pearson sends out tangy salt and pepper prawns, scallops, whiting and much more (there's also a grassy park across the road to eat in). Sue also offers weekly cooking demonstrations, guided food tours and, through 2 Birds & A Squid Catering, can deliver exquisite dinners for up to 20 guests to your choice of island locale.

With every year the **Kangaroo Island Farmers' Market** grows in stature. Held at the picturesque Penneshaw Oval, it's a great way to connect with such delights as Charing Cross's crunchy sourdough

Above (left to right): tasting platters at Chapman River Wines, Antechamber Bay; cones of fresh fish ready to go at The Rockpool Cafe, Stokes Bay; Seal Bay Conservative Park at dawn, and with Australian sea lions at play

breads, Kangaroo Island Source's curry pastes and spice rubs, South Rock Lamb, and Sea Dragon Organics' kasundi and dahl. Worthy of note is that ferry operator Sealink offers discounted fares on market days.

The Dudley Peninsula's cool high country is one of the island's top grape-growing areas. Close by the east coast's stunning Antechamber Bay, **Chapman River Wines** has a quirky and creative cellar door serving platters of local cheese, cured meats, salads and dips with their house-made sesame crackers. Meanwhile, on the opposite side of the peninsula, a hilltop perch gives visitors to **Sunset Wines** outstanding views across Eastern Bay all the way to the town of American River.

As well as big nature highlights such as Seal Bay and Admirals Arch (notable for their colonies of Australian sea-lions and New Zealand fur seals), the westward trek across the island also includes food highlights. **Clifford's Honey Farm** has a down-home feel and a range of KI honey, and honey ice-cream, from the world's only pure strain of Ligurian bee. Just

inland from Vivonne Bay, **The Marron Cafe** showcases the versatility of this freshwater crayfish, which is farmed on site (tours available). Marron dishes incorporate home-grown native herbs such as lemon myrtle and mountain pepper, plus menu options for non-crustacean diners.

Way out west in Flinders Chase National Park's visitor centre, **Chase Cafe** serves excellent baguettes together with freshly caught grilled garfish and whiting. Overlooking sugar gum woodland, the outdoor courtyard gets you in the nature mood. For evening dining **Nicolas Baudin Restaurant** (part of Kangaroo Island Wilderness Retreat) gives deft French and Asian flavours to island fare, such as seared kangaroo with Sichuan glaze and seasonal seafood treats such as oysters tweaked with dill and chardonnay jelly.

Of the beautiful beaches of KI's north coast, Stokes Bay is a favourite haunt and is also home to two handy eateries. **The Rockpool Cafe** has the air of an unassuming boatshed but the kitchen turns out some of the snappiest seafood on the island with proper house-made tartare sauce. Up the hill overlooking the bay, **Stokes Bar & Grill** does generous seafood platters and chargrilled steaks against a magnificent backdrop of the north coast.

The northern coast and plateau country is another prime grape-growing district. After falling in love with KI on his honeymoon, French winemaking legend Jacques Lurton was inspired to establish **Islander Estate** – the island's only winery given a five-star gong by James Halliday. Wine styles include several intriguing multi-varietal blends employing varieties such as cabernet franc, malbec, grenache, semillon and viognier (winery visits are by appointment only). Closer to Kingscote, the cellar door of **Bay of Shoals Wines** has a real maritime feel with its nautical relics and bay vistas. Top-rated wines include their estate-grown riesling – a made-in heaven marriage with the ubiquitous local whiting. For a very different selection of tipples, visit **Kangaroo Island Spirits**, a boutique distillery with a range of island inspired liqueurs (*see* feature, p. 280).

As the island's major centre, Kingscote is a busy produce hub. Just out of town at Cygnet River the **Island Pure Sheep Dairy** is a must-see. While this producer's haloumi and feta are justly famous, be sure to sample the creamy richness of their Spanish-style manchego. Also, when it's available, the sheep's ricotta is a sublime partner for tomato and basil salads. Kingscote, the site of the first official European settlement, is beside the sea so

fishing is a prominent industry. A Caltex service station might be an unlikely venue for a fish shop but **Kangaroo Island Fresh Seafood** lives up to its name with a full-on filleting table behind the counter preparing local catches of whiting, garfish and snapper. They also do topnotch takeaways as well. For all things lobster **Ferguson Australia** is open over the summer months for fresh-caught crayfish, prawns and other seafood delicacies. Tours of the production facility are available and lookout for their range of delicious lobster oils and sauces. Also in town, award-winning organic honeys – reflecting the character of different plant communities – are available for tasting and purchase at **Island Beehive**, one of the island's major producers. And be sure to try Tracey Zealand's sublime honeycomb ice-cream.

Popular Kingscote eateries include main street venues such as **Rogers Deli** for cakes and coffee, and **Restaurant Pizza Cafe Bella**, which does inventive pizzas such as their spiced lamb and goat's cheese special, plus fine seafood creations such as seared local kingfish with pickled Asian greens. Both the town's pubs, the **Ozone Hotel** and the **Queenscliffe Hotel**, incorporate a growing mix of local produce in their bistro-style menus. Grills and seafood are the standouts and the Ozone's historic seafront location and open-air dining make it a favourite watering hole for island visitors.

Below: panoramic view of Islander Estate's vineyard at Parndana
Opposite (clockwise from top left): cellar door relaxation at Chapman River Wines, Antechamber Bay; Ozone Hotel, Kingscote; Andermel marron and accompaniments at False Cape's Sorrento's Restaurant, Penneshaw

Island spirits

Kangaroo Island Spirits near Kingscote

South Australia's first and only boutique distillery may only be three years old, yet **Kangaroo Island Spirits** has already won plaudits aplenty for its ingenious range of liqueurs. It's a classic tale of island-inspired innovation. 'Our focus is on products infused with local flavours', says pioneer Jon Lark, 'and visitors enjoy the creative fun of what we do.' The liqueurs are a very different expression of KI's essence, with styles including limoncello, anisette, ginger and lime, pink lily strawberry and zenzerino – a tangy ginger and orange brew. One of their most popular products incorporates the flavours of roasted walnuts and Ligurian honey to create a luscious and spicy dessert liqueur. Always on the lookout for new styles, the ever-inventive Jon and his wife, Sarah, have recently added a vintage gin (using native island juniper) and vodkas, infused with KI samphire and chilli, to their range. Located just ten minutes from Kingscote, the rustic charm of the distillery's cellar door is the place to try and buy the complete range, or just enjoy a coffee or cocktail of choice. Products are also available online and at bottle shops and outlets across the island.

Contacts for Kangaroo Island

EATERIES

Chase Cafe: Flinders Chase Visitor's Centre, Flinders Chase National Park; (08) 8559 7339

Dudley Wines Cellar Door and Cafe: Cnr North Tce and Thomas Wilson St, Penneshaw; (08) 8553 1333; www.dudleywines.com.au

Fish: North Tce, Penneshaw; (08) 8553 1177; www.2birds1squid.com

Hog Bay Hotel (Penneshaw Hotel): North Tce, Penneshaw; (08) 8553 1042

Marron Cafe: Harriet Rd, Central Kangaroo Island (nr Vivonne Bay); (08) 8559 4114; www.andermel.com

Nicolas Baudin Restaurant: Kangaroo Island Wilderness Retreat, cnr South Coast Rd and West End Hwy; (08) 8559 7275; www.kiwr.com

Ozone Hotel: The Foreshore, cnr Commercial St and Chapman Tce, Kingscote; (08) 8553 2011; www.ozonehotel.com

Queenscliffe Hotel: Main St, Kingscote; (08) 8553 2254

Restaurant Pizza Cafe Bella: 54 Dauncey St, Kingscote; (08) 8553 0400; www.restaurantbella.com.au

Rogers Deli: Main St, Kingscote; (08) 8553 2053

Sorrento's Restaurant: Kangaroo Island Seafront Resort, North Tce, Penneshaw; (08) 8553 1028; www.seafront.com.au

Stokes Bar and Grill: North Coast Rd (east of Stokes Bay carpark); (08) 8559 2200

The Rockpool Cafe: North Coast Rd, Stokes Bay; (08) 8559 2277

MARKETS

Kangaroo Island Farmers' Market: Lloyd Collins Reserve, Penneshaw; 1st Sun each month, morning; (08) 8553 1185 or 0412 194 840

GOURMET PRODUCE

Clifford's Honey Farm: Elsegood Rd, MacGillivray; (08) 8553 8295; www.cliffordshoney.com.au

Ferguson Australia: 48 Kohinoor Rd, Kingscote; (08) 8346 8764 or 0418 819 403; www.fergusonaustralia.com

Island Beehive: Main Rd, Kingscote; (08) 8553 0080; www.island-beehive.com.au

Island Pure Sheep Dairy: Gum Creek Rd, Cygnet River; (08) 8553 9110

Kangaroo Island Fresh Seafoods: Caltex Fuel Complex, 26 Telegraph Rd, Kingscote; (08) 8553 0177

WINERIES/DISTILLERIES

Bay of Shoals Wines: Cordes Rd, Kingscote; (08) 8553 0289; www.bayofshoalswines.com.au

Chapman River Wines: off Cape Willoughby Rd, Antechamber Bay; (08) 8553 1371

Dudley Wines: see Eateries

False Cape Wines: Sorrento's Restaurant (cellar door), North Terrace, Penneshaw; (08) 8553 1028; www.lakebreeze.com.au

Islander Estate: Bark Hut Rd, Parndana; (08) 8553 9008; www.iev.com.au

Kangaroo Island Spirits: Playford Hwy, Kingscote; (08) 8553 9211; www.kispirits.com.au

Sunset Wines: Hog Bay Rd, Penneshaw; (08) 8553 1378; www.sunset-wines.com.au

COOKING SCHOOLS

Fish: see Eateries

Below: drying fruit at Loxton

Opposite (top to bottom): roadside fruit stalls are common in the Riverland region; misty morning on the Murray River

Riverland

Plump peaches and apricots, crunchy almonds, fruity olives, juicy oranges and grapes by the truck load – for sheer output of produce no other South Australian region can match the Riverland. On the face of it, this harvest is simply a case of good farming land, sunshine galore and, of course, a generous ration of River Murray water. Yet behind the commercial success of the vast orchards and vineyards there's also a fascinating tale of hard-working families with a flair for food. Over the past 60 years the Italian, Greek, Indian and Vietnamese immigrant communities have brought to the region both new farming traditions and a rich mix of cuisines.

This contribution is most evident at low-key roadside stalls and farmers' markets where you can be bedazzled by the wood-oven breads, sauces, relishes, curry pastes, smoked meats and array of home-grown organic vegetables. But such diversity is also reflected in many emerging businesses such as **Kingston Estate Wines**, the creation of the Moularadellis family. Located in the centre of this region at Kingston-on-Murray, their cellar door showcases an impressive selection of wines and multi-regional blends – be sure to sample some of their top-flight Echelon range, especially the

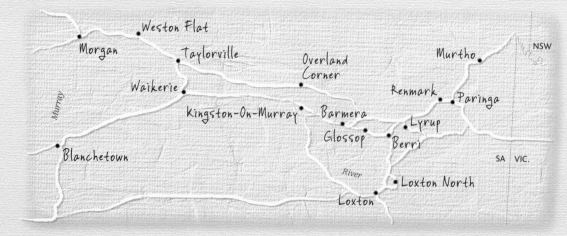

Festivals

Riverland Harvest Festival and Great Grape Stomp: family fun, food and entertainment; Balfour–Olgivy Rd, Loxton Nth; late Mar; (08) 8584 1369

Riverland Food and Wine Festival: Riverview Dr, Berri; mid-Oct; (08) 8582 3309; www.riverlandwine.org.au

Riverland Renaissance Festival: wine, food and sports; various venues, Berri; Oct; 0412 279 219

Where to stay

Mill Cottage: charming and spacious 1920s villa; 2 Mill Rd, Loxton; (08) 8584 5206; www.millcottage.com.au

Paringa House B&B Stone Cottages: traditional cottage-style rooms; 1 Museum Dr, Paringa; (08) 8595 5217; www.paringahouse.com.au

Riverbush Cottages: homestead-style units in natural bushland; Old Sturt Hwy, Berri; (08) 8582 3455; www.riverbushcottages.com.au

Thiele's Heritage B&B: charming cliff-top farmhouse; Casson Av, Loxton North; 0402 837 012; www.thielesbandb.com.au

dark-berry intensity of the petit verdot. North of town, **Banrock Station**'s Wine & Wetland Centre is an acclaimed meeting place for wine, food and nature. Australian native herbs and flavours really punctuate the menu choices here. Grazing platters have such regional tastes as river mint tomatoes, olives and emu ham, while mains include quandong-glazed kangaroo fillet, and South Australian mulloway tweaked with locally grown capers, lemon myrtle and samphire.

Across the river, the **Overland Corner Hotel** is an authentic historic landmark from Australia's droving past. Dating from 1859, this stone pub continues to welcome travellers with tasty country pub food. Still on the northern side of the Murray, but way out west towards Morgan and some 50 kilometres north-west of Taylorville, at Weston Flat, **Mallyons on the Murray** is another old watering hole reborn as a bush cafe and gallery. Organic home-grown produce is at the heart of the experience and the cafe's fresh salads, pies, quiches and lush fruit desserts. The signature, year-round dish is a plate of Weston Flat pancakes lathered in jam and cream.

By contrast **Cragg's Creek Cafe**, upstream at Berri, is an ultra-modern cellar-door and versatile eatery with echoes of the owner's Greek heritage. Serving great coffee and juices, it's a handy breakfast and snack spot right on the water's edge. It is also an

ideal lunch venue – a place to linger on the deck and enjoy the wines and the tranquil river views. The tempting selection of lunchtime tapas plates includes homemade Greek dips, lamb shashlik, couscous and watercress salad with blue cheese and wattle-seed balsamic.

A third of Australia's wine is produced in the Riverland and Berri is at the heart of the action with the biggest winery in the land, **Berri Estates**, just out of town. Look out for smaller producers such as **Salena Estate** with an excellent range of medal-winning organic wines and their flagship red Bookpurnong Hill Bin 267. Renmark is the other big wine centre, with family-owned **Angove** among the leading lights. Their portfolio encompasses many fine regional and multi-varietal blends. For beer-lovers, the locally brewed Amazon Ale is a rich, full-bodied golden ale handcrafted by **Woolshed Brewery**, open by appointment. For waterfront dining head to the Renmark Club, where the **River's Edge Restaurant** harnesses great local produce to create Mediterranean-inspired dishes such as pumpkin, almond and gorgonzola tart, and lamb cutlets partnered with wilted saltbush leaves and local vincotto. Even the desserts get the bushfood treatment, with choices including wattle-seed pavlova and quandong crumble.

Below: wetland views at Banrock Station, Kingston-on-Murray

Contacts for Riverland

EATERIES

Banrock Station: Holmes Rd, Kingston-on-Murray; (08) 8583 0299;
www.banrockstation.com.au

Cragg's Creek Cafe: Riverview Dr, Berri;
(08) 8582 4466

Mallyons on the Murray: Morgan–Renmark Rd, Weston Flat via Morgan;
(08) 8543 2263

Overland Corner Hotel: Old Coach Rd,
Overland Corner; (08) 8588 7021

River's Edge Restaurant: Renmark Club,
Murray Ave, Renmark; (08) 8586 6611

MARKETS

Barmera Main Street Markets: Barwell
Ave; Sun; 0428 152 235

Riverland Farmers' Market: Senior
Citizen's Hall, Crawford Tce, Berri; Sat
morning; (08) 8582 4864;
www.riverlandfarmersmarket.org.au

WINERIES

Angove: Bookmark Ave, Renmark;
(08) 8580 3148;
www.angoves.com.au

Banrock Station: see Eateries

Berri Estates: Old Sturt Hwy, Glossop;
(08) 8582 0340

Kingston Estate Wines: Sturt Hwy,
Kingston-on-Murray; (08) 8583 0500;
www.kingstonestatewines.com.au

Salena Estate Wines: Loxton–Berri Rd,
Lyrup; (08) 8584 1333;
www.salenaestate.com.au

BREWERIES

Woolshed Brewery: Wilkinson Rd,
Murtho via Renmark; (08) 8595 8037;
www.woolshedbrewery.com.au

Above and below: gnarled vines at Renmark's
Angove, and wine barrels in the winery's cellar

Below: a glass of red at
Boston Bay Wines, Port
Lincoln

Opposite (top to
bottom): southern rock
lobster on the menu at
The Marina Bistro, Port
Lincoln; hauling in the
day's catch of southern
bluefin tuna at
Port Lincoln

Eyre Peninsula

Remote islands, sheltered bays and long, lonely beaches make this one of
South Australia's most dramatic attractions. The peninsula is huge – in fact,
not much smaller than Tasmania – yet remains sparsely populated and
surprisingly remote. There's a wild, outback feel to its shores. For
lovers of surf, solitude and, especially seafood, the 'west coast' feels like
paradise found.

Port Lincoln is the hub of the action. Home to Australia's largest fishing
fleet, this appealing town has one of the country's finest natural harbours,
one that locals proudly boast is three times the size of Sydney's. Here you
can revel in almost every conceivable form of marine delicacy, plucked
fresh from the surrounding Southern Ocean waters – southern bluefin tuna,
oysters, squid, octopus, abalone, prawns, scallops, mussels, crabs, southern
rock lobster, King George whiting, yellow-tail kingfish and many other
deepwater scalefish species are all seasonally available. Few other ports in
the world offer greater quality and diversity.

Fishing is a way of life all along the peninsula's shores and in the
scattered coastal towns. From Cowell and Elliston to Streaky Bay and

Ceduna

Wirrulla

Streaky Bay

Minnipa

Elliston

Lock

Cleve

Cowell

Eyre
Peninsula

GREAT
AUSTRALIAN
BIGHT

Tumby
Bay

SPENCER
GULF

Coffin Bay

Port Lincoln

Festivals

Tunarama Festival: Foreshore, Tasman Tce, Port Lincoln; Jan (Australia Day weekend); (08) 8682 1300; www.tunarama.com.au

Fresh Fish Place Zonta Port Lincoln Long Lunch: various Port Lincoln venues; end May; 1300 788 378

Ceduna Oysterfest: O'Loughlin Tce; 1st weekend in Oct; (08) 8625 3407; www.oysterfest.org

Where to stay

Bay 10 Holiday House: relaxing beachfront villas; 24 Lincoln Hwy, Port Lincoln; (08) 8682 4861; www.bay10accommodation.com

Belle Vista: beautifully restored 1937 bungalow; 12 Normandy Pl, Port Lincoln; (08) 8683 0180

Sheoak East Side: luxury two-storey apartments; 257 Esplanade, Coffin Bay; 0427 844 568

Tanonga Luxury Eco Lodges: self-contained stylish eco lodge; Charlton Gully, Port Lincoln; 0427 277 417; www.tanonga.com.au

The Anchorage Holiday Apartment: waterfront units with stunning views; 6/33 South Point Dr, Port Lincoln; (08) 8683 0992; www.anchorageapartment.com.au

Ceduna there are oyster farms, aquaculture projects and active fishing fleets, many of which invite travellers to observe work in progress and enjoy the fruits of their labours. For those who like to 'catch and cook' there are fishing charters and a string of outstanding surf-fishing beaches, famed for their hauls of salmon and mulloway. Meanwhile, away from the coast, this is wool and wheat farming country on a grand scale. That means no-fuss rural towns with the hospitality of traditional country pubs and family-run bakers and butchers.

One way to get into the swing of things is to join one of the on-water tours in and around Port Lincoln. Peter Dennis of **Triple Bay Charters** guides you across beautiful Boston Bay to visit aquaculture and tuna-farm operations, with opportunities to enjoy a taste of bluefin tuna sashimi along the way. Charters depart from the Marina Hotel Pontoon. Back on dry land, the **Port Lincoln Fresh Fish Company** offers tours of its fish processing facility, with tempting samples of smoked fish, pickled calamari, octopus and soused scallops. The company's retail outlet presents one of the town's biggest selections of fresh seafood and, for canny buyers, there are even seasonal bargains such as bags of lobster 'spiders'.

No surprise to find the ocean harvest is the main attraction on menus all around town. Among local eateries **Del Giorno's** is a genuine highlight and a tribute to Kris Binder's vision for advancing fresh local produce. There's lively Italian-influenced food here at any time of day and, among the pizza and pasta dishes, there's a strong seafood showing. Dishes such as the tuna steaks with tomato salsa and lime butter, and Kinkawooka mussels in a chilli and garlic broth, are packed with vivid flavours and freshness. Just out of town **The Marina Bistro** is hugely popular among boaties and locals. You can't get any more seaside than this: with a long dining deck overhanging the marina, there is always the sound of lapping water emanating from below. The bistro's menu spans a huge range of dishes, with

many choices for oyster lovers and piquant dishes such as lemon pepper calamari and prosciutto-wrapped kingfish tossed with chilli cream. New on the scene is **Lincoln Goodies**, which purports to provide the 'finest of ocean and Eyre'. With a selection of gourmet produce on sale, this deli-cum-cafe serves light lunches and snacks.

Port Lincoln also has a small, but emerging community of wine producers. Look out for hometown labels such as **Lincoln Estate** and **Delacolline Estate Wines**. The latter's cellar door has an alfresco deck where you can enjoy a cheese platter, light lunch or just indulge in their signature lavender and honey panna cotta. The winery is also a lavender farm and various lavender products are on sale, including oils and hand creams. At local wine trailblazer **Boston Bay Wines**, the cellar door offers tastings of the Ford family's full complement of varietals, including their acclaimed riesling – a winning seafood partner – and award-winning shiraz. The district's mild maritime climate also favours Bordeaux-style wines such as cabernet sauvignon and merlot.

Further afield **The Oysterbeds** is an aptly named seaside cafe at Coffin Bay, a short hop across the peninsula from Port Lincoln. The dreamy view across the bays are the only incentive necessary to tuck into a plate of local oysters, either natural or accompanied with a range of tasty flavour embellishments. However, there are more than just molluscs on offer: prawns, lobster, tuna and other fish also appear on the menu depending on the season. It's a much longer haul up the coast to Streaky Bay but the creative cuisine at the **Mocean Cafe Restaurant** makes it worthwhile. This waterfront cafe has more than a dash of outback charm and chef Hardy Weyrauch offers an inspired all-day menu of tapas plates and seafood. As evening approaches more intricate dishes such as poached abalone with soy and wasabi dressing, a fish tagine and king prawn laksa take centre stage.

Above (left to right): dining on the deck at
Mocean Cafe Restaurant, Streaky Bay; shucking
oysters at Coffin Bay

Contacts for Eyre Peninsula

EATERIES

The Oysterbeds: 61 Esplanade, Coffin Bay;
(08) 8685 4000

Del Giorno's: 80 Tasman Tce, Port Lincoln;
(08) 8683 0577; www.delgiornos.com.au

The Marina Bistro: 13 Jubilee Dr, Port
Lincoln; (08) 8682 6141

Mocean Cafe Restaurant: 30 Alfred Tce,
Streaky Bay; (08) 8626 1775

STORES

Lincoln Goodies: 2/17 Porter St, Porter St
Plaza, Port Lincoln; (08) 8683 1600 or
0404 589 927

Port Lincoln Fresh Fish Company:
20 Proper Bay Rd, Port Lincoln;
(08) 8682 2166;
www.portlincolnseafood.com.au

Triple Bay Charters: Peter Dennis,
84 Monash Rd, Port Lincoln; (08) 8682 4119
or 0429 824 119;
www.triplebaycharters.net.au

MARKETS

Cowell Lions Club Street Market: Main
St; 1st Sun each month, morning (Oct–Apr);
(08) 8629 2606

***Eyre Peninsula Farmer and
Fishermen's Market Cleve:*** Ruddall Rd;
Tues–Thurs; 0419 295 780;
www.eyrepeninsulafarmersmarket.com.au

WINERIES

Boston Bay Wines: Lincoln Hwy,
Port Lincoln; (08) 8684 3600;
www.bostonbaywines.com.au

Delacolline Estate Wines: 31 Whillas Rd,
Port Lincoln; (08) 8682 4000;
www.delacollinewines.com.au

Lincoln Estate: 22 Lincoln Hwy,
Port Lincoln; (08) 8683 4033;
www.lincolnestatewines.com.au

Western Australia

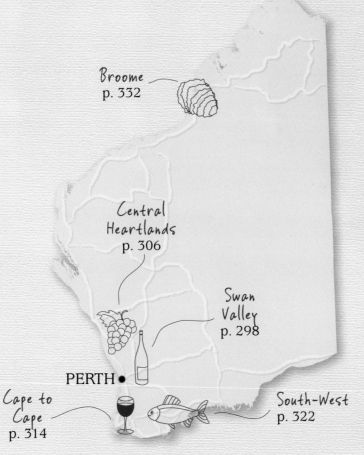

Broome
p. 332

Central
Heartlands
p. 306

Swan
Valley
p. 298

PERTH ●

Cape to
Cape
p. 314

South-West
p. 322

Left: long timber jetty
at Busselton, Cape
to Cape

Above (left to
right): wine barrels
at Margaret River's
Brookland Valley, Cape
to Cape; sensational
seafood on the shores
of Cable Beach,
Broome; vineyards
at Picardy near
Pemberton,
South-West

Overleaf: the pub
scene is thriving
in Perth

Perth

There's a distinct buzz in the Perth air
as the community develops a greater
appreciation of food, wine and beer.

Perth ~ an overview

In the most isolated city on earth, there's a saying that 'WA' is an acronym for 'wait awhile'. Not even the most zealous local will deny that Perth, in relation to its eastern counterparts, is a little behind the eight ball, particularly in cultural circles. However, there has been a breakthrough with the deregulation of licensing laws and now restaurants are allowed to serve alcohol without food. As a result, many little bars have opened and interestingly enough some of these offer menus on a par with any good restaurant. The flow-on effect has seen patrons socialising any night of the week and, combined with a surge in population from the mining boom, eateries are filling up at a dramatic rate. There's a distinct buzz in the Perth air as the community develops a greater appreciation of food, wine and beer. And it is not only restaurants that are benefiting but also gourmet outlets, which are busier than ever.

Opposite (left to right): fresh fish and chips by the water at Fremantle; relaxed waterside dining space at Matilda Bay Restaurant, Crawley
Below right: the popular cappuccino strip at Fremantle

OUTER-CITY GOURMET EXPERIENCES

* Boatshed Market
* Clarkes of North Beach
* Hippo Creek African Grill
* Kalamunda Farmers' Market
* Matilda Bay Restaurant
* Maya Indian
* Mondo Di Carne
* Pata Negra
* Spanish Flavours Wembley
* Yee Seng Oriental Supermarket

See following pages...

Outer-city gourmet experiences

Here are some very good restaurants, markets and provedores outside the CBD but well worth the slight detour.

Above (left to right): a Spanish fan on display, and all things Spanish for sale, at Spanish Flavours Wembley; seductive lemon grass panna cotta dessert at Matilda Bay Restaurant, Crawley; gourmet products at Mondo Di Carne, Inglewood

Boatshed Market: a one-stop shop for cheese, deli goods, fruit, vegetables, seafood, baked goods, meat and gourmet ingredients; 40 Jarrad St, Cottesloe; (08) 9284 5176; www.boatshedmarket.com.au

Clarkes of North Beach: the state's most revered BYO restaurant; 97 Flora Tce, North Beach; (08) 9246 7621; www.clarkesofnorthbeach.com.au

Hippo Creek African Grill: African-inspired premium meat dishes, including aged steak, certified Australian Angus beef and MSA certified Australian beef; **Hippo Creek Hillary**, Shop 203, Sorrento Quay Boardwalk, Hillarys Boat Harbour, 58 Southside Dr, Hillarys, (08) 9447 2238; **Hippo Creek Scarborough**, 251 West Coast Hwy, Scarborough, (08) 9245 8004

Kalamunda Farmers' Market: a true farmers' market where stallholders sell what they grow, catch, pickle, preserve, or bake themselves using only local seasonal produce; Town Square, Barber St, Kalamunda; 1st Sat each month; (08) 9257 2266

Matilda Bay Restaurant: aged beef and seafood at its waterside best; 3 Hackett Dr, Crawley; (08) 9423 5000; www.matbay.com.au

Maya Indian: authentic longstanding Indian cuisine on Fremantle's buzzing cappuccino strip; 75–77 Market St, Fremantle; (08) 9335 2796; www.mayarestaurant.com.au

TRUFFLE PRODUCTS

Mondo Di Carne: premier butchers,
caterers, cooking school extraordinaire;
824 Beaufort St, Inglewood;
(08) 9371 6350; www.mondo.net.au

Pata Negra: embrace that Moorish feeling
with Middle Eastern and Spanish tapas;
26 Stirling Hwy, Nedlands; (08) 9389 5517;
www.patanegra.com.au

Spanish Flavours Wembley: for all those
elusive and not so elusive Spanish products;
Shop 17, 350 Cambridge St, Wembley;
(08) 9284 1313

Yee Seng Oriental Supermarket:
family-run business for all your Asian
culinary needs, fresh produce and kitchen
equipment; Megaplex Business Centre,
36 Hulme Crt, Myaree; (08) 9330 9096

Swan Valley

When Captain James Stirling stumbled across the Swan Valley in 1827, he was greeted by a bush landscape rather than the present-day chequered vineyards, meadows of wildflowers and jovial patrons. After his arrival the land was developed into agricultural estates, which in the 1920s European immigrants transformed into the state's oldest wine region. Much of the valley's ethnic heritage is evident and any tour of the region reveals the work of Italian, Spanish, French and German families. Also known as Perth's Valley of Taste, this is a place brimming with wineries, restaurants, breweries, and accommodation options. Located just 30 minutes from the capital city, the Swan Valley provides the ideal escape for a day or two or an even longer stay.

The 32-kilometre self-drive option is a popular way to explore the valley, taking the West Swan Road from Guildford to Upper Swan before looping back down along the Great Northern Highway. On the way you pass through the small localities of Caversham, West Swan, Henley Brook, Belhus, Upper Swan, Baskerville, Millendon, Herne Hill, Middle Swan and Midland. The region is renowned for its chardonnay, shiraz, chenin blanc and verdelho, and boasts over 40 wineries, of which Houghton and Sandalford are the best known. However, those who take the time will find many more wine and gourmet treasures in this picturesque valley so close to the city of Perth.

At Caversham you should stop and be wooed by the passion of Kiran and Kelli Mainwaring of the much-awarded **Dear Friends** restaurant. This dynamic husband and wife duo have used their travels through Europe and Asia as inspiration for a menu comprising dishes such as Andalusian paella with rabbit or oriental-style suckling pig. If the à la carte list presents too many options then go for the degustation menu. Naturally the wine list includes many drops from the region as well as from the state's South-West, along with some Barossa Valley and international labels. Also look for rare and limited release wines such as the Henschke Hill of Grace Shiraz or a 1987 Penfolds Bin 95 Grange Shiraz. As well as serving lunch this is one of the few places open for dinner in the valley (Wednesday–Sunday).

Festivals

Taste of the Valley: food festival; throughout Swan Valley; Feb; (08) 8 9379 9400; www.swanvalley.com.au

Seafood and Shiraz Weekends: 8 venues in Swan Valley; 1st and 2nd weekends in July; (08) 9379 9400; www.swanvalley.com.au

Mundaring Truffle Festival: end July/early Aug; (08) 9290 6655; www.mundaringtrufflefestival.com

Spring in the Valley: wine, food and beer; various Swan Valley venues; Oct; (08) 9379 9400; www.swanvalley.com.au

Where to stay

Strelley Brook Cottage: self-contained restored heritage cottage; 90 Lefroy St, Herne Hill; (08) 9296 1876; www.strelleybrook.com.au

Swan Valley Oasis Resort: lodge and chalet rooms; 10 250 West Swan Rd, Henley Brook; (08) 9296 5500; www.swanvalleyoasis.com

The Vines Resort & Country Club: a golfer's dream; Verdelho Dr, The Vines; (08) 9297 3000; www.vines.com.au

Thie My Chree Retreat: self-contained two-bedroom cottages; 255 Lefroy Ave, Herne Hill; 0421 162 336; www.thiemychreeretreat.com.au

You can keep the fiesta spirit flowing in typical European tradition compliments of **Pinelli** winery just across the road. Their notable and fruity 2009 Family Reserve Verdelho and the strawberry and raspberry blended 2009 Breanna Rosé are the result of winemaking since 1980. Available in many varietals are 2-litre-bottle house wines, ideal for extended family gatherings.

Fancy a concert on the lawn, a contemporary Australian meal or just a tasting at the cellar door? You will find all three at **Sandalford Wines**, which is celebrating 170 years of operation. The Element Range is not only easy drinking, but it is also light on the wallet. Or perhaps sample the limited release Prendiville Reserve, named after the owners of the winery, or the Sandalera, which is based on a rich Pedro Ximenez, a sherry originating from Spain. If just sampling the wine isn't enough then join a 'winemaker for a day' tour.

If chocolate addicts are twitching, the **Margaret River Chocolate Company – Swan Valley** will be the saviour, particularly for the free samples. Since the opening of the original Margaret River factory's second outlet in the valley, with **The Chocolate Cafe** on site (open daily), patrons have been tucking into light lunches and all things chocolate – cakes,

desserts, fondues and drinks. The chocolate shop stocks all kinds of delights from handmade truffles to assorted chocolate-coated delicacies, allowing you the privilege of taking such morsels away to indulge upon in private.

At Henley Brook you will find the enchanting **Little River Winery and Restaurant**, with its picturesque vineyard views of old shiraz and chardonnay vines. Open every day except Thursday, you can dine on such fare as coq au vin, beef bourguignon or a slow-cooked lamb pie topped with puff pastry, possibly followed by a tempting tarte tatin or an old-fashioned rhubarb and strawberry crumble. Applying French winemaking techniques, the Little River's label includes the French-style dessert wine Noble Classic 2007 and the Viognier-Marsanne 2007.

In this immigrant-influenced valley, the Darling Ranges hovering in the distance are a reminder that Australian soil is still underfoot. No more so than at the **Black Swan Winery & Restaurant**, where floor-to-ceiling windows allow panoramic views of vineyards and sweeping rural scenes. Extracted from 70-year-old vines, the wine maintains its quality by harvesting and sorting the fruit by hand. Although compact in selection, the most popular choice from

Below (left to right): chocolate-coating process at Mondo Nougat, Herne Hill; wine aging in the barrel at Talijancich, Herne Hill; table setting, and one of chef Alain Fabregues' creations, at Mundaring's Loose Box Restaurant

the wine list is the rosé and the 2004 Cabernet Franc, a full-bodied rare variety of the Swan Valley. Chef Jamie Skinner spoils his devotees with local produce, estate-grown vegetables and imported delicacies such as wagyu beef, Coffin Bay oysters and Kurobuta pork – the crowd-pleasing black pig 'coteletta' (a derivation of the French veal cutlet or côtelette), is served with potato gratin, celeriac remoulade, rocket and lemon. Lunch is a daily affair while dinner is available Wednesday–Saturday.

In the tradition of a German beer hall, **Elmar's in the Valley** can seat an impressive 400 diners in one sitting. They all come to devour the bratwurst sausages, pork schnitzel, kassler smoked pork chop and, Elmar's specialty, the heart-stopping pork shank. The extensive lawn area to the rear often features families relaxing and the odd patron resting after over-indulging in the hearty fare, and throughout the year the area becomes a venue for live concerts and events. Other breweries to visit in the valley are **Duckstein**, which now also has a slick operation in Margaret River, and **Ironbark**, **Feral Brewing Company** and **Mash Brewery**.

Spanning over 20 hectares, **Edgecombe Brothers** has been a prominent player in the valley since 1925, and its casual cafe (open daily) serves up wholesome food with its rustic views. Even the air seems to smell fresher here and the menu brims with seasonal produce grown on site such as asparagus, tomatoes, eggs, melons, pumpkins, olives and grapes. Check out the 2007 Old Vine Shiraz and the limited edition Premium Muscadelle. You can also stock up on a range of gourmet treats at the cellar door, including preserves, jams, fruit butters and curds, olive oils and sun-dried fruits. During the asparagus season (September–March) people come from near and far to buy the estate-grown green and purple asparagus.

Renowned for verdelho, fortified wine, and a liqueur muscat considered to be one of the best around, **John Kosovich Wines** planted its first vines in 1922. They've had plenty of time to master their craft and the hand harvesting and small volumes produced ensure the integrity of the wines. Open daily, the family-owned boutique operation features an underground tasting room dating back to the vineyard's foundation year.

Not only is the state-of-the-art **Olive Farm Wines** cut into a hill, it is etched into Perth's viticultural history. Established in 1829, the family-run operation is the state's longest running winery; although its relocation from South Guildford to the heart of the valley is a recent endeavour. The new stylish building

makes use of Western Australian materials, with bench tops of jarrah and walls of Karratha stone. Winemaker Anthony Yurisich has had plenty of time to perfect the Olive Farm tradition and the wine list is naturally extensive. The Olivine sparkling range will put a bubble in your stride: along with the traditional white méthode champenoise, the range includes a pink variety made from shiraz grapes, and others made from merlot and tempranillo.

Awards aside, **Talijancich** at Herne Hill remains true to its humble 1932 beginnings with its rustic cellar door. Most famous for its fortifieds, the white liqueurs served on ice during the warmer months are a refreshing treat and the rich-flavoured reds are luscious year-round. The vintage verdelho has been nominated as one of the best in the country, but the 1965 Solero Pedro Ximenez, aged for some 25–30 years, and the 1961 Solero Reserve Muscat really shine.

Named after the small bird that graces the Swan River, **Sittella Winery and Cafe** regally presides over its cascading vineyards. With rendered walls and floor-to-ceiling windows, the restaurant boasts one of the best valley views in the region – reminiscent of a languid summer's day in many a European wine region. Chef Mike Price draws upon his 30-year experience in major London hotels and Michelin Star–rated restaurants in Paris and the south of France to create a menu that includes the ever-popular dishes of freshly shucked oysters, seafood

and sweet potato chowder, and sautéed scallops and spice-rubbed pork belly with rum roast pineapple, chilli coriander and ginger relish. And that's just for starters. You could follow up with garlic-crusted rack of lamb alongside whipped potatoes with mint pesto and port wine jus, or try the grilled kangaroo fillet with beetroot relish. And if this is not enough, choose a tempting dessert to be savoured with one of Sittella's fortifieds, perhaps the Liqueur Verdelho or Pedro Ximenez. At Sittella connoisseurs have a wide range of varietals to choose from (particularly as the winery boasts a vast number of wine awards), including sparkling chardonnay, reserve semillon, and muscat Alexandria (frontignac).

Squishy nougat-oozing honey and almond or a slow-cooked crunchy variety are what **Mondo Nougat** is all about. Embracing its Italian roots, the family-run business employs a simple recipe based on authentic ingredients such as lemon, orange, cherry and chocolate. You can take away heavenly Mondo Creme de Nougat to spread, dip or cook with, or feast on the homemade cakes, biscotti and gelato at the casual cafe. If you have indulged yourself here it would be easy to fly right by the **Jarrah Ridge Winery** on the Great Northern Highway, but then you'd miss out on their Reserve Shiraz or the 2009 Classic White. Jarrah Ridge supports many fundraising organisations and wines are particularly well priced (ranging from $13 to $28), which makes it a rare find in this competitive market.

Below (left to right): Elmar's in the Valley, Henley Brook; freshly made nougat at Mondo Nougat, Herne Hill; Julian James Reserve Muscat 1961 Solero, Talijancich, Herne Hill; Olive Farm Wines, Millendon; liqueurs and spirits on display at Loose Box Restaurant, Mundaring

Houghton, as befits one of Australia's most famous wineries, is set in stunning grounds planted with jacaranda trees, Norfolk pines and towering eucalypts, which attract a variety of birds and flocks of picnickers. Winemaking started here in 1836 and the range includes many varietals, from chardonnay to viognier and tempranillo, and showcases these under such labels such as Jack Mann, Museum and the Stripe Range, which includes the legendary Stripe White Classic (formerly Houghton's White Burgundy). Beneath the vine-covered pergola, the cafe is open daily and the brimming platters to share are the perfect excuse to linger, especially as the kids' lunch boxes and extensive grounds will keep the little ones content. Bountiful offerings of antipasto, beef kofte, cheeses and seafood delicacies can be followed with soups and savoury tarts then perhaps a pasta or a steak sandwich. Throughout the year Houghton hosts performances by local and international artists and year-round the underground art gallery exhibits paintings, sculptures and exquisite handicrafts.

Leaving the valley may require a little pick-me-up for the journey home and a delectable cone from the **Junction Ice Creamery** in Midland should extend the feeling of decadence, or perhaps call in to the store next door, **Midland Junction Fresh Markets**, to stock up on fresh produce and gourmet treats. And, just when you thought there could not be more, you enter the historic town of Guildford where the tantalising aroma of grilled burgers from **Alfred's Kitchen** will encourage you to stop. Established since 1946, this is Perth's longest standing roadside hamburger joint. With 40 styles to choose from and their famous pea and ham soup, patrons drive from all over the metropolitan area. On Friday and Saturday nights the place stays open until 3am and you never know who you might be sharing late-night tales with by the blazing fire.

At Midland you could decide it is worth taking the ten-minute drive eastwards to visit **Darlington Estate Winery** (*see* feature, p. 304) or even travelling a little further to the famous **Loose Box Restaurant**, nestled in the Perth Hills at Mundaring. Food lovers will continue to argue over whether the Loose Box is the best restaurant in town. Chef Alain Fabregues charms with a degustation menu that includes shelled yabby tails served warm on a saffron emulsion with slow-cooked tomatoes and thin crepes spread with almond and vanilla frangipane served with a bitter chocolate sauce. Many of the ingredients are grown on site and it's common to see the staff wandering out into the rambling grounds to pick herbs. The wine list is extensive and includes French classics not found in many Perth restaurants. Book during the Mundaring Truffle Festival and you will be fortunate enough to sample truffles at one of the restaurant's special dinners.

Wine

Meet the Osbornes of Darlington Estate Winery

The owners of the Darlington Estate Winery, Andy and Michelle Osborne, are justly proud of their 2008 Sparkling Shiraz and 2008 Sparkling Pinot/Chardonnay, which were medal winners at the Perth Hills and Swan Valley Wine Awards in 2009. Winemaker Menno Bakkers works his magic on the 16-hectare estate to produce wines that improve year after year. Michelle's passion is entertaining and customers are welcomed into her restaurant as if it's her home dining room. Behind this effervescent host is chef Aaron Free, creating a Mediterranean–Australian cuisine that competes with any urban restaurant, both in its innovativeness and value for money. On a menu featuring house-baked breads and estate-grown vegetables, you might start with house-made spinach and ricotta gnocchi with rich tomato and sage sauce and Grana Padano then follow up with the popular sage and pistachio crusted lamb rack on olive and rocket potatoes with minted pea purée. Hopefully you will have space for the chocolate tart with espresso ice-cream and cherry compote. The restaurant is open Wednesday–Sunday for lunch, Friday–Saturday for dinner and Sunday for breakfast. A new cellar door offers the chance to sample local produce as well as the estate wines and purchase a range of local delicacies and gourmet gift baskets. And the winery seems guaranteed of longevity. As Michelle says, 'Our three sons are the cornerstone of our business – a future winemaker, a chef and a restaurant manager. Our future is predetermined.'

Contacts for Swan Valley

EATERIES

Alfred's Kitchen: Cnr Meadow and James sts, Guildford; (08) 9377 1378; www.alfredskitchen.com.au

Black Swan Winery & Restaurant: 8600 West Swan Rd, West Swan; (08) 9296 6090; www.blackswanwines.com.au

Darlington Estate Winery: 1495 Nelson Rd, Darlington; (08) 9299 6268; www.darlingtonestate.com

Dear Friends: 100 Benara Rd, Caversham; (08) 9279 2815; www.dearfriends.com.au

Edgecombe Brothers: Cnr Gnangara and West Swan rds, Henley Brook; (08) 9296 4307; www.edgecombebrothers.com.au

Houghton cafe: Dale Rd, Middle Swan; (08) 9274 9543; www.houghton-wines.com.au

Little River Winery and Restaurant: 6 Forest Rd; Henley Brook; (08) 9296 4462; www.littleriverwinery.com

Loose Box Restaurant: 6825 Great Eastern Hwy, Mundaring; (08) 9295 1787; www.loosebox.com.au

Mondo Nougat: see Gourmet Produce

Sittella Winery and Cafe: 100 Barrett St, Herne Hill; (08) 9296 2600; www.sittella.com.au

The Chocolate Cafe: see Gourmet Produce/Margaret River Chocolate Factory – Swan Valley

STORES

Midland Junction Fresh Markets: Cnr Great Eastern Hwy and Morrison Rd, Midland; (08) 9250 1205

MARKETS

Kalamunda Farmers' Market: Town Square, Barber St, Kalamunda; 1st Sat each month; (08) 9257 2266

Midland Farmers' Market: Old Great Northern Hwy; Sun; (08) 9576 1234 or (08) 9572 1541

GOURMET PRODUCE

Darlington Estate Winery: see Eateries

Edgecombe Brothers: see Eateries

Junction Ice Creamery: 380 Great Eastern Hwy, Midland; (08) 9274 1013

Margaret River Chocolate Factory: 5123 West Swan Rd, West Swan; (08) 9250 1588; www.chocolatefactory.com.au

Mondo Nougat: 640 Great Northern Hwy, Herne Hill; (08) 9296 0111; www.mondonougat.com.au

WINERIES

Black Swan Winery & Restaurant: see Eateries

Darlington Estate Winery: see Eateries

Edgecombe Brothers: see Eateries

Houghton: Dale Rd, Middle Swan; (08) 9274 9540; www.houghton-wines.com.au

Jarrah Ridge Winery: 651 Great Northern Hwy, Herne Hill; (08) 9296 6337; www.jarrahridge.com.au

John Kosovich Wines: 180 Memorial Ave, Baskerville; (08) 9296 4356; www.johnkosovichwines.com.au

Little River Winery and Restaurant: see Eateries

Olive Farm Wines: 920 Great Northern Hwy, Millendon; (08) 9296 4539; www.olivefarmwines.com

Pinelli: 30 Bennett St, Caversham; (08) 9279 6818; www.pinelliwines.com.au

Sandalford Wines: 3210 West Swan Rd, Caversham; (08) 9374 9374; www.sandalford.com

Sittella Winery: see Eateries

Talijancich: 26 Hyem Rd, Herne Hill; (08) 9296 4289; www.taliwine.com.au

BREWERIES

Duckstein Brewery: Lot 9720 West Swan Rd, Henley Brook; (08) 9296 0620; www.duckstein.com.au

Elmar's in the Valley: 8731 West Swan Rd, Henley Brook; (08) 9296 6354; www.elmars.com.au

Feral Brewing Company: 152 Hadrill Rd, Baskerville; (08) 9296 4657; www.feralbrewing.com.au

Ironbark Brewery: 55 Benara Rd, Caversham; (08) 9377 4400; www.ironbarkbrewery.com.au

Mash Brewery: 10 250 West Swan Rd, Henley Brook; (08) 9296 5588; www.mashbrewing.com.au

Central Heartlands

Encompassing the rolling green hills, citrus orchards, vineyards and olive groves of the Moore River region and the Chittering Valley in the west and a picturesque section of the Avon Valley between Toodyay and Clackline in the east, this region is located to the north and north-east of Perth. Linking the western and eastern areas of the region is the Julimar State Forest, an area of majestic wandoo trees – white-barked eucalypts endemic to Western Australia. Due to its far-flung locations, a tour of this region requires some careful planning: two of the recommended places to visit are situated on or near the Wanneroo Road in the west; the Chittering Valley, part of the larger Moore River region, has a 76-kilometre wine trail that winds around the hills from Bullsbrook to Gingin; north-west of Gingin there is a cluster of olive groves while some 50 kilometres north-east of Bindoon is Australia's only monastic town, founded by Spanish Benedictine monks in 1846; and, finally, a 50-kilometre drive eastwards through the hardwood forest leads to the historic town of Toodyay, and south of here are several noteworthy wineries, organic honey and olive oil producers and an emu farm.

If you decide to start in the west, take the Wanneroo Road from Perth to reach **Paul Conti Wines** at Woodvale, just south of Wanneroo. It has been on the wine circuit since the family immigrated from Sicily 60 years ago. With several ranges to choose from, the Nero Sparkling Shiraz and the Fronti Late Harvest Muscat 2009 (aka Conti's Fronti) are both popular drops. The family's warm Sicilian hospitality is evident in the on-site **Conti's Restaurant**, a homely elegant dining space housed in their charming original 1928 homestead. The extensive French–Australian menu includes local specialties of beef (a choice of five dishes), lamb, venison, duck, kangaroo and emu. You can enjoy lunch here Wednesday–Friday and dinner Tuesday–Saturday.

Some 25 kilometres north, **Jumanga Olives** is located along the Old Yanchep Road. This is one of several prominent olive-growing estates in the Moore River region. The family-run business sells their extra virgin olive oil and table olives through local outlets and from their Carabooda olive grove (open Wednesday for olive oil and table olive tasting). The property also

Festivals

York Gourmet Food and Wine Festival: showcasing the Swan and Avon valleys' produce; York Town Hall; end June; (08) 9641 1177

Where to stay

Amirage: cosy B&B in rural setting; 1654 Gingin Brook Rd, West Gingin; (08) 9575 7646 or 0411 277 500; www.amiragerestaurantbb.com.au

New Norcia Hotel: simple rooms in grand surrounds; Great Northern Hwy, New Norcia; (08) 9654 8034; www.newnorcia.wa.edu.au/ accommodation/new-norcia-hotel/

White Dog Farm: boutique B&B amid vines; 2035 Chittering Rd, Lower Chittering; (08) 9571 8880; www.whitedogfarm.com.au

Willowbrook Farm Tearooms and Caravan Park: friendly park in rural setting; 1679 Gingin Brook Rd, West Gingin; (08) 9575 7566

307

Above (left to right): Central Heartlands vines; Abbey Church at Australia's only monastic town, New Norcia; Stringybark Winery, Lower Chittering

holds olive oil workshops, run in association with the University of Western Australia. From Jumanga you can wind your way across country to Bullsbrook, the starting point for the Chittering Valley Wine Trail.

If you started out early from Perth, **The Mean Bean Cafe** in Bullsbrook will be a welcome sight and should cure the caffeine shakes before you head off along Chittering Road. The Chittering Valley has eight major wineries where you can sample what the region is best known for: shiraz, verdelho, grenache, viognier, chenin blanc and chardonnay. And the views are beautiful – you could be mistaken for thinking you're driving through a Frederick McCubbin landscape – with sunburnt rural scenes in summer, spectacular shows of wildflowers in spring, and year-round vistas of vineyards, olive groves and orchards.

Kyotmunga Estate, on Chittering Valley Road, offers wine-tasting (try their signature shiraz) and laid-back dining overlooking the spectacular Avon Valley National Park. Open weekends for Devonshire teas and lunch, you can enjoy light food platters of

dolmades, cheese, olives, fresh bread, extra-virgin olive oil and dukkah spice mixture – accompanied by entertainment from the resident Jack Russells. The olive oil and dukkah are made on the premises and are available for tasting and purchase (along with mandarins in season). The property comprises some 3 hectares of wine grapes and 200 olive trees.

Back on Chittering Road, nestled amid row after row of vineyards, is the rustic **Stringybark Winery & Restaurant** (open Wednesday–Sunday for lunch and dinner). Stone and timber adorn the rustic dining room, where wine suggestions accompany hearty serves of traditional favourites such as rack of lamb, bangers and mash, roast of the day, duck and Atlantic salmon. One of the oldest vineyards in the Chittering Valley and producing only a limited quantity of wine annually (the cabernet shiraz is popular), it is worth stopping here particularly in warm weather when patrons make the most of the deck and those rolling vineyard views.

In the small locality of Lower Chittering two wineries are worth checking out. Taking advantage of

the Mediterranean climate, **Western Range Wines** has produced an outstanding Goyamin Pool Old Vine Grenache and Julimar Shiraz Viognier. The vineyard's wine range is stocked in restaurants and outlets all over the state, which gives an indication of the popularity of the label. Established in 1998, this relative newcomer to the valley holds NASAA/IFOAM certification for the production of organic wines to appeal to a growing demand in Europe and Australia. Light meals and hampers are available on site. Down the road is the small **White Dog Farm Fine Wines**, which has developed from humble beginnings to its present-day production of a limited quantity of wine, and boutique accommodation (see Where to stay). The compact wine list includes the pink bubbles of the 2005 Reserve Méthode Champenoise, a 2006 Méthode Traditionalle, 2007 Cabernet Merlot and 2007 Z Light Red. You can also pick up some of the award-winning estate-grown extra virgin olive oil while you are here.

Once back on the Great Northern Highway you head north to Bindoon. West of town is

Briery Estate, a welcoming spot to throw down your rug and have a picnic, especially if it's during the jam session on the last Sunday of the month. Offering a range of white and red varietals, the 2005 First Furmint was a trophy winner for a best alternative white wine. And, if you need a pit stop after all that wine-tasting, take a break in town at the Bindoon Roadhouse or the bakery. Or ring ahead to arrange a tour of **Apricot Acres Farm** just north of town, off the Bindoon–Moora Road. In season this family-run business has sales of fresh fruits, along with dried fruits and honey. Not far away, the wine trail continues at **Halina Brook Estate**, which aims to please with its crisp fruity flavours. Long-established vines, some around 60 years old, surround the rustic cellar door, actually a converted shearing shed with uninterrupted views over the estate. Visitors are most welcome to come and enjoy wine-tasting in this idyllic rural setting.

You now need to head for Gingin along Mooliabeenee Road. On the way the stylish contemporary winery building at

Riseborough Estate, perched on a hilltop overlooking the surrounding valleys, is hard to miss. The estate is justly proud of the success of its red wine range, which includes its signature 2004 Cabernet Sauvignon. The gift shop sells cheese, olive products and ice-cream (you are invited to picnic in the shade of a flowering gum) and above the cellar door a gallery showcases contemporary sculpture exhibitions, where the art works must compete with the glorious views. Before driving into Gingin you can visit Jylland Vineyard on the southern outskirts of town. With its name harking back to the owner's Scandinavian heritage, this winery is noted for its zesty chenin blanc and a honeyed verdelho. Amid panoramic rural vistas you can settle in with a gourmet platter, especially if you're treated to one of the regular jazz or classical performances hosted by the estate.

If you are feeling like some hearty fare and a beer, the Gingin Hotel is the epitome of outback Australiana, priding itself on its old-fashioned country hospitality. The two-storey building with its wide verandahs overhanging the street also provides accommodation in upstairs rooms and motel-style units. As well as an extensive range of takeaway meals, the in-house dining room offers an impressively large menu that covers all bases, from burgers and light meals to meat and three veg, pie of the day, seafood dishes, a range of pasta creations and a kids' menu. The dessert list will have you in a time warp as you choose between old favourites such as ice-cream Sunday, banana split, cheesecake and pavlova. However, try to save space for something else sweet as west of town, along Gingin Brook Road, you should call in to West Coast Honey for tastings, ice-cream, and other indulgences.

There is more on offer nearby at Amirage Restaurant where, in keeping with the European tradition of the region, guests are welcomed with open arms and a kiss on each cheek. Situated within magnificent gardens, this eatery prides itself on using local produce wherever possible; in particular, the steak, olive oil and olives are sourced from within the valley. The menu has a European influence as a result of owner June Reith spending many years on the Continent. She has created a friendly community atmosphere by hosting many functions and charity events, and with picturesque gardens, a billabong with a fountain and abundant wildlife, this

is an ideal spot for the whole family to enjoy. Open Thursday–Sunday for lunch and dinner, you could extend your stay at the on-site B&B (see Where to stay) and go stargazing at the nearby Gravity Discovery Centre.

Next day you could pop into Willowbrook Farm Tearooms for a spot of morning or afternoon tea under the pergola of an old homestead built in 1874. Or stay awhile for something more substantial (open Thursday–Sunday for breakfast and lunch) at this picturesque property some 20 kilometres from Gingin. The farm includes a caravan park (see Where to stay), pioneer cemetery (where the original owners are buried), shady trees, wildflowers in spring and roaming farm animals.

Gingin is at the centre of the Moore River region, which is home to over 70 per cent of the state's olive trees. Ten kilometres north of town is Green Gold Farm Olive Estate, which produces extra virgin olive oil for bulk sales (a minimum quantity of 20 litres applies to farm purchases). Further north, on Orange Springs Road south-east of the township of Regans Ford, are Fini Olives with its many varieties, and Regans Ridge, an organically managed grove that produces ten different olive varieties. This property is open for tastings and sales by prior arrangement at weekends. Numerous olive groves dot the landscape throughout this area but many are not open to the public except by appointment so call before you visit.

At this point in time, you have to decide on where to go next. A visit to the monastic town of New Norcia (see feature, p. 312), which lies to the east, is highly recommended. When you reach the Great Northern Highway you turn left and head north. You can stay in town at the historic New Norcia Hotel (see Where to stay), or simply lounge on the impressive verandah for lunch, dinner or drinks. The atmosphere is informal and the Sunday-night roast is popular, as are the barbecues in summer. Try a glass of New Norcia Abbey Ale, a traditional ale laced with the scents of fruit and spice. A stroll around the town to admire the magnificent architecture before or after your meal is a must.

Alternatively you may wish to drive south-eastwards to visit the pretty Avon Valley. If you take the forest-fringed Julimar Road you can stop halfway to Toodyay at Esslemont Estate, which specialises in the production of premium organic extra virgin olive oil. The olive trees are grown organically (no chemical sprays or fertilisers) then hand-picked and pressed in a certified organic press. Centrally located between the wine and olive properties of the Chittering Valley and the picturesque delights of the Avon Valley, an overnight stay in one of the two cottages here allows time to take in the many attractions of the region. The farmstay accommodation is self-contained, dog-friendly and is available during weekends and holidays. This pleasant spot 20 kilometres west of Toodyay is surrounded by the 36 000-hectare Julimar State Forest, which stretches from Toodyay to Gingin.

On the western outskirts of the quaint town of Toodyay you can discover shades of Provence at **Oliomio**. This is an olive and lavender farm, producing olive oils, table olives, tapenade, handcrafted oil soap and lavender products. On the southern side of town honey lovers in particular will be happy with the four varieties of organic honey at the **Bee Happy Apiaries & Candle Co**. Further south is **Coorinja Vineyard**, one of the oldest wineries in the state. Established in the 1870s, it has perfected the art of fortified-wine production with tasty port, marsala, muscat and a unique ginger wine.

About halfway between Toodyay and Clackline is the **Free Range Emu Farm**, which sells emu products including cuts of emu meat – ideal for barbecuing. Another 10 kilometres south and really off the beaten track is the rural retreat of **Avonbrook Wines**. If it seems very remote then why not stay the night in one of the comfortable B&B studio rooms? The boutique winery, open Thursday–Sunday and public holidays, produces wines such as chardonnay, verdelho, vintage shiraz and a sweet shiraz that is served chilled. Its fruity shiraz and rich ports and liqueurs, for which it is generally known, can all be enjoyed while savouring the creamy delights of one of the gourmet cheese platters. There is also coffee and cake and local products for sale.

Below: Chittering Valley vines nestle in between the surrounding hills

New Norcia Benedictine Community

In 1846 Spanish Benedictine monks established a mission 132 kilometres north of Perth in the secluded Moore Valley in an attempt to help the local Aboriginal population. Today, the handsome and imposing Spanish-inspired buildings, surrounded by the gum trees and dry grasses of the wheat belt, provide a most unexpected vista. The town still operates as a monastery and is Australia's only monastic town. It is also a treasure trove of art, artefacts and European culture and is Western Australia's oldest and finest living museum. Over the past 150 years, the monks here have been farmers, purveyors of wine, and makers of olive oil (the grove was established in 1886 and today Spanish methods are still employed to produce extra virgin olive oil from more than 600 trees). The monks also established an orchard and grew enough vegetables to support their community. However, it was their breadmaking that received national acclaim, these days run by New Norcia Bakeries, a private company, in agreement with the Benedictine community. Using the original wood-fired flour mill, the bakery turns out all things nutty and spice – try the nutcake, biscotti, pan chocolatti and the extensive bread range (sample the raisin and walnut sourdough, which is divine with a slathering of gooey cheese, or the other sourdough varieties of fig and fennel, and the olive, rosemary and sun-dried tomato). New Norcia bakery products are available in town from the **New Norcia Gift Shop** (along with wine, ale, honey and olive oil), and at Mount Hawthorn, Subiaco and many other metropolitan outlets (see website for details).

Contacts for Central Heartlands

EATERIES

Amirage Restaurant: 1654 Gingin Brook Rd, West Gingin; (08) 9575 7646 or 0411 277 500; www.amiragerestaurantbb.com.au

Conti's Restaurant: Paul Conti Wines, 529 Wanneroo Rd, Woodvale; (08) 9409 1516; www.paulcontiwines.com.au

Gingin Hotel: 5 Jones St, Gingin; (08) 9575 2214; www.ginginhotel.com.au

New Norcia Hotel: Great Northern Hwy, New Norcia; (08) 9654 8034; www.newnorcia.wa.edu.au/ accommodation/new-norcia-hotel/

Stringybark Winery & Restaurant: 2060 Chittering Rd, Lower Chittering; (08) 9571 8069; www.stringybarkwinery.com.au

The Mean Bean Cafe: 2542 Great Northern Hwy, Bullsbrook; (08) 9571 2972

Willowbrook Farm Tearooms and Caravan Park: 1679 Gingin Brook Rd, West Gingin; (08) 9575 7566

MARKETS

Bindoon Markets: home-grown produce, art and craft; Seventh Day Adventist Church Centre, cnr Edmonds Pl and Great Northern Hwy; last Sun each month; (08) 9576 1100

York Mill Markets: art, craft, collectibles and regional food; York Mill, 10 Henrietta St; every weekend; (08) 9641 2900; theyorkmill.com.au

GOURMET PRODUCE

Apricot Acres Farm: 124 Toy Rd, Bindoon; (08) 9576 1030

Bee Happy Apiaries & Candle Co: 63 Sandplain Rd, Toodyay; (08) 9574 2857; www.beehappy.com.au

Esslemont Estate: Lot 513 Timberden Dr, Toodyay; (08) 9574 5419; www.esslemontestate.com

Fini Olives: 237 Orange Springs Rd, Gingin; (08) 9655 0091; www.finiolives.com.au

Free Range Emu Farm: 680 Clackline Rd, Toodyay; (08) 9574 1415; www.emufarm.iinet.net.au

Green Gold Farm Olive Estate: 69 Hancock Place, Gingin; (08) 9575 1067

Jumanga Olives: 360 Old Yanchep Rd, Carabooda; (08) 9561 2411

Kyotmunga Estate: see Wineries

New Norcia Gift Shop: New Norcia Museum and Art Gallery, Great Northern Hwy, New Norcia; (08) 9654 8056; newnorcia.wa.edu.au

Oliomio: 439 Parkland Dr, Toodyay; (08) 9574 5786; members.iinet.net.au/~oliomio/

Regans Ridge: 436 Orange Springs Rd, Gingin; (08) 9402 0298; www.regansridge.com.au

West Coast Honey: 172 Gingin Brook Rd, Gingin; (08) 9575 1250; www.westcoasthoney.com.au

WINERIES

Avonbrook Wines: 245 Benrua Rd, Clackline; (08) 9574 1276 or 0400 832 933; www.avonbrookwines.com.au

Briery Estate: 37 Briar Lane, Bindoon; (08) 9576 1417; www.brieryestatewines.com

Coorinja Vineyard: Toodyay Rd, Toodyay; (08) 9574 2280

Halina Brook Estate: 682 Bindoon– Moora Rd, Bindoon; (08) 9576 2030 or 0429 117 741

Jylland Vineyard: 77 Ashby Rd, Lennard Brook (via Gingin); (08) 9575 1442; www.jylland.com.au

Kyotmunga Estate: 287 Chittering Valley Rd, Lower Chittering; (08) 9571 8001; www.kyotmunga.com.au

Paul Conti Wines: 529 Wanneroo Rd, Woodvale; (08) 9409 9160; www.paulcontiwines.com.au

Riseborough Estate: Lot 21 Peterson Rise, Gingin; (08) 9575 1211; www.riseborough.com.au

Stringybark Winery & Restaurant: see Eateries

Western Range Wines: 1995 Chittering Rd, Lower Chittering; (08) 9571 8800; www.westernrangewines.com.au

White Dog Farm Fine Wines: 2035 Chittering Rd, Lower Chittering; (08) 9571 8880; www.whitedogfarm.com.au

Cape to Cape

Ask any Perth locals where they go for an escape and chances are they will say 'down south'. Of course this could mean any number of southern destinations but the Cape to Cape region has been popular for longer than the average surfie has ridden its waves. Including the towns and environs of Yallingup, Cowaramup, Gracetown, Prevelly, Margaret River, and Augusta in the south, it is a region of great natural beauty, with beaches, caves and walking trails to appeal to the energetic. However, the region's reputation as one of Australia's best wine regions is what has really put it on the gourmet trail. The most popular varietals here include sauvignon blanc, semillon, merlot, cabernet sauvignon, shiraz, rosé and chenin blanc. There are over 150 producers in the area so if it is your first visit you should call into the Margaret River Regional Wine Centre at Cowaramup, a one-stop centre for tastings, sales and in-depth information on local wines and wineries.

Yallingup in the region's north has long been known for its magnificent limestone caves and world-class surf breaks. In town art and craft galleries abound but for an organic sourdough like no other, start your gourmet journey at the **Yallingup Woodfired Bakery**. The ovens are built from volcanic stones heated by a wood fire and the loaves are slow-cooked on hot stones. If the idea of learning how to wood-fire your own bread has you salivating then book yourself into a Mad About Food cooking course at **Wildwood Valley**, south of town. Specialising in Tuscan and Thai cooking, day classes and residential weekend packages are available.

With vineyard views and lush forest, **Clairault** has flung open its glass doors to nature and lovers of fine food. Start the experience with a tasting at the cellar door before moving onto drunken king prawns, boneless pork shank or rabbit and black pudding terrine, which are the handiwork of chef Tim Taylor. Or opt for the degustation menu with each course matched with estate-grown wine.

There's much to rave about at **Cape Lodge**, and the restaurant is no exception since it was voted among the Top Ten in the World for Food in *Conde Naste Traveller*'s Gold List in 2008. The menu changes daily and could include rare roasted Margaret River Venison or handmade crab tortellini with sweetcorn purée and truffle burnt butter. The wine list

Tropfest Film Festival: movies under the stars; Madfish Wines, Miamup Rd, Cowaramup; Mar; (08) 9756 5200; www.madfishwines.com.au

Margaret River Wine Region Festival: various venues; Apr; (08) 9757 9330; www.margaretriverfestival.com

Margaret River Olive Festival: Duckstein at Saracen Estates, 3517 Caves Rd, Wilyabrup; end June; (08) 9755 6500 or (08) 9755 6206

Geographe Crush Food & Wine Festival: Bicentennial Sq, Bunbury; Nov; (08) 9228 9166; www.cmsevents.com.au

Where to stay

Cape Lodge: ultra-luxury rooms and suites; 3341 Caves Rd, Wilyabrup; (08) 9755 6311; www.capelodge.com.au

Merribrook Retreat: villas surrounded by forest teeming with birdlife; Armstrong Rd, Gracetown; (08) 9755 5599; www.merribrook.com.au

Moondance Lodge: up-market suites; Spencer Rd, off Caves Rd, Margaret River; (08) 9750 1777

Redgate Farmstay: family-friendly farm; 81 Redgate Rd, Witchcliffe; (08) 9757 6400; www.redgatefarmstay.com.au

Wildwood Valley: rural B&B and private cottages; 1481 Wildwood Rd, Yallingup; (08) 9755 2120; www.wildwoodvalley.com.au

includes 150 premium and vintage wines. There is also the opportunity to learn from executive chef Tony Howell by attending one of his cooking classes. Restaurant bookings are essential, but a meal here is worth the expense if only to brag that you've experienced the sublime. (*See* also Where to stay).

Until the establishment of the slick **Duckstein Brewery at Saracen Estates**, breweries in the region were raucous affairs. However, do not think for a minute that the atmosphere at Duckstein will be retiring. Check out the tasting tray to sample the whole range of brews. The food menu includes not only the standard fare of chicken, seafood and meat, but also German specialties that shine with hearty goodness – pork shank, huge veal schnitzels and the popular Brewer's Pan with kassler smoked pork cutlets, bratwurst sausages, pan-fried potatoes and a mountain of sauerkraut. You are assured of a traditional German-style dining experience. The brewery is situated on the premises of **Saracen Estates** winery, and at the cellar door the indulgence continues with a zippy range of whites and reds and in particular the 2007 Cabernet Merlot. In summer diners seek out a window seat overlooking the vast twinkling lake complete with an island, while in the cooler months spots by the fire are particularly popular. Those travelling with children will appreciate the state-of-the-art playground. In nearby Puzey Road, **Bootleg Brewery** has been on the tourist trail since its opening in 1994. A hearty lunch of a stockman's pie or burger with fries matches well with their lagers, ales and the Czech-style Wils Pils.

With chef Bradley Hornby applying molecular gastronomy techniques without a science laboratory at his talented fingertips, every single item on the compact menu at **Knee Deep** winery is tempting. For starters try the variations of Donnybrook pear with goat's curd or the sous vide of Plantagenet pork belly with duck leg croquette, perhaps followed by cabernet-braised beef cheek with house-made pasta and parsnip cream. The petite wine range includes three wines named after the owners' daughters. Not far away **Moss Wood**, known for its flagship cabernet sauvignon and dessert wines, selected its Wilyabrup location wisely in the 1980s for its premium grape-growing conditions and it paid off. The cellar door is open by appointment only, but the limited release 1996 vintage is worth the splurge.

Heading south along Caves Road those endless vineyard views from **Cullen Wines** will surely justify an afternoon of relaxing over lunch, and depending on the season you could be treated to Shark Bay scallops, pork belly or crispy confit duck. The Cullen family have been dedicated to producing wine for the past 40 years so it's no wonder the extensive wine list includes flagship labels named after their makers: Kevin John Chardonnay and Diana Madeline Cabernet Sauvignon Merlot. While these two wines may be out of your price bracket, the rest of the range including the Mangan blend of malbec, petit verdot and merlot still offer much complexity. The vineyard has been certified as organic since 2003.

You have been driving through the Wilyabrup Valley, the premier subregion of Margaret River where the region's first vines were planted. And not

Below (left to right): evening at Cullen Wines, Cowaramup; beer and wine at Duckstein Brewery at Saracen Estates, Wilyabrup; a degustation delight at Clairault, Wilyabrup; cabernet sauvignon at Vasse Felix, Cowaramup; fresh oysters at Settlers Tavern, Margaret River; tasting platter at Sea Gardens, Prevelly Park

far from Cullen Wines is the region's oldest winery, **Vasse Felix**. Here you will experience the handcrafted wines, the quintessential vineyard and forest views, the on-site art gallery's exhibits and the innovative restaurant menu that define this winery. Overlooking the original 1967 plantings, you can feast on rabbit, duck and barramundi in the timber and stone building (open for lunch daily), savouring the thought that this restaurant has been acclaimed the finest regional restaurant in Western Australia. The five labels of Heytesbury, Estate, Classic, Theatre and Specialty should satisfy even the fussiest of wine drinkers, and the free weekday winery tours at 11am will please those curious to find out how this renowned establishment makes its wines.

Also in the Wilyabrup Valley is **Hay Shed Hill** winery, most famous for its easy drinking Pitchfork series, in particular the Late Harvest 2009. The full-bodied Block series is also gaining ground. A visit to this compact winery is highly recommended and, wines apart, its gourmet deli is a place where gourmet dreams are realised. Displayed in the recently opened **Hay Shed Deli Cafe** is an irresistible array of estate-made, local and international gourmet products, including cured meats, exceptional cheeses and marinated vegetables. The cafe, open for breakfast and lunch, serves up a mass of tapas-style dishes to share, such as grilled chorizo with Persian feta, or more substantial offerings such as hearty soups perhaps followed by house-baked pita filled with lamb kofte, roasted marinated eggplant, tomato relish and tahini yoghurt. Gourmet pizzas are also on offer, to eat in or take away. And, reassuringly, they ask that

you be patient while your food is prepared as it is all 'made from first principles with passion and pride'.

South-eastwards towards Cowaramup and high on a hill, surrounded by tall marri and karri trees, and approached via a birch-lined drive, stands the impressive **Howard Park** winery (also producer of **Madfish Wines**). Inside the building the soaring ceilings of the contemporary cellar door overhang a spacious area where you can taste the full Howard Park/Madfish wine range. If you are feeling spritely you could start the day with a breakfast tipple of the 2009 Madfish Moscato, made from muscat, gewürztraminer and riesling grapes, seductively described as displaying 'a distinctive pink blush'. The Howard Park collection of wines includes their Single Vineyard Series, developed to highlight the distinctive regional characteristics of shiraz and cabernet sauvignon. The summer months bring gourmet occasions and art events to the estate.

For chocolate lovers, a slight detour to Metricup (north-east of Cowaramup) is mandatory to visit the **Margaret River Chocolate Factory**, a mecca for all things chocolate. Thankfully there is a lawn area for hyped-up children to unwind and for over-indulgent adults to flop. Around the corner and surrounded by vineyards, an organic olive grove and thriving vegetable gardens, **Margaret River Providore** is housed in a rammed earth building. Here you will find an overwhelming range of cookbooks, cheeses, sauces, spreads, vinegars, meat rubs, exotic rice mixes, preserves, and oils pressed from the 1000 trees that make up the on-site olive grove. The cafe sources most of its ingredients from the property and

bakes daily, and the menu includes slow-cooked items and the likes of homemade gnocchi with burnt butter and organic sage, accompanied by wine from the adjacent **Coward & Black Vineyards**.

The charming dairy town of Cowaramup lies just ten minutes north of Margaret River and is home to the tooth-achingly sweet lolly shop, **Candy Cow**. Next door is the **Margaret Riviera**, full to the brim of gourmet goodies including handmade pasta, venison, ostrich, olive oils, Yallingup wood-fired bread and cheese. If you head west towards Gracetown, there is more olive oil available at **Olio Bello**, which produces organic estate-pressed oils from their 130-hectare olive grove. Nearby is **Margaret River Venison** offering an array of emu, kangaroo, and venison cuts and products, including biltong.

Margaret River, one of the best-known towns in Western Australia, is synonymous with world-class wines, magnificent coastal scenery, excellent surfing beaches and spectacular cave formations. The pretty township lies on the Margaret River and provides a pleasant spot to take a break. You can stock up on any number of elusive exotic ingredients at **The Larder**, as well as healthy take-home meals, or book in for one of their cooking classes. If you are particularly hungry, the meals at the **Settlers Tavern** arrive at the table in huge over-sized serves. Alternatively, at the other end of the restaurant spectrum, **Must** is an alluring place with a long list of awards after only being operational for a year (it is certainly living up to the reputation of its sister restaurant in Perth). The bistro-style menu uses ingredients sourced locally, including its renowned dry aged beef, Jarrahdene Free Range Pork (reared just several kilometres away), and a dish comprising angel hair pasta tossed with blue manna crab that has remained on the Perth menu for years due to its popularity. The wine list is literally bible-size and it's best to put yourself in the sommelier's expert hands. This restaurant is one of the few places in the region open nightly and the cocktail bar is a slice of urban chic in the country.

Approaching the coast, **Cape Mentelle** vineyard is guaranteed to please regardless of your wine leanings. Even its reasonably priced classic red and white make for good drinking but for something special try the rich zinfandel, which is unique to the area and is almost like drinking liquid Christmas cake. The coastal area of Prevelly Park has **Sea Gardens** cafe and

restaurant, renowned for its trifecta of attractions – ocean views, friendly service and delicious fare (open daily for breakfast, lunch and dinner). The vibe may be casual but the food is seriously good under the watchful eye of talented French chef Gilles England-Brassy. Start the day with poached eggs with Blue Cow feta and avocado, and coffee to follow – the cafe is rumoured to have the best coffee in the region and a caffeine fix is available at all hours – or perhaps end the day over a gourmet pizza, tandoori chicken or a seafood dish laced with garlic and served with onion, tomato, mushroom and olives.

Situated in a Cape Dutch-style building set in formal gardens is the opulent dining room of **Voyager Estate**. Because it showcases irresistible delights of the region such as grilled Pemberton marron, venison chorizo, lamb loin, or a trilogy of seafood with the seafood assiette, many diners opt for the degustation menu. To accompany the food try the tasting sample called Take Flight, which comprises 50-millilitre shots of either white or red wines.

As well as a world-wide name for hosting performances by international artists and entertainers, **Leeuwin Estate** has a long history of fine wine, gourmet food and artworks all set in idyllic surrounds. There is a renowned wine range called the Art Series, with bottle labels featuring artwork commissioned by the estate. The chardonnay with its creamy, buttery finish is particularly worth purchasing and cellaring. In the restaurant with its unusually long jarrah wood tables, the menu includes the many local delicacies of the region including marron, lamb and venison and an intensely rich dessert of churros with a Pedro Ximenez sherry chocolate sauce.

Yahava Koffee Works has relocated to new premises, just south of Margaret River on the corner of the Bussell Highway and Rosa Brook Road, and has a range of coffees – any one of which is sure to give caffeine addicts a fix. The beans are sourced internationally and to give you an idea of how seriously this place takes its coffee, there is an X-rated variety. You can enjoy a cup or two on site or grab a stash for later. Finally, a pleasant way to end a gourmet tour of this bountiful region is with marron and wine at **Witchcliffe Estate**. The cellar door offers a long list of wines including a chardonnay that complements marron perfectly (the marron can be purchased next door and eskies and ice are for sale if you want to take it away).

Bushfoods

Indigenous foods and culinary innovations

Indigenous Australian culture has developed over centuries, based on a deeply spiritual connection to the land. In the south-western area of Western Australia the Noongar clan made its home; living as hunter-gathers when Europeans arrived, their diet comprised a vast range of produce they collected such as vegetables, roots, herbs, fruit, nuts, eggs and honey, along with the flesh of hunted animals such as snakes, goannas, emus, kangaroos, fish and birds. The land was bountiful but the ingredients frequently required complex preparation before being safe and correctly flavoured for consumption. Contemporary Australia has learned much from this Indigenous culinary heritage. Many of the ingredients are stocked at gourmet outlets and supermarkets: paperbark, when used to wrap seafood and meat, imparts a delicate smoky flavour during cooking in a slow oven or over hot coals; quandongs have a nectarine-and-peach-like flavour, only tarter, and are ideal in savoury sauces for meats such as lamb and kangaroo; lemon myrtle has a strong lemon flavour and is great for seasoning fish and sweet and savoury sauces; and lotus is a water lily whose leaves, root and seeds featured in the diet of Indigenous Australians and is frequently seen today in Asian cuisine. There are a few places where you can sample some products made from a few of these and other bushfoods. The **Berry Farm** has jams, preserves, pickles, sauces, dressings, naturally fermented vinegars, and fruit wines and liqueurs; Margaret River Venison offers emu and kangaroo; and Witchcliffe Estate sells fresh marron. If you'd like to explore Indigenous cuisine further, join a specialist guide from Bushtucker River and Winery Tours; call (08) 9757 9084 for details (www.bushtuckertours.com). The Wardan Aboriginal Centre, established by the Wardandi people as a place to share their culture with the community, conducts guided walking tours through the bush to uncover ingredients such as witchetty grubs and sea celery. The centre is in Injidup Springs Road in Yallingup; call (08) 9756 6566 for details or see their website (www.wardan.com.au).

Contacts for Cape to Cape

EATERIES

Bootleg Brewery: *see* Breweries

Cape Lodge: 3341 Caves Rd, Wilyabrup;
(08) 9755 6311; www.capelodge.com.au

Clairault: 3277 Caves Rd, Wilyabrup,
Margaret River; (08) 9755 6655;
www.clairaultwines.com.au

Cullen Wines: *see* Wineries

Duckstein Brewery at Saracen Estates:
see Breweries

Hay Shed Deli Cafe: Hay Shed Hill,
Harmans Mill Rd, Wilyabrup;
(08) 9755 6046; www.hayshedhill.com.au

Knee Deep: Lot 61 Johnson Rd, Wilyabrup;
(08) 9755 6776;
www.kneedeepwines.com.au

Leeuwin Estate: *see* Wineries

Margaret River Providore: *see* Gourmet
Produce

Must: 107 Bussell Hwy, Margaret River;
(08) 9758 8877; www.must.com.au

Sea Gardens: Lot 103, 9 Mitchell Dr,
Prevelly Park; (08) 9757 3074;
www.seagardens.com.au

Settlers Tavern: 114 Bussell Hwy,
Margaret River; (08) 9757 2398;
www.settlerstavern.com

Vasse Felix: Cnr Caves Rd and Harmans Rd
South, Cowaramup; (08) 9756 5050;
www.vassefelix.com.au

Voyager Estate: Lot 1 Stevens Rd,
Margaret River; (08) 9757 6354;
www.voyagerestate.com.au

STORES

Candy Cow: 3 Bottrill St, Cowaramup;
(08) 9755 9155; www.candycow.com.au

Margaret River Regional Wine Centre:
9 Bussell Hwy, Cowaramup; (08) 9755 5501;
www.mrwines.com

Yahava Koffee Works: Cnr Bussell Hwy
and Rosa Brook Rd, Margaret River;
(08) 9757 2900; www.yahava.com.au

Yallingup Woodfired Bakery: Cnr
Biddles and McLachlan rds, Yallingup;
(08) 9756 6306

MARKETS

Margaret River Farmers' Markets:
Tunbridge St, Margaret River; various dates;
www.margaretriver.com

GOURMET PRODUCE

Hay Shed Deli Cafe: *see* Eateries

Margaret River Chocolate Factory:
Cnr Harmans Mill and Harmans
South rds, Metricup; (08) 9755 6555;
www.chocolatefactory.com.au

Margaret River Providore: 448 Harmans
South Rd, Wilyabrup; (08) 9755 6355;
www.providore.com.au

Below (left to right): gourmet treats to go at
The Larder, Margaret River; Yahava Koffee Works,
Margaret River; wine barrels at Brookland Valley
Estate, Margaret River; vines at Cape Mentelle,
Margaret River

Margaret River Venison: Caves Rd, Margaret River; (08) 9755 5028; www.mrvenison.com

Margaret Riviera: 4 Bottrill St, Cowaramup; (08) 9755 9333

Olio Bello: Cnr Cowaramup Bay and Caves rds, Cowaramup; (08) 9755 9771

The Berry Farm: RMB 222 Bessell Rd, Margaret River (15 km south-east of town); (08) 9757 5054; www.theberryfarm.com.au

The Larder: 2/99 Bussell Hwy, Margaret River; (08) 9758 8990; www.larder.biz

WINERIES

Cape Mentelle: 331 Wallcliffe Rd, Margaret River; (08) 9757 0888; www.capementelle.com.au

Clairault: see Eateries

Coward & Black Vineyards: 448 Harmans South Rd, Wilyabrup; (08) 9755 6355; www.providore.com.au

Cullen Wines: Caves Rd, Cowaramup; (08) 9755 5277; www.cullenwines.com.au

Hay Shed Hill: Harmans Mill Rd, Wilyabrup; (08) 9755 6026; www.hayshedhill.com.au

Howard Park/Madfish Wines: Lot 2948 Miamup Rd, Wilyabrup, Cowaramup; (08) 9756 5200; www.howardparkwines.com.au and www.madfishwines.com.au

Knee Deep: see Eateries

Leeuwin Estate: Stevens Rd, Margaret River; (08) 9759 0000; www.leeuwinestate.com.au

Moss Wood: 926 Metricup Rd, Wilyabrup; (08) 9755 6266; www.mosswood.com.au

Saracen Estates: 3517 Caves Rd, Wilyabrup; (08) 9755 6099; www.saracenestates.com.au

Vasse Felix: Cnr Caves Rd and Harmans Rd South, Cowaramup; (08) 9756 5055; www.vassefelix.com.au

Voyager Estate: see Eateries

Witchcliffe Estate: Wickham Rd, Witchcliffe; (08) 9757 6279

BREWERIES

Bootleg Brewery: Puzey Rd, Wilyabrup, Margaret River; (08) 9755 6300; www.bootlegbrewery.com.au

Duckstein Brewery at Saracen Estates: 3517 Caves Rd, Wilyabrup; (08) 9755 6500; www.duckstein.com.au

COOKING SCHOOLS

Cape Lodge: 3341 Caves Rd, Wilyabrup; (08) 9755 6311; www.capelodge.com.au

The Larder: 2/99 Bussell Hwy, Margaret River; (08) 9758 8990; www.larder.biz

Wildwood Valley: 1481 Wildwood Rd, Yallingup; (08) 9755 2120; www.wildwoodvalley.com.au

Below: Denmark Farmhouse Cheese

Opposite (top to bottom): remotely situated, The Lily restaurant in Stirling Range National Park; picture-postcard setting at Picardy, Pemberton

South-West

Tucked away in a cool, well-watered area in the southern corner of Western Australia is a pocket of towering old-growth forests, the only forests in this sun-scorched state. Forests of karri, one of the world's tallest trees, are found in the wetter areas, from Manjimup to Walpole. Near Pemberton, 4000 hectares of old-growth karri forest are protected within national parks. The Valley of the Giants, east of Walpole, is home to towering red tingle trees. However, in addition to majestic forest scenery, the South-West has a picturesque coastline dotted with secret inlets, a number of growers producing unique gourmet products, and a thriving wine-producing industry – the Great Southern Wine Region takes in the areas around Denmark, Albany and Mount Barker, and to the west a cluster of vineyards around Pemberton have won international acclaim. Although this is a longer journey from Perth than the ever-popular Margaret River/Cape to Cape region, you will not be disappointed. Perhaps stay in one or two of the suggested accommodation options (*see* Where to stay) along the way and allow time to explore and discover the region's hidden gems.

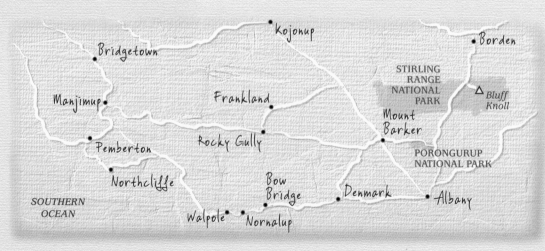

Festivals

Mount Barker D'vine Wine Festival: fine wine, food and music; Goundrey Wines, Mount Barker; Jan; (08) 9892 1777

Great Southern Taste Festival: food and wine; Feb–Mar; (08) 9844 1912; www.greatsoutherntastewa.com

Truffle Affaire: truffle festival including long lunch; The Wine & Truffle Co, Seven Day Rd, Manjimup; May; (08) 9777 2474; wineandtruffle.com.au

Cambinata Yabbies Extravaganza: regional food festival; Collie Lake, King Rd, Kukerin; Oct; (08) 9864 6054; www.cambinatayabbies.com.au

Manjimup Cherry Harmony Festival: Dec; www.cherryfestival.com.au

Where to stay

Cape Howe Cottages: private, contemporary luxury; 322 Tennessee Rd South, Lowlands Beach; (08) 9845 1295; www.capehowe.com.au

Pensione Verde: organic accommodation and meals; 31 South Coast Hwy, Denmark; (08) 9848 1700; www.denmarkaccommodation.com.au

Salitage Winery: luxury retreat; Vasse Hwy, Pemberton; (08) 9776 1195; www.salitage.com.au

Stirling Range Retreat: ideal for adventure enthusiasts; Chester Pass Rd, Borden; (08) 9827 9229; www.stirlingrange.com.au

The Rocks: historic B&B; 182–188 Grey St, Albany; (08) 9842 5969; www.therocksalbany.com.au

Tree Elle Retreat: spacious B&B in self-contained houses (*see* feature, p. 329); South Coast Hwy, Bow Bridge; (08) 9840 8471; www.treeelle.com

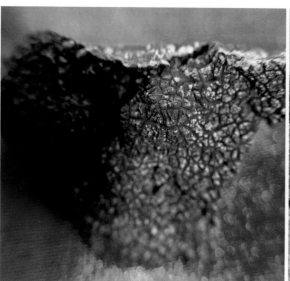

Above (left to right): slivers of the 'black diamond' of truffles adorn dishes at Gourmet Truffle Cafe, Manjimup; vines at The Lake House, Denmark; Galafrey Wines, Mount Barker; Lost Lake Winery, Pemberton

Three hundred kilometres south of Perth via the South Western Highway is the historic timber town of Manjimup. South of town (some 7 kilometres) you must not miss the property of **The Wine & Truffle Co**. A pioneer in the Australian truffle trade, this company cultivates the exotic fungi, including the highly prized black truffle (the 'black diamond') so sought after by restaurant kitchens across the nation. In season you can even join a truffle hunt. At the on-site **Gourmet Truffle Cafe** the menu tantalises with slithers of truffle over handmade pasta, a supple scallop or a sliver of asparagus. Alternatively start with the truffle-infused brie arancini and follow with their signature wine and truffle beef pie or perhaps the truffle butter glazed marron. And the added bonus is that you can buy a vast array of gourmet truffle products to take home. The cafe is also the cellar door for the company-produced Truffle Hill wines so let the seduction continue with tastings of sauvignon blanc semillon (check out the Truffle Hill Sauvignon Blanc Semillon 2009, a trophy winner for the best

white blend), riesling, chardonnay, shiraz, merlot and rosé.

Nearby on the same road is **Fonty's Pool**, one of the Pemberton area's renowned wineries. You could be forgiven for wondering if picturesque scenery has anything to do with producing happy grapes. The region's cool climate makes it ideal for growing pinot noir, chardonnay and merlot grapes. Fonty's Pool produces a wide range of varietals and is a consistent award winner – the latest accolade is the inclusion of the 'well-priced' Fonty's Pool Sauvignon Blanc Semillon 2009 in the Gourmet Traveller Wine 100 Top New Release Wines, announced February/March 2010.

Some 15 kilometres south of Manjimup, the Vasse Highway leads south-east to Pemberton. Four kilometres from the turn-off, amid the karris of the Eastbrook Valley, is **Lost Lake Winery**. Here you can feast on fresh marron, Pemberton trout and pork belly in the cedar and limestone barn-style restaurant and cellar door. The 2008 Single Vineyard Pinot is a favourite and the chilled Honey Merlot is a mix of cherry and berry quirkiness. A little further

along the highway those towering karris outdo themselves at **Salitage Winery**. With two outstanding wine collections in their wine stable, the Salitage and Treehouse ranges, the family-run winery is the result of 30 years experience in the industry. You can stay here in forested seclusion in one of their fully self-contained luxury suites (*see* Where to stay), fitted out with red gum furniture handcrafted from estate-grown marri trees. Nearby, on the corner of the Vasse Highway and Eastbrook Road, **Picardy** is another must-visit winery. Old-world chardonnay and complex shiraz have really put the estate on the wine circuit, and the 2005 vintage is sublime.

If you plan to stay in this area, the charming town of Pemberton has much to offer. In earlier times, before electricity came to the region, the Pemberton Mill was powered by batteries, which were housed in the 1911 building where the **Shamrock Restaurant** has been operational since the 1970s. The restaurant retains much of its historic charm, and food-wise is best known for its steaks and marron and trout platters for two. Just north of town all those

hankering for a beer will appreciate **Jarrah Jacks Brewery** and the attached **Woodsmoke Cafe**. And do not think you will be offered the standard brewery-type fare; instead find dishes on the menu such as provincial duck sausage, Pemberton trout dip and chicken and mushroom roulade.

Surrounded by more of those magnificent karri trees, patrons fish for their own lunch at the **King Trout Restaurant and Marron Farm**, situated at the intersection of Old Vasse and Northcliffe roads. This makes for a great family activity and fishing aficionados can try out the special fly-fishing dam. As you'll be catching your meal, freshness is guaranteed and while the chef cooks up your catch you can sample the smoked trout or smoked trout pâté and marron. Rods can be hired and tours are available. It's BYO so bringing your own bottle of Pemberton wine shouldn't be too hard to do in this neck of the woods.

Back on the South Coast Highway, head south for Walpole and beyond. Hearty fare and charming service are on the menu at **Nornalup Tea House**,

326

nestled within tall timber country. The menu includes fresh seafood, steak, and gamy fare such as kangaroo and rabbit. The wine list includes many local favourites and a range of Bridgetown ciders. A little further along the highway, if you're craving something as basic as a caffeine fix, a homemade hamburger or need to stock up on some essentials and not-so essential marron, then drop into the **Bow Bridge Roadhouse**.

About halfway between Walpole and Denmark, **Old Kent River** winery is the place to forget about time and settle into the slow food cafe. Graze on their home-reared marron and estate-grown lamb, perhaps with a glass of sparkling Diamondtina from the compact wine list – this taste of bubbles matches perfectly with the marron. Before the run in to Denmark, a stop at **Bartholomews Meadery** will add some sweetness to your journey with their outstanding honey wines and products, and ice-creamery. A beehive in operation can be seen from a glass-viewing area, which will fascinate the whole family.

At this point you may want to think about staying in Denmark so you can plan your visits to the wineries of Great Southern – clustered around Denmark, Albany, and Mount Barker and surrounds to the north. To indulge in a food and wine experience, check into **Pensione Verde** in Denmark. This is an organic cooking school where students learn the techniques of slow cooking and matching cheese and wine –you may even be treated to the expertise of guest chefs. Each of the charming rooms has food-inspired names, and the cooking school is a member of the international Slow Food Movement (www.slowfood.com). Also in town is **The Source Real Food Store**, offering organic and fresh produce and some exotic goodies. If you missed out on a cooking class then **Six Triple Three** serves up homemade fare in intimate surroundings.

On the western side of Denmark are the wineries of Lake House, Forest Hill, Rickety Gate and Ducketts Mill. At **The Lake House** (5 kilometres from town), the restaurant's idyllic lakeside setting is the perfect spot to enjoy a vineyard platter for two, including

Above (left to right): wines of Picardy near Pemberton; the far-flung winery of Alkoomi at Frankland; a Dutch windmill at The Lily evokes European origins, Stirling Range National Park

one platter deemed fit for royalty. Also on offer to take away are 'flavours from the vine', the estate-produced Vino Food range, which includes many wine-inspired temptations, such as the beetroot and shiraz relish or the rocky road with red wine jelly. Look for these products in stores as you travel around the region. Not far from The Lake House, the boutique **Forest Hill Vineyard** located off the South Coast Highway is the state's oldest cool-climate vineyard – its wines are considered some of the best in Western Australia. The winery's restaurant, **Greenpool**, has a slick dining room featuring lots of timber, stone and glass, designed to capture the lovely views of green pastures. The constantly evolving menu focuses on freshwater crustaceans and seafood, regional tasting plates and sizzling selections from the chargrill. A well-priced degustation menu matched with Forest Hill estate wines takes out the cumbersome task of making any kind of a decision.

North-west of town on Scotsdale Road, **Rickety Gate** probably selected its location for its ideal grape-growing conditions rather than for the rolling picturesque views of the Bennett Ranges. Winemaker John Wade produces a range of reds and whites including a sparkling shiraz and an 'unoaked' chardonnay, a varietal for which the region is well known. Also on Scotsdale Road and with 8 hectares of vines producing fruity whites, deep reds and a rich range of fortified wines, **Ducketts Mill Wines** is a popular pit stop. On site is **Denmark Farmhouse Cheese** producing handmade cheeses, fudge, and ice-cream to keep the children entertained while you work your way through that extensive wine list.

To explore the eastern part of this region head out along the highway to Albany. On the way pop in to **Eden Gate Blueberry Farm** for some muffins, ice-cream, jams, preserves and port or you might enjoy the exercise and opt to pick your own berries. The township of Albany has been likened to the English town of Brighton, and no more so than at the **Earl of Spencer**, which resembles an English corner pub. Established in 1874 and with cosy fireplaces and a lively beer garden, the popular watering hole serves hearty pub fare. A short walk down towards the Princess Royal Harbour is **Rustler's**, a popular spot for families and carnivores to tuck into juicy steaks. If romance is in the air choose a moonlit night to walk to the waterfront's **Wild Duck Restaurant**. On a par with any city eatery, intimate lighting and filmy curtains add to the seduction of diners as they feast on decadent duck and other gamy and seafood combinations.

Located right beside Princess Royal Harbour is the boutique **Great Southern Distilling Company**. The main aim here is the production of premium single malt whisky but they also produce flavoured vodka and brandy, gin, grappa and absinthe. Even if you're not a spirits drinker, the funky cafe serves a mean coffee, compliments of the Naked Bean. Beer lovers are not forgotten in town either, and drinkers of a brew or two can head for the **Tanglehead Brewing Company**, which also overlooks the harbour.

Saturday mornings are abuzz on Collie Street at the **Albany Farmers' Market**, where farmers sell home-grown and home-reared products, including crustaceans, fish, game, cheese, fruit, vegetables and olive oils. And if there is not enough for you here, head 23 kilometres east of Albany along Two Peoples Bay Road to **Albany Marron Farm & Nippers Cafe**, which serves all things marron, including yabby sushi, and rainbow trout. The petting farm will keep the young ones amused while you relax and have a civilised lunch.

North-east of town, the Wignall family have been experimenting with pinot noir, chardonnay and sauvignon since the early 1980s and have won countless awards for their product. January brings thousands of revellers to **Wignalls** for the Vintage Blues Music Festival. Further to the north-east (15 kilometres from Albany), **Montgomery's Hill Vineyard** may be one of the most remote vineyards in the state but it is certainly worth a visit for its award-winning wines and stunning scenery. The vineyard's chardonnay and shiraz have won multiple awards over the last decade and at the 2009 Qantas Wine Show of WA, Montgomery's Hill won gold for its 2009 Sauvignon Blanc.

Some 50 kilometres north-west of Albany lies the town of Mount Barker, surrounded by vineyards and, to the east and north-east, the national parks of Porongurup and Stirling Range respectively. Adventurers and hiking enthusiasts will want to head out to the latter, where accommodation is available at the Stirling Range Retreat (see Where to stay). Meals are on offer at **The Lily**, close to the highest point of the range at Bluff Knoll. The wholemeal spelt bread is stone-ground milled and baked on site and accompanies much of the European-style menu.

A few kilometres north-west of Mount Barker, **Galafrey Wines** serves its platters with views of the Porongurups and Stirling Ranges. This area is well known for its riesling and you should try it here, along with the La De Da, a champagne-style wine made from riesling grapes. Nearby, to the south-west, is the renowned **Goundrey Wines**. Light whites and ruby reds are part of the Homestead and Goundrey-G ranges, and the G Sauvignon Blanc Semillon is definitely one to try.

The Frankland River area, around 85 kilometres north-west of Mount Barker, is home to **Alkoomi**, located 11 kilometres west of the Frankland River township. The vineyard, one of the earliest in the area, was established in 1971 with plantings of riesling, cabernet sauvignon, shiraz and malbec grape varieties but today produces a much wider variety of wines, bottled under three main labels: Alkoomi Icon Wines, Alkoomi Black Label and Alkoomi White Label. The output here is considerable, with a large portion exported overseas. You can stay on the property in self-contained chalets, but if you do not make it to the Frankland River area, call into their Albany Cellar for a tasting (open daily).

Accommodation

Tree Elle Retreat at Bow Bridge

The 11-hectare Tree Elle Retreat property, situated between Walpole and Denmark, has a distinctive magical quality. The moment you drive through the gates you are transported into a picturesque world of lush landscaped potager gardens, shimmering silver birch forests, groves of apple, fig, plum, peach, mulberry and orange trees, and a help-yourself organic vegetable and herb garden. Upon entering your modern self-contained chalet you'll be greeted with the aroma of baking bread and a kitchen that is sure to inspire greatness, even if it's just to smear jam all over slices of that warm loaf. A well-stocked pantry includes plenty of ingredients to whip up a feast, although you'll be sure to collect your own gourmet delights from the area, including marron, truffles, cheese, berry products and of course the regional wine. It's a common sight to see guests wandering around the grounds with baskets brimming with fresh garden produce; while others can be found indulging in coffee and treats in the secluded coffee 'nook', breathing in the subtle smells of old-fashioned roses and the heady perfume of cascading jasmine. One of the most frequent comments written by guests in the guest book is that no matter how long they stay, it never seems long enough. For contact details, *see* Where to stay.

Contacts for South-West

EATERIES

Albany Marron Farm & Nippers Cafe:
304 Two Peoples Bay Rd, Albany;
(08) 9846 4239;
www.albanymarronfarm.com.au

Earl of Spencer: Cnr Earl and Spencer sts,
Albany; (08) 9841 1322;
www.earlofspencer.com.au

Gourmet Truffle Cafe: The Wine & Truffle
Co, Seven Day Rd, Manjimup;
(08) 9777 2474; wineandtruffle.com.au

Greenpool: Forest Hill Vineyard, South
Coast Hwy, Denmark; (08) 9848 1922

**King Trout Restaurant and Marron
Farm:** Cnr Northcliffe and Old Vasse rds,
Pemberton; (08) 9776 1352

Lost Lake Winery: see Wineries

Nornalup Tea House: 6684 South Coast
Hwy, Nornalup; (08) 9840 1422;
www.nornalupteahouse.com.au

Old Kent River: South Coast Hwy
(nr Bow Bridge), Rocky Gully;
(08) 9855 1589; www.oldkentriver.com.au

Rustler's: 63 Frederick St, Albany;
(08) 9842 2454

Shamrock Restaurant: 18 Brockman St,
Pemberton; (08) 9776 1186;
www.shamrockdining.com.au

Six Triple Three: 4 Brazier St, Denmark;
(08) 9848 3333

The Lake House: see Wineries

The Lily: 9793 Chester Pass Rd, Stirling
Range National Park; (08) 9827 9205,
www.thelily.com.au

Wild Duck Restaurant: Shop 5, 112 York
St, Albany; (08) 9842 2554

Woodsmoke Cafe: Lot 2 Kemp Rd,
Eastbrook, Pemberton; (08) 9776 0225;
www.jarrahjacks.com.au

STORES

Bow Bridge Roadhouse: Great Southern
Hwy, Bow Bridge; (08) 9840 8062;
www.valleyofthegiants.com.au/bowbridge/

The Source Real Food Store: Fig Tree Sq,
27 Strickland St, Denmark; (08) 9848 1183

MARKETS

Albany Farmers' Market: Collie St,
Albany; (08) 9841 4312;
www.albanyfarmersmarket.com.au

GOURMET PRODUCE

Bartholomews Meadery: 2620 South
Coast Hwy, Denmark; (08) 9840 9349;
www.honeywine.com.au

Denmark Farmhouse Cheese:
1678 Scotsdale Rd, Denmark;
(08) 9840 9844;
www.denmarkfarmhouse.com.au

Eden Gate Blueberry Farm: 685 Eden
Rd, Albany; (08) 9845 2003;
www.edengate.com.au

**Gourmet Truffle Cafe and Cellar
Door:** The Wine & Truffle Co, Seven Day Rd,
Manjimup; (08) 9777 2474;
wineandtruffle.com.au

**King Trout Restaurant and Marron
Farm:** see Eateries

Vino Foods: see Wineries/The Lake House

WINERIES/MEADERIES

Alkoomi: 1141 Wingebellup Rd, Frankland, (08) 9855 2229; **Alkoomi Albany Cellar**, 225 Lower Stirling Tce, Albany, (08) 9841 2027; www.alkoomiwines.com.au

Bartholomews Meadery: 2620 South Coast Hwy, Denmark; (08) 9840 9349; www.honeywine.com.au

Ducketts Mill Wines: 1678 Scotsdale Rd, Denmark; (08) 9840 9844; www.duckettsmillwines.com.au

Fonty's Pool: Seven Day Rd, Manjimup; (08) 9777 0777; www.fontyspoolwines.com.au

Forest Hill Vineyard: *see* Eateries/ Greenpool

Galafrey Wines: 432 Quangellup Rd, Mount Barker; (08) 9851 2022; www.galafreywines.com.au

Goundrey Wines: Muirs Hwy, Mount Barker; (08) 9892 1777; www.goundreywines.com.au

Lost Lake Winery: Lot 3 Vasse Hwy, Pemberton; (08) 9776 1251 or 0411 254 524; www.lostlake.com.au

Montgomery's Hill Vineyard: 45 805 South Coast Hwy (East), Kalgan River via Albany; (08) 9844 3715; www.montgomeryshill.com.au

Old Kent River: *see* Eateries

Picardy: Cnr Vasse Hwy and Eastbrook Rd, Pemberton; (08) 9776 0036; www.picardy.com.au

Rickety Gate: 1949 Scotsdale Rd, Denmark; (08) 9840 9503; www.ricketygate.com.au

Salitage Winery: Vasse Hwy, Pemberton; (08) 9776 1771; www.salitage.com.au

The Lake House: 106 Turner Rd (off Mt Shadforth Dr), Denmark; (08) 9848 2444; www.lakehousedenmark.com.au

Truffle Hill: *see* Gourmet Produce/ Gourmet Truffle Cafe and Cellar Door

Wignalls: 448 Chester Pass Rd, Albany; (08) 9841 2848; www.wignallswines.com.au

BREWERIES/DISTILLERIES

Great Southern Distilling Company: 252 Frenchman Bay Rd, Robinson, Albany; (08) 9842 5363; www.distillery.com.au

Jarrah Jacks Brewery: Lot 2 Kemp Rd, Pemberton; (08) 9776 1333; www.jarrahjacks.com.au

Tanglehead Brewing Company: 72 Stirling Tce, Albany; (08) 9841 1733

COOKING SCHOOLS

Pensione Verde: 31 South Coast Hwy, Denmark; (08) 9848 1700; www.denmarkaccommodation.com.au

Below (left to right): fresh bread at Albany Farmers' Market; the home of Denmark Farmhouse Cheese; Lost Lake Winery near Pemberton

Broome

The historic Kimberley town of Broome, 2000 kilometres north of Perth, is distinguished by its pearling history, cosmopolitan character and its spectacular natural assets: white sandy beaches, turquoise waters and red soils. In the evening the sinking sun casts hues of red and gold over the creamy sands of Cable Beach. As the moon gently rises to meet the night at Roebuck Bay, silver reflects across the mudflats creating an illusion of a long shimmery staircase. This natural phenomenon is known as the Staircase to the Moon, a thrice-monthly occurrence during March–October. The surreal beauty of Broome and its laid-back vibe attracts visitors in droves and gourmands won't go hungry as the old pearling town serves up an eclectic mix of Asian and European tastes — and at sunset cocktails are mandatory, their vibrant colours reflecting the tones of the Kimberley landscape.

Just out of town, **Matso's Broome Brewery** is an institution and the perfect initiation into Broome time. Start with a tasting of the award-winning boutique beers, including a spicy ginger beer and a chilli and mango variety. The menu ranges from breakfast fare and bar snacks to a substantial dinner of steak, kangaroo or local seafood, all well matched to

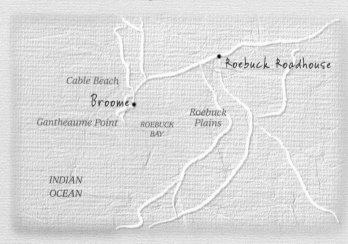

Above: cultured pearls from Broome
Opposite (top to bottom): a Sunday market in Broome; camel rides on Broome's famous Cable Beach

Broome Mango Festival:
3-day mango festival; Nov;
0439 963 339

Where to stay

Bungalow Broome: one-bedroom
retreat; 3 McKenzie Rd, Broome;
0417 918 420;
www.thebungalowbroome.com.au

Cable Beach Resort: resort rooms
and villas; Cable Beach Rd, Cable
Beach; (08) 9192 0400;
www.cablebeachclub.com

McAlpine House: historic luxury;
55 Herbert St, Broome;
(08) 9192 3886;
www.mcalpinehouse.com.au

**Moonlight Bay Suites & Bayside
Apartments:** self-contained
accommodation; 51 Carnarvon St,
Broome; (08) 9195 5200;
www.mlb.broomeaccommodation.
com.au

the local brew. Just around the corner, soft-shell crab, kangaroo, duck, oysters and barramundi all star at **Black Pearl Restaurant**.

The influence of Asian ancestry is evident from several outlets in town including **Azuki Japanese Fusion**, which offers a fusion breakfast menu like no other. Start the day with silken tofu and sweetcorn buttermilk pancake, a breakfast bento box and tempura sweet potato hash browns with shiitake mascarpone. Azuki is also open for lunch and dinner and a takeaway menu is on offer as well.

Heading towards Cable Beach, the inauspicious location of **Cafe Carlotta** cleverly disguises what lies within, keeping away drop-ins, which suits the locals who appreciate the importance of booking. The Italian menu includes handmade pasta, wood-fired pizza, venison and seafood. Alfresco dining takes advantage of those balmy nights and the takeaway menu will recompense those who didn't think to book. Situated across the road from the Cable Beach Club is the **Old Zoo Cafe**, housed in the original feed-house of the Pearl Coast Zoological Gardens. The Kimberley Tasting Plate includes pearl meat, barramundi, crocodile, kangaroo and emu. The menu has an Asian influence with duck and hoi son shiitake mushroom spring rolls, char sui quail and

the European flavours of slow-cooked beef cheeks and a shiitake mushroom risotto.

It would take you some time to work your way through all the mango wines and liqueurs at the **Mango Place**, situated 18 kilometres out of town, but the wood-fired pizza, mango ice-cream and fudge ensure that you have plenty of food to counteract the effects of the beverages. End your day at the **Zeebar** with high-end bubbles of the Dom kind, and a range of Australian and international wine labels and cocktails. The slinky nightspot offers a gig guide, Monday night Barramondays (barramundi served two ways), and the Mediterranean menu includes sharing plates and tapas.

For those wanting a more far-flung experience, charter a flight from Broome and fly to **Faraway Bay**, a luxurious resort only accessible by sea, or by air from Kununurra. The resort holds a number of cooking classes during the year: Kimberley Cooking School (generally once a year in May), focusing on the preparation of fresh local produce; Bush Tucker and Camp Oven Cooking School (June/August), featuring the collecting and preparation of bushfoods; and Pete Evans Celebrity Cooking School (October). Contact the resort or see the website for further details.

Below (left to right): Matso's Broome Brewery; mango wines, liqueurs and all things mango on offer at Mango Place outside of Broome township

Contacts for Broome

EATERIES

Azuki Japanese Fusion: Shop 1, Napier Tce, Chinatown, Broome; (08) 9193 7211

Black Pearl Restaurant: 63 Robinson St, Broome; (08) 9192 1779

Cafe Carlotta: Jones Pl, Broome; (08) 9192 7606; www.cafecarlotta.com.au

Matso's Broome Brewery: 60 Hamersley St, Broome; (08) 9193 5811; www.matsos.com.au

Old Zoo Cafe: 2 Challenor Dr, Cable Beach; (08) 9193 6200; www.zoocafe.com.au

Zeebar: 8 Sanctuary Rd, Cable Beach; (08) 9193 6511; www.zeebar.com.au

MARKETS

The Broome Courthouse Markets: food stalls; Broome Courthouse, cnr Frederick and Hamersley sts; Sat and Sun; (08) 9192 2222

WINERIES

Mango Place: Lot 4, Kanagae Dr, 12 Mile, Broome; (08) 9192 5462; www.mangowine.com.au

BREWERIES

Matso's Broome Brewery: 60 Hamersley St, Broome; (08) 9193 5811; www.matsos.com.au

COOKING SCHOOLS

Faraway Bay Cooking Schools: Faraway Bay, PO Box 901, Kununurra; (08) 9169 1214 or 0417 986 614; www.farawaybay.com.au

Right: a seafood feast on the sands at Cable Beach

Queensland

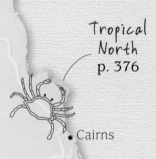

Tropical
North
p. 376

• Cairns

Sunshine
Coast
p. 364

Gold Coast
and hinterland
p. 344

Granite
Belt
p. 356

BRISBANE

Scenic
Rim
p. 352

Left: Palm Cove in the Tropical North

Above (left to right): intimate setting at Nautilus in Port Douglas, Tropical North; lavish style at Palazzo Versace in Main Beach, Gold Coast and hinterland; Thai cuisine shines at the Spirit House in Yandina, Sunshine Coast

Overleaf: fresh seafood dominates in Brisbane

Brisbane

Brisbane's food scene is defined by Moreton Bay and dining out is very much about seafood, whether it is wrapped in paper and eaten on a bench beside the lazy winding river or on a stylish restaurant deck overlooking a riverside marina.

Brisbane – an overview

Brisbane's food scene is defined by Moreton Bay and dining out is very much about seafood, whether it is wrapped in paper and eaten on a bench beside the lazy winding river or on a stylish restaurant deck overlooking a riverside marina. In an imitation of Melbourne trends, the city is also now rediscovering its laneways – in this area it is still finding its culinary identity, but you can be sure there'll be something fishy there.

The inner city retains its wide-ranging eating precincts. Paddington has the long-established restaurants on Caxton Street and Latrobe and Given terraces, with excellent Indian, French and contemporary Australian eateries. At New Farm the mood is relaxed with apartment dwellers patronising some great bistro bars and the many small local eateries serving Japanese, modern Australian and French, and southern Asian food. At the Brisbane Powerhouse bars and restaurants are as hip as you would expect from a theatre complex. Fortitude Valley has always been a mix of Italian coffee bars, casual Italian restaurants and Chinese cafes. Despite the large Chinatown Mall, the epicentre of Asian food has left town for the outer suburbs although there are still good Asian restaurants here. With a few notable exceptions the Italian restaurants have also gone. The once gritty Valley has taken on a few airs and graces with the emergence of stylish up-market restaurants, especially at the Emporium complex. James Street is the place to go to drink cocktails and wine. South Bank's Grey Street, now with river views, has a mix of bustling Turkish places, bars and bistros serving Mod Oz food, and laid-back eateries offering Japanese, French, Vietnamese, Chinese and Italian fare, while the Queensland Cultural Centre has great cafes for lunch. And finally, despite more recent arrivals from Vietnam, West End has never really lost its Greek ambience.

OUTER-CITY GOURMET EXPERIENCES

* Cinco
* Jan Power's Farmers' Markets
* Landmark
* Liquorish
* Morgans Seafood Restaurant and Teppanyaki Room
* My'ooz
* Restaurant Lurleen's
* Rhubarb Rhubarb
* The Summit Restaurant
* Yum Yum Peking Duck

See following pages...

Outer-city gourmet experiences

Here are some good restaurants and markets outside the CBD but well worth the detour.

Above (left to right):
bugs and crabs on sale at Morgans' seafood market, and cooked bugs at the company's Scarborough restaurant; The Summit Restaurant for the views, Mount Coot-tha; food from Eritrea is the feature at Mu'ooz, Moorooka

Cinco: superb food from owner-chef Peter Stubbs who spent years in the Northern Hemisphere cooking for the world's wealthiest and most celebrated people before coming home to Brisbane to open his own place; 589 Old Cleveland Rd, Camp Hill; (07) 3843 6666; www.cincobistro.com

Jan Power's Farmers' Markets: at various locations including Queen St Mall, City, Wed; Blackwood St, Mitchelton, 1st Sun each month, morning; Powerhouse, 119 Lamington St, New Farm, 4th and 2nd Sat each month, morning; Esplanade, Manly, 3rd Sat each month, morning; 0439 999 009; www.janpowersfarmersmarkets.com.au

Landmark: the weekend yum cha is to queue for, and you almost certainly will have to; Sunnybank Plaza, cnr Mains Rd and McCullough St, Sunnybank; (07) 3344 3288

Liquorish: from its tapas to its degustation, its cocktail bar to its French-influenced contemporary Australian meals, this place entices diners from near and far and at all hours of the day; 2/140 Oxford St, Bulimba; (07) 3399 1520; www.liquorishbistro.com.au

Morgans Seafood Restaurant and Teppanyaki Room: alfresco dining on the deck, feasting on fresh seafood – bugs, blue swimmer crab, oysters and prawns – overlooking the trawlers that bring in their catches from Moreton Bay; also includes teppanyaki room, sushi and oyster bar, seafood market and more; well worth the 40-kilometre trek from the city; Bird Of Passage Pde, Scarborough; (07) 3203 5744; www.morganseafood.com.au

Mu'ooz: offers delicately spiced and distinctive food of Eritrea as well as giving training, work experience and employment to refugee women from Africa; Lower level, Ranchhod Arcade, 197–201 Beaudesert Rd, Moorooka; (07) 3255 8992; www.muooz.com.au

Restaurant Lurleen's: vineyard restaurant where, to put you in the picture, renowned chef Andrew Mirosch serves up mains such as a caviar duo of Iranian Osetra sturgeon and Australian caviar and Yarra Valley salmon pearls, and a single dish dessert of hot mango soufflé crepe with mango and lime compote and macadamia praline ice-cream; easy 50-kilometre drive; 850–938 Mt Cotton Rd, Mount Cotton; (07) 3206 2999; www.sirromet.com/restaurant-lurleens.html

Rhubarb Rhubarb: since it opened in 2001, diners have kept coming back for more great French food at this small BYO; 85 Kent Rd, Wooloowin; (07) 3857 5118

The Summit Restaurant: year-round seafood from seared scallops to grilled prawns, spanner crab risotto, Darling Downs Black Angus beef and oven-roasted grain-fed lamb rump; panoramic views over Brisbane to Moreton Bay and the Glasshouse Mountains; 1012 Sir Samuel Griffith Dr, Brisbane Lookout, Mount Coot-tha; (07) 3369 9922; www.brisbanelookout.com

Yum Yum Peking Duck: people travelled 15 kilometres from the city to eat the Chinese and Vietnamese food at this Darra institution before the advent in 2010 of a second restaurant at New Farm; 5/146 Scotts Rd, Darra, (07) 3217 0188; 876 Brunswick St, New Farm, (07) 3254 3280

Gold Coast and hinterland

Tamborine
Sanctuary Cove
Eagle Heights
Upper Coomera
CORAL SEA
North Tamborine
Mount Tamborine
Nerang
Main Beach
Surfers Paradise
Gold Coast
Broadbeach
Miami
Burleigh Heads
Tallebudgera
Coolangatta
QLD   NSW

The Gold Coast, the epitome of everything that is big, brash and gold in Queensland, is only an hour's drive from Brisbane. The place was built on a dream – a surfer's paradise – when Jim Cavill built a hotel there in the 1930s and, as a drawcard, advertised the place as having the best surf beaches in the world. Today it is the country's biggest and best-known holiday region. Stretching out along the golden shoreline is a string of interconnected population centres, from the resort hotel village of Sanctuary Cove in the north to the long-established old Queensland town of Coolangatta in the south. You can cross the state border between Coolangatta and the Tweed in New South Wales by crossing the street – and remain oblivious to the fact that you have exited the Sunshine State.

With a population of almost 600 000, the Gold Coast is Australia's sixth largest population centre and therefore attracts restaurateurs who are used to providing a constantly high level of food and service to keep local customers coming back to their tables. At the main hotspots of Southport, Main Beach, Surfers Paradise, Broadbeach and Burleigh Heads there is a huge variety of restaurants, understandable since the region attracts around 10 million visitors a year, nearly half of them from overseas. Its tourist accommodation ranges from the world's first designer-labelled hotel, Palazzo Versace, to hostels and two-star apartment blocks. So, on the coastal strip, when choosing a dining venue, keep in mind that restaurants generally reflect the standards of the surrounding hotels and apartments.

The Gold Coast hinterland, by contrast, is a world of misty green mountains and World Heritage rainforests. The most vibrant spot for food lovers is in the thickly forested Tamborine Mountain area, where tiny hillside villages produce cheese, wine and beer. On the coast's wall-to-wall high-rise strip there's no room for growing much more than a balcony-based potted plant.

Friday afternoons in summer see the eight-lane Pacific Motorway a mass of city-weary workers heading from Brisbane to the coast to escape the heat. Try and plan your trip at a more civilised day and hour and during the milder months (May–October). At Upper Coomera (exit off the highway soon after Dreamworld) you can make your first stop at **Thumm Estate**.

Festivals

A La Carte in the Park: showcasing diversity of local cuisine; Lionel Perry Park, Surfers Paradise; May; (07) 5584 3700; www.surfersparadisefestival.com

Eat Week: various Surfers Paradise restaurants; June; (07) 5584 3700; www.surfersparadisefestival.com

Great Aussie BBQ: Eileen Peters Park, The Esplanade, Surfers Paradise; June; (07) 5584 3700; www.surfersparadisefestival.com

Broadbeach Restaurant Week: set-price meals in 25 restaurants; July; broadbeachgc.com

Broadbeach Jazz and Food Festival: various locations; Aug; (07) 5539 8416; broadbeachgc.com

Tastes of Gold Coast: celebrity-chef demonstrations and dinners; various venues; Aug–Sept; (07) 5581 7473; www.tastesofgoldcoast.com.au

Where to stay

Palazzo Versace: designer luxury hotel; 94 Seaworld Dr, Main Beach; (07) 5509 8000; www.palazzoversace.com

Q1 Resort and Spa: world's tallest residential tower; Cnr Surfers Paradise Blvd and Hamilton Ave, Surfers Paradise; (07) 5630 4524; www.q1.com.au

Songbirds in the Forest: luxury villas in rainforest; Tamborine Mountain Rd, North Tamborine; (07) 5545 2563; www.songbirds.com.au

The Polish Place: chalets with log fires and mountain views; 333 Main Western Rd, Mount Tamborine; (07) 5545 1603; www.polishplace.com.au

Here Robert Thumm, son of one of the Barossa's great winemaking families and founders of Chateau Yaldara, continues a 300-year family heritage of viticulture and winemaking in Germany and Australia. The wine list is wide-ranging and includes Thumm's private label and the justifiably famous Thumm's port. The on-site restaurant in a bushland setting has light and affordable meals, with offerings such as the Pruner's Picnic for two, comprising a platter of olives, charred capsicum, parma ham or the chef's pâté, sun-dried tomatoes, artichoke hearts and frozen grapes (a house specialty). Perhaps match this with the Thumm Estate Sparkling Rosé. Alternatively there is more hearty fare, such as wagyu beef and thick-cut chips, Moroccan-spiced chicken with couscous, or crispy skin wild snapper fillets. The restaurant is open daily for lunch, but if you are planning ahead keep in mind that it is famous for its great Sunday breakfasts.

Now you can head for that famous coast, on highway or byway. At Southport's Main Beach you should try and schedule a meal at the much-awarded **Ristorante Fellini**. It is impossible not to be dazzled, first by the sparkling Broadwater vistas then by the fact that for all its rave reviews and its Philippe Starck transparent polycarbonate Louis Ghost chairs, this is an Italian family restaurant – although in the way perhaps that Buckingham Palace

is a family home. The Percuoco family – Tony, his sister Anna Cacace and brother Carlo – work in partnership with pasta master Raffaele Di Benedetto and executive chef Richard Burt to produce Neapolitan- and Tuscan-influenced food as modern as tomorrow and as traditional as generations of an Italian food-loving family (is there any other kind?) can produce. Perhaps start with rollata di caprino (goat's cheese rolled with fire-roasted capsicum, fried eggplant slivers, basil, and more ...) or ravioli di anatra (filled with roasted duck and vegetables cooked in a butter and sage sauce), move on to a main of scaloppine alla caprese made with Green Mountain's veal, then finish with a double cream and vanilla bean panna cotta. If all this sounds way too much, or you have arrived at the wrong time of day, buy some fresh handmade pasta at **Pastificio Fellini** to take home. There is an infinite selection of fresh, dry and filled pasta, and a range of five classic sauces and some other special offerings, including the house-made balsamic vinegar.

When it comes to being very grand about your food and its setting there are two standout choices in this region – Vanitas at Palazzo Versace where even the Versace tableware deserves special attention, and **Absynthe** at the world's tallest residential tower, Q1 (*see* Where to stay). At Absynthe, chef Meyjitte Boughenout, with a

Below (left to right): outdoor dining at Oskars on Burleigh, Burleigh Heads; pork belly and scallops at RockSalt, Broadbeach; glitz and glamour in the lobby, and poolside accommodation, at Palazzo Versace, Main Beach

background in European Michelin-starred restaurants, presents adventurous French fare displaying Australian contemporary influences, while still managing to remain true to his classical roots. Slow-cooked fish is not the norm in Australian restaurants; Boughenout does it with sea bass, accompanied by candied celeriac, confit tomato and sautéed cepes. He also challenges preconceptions of what goes with what with a dish of lightly cured ocean trout, white chocolate cannelloni and a pomegranate reduction.

You will need to polish up your bling before anchoring yourself to a silken-covered Versace chair at **Vanitas** at Palazzo Versace (*see* Where to stay). Order the degustation and settle in for a good long read of the wine list while you check your credit card limit. You wouldn't be here if you didn't want to throw caution to the winds and enjoy. Of course the contemporary Australian food is good and if you don't overdo the drinks it is no more expensive than any other uber-eatery for the rich, famous and aspirational. As a bonus you might do some quiet celebrity spotting. But if you're only after a small indulgence, tea and scones in the hotel lobby is almost as exclusive.

Ten minutes drive and a world away on Chevron Island is **Shimbashi – Soba So Good**, where you will find Yoshi Shibazaki, one of a small number of Japanese chefs to complete ten years of training to attain the title of Soba Master. He is believed to be the only Soba Master working in Australia and his 40-seat restaurant is a simple, affordable and friendly mecca for the gluten-intolerant and people who eat for their health as well as those who simply love the taste of Soba noodles. Watch Yoshi at work making noodles with Tasmanian organic buckwheat and eat the fresh noodles hot or cold, with soup, vegetables, meat, seafood, sashimi, tempura or deep-fried as chips. This place is testament to the fact that not everything exclusive and a little exotic is expensive.

RockSalt restaurant is in the interesting Broadbeach dining precinct, only 6 kilometres from the heart of Surfers Paradise but with much more of a local atmosphere and with a little less beachfront high-rise development. Co-owners Amy and Matt Jefferson have the youthful courage and energy to call themselves simply 'modern' and this leaves plenty of room to range at will between genres, relying on quality food and treating it with imagination and flair. Soft shell crabs are morsels of sheer delight in Moroccan spices, crisp-fried and served with mint yoghurt, tomato, rocket, lemon and chickpea salad. Matt plays with textures in an entrée of seared scallops served with crisp-fried bread, lardons and herbs. And just when you are wondering

why they are served in a bowl, your waiter adds a potato and leek broth and the flavours stand to attention. Order the Tasting Menu to see just how far a young, smart and game chef will go to tease your palate.

Not far away, **Kurrawa Surf Club**'s bistro is a popular spot for visitors and locals alike looking for well-prepared food. Here is fare to suit any taste from hearty lamb shank dishes to light meals and snacks. Eat on the balcony overlooking the ocean or in the air-conditioned restaurant but make sure you leave room for the cakes.

There has been an Oskars on the Gold Coast for nearly three decades and, since it opened in 1997, **Oskars on Burleigh** is as close as you'll get to surfside dining on the coast, apart from some of the successful mid-range surf life saving club eateries. Seafood is a specialty here, with menus changing daily depending on what's available from long-established sources – from as close by as Moreton Bay and Hervey Bay to as far afield as Western Australia for crayfish. Even though it is only kilometres away you can look northwards from the restaurant and see the distinctive Surfers Paradise skyline. In winter you might see whales cruise past.

For a change of tempo and environment the Gold Coast hinterland beckons those who just want to get away from all that glitz and glamour. Only around

15 kilometres inland from Burleigh yet in an utterly different setting you can learn to grow organic food and cook healthy meals during a three-day retreat at **Gwinganna Lifestyle Retreat** at Tallebudgera. Organic meals and snacks throughout the day are delicious and portions are generous. Pampering body treatments, luxurious accommodation and a bushland setting with views to the coast take the sting out of the limits guests are asked to accept on the consumption of alcohol and coffee. You can also take daytrips to other parts of the surrounding hinterland if you wish.

There are several ways to get from Tallebudgera to the Tamborine Mountain area. Either scoot along the M1 to the Beaudesert–Nerang Road or take a longer but more picturesque drive via Beechmont to Mount Tamborine. Just north of town, at **The Polish Place**, the food, wildlife and spectacular mountain views are as enjoyable, hearty and generous as the hosts, Phil and Ania Sowter. Their à la carte offerings, served indoors and out, include such Polish delights as Polski Bigos – sauerkraut cooked with different meats, porcini mushrooms, prunes and herbs, and served with Polish sausage. Vegetarians might enjoy the vegetarian pierogi (Polish dumplings) – made up of sauerkraut and porcini mushrooms wrapped in pastry and boiled, served topped with a creamy porcini and onion sauce. There are plenty of Polish

Below (left to right): Mount Tamborine Brewery, North Tamborine; the stylish interior of Absynthe restaurant, Surfers Paradise; dessert with flair at RockSalt, Broadbeach; sit in Louis Ghost chairs at Ristorante Fellini, Main Beach

vodkas and beers on the drinks list to keep you warm at this mountainside eyrie. Open daily for lunch and Friday–Saturday for dinner, there is also accommodation (*see* Where to stay) on offer in spacious, beautifully appointed timber chalets looking across the mountain ranges.

Nearby at North Tamborine is **Witches Falls**, where winemaker Jon Heslop is producing some excellent limited release varieties, in particular pinot noir, grenache and marsanne using Granite Belt grapes. His 2007 Syrah is on the wine list for Queensland parliamentary functions. And spirit drinkers can get a lift around the corner in Beacon Road at **Tamborine Mountain Distillery**, where there are a multitude of chemical-free schnapps, gins and vodkas to try, many of which come from the fruits grown on the farm. Try the multifaceted choc'n'chilli liqueur, macadamia nut liqueur or the zany Turkish delight liqueur. Under the Australian Vodka Company brand, the distillery also produces a multi-award-winning herbal liqueur, and a 2 Rooz range of flavoured vodkas, including lemon myrtle leaf, forest peppermint and eucalyptus gum leaf.

On the other side of town, in the small locality of Eagle Heights, is the must-visit **Witches Chase Cheese Company** (*see* feature, p. 350), where a business that started from humble beginnings has grown from strength to strength. About ten minutes drive from here, along Tamborine Mountain Road, is the sublime **Songbirds in the Forest**. This is an exquisite restaurant and rainforest retreat in a setting that lives up to its lyrical name. Chef Duncan Elliott uses organic produce wherever possible, because 'it is better tasting, better for you, better for the environment'. The very diverse menu features wild pigeon, pork, lamb, beef and fish, all cooked in interesting ways and displaying some interesting combinations. A roasted pork rack is served with sauce tagine, whipped sesame honey, couscous and leeks vinaigrette, while baby barramundi comes with roast chicken wings, chive dumplings, melted onions, smoked mussel and brown bread sauce. But a peanut butter and jam sandwich for dessert? Now that shows a brave chef in the face of the sometimes ludicrous fantasies of haute cuisine practitioners. You would be hard put to guess at what it might contain, so stop reading now if you don't want to know until you taste. It's actually a brown bread parfait with peanut butter ice-cream served usually with a raspberry cloud. In summer the cloud is made of grapes. Eat here (open daily for lunch and Thursday–Saturday for dinner) and you will almost certainly want to retire to one of the six luxury two-person villas (*see* Where to stay) and next day succumb to meditation, massage or yoga.

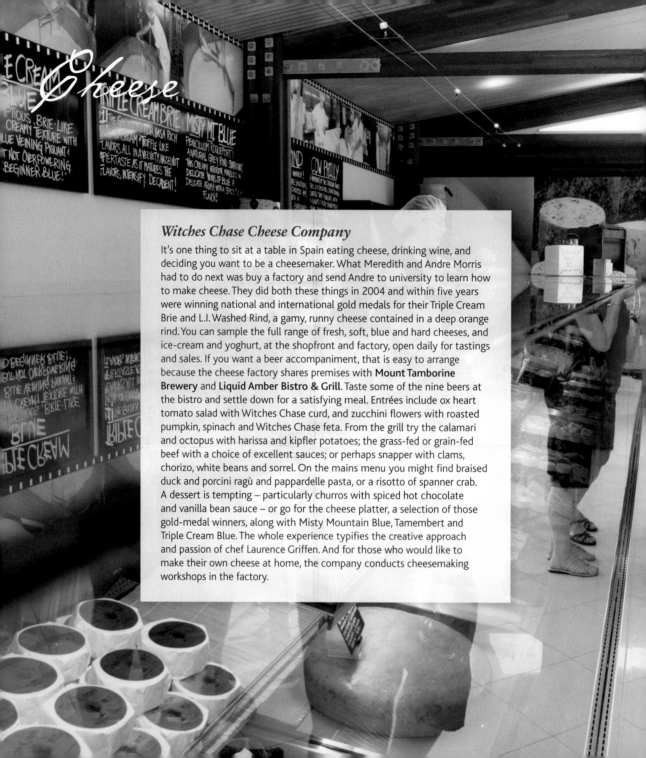

Cheese

Witches Chase Cheese Company

It's one thing to sit at a table in Spain eating cheese, drinking wine, and deciding you want to be a cheesemaker. What Meredith and Andre Morris had to do next was buy a factory and send Andre to university to learn how to make cheese. They did both these things in 2004 and within five years were winning national and international gold medals for their Triple Cream Brie and L.I. Washed Rind, a gamy, runny cheese contained in a deep orange rind. You can sample the full range of fresh, soft, blue and hard cheeses, and ice-cream and yoghurt, at the shopfront and factory, open daily for tastings and sales. If you want a beer accompaniment, that is easy to arrange because the cheese factory shares premises with **Mount Tamborine Brewery** and **Liquid Amber Bistro & Grill**. Taste some of the nine beers at the bistro and settle down for a satisfying meal. Entrées include ox heart tomato salad with Witches Chase curd, and zucchini flowers with roasted pumpkin, spinach and Witches Chase feta. From the grill try the calamari and octopus with harissa and kipfler potatoes; the grass-fed or grain-fed beef with a choice of excellent sauces; or perhaps snapper with clams, chorizo, white beans and sorrel. On the mains menu you might find braised duck and porcini ragù and pappardelle pasta, or a risotto of spanner crab. A dessert is tempting – particularly churros with spiced hot chocolate and vanilla bean sauce – or go for the cheese platter, a selection of those gold-medal winners, along with Misty Mountain Blue, Tamembert and Triple Cream Blue. The whole experience typifies the creative approach and passion of chef Laurence Griffen. And for those who would like to make their own cheese at home, the company conducts cheesemaking workshops in the factory.

Contacts for Gold Coast and hinterland

EATERIES

Absynthe: Q1 Building, cnr Surfers Paradise Blvd and Hamilton Ave, Surfers Paradise; (07) 5504 6466; www.absynthe.com.au

Kurrawa Surf Club: Old Burleigh Rd, Broadbeach; (07) 5538 0806; www.kurrawasurf.com.au

Liquid Amber Bistro & Grill: 165–185 Long Rd, North Tamborine; (07) 5545 2032; www.witcheschasecheese.com.au

Oskars on Burleigh: 43 Goodwin Tce, Burleigh Heads; (07) 5576 3722; www.oskars.com.au

Ristorante Fellini: Waterfront level, Marina Mirage, Seaworld Dr, Main Beach; (07) 5531 0300; www.fellini.com.au

RockSalt: Shop 12, Aria, Albert Ave, Broadbeach; (07) 5570 6076; www.rocksaltmoderndining.com.au

Shimbashi – Soba So Good: Shop 2, 54 Thomas Dr, Chevron Island; (07) 5504 6404

Songbirds in the Forest: Lot 10 Tamborine Mountain Rd, North Tamborine; (07) 5545 2563; www.songbirds.com.au

The Polish Place: 333 Main Western Rd, Mount Tamborine; (07) 5545 1603; www.polishplace.com.au

Vanitas: Palazzo Versace, 94 Seaworld Dr, Main Beach; (07) 5509 8000; www.palazzoversace.com

MARKETS

Carrara Markets: Cnr Gooding Dr and Manchester Rd; Friday morning, Sat–Sun; (07) 5579 9388; www.carraramarkets.com.au

Organic Gold Coast Farmers' Market: Miami State High School, Gold Coast Hwy; Sunday morning; (07) 3358 6309 or 1300 668 603; www.gcorganicmarket.com

Tamborine Country Markets: Showground, Main Western Rd; 2nd Sunday each month, morning; (07) 5545 2155; www.tamborinemtncc.org.au

GOURMET PRODUCE

Pastificio Fellini: Marina Mirage, Seaworld Dr, Main Beach; (07) 5531 0300; www.fellini.com.au

Witches Chase Cheese Company: 165–185 Long Rd, Eagle Heights, North Tamborine; (07) 5545 2032; www.witcheschasecheese.com.au

WINERIES

Thumm Estate: 87 Kriedeman Rd, Upper Coomera; (07) 5573 6990; www.thummestate.com

Witches Falls: 79 Main Western Rd, North Tamborine; (07) 5545 2609; www.witchesfalls.com.au

BREWERIES/DISTILLERIES

Mount Tamborine Brewery: 165–185 Long Rd, North Tamborine; (07) 5545 2032; www.mtbeer.com

Tamborine Mountain Distillery: 87–91 Beacon Rd, North Tamborine; (07) 5545 3452; www.tamborinemountaindistillery.com

COOKING SCHOOLS

Gwinganna Lifestyle Retreat: 192 Syndicate Rd, Tallebudgera; 1800 219 272; www.gwinganna.com.au

Witches Chase Cheese Company: see Gourmet Produce

Scenic Rim

It is ironically apposite that Queensland's Lost World is in the Scenic Rim region, where the rugged mountain ranges and picturesque small towns struggle for attention against the magnetic glitz of the Gold Coast and the enticing bustle of the city of Brisbane. The Scenic Rim is roughly equidistant from both – a 90-minute drive (via Beaudesert) from either direction will take you to Darlington, a good place to start.

There are many charms for those who love small rural towns with classic country pubs and roadside farm stalls and the region is attracting many Brisbane food and nature lovers looking for a change of pace. There are two cooking schools, two luxury resorts, vineyard restaurants and eight national parks. If you head south from Brisbane on the Mount Lindsay Highway and turn off to Darlington, you can stay at **Worendo Cottages** (*see* Where to stay) and take rainforest walks, find the Lost World Valley, fish in the dam, swim in rockpools, feed farm animals, pick olives from the property's olive grove or simply eat, drink and relax beside a warm fire. At Worendo's on-site **Wild Lime Cooking School**, you can learn to use native foods in Asian and Mediterranean dishes (bookings essential).

Above: a relaxing breakfast before a morning on the working cattle property at Lillydale Host Farm, Mount Barney

Opposite (top to bottom): gracious Spicers Peak Restaurant at Maryvale; lavender at Kooroomba Vineyard's on-site lavender farm, Mount Alford

Festivals

A World Apart: showcases food and wine of Mount Barney area; various locations; May; (07) 5544 3233; scenicrimescapes.com.au

Art in the Olives Festival: artisan stalls, gourmet food and wine-tasting; Worendo Olive Grove (*see* Gourmet Produce); May; lostworldvalley.com

Where to stay

Lillydale Host Farm: working cattle property; 821 Upper Logan Rd, Mount Barney; (07) 5544 3131; www.lillydale.com.au

Spicers Hidden Vale: luxury cattle property with fine dining; 617 Mount Mort Rd, Grandchester; 1300 179 340; www.spicershiddenvale.com.au

Spicers Peak Lodge: luxury lodge on mountaintop; Wilkinsons Rd, Maryvale; 1300 253 103; www.spicerspeaklodge.com.au

Wiss House B&B: heritage-listed home with contemporary service; 7 Ann St, Kalbar; (07) 5463 9030; wisshouse.com.au

Worendo Cottages: B&B tree house/cottage with mountain views; 97 Cedar Glen Rd, Darlington; (07) 5544 8104; www.worendo.com

From here wind your way west through the rich green countryside, back onto the Mount Lindsay Highway and south to Rathdowney and **Classi di Cucina Italiana**. Here people love to cook and eat at Pietro and Desley Agnoletto's monthly pizza and pasta cooking classes, where the wood-fired pizza oven is a popular attraction. Or book a five-course Veneto banquet for yourself and friends at their place or yours – if you are staying locally.

If you want to discover something about the winegrowing in this region head towards Mount Alford (turn off the Boonah–Rathdowney Road just before Boonah) to visit **Kooroomba Vineyard**, with its cellar door open for tastings Wednesday–Sunday. At **Kooroomba Vineyard Restaurant** chef Mark Naoum changes his menu of contemporary Australian–Mediterranean cuisine to match what is available locally. One constant is the ice-cream made with cream infused with the property's own lavender and served with a tart, fresh berry compote. Lavender changes its flavour with the seasons, a good excuse to go back for more at another time of the year. The estate is also a lavender farm and lavender products are sold on site.

North-west of Boonah, in tiny Kalbar, historic buildings have miraculously survived the challenges of development despite it being only 70 kilometres from rampantly expanding Brisbane. The lovely old **Royal Hotel** has maintained its original architecture but refurbished the kitchen and dining rooms and added an outdoor deck. Lunches are most popular here and usually booked out on weekends by holidaymakers and locals. Dishes include grass- and grain-fed steaks from the local butchery at Fassifern, which has its own feed lot, and makes sausages to recipes provided by chef Jason Somers. Because the area is fertile, the kitchen uses local vegetables in season. It may not win any national gourmet awards but the hotel is a good example of cutting down

food air miles and keeping prices modest without sacrificing quality.

From here take the Cunningham Highway south-west towards Maryvale. Spicers Peak Lodge (*see* Where to stay) sits in a beautiful wilderness area at the summit of a steep and winding unsealed 12-kilometre road, slippery when wet. Many guests arrive by helicopter. Only house guests at this luxury mountain-top retreat can enjoy the full repertoire of meals at **Spicers Peak Restaurant**, but it has recently opened to visitors for the seven-course degustation dinner as well as the five-course lunch. Menus change daily at the whim of the chef or at the behest of the pampered guests staying in the ten lodges, but choices can include assiette of white rabbit, milk-poached veal with roast fennel and porcini beurre blanc, seared tuna with sorbet and salad or whole roast quail with broad beans and semi-dried grapes.

Return to Boonah and drive north along the Cunningham Highway for an hour to **Cotton's Restaurant** at Spicers Hidden Vale (*see* Where to stay). The signature steak, the Kumamoto wagyu beef, is raised on the property and is used even in the burgers on the small lunch menu, along with that old 1960s favourite surf and turf, although it gets an upgrade with a 200-gram sirloin fillet served with bug tails and galliano cream. Dinner is à la carte and still has plenty of beef – grilled or as slow-cooked cheek – along with the standard choices of meat and poultry. These include maple syrup glazed duck breast with orange braised red cabbage compote and duck prosciutto, and a rabbit trio of ballotine of loin with beetroot tart, sticky faggot (in this case finely minced and larded leg meat from the rabbit), scallop and oyster mushroom duxelles and a warm salted rabbit salad with cherry brandy sauce.

Contacts for Scenic Rim

EATERIES

Cotton's Restaurant: Spicers Hidden Vale, 617 Mount Mort Rd, Grandchester; (07) 5645 5900; www.spicershiddenvale.com.au

Kooroomba Vineyard Restaurant: 168 F.M. Bells Rd, Mount Alford via Boonah; (07) 5463 0022; www.kooroomba.com.au

Royal Hotel: Cnr George and Edward sts, Kalbar; (07) 5463 7188

Spicers Peak Restaurant: Spicers Peak Lodge, Wilkinsons Rd, Maryvale; 1300 253 103; www.spicerspeaklodge.com.au

GOURMET PRODUCE

Worendo Olive Grove: 97 Cedar Glen Rd, Darlington; (07) 5544 8104; www.worendo.com

WINERIES

Kooroomba Vineyard: *see* Eateries

COOKING SCHOOLS

Classi di Cucina Italiana: 111 Douglas Rd, Rathdowney; (07) 5544 1008

Wild Lime Cooking School: Worendo, 97 Cedar Glen Rd, Darlington; (07) 5544 8104; www.worendo.com

Above (top to bottom): Spicers Peak Restaurant, and the deck of a private lodge, at Spicers Peak Lodge, Maryvale

Granite Belt

The Granite Belt is between 800 and 1000 metres above sea level and centred on Stanthorpe, three hours drive south-west of Brisbane and the coldest town in Queensland. On the western spine of the Great Dividing Range, the region's spectacular granite outcrops have given it two national parks, Girraween and Sundown. It is a scenic and delicious place to visit. Go there in spring for berries and cherries and fields of lavender. In summer and autumn there are crisp fresh apples and pears, grapes and stone fruit. In autumn, apricots and figs are added to the abundance on sale at roadside stalls. All the wineries and restaurants are quite close to the New England Highway, beginning in the north at Cottonvale and continuing almost to the New South Wales border at Wallangarra. The main street of the major town of Stanthorpe runs parallel with the highway.

Although its medal tally shows that the Granite Belt can match a lot of better known cool-climate wine regions it has had to face the undeniable challenges presented by its location and comparatively late start in the industry. Rather than fighting the battle for recognition on that one front, the region's winemakers are diversifying into dozens of different grapes. They've done this in part by being early adapters of alternative grape varieties that, while familiar to Europeans, are still regarded as rather 'strange birds' by many Australians. In a flight of marketing brilliance the small winemakers got together and drew up a Strange Bird trail for tourists looking for alternatives to the dominant grapes grown by the big winemakers elsewhere in the country. An exponent of the region's wines, Darby Higgs, on his website (www.vinodiversity.com), lists 38 Granite Belt growers planting almost as many varieties.

It certainly has the terroir, with free-draining decomposed granite soil, spring rains, cold winters and moderately hot summers with cool nights. Add to these attributes a strong Italian culture and you have a fine place for eating, drinking and making merry – this last with musical events such as opera and jazz and Italian feasts in the vineyards. June, July and August barely have enough days in them to accommodate winter festivities. There are so many Christmas in July dinners and events that it's a wonder there's a turkey left standing. Almost every weekend there is a vineyard festival.

Festivals

Sicilian Vintage Lunch: grape stomping and Italian food; Golden Grove Estate, Ballandean; Feb; (07) 4684 1291; www.goldengroveestate.com.au

Jazz in the Vineyard: food and jazz; Ballandean Estate; Aug; (07) 4684 1226; www.ballandeanestate.com

Australian Small Winemakers Show: Stanthorpe Showgrounds; Oct; (07) 4681 4482; www.asws.com

Shakespeare under the Stars: theatre and muscat; Bungawarra Wines, Bents Rd, Ballandean; Oct; (07) 4684 1128; www.bungawarrawines.com.au

Where to stay

Diamondvale B&B Cottages: luxury in a bush setting; 26 Diamondvale Rd, Stanthorpe; (07) 4681 3367; www.diamondvalecottages.com.au

Granite Gardens Luxury Cottages: luxury amid 4 ha gardens; 90 Nicholson Rd, Thorndale; (07) 4683 5161; www.granitegardens.com.au

Ridgemill Estate: funky self-contained cabins; 218 Donges Rd, Severnlea; (07) 4683 5211; www.ridgemillestate.com

The Trainhouse: quirky ensuite accommodation; Harrington Glen Vineyard, 88 Townsend Rd, Glen Aplin; (07) 4683 4388; www.harringtonglenwines.com.au

Vineyard Cottages and Cafe: 28 126 New England Hwy, Ballandean; (07) 4684 1270; www.vineyardcottages.com.au

Above (left to right):
cellar door of Ridgemill
Estate, Severnlea;
chocolate extravaganza
at Bella Rosa's Tea
Rooms, Thulimbah;
the entrance to
Boireann Wines, The
Summit; fresh fruit at
Stanthorpe's twice-
monthly Market in
the Mountains

The first winery you strike coming from the north is **The Heritage** near Cottonvale, which produces mainly sweet wines from chardonnay grapes. The advantages of being small and family-owned meant they could adapt in 2007 when there was a particularly dry vintage; the result was the production of their award-winning The Heritage Estate Reserve Granite Belt Chardonnay 2007. The cellar door's log fire is a great spot in winter and there are light meals available at the cafe.

At Thulimbah, **Bella Rosa's Tea Rooms** offers chocolate-making classes (held on the first Saturday of each month or by arrangement), as well as a garden centre and cottage accommodation. The Tea Rooms serve breakfast, lunch, high tea (they're famous for their cakes) and dinner (reservations essential). They offer reasonably priced four- and five-course set menus. On winter nights you can tuck into soups, roast dinners, and apple crumbles with custard or butterscotch sauce.

At a high altitude, near the aptly named township of The Summit, the small and picturesque

16-hectare **Boireann Wines** produces red table wines using open fermentation, basket-pressing and barrel-ageing before bottling. Try the highly regarded shiraz viognier. Grapes include barbera, nebbiolo, mourvèdre, merlot, shiraz and cabernet sauvignon. The vineyard's hands-on care and attention has won the praise of some of Australia's most-respected wine writers.

Just out of Stanthorpe, Vivienne Abeywardena of **Vivienne's Cottage** produces Sri Lankan curry powders, chutneys, jams, novelty cakes and gift baskets. Her recipe book, *Mixing Cultures*, and her cooking classes (held monthly or by arrangement) use easy-to-follow recipes based on the traditional cooking of her Sri Lankan family, but using ingredients readily available in supermarkets. Not far from here, **Banca Ridge** is a winery that exists ostensibly to provide training to students of the Queensland College of Wine Tourism. Under the watchful eye of a professional winemaker, grapes are grown and wine produced by students from Stanthorpe State High School (who sell their own

range under the Banca Ridge label) and elsewhere. The enterprise started in 2000 with plantings of merlot and marsanne grapes and has rapidly expanded. **Banca Ridge Cellar Door and Bistro** is a pleasant spot for lunch (open Tuesday–Sunday), overlooking the mountains and serving modern Australian food prepared and served by hospitality students during their training 'on the job'. This is also a place where visitors can learn, along with the students, at cooking schools held at quarterly intervals during the year. What is taught depends on the curriculum and includes Asian, Thai, Greek, Italian and New Orleans cuisines.

Backtrack to the highway and follow the signs to Amiens, so named because it was initially a soldier settlement location for World War I veterans who served on the Western Front near the French city of the same name. Here **Robert Channon Wines** is a star of the region for its award-winning verdelho – the 2009 is a gold-medal winner and was selected as the Queensland Parliament's 150th anniversary white wine. The winery has also taken out awards for pinot gris, chardonnay, shiraz cabernet and cabernet sauvignon. At the estate's **Singing Lake Cafe** lunch is a daily affair, with hearty soups, pies, chicken curry, braised beef cheeks, confit duck and pasta dishes. Sunday breakfasts are particularly popular and there are special events, occasional cooking classes and dinners in the restaurant overlooking the lake, and concerts, jazz and opera in the purpose-built (and humorously called) Swigmore Hall.

A little further south towards Severnlea is another award winner, **Ridgemill Estate**, recognised at national and international wine shows. Look in particular for its 2005 and 2006 tempranillo, 2005 merlot, 2005 Black Dog Cabernet Sauvignon and 2005 Reserve Chardonnay. All have won awards and high praise. Not bad considering the first vines – cabernet, shiraz, chardonnay and merlot – were planted in 1998. Tempranillo was planted in 2000 and saperavi, lagrein and viognier in 2005.

At Glen Aplin you can buy olives, olive oil, three varieties of tapenade (from black and green olives and sun-dried tomatoes) or even an olive tree at

Mount Stirling Olives. Here the olives are processed on the property within 24 hours of being picked and it really shows in the quality of the products, including a marvellous extra virgin cold pressed olive oil. Just past Glen Aplin, you can stay overnight at **Harrington Glen Vineyard** and sample some of their good red wine. The unusual thing here is that you'll be sleeping in a house that is also a train. The Trainhouse (see Where to stay) is built above, around and within a Victorian Railways carriage and includes three ensuite queen bedrooms, as well as a deck with views, and all mod cons. Here the cabernet sauvignon has been consistently praised by judges and critics and its winemaker, Stephen Oliver, was a finalist in the 2009 Wine Society Young Winemaker of the Year award and is the only Queenslander to have made the list in its nine-year history.

Some 6 kilometres south of Glen Aplin, the **Cellar Door Cafe** at **Mason Wines Vineyards** makes a pleasant lunch stop for the bruschetta alone, with its homemade basil, parmesan and pine-nut pesto. For a hearty meal you can eat gluten-free pork, beef and sausages from Hawker Brothers or a wondrously rich beef and shiraz hot pot of slow-cooked rump steak and shiraz gravy topped with puff pastry, served with mashed potatoes and mushy peas.

Accommodation in this region is small, privately operated and distinctive and often attached to a vineyard and restaurant. As you enter Ballandean, the **Vineyard Cafe** at **Vineyard Cottages and Cafe** (see Where to stay) is a case in point and a good place to try a variety of local wines by the glass, matched with local seasonal ingredients such as trout, beef, lamb, asparagus, berries, and stone fruit. Housed in an old church, the cafe restaurant is open to cottage guests daily and to outside visitors for dinner Friday–Saturday. Main-course dishes display Asian influences in mains such as the fillet of lamb in nori and tempura served on roasted eggplant and Asian greens with a soy-based sauce and wasabi. The small cottages are beautifully furnished and very private if you feel like staying awhile.

Take the Eukey Road from Ballandean to **Hidden Creek**, where there's a special interest in Mediterranean and European wine styles, hardly surprising since owners include wine commentator and Master of Wine Andrew Corrigan, who knows a thing or two about these things, plus award-winning winemaker Jim Barnes. The award winners on the wine front include viognier and tempranillo.

A little further along the same road, **Symphony Hill Wines** is one of the leading wineries of the region with third-generation winemaker Mike Hayes producing excellent cabernet sauvignon, merlot, shiraz and sauvignon blanc, particularly the 2007 vintage. The 2003 Reserve Shiraz won Queensland's first-ever gold medal at the 2005 Sydney Royal Wine Show and was the second highest scoring wine, after Tyrrell's Vat 1 Semillon.

At **Golden Grove Estate,** along the road from Ballandean towards Sundown National Park, father and son winemaking team Sam and Ray Costanzo have taken out too many awards to list. The much-praised shiraz, castalina, tempranillo and durif are all excellent. The latest plantings include vermantino from Sardinia and nero d'avola from Sicily. Just around the corner from here, meet one of the region's wine-pioneering families, the Puglisis, at the **Barrel Room Cafe**, attached to their cellar door at **Ballandean Estate** (see feature, p. 362). The cafe offers good, hearty Italian home cooking, with wholesome pasta dishes of carbonara, bolognaise, linguine with smoked salmon and pumpkin ravioli, or try the cabernet beef pie or share an antipasto platter. Anyone lucky enough to book one of the 70 tickets available to their annual Gamekeepers Dinner in September is urged to come with an empty stomach and a sense of adventure to enjoy five courses of game and the estate's best wines. In 2008, in an initiative to support local producers, Ballandean opened **The Gourmet Food Gallery**, where an impressive range of local gourmet products, along with some specialties from elsewhere, can be tasted and purchased.

Opposite (top to bottom): chocolate treats at Ballandean Estate, Ballandean; admiring the vines at Golden Grove Estate, Ballandean; sunset vineyard views from one of the cabins at Ridgemill Estate, Severnlea

Wine

Family-owned Ballandean Estate

Queensland's reputation as a tropical paradise (beautiful one day, perfect the next) has often seen it dismissed as being too hot for winegrowing. But don't say that to Angelo Puglisi whose Ballandean Estate in the Granite Belt is the state's longest-running and largest family-operated winery.

'We can tell you about cold,' he says. 'Those people in so-called cool climates in the south, they have four or five weeks of bushfire season, we don't. They get days and days of 45-degree heat, we don't. We'd be unlikely to get 38 degrees one day a year.'

Sundown Valley Vineyards (it was renamed Ballandean Estate in 1988) began producing wine in 1932, made from table grapes grown on the family farm. The first wine grapes were planted elsewhere in the region in 1965 and in the late 1960s third-generation family members Angelo and Mary Puglisi replanted their estate with wine grapes. The cellar door opened in 1970 and, in 1977, Angelo drew attention to the district when he was awarded a Churchill Fellowship to study European winemaking techniques. Today Ballandean's signature styles are viognier, sylvaner, shiraz and semillon/sauvignon blanc. The latter — a classic cool-climate wine — has taken out numerous awards and the 2008 vintage alone has won two gold medals. There are 25 varieties under cultivation here and more to come. In 2009 the family planted fiano, a Sicilian white varietal, and saperavi, a rich red wine grape from Georgia. The first wine won't be made before 2012. 'You have to have patience in this business or you'll fall apart,' Angelo says.

Contacts for Granite Belt

EATERIES

Banca Ridge Cellar Door and Bistro:
22 Caves Rd, Stanthorpe; (07) 4685 5050;
www.usq.edu.au/qcwt/cellardoor

Barrel Room Cafe: Ballandean Estate,
354 Sundown Rd, Ballandean;
(07) 4684 1226;
www.ballandeanestate.com

Bella Rosa's Tea Rooms: 357 Granite Belt
Dr, Thulimbah; (07) 4685 2367;
www.bellarosas.com.au

Cellar Door Cafe: Mason Wines,
27850 New England Hwy, Glen Aplin;
(07) 4684 1341; www.masonwines.com.au

Singing Lake Cafe: see Wineries/Robert
Channon Wines

The Heritage cafe: see Wineries/The
Heritage

Vineyard Cafe: Vineyard Cottages and
Cafe, 28 126 New England Hwy, Ballandean;
(07) 4684 1270;
www.vineyardcottages.com.au

MARKETS

Market in the Mountains: Stanthorpe
Civic Centre, cnr Marsh and Lock sts; 2nd
and 4th Sun each month, morning;
0417 760 529;
www.marketinthemountains.org

GOURMET PRODUCE

Mount Stirling Olives: Collins Rd, Glen
Aplin; (07) 4683 4270;
www.mtstirlingolives.com.au

The Gourmet Food Gallery: see
Wineries/Ballandean Estate

Vivienne's Cottage: 96 Mt Tully Rd,
Stanthorpe; (07) 4681 0227 or
0403 351 968; www.viviennescottage.com

WINERIES

Ballandean Estate: 354 Sundown Rd,
Ballandean; (07) 4684 1226;
www.ballandeanestate.com.au

Banca Ridge Winery: 22 Caves Rd,
Stanthorpe; (07) 4685 5050;
www.usq.edu.au/qcwt/bancaridge

Boireann Wines: 26 Donnellys Castle Rd,
The Summit; (07) 4683 2194;
www.boireannwinery.com.au

Golden Grove Estate: Sundown Rd,
Ballandean; (07) 4684 1291;
www.goldengroveestate.com.au

Harrington Glen Vineyard: 88
Townsend Rd, Glen Aplin; (07) 4683 4388;
www.harringtonglenwines.com.au

Hidden Creek: Eukey Rd, Ballandean;
(07) 4684 1383; www.hiddencreek.com.au

Ridgemill Estate: 218 Donges Rd,
Severnlea;(07) 4683 5211;
www.ridgemillestate.com

Robert Channon Wines: 50 Amiens Rd,
Stanthorpe; (07) 4683 3260;
www.robertchannonwines.com

Symphony Hill Wines: 2017 Eukey Rd,
Ballandean; (07) 4684 1388;
www.symphonyhill.com.au

The Heritage: Granite Belt Dr, Cottonvale;
(07) 4685 2197; www.heritagewines.com.au

COOKING SCHOOLS

Banca Ridge: Queensland College of Wine
Tourism, 22 Caves Rd, Stanthorpe;
(07) 4685 5050; www.usq.edu.au/qcwt

Bella Rosa's Tea Rooms: see Eateries

Robert Channon Wines: see Wineries

Vivienne's Cottage: see Gourmet Produce

Sunshine Coast

Boreen Point • Lake Cootharaba
Noosa Heads
Noosaville
Sunshine Beach
Eumundi
Peregian Beach
Yandina
CORAL SEA
Bli Bli
Nambour
Maroochydore
Palmwoods
Mooloolaba
Maleny
Warana
Bald Knob
Caloundra

In contrast to the Gold Coast's high-rise towers, theme parks and luxury hotels that all compete for location and attention, the Sunshine Coast, particularly the hinterland and the northern coastal strip, is quieter, less in-your-face, and its hidden gems are happy with their seclusion. In the gourmet food stakes the Noosa area is still the main event, but you'll find good eating in most towns, whether on the 65-kilometre coastline that stretches from Noosa Heads in the north to Caloundra in the south or in the picturesque hinterland from Eumundi to Maleny. Food producers and chefs work together and there are more cooking schools here than in any other gourmet region in the state.

Noosa Heads – or simply 'Noosa' as it is known – is at the centre of a gourmet food enclave of villages that merge into one another around the waterways and national parks of the area. Noosa faces the calm waters of Laguna Bay, its safe-swimming beach a drawcard for families. Over the hill to the south is the commercial hub of Noosa Junction and to the east, on the other side of the much-trekked Noosa National Park, is Sunshine Beach, a small conglomerate of shops, restaurants, beach shacks, apartments and luxury holiday homes, all happily co-existing and vying for views of its superb surf beach – with kilometres of white sand stretching southwards to Coolum and beyond. On the western side of Noosa, on a backwater of the Noosa River, is Noosa Sound, then further west Noosaville, where an eclectic mix of eateries, cafes, shops and holiday rentals stretches out along the southern bank of the river's wide expanse.

If you have chosen to stay in Noosa, begin your culinary journey in its famous Hastings Street, where for years **Berardo's Restaurant and Bar** has been regarded as one of Australia's best regional dining spots. This is the Noosa restaurant for a special night out, with an elegant casual dress code. Chef Shane Bailey produces exquisite modern Australian food combinations using local produce extensively – from the vegetables to the fish, prawns and organic poultry. As well as à la carte offerings, seven-course degustation menus show off the chef's best of the best. Co-owner Jim Berardo is a founder and the director of the Noosa Food & Wine Festival where well over 100 of Australia's top chefs, winemakers, food and wine

Festivals

Sunshine Coast Food Show:
Novotel Twin Waters, Ocean Dr,
Maroochydore; Feb;
(07) 5448 8000 or 1800 072 277;
www.twinwatersresort.com.au

Noosa Food & Wine Festival:
over 100 events; Apr/May;
(07) 5455 4455;
www.celebrationofaustralianfood
andwine.com.au

Tierra Madre: slow food events;
various Sunshine Coast venues;
Dec; 0439 944 690;
www.slowfoodsunshinecoast.org.au

Where to stay

Aegean Apartments: near beach;
14 River Espl, Mooloolaba; (07) 5444 1255;
www.aegeanmooloolaba.com.au

Amytis Gardens Retreat: luxury
cabins; 51 Malone Rd, Maroochydore;
(07) 5450 0115;
www.amytisgardens.com

Frog House B&B: modern ensuites;
73 Mountain View Rd, Maleny;
(07) 5499 9055;
www.thefroghouse.com.au

Lake Weyba Cottages: luxurious
lakeside cottages; 79 Clarendon Rd,
Peregian Beach; (07) 5448 2285;
www.lakeweybacottages.com

Sheraton Noosa Resort and Spa:
five-star hotel; 14–16 Hastings St, Noosa
Heads; (07) 5449 4888;
www.starwoodhotels.com/sheraton

Spicers Clovelly Estate:
intimate retreat; 68 Balmoral Rd,
Montville; 1300 252 380;
www.spicersgroup.com.au

Above (left to right):
pan-fried scallops with
pickled vegetables at
Spirit House, Yandina;
evening light at Wasabi,
Noosa Sound; Gallery
Gourmet's colourful
display at the Noosa
Farmers' Market,
Noosaville; dining
with a view at The
Boat Shed Restaurant,
Cotton Tree

writers and critics cater to the enthusiastic diners
who converge each year for the three-day event. A
highlight is at Berardo's where nine chefs prepare a
nine-course degustation using winning foods from
the annual Great Australian Produce Awards.

Berardo's Bistro on the Beach is more casual, but
still focuses on local ingredients with a blackboard
menu that reflects the best food available on the
day. Jim Berardo and co-owner Greg O'Brien like to
say the restaurant is just a towel length from the
sand and they aren't exaggerating. Thanks to its
floor-length sliding windows it is like picnicking on
the beach but much more comfortable.

Some holidaymakers love the Hastings Street
beachfront location of **Bistro C** so much they go
there for breakfast, lunch and dinner on the same
day. If you remember that epicurean pleasures are
not just about food, but total sensual hedonism that
can include bobbing gently in the ocean between
drinks and eats without having to move far from
your towel then you'll love this place. Cocktails are
disparate and delicious, wines by the glass are from
France, Germany and Australia, the beer selection is
wide and digestifs a very reasonable price on a list
that runs from amaretto to Jägermeister. Menus
change daily from breakfast to brunch, lunch,
afternoon snacks and dinner. You might find the
beer-battered snapper and chips a perfect
complement to a swim and a lunchtime beer.

Finally, no visit to Noosa is complete without
sampling an ice-cream from **Massimo's Gelateria** in
Hastings Street. Savour the flavours that see
returning customers beating a path to this Italian
vendor's door. This is reputedly the best gelato you
will find outside Italy. Make the journey and decide
for yourself!

At the spectacular Sunshine Beach, long-time
Noosa restaurateur Leonie Palmer will greet you at
the door and welcome you 'home' to **Coconut
Grove**. The rustic Mediterranean food is excellent
and because the menu changes constantly with the
season and availability you can ask to have it faxed
or emailed to you before you arrive. There is a
charming subtropical plantation ambience with

plenty of white louvres to control and direct the breezes off the ocean, although there is air-conditioning for when those stupefying humid Queensland late summer days come along. The separate wine bar has a range of Australian, French and Italian wines by the glass that won't break the bank. Enjoy them with cheeses and house-made terrine and bread. Leonie and husband Stef were restaurant pioneers in Hastings Street when they started Palmer's in 1985 in what is now Berardo's.

After six wildly successful years at Sunshine Beach, **Wasabi** moved in 2009 to Noosa Sound on the Noosa River, a dining hotspot that, along with neighbouring Noosaville, some say now outshines Hastings Street for quality and variety. Chef Shinichi Maeda grew up in a village on Japan's Hokkaido Island where fresh fish is a large part of the diet. He trained in the Ginza district and moved to Australia in 2003, at the age of 24, as executive chef at Wasabi. Now a part owner of Wasabi, Maeda continues to produce some of the most highly awarded Australian high-end Japanese food, from

entrées, perfect to share, to a seven-course tasting menu or omakase (chef's choice).

Down the road at Noosaville, **Blue Angel** chef Daniel Mosedale is also the president of the long-running Slow Food Convivium so you can be sure of the quality of the products he uses in his modern Australian menu. His talent is undeniable when you consider he has cooked in some of the greatest restaurants in Europe, the US and Australia, among them Philippe Chavant's La Tour Rose in Lyon. He established Blue Angel with his wife Angela in 2006, proclaiming, 'Our focus is to highlight the amazing produce available in the local area.' A meal here is a sumptuous affair. For entrée you may find citrus-cured Hervey Bay scallops with labna, avocado, chilli olive oil and sumac, or a double-baked Roquefort soufflé with poached quince, almonds, truffled honey and wild rocket. Mains may include a roast saddle of lamb with organic garlic and thyme, caramelised sweetbreads, buttered new season peas, baby onions, barrel-aged feta and mint, or perhaps confit Dakota Vale duck leg with sticky

Above (left to right):
a delectable dish at
Blue Angel, Noosaville;
a display of creative
flair at Spirit House,
Yandina; Spicers
Clovelly Estate
at Montville

French lentils, roast baby fennel, parsnips and cumquats. Mosedale also makes time to conduct regular cooking classes at the restaurant, an endeavour that further supports local growers, farmers and fishermen.

Definitely worth leaving the beach for, **River House** is a great restaurant with an international wine list but a very firmly local menu. Glass shutters welcome the Noosa River breeze inside the stylish split-level dining room of this Noosaville establishment (open Sunday for lunch, daily for dinner). Expect a real eating treat here, where the evening menu isn't printed until chef David Rayner has organised the freshest and best local supplies of the day. For vegetarians, the freshness and variety of products from local growers is a real plus. The innovative menu evolves daily and typically may comprise two way duck (seared breast, confit leg spring roll, Thai-style red curry, green beans and smoked eschalots) or pan-seared sea bass with fresh figs and braised fennel. Desserts are suitably decadent and you may find that the pavlova roulade

with fresh cream, black figs and strawberry salad is simply irresistible.

Also at Noosaville, **Belmondos Fresh Food Market** does more than merely sell gourmet foods from all over the world, including local delicacies. Its staff are well educated in food and its preparation and can help you select a cheese platter or sort out what goes with what, suggesting some combinations you'd never have thought of on your own.

North of Noosaville at Boreen Point in the Lake Cootharaba area, **Kabi Organic Golf Course and Orchard** is the place to buy juices and fruits including oranges, mandarins, lemons, limes, grapefruit, tangelos, pomelos, lemonades, kaffir limes, custard apples, nashi pears, longans, olives and starfruit at the club house bar, which opens daily and serves lunch on Sundays.

If you travel some 20 kilometres eastwards from Noosa to Eumundi, you'll find Queensland's most famous market selling everything from produce (Wednesday is best for food) and clothes to sturdy handmade peg baskets and ironing boards. Here you

will also find Andrew Hickinbotham, an enthusiastic third-generation winemaker with degrees from Australian and French universities. Visit his **Eumundi Winery** from Wednesday to Sunday when there is live music or buy from his stall at the market. Andrew says Mediterranean grape varieties thrive in the region's red volcanic soils. His plantings include alabarino, verdelho, shiraz, tempranillo and refosco. He plants disease-resistant vines and uses minimum levels of fungicides. If you have a taste for old-world wines made with a clean, green and modern approach this is your kind of place.

While in Eumundi you must seek out the unprepossessing shopfront at the chocolate factory of **Cocoa Chocolat**, tucked away in a backstreet. Once inside be seduced by chocolatier Louisa Raven's exquisite handcrafted chocolates and truffles, made using the finest Belgian couverture, King Island cream and butter, and locally sourced ingredients. Lose yourself in a range of pistachio cremes, passion fruit hearts, crème de menthe truffles and hazelnut pyramids, to name just a few

of the chocolate delicacies on offer here. The shop is open daily Monday–Saturday and Sunday until 2pm; a Noosa outlet is housed at the Sheraton Noosa Resort in Hastings Street.

From Eumundi it is an easy drive south to Yandina. Walk through the front gate of the **Spirit House** and into an Asian garden of singing bamboo and thriving ginger plants that leads you to a store packed with **Thai Epicurean Products** made by the chefs (take-home Thai-style meals, condiments and ice-cream), along with their two recipe books. At the restaurant, tables surround a pond and the contemporary Thai food is vibrant with the fresh tastes of just-picked ginger, lemongrass, turmeric, chilli, kaffir lime and more. Some of the daily cooking schools here book out as much as four months ahead with enthusiasts eager to learn how to cook the many variations of Thai food from royal to epicurean to essential to fast but fabulous.

Ginger is one of the earth's most useful plants, good for eating and good for health and Buderim ginger is recognised world-wide for its high quality.

Above (left to right):
The Boat Shed
Restaurant, Cotton
Tree; well-stocked
shelves at Belmondos
Fresh Food Market
store, Noosaville;
handcrafted Swiss-style
cheeses at Fromart

The **Buderim Ginger Cooking School** is at Yandina
and is about more than just the remarkable rhizome,
with visiting celebrity chefs offering classes on
culinary dishes from around the world as well as
seasonal classes featuring regional produce. You can
buy **Buderim Ginger** products here at the large
visitor complex, including crystallised ginger, ginger
preserves, confectionery, syrups and non-alcoholic
ginger wine.

From Yandina you might want to leave the
hinterland for a while and return to the coast for a
breath of sea air at Maroochydore. One of the great
assets of this part of the coast is the calm water of
the Maroochy River, a happy fishing and boating
ground for many. A constantly changing menu keeps
the locals coming back to **The Wine Bar Restaurant**
to enjoy modern Australian food prepared by owner
and chef Tony Kelly. The riverfront location keeps
them lingering long over a wine list that includes the
good and the great of the best of Champagne and
some very desirable pinot noirs from New Zealand,
Australia and Burgundy.

At the river's mouth at Cotton Tree, **The Boat
Shed Restaurant** is a long-time local favourite with
good reason. The food is a combination of Asian and
Mediterranean flavours that have attracted
dedicated fans for years and the ambience is pure
coastal magic. Before or after a meal, relax on a
daybed or loll in one of the comfy cane lounges on
the grassy riverbank and watch as pelicans fish and
kids dive into the safe blue waters at its edge.

If you believe too much sumac is never enough
and that there can never be too much smoked red
pepper in your chorizo then the modern Spanish
menu at **Ba Vigo** at Cotton Tree is for you. As in Vigo
itself in Galicia, seafood rules the mains, although
the restaurant's signature dish is green chilli crusted
spatchcock with mint and pomegranate molasses. As
an extra bonus, the Spanish wine is excellent and
available by the glass or bottle.

Also at Cotton Tree, at **How to Cook**, chef and
home economics teacher Iris Windsor makes it easy
for beginners because of her enthusiasm for cooking,
her teaching experience and a kitchen shop

chock-full of must-have cooking aids from knives to saucepans and more. There is also a licensed cafe and a gourmet deli here. Cooking demonstrations are held every Friday for a very low price and weekly hands-on classes cover a wide range of skills from cake making and decorating to knife skills, and the rudiments of Moroccan, Asian and Italian cooking and cuisine. If you need a break from all this gourmet food, drive just 10 minutes from Maroochydore to the **Sunshine Coast Brewery** to taste its bitters, ales, lagers and wheat beers.

South of Maroochydore is the once quiet and now buzzing centre of Mooloolaba with one of the best and safest beaches on the Sunshine Coast, just across the road from its cafes and bars. Around the corner from the beachfront, the trawlers bring their daily catch of the famous Mooloolaba prawns into the harbour. Mooloolah River Fisheries operates the **Mooloolaba Fish Market**, where you can buy fresh or cooked seafood. Alternatively, in the same complex, you can feast on succulent lobster, plump scallops, oysters natural, Mornay or Kilpatrick, and a

vast range of other shellfish, crustaceans and scalefish at **The Deck** restaurant.

Not far down the road you can also eat at **Fish on Parkyn**, a large, airy and open-sided restaurant that lives up to its location with a great variety of fresh fish. The entrée platter is a good taster, especially for the parmesan-crumbed oysters that will leave you asking for more. The crab pikelet entrée is another winner and rarely has a crispy whole reef fish looked and tasted as good as when it faces square on to you from a swimming position in a bed of jasmine rice. Non-fish eaters won't be disappointed, with a confit of Bendelle duck served with Stilton and potato mash and prime eye fillet with an excellent cauliflower Stilton and Yorkshire pudding.

Head for the hills along Old Maroochydore Road to the cute little town of Palmwoods and the simply tasty and healthy **Sister Organic Cafe**. Owner Hayley Robinson has cooked at Montes in London with Ben O'Donahue and Jamie Oliver. So why has she gone, as she puts it, from cosmopolitan to composting and making sandwiches and salads instead of showing off her more sophisticated culinary skills? The answer is that in 2003 a diagnosis of Hodgkin's lymphoma led to lifestyle and dietary changes and the opening in 2005 of this first Sister. There's now a twin sister at Maroochydore. The special thing about Hayley's food is its fresh, natural goodness and taste and that is something, like good health, that she came to the Sunshine Coast to find.

If you backtrack 6 kilometres north-east from Palmwoods to Kiels Mountain, you will find **Amytis Gardens Retreat and Spa**. At the cooking school here you can learn to create European-style chocolates or master Italian cooking techniques, from making homemade pasta to creating the perfect tiramisu. Accommodation is available in luxury cabins (*see* Where to stay). On the other side of the highway, north-west of Palmwoods, **On the Ridge Cooking School** is located on the Blackall Range Tourist Drive between Nambour and Mapleton. This place aims 'to take the mystery out of cooking', teaching basic principles and techniques using the local produce wherever possible.

From Mapleton you can wind your way along the ridges of the Blackall Range to Maleny. This is picturesque mountain country and Maleny is the epicentre of country style, with old-fashioned storefronts harbouring all things desirable to urbanites who cannot live without coffee, cakes, organics and meals available on demand from breakfast to beyond sundown. The town is sometimes referred to as 'Noosa in the Mountains' because it has attracted a well-off bunch of tree changers with more highly developed and highly apparent green and social consciousness than the showy sybarites by the sea. Even the local **IGA Supermarket** conscientiously stocks extensive local clean and green produce.

In a Maleny back street and surrounded by gardens, **Pomodoras On Coral** looks like a private home, serves restaurant-quality food at cafe prices, is quite a local hub of Maleny's community activity and holds regular degustations of local products. It's a long way from the Sheraton Park Tower in Knightsbridge where owners Jodi and Chris Bond met as co-workers but their background is reflected in the European-style dinner menus. Lunches run to burgers and salads.

On the south-eastern side of town, off the Landsborough–Maleny Road, Thai cooking is taught at **The Tamarind** on both day courses and weekend retreats, where many couples book packages for classes and accommodation in beautifully appointed bungalows on the 4-hectare property that overlooks rainforest and a waterfall. There is also a licensed restaurant here.

Further down the road, at Bald Knob, is one of the more recent additions to the regional gourmet scene. A restaurant on the Sunshine Coast has to meet high expectations on food quality to succeed and in 2007 sommelier Steve Heffernan and chef Kieran Reekie rose to the challenge with **Reserve Restaurant**. Housed in a replica of an old colonial Queenslander, dining here is an experience too good to miss. The entrée menu is so varied and intriguing that it's tempting to simply work your way through that and ignore the mains. Typical of the delights to be found in the entrée list are steamed and fried Mooloolaba prawn dumplings with pickled daikon and sesame mayonnaise; sticky anise beef cheek with glazed pumpkin purée and sesame tuille; and twice-baked soufflé of white truffle oil with fresh goat's curd and wild mushroom salad.

Local produce

Noosa Farmers' Market at Noosaville

The Sunshine Coast was a food bowl for south-east Queensland until international factory farming and industrial food production convinced many producers it was uneconomical to continue small-scale farming and processing. But the consumer shift to clean, green food production has seen a new generation producing high-quality food in a sustainable fashion here. With its subtropical climate and volcanic soils, the coast, and particularly its hinterland, is once again renowned for its produce. 'There has been a huge renaissance across the board,' says Julie Shelton of the Sunshine Coast Slow Food Convivium. The best way to find the region's gourmet products in one place is to visit **Noosa Farmers' Market** at Noosaville, where chefs arrive at first light before stallholders have had a chance to set up. Locals are on the doorstep at opening time to buy cheese, poultry, fish, meat, fruit and vegetables. There are still some things left for late-rising holidaymakers, not the least of which are the French breads, pastries, cakes, duck rillettes, pâté and terrines of Montpelier-born Anne Calvet at **French Sin**, her market stand that includes a kitchen with ovens working overtime (products also available at Belmondos; *see* Stores). Also look for **Ceas Spanner Crab** in the shell or in handy packs of shelled meat; handcrafted Swiss-style cheeses from **Fromart**; refreshing lime cordial made with kaffir lime and ginger from **Noosa Lime Co**; and smoked fish from Greg and Sue Rasmusen of **Noosa River Smokehouse**, who produce smoked trout, salmon, snapper, eel and more from their kitchen at Belmondos store in Noosaville.

Contacts for Sunshine Coast

EATERIES

Ba Vigo: 3/27 Cotton Tree Pde, Cotton Tree; (07) 5479 1000

Berardo's Bistro on the Beach: Boardwalk, On the Beach complex, Noosa Heads; (07) 5448 0888; www.berardos.com.au/berardos_bistro.html

Berardo's Restaurant and Bar: 52 Hastings St, Noosa Heads; (07) 5447 5666; www.berardos.com.au/ber_rest/home.htm

Bistro C: 49 Hastings St, Noosa Heads; (07) 5447 2855; www.bistroc.com.au

Blue Angel: 235 Gympie Tce, Noosaville; (07) 5473 0800; www.blueangelrestaurant.com.au

Coconut Grove: 8/46 Duke St, Sunshine Beach; (07) 5449 2333; coconutgrovebistro.com

Fish on Parkyn: 25 Parkyn Pde, Mooloolaba; (07) 5444 4711; www.fishonparkyn.com.au

How to Cook: see Cooking Schools

Massimo's Gelateria: 75 Hastings St, Noosa Heads; (07) 5474 8022

Pomodoras On Coral: 34 Coral St, Maleny; (07) 5429 6543

Reserve Restaurant: 840 Landsborough–Maleny Rd, Bald Knob; (07) 5435 2288; www.reserverestaurant.com.au

River House Restaurant: 301 Weyba Rd, Noosaville; (07) 5449 7441; www.riverhouserestaurant.com.au

Sister Organic Cafe: 18–20 Margaret St, Palmwoods, (07) 5445 0655; 1/13 The Esplanade, Cotton Tree, (07) 5479 4911; www.sister.com.au

Spirit House: 20 Ninderry Rd, Yandina; (07) 5446 8994; www.spirithouse.com.au

The Boat Shed Restaurant: The Esplanade, Cotton Tree; (07) 5443 3808; www.theboatshed.com.au

The Deck: see Gourmet Produce/Mooloolaba Fish Market

The Tamarind: see Cooking Schools

The Wine Bar Restaurant: 4–8 Duporth Ave, Maroochydore; (07) 5479 0188; thewinebarrestaurant.com.au

Wasabi: 2 Quamby Place, Noosa Sound; (07) 5449 2443; www.wasabisb.com

STORES

Belmondos Fresh Food Market: 59 Rene St, Noosaville; (07) 5474 4404; www.belmondos.com

IGA Supermarket: 26 Maple St, Maleny; (07) 5494 2257; www.malenyiga.com.au

MARKETS

Eumundi Market: 80 Memorial Dr; Wed and Sat mornings; (07) 5442 7106; www.eumundimarkets.com.au

Noosa Farmers' Market: Aussie Rules Football Grounds, Weyba Rd, Noosaville; Sun morning; 0418 769 374; www.noosafarmersmarket.com.au

GOURMET PRODUCE

Buderim Ginger: 50 Pioneer Rd, Yandina; (07) 5446 7100; www.buderimginger.com.au

Ceas Spanner Crab: Southern Cross Fisheries, 9 Production Ave, Kawana Waters; (07) 5493 3999; www.ceascrabpak.com

Cocoa Chocolat: 6 Etheridge St, Eumundi; Sheraton Noosa Resort & Spa, 14 Hastings St, Noosa; (07) 5442 7841 or 0406 494 496; www.cocoachocolat.com.au

French Sin: 0417 630 775

Fromart: 0408 725 349; www.fromart.com.au

Kabi Organic Golf Course and Orchard: 59 Kabi Rd; Boreen Point; (07) 5485 3494; www.kabigolf.com.au

How to Cook: see Cooking Schools

Massimo's Gelateria: 75 Hastings St, Noosa Heads; (07) 5474 8022

Mooloolaba Fish Market: Lot 201, Parkyn Pde, Mooloolaba; (07) 5452 4600; www.mooloolahfish.com.au

Noosa Lime Co: (07) 5449 8990; www.noosalimeco.com.au

Noosa River Smokehouse: 59 Rene St, Noosaville; 0400 551 378; www.noosariversmokehouse.com

Thai Epicurean Products: see Eateries/ Spirit House

WINERIES

Eumundi Winery: 310 Memorial Dr, Eumundi; (07) 5442 7444; www.eumundiwinery.com.au

BREWERIES

The Sunshine Coast Brewery: 13 Endeavour Dr, Kunda Park; (07) 5476 6666

COOKING SCHOOLS

Amytis Gardens Retreat and Spa: 51 Malones Rd, Kiels Mountain; (07) 5450 0115; www.amytisgardens.com

Blue Angel: see Eateries

Buderim Ginger Cooking School: 50 Pioneer Rd, Yandina; (07) 5446 7100; www.buderimgingercookingschool.com.au

How to Cook: 68 Sixth Ave, Cotton Tree; (07) 5443 6210; www.howtocook.com.au

On the Ridge Cooking School: 183 Kureelpa Falls Rd, Kureelpa; (07) 5441 3715; www.ontheridge.com.au

Spirit House: 20 Ninderry Rd, Yandina; (07) 5446 8977 or 0427 468 977; www.spirithouse.com.au/school

The Tamarind: 88 Obi Lane Sth, Maleny; (07) 5429 6922; www.thetamarind.com.au

Below (left to right): wicked dessert at Blue Angel, Noosaville; cheese varieties at Belmondos Fresh Food Market store, Noosaville; expansive grounds at Spicers Clovelly Estate, Montville; miang of ocean trout and scallop roe at Spirit House, Yandina

Tropical North

Cape Tribulation
Daintree
Cow Bay
DAINTREE NATIONAL PARK
Port Douglas
Oak Beach
Palm Cove
Kuranda
Cairns
Mareeba
Dimbulah Walkamin Gordonvale
Tolga
Atherton Yungaburra
Malanda
Millaa Millaa
Innisfail

If you had to choose one word to describe Tropical North Queensland it would have to be 'exotic'. It is another country, even for most Australians, with its deep green rainforests and cloud-shrouded misty mountains. It has a strong Italian heritage, due to the migration of canecutters, after both world wars, initially to Innisfail and Ingham, respectively 70 kilometres and 230 kilometres south of Cairns. These towns are generally still strongholds of Italian cuisine and culture. Many canecutters ultimately moved north to Cairns and its hinterland, where they established their own properties, first to grow coffee then tobacco. Now they have returned to coffee production, and many are also engaged in growing tea, as well as fruit for making liqueurs. While the coastal strip has many excellent restaurants, the Cairns Highlands, better known locally as the Atherton Tablelands, are at the heart of primary production.

The following look at the gourmet hotspots of the region starts at Innisfail and takes you in a loop around the Palmerston Highway through Millaa Millaa and Malanda to Atherton on the Kennedy Highway, which leads on to Mareeba then Kuranda. From here the trail heads north along the Captain Cook Highway to Daintree, takes a fascinating look at a tropical fruit farm near Cape Tribulation then returns along the coast, stopping off at the holiday resort towns of Port Douglas and Palm Cove before ending in Cairns for a look at the gourmet scene in this self-proclaimed 'capital' of the north.

The Palmerston Highway from Innisfail runs through the Wet Tropics World Heritage section of the southern highlands. Here waterfalls rush and dive, tea plantations nestle in the foothills and the local wildlife travels via rope skywalks strung above the road. At East Palmerston keep an eye out for the honesty box on the roadside where you can buy fine leaf black **Nucifora Tea** grown by Sybbie Nucifora in the adjacent fields. This laid-back attitude to retail is typical of an area where production comes first and tourism a long second and it makes the area a very genuine place to visit, without billboards or overt signage dragging your attention away from the natural beauty and richness of the land. If you miss the roadside box, Nucifora Tea is also on sale at local shops.

Festivals

Feast of the Senses: food festival; Innisfail; Mar; 0413 010 625; www.feastofthesenses.com.au

Australian Italian Festival: food, music and fun; Ingham Showgrounds; May; (07) 4776 5288; www.australianitalianfestival.com.au

Champagnes of France: Reef House Restaurant, 99 Williams Espl, Palm Cove; June; (07) 4055 3633; www.reefhouse.com.au

Where to stay

Daintree Eco Lodge: world's leading eco lodge; 20 Daintree Rd, Daintree; (07) 4098 6100; www.daintree-ecolodge.com.au

Eden House Retreat and Mountain Spa: luxury cottages and villas; 20 Gillies Hwy, Yungaburra; (07) 4089 7000; www.edenhouse.com.au

Shangri-La: luxury hotel on marina; Pierpoint Rd, Cairns; 1300 733 274; www.cairnsshangrilahotel.com.au

Thala Beach Lodge: secluded deluxe bungalows; Private Rd, Oak Beach (nr Port Douglas); (07) 4098 5700; www.thalabeach.com.au

The Sebel Reef House & Spa: small luxury hotel; 99 Williams Espl, Palm Cove; (07) 4055 3633; www.reefhouse.com.au

Above (left to right): exotic chocolate dessert, and entrance to Ochre Restaurant, in Cairns; tea-producing plant Camellia sinensis at the Nerada Tea factory at Malanda; beautifully presented dish of steamed coral trout fillet with a pickled watermelon, cucumber and lobok salad and a Thai fried nahm jim dressing at 2 Fish Seafood Restaurant, Port Douglas

At Milla Milla, further along the highway, the folks at **Mungalli Creek Dairy** call their cheesery and teahouse **Out of the Whey**. It is out of the way too, because you leave the highway on a tiny road and after several curves and under the disinterested gaze of many cows you begin to wonder if you've taken a wrong turn. Then, without fanfare, there's the teahouse in the middle of the cow paddocks, an ideal spot for homemade lunches and morning and afternoon teas. Set aside all thought of cholesterol counts and tuck into a pie made of three different cheeses, or leaven the dairy products with some spinach with your feta in a spanakopita. Follow up with a Quark cheesecake and worry about your arteries tomorrow. Mungalli dairy is certified A Grade Demeter Biodynamic so surely its cheeses can't be bad for you. The dairy produces a vast array of milks, yoghurts, cheese and ice-cream and there are plenty of free tastings.

From here take the Malanda Road and turn right just before the township to the **Nerada Tea** factory, a name probably familiar from supermarket shelves

although you might not have known this is the world's biggest processor of Australian-grown *Camellia sinensis* – that's the bush, also known as the Chinese rose, that produces both green and black tea. In town, the **Malanda Dairy Centre** is part a museum-style tribute to dairy-industry pioneers, and part retail store, selling local coffee, tea, fruit, vegetables, meats and cheese. A restaurant is open for breakfast and lunch and third-generation dairy farmers provide well-informed guided tours of the factory that processes milk and cheese.

Yungaburra, a tiny town that is heritage listed, can also be accessed from Cairns via the winding and picturesque Gillies Highway from Gordonvale. At Yungaburra some people say the boy from Zuoz, Nick Crameri, also deserves a heritage listing for keeping alive his own exuberant Swiss culture at **Nick's Restaurant and Yodeller's Bar**. He trained as a chef in five-star hotels in Europe so the food preparation is skilful. Harking back to the cuisine of his homeland, Nick makes excellent pasta and his Mountaineers Meat Platter of bündnerfleisch and

coppa salami would bring tears of joy to a Swiss mother's eyes. If you're allergic to cow bells and accordion music, avoid Saturday nights, although a bar well stocked with schnapps, grappa, and European and Aussie beers has turned many a silent diner into an unexpected yodeller. 'I can usually tell whether diners would prefer to eat in a quiet place, or maybe be happy for me to bring out the accordion,' Nick says. Follow the sounds of yodelling and Swiss bells at the weekend **Yungaburra Market** (on the fourth Saturday each month) to try some flavoursome bratwurst with all the trimmings at Nick's Sausage Van.

Take the Atherton Road to the **Gallo Dairyland Centre**. The Gallo family had been running a dairy for 70 years without changing much until a European business partner introduced them to Swiss couverture for handmade chocolates and European cheesemaking. Now the cows have to share the limelight with the products of their udders being served in the Gallo cafe in various, mainly lactose-free, guises. The dairy's version of gorgonzola, the

lactose-free Gallozola, is a marvel of pungency with a creamy texture. You can even show your appreciation of the cows by observing the daily milking (3–5pm).

Travel north from Atherton on the Kennedy Highway and stop for lunch or morning and afternoon tea at the **Tolga Woodworks Gallery & Cafe**. It sells well-crafted wood sculptures and its cafe serves home-baked cakes and beautifully prepared fresh Thai, Greek and Tuscan salads, Mediterranean-style vegetable dishes and brilliant soups, all perfect accompaniments to the baked-on-the-premises bread – in a wood-fired oven of course.

Mareeba is in the Dry Tropics of the Cairns Highlands and the centre of Australian coffee growing. Ten minutes before you arrive there, the **Mt Uncle Distillery** is a banana, avocado and macadamia plantation that makes plum, banana, mulberry, coffee and marshmallow liqueurs and a lime cello and lemon cello. Its **Bridges Cafe Tearoom** serves over 50 types of tea to try and buy, and light lunches are served in the licensed premises. At

Above (left to right):
oyster shooters at 2
Fish Restaurant, Port
Douglas; tropical
colours mark the
interior of Harrisons
at Port Douglas; a
work of 'food art' at
Salsa Bar and Grill
at Port Douglas;
duck breast at Ochre
Restaurant in Cairns

Mareeba, the **Australian Coffee Centre**'s Skybury Plantation produces more than half of Australia's coffee and has a highly sophisticated processing system that has made it a successful niche exporter to some very demanding markets in the United Kingdom and Europe. At the other end of the scale, Bruno Maloberti's **North Queensland Gold Coffee** is an artisan operation where the beans are hand-sorted by Bruno's wife, Luisa, and carefully tended in an antique roaster by their daughter Maria. Look for a small handwritten sign on the gate and mind you don't run over the hens on the driveway. It is interesting to compare the excellent results achieved from two very different processes.

Just past Mareeba, the Nastasi family not only operates one of Far North Queensland's biggest commercial mango plantations but its **Golden Pride Wineries** also made the world's first mango wine in 1999 from plump juicy Kensington Red Mangoes. Visit the plantation, set aside your wine prejudices and taste the wines that now include citrus cellos, mango port and mango liqueur. Just as Europeans

have been making their own traditional fruit brews for years (think about those homemade fruity firewaters produced with a flourish to visitors in France and Italy), these fruit wines are a uniquely Aussie tipple, only here they are made on a commercial scale.

Stay on the Kennedy Highway and head north-east through spectacular countryside to Kuranda. Here cooks will want to shop at the **Village Herb Farm** where a huge range of culinary herbs is grown, mostly using hydroponic methods. The weekend **Speewah Food Market**, 6 kilometres before you arrive in Kuranda, offers great value in avocados, mangos, bananas, pawpaws, citrus, herbs, unusual tropical fruits, honey, organic produce and fresh fish as well as home-cooked goodies.

From Kuranda you head way up north to the world-renowned Daintree Eco Lodge (*see* Where to stay) and its **Julaymba Restaurant**. You're in crocodile country now so it seems only reasonable to eat some (they wouldn't hesitate to return the compliment given half the chance). Julaymba serves

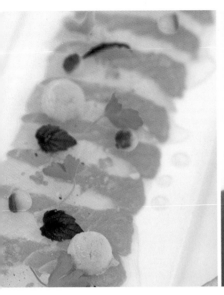

smoked croc in a salad of cucumber, honeydew, chilli, Vietnamese mint, red onion and heart of palm, all with a ginger and mirin dressing. Because of its close relationship with the local Kuku Yalanji people, the restaurant is able to feature a larger than usual range of freshly harvested Indigenous rainforest foods. Lemon myrtle is used with great success on several savoury dishes including a fettuccini tossed with rainforest mushrooms.

At Cubbagudta (it means 'rainy place' in the language of the Kuku Yalanji) Plantation the Nicholas family has been growing tea since 1978. **Daintree Tea** is grown and packaged here and you can visit and take tours but only by prior arrangement. You can buy the tea online and in local stores. It is fine-leafed, delicate and so delicious you can almost taste the fresh falling rain when you brew a pot. A final excursion from here is to Cape Tribulation. Take your vehicle on the cable ferry across the Daintree River to the **Cape Trib Exotic Fruit Farm**, which also has B&B accommodation. Roads are narrow and winding so drive with care. At the farm you can try

many of those exotic tropical fruits that you have only read about (*see* feature, p. 384).

From Daintree you can drive south and towards the coast to the famous foodie town of Port Douglas. The first and finest restaurant, **Nautilus**, has a star-studded history. The wealthy and powerful eat here, most famously in 1996 when Bill and Hillary Clinton dined at the restaurant. Eat under the stars in a rainforest setting on a soft tropical night and don't even think about the prices, because Nautilus is special-occasion dining at its most romantic. No children are allowed, service is faultless and chef Steve Ritchie watches intently over food leaving the kitchen to ensure its perfection, whether it is fish, duck, fillet of beef, or a lime, coconut and ginger crème brûlée.

Although fish is also on the menu at **Harrisons**, the owner-chef Spencer Patrick brings a particular flair to meat dishes, thanks to years of experience in Michelin-starred restaurants in London. If you've always lusted for a really good chateaubriand then this is where you'll find it with Victorian Black Angus served with caramelised onions, bone marrow, green beans, truffle mash, red wine jus and sauce béarnaise. The signature dish as far as regulars are concerned is the ox cheek nine-hour red-wine braise with pommes Sardiniere and sauce Bordelaise.

There are more seafood delights at **2 Fish Seafood Restaurant** in the heart of town. Talented chef Tommy Young won a prestigious award for excellence in 2010 so the food must be exceptional. And don't forget to try one of the cocktails while you are there. If you can make a booking ahead of the enthusiastic locals, you're in for a treat behind the timber-slatted louvres of **Salsa Bar and Grill**, where you can dine on the likes of jambalaya, baharat-crusted kangaroo loin and palm sugar and lemongrass oven-baked chicken breast. Decor is simple, there's no silver service or white linen, just good food and a thoroughly tropical laid-back vibe.

Further south again on the way to Cairns, Palm Cove is a major spa resort centre and offers many five-star dining experiences. One of the earliest and still among the best is **Reef House Restaurant** (part of The Sebel Reef House & Spa, *see* Where to stay) where the waterfront ambience is unmistakably Australian – the restaurant is surrounded by 300-year-old heritage-listed melaleuca trees. With entrée choices such as teppanyaki sea scallop, Vietnamese spanner crab salad, Mediterranean sardine crostini and Japanese beef tataki it can be a challenge to move on to the next course. But the mains are equally diverse and although fish rules here it doesn't have the field to itself with choices such as roast ras el hanout lamb rib eye with prune blini, pumpkin skordalia and dukkah and black label eye steak with gratin potato, pea purée, horseradish sabayon and red wine jus. The wine list includes several varietals that are ideally suited to the tropics, something often overlooked by sommeliers. The resort has a Champagnes of France event in June.

Nu Nu put Palm Cove on the national gourmet map around 2005 and hasn't stopped winning praise and prizes since thanks to its contemporary Mediterranean- and Asian-inspired preparation of fresh ingredients. With its drapes billowing gently in the breeze from the Coral Sea this is a place to relax and forget the rules of everyday life as applied to food. Even breakfast is a spectacular event if you can handle the likes of mud-crab omelettes in the morning. Co-owners Jason Rowbottom and chef

Nick Holloway describe their food as 'exuberant' and the eight-course tasting menu shows just how far they will go to surprise and delight. It might begin with a fresh Tasmanian truffle, leek and talleggio pie and run through treats such as the Millionaire's Salad, featuring local hearts of palm as well as feeding the soul with Za'atar spiced sesame crusted chicken livers, labna and green harissa broth.

In Cairns, you can match beer to food at the **Blue Sky Brewery** with hearty meals of seafood, pasta, steak, burgers and salads and, naturally, foods cooked in beer, from mussels sautéed in Woody ale to True Blue Stout beer sorbets. If you missed any distilleries in the highlands, you'll probably find their products here. There are daily tours to watch the craftsman-like brewers at work producing the goods that have picked up silver and bronze awards at the Australian International Beer Awards. Patrons tend to be young and enthusiastic and it's a popular backpacker spot.

Bayleaf Balinese Restaurant owner Klaus Ullrich has worked in leading hotels throughout the world since beginning his career in Austria. But it was his two years at the Sheraton Nusa Dua in Bali that led him to open Cairns' only Balinese restaurant. This is the real deal, with all the chefs trained at the Bumbu Bali Restaurant & Cooking School in Bali, and while the cuisine is Balinese they often use native Australian ingredients – crocodile for instance – in food that really suits the climate. The restaurant is part of the Bay Village Tropical Retreat.

Ochre Restaurant is the must-go-to restaurant for corporate types. It has won many national awards since it was established in 1994 and chef Craig Squire is in demand around the world by chefs keen to learn more about Australian food flavourings and how to use them in contemporary dishes. If you've been intrigued by the products you've seen in the region, Ochre has two excellent tasting menus that utilise most of them. If you choose the à la carte, leave room for dessert so you can savour the pungent lemongrass and lime flavour of lemon myrtle in a panna cotta with mango coulis.

Given the amount of produce in the region it's no surprise that food markets abound. In Cairns visit **Rusty's Bazaar** and **Farmgate Markets** for food. **Cairns Ocean Products** is close to the city and has a huge range of local seafood for sale, including wild prawns, reef fish and barramundi. It also packs and seals airline-approved foam chillers.

Opposite (top to bottom): feuilletté of asparagus at Harrisons in Port Douglas; eye-catching crab at Ochre Restaurant in Cairns; the Australian Coffee Centre at Mareeba

Tropical fruits

From the abiu to the zapote blanco

If you think that achacha is a Latin American dance, you have a lot to learn about fruit. Tropical North Queensland is the place to educate yourself in this fascinating field of produce that often looks as spectacular as it tastes. Do you like your sapote black or white? The black variety (aka black persimmon) tastes like chocolate pudding and the white sapote (or casimiroa; zapote blanco in its native Mexico) like vanilla custard. From the abiu to the avocado, the salak (its creamy yellow flesh has a flavour suggestive of pineapple) to the sapadilla (a yellow-brown flesh with a caramel or brown sugar taste) and right down to the vanilla bean, there's hardly a letter of the alphabet untouched in the list of fruit growing here. Many varieties are too delicate to ship to capital city markets in far away Australian cities so it's well worth a visit to see and try them where they grow. If possible make that journey north of Daintree to the Cape Trib Exotic Fruit Farm. Otherwise, look for the use of these fruits at restaurants in the region, particularly in cakes, desserts, sauces, custards and cocktails. And the achacha? It is orange-skinned and its pearly white flesh starts with a rush of delicate sweetness on the palate and finishes with a lemony tartness that may well make you feel like dancing for joy.

Contacts for Tropical North

EATERIES

2 Fish Seafood Restaurant: Wharf St, Port Douglas; (07) 4099 6350; www.2fishrestaurant.com.au

Bayleaf Balinese Restaurant: 227 Lake St, Cairns; (07) 4051 4622; www.bayvillage.com.au

Blue Sky Brewery: *see* Breweries

Bridges Cafe Tearoom: *see* Wineries/Distilleries/Mt Uncle Distillery

Harrisons: 22 Wharf St, Port Douglas; (07) 4099 4011; www.harrisonsrestaurant.com.au

Julaymba Restaurant: Daintree Eco Lodge, 20 Daintree Rd, Daintree; (07) 4098 6100 or 1800 808 010; www.daintree-ecolodge.com.au

Malanda Dairy Centre: *see* Stores

Nautilus: 17 Murphy St, Port Douglas; (07) 4099 5330; www.nautilus-restaurant.com.au

Nick's Restaurant and Yodeller's Bar: 33 Gillies Hwy, Yungaburra; (07) 4095 3330; www.nicksrestaurant.com.au

Nu Nu: 123 Williams Espl, Palm Cove; (07) 4059 1880; www.nunu.com.au

Ochre Restaurant: 43 Shields St, Cairns; (07) 4051 0100; www.ochrerestaurant.com.au

Out of the Whey: *see* Gourmet Produce/Mungalli Creek Dairy

Reef House Restaurant: 99 Williams Espl, Palm Cove; (07) 4055 3633; www.reefhouse.com.au

Salsa Bar and Grill: 26 Wharf St, Port Douglas; (07) 4099 4922; www.salsaportdouglas.com.au

Tolga Woodworks Gallery & Cafe: Kennedy Hwy, Tolga; (07) 4095 4488; www.tolgawoodworks.com.au

STORES

Malanda Dairy Centre: 8 James St, Malanda; (07) 4095 1234

MARKETS

Farmgate Markets: Pier Shopping Centre, Pierpoint Rd, Cairns; Sat

Rusty's Bazaar Market: 64 Sheridan St, Cairns; Fri morning, Sat–Sun; (07) 4051 5100; www.rustysmarkets.com.au

Speewah Food Market: Speewah (nr Kuranda); Sun; (07) 4093 0361

Yungaburra Market: 19 Eacham Rd; 4th Sat each month, morning; (07) 4095 2111; www.yungaburramarkets.com

GOURMET PRODUCE

Australian Coffee Centre: Skybury Plantation, 94–136 Ivicevic Rd, Mareeba; (07) 4093 2194; www.skybury.com.au

Cairns Ocean Products: Comport St, Portsmith; (07) 4031 3277; www.cairnsoceanproducts.com.au

Cape Trib Exotic Fruit Farm: Lot 5 Nicole Dr, Cape Tribulation; (07) 4098 0057; www.capetrib.com.au

Daintree Tea: Cape Tribulation Rd, Cow Bay; (07) 4098 9139; www.daintreetea.com

Gallo Dairyland Centre: Malanda Rd, Atherton; (07) 4095 2388; www.gallodairyland.com.au

Mungalli Creek Dairy: 251 Brooks Rd, Millaa Millaa; (07) 4097 2232; www.mungallicreekdairy.com.au

Nerada Tea: Visitor Centre, 933 Glen Allyn Rd, Malanda; (07) 4096 8328; www.neradatea.com.au

North Queensland Gold Coffee: Wheelbarrow Way, Dimbulah; (07) 4093 2269; www.nqgoldcoffee.com.au

Nucifora Tea: 2402 Palmerston Hwy, East Palmerston, Innisfail; (07) 4061 8151 or 0418 456 309; www.nuciforatea.com.au

Village Herb Farm: 8 Green Hills Rd; Kuranda; (07) 4093 7482; www.villageherb.com.au

WINERIES/DISTILLERIES

Golden Pride Wineries: 227 Bilwon Rd, Mareeba; (07) 4093 2750; www.goldendrop.com.au

Mt Uncle Distillery: 1819 Chewko Rd, Walkamin; (07) 4086 8008; www.mtuncle.com

BREWERIES

Blue Sky Brewery: 34–42 Lake St, Cairns; (07) 4057 0500; www.blueskybrewery.com.au

Tasmania

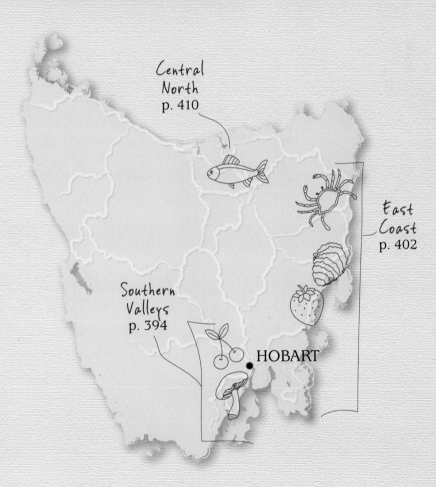

Central
North
p. 410

East
Coast
p. 402

Southern
Valleys
p. 394

HOBART

Left: iconic Tasmanian scene at Dove Lake, Cradle Mountain–Lake St Clair National Park

Above (left to right): wine barrels at Pipers Brook/Kreglinger, Central North; The Agrarian Kitchen cooking school at Lachlan, Southern Valleys; seafood with ocean views from The Bay Restaurant at Freycinet Lodge, East Coast

Overleaf: market-fresh produce at Salamanca Market, Hobart

Hobart

Every weekend Hobart markets offer
an amazing variety of tempting produce
including just-pulled baby carrots,
vibrant radishes and baby beets.

Hobart ~ an overview

Any tour of Hobart's gourmet scene must include a visit to its beautiful waterfront. On and around the docks there are seafood eateries for every taste. Floating fish punts and bustling wharf-side takeaways sell paper cones of crisply battered fish and chips, while fine-dining restaurants serve Tasmania's famed blue-eye trevalla and lobster (in season) with harbour-side views. At weekends, at Salamanca Place and elsewhere, bustling markets offer an amazing variety of tempting produce, arts and crafts, and the chance to meet primary producers and local artisans. In the lanes around Salamanca Place are Greek, Vietnamese, Indian and Italian restaurants doing brisk business amid the hustle and bustle of the busy tourist precinct with hip cafes and wine bars adding to the mix, while on the hill behind there are top-class restaurants in Battery Point's historic cottages.

Dining options in the CBD are limited outside office hours so for night-time eateries head to cosmopolitan North Hobart. Here you'll find everything from noodles and tapas to lip-tingling vindaloo and elegant degustation plates, all in a three-block section where the partying goes on into the wee small hours. Hobart's unofficial Chinatown in Sandy Bay caters for every budget and every international palate with Italian and Asian eateries, chic bistros and a seafood cafe, while down the road at picturesque Lower Sandy Bay gourmet pizzas come sizzling from a tiny beachfront eatery's wood-fired oven and an excellent restaurant beguiles seafood lovers with its stunning food and views.

OUTER-CITY GOURMET EXPERIENCES

* Eating on the Edge
* Hill Street Grocer
* Howrah Garden Centre
* Jean Pascal Patisserie
* Pear Ridge
* Taroona Lounge Bar
* The Beach Restaurant
* The Foodstore
* The Source
* The Station Cafe

See following pages...

Outer-city gourmet experiences

Here are some very good restaurants and up-market grocers just out of the city proper but well worth the detour.

Above (left to right): fresh breads at Hill Street Grocer, Lauderdale; cosy interior of The Station Cafe, Mount Nelson; eye-catching ceiling above the stairs leading to The Source, Berriedale; peaceful setting at Eating on the Edge, Lauderdale; captivating signage at Howrah Garden Centre, Rokeby

Eating on the Edge: modern family restaurant with a reputation for excellent veal scaloppine marsala, great pizzas and yummy Italian ices; 13 North Tce, Lauderdale; (03) 6248 7707; www.eatingontheedge.com.au

Hill Street Grocer: epicurean grocer with grind-your-own coffees and a glass counter filled with salads, panini and cakes; 528 South Arm Rd, Lauderdale; (03) 6248 6221; www.hillstreetgrocer.com

Howrah Garden Centre: looks like a regular grocer but stocks handmade black cherry jam, Heritage honey, Manna Bakehouse breads and Tasmanian farmhouse milk; 469 Rokeby Rd, Rokeby; (03) 6247 9570; www.howrahgardencentre.com.au

Jean Pascal Patisserie: with garlic butter snails on the menu, good coffee and chocolate-filled éclairs, this is a lovely European-style cafe where you would least expect it; 34 Cambridge Rd, Bellerive; (03) 6244 1077; www.jeanpascal.com.au

Pear Ridge: this light-filled modern bistro has a menu of up-market dishes but the family favourite is fish and chips; 1683 Channel Hwy, Margate; (03) 6267 1811; www.pearridge.com.au

Taroona Lounge Bar: a contemporary glass-walled bistro in the beautiful Art Deco Taroona Hotel, where you can lounge on the couches to share a huge wood-fired pizza or dine at a table with views over the leafy riverside suburbs. The usual bistro favourites are here – chargrilled steak and pesto-stuffed chicken breast – and they also do a great paella, but the serves are

generous so be sure to leave room for a slice of the wicked dessert cakes; 178 Channel Hwy, Taroona; (03) 6227 8886; www.taroonalounge.com.au

The Beach Restaurant: tables at high-tide level, couches around the wood heater, a well-stocked wine bar and a menu of duck, eye fillet and pizza ensure this casual bistro is always busy; 14 Ocean Espl, Blackmans Bay; (03) 6229 7600; www.thebeachrestaurant.com.au

The Foodstore: a busy supermarket and deli with a nice selection of Tasmanian wines and the complete range of Moo Brew beers; 19 Clarence St, Bellerive; (03) 6244 2927; www.thefoodstorecom.au

The Source: contemporary glass-walled restaurant serving fine Tasmanian seafood, meats and game and famed for its delicious cioccolati plate – a threesome of chocolate delights; Moorilla Estate, 655 Main Rd, Berriedale; (03) 6277 9900; www.moorilla.com.au

The Station Cafe: on top of suburban Mount Nelson this cute restaurant has superb views over the Derwent Estuary and does great homemade feta and veggie quiche; 700 Nelson Rd, Mount Nelson; (03) 6223 3407; www.signalstationcafe.com

Southern Valleys

It is Hobart's good fortune to be at the centre of three incredibly rich food-producing valleys and travellers will find epicurean delights in every direction. In the Huon Valley and D'Entrecasteaux Channel, a diverse world of gourmet producers is within an easy day's drive, while the Derwent Valley's lush small fruit orchards and the Coal River Valley's vineyards should not be missed.

Huonville in the Huon Valley is the gateway to a food-lovers universe. In town the best eating is seafood and you can have it fresh and crisply battered in a takeaway box at the floating **Boat House Cafe** (open Wednesday–Sunday) or delicately sauced from white damask table settings at **Huon Manor** (open Monday–Saturday), while down the road at Franklin, **Petty Sessions** gourmet cafe offers a famously delicious abalone chowder with a chunk of crusty sourdough every day of the week.

The Huon Valley's chilly climate is perfect for pinot noir, giving the ice queen of wine grapes the long slow ripening it loves. A handful of wineries here produce excellent intensely flavoured aromatic pinots. One of the best is **Home Hill Winery**, just west of Huonville. It's a bit of a surprise when you first come across stunning 21st-century architecture in such old-world rural surroundings, but as you get closer it becomes apparent the building is made from the valley itself – a vast rammed earth and Huon pine glass-fronted space with views to the distant Sleeping Beauty Mountain. This 5-hectare boutique vineyard produces sparkling wines, chardonnays, a late harvest sticky dessert wine and a velvety pinot that recently beat the best of South Africa, New Zealand and Australia. At Home Hill's contemporary à la carte restaurant the menu is short and seasonal, with each locally sourced dish perfectly matched with an estate wine. The restaurant is open daily for lunch, Friday–Saturday for dinner and Saturday–Sunday for breakfast.

A few kilometres from the highway beside the river at Glen Huon, decades of devotion to the dark art of mushroom growing have come to fruition for Warwick Gill and Michael Brown and their team at **Huon Valley Mushrooms,** and they are now the biggest gourmet producer in Australia. They cultivate a weird and wonderful array of edible fungi from buttons,

Southern and East Coast Open Vineyards Weekend: Feb; for brochure phone (03) 6223 3770

Richmond Village Fair: music, fun and gourmet food; village green; Mar; 0408 459 026; www.richmondvillagefair.com

Taste of the Huon: food festival; Ranelagh Showground, Lucaston Rd, Ranelagh; Mar; www.tasteofthehuon.com

Derwent Valley Autumn Festival: food and wine festival; The Esplanade, New Norfolk; Apr; (03) 6261 8512; www.derwentvalley.tas.gov.au

Hopfest: beer, bratwurst and sauerkraut; New Norfolk Memorial Hall; Apr; 0417 522 643

Where to stay

Anstey Barton: ultra-luxurious waterside mansion; 82 Ferry Rd, Kettering; (03) 6267 4199; www.anstey-barton.com.au

Hartzview Homestead: country homestead amid bush and vines; 70 Dillons Rd, Gardners Bay; (03) 6295 1723; www.hartzview.com.au

Herons Rise: rustic vineyard cabins; 100 Saddle Rd, Kettering; (03) 6267 4339; www.heronsrise.com.au

Riverside: stylish riverside house; 35 Graces Rd, Glaziers Bay; (03) 6295 1952; www.huonriverside.com.au

Tynwald: riverside mansion and restaurant; 1 Tynwald Rd, New Norfolk; (03) 6261 2667; www.tynwaldtasmania.com

caps and open flats of *Agaricus bosporus* – or 'whites' for those in the know – to Swiss browns, shiitake and shimeji. With the right spells and a good deal of research they'll soon be growing the matsutake too, supplying the Japanese market in the off-season at a cool $1500 a kilogram. Visits to their dark damp growing rooms, where bags of bulging fungi are piled five high, are by appointment with 24-hours notice.

From Huonville it's a 40-kilometre scenic drive to the valley's most southerly winery. At tiny **St Imre Vineyard**, Hungarian winemaker Paul Molnar and his mob of pest-hungry chickens tend vines that can be snow-covered in the depths of winter. In the warmth of his little tasting room (open Wednesday–Sunday) you can sample his full-bodied Bull's Blood, a preservative-free earthy blend of pinot noir, gamay and baco noir made without filtering, its clarity achieved through racking alone.

Across the Huon estuary at Cradoc, Sharon and Michael Vishacki's **Panorama Vineyard** captured attention in 2001 when it set a remarkably high price for a pinot noir – and sold out in weeks. Half a dozen 2003 Reserve Pinot Noir (Limited Edition) will set you back more than $1000 but you can pick up a very good non-reserve pinot or cool-climate riesling for a more modest outlay. The cellar door is open daily.

At nearby Glaziers Bay there's a farm you'd think is more suited to the hills of Kashmir or Spain. From neatly tended rows the purple blooms of *Crocus sativus* are gathered in autumn and when each flower's three orange stigmas are carefully plucked out and dried, they fetch more than gold, gram for gram. **Tas-Saff** sea-changers Terry and Nicky Noonan began the venture in 1991 after hunting down and finally paying $14.95 for a tiny phial of saffron for a paella dinner they were planning. Today their grade one product is distributed by Hoyts and paella cooks all over Australia will find it in their local supermarket. Visits here are by appointment.

In recent years Cygnet has become a foodie's destination and **Red Velvet Lounge** is the place that started it. Overseen by chef Steve Crumper, it's part boutique food store and part funky eclectic restaurant, with a clientele of knowing gourmets, vegan hippies and ladies doing lunch. Crusty sourdoughs, exquisite cakes and a menu of exciting local dishes tempt the adventurous palate as well as the more conventional. Expect salmon cakes with garlic aioli, or black pudding lying on a sweet red sauerkraut bed. In winter, wine pot pie is always a favourite, as is baked apple with butterscotch sauce and vanilla ice-cream. Apart from breakfast and lunch daily, they do dinner on Friday and Saturday nights.

A vineyard making a name for its fruit liqueurs is **Hartzview** in the hills between Cygnet and Woodbridge. The idea in the tasting room is to sip every fruity hue from honey mead and ruby-red

Below (left to right): Red Velvet Lounge, Cygnet; berries and ice-cream at Taste of the Huon food festival at Ranelagh; Stefano Lubiana Wines, Granton; barley harvest at Two Metre Tall Company, Hayes; modern art sculptures at Peppermint Bay, Woodbridge; vines at Bruny Island Premium Wines, Lunawanna

raspberry liqueur to the blackcurrant intensity of cassis. In the glass-fronted cafe there are excellent handmade pies, and the slow-cooked lamb is a perfect match to their pinot noir. You can stay here in the beautiful country homestead (*see* Where to stay).

South of Woodbridge overlooking Bruny Island, **d'meure wines** is a pocket-sized low-yield vineyard bathed in a quality of light owner Dick Meure says is discernable even in the glass. Meure's close-planted vines produce lively pinots and intense chardonnays, which have earned d'meure the five-star rating reserved for consistently exemplary wineries. Visits here are by appointment.

Nearby, an unsealed track leads a few hundred metres to Diane Rae's sheep's milk cheesery. Her 'girls' – a flock of East Friesland milking sheep – were originally a lawn-mowing sideline to Rae's vineyard but now they are the stars of **Grandvewe Cheeses**. Their milk is transformed into a traditional manchego, or a truffly soft cheese wrapped in vine leaves or dusted with wood ash. These are all available at the cheesery (open Wednesday–Monday) where you can meet the girls as well.

At nearby Woodbridge there is one food experience every visitor to Tasmania should have. **Peppermint Bay** dining room and terrace cafe is a modern glass-fronted restaurant complex set in a garden dotted with outdoor art. Inspired by Tasmania's regional produce (and herbs straight from the on-site

garden), a meal here might include confit of Huon ocean trout with Macquarie Harbour flying fish roe and a luscious dessert of crème caramel with Glaziers Bay saffron. If driving is not an option there are gourmet cruises from Hobart's waterfront, which will take you there in a high-speed catamaran and impress you with the channel's marine life along the way.

If you are in the Woodbridge area, do make time to cross over by ferry from Kettering to Bruny Island. Before you depart, stop off at Kettering's **Mermaid Cafe**, where large scones and more substantial fare are served with a smile while you admire the fantastic views. Once on Bruny, head to the Bruny Island Cheese Company's Great Bay cafe (*see* feature, p. 399), where you can sip a glass of the island's own – and Australia's most southerly – premium wine from **Bruny Island Premium Wines** at nearby Lunawanna. Practically next door to the cafe, the **Get Shucked** roadside van sells fantastically fresh oysters, while just down the road at Adventure Bay there is **Bruny Island Providore**, the outlet for Hiba's beautiful handmade fudge, and sweet mixed berries in champagne with double cream at **Bruny Island Berry Farm**.

Heading north out of Hobart's suburbs, the dry hills at Granton are the chosen location for **Stefano Lubiana Wines**, one of Australia's finest European-style wine producers. Steve Lubiana brings five generations of winemaking art to creating a

premium Australian sparkling wine, and his vision is realised in the $100-a-bottle 'Prestige' traditional méthod champenoise. Gorgeous floral rieslings and a creamy chardonnay derived sur lie are other boutique creations you can taste here (they are open Sunday–Thursday).

Further into the valley, Sydney escapees Rodney Dunn and Séverine Demanet nurture the award-winning **Agrarian Kitchen** cooking school at Lachlan, where they have given a 19th-century schoolhouse a second life sharing their slow food philosophy. Amid tall English trees and a tangle of Paul Healey-designed organic potager beds are 60 types of heirloom tomatoes, 37 varieties of fruit trees and a gaggle of livestock from geese to Saddleback pigs. Dunn's expertise – he was trained under Tetsuya Wakuda – infuses his dream to create an antipodean River Cottage and his students are guided through a day that begins with foraging and ends with a communal feast as a grand finale.

Also paying homage to the slow food tradition, **Two Metre Tall Company** is a brewery across the Derwent at Hayes, which nurtures its beer from the ground up. Ex-winemaker Ashley Huntington creates his tasty authentic beers from hops and barley he grows himself, and even insists on installing traditional hand pumps wherever it is served. On every second Friday (September–April) Huntington and his partner Jane run 'Friday at the Farm Bar' where, among fellow beer connoisseurs, you can enjoy their wintery Huon Dark Ale made from five different barley malts and unfiltered apple juice or have a TMT Cleansing Ale. Huntington has recently added traditional bottle-fermented cider to his ever-expanding range after discovering an old orchard of Sturmer Pippin cider apples in the Huon Valley.

The Derwent Valley's rural picture-postcard landscape is blessed with fertile river flats and deep rich soils perfect for a luscious variety of small fruits. December, January and February are the best months to find premium hand-picked cherries for sale from picking sheds at **Fallowfield Orchard** at Malbina, **Orchard Place** at Hayes and **Styx River Cherries** at Bushy Park.

Raspberries are the other sought-after seasonal berries you'll find here in abundance. Look out for the summer Tullameens, Chillawacks and the deeply flavoured autumn varieties. **Westerway Raspberry Farm**'s team of international backpacker pickers begin their season around the end of November – then there are berries for sale by the punnet or by the bucket for jam as well as the deliciously tangy handmade jam itself. The shed door sales operate daily December–January.

The Coal River Valley east of Hobart has more cellar doors than any other part of the state. With a measured ripening capacity matching that of Bordeaux and Burgundy, it is no surprise that the valley grows a quarter of Tasmania's cool-climate wines. **Meadowbank Estate** is the valley's flagship. First planted in 1974 when Tasmania's vineyards could be counted on your fingers, they now specialise in sauvignon blanc and pinot gris, balancing the depth and structure of their maritime-climate Cambridge vines with the fruity zing of grapes from the more continental environment of their other plantings in the Derwent Valley. Their impressive tasting centre (open daily) is designed to indulge all the senses with an à la carte restaurant, local artist Tom Samek's amusing portrayal of the wine industry, classical music recitals and, of course, excellent cool-climate wines, including a popular méthod champenoise.

At the northern end of the valley, the small **Domaine A/Stoney Vineyard** is famed for its classic cabernet sauvignon and sauvignon blanc. Domaine has only 20 hectares of vines, closely planted and meticulously tended by Swiss winemaker Peter Althaus. In 1997 this tiny vineyard brought three international gold medals home and in the years since has wowed judges world-wide. The Domaine A 2001 Fume Blanc is a standout oaked sauvignon blanc and the 2003 has been called 'sauvignon blanc on steroids'. The cellar door is open Monday–Friday.

The wines of the Coal River region are gathered in one marvellous place at the **Richmond Wine Centre**. You'll find organic European-style fragrant cool-climate riesling, zesty sauvignon blanc and spicy aromatic gewürztraminer from **Craigow Vineyard** and **Frogmore Creek**, as well as **Bream Creek Vineyard**'s multi-award-winning pinot noirs.

Cheesemaker Nick Haddow

An island without a single dairy might not be the best place to run a cheesemaking business, but Bruny is an island like no other and artisan cheesemaker Nick Haddow draws inspiration from his unashamed love for this place. 'There's magic here,' he says.

Haddow arrived in Tasmania with a passion for cheese. He had learned the cheesemaker's craft with skilled makers in Italy, France and the United Kingdom and, after a stint managing Richmond Hill Cafe & Larder in Melbourne and time making cloth-matured cheddar at Pyengana Dairy Company in Tasmania's north-east, he founded **Bruny Island Cheese Co** on his beloved island. The output from Haddow's factory is small by industry standards but these are feisty, personality-packed cheeses, each carrying a strong sense of place. 'I make the cheeses I most want to eat and they are an expression of where they are made,' says Haddow.

At the cellar door at Great Bay you'll be captivated by Haddow's creations. There is the voluptuous, pungent and simply named 1792; an oozing soft white cow's milk cheese called Saint; and Pan, a nutty firm blue made from goat's milk. Two other varieties, Oen and The Pressings, are made to bask in the glow of a good Tasmanian pinot noir, another of Haddow's passions (during the cheesemaking process, Oen is washed in pinot noir before being wrapped in vine leaves; with The Pressings, the new rind is rubbed with pinot noir grape pressings from the nearby vineyard). At the company's **Great Bay cafe** you can taste them all and more with still-warm wood-fired sourdough followed by homemade ice-cream.

Contacts for Southern Valleys

EATERIES

Boat House Cafe: The Esplanade, Huonville; (03) 6264 1133

Great Bay cafe: see Gourmet Produce/ Bruny Island Cheese Co

Hartzview Vineyard: see Wineries

Home Hill cafe: see Wineries/Home Hill Winery

Huon Manor: 1 Short St, Huonville; (03) 6264 1311; www.huonmanor.com.au

Meadowbank Wines: see Wineries

Mermaid Cafe: 81 Ferry Rd, Kettering; (03) 6267 4494

Peppermint Bay: 3435 Channel Hwy, Woodbridge; (03) 6267 4088; www.peppermintbay.com.au

Petty Sessions: 3445 Huon Hwy, Franklin; (03) 6266 3488; www.pettysessions.com.au

Red Velvet Lounge: 24 Mary St, Cygnet; (03) 6295 0466; www.theredvelvetlounge.blogspot.com

STORES

Bruny Island Providore: 53 Adventure Bay Rd, Bruny Island; (03) 6293 1456; www.hiba.com.au

Red Velvet Lounge: see Eateries

Richmond Wine Centre: 27 Bridge St, Richmond; (03) 6260 2619; www.richmondwinecentre.com.au

MARKETS

Cygnet Growers' Market: Cygnet Town Hall, Mary St; 1st and 3rd Sun each month; 0488 006 873

Dover Farmers' Market: Dover Old School, Main Rd; 2nd Sun each month; (03) 6297 6358

Franklin Growers' Market: Franklin Palais, Main Rd; last Sun each month, morning; (03) 6297 9923

Geeveston Farmers' Market: Brady St; 2nd Sun each month, morning; (03) 6297 9913

Huonville Farmers' Market: Coolstore Rd; 1st and 3rd Sun each month; (03) 6266 3477

Judbury Farmers' Market: Judbury Community Hall, Judbury Park; 2nd Sun each month, morning; (03) 6266 0262

GOURMET PRODUCE

Bruny Island Berry Farm: 526 Adventure Bay Rd, Bruny Island; (03) 6293 1055; www.brunyislandberryfarm.com.au

Bruny Island Cheese Co: 1807 Main Rd, Great Bay; (03) 6260 6353; www.brunyislandcheese.com.au

Fallowfield Orchard: 1042 Lyell Hwy, Malbina; 0438 613 650

Get Shucked: 1650 Bruny Island Main Rd, Great Bay; 0428 606 250; www.getshucked.com.au

Grandvewe Cheeses: 59 Devlyns Rd, Birchs Bay; (03) 6267 4099; www.grandvewe.com.au

Huon Valley Mushrooms: 850 Main Rd, Glen Huon; (03) 6266 6333

Orchard Place: 2261 Lyell Hwy, Hayes; (03) 6261 3706

Styx River Cherries: 42 Kenmore Rd, Bushy Park; (03) 6238 2035

Tas-Saff: 155 Dillons Hill Rd, Glaziers Bay; (03) 6295 1921; www.tas-saff.com.au

Westerway Raspberry Farm: Westerway Town Centre, Westerway; 0447 010 701

WINERIES

Bream Creek Vineyard: Bream Creek; 0419 363 714; www.breamcreekvineyard.com.au

Bruny Island Premium Wines: 4391 Main Rd, Lunawanna; (03) 6293 1088; www.brunyislandwine.com

Craigow Vineyard: 528 Richmond Rd, Cambridge; (03) 6248 5379; www.craigow.com

d'meure wines: 16 Fleurtys La, Birchs Bay; (03) 6267 4483; www.dmeure.com.au

Domaine A/Stoney Vineyard: 105 Tea Tree Rd, Campania; (03) 6260 4174; www.domaine-a.com.au

Frogmore Creek: 20 Denholms Rd, Cambridge; (03) 6248 5844; www.frogmorecreek.com.au

Hartzview Vineyard: 70 Dillons Rd, Gardners Bay; (03) 6295 1623; www.hartzview.com.au

Home Hill Winery: 38 Nairn St, Ranelagh; (03) 6264 1200; www.homehillwines.com.au

Meadowbank Estate: 699 Richmond Rd, Cambridge; (03) 6248 4484; www.meadowbankwines.com.au

Panorama Vineyard: Cygnet Coast Rd, Cradoc; (03) 6266 3482; www.panoramavineyard.com.au

St Imre Vineyard: 6900 Huon Hwy, Dover; (03) 6298 1781; www.stimrevineyard.com.au

Stefano Lubiana Wines: 60 Rowbottoms Rd, Granton; (03) 6263 7457; www.slw.com.au

BREWERIES

Two Metre Tall Company: 2862 Lyell Hwy, Hayes; (03) 6261 1930; www.2mt.com.au

COOKING SCHOOLS

The Agrarian Kitchen: 650 Lachlan Rd, Lachlan; (03) 6261 1099; www.theagrariankitchen.com

Below (left to right): historic Richmond Bridge is a major tourist attraction in the region; wine barrels at Stefano Lubiana Wines, Granton; waterfront atmosphere at Mermaid Cafe, Kettering; country-cottage setting at The Agrarian Kitchen cooking school, Lachlan; a seductive Birchs Bay blonde at Grandvewe Cheeses, Birchs Bay

East Coast

Map labels:
Pyengana
St Helens
Binalong Bay
Scamander
Four Mile Creek
Bicheno
Cranbrook
FREYCINET NP
Swansea
Swanwick
Rocky Hills
Coles Bay
Triabunna
Orford
Spring Bay
Sorell
Bream Creek
Dodges Ferry
Dunalley
TASMAN SEA
Taranna

Tasmania's East Coast region is the state's premier seaside destination and boasts exquisite coastal scenery, historic sites, a lush hinterland and, offshore, a rich marine environment. It also has a wealth of gourmet produce and is a great destination for food lovers. A gourmet meander around the Tasman Peninsula and then 'up the coast' from Sorell to St Helens reveals a larder of mouth-watering delights from small fruits to seafood, and some excellent wineries.

After leaving Hobart, your first stop should be Barilla Bay east of Cambridge. There's a story around that Pacific oysters came to Australia by accident in a smelly crate that was landed at Hobart airport as part of Japanese war reparations, and after days on the tarmac was tipped into Barilla Bay just to be rid of it. Fast forward to 1980, and the bay — now full of flourishing oysters — became the inspiration for Peter Forrest's shellfish farming venture. Whether they got here by accident or by design in a CSIRO trial, seafood lovers are happy they did and **Barilla Bay Oyster Farm**, next door to Hobart airport, is now a gourmet complex where you can dine à la carte (Thursday–Monday), tour the farm or head on your way with a box of just-shucked juicy bivalves and Barilla's unique oyster stout (retail outlet open daily). East of Barilla Bay is Sorell. **The Sorell Providore** is a bright and breezy deli and restaurant where you can taste test the epicurean delights of each region. Before leaving town a must-visit is **Sorell Fruit Farm**. December is best for the sweetest Van or Stella cherries and the first flush of large orange-red Alinta strawberries. There's a nice cafe here that is famous for its savoury mushroom-topped bruschetta, homemade dips and delicious berry desserts.

Sorell is a decisive moment. Do you turn left to the sun-drenched East Coast holiday towns or right to the Tasman Peninsula's gothic seacoast and Port Arthur historic site? If you take the latter option, on your way to Port Arthur be sure to stop at tiny Dunalley for exquisite seafood. The unassuming **Dunalley Fish Market** only sells local produce, so there's no doubting its quality. Their fish is filleted on site, lobsters are cooked daily and they don't open the oysters until you order them. Oysters and crayfish for two will not break the bank so you can indulge afterwards in one of

Festivals

Southern and East Coast Open Vineyards Weekend: multiple venues; Feb; (03) 6223 3770

Bream Creek Show: includes giant pumpkin contest; (03) 6253 5718; Marion Bay Rd, Copping; Mar; www.breamcreekshow.com.au

From France to Freycinet Festival: celebrates Tasmanian–French links; Swansea–Triabunna area; May; www.fromfrancetofreycinet.com.au

Where to stay

Avalon Coastal Retreat: ultra-chic cliff-top villa; 11 922 Tasman Hwy, Rocky Hills; 1300 361 136; www.avaloncoastalretreat.com.au

Beachbreaks: glass-fronted beach house; 357 Marion Bay Rd, Bream Creek; (03) 6253 5476; www.beachbreaks.com.au

Bed in the Treetops: tree-top pole house overlooking Bay of Fires; 701 Binalong Bay Rd, Binalong Bay (03) 6376 1318; www.bedinthetreetops.com.au

Freycinet Beach Apartments: architect-designed and minimalist; Meika Crt, Swanwick; 0428 245 336; www.freycinetbeach.com.au

Saffire: exclusive all-suite sanctuary; Coles Bay Rd, Coles Bay; 1800 723 347; www.saffire-freycinet.com.au

Dunalley Bakery's huge vanilla slices. The local Dunalley Hotel has a well-earned reputation for great pub seafood, and in the old cannery there's a modern eatery also showcasing local fare, the Dunalley Waterfront Cafe, with a maritime outlook.

At the high-drama entrance to Tasman Peninsula amid sea cliffs, blowholes and surf beaches, The Mussel Boys Restaurant offers a scintillating flavour-driven menu of excellent local fare. Fresh oysters come to you still dripping from their watery cage across the road. Add mussels, venison, quail, wallaby, octopus and local fish from suppliers all within a few kilometres and you can tour the peninsula from your table with their signature Seven Natural Wonders tasting menu. There's an excellent Tasmanian-focused wine list and stylish luxury accommodation on site.

The route north from Sorell hits the coast at Orford then heads happily towards the sun along Tasmania's east coast. It would be difficult to find a better drive for stunning coastal scenery, but particularly for the restaurants, seafood cafes and roadside eateries scattered along its length. Orford is an obvious spot for a break with a couple of casual eateries where you can settle in with a wild scallop and hot-smoked salmon pizza and a chilled Tasmanian chardonnay, or just a pile of crispy fish and chips. Try The Gateway Cafe Orford for meals

using local produce, a modest eatery Just Hooked where you can eat in or take away great fish and chips, or Scorchers By The River Gallery Cafe, a relaxed sort of place serving good comfort food.

The next stop for shellfish devotees must be Spring Bay Seafoods just out of Triabunna. Signs on the highway point the way to this little-known factory shop (open Monday–Friday), where you'll find the deepwater blue mussels that grace Kylie Kwong's restaurant menus. Fresh oysters, abalone, and scallops are here in season too. Further north, on an isolated stretch of coast south of Swansea, Piermont Restaurant has a growing reputation and swag of awards for its skilful modern takes on European-style dishes. Along with local seafood creations such as Tasmanian sea-run trout and vongole clams there are dishes using rabbit, venison, duck and pork. They have secluded, rustic accommodation in eco-friendly retreat cottages, and have added a cooking school teaching preparation of game meats, breadmaking and the art of holding a stress-free dinner party.

Approaching Swansea watch out for the turn-off to Kate's Berry Farm. From her hillside tearooms there are views all the way to Freycinet, but the real reason to visit is a wickedly indulgent Devonshire tea. Crisp Belgian waffles drenched in poached berries and sticky fruit tarts made with every berry

Below (left to right): fresh Tasmanian salmon topped with rocket salad at Angasi, Binalong Bay; Palate's dining area, and the seascape view of The Hazards visible from your table, at Saffire, Coles Bay

you can think of from youngberries to Himalayan blackberries make this a must-stop even if it's nowhere near afternoon-tea time. Kate planted every vine and cane and now her farm produces delectable jams – including Cointreau- or Grand Marnier-infused R-rated 'adult jams' – and sauces, pure strawberry juice 'Bubbly Enhancer', sensational fruity ice-creams and handmade chocolate packed with local walnuts or berries.

The sleepy seaside town of Swansea is at the centre of a gourmet universe of high-quality farm produce, excellent wines and abundant seafood. John and Lee Bailey's **The Banc** sets the tone, beguiling guests with exquisitely cooked local fare and the warmest of welcomes. Even in the garden's beautiful alfresco area or the more formal candlelit 'vault', the food is the star attraction, created with skills honed in London's Dorchester and Singapore's Raffles. Expect sashimi of marlin or suckling pig with braised cabbage and apple sauce, a bento-box of Asian-inspired tasting morsels, a no-holds-barred green chicken curry or their signature dish of melt-in-your-mouth slow-cooked abalone. Swansea's **Trellis** is a bustling tapas-style bistro and wine bar showcasing **Spring Vale Vineyard**'s lovely pinots and gewürztraminers, which can also be sampled at the source – the Lyne family's 1842 convict-built cellar door on their nearby Cranbrook vineyard.

Between Swansea and Bicheno the road briefly leaves the coast and winds through dry inland hills where Freycinet and Coombend's trellised vineyards lie tucked into a natural heat-trapping amphitheatre. **Freycinet Vineyard** was planted in 1979 and it remains in the Bull family with Tasmania's first oenology graduate, Lindy Bull, and her winemaker partner, Claudio Radenti, blending their skills in a vineyard regarded by some as Tasmania's best. In the sheltered warmth of its valley, Freycinet's reds ripen to an unusually deep colour making wines with powerful intensity infused with a dinner party of flavours. Black olive, herbs, plum, blackcurrant and chocolate have all been described in the complex 2006 Cabernet Merlot, and citrus, honeysuckle, fig, strawberry and crème brûlée in the award-winning 2000 Radenti Sparkling Pinot Noir Chardonnay. Visit the vineyard and sample Freycinet's standout estate wines, including the pinot noir and chardonnay served to Qantas first class international passengers. Nearby, **Coombend Wine Centre**'s olive oils, wines and locally grown walnuts can also be tasted and purchased at its cellar door just off the highway.

The side trip off the Tasman Highway to Freycinet is a feast for all the senses. **The Bay Restaurant** at Freycinet Lodge offers enchanting views across sheltered bays and craggy mountain peaks and sources its inspiration and menu from the sea.

Seafood and game dishes are served up with flavoursome accompaniments. For a different experience of the bay's gourmet marine delights, the Wineglass to Wine Glass tour takes you on an intimate guided exploration deep into the national park. The trek up to the Wineglass Bay lookout is amply rewarded with a beachside banquet of abalone, rock lobster, quail and beef matched to cool-climate wines on Hazards Beach.

Another sensory indulgence is the oysters-on-the-bay cruise to **Melshell Oysters**' farm where you can taste and learn or just enjoy bubbly and cheese with some lovely scenery as you drift past the suitably named Picnic Island. You can also visit the farm gate to pick up some oysters (take the Dolphin Bay Road from Swansea and turn on to Yellow Sandbanks Road; the farm is at the end of the cul-de-sac just past the jetty).

Back at Coles Bay, head to **Freycinet Marine Farm** where shellfish are brought in daily from their own leases in the bay and crates of rock lobsters are landed – still jumping – from local fishers. At their tasting room's cheerful alfresco eatery, grab a table for a splurge on half a dozen fresh creamy oysters or a bowl of garlic scallops. At the other extreme there is the ultra-luxurious Saffire, where ex-Lillianfels chef Hugh Whitehouse sources the best of the best for his cuisine at the resort's fine-dining restaurant **Palate**.

Degustation courses are matched with wines and the à la carte menu is not all about southern rock lobster; Cape Grim pasture-fed beef is a slow-braised oxtail with celeriac purée, pearl onions, spinach, mushrooms and Tasmanian black truffle butter. The resort's guests can also hunt and gather their own gourmet tucker with a helicopter fly-fishing tour to a pristine highland lake and on return join Whitehouse for a private cooking and tasting masterclass.

The highway meets the coast again at the little fishing village of Bicheno, which is becoming a foodie destination in its own right. Besides the **Blue Edge Bakery and Cafe**, a bustling modern place, and an astoundingly good butcher at **Sir Loin Breier**, who smokes his own bacon and will cut it for you in heart-achingly thick slices, **Cyrano Restaurant** has a reputation for authentic French provincial cuisine with classic dishes such as scallop au gratin. Further north, on the White Sands estate, beside an ocean as blue as its label, **Ironhouse Brewery** was named for the coast's first corrugated iron house. Brewer Michael Briggs' flagship pale ale is a prizewinner recognised for its fine citrusy hop-driven flavours. Tastings of all the Ironhouse brews can be enjoyed at **White Sands Resort** restaurant during each lunch and dinner service. This venue is consistently recognised as one of the best seafood restaurants in Tasmania (try the salt and pepper squid).

Below (left to right): White Sands Resort, Four Mile Creek; fresh East Coast crayfish; romantic setting for two at The Bay Restaurant at Freycinet Lodge, Freycinet National Park; oysters, salmon, scallops and leafy greens typify East Coast cuisine

Up the coast along a country road just south of Scamander (blink and you'll miss the turn-off), Denis and Ann Buchanan tend the fabulous **Eureka Farm**, where 3500 fruit trees and thousands of berry bushes and plants produce the ingredients for Ann's award-winning products. The main crop is apricots and their Italian-style apricot ice-cream is luscious, but they're also famous for glisteningly sweet summer puddings and chocolate raspberry-topped pavlovas. You can't leave without an armload of gourmet fruity jams and sauces.

St Helens is the game-fishing heart of Tasmania and one of the most sparkling fresh seafood eateries in town is **Latris**, a glass-fronted restaurant complex named for the stripy trumpeter *Lateris lineata*. The menu here is one of exquisite and contemporary Asian-inspired offerings.

A few minutes out of town, **Angasi** restaurant is particularly highly rated. Seasonal produce is everything here and the menu leans towards seafood (rock lobster five ways, for example) and game. In season there are native Angasi oysters (*see* feature, p. 408) – bigger and bolder than their Pacific cousins – an oyster-lover's oyster, and not for the faint-hearted. Shaped more like a scallop than the Sydney rock or Pacific oysters that we all know and love, the flat shells of Ostrea angasi can be as big as a saucer and as thick as one too. Inside, the fine-textured 'meaty' flesh packs a punch with a smoky, earthy flavour. The restaurant is also famous for its fine and adventurous regional cuisine and spectacular location at Binalong Bay. For the more adventurous gourmands, Angasi's bold cuisine extends to muttonbird or 'yolla', served as a terrine tempered with apple, sage and date chutney. The muttonbird chick, a traditional food of Tasmania's Aboriginal people, has an oily flinty flavour derived from the bird's marine diet. It is becoming a gourmet 'wild food' ingredient and the harvest is sanctioned and controlled by Parks and Wildlife.

Inland from the glistening beaches a verdant hinterland nourishes **Pyengana Dairy**, a half-hour's drive west of St Helens. Crumbly cloth-matured cheddars have been made in the district for 100 years and fourth-generation dairyman Jon Healy has revived the skills his grandfather used to make Pyengana's flagship cheddar. To produce the sweet grassy cheddar wheels, curd is toughened by stirring, hand-torn, pressed in an antique cheese-press and cloth-matured for twelve months in unbleached muslin. Three tonnes of this crumbly cheddar is sold every year, and Pyengana has a trophy case of prizes. If there's a whiff of wood smoke in the air visitors at the tasting rooms and cafe know a fresh batch is on the go because Healey's devotion to tradition extends to warming the milk in a wood-fired boiler.

Oysters

Panko-crumbed Angasi oysters

This dish of Panko-crumbed Angasi oysters is served with carrot, wasabi
and wombok noodles, and ginger caramel.

1 cup milk
1 egg
1 litre cottonseed oil
1 large carrot
knob of butter
1 tablespoon freshly grated wasabi
1 tablespoon freshly grated ginger
Small handful wombok (Chinese cabbage) julienne
1 cup orange juice
½ cup fine caster sugar
3 Angasi oysters
1 cup rice flour
1 cup Panko Breadcrumbs (Japanese-style breadcrumbs)

Combine the milk and egg in a bowl to form an egg wash. Heat the oil in
a heavy-based saucepan to 180°C. Using a mandolin, cut the carrot into
20 cm julienne strips or 'noodles'. Heat a small knob of butter in a pan and
add the grated wasabi and half the ginger then cook until you can smell
the full aroma. Add the carrot and wombok julienne and half the orange
juice. Simmer for 2 minutes then remove from the heat. Dry 'roast' the
sugar in a heavy-based pan until it starts to melt. Add the rest of the ginger
and orange juice then cook until golden brown. Coat the oysters in the rice
flour, then the egg wash and then the Panko crumbs. Drop the crumbed
oysters into the hot oil and cook until golden brown. Form the vegetable
noodles into a nest shape, place the hot oysters on the side and drizzle
with the ginger caramel.

Pictured here are other Angasi oyster favourites.

Contacts for East Coast

EATERIES

Angasi: 64A Main Rd, Binalong Bay; (03) 6376 8222; www.angasi.com.au

Barilla Bay Oyster Farm: *see* Gourmet Produce

Blue Edge Bakery and Cafe: *see* Stores

Cyrano Restaurant: 77 Burgess St, Bicheno; (03) 6375 1137

Dunalley Fish Market: 11 Fulham Rd, Dunalley; (03) 6253 5428

Dunalley Hotel: 210 Arthur Hwy, Dunalley; (03) 6253 5101

Dunalley Waterfront Cafe: 4 Imlay St, Dunalley; (03) 6253 5122

Eureka Farm: *see* Gourmet Produce

Freycinet Marine Farm: *see* Gourmet Produce

Just Hooked: 49 Tasman Hwy, Orford; (03) 6257 1549

Kate's Berry Farm: 12 Addison St, Swansea; (03) 6257 8428; www.katesberryfarm.com

Latris Restaurant: Marine Pde, St Helens; (03) 5376 1170

Palate: Saffire Freycinet, 2352 Coles Bay Rd, Coles Bay; 1800 723 347; www.saffire-freycinet.com.au

Piermont Restaurant: Piermont Retreat, 12 990 Tasman Hwy, Swansea; (03) 6257 8131; www.piermont.com.au

Scorchers By The River Gallery Cafe: 1 Esplanade, Orford; (03) 6257 1033

Sorell Fruit Farm: *see* Gourmet Produce

The Banc: Cnr Franklin and Maria sts, Swansea; (03) 6257 8896; www.thebancrestaurant.com.au

The Bay Restaurant: Freycinet Lodge, Freycinet National Park; (03) 6225 7016 or 1800 420 155; www.freycinetlodge.com.au

The Gateway Cafe Orford: 1 Charles St, Orford; (03) 6257 1539

The Mussel Boys Restaurant: 5927 Arthur Hwy, Taranna; (03) 6250 3088; www.themusselboys.com.au

The Sorell Providore: *see* Gourmet Produce

Trellis: 26 Franklin St, Swansea; (03) 6257 9095

White Sands Resort: 21 554 Tasman Hwy, Ironhouse Point, Four Mile Creek; (03) 6372 2228; www.white-sands.com.au

STORES

Blue Edge Bakery and Cafe: 55 Burgess St, Bicheno; (03) 6375 1972

Dunalley Bakery: 135 Arthur Hwy, Dunalley; (03) 6253 5604

Sir Loin Breier: 57 Burgess St, Bicheno; (03) 6375 1182

MARKETS

Dodges Artisans and Farmers' Market: The Boat Park, Dodges Ferry; 1st Sun each month in summer; (03) 6265 8050

GOURMET PRODUCE

Barilla Bay Oyster Farm: 1388 Tasman Hwy, Cambridge; (03) 6248 5458; www.barillabay.com.au

Eureka Farm: 89 Upper Scamander Rd, Scamander; (03) 6372 5500

Freycinet Marine Farm: 1784 Coles Bay Rd, Coles Bay; (03) 6257 0140; www.freycinetmarinefarm.com

Kate's Berry Farm: *see* Eateries

Melshell Oysters: 1 Yellow Sandbanks Rd, Dolphin Sands; (03) 6257 0269; melshelloysters.com

Pyengana Dairy Company: St Columba Falls Rd, Pyengana; (03) 6373 6157

Sorell Fruit Farm: 174 Pawleena Rd, Sorell; (03) 6265 3100; www.sorellfruitfarm.com

Spring Bay Seafoods: 488 Freestone Point Rd, Spring Bay; (03) 6257 3614; www.springbayseafoods.com.au

The Sorell Providore: 21 Gordon St, Sorell; (03) 6265 2444

WINERIES

Coombend Wine Centre: 16 017 Tasman Hwy, Bicheno; (03) 6257 8881; www.coombend.com.au

Freycinet Vineyard: 15 919 Tasman Hwy, Cranbrook; (03) 6257 8574; www.freycinetvineyard.com.au

Spring Vale Vineyard: 130 Spring Vale Rd, Cranbrook; (03) 6257 8208; www.springvalewines.com

BREWERIES

Ironhouse Brewery: White Sands Estate, 21 554 Tasman Hwy, Four Mile Creek; (03) 6372 2228; www.ironhouse.com.au

COOKING SCHOOLS

Piermont Retreat: Piermont Restaurant, 12 990 Tasman Hwy, Swansea; (03) 6257 8131; www.piermont.com.au

Below: stylishly packaged confectionery from House of Anvers, Latrobe

Opposite (top to bottom): matching food and wines at Josef Chromy, Relbia; picturesque Deloraine, located in the heart of the Central North

Central North

The Central North region is the heart of Tasmania's gourmet world. In the east of this region are the wineries around Pipers Brook and to the west of here is the Tamar Valley, a wine area that makes exceptional cool-climate reds and sparkling wines. In the south-east is Evandale, and just to its north the state's second largest city, Launceston, with a flourishing and diversified food scene. The farming country to the west of Launceston is dotted with gourmet concerns producing a feast of delicacies from smoked salmon and venison to chocolates and farmhouse cheese. The suggested trail extends as far west as Mole Creek before winding its way back north to Devonport.

The city of Launceston lies nestled in northern hilly country where the Tamar, North Esk and South Esk rivers meet. It is a city of contrasts, where modern marinas meet graceful Georgian and Victorian streetscapes. One of its gourmet claims to fame is that it has Australia's oldest sweet shop. Gourlays lolly factory has been making toffee bars, acid drops and milkshake syrups for 108 years and, in its Launceston **Gourlays Sweet Shop**, a wall of help-yourself lolly jars challenges the self-control of young and old alike.

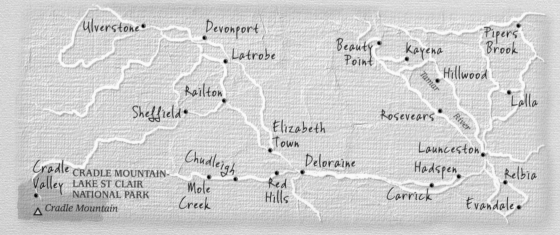

Map showing: Ulverstone, Devonport, Latrobe, Beauty Point, Kayena, Pipers Brook, Hillwood, Railton, Sheffield, Lalla, Rosevears, Elizabeth Town, Chudleigh, Deloraine, Launceston, Cradle Valley, CRADLE MOUNTAIN-LAKE ST CLAIR NATIONAL PARK, Mole Creek, Red Hills, Hadspen, Relbia, Carrick, Evandale, △ Cradle Mountain, Tamar River

Festivals

Festivale: food and wine festival; City Park, Launceston; Feb; (03) 6334 9990; www.festivale.com.au

Agfest: Carrick; May; www.agfest.com.au

Tastings at the Top: fine food and wine; Cradle Mountain Lodge, 4038 Cradle Mountain Rd, Cradle Mountain; June; (03) 6492 2100; www.cradlemountainlodge.com.au/assets/tastings_at_the_top.html

Chocolate Winterfest: Latrobe; July; (03) 6421 4650; www.chocolatewinterfest.com.au

Where to stay

Kateland Manor Estate: luxury private manor; 170 West Arm Rd, Beauty Point; 0418 128 742; www.kateland.com.au

Peppers Calstock: 19th-century boutique hotel; Highland Lakes Rd, Deloraine; 1300 987 600; www.peppers.com.au

Red Feather Inn: French-style provincial hotel; 42 Main St, Hadspen; (03) 6393 6506; www.redfeatherinn.com.au

Rosevears Vineyard Retreat: chalet apartments; 1A Waldhorn Dr, Rosevears; (03) 6330 1800; www.rosevears.com.au

TwoFourTwo: hip apartments; 242 Charles St, Launceston; (03) 6331 9242; www.twofourtwo.com.au

Above (left to right): barrels at the entrance to Pipers Brook/ Kreglinger; sun-ripened apples, synonymous with Tasmania; Central North landscape with the vineyard of Josef Chromy Wines in the foreground, Relbia

Another Launceston institution is **J Boag & Son Brewery**. When the first James Boag started brewing here it was called Esk Brewery but he and his son (the second James Boag) made such a name for themselves that by 1883, when they took over the company, it was already widely known as Boags. Launcestonians are fiercely proud of the local brew and they'll tell you there is no better match to a meal of fish and chips than a chilled Boags Premium. The brewery consistently wins accolades for its boutique beers too, particularly the pale gold hoppy St George Lager. Tours and tastings begin and end at the nearby Tamar Hotel, which is even older than the brewery.

An easy stroll from Boags, in the old Art Deco premises of Luck's butchery, **Black Cow Bistro** is a steak restaurant that unashamedly worships quality produce and skilled preparation both on and off the farm. Ex-Stillwater chef Craig Will sources local premium beef and presents a menu giving the whole story of your dinner from beginning to end. The prime steer eye fillet, produced by Swift just down the road at Longford, comes topped with a puck of shallot and red wine-infused butter, and if it is accompanied by a local pinot noir it is a beef connoisseur's heaven.

If you could conjure up a perfect place to spend a day exploring premium wineries the Tamar Valley would be it. With cellar doors along both sides of the Tamar and South Esk rivers, superb restaurants and sensational views around every corner, few wine regions can match it. Add a bubbly detour to Tasmania's 'champagne' country east of Pipers River to visit the extraordinary Jansz Tasmania Wine Room and Interpretation Centre at **Jansz Tasmania** vineyard, **Pipers Brook/Kreglinger** cellar door, and **Dalrymple** and **Delamere** vineyards and you have a magical wine-lover's expedition.

The Tamar Valley's climate and pinot noir are made for each other. At their best the Tamar's terroir-driven pinots are complex, fruity and voluptuous with raspberry-and-cherry-scented wines from the lower valley and heady, darker truffly notes in those grown upriver. There is also elegant fresh riesling and sauvignon blanc. **The Pinot Shop** in

Launceston brings together the world's largest collection of Tasmanian wines, focusing on the state's gorgeous pinot noirs and their cousins pinot gris and grigio, while other varieties earn a place on their shelves if they're good enough.

On the western side of the Tamar, winemaker Andrew Pirie produces chardonnay and riesling from sun-drenched blocks where the harvest comes in two weeks earlier than other parts of the valley. Take the steep drive to **Rosevears Vineyard** cellar door for tastings of the large Tamar Ridge range (including the fine **Tamar Ridge Kayena Vineyard**'s sauvignon blanc, which stand ups against those from Bordeaux and Marlborough). There is luxury chalet accommodation at Rosevears too, but the standout attraction is the superb **Estelle Restaurant** with its famous bird's eye view of the valley. In keeping with their philosophy, the produce is local and always top quality, and the menu changes with the seasons to highlight Rosevears estate's current vintages.

Downriver one of the smaller players in the wine industry is **Goaty Hill**, the shared passion of six friends, which makes deliciously spicy, fruity pinots and citrusy mineral sauvignon blancs. Across the cantilevered Batman Bridge on the Tamar's cooler eastern side, at Hillwood, another small vineyard is the family-owned **Three Wishes**, producing award-wining premium chardonnay, riesling and earthy pinot noir from low-yielding blocks with minimal chemical input.

In the nearby hills at Lalla, Tasmania's modern wine industry was born in 1956 when French migrants and fifth-generation winemakers Jean and Cecile Miguet planted their first vines in a spot found by testing the soil with a thermometer. Their vision endures at **Providence**, which now produces premium estate chardonnay, riesling, pinot noir and semillon. Two outstanding releases are the fruity, full-bodied 2004 Miguet Reserve Pinot Noir made from the original vines and a gold-medal-winning 2005 Madame Miguet Reserve Chardonnay named for Cecile, who died in 2005 a few weeks before her 100th birthday. The cellar door, just out of Lilydale, stocks their own and the state's best wines.

Josef Chromy is a more contemporary wine pioneer. His early vintages of riesling and pinot noir grown on the sun-trapping hills of Relbia, south of Launceston, raised the bar in Tasmania, and he continues to set the standard. The 2007 Botrytis Riesling took all before it to win best in show at the Sydney International Wine Competition. In its Zen landscape of parallel trellises, the **Josef Chromy Cellar Door Cafe** serves a range of lunch dishes as well as a tasting plate matching East Coast oysters to a chilled riesling, and truffle-infused brie drizzled in quince sauce to an aromatic gewürztraminer.

Further south, Tim and Julie Barbour's **Tasmanian Gourmet Sauce Company** is a tiny sauce and condiment-making business run from the kitchen of their pretty Victorian home near Evandale. In their tasting room you'll find glossy homemade crab-apple jam, rich berry dessert sauces, zingy lip-smacking tomato relish and a pale yellow creamy pepperberry mustard, all made with Tasmanian produce, some harvested from the Barbours' cottage orchard.

West of Launceston winemaking takes a back seat to a delicious variety of other gourmet products. Showcasing them all is Hadspen's **Red Feather Inn**. Behind its Georgian facade this 1843 coaching inn has been reborn by owner Lynne Nettlefold as an exquisitely indulgent French provincial hotel and cooking school. Gourmands can join chef Lee Christmas for two days of charcuterie classes, celebrating the life of a Wessex saddleback, or prepare their own feast from a weekend of hunting and gathering in the wilds of Tasmania.

The lush farmland between Deloraine and Mole Creek is a gourmet hotspot. At Mole Creek the **R. Stephens Tasmanian Honey** factory shop (open daily in summer; Wednesday–Sunday in winter) will fill your container with sweetly aromatic pasture honey, or the holy grail of honey connoisseurs – the spicy piquant leatherwood honey from hives trucked to Tasmania's remote rainforests. Nearby **Chudleigh Honey Farm** (closed Sunday) has a dip-and-taste bar of less conventional honeys with flavours from chocolate to aniseed. While these might not seduce purists, their honey ice-cream will.

Mole Creek is also home to **Springfield Deer Farm**. Fallow deer were introduced into Tasmania in 1836 and there is a hunting season but wild venison cannot be served in restaurants. Springfield's naturally fed farm-raised venison is a superb alternative and the farm sells fresh cuts, pastrami, hams and pies as well as providing roasted dinners to guests who stay in its homely on-site cottage.

A short distance off the Mole Creek road, south of Red Hills at the exact latitude of 41 degrees south, an unlikely enterprise combines organic principles, traditional Chinese herbs, a smokehouse and a network of ponds alive with salmon – creating **41 Degrees South Aquaculture**, a farm like no other. As Ziggy and Angelika Pyka's quirky dream to grow ginseng took root, they were inspired by the property itself to extend its natural wetlands into an ecologically sustainable salmon farm. At the salmon and ginseng farm the salmon have been the success story, especially the way the owners hot-smoke them over blackwood chips to tender flaky pinkness. When

Below (left to right): treats and gourmet produce on show at House of Anvers, Latrobe; tasting room at Seven Sheds Brewery Meadery & Hop Garden, Railton; panoramic view across the vineyard at Pipers Brook/Kreglinger

you've wandered around the ponds, fed the eco-certified fish, glimpsed a platypus and learned a thing or two about ginseng – and wasabi – you must head to the shop and tearooms. There's energy-boosting ginseng in an array of disguises from dried chips to chewy nougat but salmon rillettes are the star of the show. Brined, herbed and hot-smoked salmon is shredded and potted with butter, lemon, Westhaven yoghurt and Tasmanian pepperberries in a combination that just cries out for a crusty baguette.

Back on the Bass Highway, midway between Deloraine and Elizabeth Town, a foodie must-stop destination is **Christmas Hills Raspberry Farm Cafe**. If you can, get there for breakfast, as do some travellers from the Bass Strait ferry who are sometimes waiting in the carpark for the place to open. Every plate – savoury and sweet – is piled, drizzled and stuffed with delicious raspberries. They're hidden in crepes, minced into sausages, disguised under chocolate and smashed into ice-cream. And if that's not enough there are house-made jams and sauces to go.

Further along the highway, 4 kilometres north of Elizabeth Town, is **Ashgrove Cheese**, where most of the action is not at the viewing window of the cheese-maturing room but around the well-stocked tasting rotunda. Start a cheese-tasting circuit with a cube of creamy Golden Valley or lavender-infused club cheese and finish with a palate-tingling Crumbly Tasty or Wild Wasabi. The deli has a variety of cheese packs and a nice range of local wines, olives and chutneys to take on the road for later. The on-site cafe serves light meals all day.

A side trip worth doing takes in a few places along the Railton Road, and you can take this route through to Latrobe. The turn-off from the highway is at Elizabeth Town. At **Elgaar Farm** Josef and Antonia Gretschmann produce certified organic cream-topped milk, natural pure yoghurts, cultured butter and velvety mascarpone with the help of their small herd of jersey cows, each known by name. There's no farm gate but their glass-packed products can be found in gourmet retailers throughout Tasmania (and Victoria) so look for them as you travel through the region.

At **Seven Sheds Brewery Meadery & Hop Garden** at Railton, Willie Simpson and Catherine Stark have turned their passion for home brewing into a way of life. With an eye on sustainability and food miles they source coastal grain malted in Devonport, grow their own hops and use local honeys, while the spent grain is fed to local cattle and the yeast lees to pigs. Seven Sheds' medal-winning blackcurrant-and-pepperberry-infused Melomel might be an acquired taste but their flagship Kentish Ale is a popular brew and can be found on tap at Cradle Mountain Chateau.

Before reaching Devonport there is one more foodie stop not to be missed. On the Bass Highway just north of Latrobe, in a quaint roadside bungalow, Belgian chocolatier Igor Van Gerwen makes mouth-watering fudges and truffles enrobed in fine couverture chocolate. While there is a viewing window, the **House of Anvers** is a place to taste not watch. A mug of chilli hot chocolate and a little bag of mocha walnut fudge or a warm chocolate croissant fresh from the oven is an unbeatable way to wrap up any gourmet tour.

Black gold

Truffle growing near Mole Creek

Emerging from the earth as a dark warty clod, a freshly dug truffle hardly looks appetising but these revered fungi exude such an indescribably unique flavour that they top the list of the world's most expensive natural foods. Their powerful pungency apparently mimics the sexual pheromones of pigs, but shaved over softly scrambled eggs, infused into creamed butter or slipped under the skin of a roast chicken they impart a seductive aromatic earthiness. Europe's most-prized truffles are grown in south-west France at the same latitude north as Tasmania is south – where wet spring rains and cold winters allow the truffles to set and mature. Inspired by this and banking on good fortune, pioneer growers Duncan Garvey and Peter Cooper planted their first *Tuber melanosporum* in 1993. A long six years later, in the winter of 1999, the fruits of their vision were detected by a truffle-sniffing dog and Tasmania's truffle industry was born. From the cold Tasmanian soil ripe truffles are wrapped in tissue, encased in glass and high density foam and packed off to the finest gastronomic restaurants of Tokyo and Paris. There is interest from other places also, especially since another Tasmanian export, Princess Mary of Denmark, received a hand-delivered consignment in 2007. A stone's throw from Tasmania's first successful truffiere at Mole Creek near Deloraine another pioneer grower, Tim Terry, is now cultivating summer truffles too. Visit his plantation shop or in season match your nose to a trained Springer spaniel on a truffle-hunting tour, but you must book ahead. **Truffles Australis** at Red Hills is open for truffle hunts June–September and January–March (bookings essential).

Contacts for Central North

EATERIES

41 Degrees South Aquaculture: see Gourmet Produce

Black Cow Bistro: Cnr George and Paterson sts, Launceston; (03) 6331 9333; www.blackcowbistro.com.au

Christmas Hills Raspberry Farm Cafe: 9 Christmas Hills Rd, Elizabeth Town; (03) 6362 2186; www.raspberryfarmcafe.com

Estelle Restaurant: see Wineries/ Rosevears Vineyard

Josef Chromy Cellar Door Cafe: 370 Relbia Rd, Relbia; (03) 6335 8700; www.josefchromy.com.au

STORES

Gourlays Sweet Shop: 147 Paterson St, Launceston; (03) 6331 4730

The Pinot Shop: 135 Paterson St, Launceston; (03) 6331 3977; www.pinotshop.com

MARKETS

Evandale Market: Falls Park, Logans Rd, Evandale; Sun; (03) 6391 9191

GOURMET PRODUCE

41 Degrees South Aquaculture: 323 Montana Rd, Deloraine; (03) 6362 4130; www.41southtasmania.com

Ashgrove Cheese: 6173 Bass Hwy, Elizabeth Town; (03) 6368 1105; www.ashgrovecheese.com.au

Chudleigh Honey Farm: 39 Sorell St, Chudleigh; (03) 6363 6160; www.thehoneyfarm.com.au

Elgaar Farm: 17 Railton Rd, Elizabeth Town; (03) 6368 1126; www.elgaarfarm.com.au

House of Anvers: 9025 Bass Hwy, Latrobe; (03) 6426 2958; www.anvers-chocolate.com.au

R. Stephens Tasmanian Honey: 25 Pioneer Dr, Mole Creek; (03) 6363 1170; www.leatherwoodhoney.com.au

Springfield Deer Farm: 20 Azels Rd, Mole Creek; (03) 6363 1282; www.springfielddeerfarm.com

Tasmanian Gourmet Sauce Company: 174 Leighlands Rd, Evandale; (03) 6391 8437; www.gourmetsauce.com.au

Truffles Australis: 844 Mole Creek Rd, Red Hills; 0407 523 552

WINERIES

Dalrymple Vineyards: Pipers Brook Rd, Pipers Brook; (03) 6382 7229; www.dalrymplevineyards.com.au

Delamere Vineyards: 4238 Bridport Rd, Pipers Brook; (03) 6382 7190; www.delamerevineyards.com.au

Goaty Hill: 530 Auburn Rd, Kayena; 1300 819 997; www.goatyhill.com

Jansz Tasmania: 1216B Pipers Brook Rd, Pipers Brook; (03) 6382 7066; www.jansztas.com

Josef Chromy: see Eateries

Pipers Brook/Kreglinger: 1216 Pipers Brook Rd, Pipers Brook; (03) 6382 7527; www.kreglingerwineestates.com

Providence: 236 Lalla Rd, Lalla; 1800 992 967 or (03) 6395 2088; www.providence.com.au

Rosevears Vineyard: 1A Waldhorn Dr, Rosevears; (03) 6330 1800; www.rosevears.com.au

Tamar Ridge Kayena Vineyard: 653 Auburn Rd, Kayena; (03) 6394 1114; www.tamarridge.com.au

Three Wishes Vineyard: 655 Craigburn Rd, Hillwood; (03) 6331 2009 or 0410 754 728; www.threewishesvineyard.com

BREWERIES

Boags Centre for Beer Lovers: Tamar Hotel, 39 William St, Launceston; (03) 6332 6300

J Boag and Son Brewery: 21 Shields St, Launceston; www.boags.com.au

Seven Sheds Brewery Meadery & Hop Garden: 22 Crockers St, Railton; (03) 6496 1139; www.sevensheds.com

COOKING SCHOOLS

Red Feather Inn Cooking & Lifestyle School: 42 Main St, Hadspen; (03) 6393 6506; www.redfeatherinn.com.au

Festival Calendar

January

NEW SOUTH WALES

Guyra Lamb & Potato Festival: see New England Tablelands, p. 77

Oysters in the Vines: Port Macquarie; *see* Southern Holiday Coast, p. 53

VICTORIA

Mornington Peninsula International Pinot Noir Celebration: biennial event, odd-numbered years; *see* Mornington Peninsula, p. 135

New Year's Day Races: Hanging Rock; *see* Macedon and Spa Country, p. 155

Portarlington Mussel Festival: see Geelong and Bellarine, p. 179

SOUTH AUSTRALIA

Cape Jaffa Seafood and Wine Festival: see Limestone Coast, p. 259

Crush Adelaide Hills Wine & Food Festival: see Adelaide Hills, p. 239

Kangaroo Island Gourmet Gallop: Cygnet River; *see* Kangaroo Island, p. 275

Tunarama Festival: Port Lincoln; *see* Eyre Peninsula, p. 287

WESTERN AUSTRALIA

Mount Barker D'vine Wine Festival: see South-West, p. 323

February

NEW SOUTH WALES

Annual Grape Stomp: Wauchope; *see* Southern Holiday Coast, p. 53

VICTORIA

A Palate of Passions: West Gippsland (Feb–Mar); *see* Gippsland, p. 145

Boolarra Folk Festival: see Gippsland, p. 145

Grampians Jazz Festival: Halls Gap; *see* Grampians and surrounds, p. 199

Harvest Picnic: Hanging Rock; *see* Macedon and Spa Country, p. 155

Regional Producers Day: Daylesford; *see* Macedon and Spa Country, p. 155

Wood, Wine & Roses Festival: Heywood; *see* South-West Coast, p. 189

SOUTH AUSTRALIA

Seafari Beachport Festival: Beachport; *see* Limestone Coast, p. 259

Taste the Limestone Coast Festival: Naracoorte; *see* Limestone Coast, p. 259

WESTERN AUSTRALIA

Great Southern Taste Festival: various venues (Feb–Mar); *see* South-West, p. 323

Taste of the Valley: see Swan Valley, p. 299

QUEENSLAND

Sicilian Vintage Lunch: Ballandean; *see* Granite Belt, p. 357

Sunshine Coast Food Show: Maroochydore; *see* Sunshine Coast, p. 365

TASMANIA

Festivale: Launceston; *see* Central North, p. 411

Southern and East Coast Open Vineyards Weekend: see Southern Valleys, p. 395, and East Coast, p. 403

March

NEW SOUTH WALES

Nosh on the Namoi: see New England Tablelands, p. 77

Taste of Sydney: Centennial Park, Sydney

Wine & Waves Festival: Newcastle; *see* Central Coast and Newcastle, p. 37

VICTORIA

Ballarat Begonia Weekend: see Ballarat and Pyrenees, p. 163

Harcourt Applefest: see Northern Goldfields, p. 171

Inverloch Food and Wine Festival: see Gippsland, p. 145

Jindi Harvest of Gippsland: see Gippsland, p. 145

Lake Bolac Eel Festival: see Grampians and surrounds, p. 199

Lara Food and Wine Festival: see Geelong and Bellarine, p. 179

Melbourne Food and Wine Festival: various Melbourne venues

Mildura Wentworth Arts Festival: see Mildura and environs, p. 207

Ocean Grove Apple Fair: see Geelong and Bellarine, p. 179

Peninsula Piers and Pinots: see Mornington Peninsula, p. 135

Port Fairy Folk Festival: see South-West Coast, p. 189

Tastes of Rutherglen: see North East, p. 211

Wallington Strawberry Fair: see Geelong and Bellarine, p. 179

SOUTH AUSTRALIA

Riverland Harvest Festival and Great Grape Stomp: Loxton North; *see* Riverland, p. 283

WESTERN AUSTRALIA

Tropfest Film Festival: Cowaramup; *see* Cape to Cape, p. 315

QUEENSLAND

Feast of the Senses: Innisfail; *see* Tropical North, p. 377

TASMANIA

Bream Creek Show: Copping; *see* East Coast, p. 403

Richmond Village Fair: see Southern Valleys, p. 395

Taste of the Huon: Ranelagh; *see* Southern Valleys, p. 395

Easter

NEW SOUTH WALES

La Festa: Griffith; *see* Riverina and Murray, p. 107

VICTORIA

Bendigo Winemakers' Festival: see Northern Goldfields, p. 171

Maldon Easter Fair: see Ballarat and Pyrenees, p. 163

Queenscliff Seafood Festival: see Geelong and Bellarine, p. 179

Stawell Easter Gift: see Grampians and surrounds, p. 199

April

NEW SOUTH WALES

Bathurst Harvest Festival: see Central Tablelands, p. 27

Festival of the Falling Leaf: Tumut; *see* Snowy Mountains and Capital Country, p. 99

Harvest Festival: see Snowy Mountains and Capital Country, p. 99

Hunter Uncorked at Pyrmont: see Hunter Valley, p. 45

Orange FOOD Week: see Central Tablelands, p. 27

VICTORIA

Bright Autumn Festival: (end Apr – early May); *see* Alpine Lowlands, p. 221

Mount Avoca Races: see Ballarat and Pyrenees, p. 163

Mount Beauty Music Festival: see Alpine Lowlands, p. 221

Southern Grampians Promenade of Sacred Music: Hamilton; *see* Grampians and surrounds, p. 199

SOUTH AUSTRALIA

Barossa Vintage Festival: biennial event, odd-numbered years; *see* Barossa and Eden valleys, p. 247

Tasting Australia: 8-day festival (end Apr – early May); various venues, Adelaide and South Australia

WESTERN AUSTRALIA

Margaret River Wine Region Festival: see Cape to Cape, p. 315

QUEENSLAND

Celebration of Australian Food and Wine Noosa style: Noosa area (late Apr – early May); *see* Sunshine Coast, p. 365

TASMANIA

Derwent Valley Autumn Festival: New Norfolk; *see* Southern Valleys, p. 395

Hopfest: New Norfolk; *see* Southern Valleys, p. 395

May

NEW SOUTH WALES

Autumn Harvest Food & Wine Festival: Mount Tomah; *see* Hawkesbury and surrounds, p. 14

Lovedale Long Lunch: *see* Hunter Valley, p. 45

Moree on a Plate: *see* New England Tablelands, p. 77

Narooma Oyster Festival: *see* South Coast, p. 91

Slice of Haven Food & Wine Festival: Laurieton; *see* Southern Holiday Coast, p. 53

VICTORIA

Ballarat Heritage Weekend: *see* Ballarat and Pyrenees, p. 163

Grampians Grape Escape: Halls Gap; *see* Grampians and surrounds, p. 199

Kellybrook Cider Festival: *see* Yarra and Dandenongs, p. 123

Mildura Cup Carnival: *see* Mildura and environs, p. 207

SOUTH AUSTRALIA

Clare Gourmet Weekend: *see* Clare Valley, p. 255

Fresh Fish Place Zonta Port Lincoln Long Lunch: *see* Eyre Peninsula, p. 287

WESTERN AUSTRALIA

Truffle Afaire: Manjimup; *see* South-West, p. 323

QUEENSLAND

A La Carte in the Park: Surfers Paradise; *see* Gold Coast and hinterland, p. 345

A World Apart – Discover the Hidden Tastes of Mt Barney: *see* Scenic Rim, p. 353

Art in the Olives Festival: Darlington; *see* Scenic Rim, p. 353

Australian Italian Festival: Ingham; *see* Tropical North, p. 377

TASMANIA

Agfest: Carrick; *see* Central North, p. 411

From France to Freycinet Festival: Swansea–Triabunna area; *see* East Coast, p. 403

Savour Tasmania: international chefs create degustation feasts; Hobart and other locations

June

NEW SOUTH WALES

Capital Country Truffle Festival: *see* Snowy Mountains and Capital Country, p. 99

Cool Flavours Festival: *see* Southern Highlands, p. 83

Hunter Valley Wine and Food Month: *see* Hunter Valley, p. 45

Shoalhaven Winter Wine Festival: *see* South Coast, p. 91

UnWINEd in the Riverina: *see* Riverina and Murray, p. 107

Yulefest: Blue Mountains (June–Aug); *see* Blue Mountains and beyond, p. 17

VICTORIA

Good Food and Wine Festival: Exhibition Centre, Melbourne

Kyneton Olive Oil Harvest: *see* Macedon and Spa Country, p. 155

Loch Village Food & Wine Festival: *see* Gippsland, p. 145

Rutherglen Winery Walkabout: *see* North East, p. 211

Smaller Wineries Shortest Lunch: see Yarra and Dandenongs, p. 123

Trails, Tastings & Tales: Glenrowan; see North East, p. 211

Winter Wine Weekend: see Mornington Peninsula, p. 135

SOUTH AUSTRALIA

Fabulous Fortifieds: Sevenhill; see Clare Valley, p. 255

Kuitpo Continuous Picnic: see Adelaide Hills, p. 239

Sea & Vines: McLaren Vale; see Fleurieu Peninsula, p. 267

Stew and Shiraz: Marananga; see Barossa and Eden valleys, p. 247

WESTERN AUSTRALIA

Margaret River Olive Festival: Wilyabrup; see Cape to Cape, p. 315

York Gourmet Food and Wine Festival: see Central Heartlands, p. 307

QUEENSLAND

Champagnes of France: Palm Cove; see Tropical North, p. 377

Eat Week: Surfers Paradise; see Gold Coast and hinterland, p. 345

Great Aussie BBQ: Surfers Paradise; see Gold Coast and hinterland, p. 345

TASMANIA

Tasmanian Red Wine Weekend: 1st weekend of month; Hobart

Tastings at the Top: Cradle Mountain; see Central North, p. 411

July

NEW SOUTH WALES

Central Ranges Truffle Festival: Orange; see Central Tablelands, p. 27

Chilli Festival: Sawtell; see Coffs Harbour and hinterland, p. 61

Good Food and Wine Festival: 1st weekend of month; Convention & Exhibition Centre, Sydney

VICTORIA

Mildura Writers Festival: see Mildura and environs, p. 207

SOUTH AUSTRALIA

Willunga Almond Blossom Festival: see Fleurieu Peninsula, p. 267

WESTERN AUSTRALIA

Good Food and Wine Festival: 1st weekend of month; Convention Exhibition Centre, Perth

Mundaring Truffle Festival: Mundaring (end July – early Aug); see Swan Valley, p. 299

Seafood and Shiraz Weekends: see Swan Valley, p. 299

QUEENSLAND

Broadbeach Restaurant Week: see Gold Coast and hinterland, p. 345

TASMANIA

Chocolate Winterfest: Latrobe; see Central North, p. 411

August

NEW SOUTH WALES

Fireside Festival: Canberra region; see Snowy Mountains and Capital Country, p. 99

Mudgee Wine and Food Fair at Balmoral: see Blue Mountains and beyond, p. 17

Tweed Valley Banana Festival: Murwillumbah; see Tropical North Coast, p. 69

VICTORIA

Mildura Masters Games: biennial event, odd-numbered years; see Mildura and environs, p. 207

Taste of Melbourne: last weekend of month; Royal Exhibition Building

Festival Calendar continued

SOUTH AUSTRALIA

Barossa Gourmet Weekend: Tanunda; *see* Barossa and Eden valleys, p. 247

Zema Estate's Great Cabernet Experience: Coonawarra; *see* Limestone Coast, p. 259

QUEENSLAND

Broadbeach Jazz and Food Festival: *see* Gold Coast and hinterland, p. 345

Jazz in the Vineyard: Ballandean Estate; *see* Granite Belt, p. 357

Tastes of Gold Coast: various venues (end Aug – early Sept); *see* Gold Coast and hinterland, p. 345

September

NEW SOUTH WALES

Gate to Plate: Grafton; *see* Coffs Harbour and hinterland, p. 61

Gourmet in the Glen: Glen Innes; *see* New England Tablelands, p. 77

Mudgee Fine Food Awards: *see* Blue Mountains and beyond, p. 17

Mudgee Wine Festival: *see* Blue Mountains and beyond, p. 17

Toast Urunga Food and Wine Festival: *see* Coffs Harbour and hinterland, p. 61

VICTORIA

Classics in Wartook Valley: *see* Grampians and surrounds, p. 199

Discover Dunkeld: *see* Grampians and surrounds, p. 199

Melba Festival: *see* Yarra and Dandenongs, p. 123

Mildura Country Music Festival: Mildura (Sept–Oct); *see* Mildura and environs, p. 207

October

NEW SOUTH WALES

Cool Creek Rhythms: Coffs Harbour; *see* Coffs Harbour and hinterland, p. 61

Hunter Valley Semillon & Seafood: *see* Hunter Valley, p. 45

IDS Trust Sydney Food & Wine Fair: last Sat of month; Hyde Park North, Sydney

Murrumbateman Moving Feast: *see* Snowy Mountains and Capital Country, p. 99

Orange Wine Week: *see* Central Tablelands, p. 27

Snowy Mountains Regional Food Fair: Dalgety; *see* Snowy Mountains and Capital Country, p. 99

Sydney International Food Festival: various Sydney venues

Tastings of the Hastings: Port Macquarie; *see* Southern Holiday Coast, p. 53

Terrigal Food & Wine Fair: Terrigal Haven; *see* Central Coast and Newcastle, p. 37

VICTORIA

Bendigo Heritage Uncorked: *see* Northern Goldfields, p. 171

Birregurra Weekend Festival: *see* South-West Coast, p. 189

Bright Spring Festival: *see* Alpine Lowlands, p. 221

Heathcote Wine and Food Festival: *see* Northern Goldfields, p. 171

Mildura Jazz, Food & Wine Festival: *see* Mildura and environs, p. 207

October Pinot Week: *see* Mornington Peninsula, p. 135

Pyrenees Escapade: *see* Ballarat and Pyrenees, p. 163

Shed Fest Wine Festival: various Warburton Hwy winery sheds; *see* Yarra and Dandenongs, p. 123

Swiss Italian Festa: Hepburn Springs; *see* Macedon and Spa Country, p. 155

SOUTH AUSTRALIA

Ceduna Oysterfest: *see* Eyre Peninsula, p. 287

Coonawarra Cabernet Celebrations: Coonawarra; *see* Limestone Coast, p. 259

Fleurieu Folk Festival: Willunga; *see* Fleurieu Peninsula, p. 267

Good Food and Wine Festival: 1st weekend of month; Event Exhibition Centre, Adelaide

Kangaroo Island Art Feast: see Kangaroo Island, p. 275

Meadows Country Fair: see Adelaide Hills, p. 239

Riverland Food and Wine Festival: Berri; *see* Riverland, p. 283

Riverland Renaissance Festival: Berri; *see* Riverland, p. 283

Vintner's Picnic: Clare; *see* Clare Valley, p. 255

WESTERN AUSTRALIA

Cambinata Yabbies Extravaganza: Kukerin; *see* South-West, p. 323

Spring in the Valley: see Swan Valley, p. 299

QUEENSLAND

Australian Small Winemakers Show: Stanthorpe; *see* Granite Belt, p. 357

Shakespeare under the Stars: Ballandean; *see* Granite Belt, p. 357

NEW SOUTH WALES

Bitter & Twisted International Boutique Beer Festival: East Maitland; *see* Central Coast and Newcastle, p. 37

Eurobodalla Slow Food Celebration: Moruya; *see* South Coast, p. 91

Hunter Uncorked Balmoral: see Hunter Valley, p. 45

Tastes of the Bay Food & Wine Festival: Nelson Bay; *see* Southern Holiday Coast, p. 53

Tenterfield Food & Wine Festival: see New England Tablelands, p. 77

Wine, Roses and all that Jazz: Capital Country wineries; *see* Snowy Mountains and Capital Country, p. 99

VICTORIA

Budburst: Macedon Ranges; *see* Macedon and Spa Country, p. 155

Queenscliff Music Festival: see Geelong and Bellarine, p. 179

Toast to the Coast: Geelong; *see* Geelong and Bellarine, p. 179

WESTERN AUSTRALIA

Broome Mango Festival: see Broome, p. 333

Geographe Crush Food & Wine Festival: Bunbury; *see* Cape to Cape, p. 315

QUEENSLAND

Good Food and Wine Festival: 1st weekend of month; Convention & Exhibition Centre, Brisbane

TASMANIA

Royal Hobart International Wine Show Public Tasting: Australia's largest public wine-tasting; Glenorchy

Tasmanian Beerfest: 2nd weekend of month; Princes Wharf Shed No. 1, Hobart

December

NEW SOUTH WALES

Young Cherry Festival: see Central Tablelands, p. 27

WESTERN AUSTRALIA

Manjimup Cherry Harmony Festival: see South-West, p. 323

QUEENSLAND

Tierra Madre: see Sunshine Coast, p. 365

TASMANIA

The Taste Festival: Tasmania's biggest food week (late Dec – Jan); Hobart waterfront

The Publisher would like to acknowledge the following individuals and organisations:

Publications manager
Astrid Browne
Project manager
Melissa Krafchek
Editor
Helen Duffy
Writers
Sally Hammond (New South Wales and Victoria's South-West Coast), Tricia Welsh (Victoria), Quentin Chester (South Australia), Carmen Jenner (Western Australia), Liz Johnston (Queensland), Sue Medlock (Tasmania)
Internal page design
Stephen Smedley, tonto design
Cover design
Philip Campbell Design
Layout
Mike Kuszla, J&M Typesetting
Cartography
Emily Maffei
Pre-press
PageSet Digital Print & Pre-press
Photography credits
Front cover: vineyard in the Hunter Valley, New South Wales (Australian Scenics); coastal sea-farmed abalone, French breakfast radishes, sea lettuce, samphire, black garlic, petals of sea rocket and radish flowers, served with a shellfish consommé at Merrijig Inn, South-West Coast, Victoria (Tim James)
Back cover: Campari bottles (Explore Australia Publishing)
Title page: tasting platter and wine at Stillwater at Crittenden, Mornington Peninsula, Victoria (Courtesy of Stillwater at Crittenden)

Internal images (left to right, clockwise from top to bottom, where multiple images appear on a page):
Preliminary pages
ii–iii (a) Courtesy of The Stag Restaurant (b) Courtesy of Absynthe (c) Courtesy of Warrenmang Vineyard & Resort (d) Courtesy of Grandvewe Cheeses (e) Lisa Lovick; iv (a) Freedom Garvey (b) Adam Bruzzone (c) Courtesy of Clairault Winery & Restaurant (d) Courtesy of Pipers Brook/Kreglinger
New South Wales
viii Great Lakes Tourism/TNSW; 1 (a) Chris Elfes Photography (b) Gecko Photographics Orange (c) Courtesy of Paperbark Camp; 2–3 © photolibrary. All rights reserved; 4–5 (a) Courtesy of Jonah's (b) Sally Mayman/TNSW (c) Sydney Seaplanes/TNSW; 6 (a) Courtesy of Barrenjoey House (b) Courtesy of Cottage Point Kiosk; 7 (a) Courtesy of Brasserie Bread Bakery Cafe (b) Michela Boncagni; 8 Melanie Helliwell; 9–10 GH; 11 (a) Gina Porteous (b) GH; 13 (a) Courtesy of Sun Masamune (b) GH (c) Paul Blackmore/TNSW; 14 Jeff Drewitz; 16 Courtesy of The Conservation Hut; 17 (a) TNSW (b) Courtesy of Echoes Boutique Hotel and Restaurant; 18 Courtesy of Fresh Espresso and Food Bar; 19 (a) Nick Rains/TNSW (b) Hamilton Lund/TNSW; 20 (a) Courtesy of Echoes Boutique Hotel and Restaurant; 21 (a) Peter Solness (b) Courtesy of Glenella Guesthouse; 22 (a) Courtesy of Glenella Guesthouse (b) Adam Taylor/Tourism NSW; 23 ©iStockphoto.com/rubenhi; 25 (a) Courtesy of Roth's Wine Bar (b) Graham McCarter (c) Courtesy of Silk's Brasserie; 26 (a) Gecko Photographics Orange; 27 (a) Lisa Lovick (b) RegionalShowcase.com.au; 28 (a) Peter Gumpert (b) Courtesy of Cowra Japanese Garden; 29 (a) Courtesy of Grove Estate Wines (b) Bob Henry; 30 (a) Justin Smith (b) Lisa Lovick; 31 (a) Courtesy of Urban Graze Millthorpe (b) Evolving Images/TNSW; 32 (a) Lisa Lovick (b) & (c) Courtesy of Taste Canowindra; 33 GH; 35 (a) Lisa Lovick (b) Courtesy of Neila; 36 GH; 37 (a) Bella at Killcare (b) Anson Smart; 38 (a) Anson Smart (b) Newcastle Tourism/TNSW; 39 (a) Courtesy of rocksalt (b) Anson Smart; 41 TNSW; 42 Sonia Franckin; 43 (a) Newcastle Tourism (b) Courtesy of Firescreek Fruit Wines; 45 (a) Chris Elfes Photography (b) Mike Newling/TNSW; 46 (a) Chris Elfes Photography (b) Courtesy of Margan Family Wines; 47 (a) Chris Elfes Photography (b) Paul James; 49 Courtesy of Margan Family Wines; 51 (a) TNSW (b) Courtesy of Margan Family Wines; 53 (a) Courtesy of Cassegrain Wines (b) Courtesy of M Bistro and Bar; 54 (a) Courtesy of Peppers Anchorage (b) GH; 55 (a) GH (b) Courtesy of Bago Vineyards; 56 Courtesy of Cassegrain Wines; 57 (a) Courtesy of M Bistro and bar (b) GH; 58 GH; 61 (a) David Carse, Waterfall Way Designs (b) Courtesy of Fiasco Ristorante + Bar; 62 (a) ST Images (b) David Carse, Waterfall Way Designs; 63 (a) Rae Dawson – Courtesy of No 2 Oak Street (b) Courtesy of Bonville Golf Resort; 64–5 (a) Bruce Postle (b), (c) & (d) GH; 66 GH; 69 (a) Courtesy of Eltham Valley Pantry (b) Sharyn Cairns/TNSW; 70 (a) Courtesy of Eltham Valley Pantry (b) Courtesy of Mavis's Kitchen & Cabins @ Mt Warning; 71 (a) Courtesy of Zentveld's Australian Coffee (b) Courtesy of Byron Bay Chilli Co.; 73 Courtesy of Mavis's Kitchen & Cabins @ Mt Warning; 75 Brett Boardman; 76 Simon Scott; 77 GH; 79 (a) Courtesy of Deetswood Wines (b) Simon Scott; 80 ©iStockphoto.com/pederk; 81 (a) Courtesy of Petersons Armidale Winery & Guesthouse (b) Courtesy of Deetswood Wines; 82 Courtesy of Small Cow Farm; 83 (a) Courtesy of Bluemetal Vineyard (b) Belinda Borbely; 84 (a) Courtesy of Zweefers Great Cakes (b) Belinda Borbely; 85 (a) Julie Stone (b) Courtesy of Joadja Winery; 87 North Sullivan/TNSW; 89 (a) Courtesy of Tumbling Waters Retreat (b) Courtesy of Blue Bowl Brown Sugar (c) Courtesy of Zweefers Great Cakes; 91 (a) Mike Newling/TNSW (b) Courtesy of Bannisters; 92 (a) Courtesy of On The Pier (b) Courtesy or Silos Estate & Wileys Creek (c) Courtesy of Paperbark Camp; 93 Courtesy of Valley Edge; 95 EAP; 97 (a) Lorraine Cordeaux Photography (b) Courtesy of ABC Cheese Factory; 99 (a) Courtesy of Shaw Vineyard Estate (b) Kate Luke; 100 (a) CJ (b) Barb Uil; 101 (a) & (b) Courtesy of Thredbo Valley Distillery; 102 (a) CJ (b) Courtesy of Thredbo Valley Distillery; 103 (a) Courtesy of Goulburn Brewery (b) Courtesy of www.schonegg.com.au; 104 Paul Foley, Lightmoods/TACT; 107 (a) Andrew Chapman (b) Courtesy of Wilga Park Cottage; 108 (a) Courtesy of Wollundry Grove (b) Jay Beaumont; 109 Andrew Chapman; 111 (a) Courtesy of Casella Wines (b) Andrew Chapman (c) Jay Beaumont (d) Ginette DeMarco; 112 Paul Foley/TNSW
Victoria
114 Paoli Smith/TVIC; 115 (a) Courtesy of The Pickled Sisters Cafe (b) Courtesy of TarraWarra Estate; 116–17 EAP; 118–19 (a) Ben King/TVIC (b) David Hannah/TVIC (c) EAP (d) Mark Chew/TVIC; 120 (a) Chris Scott (b) Courtesy of Oasis Bakery; 121 (a) & (b) Colin Page; 122 Courtesy of Rochford Wines; 123 (a) Courtesy of Yarra Valley Dairy (b) Courtesy of TarraWarra Estate; 124 Courtesy of Vines Restaurant at Helen's Hill; 125 (a)

Anthony & Robina Summers, Upfront Pictures (b) Tizia May; 126 (a) Courtesy of Chateau Yering (b) Courtesy of Yarra Valley Dairy; 127 Courtesy of Bulong Estate; 128 (a) Courtesy of Mandala Wines; 128 (b) Courtesy of Chateau Yering; 129 (a) Courtesy of Chateau Yering (b) Robert Hock Photography; 131 Courtesy of the Yarra Valley Regional Food Group; 134 Courtesy of Sunny Ridge Strawberry Farm; 135 (a) Peter Dunphy/TVIC (b) Courtesy of La Petanque; 136 Courtesy of Stillwater at Crittenden (c) Courtesy of Mornington Peninsula Chocolates; 137 (a) Jacquie Melville (b) Courtesy of La Petanque; 138 Courtesy of Max's at Red Hill Estate; 139 (a) Courtesy of Red Hill Brewery (b) Courtesy of La Petanque; 140–1 Earl Carter; 143 Courtesy of Max's at Red Hill Estate; 144 Cathrine Sutherland/TVIC; 145 (a) Courtesy of Destination Gippsland (b) Courtesy of Brandy Creek Winery; 146 (a) Courtesy of Destination Gippsland; 146 (b) & 147 Courtesy of the West Gippsland Regional Tourism Association; 148 (a) Courtesy of The Outpost Retreat (b) Courtesy of Grand Ridge; 149 (a) Courtesy of Culinaire (b) Courtesy of Tinamba Hotel; 151 Courtesy of Capra Organic Goat Cheese; 154 Courtesy of Ellender Estate; 155 (a) Tim Burder (b) Courtesy of Lake House Daylesford; 157 (a) Courtesy of Farmers Arms Hotel (b) Simon Grffiths; 159 Courtesy of Lake House Daylesford; 160 (a) Carol White (b) Courtesy of Royal George Hotel; 161 (a) Sandy Scheltema (b) Courtesy of Ellender Estate (c) Courtesy of Holgate Brewhouse; 163 (a) & (b) Peter Dunphy/TVIC; 164 Courtesy of Warrenmang Vineyard & Resort; 165 (a) Courtesy of The Good Table (b) Courtesy of Blue Pyrenees Estate; 167 Courtesy of Warrenmang Vineyard & Resort; 169 (a) Courtesy of Blue Pyrenees Estate (b) David Mitchiner/TVIC; 170 Courtesy of Heathcote Winery; 171 Anthony Webster, Imagine Pictures; 172 (a) Courtesy of Green Olive (b) Courtesy of The Redesdale; 173 City of Greater Bendigo; 174 (a) Anthony Webster, Imagine Pictures (b) Courtesy of Cellar & Store (c) Courtesy of Green Olive; 175 (a) Courtesy of Water Wheel Vineyards (b) Courtesy of The Redesdale; 176 ©iStockphoto.com/steps; 178–80 (a) Mark Chew/TVIC; 180 (b) Courtesy of Bellarine Estate; 181 (a) Mark Chew/TVIC (b) Courtesy of Wineries of Victoria; 183 (a) Courtesy of La Madre Bakery (b) Courtesy of Wineries of Victoria (c) Mark Chew/TVIC; 184 (a) Courtesy of Barrgowan Vineyard (b) Trevor Cook; 185 Adrian Lander; 187 Andrew Paoli/Great Ocean Road Marketing/TVIC; 188 Courtesy of Chris's Beacon Point Restaurant & Villas; 189 Tim James; 190 (a) Zoe Geshen (b) Courtesy of Chris's Beacon Point Restaurant & Villas; 191 (a) Bernie Phelan Photography (b) Mark Roper; 192 (a) Gemma Carman (b) Courtesy of Bridgewater Bay Cafe; 193 (a) Courtesy of Pippies by the Bay (b) Courtesy of Gentle Annie Berry Gardens; 195 George Biron, Sunnybrae Birregurra; 197 (a) Courtesy of Pronto Fine Food Merchants (b) Courtesy of Pennyroyal Raspberry Farm; 198 Courtesy of Royal Mail Hotel; 199 Southern Grampians Shire/TVIC; 200 (a) Anthony Kumnick (b) Southern Grampians Shire/TVIC; 201 Southern Grampians Shire/TVIC; 203 Courtesy of Royal Mail Hotel; 204 (a) Southern Grampians Shire/TVIC (b) Courtesy of Mount Cole Wineworks; 205 (a) Southern Grampians Shire/TVIC (b) Courtesy of Royal Mail Hotel; 207 Courtesy of Stefano's Cafe & Restaurant; 208 (a) & (b) Darren Seiler Photography (c) Courtesy of Oak Valley Estate; 209 (a) Courtesy of Stefano's Cafe & Restaurant (b) Rob Blackburn/TNSW (c) Darren Seiler Photography; 210 Courtesy of Campbell's Wines; 211 (a) Courtesy of The Pickled Sisters Cafe (b) Gavin Hansford/Bushfire Recovery/TVIC; 212 (a) Courtesy of The Pickled Sisters Cafe (b) 210 Courtesy of Campbell's Wines; 213 (a) Gavin Hansford/TVIC (b) Courtesy of Campbell's Wines; 214 Jamie Durrant; 215 (a) & (b) Courtesy of The Pickled Sisters Cafe; 216 (a) Courtesy of Vintara Winery & Restaurant (b) & (c) Jos Weemaes; 217 Courtesy of Beechworth Honey; 219 (a) Courtesy of The Pickled Sisters Cafe (b) Peter Dunphy/North East Victoria Tourism/TVIC; 220 Gavin Hansford/Bushfire Recovery/TVIC; 221 Peter Dunphy/North East Victoria Tourism/TVIC; 222 (a) Peter Dunphy/Victoria's High Country Campaign Committee/TVIC (b) Courtesy of Lindenwarrah at Milawa; 223 (a) Jamie Durrant (b) Mojo Partners/TVIC; 224 (a) Peter Bennett (b) Peter Dunphy/North East Victoria Tourism/TVIC; 225 (a) Jamie Durant (b) Peter Dunphy/North East Victoria Tourism/TVIC; 226 (a) Peter Dunphy/Victoria's High Country Campaign Committee/TVIC (b) Peter Dunphy/North East Victoria Tourism/TVIC; 227 Dean Cambray; 229 (a) Jamie Durant (b) Peter Bennett
South Australia
230 MK; 231 (a) Samuel Collins (b) Australian Scenics; 232–3 EAP; 234–5 (a) SATC (b), (c) & (d) Matt Nettheim/SATC; 236 (a) Courtesy of Dhaba (b) The Spice Kitchen (b) Matt Nettheim/SATC; 237 (a) Courtesy of Utopia @ Waterfall Gully (b) Rosey Boehm; 239 (a) Courtesy of Golding Wines (b) Courtesy of Petaluma Wines; 240 (a) Drew Lenman, Orange Lane Studios (b) Courtesy of Petaluma Wines; 241 (a) Brett Sheriden/SATC (b) & 243 Courtesy of Udder Delights Cheese Cellar; 244 (a) Brett Sheriden/SATC (b) Courtesy of Sticky Rice Cooking School (c) Courtesy of Howard Vineyard; 245 (a) Courtesy of Hahndorf Hill Winery (b) Brett Sheriden/SATC (c) Samuel Collins; 246 Courtesy of Pernod Ricard Pacific; 247 (a) Tony Lewis (b) Dragan Radocaj; 248 (a) Courtesy of Grant Burge Wines (b) Courtesy of Blond Coffee & Store; 249 (a) Tony Lewis (b) Courtesy of Langmeil Winery; 251 (a) Dragan Radocaj (b) Courtesy of Barossa Grape & Wine; 252 Courtesy of Charles Melton Wines; 255 (a) © photolibrary. All rights reserved. (b) MK; 256 (a) Courtesy of Grosset Wines (b) Vanessa Size; 257 Courtesy of Mitchell Wines; 259 (a) Tony Lewis (b) MK; 260 (a) MK (b) Courtesy of Rymill Coonawarra; 261 (a) Matilda Innes (b) Courtesy of Wynns Coonawarra; 262 (a) Courtesy of Katnook Estate, Coonawarra (b) Dru Reschke; 264 Joanna Fincham; 266 Marie Watt; 267 (a) Marie Watt (b) Neale Winter/SATC; 268 (a) Marie Watt (b) John Kruger; 269 Courtesy of Coorong Vineyards; 271 (a), (b) & (c) Marie Watt (d) Courtesy of Flying Fish Cafe; 272 John Kruger; 274 QC; 275 (a) Daniel Noone (b) & 276 QC; 277 (a) QC (b) Matt Nettheim/SATC; 278 Daniel Noone; 279 (a) QC (b) Brett Sheriden (c) Jaba Multi Media; 280 QC; 282 Bill Bachman/Alamy; 283 (a) © photolibrary. All rights reserved. (b) Neale Winter/SATC; 284 © photolibrary. All rights reserved. 285 Courtesy of Angove Family Winemakers; 286 Randy Larcombe; 287 (a) Matt Nettheim/SATC (b) John White Photos/Alamy; 289 (a) Courtesy of Mocean Cafe (b) John Hay/Lonely Planet Images
Western Australia
290 © photolibrary. All rights reserved; 291 (a) Courtesy of Brookland Valley (b) John Hay/Lonely Planet Images (c) Christian Fletcher; 292–3 EAP; 294 Greg Elms/Lonely Planet Images; 295 (a) Simon Pynt Photography (b) Greg Elms/Lonely Planet Images; 296 CJ; 297 (a) Simon Pynt Photography (b) CJ; 299 (a) Courtesy of Loose Box (b) Orien Harvey/Lonely Planet Images; 300 (a) Courtesy of Mondo Nougat (b) Courtesy of Talijancich Wines; 301 Courtesy of Loose Box; 302 (a) Courtesy of Elmar's in the Valley (b) Courtesy of Mondo Nougat (c) Courtesy of Talijancich Wines; 303 (a) Michael Yurisich (b) Courtesy of Loose Box; 304 & 307 (a) CJ (b) Courtesy of Western Range Wines; 308 (a) CJ (b) Steven David Miller/AUSCAPE; 309–11 CJ; 312 Frances Andrijich©/Wildlight; 315 (a) CJ (b) Courtesy of Cape Lodge; 316 (a) Frances Andrijich Photography (b) Oliver Marill (c) Courtesy of Clairault Winery & Restaurant; 317 (a) Courtesy of

Vasse Felix (b) Courtesy of Settlers Tavern Margaret River (c) Courtesy of Jam Revolution; 319 Courtesy of Bushtucker River & Winery Tours; 320 (a) Freedom Garvey (b) CJ; 321 (a) Courtesy of Brookland Valley Estate (b) Courtesy of Cape Mentelle; 322 Courtesy of Denmark Farmhouse Cheese; 323 (a) Courtesy of The Lily Dutch Windmill (b) Christian Fletcher; 324 (a) CJ (b) Courtesy of The Lake House Denmark; 325 (a) Courtesy of Galafrey Wines (b) Karen Masters; 326 (a) Jodie Pannell (b) Clare Day; 327 Courtesy of The Lily Dutch Windmill; 329 Courtesy of TreeElle Retreat; 330 (a) CJ (b) Courtesy of Denmark Farmhouse Cheese; 331 Karen Masters; 332 Penny Tweedie/Alamy; 333 (a) Jiri Lochman/Lochman Transparencies (b) Graeme & Margaret Herald/EAP; 334 (a) Courtesy of Matso's Broome Brewery (b) Kanagae Estate Mango Place; 335 John Hay/Lonely Planet Images
Queensland
336 Peter Lik/TQ; 337 (a) Alison George, Catseye Productions (c) Courtesy of Palazzo Versace (c) Courtesy of Spirit House; 338–9 Ezra Patchett/TQ; 340–1 (a) Ezra Patchett/TQ (b) & (c) Paul Ewart/TQ (d) Peter Lik/TQ; 342 (a) Ezra Patchett/TQ (b) TQ; 343 (a) Murray Waite & Associates/TQ (b) Courtesy of Mu'ooz; 345 (a) Courtesy of Absynthe (b) Murray Waite & Associates/TQ; 346 (a) Murray Waite/TQ (b) Courtesy of Rocksalt; 347 Courtesy of Palazzo Versace; 348 (a) Courtesy of Louise Carroll Marketing (b) Courtesy of Absynthe; 349 (a) Courtesy of Rocksalt (b) Courtesy of Ristorante Fellini; 350 Courtesy of Louise Carroll Marketing; 352 Darren Jew/TQ; 353 (a) Courtesy of Spicers Hidden Vale (b) Paul Ewart/TQ; 355 Courtesy of Spicers Peak Lodge; 357 (a) Ray Cash/TQ (b) TQ; 358 (a) Courtesy of Ridgemill Estate (b) Nat Burton; 359 (a) Courtesy of Boireann Winery (b) TQ; 361 (a) Ezra Patchett/TQ (b) Exposure/TQ (c) Courtesy of Ridgemill Estate; 362 Courtesy of Ballandean Estate; 365 (a) Courtesy of Blue Angel (b) Courtesy of Spirit House; 366 (a) Courtesy of Spirit House (b) Courtesy of Wasabi; 367 (a) Courtesy of Gallery Gourmet (b) Lisa Downie; 368 (a) Philip Morgan (b) Courtesy of Spirit House; 369 Courtesy of Spicers Clovelly Estate; 370 Lisa Downie; 371 (a) Courtesy of Belmondos Retail (b) Courtesy of Fromart; 373 Courtesy of Noosa Lime Co.; 374 (a) Courtesy of Blue Angel (b) Courtesy of Belmondos Retail; 375 (a) Courtesy of Spicers Clovelly Estate (b) Courtesy of Spirit House; 377 (a) Alison George, Catseye Productions (b) Courtesy of Harrisons; 378 Courtesy of Ochre Restaurant; 379 (a) Courtesy of Nerada Tea (b) & 380 (a) Courtesy of 2 Fish Restaurant Port Douglas – Head Chef Tommy Young (b) Courtesy of Harrisons; 381 (a) Perrin Clarke (b) Courtesy of Ochre Restaurant; 383 (a) Courtesy of Harrisons (b) Courtesy of Ochre Restaurant (c) Courtesy of Skybury; 384 Glenn Weiss/TQ
Tasmania
386 George Apostolidis/TTAS; 387 (a) Courtesy of Pipers Brook/Kreglinger (b) Amanda McLauchlan (c) Courtesy of Pure Tasmania; 388–9 © photolibrary. All rights reserved; 390–1 (a), (b) & (c) SM (d) Southern Cross Television/TTAS; 392 SM; 393 (a) MK (b) & (c) SM; 395 (a) Courtesy of Grandvewe Cheeses (b) Amanda McLauchlan; 396 (a) & (b) SM (c) Adrian Lander; 397 (a) Courtesy of Two Metre Tall Company (b) MK (c) Bernice Woolley; 399 SM; 400 (a) SM (b) Adrian Lander; 401 (a) SM (b) Amanda McLauchlan (c) Courtesy of Grandvewe Cheeses; 403 (a) Garry Moore/TTAS (b) Courtesy of Pure Tasmania; 404 (a) Courtesy of Angasi (b) & 405 Courtesy of Saffire; 406 (a) Courtesy of Ironhouse Brewery (b) SM; 407 (a) Courtesy of Pure Tasmania (b) Garry Moore/TTAS; 408 Courtesy of Angasi; 410 Courtesy of House of Anvers; 411 (a) Rob Burnett (b) SM; 412 (a) Courtesy of Pipers Brook/Kreglinger (b) SM; 413 Rob Burnett; 414 (a) Courtesy of House of Anvers (b) Courtesy of Seven Sheds Brewery, Meadery & Hop Garden; 415 Courtesy of Pipers Brook/Kreglinger; 416 ©iStockphoto.com/kcline

Abbreviations
CJ Carmen Jenner
EAP Explore Australia Publishing
GH Gordon Hammond
MK Melissa Krafchek
QC Quentin Chester
SATC South Australian Tourism Commission
SM Sue Medlock
TNSW Tourism New South Wales
TQ Tourism Queensland
TTAS Tourism Tasmania
TVIC Tourism Victoria

Explore Australia Publishing Pty Ltd
85 High Street
Prahran, Victoria 3181, Australia

Explore Australia Publishing Pty Ltd is a division of Hardie Grant Publishing Pty Ltd

Published by Explore Australia Publishing Pty Ltd, 2010

Concept, text, maps, form and design © Explore Australia Publishing Pty Ltd, 2010

ISBN 13 978 1 74117 347 5

10 9 8 7 6 5 4 3 2 1

Printed and bound in China by C & C Offset Printing Co. Ltd

Publisher's Note: Every effort has been made to ensure that the information in this book is accurate at the time of going to press. The publisher welcomes information and suggestions for correction or improvement. Email: info@exploreaustralia.net.au

Publisher's Disclaimers: The publisher cannot accept responsibility for any errors or omissions. The representation on the maps of any road or track is not necessarily evidence of public right of way. The publisher cannot be held responsible for any injury, loss or damage incurred during travel. It is vital to research any proposed trip thoroughly and seek the advice of relevant state and travel organisations before you leave.